By Lawrence I. Lipking

The Ordering of the Arts in Eighteenth-Century England   1970

By A. Walton Litz

James Joyce's Dubliners (WITH ROBERT SCHOLES)   1969
Jane Austen   1965
Modern American Fiction: Essays in Criticism   1963
The Art of James Joyce   1961; REVISED 1964

MODERN
LITERARY
CRITICISM
1900–1970

MODERN LITERARY CRITICISM 1900–1970

Edited by

LAWRENCE I. LIPKING

Department of English, Princeton University

and

A. WALTON LITZ

Department of English, Princeton University

ATHENEUM   *NEW YORK*

1972

PREFACE

Perhaps no age of literary criticism has enjoyed such prestige and authority as the twentieth century. Twenty years ago, when Randall Jarrell complained that we were living in an age of criticism, all the facts seemed to bear him out. Literary magazines were dominated by the critical arguments of warring schools, the universities had made a home for critics, and a series of anthologies and histories of criticism seemed to enshrine a main line and orthodoxy of the modern movement. Nor has the situation altogether changed today. Looking back on the achievements of modern literary criticism, we see a period as rich and diverse, as thronged with its own classics, as any in the past.

What has changed, however, is our sense of that period. Twenty years ago, many anthologists and historians thought that modern criticism had reached a true culmination, that many of the age-old questions about literature were at the point of being solved. Today the nature of literary criticism seems far more fluid, and far more exciting. New critical movements have arisen to challenge or bypass the old, important new critics like Northrop Frye have helped to revise our views of the nature of criticism itself, and the embattled critics of the earlier twentieth century, men such as Pound and Eliot and the still vigorous I. A. Richards, have become less controversial than classic, the progenitors of a criticism whose strength is the number of questions it continues to ask. From our present-day perspective, modern literary criticism is valuable because it opens so many windows; it has not ended but begun a search for a better understanding of literature. We think that the time has come to take stock of that understanding.

As every teacher of an introductory course in literary criticism knows, it is easy to make large claims for the richness and importance of modern literary criticism, but extremely difficult to substantiate these claims from the existing anthologies. The major documents of literary criticism from Aristotle through the nineteenth century are available in a number of comprehensive volumes, but most collections of twentieth-century criticism fall into two unsatisfactory categories: they are either general surveys in which the major figures of the century are thinly represented, or specialized collections emphasizing a particular method or critical movement. As a result, the teacher must choose between treating the modern period in anticlimactic fashion or constructing his syllabus from an awkward combination of assigned texts and library resources. The editors of *Modern Literary Criticism* have taught undergraduate and graduate courses in the history of literary criticism for over a decade, and the idea for a new anthology grew directly out of our frustration with the available texts.

Our primary aim in making this new collection has been to reprint a body of criticism large enough to support an entire course, and broad enough in range to accommodate a variety of classroom approaches: to this end we have organized the volume around selections from four major critics which are much more extensive than those found in other anthologies, and which should give the reader a clear understanding of each critic's significant contributions. Throughout the process of selection we have kept the immediate needs of undergraduate students and teachers foremost in mind, but we hope that we have also produced a collection which can be of service at the graduate level. Whether used as a supplement to the standard historical anthologies or as a sourcebook for intensive study in modern criticism, this anthology should provide the fundamental materials for a comprehensive treatment of twentieth-century English and American criticism.

With the goals of flexibility and broad representation constantly before us, we have avoided any arrangement that would force the reader into a narrow view of the development of modern criticism. This does not mean, however, that the editors have abandoned their own opinions on the history and significance of modern criticism: these opinions are implicit in the choice of texts, and explicit in the introductions. But our aim throughout has been to avoid polemics and partisan argument, allowing the major critics to speak for themselves at the greatest possible length.

The general design of the anthology reflects this aim. In Part One, the longest and most important section, we have tried to represent the full achievements of four indispensable critics (Pound, Eliot, Richards, Frye). Others might have merited such detailed treatment, but we feel that the choice of these particular critics can be justified on both individual and historical grounds. In effect, Part One introduces most of the crucial issues and methods which have formed the continuing debate that is modern criticism. The sections on T. S. Eliot and I. A. Richards follow a familiar historical pattern, although we believe them to be far more comprehensive and balanced than those found in other anthologies. The accomplishments of Pound and Frye, however, do not lend themselves to conventional principles of selection, and in these sections we have organized the materials around special issues or themes. The selections from Pound's voluminous criticism were chosen to support his belief that criticism is most alive when an adjunct to creation; hence most of the essays are drawn from that period (1909–1918) when Pound was the critical conscience of the new movements in poetry and prose. With Northrop Frye, on the other hand, the difficulties of selection were of a different order. *Anatomy of Criticism* possesses a dense argument and orchestrated structure that defy the anthologist, and therefore we have chosen to reprint as the heart of this section several essays later incorporated into the *Anatomy*. It is our hope that these selections will provide both a summary of the *Anatomy*'s leading themes and a rough history of Frye's progress as a critic.

In Part Two seven major critics speak of the problems and methods that are most characteristic of their work. Our aim in this section has been to represent the achievements of a number of important critics while simultaneously introducing the reader to some of the crucial problems and techniques in modern criticism. The essays are grouped so as to indicate possible connections and continuities, while other relationships are suggested in the introduction; but it must be emphasized that these patterns are deliberately provisional. Our main purpose in Part Two was to reprint a series of major essays which would lend themselves to a wide range of uses in the classroom.

Part Three, "Continental Criticism," does not pretend to be representative. Instead we have selected essays which either had a significant impact on English and American criticism, or which employ methods not yet fully assimilated into our critical tradition. Some of these continental essays can be fruitfully used in connection with the materials of Parts One and Two (e.g., Freud with Trilling, Jung with Frye, Lukács with Wilson). The gathering of essays on Flaubert serves a double purpose, indicating the scope of continental criticism while providing a brief introduction to the criticism of prose fiction. Because of its bulk and special interests, theory of fiction has been largely excluded from other parts of the anthology, but we hope that the Flaubert section will supply the reader with a useful starting point.

Part Four, "Poet-Critics," may be considered a luxury by some readers, but the editors see it as of crucial importance. It reflects our belief that the greatest English and American criticism has most often been inductive, and that the chief glory of the tradition has been the many poet-critics who have thought of criticism as a vital part of the literary tradition rather than a separate theoretical enterprise. With a few notable exceptions, the critics represented in Parts One and Two are known as creators in their own right, and when they are combined with the poet-critics of Part Four one is left with the overwhelming conviction that the greatness of modern criticism stems from its close alliance with the major literary experiments and achievements of the century. Modern literature has been so obsessively concerned with its own forms and origins that it can hardly be understood apart from the double achievement of its poet-critics.

The general plan of this anthology has been the joint work of both editors, but the responsibility for individual sections and introductions should be apportioned as follows: Part I, "Ezra Pound" and "T. S. Eliot," Part II—A. Walton Litz; Part I, "I. A. Richards" and "Northrop Frye," Parts III and IV—Lawrence I. Lipking.

A note on the style of this text: Titles in brackets are titles provided by the editors. Footnotes keyed with an asterisk are editors' notes; those keyed with a numeral are part of the original essay.

Selective Bibliography

The following works will provide the student with an overview of modern literary criticism. Those containing extensive bibliography are marked with an asterisk.

Northrop Frye, *Anatomy of Criticism* (1957). A systematic and archetypal approach to the major categories of criticism.

Stanley Edgar Hyman, *The Armed Vision* (1948). The first detailed study of the entire range of modern criticism. Contains essays on, among others, Yvor Winters, T. S. Eliot, Maud Bodkin, Caroline Spurgeon, R. P. Blackmur, William Empson, I. A. Richards, Kenneth Burke.

*Philip Stevick (ed.), *The Theory of the Novel* (1967). A comprehensive anthology of essays on the theory and practice of prose fiction. Contains a full bibliography of criticism of the novel since 1900.

Walter Sutton, *Modern American Criticism* (1963). A useful survey, with chapters on the important kinds and theories of modern criticism.

*James Thorpe (ed.), *Relations of Literary Study* (Modern Language Association, 1967). Authoritative essays on the following topics, some with detailed bibliography: Literature and History, Literature and Myth, Literature and Biography, Literature and Psychology, Literature and Sociology, Literature and Religion, Literature and Music.

*René Wellek, *A History of Modern Criticism*, Vol. IV: *The Later Nineteenth Century* (1965). The standard history of the backgrounds to twentieth-century criticism, with elaborate notes and bibliographies. Volume V, *The Twentieth Century*, is forthcoming.

*René Wellek and Austin Warren, *Theory of Literature* (1949). An essential compendium of the methods and assumptions of twentieth-century criticism. Theoretical rather than historical, it contains chapters on the various aspects of formal analysis, and on the relation of literature to other disciplines (biography, psychology, history of ideas, etc.).

William K. Wimsatt, Jr., and Cleanth Brooks, *Literary Criticism: A Short History* (1959). The final chapters cover the entire range of modern criticism.

Morton D. Zabel (ed.), *Literary Opinion in America* (revised edition, 1951). An important anthology, with a detailed introduction and elaborate appendices on "Recent Works of American Criticism" and "American Magazines Publishing Criticism."

CONTENTS

II *Modern Criticism: Problems and Methods*

III *Continental Criticism*

IV Poet-Critics

PART I

Four Major Critics

EZRA POUND

Introduction

CRITICISM, Ezra Pound once said, is written in the hope of better things. To Pound, a critical activity which does not have a direct bearing on the contemporary needs of literature is suspect and irrelevant. The job of the critic is to "Make It New," to redefine the past in the service of the present, and his aims may be seen as twofold:

1. . . . . to forerun composition, to serve as gun-sight, though there is, I believe, no recorded instance of this foresight having EVER been of the slightest use save to actual composers. I mean the man who formulates any forward reach of co-ordinating principle is the man who produces the demonstration.

2. Excernment. The general ordering and weeding out of what has been performed. The elimination of repetitions. The work analogous to that which a good hanging committee or a curator would perform in a National Gallery or in a biological museum.

   The ordering of knowledge so that the next man (or generation) can most readily find the live part of it, and waste the least possible time among obsolete issues.

   ("Date Line," 1934)

The interesting thing here is that Pound's second category, which he clearly thinks of as embodying works of lesser intensity, covers the entire range of what is conventionally called "criticism." The first aim of the critic, as Pound sees it, is "demonstration": the great critic must be the creator who not only can "excern" and reorder the literary tradition but can also validate his new vision through artistic creation. Throughout Pound's works "criticism" and "creativity" are seen as essentially the same activity; literary comment can be of immense use in educating the reader, in sharpening his sensibility, but it takes on authority only when it is validated in new creations of living literature.

In describing the "kinds" of criticism ("Date Line," 1934), Pound ranks them in ascending order of importance, and it is instructive to consider examples of each "kind" from Pound's own career.

> 1. Criticism by discussion, extending from mere yatter, logic-chopping, and description of tendencies up to the clearly defined record of procedures and an attempt to formulate more or less general principles.

The range of this category, from occasional reviewing to the theories of an Aristotle, is immense, but Pound clearly considers these activities the least important branch of "criticism." Included here would be most of his own occasional reviews, generously performed in the service of contemporary letters (one thinks of his role as promoter of Joyce, Eliot, Frost, and a host of other important figures), as well as his more general essays on critical procedure and the theory of poetic language. Together these essays provide an impressive record of critical achievement, but Pound thinks of them as the most expendable part of his work. They stemmed from his function as critic of the "moment," alive to the immediate needs of English literature: one example would be his deliberate decision (along with T. S. Eliot) to champion more formal verse in his criticism and practice as an antidote to the excesses of *vers libre*. Most of Pound's conventional criticism—his articles on Imagism and Vorticism for instance—must not be taken as statements of permanent principles but as parts of an intensive campaign to redirect and revitalize the language of English poetry *at a particular moment in time*. All of Pound's occasional criticism must be read against the background of a special literary scene, and in the context of a self-conscious desire to shape English literature to the form of his "tradition." Like Wordsworth and Coleridge in the 1800 Preface to *Lyrical Ballads*, Pound is most often writing a criticism which simultaneously "excerns" the past and looks forward to new literary achievements in which he himself is determined to play an important part.

> 2. Criticism by translation.

Under this heading would come Pound's evocative rendering of the Anglo-Saxon "Seafarer," his adaptations from the Chinese in *Cathay*, his translations and adaptations from the Latin and the Provençal. Appearing at crucial turns in his poetic career, these "translations" from one culture to another are just as much a part of his critical activity as his conventional essays, and have had at least as great an impact on the evolution of modern literature.

> 3. Criticism by exercise in the style of a given period.

The final test of a man's knowledge of English literature is his ability to recognize and recreate various traditional "styles," and Pound sees this process as an essential device for renewing the past and defining the present. *Hugh Selwyn Mauberley* is a museum of imitated styles, each playing a crucial role in Pound's anatomy of the London literary scene. Stretching from his echoes of the poets of the 'nineties and the Pre-Raphaelites to his marvelous pastiche of Elizabethan songs in "Envoi," these sections of *Mauberley* form a special view of Pound's own tradition that is far more subtle than anything in his discursive criticism.

> 4. Criticism via music, meaning definitely the setting of a poet's words; e.g., in *Le Testament*, Villon's words, and in *Cavalcanti*, I have set Guido's and Sordello's.

Whatever one may think of Pound's musical theory and his excursions into musical composition, these activities are obviously "critical," an attempt to reveal that aspect of language (*melopoeia*) "wherein the words are charged, over and above their plain meaning, with some musical property which directs the bearing or trend of the meaning" (*How to Read*). Since *melopoeia* cannot be "translated" in any usual sense of that word, Pound feels that the only way a critic can comment on this important aspect of earlier poetry is through some kind of transformation into actual music.

> 5. Criticism in new composition. For example the criticism of Seneca in Mr. Eliot's *Agon* is infinitely more alive than in his essay on Seneca.

The most important of Pound's works would fall under this category of ultimate criticism. At its deepest reaches *Hugh Selwyn Mauberley* is, for example, a profound act of criticism performed upon the foreground and background of English literature *circa* 1918, a work which has had a major impact on the view of the 'nineties and the Pre-Raphaelites taken by later critics and readers. Perhaps the finest example of "Criticism in new composition" is Canto I, which provides a masterly synthesis of "Criticism by translation" and "Criticism in the style of a given period" with radically new material. In the first section of Canto I the account of Odysseus' descent into Hell from Book XI of the *Odyssey*, as told in compressed form by a Renaissance Latin translator (Pound's direct source), is rendered by Pound in imitated Anglo-Saxon language and meter. The Anglo-Saxon style was adopted because Pound associated Old English poems such as the "Seafarer" and the "Wanderer" with the direct and robust qualities of the *Odyssey*: "Such poems are not made for after-dinner speakers, nor was the eleventh book of the Odyssey." The result is a composite form in which Pound's theme of the artist as a questing Odysseus, already developed in *Mauberley*, is presented through successive historical overlays: the world of Renaissance translation, the Anglo-Saxon epic tradition, and the *Odyssey* itself. Thus Canto I is a living illustration of one particular tradition, a bringing together of past and present, and therefore a major act of literary criticism. When all Pound's "categories" for criticism are taken into account, his entire career may be seen as one sustained critical

performance in which the poetry and the discursive prose are simply
different facets of the same complex achievement.

Turning now from the "kinds" of criticism to Pound's particular
methods as found in his essays, the first thing to note is the "comparative" nature of his writings. Robert Frost once said that "poetry is what
is lost in translation," but Pound (in an early essay called "How I Began") said that he wished to know by the time he was thirty "what part
of poetry was 'indestructible,' what part could *not be lost* by translation,
and—scarcely less important—what effects were obtainable in *one* language only and were utterly incapable of being translated." Pound's
interests were always international; he conceived of Europe as a single
literary community, and—in contrast to Frost—his major emphasis
always lay on those qualities and "virtues" of a writer which were truly
cosmopolitan, which could be "translated" in the most radical sense of
that term. In pursuing his methods of "translation" and comparison
Pound was essentially pragmatic: his method is always that of the
worker in the laboratory, trying out new combinations and looking for
evidence of new effects.

Pound's famous anecdote of Agassiz and the fish is relevant here.

No man is equipped for modern thinking until he has understood the
anecdote of Agassiz and the fish:

A post-graduate student equipped with honours and diplomas went to
Agassiz to receive the final and finishing touches. The great man offered
him a small fish and told him to describe it.

Post-Graduate Student: "That's only a sunfish."

Agassiz: "I know that. Write a description of it."

After a few minutes the student returned with the description of the
Ichthus Heliodiplodokus, or whatever term is used to conceal the common
sunfish from vulgar knowledge, family of Heliichtherinkus, etc., as found in
textbooks of the subject.

Agassiz again told the student to describe the fish.

The student produced a four-page essay. Agassiz then told him to look at
the fish. At the end of three weeks the fish was in an advanced state of de-
composition, but the student knew something about it.

(ABC of Reading, 1934)

Like Agassiz's experimental method, Pound's technique—always a pedagogical one—was to cut through received theories and examine the
actual effects of language, preferably through a process of comparison
and pragmatic classification.

As for the critical judgments which flow from Pound's comparative
studies, they depend in large measure on his hierarchy of artists.

1. *The inventors*, "discoverers of a particular process or of more than
one mode and process."

2. *The masters.* "This is a very small class, and there are very few real
ones. The term is properly applied to inventors who, apart from their
own inventions, are able to assimilate and co-ordinate a large number of
preceding inventions."

3. *The diluters.*

4. *The craftsmen,* competent practitioners in a particular kind or the "style of a period."

5. *Belles Lettres.* Those who "are not exactly 'great masters,' who can hardly be said to have originated a form, but who have nevertheless brought some mode to a very high development."

6. *Eccentrics,* the starters of crazes.

(How to Read, 1929)

It is a sign of Pound's desire to instigate new movements, to direct the evolution of literature, that he ranks the inventors above the great masters who synthesize a number of literary inventions (such as Shakespeare or Dante). In this regard, T. S. Eliot was paying Pound the highest compliment when, in the Preface to *Selected Poems* (1928), he said that "Chinese poetry, as we know it today, is something invented by Ezra Pound."

The crucial value Pound placed on "invention" and discovery is evident in his special view of the literary tradition, where the inventors play a decisive role because they are of most use to the contemporary artist. In the Preface to *The Spirit of Romance* (1910) he anticipated the argument of T. S. Eliot's famous essay, "Tradition and the Individual Talent" (1917): "All ages are contemporaneous. . . . What we need is a literary scholarship, which will weigh Theocritus and Yeats with one balance, and which will judge dull dead men as inexorably as dull writers of today, and will, with equity, give praise to beauty before referring to an almanack." And in 1933 he commented, retrospectively: "Mr. Eliot and I belong to the same school of critics, in so far as we believe that existing works form a complete order which is changed by the introduction of the 'really new' work." Like Eliot, Pound sees a reciprocal relationship between past and present, each modifying the other, with the introduction of the "really new" work of art altering the alignment of the entire tradition. Our reading of Joyce's *Ulysses,* for instance, is certainly conditioned by what we know of the *Odyssey,* but it is equally true that after reading *Ulysses* one can never understand Homer again in exactly the same way.

In his essay "Cavalcanti" Pound comments that modern man has lost the medieval talent for seeing the forms in all material things. A "medieval 'natural philosopher' " would find the modern world full of forms, but the modern scientist does not think of the shape of his subject: "The rose that his magnet makes in the iron filings [as the field of force realigns the disparate fragments], does not lead him to think of the force in botanic terms, or wish to visualize that force as floral and extant." Later this image was translated into Canto LXXIV, where it provides a perfect comment on Pound's idea of tradition:

> Hast ou' seen the rose in the steel dust
> (or swansdown ever?)
> so light is the urging, so ordered the dark petals of iron
> we who have passed over Lethe.

To see the rose in the steel dust, to discern the forms of the past (perhaps the rose of the Court of Love) in the materials of the present, is the true function of the poet-critic:

> To have gathered from the air a live tradition
> or from a fine old eye the unconquered flame
> This is not vanity.
>   Here error is all in the not done,
> all in the diffidence that faltered,

(Canto LXXXI)

The editor of the *New Age*, in which Pound's series of essays called "I Gather the Limbs of Osiris" appeared, noted that "under this heading Mr. Pound will contribute expositions and translations in illustration of the New Method in Scholarship." The "New Method" clearly owed a great deal to modern anthropology, with its emphasis on patterns of cyclic return and the presence of ancient patterns beneath the details of modern life. The title of Pound's series—an obvious allusion to Sir James Frazer's *The Golden Bough*—implies that Pound, like the Isis of Egyptian myth, will gather the fragments of the past and make them live again. The format of "I Gather the Limbs of Osiris," which blends discursive commentary with practical demonstrations (such as the translation of the "Seafarer"), is a splendid illustration of Pound's method at its best—aimed at an elite audience of those in touch with the modern movement, these essays and translations are educational in intent but free from the brash and hectoring quality which vitiated so much of his later criticism.

It is easy to see how Pound's critical methods and his idea of tradition have determined the major techniques of his poetry (or did the early poetic successes determine his critical direction?). The method of bringing past and present together through literary allusion; the technique of the *persona*, which enables the poet to speak with the voice of another age or another personality; the artistic use of various imitated or "period" styles—these and other characteristics of Pound's verse are consonant in every way with his critical aims. The moral is that his poetry and prose should be read together, and in chronological order, to gain a just perspective on his immense achievement as a twentieth-century critic.

A brief catalogue of the major figures in Pound's "great tradition," and of his glaring omissions, will give a clear sense of the values he wished to resurrect and re-embody (it is instructive to compare Pound's view of the literary past with Eliot's; see the Introduction to the following section). In the classical world Pound's admiration is directed chiefly at Homer, whose narrative drive and masterful psychology he praised; and at the Latin poets (Catullus, Ovid, Propertius) whose wit, precision, and lack of sentimentality seemed proper antidotes to the diffuseness of much contemporary verse. In the middle ages it is the troubadours, masters of intricate verse-forms and the musical phrase, that Pound most admires, along with the total honesty and realism of

Villon. In the Renaissance the major translators of Latin and Greek, who in their own time were determined to "make it new," gain Pound's greatest attention, in tandem with the masters of song and musical statement: Waller, Campion, Dowland. In the nineteenth century Pound's emphasis is on those French poets who were exponents of ironic statement (as in Laforgue) and the precise presentation of emotion (Gautier), while in England it is Browning's dramatic monologues that capture his admiration. In the foreground of English literature two groups stand out: the decadent poets of the 'nineties, exemplars of a fine disregard for public standards, and the masters of nineteenth-century prose fiction—Stendhal, Flaubert, James—who led Pound to his famous dictum, "Poetry should be at least as well written as prose," by which he meant that most contemporary verse was loose and vague in contrast to the density of a novelist like Flaubert. Among his contemporaries, Pound's unerring taste within his own generation (it was to waver with successive generations of writers) led him to single out precisely those writers whom we now associate with the heroic age of modernism: Joyce, Eliot, Wyndham Lewis, Yeats. As the eye moves through this catalogue one thing is obvious: these were the artists whom Pound found useful in the shaping of his own art, so in a sense—as Wordsworth said of the great poet—he created the taste and audience which would come to appreciate his art.

Equally revealing are the obvious omissions in Pound's list: Shakespeare and the Renaissance dramatists, the entire eighteenth century, English Romantic poetry, the great Victorians. Obviously in the process of making a new tradition and cleansing the artist's palette, a great deal of the best in older literature had to be ignored or actively denigrated (see Pound's persistent attacks on Milton, which—like Eliot's—were done with an eye toward Milton's influence on the language of poetry, but which—unlike Eliot's—were never changed after the revolution in modern poetry had taken place). Pound's "tradition" is a personal and highly pragmatic view of the past, in sharp contrast to that judicious view which gradually developed in Eliot's criticism.

If we look for a key to Pound's treatment of his literary antecedents the method of Walter Pater comes immediately to mind, since Pater believed that the most effective criticism is that "which is itself a kind of construction, or creation, as it penetrates, through the given literary or artistic product, into the mental and inner constitution of the producer, shaping his work." Compare these two passages, the first from Pater's preface to *The Renaissance*, the second from Part VI, "On Virtue," of "I Gather the Limbs of Osiris":

. . . the function of the aesthetic critic is to distinguish, to analyze, and separate from its adjuncts, the virtue by which a picture, a landscape, a fair personality in life or in a book, produces this special impression of beauty or pleasure, to indicate what the source of that impression is, and under what conditions it is experienced. His end is reached when he has disengaged that virtue, and noted it . . .

The soul of each man is compounded of all the elements of the cosmos of souls, but in each soul there is some one element which predominates, which is in some peculiar and intense way the quality or *virtù* of the individual; in no two souls is this the same. It is by reason of this *virtù* that a given work of art persists. It is by reason of this *virtù* that we have one Catullus, one Villon . . .

One is reminded of Pound's early poem, "Histrion," in which he marks "how that the souls of all men great/ At times pass through us":

> Thus am I Dante for a space and am
> One François Villon, ballad-lord and thief . . .
> This for an instant and the flame is gone.

The power of Pound's criticism derives from his ability to disengage the "virtue," the essential quality, in the poets of tradition, and to re-create it for a moment in contemporary form. It is for this talent, above all others, that he will be longest read and admired.

The choice of essays for inclusion in this section may require some explanation. We have tried to represent the major kinds and forms of Pound's criticism, from the early *Spirit of Romance* to his pedagogical texts of the 1930's, while concentrating on that period (roughly 1911–18) when his criticism was most closely tied to the crucial developments in his own verse and English poetry in general. Thus his comments on the Imagist and Vorticist movements have been reproduced at length, as central examples of his method and its importance. Perhaps no example is more revealing than Pound's repeated critical use of the circumstances that surrounded the composition of his famous *haiku*, "In a Station of the Metro," a poem which has become the *locus classicus* for Imagist theory. The origins of the poem were first described in "How I Began" (June 1913; quoted below), and repeated in the essays on "Vorticism."

For well over a year I have been trying to make a poem of a very beautiful thing that befell me in the Paris Underground. I got out of a train at, I think, La Concorde and in the jostle I saw a beautiful face, and then, turning suddenly, another and another, and then a beautiful child's face, and then another beautiful face. All that day I tried to find words for what this made me feel. That night as I went home along the rue Raynouard I was still trying. I could get nothing but spots of colour. I remember thinking that if I had been a painter I might have started a wholly new school of painting. I tried to write the poem weeks afterwards in Italy, but found it useless. Then only the other night, wondering how I should tell the adventure, it struck me that in Japan, where a work of art is not estimated by its acreage and where sixteen syllables are counted enough for a poem if you arrange and punctuate them properly, one might make a very little poem which would be translated about as follows:

> "The apparition of these faces in the
>   crowd:
> "Petals on a wet, black bough."

And there, or in some other very old, very quiet civilisation, some one else might understand the significance.

It is fascinating to compare this early account with the fuller treatment in "Vorticism." What has occurred in the interim is the intervention of Pound's developing critical theory, so that in the final account the growth of the poem illustrates his fundamental aesthetic beliefs of the time: art as an "equation" for emotions (a precursor of Eliot's "objective correlative"); poetry as a possible vehicle for the "language of color," a medium in which the effects of modern painting can be achieved; Chinese poetry as a model of concision and "simultaneity"; the " 'one-image' poem" as a "form of super-position, that is to say it is one idea set on top of another"; the great poem as a record of "the precise instant when a thing outward and objective transforms itself, or darts into a thing inward and subjective." The entire process of putting "In a Station of the Metro" to critical use is a perfect example of the affinities between practice and theory in Pound's art, and may stand as our final emblem for his unique contribution to modern criticism.

A Note on Sources

The literary criticism of Ezra Pound (1885–   ), scattered through dozens of books and little magazines, has never been properly collected. The principal source is *Literary Essays of Ezra Pound,* ed. T. S. Eliot (1954), a fine gathering which is tilted somewhat toward the axis of Eliot's own criticism. Pound's major critical publications are: *The Spirit of Romance* (1910), a series of essays on Dante and the troubadours which reflects Pound's early scholarly interests; *Pavannes and Divisions* (1918) and *Instigations* (1920), which collect the most important essays of the 1912–18 period; *How to Read* (1931), a trial run for *ABC of Reading* (1934); *Make It New* (1934), a selection of the early essays which contains much material from *Pavannes and Divisions* and *Instigations,* and which indicates the direction of Pound's critical interests in the 1930's; and *Guide to Kulchur* (1938), an eccentric but brilliant analysis of the interactions between past and present. More recent sources are *The Letters of Ezra Pound,* ed. D. D. Paige (1950); *The Translations of Ezra Pound,* ed. Hugh Kenner (1953); and *Pavannes and Divagations* (1958), a gathering of miscellaneous comment which provides a nice introduction to Pound's day-by-day literary criticism. For a complete listing of Pound's critical writings see Donald Gallup, *A Bibliography of Ezra Pound* (1963).

Pound's literary criticism has not received the scholarly attention that it deserves, probably because of its bewildering variety and the "occasional" nature of many of the essays. The best comments on Pound as critic will be found in general studies of his career, especially Hugh Witemeyer, *The Poetry of Ezra Pound: Forms and Renewal, 1908–1920* (1969); Herbert N. Schneidau, *Ezra Pound: The Image and the Real* (1969); and Donald Davie, *Ezra Pound: Poet as Sculptor* (1964). A more systematic study of Pound's critical theory and its major sources may be found in N. Christoph de Nagy, *Ezra Pound's Poetics and Literary Tradition: The Critical Decade* (1966).

From the Preface to
The Spirit of Romance (1910)

THIS BOOK is not a philological work. Only by courtesy can it be said to be a study in comparative literature.

I am interested in poetry. I have attempted to examine certain forces, elements or qualities which were potent in the mediaeval literature of the Latin tongues, and are, I believe, still potent in our own.

The history of an art is the history of masterwork, not of failures, or mediocrity. The omniscient historian would display the masterpieces, their causes and their inter-relation. The study of literature is hero-worship. It is a refinement, or, if you will, a perversion of that primitive religion.

I have floundered somewhat ineffectually through the slough of philology, but I look forward to the time when it will be possible for the lover of poetry to study poetry—even the poetry of recondite times and places—without burdening himself with the rags of morphology, epigraphy, *privatleben* and the kindred delights of the archaeological or "scholarly" mind. I consider it quite as justifiable that a man should wish to study the poetry and nothing but the poetry of a certain period, as that he should study its antiquities, phonetics or paleography and be, at the end of his labours, incapable of discerning a refinement of style or a banality of diction.

There are a number of sciences connected with the study of literature. There is in literature itself the Art, which is not, and never will be, a science.

Art is a fluid moving above or over the minds of men.

Having violated one canon of modern prose by this metaphysical generality, I shall violate another. I shall make a florid and metaphorical comparison.

Art or an art is not unlike a river, in that it is perturbed at times by the quality of the river bed, but is in a way independent of that bed. The color of the water depends upon the substance of the bed and banks immediate and preceding. Stationary objects are reflected, but the quality of motion is of the river. The scientist is concerned with all of these things, the artist with that which flows.

It is dawn at Jerusalem while midnight hovers above the Pillars of Hercules. All ages are contemporaneous. It is B.C., let us say, in Morocco. The Middle Ages are in Russia. The future stirs already in the minds of the few. This is especially true of literature, where the real time is independent of the apparent, and where many dead men are our grandchildren's contemporaries, while many of our contemporaries have been already gathered into Abraham's bosom, or some more fitting receptacle.

What we need is a literary scholarship, which will weigh Theocritus and Yeats with one balance, and which will judge dull dead men as inexorably as dull writers of today, and will, with equity, give praise to beauty before referring to an almanack.

Art is a joyous thing. Its happiness antedates even Whistler; apropos of which I would in all seriousness plead for a greater levity, a more befitting levity, in our study of the arts.

Good art never bores one. By that I mean

that it is the business of the artist to prevent ennui; in the literary art, to relieve, refresh, revive the mind of the reader—at reasonable intervals—with some form of ecstasy, by some splendor of thought, some presentation of sheer beauty, some lightning turn of phrase—laughter is no mean ecstasy. Good art begins with an escape from dullness.

The aim of the present work is to instruct. Its ambition is to instruct painlessly.

From I Gather the Limbs of Osiris

(1911-12)

IV. A BEGINNING

IN MY OPENING CHAPTER I said that there were certain facts or points, or "luminous details," which governed knowledge as the switchboard the electric circuit. In the study of the art of letters these points are particular works or the works of particular authors.

Let us suppose a man, ignorant of painting, taken into a room containing a picture by Fra Angelico, a picture by Rembrandt, one by Velasquez, Memling, Rafael, Monet, Beardsley, Hokusai, Whistler, and a fine example of the art of some forgotten Egyptian. He is told that this is painting and that every one of these is master-work. He is, if a thoughtful man, filled with confusion. These things obey no common apparent law. He confesses, if intelligent, to an ignorance of the art of painting. If he is a natural average human he hates part of the work, perhaps violently; he is attracted, perhaps, by the subjects of some of the pictures. Apart from the subject matter he accepts the Rafael, then, perhaps, the Rembrandt or the Velasquez or the Monet or the Memling, and then the Whistler or the An-

First appeared in *The New Age* (London), Dec. 21, 1911.

gelico or the Egyptian, and last the Beardsley. Or he does it in different order. He calls some ugly and some pretty. If, however, he is a specialist, a man thoroughly trained in some other branch of knowledge, his feelings are not unlike mine when I am taken into the engineering laboratory and shown successively an electric engine, a steam-engine, a gas-engine, etc. I realise that there are a number of devices, all designed for more or less the same end, none "better," none "worse," all different. Each, perhaps, slightly more fit for use under certain conditions for certain objects minutely differentiated. They all "produce power"—that is, they gather the latent energy of Nature and focus it on a certain resistance. The latent energy is made dynamic or "revealed" to the engineer in control, and placed at his disposal.

As for me—the visitor in the engine-room—I perceive "sources"—not ultimate sources, but sources—of light, heat, motion, etc. I realise the purpose and effect; I know it would take me some time really to understand the rules in accordance with which any engine works, and that these rules are similar and different with different engines.

* * *

To read a number of books written at different ages and in different tongues may arouse our curiosity and may fill us with a sense of our ignorance of the laws of the art in accordance with which they are written. The fact that every masterpiece contains its law within itself, self-sufficing to itself, does not simplify the solution. Before we can discuss any possible "laws of art" we must know, at least, a little of the various stages by which that art has grown from what it was to what it is. This is simply restatement of what ought to be in every text-book, and has nothing to do with any "new method." The handiest way to some knowledge of these "various stages" is, however, by "the new method"—that of luminous detail.

Interesting works are of two sorts, the "symptomatic" and the "donative"; thus a sestina of Pico della Mirandola, concerned for the most part with Jove and Phoebus, shows us a Provençal form stuffed with revived classicism. Camoen's "Os Lusiadas" has a similar value. In them we find a reflection of tendencies and modes of a time. They mirror obvious and apparent thought movements. They are what one might have expected in such and such a year and place. They register.

But the "donative" author seems to draw down into the art something which was not in the art of his predecessors. If he also draws from the air about him, he draws latent forces, or things present but unnoticed, or things perhaps taken for granted but never examined.

Non e mai tarde per tentar l'ignoto. His forbears may have led up to him; he is never a disconnected phenomenon, but he does take some step further. He discovers, or, better, "he discriminates." We advance by discriminations, by discerning that things hitherto deemed identical or similar are dissimilar; that things hitherto deemed dissimilar, mutually foreign, antagonistic, are similar and harmonic.

Assume that, by the translations of "The Seafarer" and of Guido's lyrics, I have given evidence that fine poetry may consist of elements that are or seem to be almost mutually exclusive. In the canzoni of Arnaut Daniel we find a beauty, a beauty of elements almost unused in these two other very different sorts of poetry. That beauty is, or would be if you read Provençal, a thing apparent, at least, a thing not to be helped or thrust upon you by any prose of mine. In the translations (to follow next week) I give that beauty—reproduced, that is, as nearly as I can reproduce it in English—for what it is worth. What I must now do—as the scholar—in pursuance of my announced "method" is to justify my use of Arnaut's work as a strategic position, as "luminous detail."

We advance by discriminations, and to Arnaut Daniel we may ascribe discriminations. The poems of Arnaut were written in Provence about 1180–1200 A.D., about a century, that is, before the love poems of Dante and of Guido. And if he, Arnaut, frequented one court more than another it was the court of King Richard "Coeur de Lion," "Plantagenet," in compliment to whose sister (presumably) he rimes to "genebres" in Canzon XVI.

"Ans per s'amor sia laurs o genebres"—"Her love is as the laurel or the broom is." The compliment is here given, presumably, to Mona Laura and the Lady Plantagenet (or, in Provençal, *Planta genebres*), or it is, may be, only in homage to the loyalty of Richard himself. After seven centuries one cannot be too explicit in the unravelling of personal allusion. To be born a troubadour in Provence in the twelfth century was to be born, you would say, "in one's due time." It was to be born after two centuries of poetic tradition, of tradition that had run in one groove—to wit, the making of canzoni. The art might have, you would say, had time to come to flower, to perfect itself. Moreover, as an art it had few rivals; of painting and sculpture there was little or none. The art of song was to these people literature and opera: their books and their theatre. In the north of France the longer narrative poems held the field against it, but the two arts were fraternal, and one guild presided over them—not a formal guild, that is, but the same people purveyed them.

Now in the flower of this age, when many people were writing canzoni, or had just written them—Jaufre Rudel, Ventadorn, Borneilh, Marvoil, de Born—Arnaut discriminated between rhyme and rhyme.

He perceived, that is, that the beauty to be gotten from a similarity of line-terminations depends not upon their multiplicity, but upon their action the one upon the other; not upon frequency, but upon the manner of sequence and combination. The effect of "lais" in monorhyme, or of a canzon in which a few rhymes appear too often, is monotonous, is monotonous beyond the point where monotony is charming or interesting. Arnaut uses what for want of a better term I call polyphonic rhyme.

At a time when both prose and poetry were loose-jointed, prolix, barbaric, he, to all intents and purposes, virtually rediscovered "style." He conceived, that is, a manner of writing in which each word should bear some burden, should make some special contribution to the effect of the whole. The poem is an organism in which each part functionates, gives to sound or to sense something—preferably to sound *and* sense gives something.

Thirdly, he discerns what Plato had discerned some time before, that μέλος is the union of words, rhythm, and music (i.e., that part of music which we do not perceive as rhythm). Intense hunger for a strict accord between these three has marked only the best lyric periods, and Arnaut felt this hunger more keenly and more precisely than his fellows or his forerunners.

He is significant for all these things. He bears to the technique of *accented* verse of Europe very much the same relation that Euclid does to our mathematics. For these things Dante honoured him in his "Treatise on the Common Speech," and he honoured him in the "Divina Commedia" for these three things and for perhaps one other—a matter of content, not of artistry, yet a thing intimate and bound in with the other three. For that fineness of Arnaut's senses which made him chary of his rhymes, impatient of tunes that would have distorted his language, fastidious of redundance, made him likewise accurate in his observation of Nature.

For long after him the poets of the North babbled of gardens where "three birds sang on every bough" and where other things and creatures behaved as in nature they do not behave. And, apart from his rhyme, apart from the experiments in artistry which led in so great part to the conclusions in the "Treatise on the Common Tongue," [1] it is this that Dante learns from him, this precision of observation and reference. "*Que jes Rozers*" sings Daniel, "*Dove l'Adige*" the other. And it will be difficult to prove that there is not some recognition and declaration of this in the passage in the Purgatorio (Canto XXVI.) where Arnaut is made to reply—

> *E vei jausen lo jorn qu'esper denan—*
> I see rejoicing the day that is before.

If this is not definite allegory, it is at least clearer than many allegories that tradition has brought to us, bound in through the "Commedia." If Dante does not here use Arnaut as a symbol of perceptive intelligence, sincere, making no pretence to powers beyond its own, but seeing out of its time and place, rejoicing in its perspicacity, we can at least, from our later vantage, find in this trait of Arnaut's some germ of the Renaissance, of the spirit which was to overthrow superstition and dogma, of the "scientific spirit" if you will, for science is unpoetic only to minds jaundiced with sentiment and romanticism—the great masters of the past boasted all they could of it and found it magical; of the spirit which finds itself most perfectly expressed and formulated in this speech which Merejkowski has set in the mouth of Leonardo da Vinci—I think on authority of the writings of the latter—when he is speaking of the artist, of the Greek and Roman classics, and of Nature: "Few men will drink from the cup when they may drink from the fountain."

---

[1] I do not mean that Dante here accepts all Arnaut's forms and fashions. Arnaut's work as we have it shows constant search and rejection.

VI. ON VIRTUE

IN AN EARLIER CHAPTER I said that interesting authors were either "symptomatic" or "donative"; permit me new diameters and a new circumscription, even if I seem near to repetition.

As contemporary philosophy has so far resolved itself into a struggle to disagree as to the terms in which we shall define an indefinable something upon which we have previously agreed to agree, I ask the reader to regard what follows not as dogma, but as a metaphor which I find convenient to express certain relations.

The soul of each man is compounded of all the elements of the cosmos of souls, but in each soul there is some one element which predominates, which is in some peculiar and intense way the quality or *virtù* of the individual; in no two souls is this the same. It is by reason of this *virtù* that a given work of art persists. It is by reason of this *virtù* that we have one Catullus, one Villon; by reason of it that no amount of technical cleverness can produce a work having the same charm as the original, not though all progress in art is, in so great degree, a progress through imitation.

This virtue is not a "point of view," nor an "attitude toward life"; nor is it the mental calibre or "a way of thinking," but something more substantial which influences all these. We may as well agree, at this point, that we do not all of us think in at all the same sort of way or by the same sort of implements. Making a rough and incomplete category from personal experience I can say that certain people think with words, certain with, or in, objects; others realise nothing until they have pictured it; others progress by diagrams like those of the geometricians; some think, or construct, in rhythm, or by rhythms and sound; others, the unfortunate, move by words disconnected

First appeared in *The New Age* (London), Jan. 4, 1912.

from the objects to which they might correspond, or more unfortunate still in blocks and *clichés* of words; some, favoured of Apollo, in words that hover above and cling close to the things they mean. And all these different sorts of people have most appalling difficulty in understanding each other.

It is the artist's business to find his own *virtù*. This virtue may be what you will:—

Luteum pede soccum, . . .
Viden ut faces
Splendidas quatiunt comas? . . .
Luteumve papauer.

It may be something which draws Catullus to write of scarlet poppies, of orange-yellow slippers, of the shaking, glorious hair of the torches; or Propertius to

Quoscumque smaragdos
Quosve dedit flavo lumine chrysolithos.
—The honey-coloured light.

Or it may be the so attractive, so nickel-plated neatness which brings Mr. Pope so to the quintessence of the obvious, with:—

Man is not a fly.

So far as mortal immortality is concerned, the poet need only discover his *virtù* and survive the discovery long enough to write some few scant dozen verses—providing, that is, that he have acquired some reasonable technique, this latter being the matter of a lifetime—or not, according to the individual facility.

Beyond the discovery and expression of his virtue the artist may proceed to the erection of his microcosmos.

"Ego tamquam centrum circuli, quae omnes circumferentiae partes habet equaliter, tu autem non sic"—"I am the centre of a circle which possesseth all parts of its circumference equally, but thou not so," says the angel appearing to Dante ("Vita Nuova," XII).

Having discovered his own virtue the artist will be more likely to discern and allow for a peculiar *virtù* in others. The erection of the microcosmos consists in discriminating these other powers and in holding them in orderly arrangement about one's own. The process is uncommon. Dante, of all men, performed it in the most symmetrical and barefaced manner; yet I would for you—as I have done already for myself—stretch the fabric of my critique upon four great positions.

Among the poets there have been four men in especial virtuous, or, since virtues are so hard to define, let us say they represent four distinct phases of consciousness:

Homer of the Odyssey, man conscious of the world outside him; and if we accept the tradition of Homer's blindness, we may find in that blindness the significant cause of his power; for him the outer world would have been a place of mystery, of uncertainty, of things severed from their attendant trivialities, of acts, each one cloaked in some glamour of the inexperienced; his work, therefore, a work of imagination and not of observation;

Dante, in the "Divina Commedia," man conscious of the world within him;

Chaucer, man conscious of the variety of persons about him, not so much of their acts and the outlines of their acts as of their character, their personalities; with the inception of this sort of interest any epic period comes to its end;

Shakespeare, man conscious of himself in the world about him—as Dante had been conscious of the spaces of the mind, its reach and its perspective.

I doubt not that a person of wider reading could make a better arrangement of names than this is, but I must talk from my corner of the things that I know; at any rate, each of these men constructed some sort of world into which we may plunge ourselves and find a life not glaringly incomplete. Of the last three we know definitely that each of them swept into his work the virtues of many forerunners and contemporaries, and that in no case do these obtrude or disturb the poise of the whole.

I believe sincerely that any man who has read these four authors with attention will find that a great many other works, now accepted as classic, rather bore him; he will understand their beauty, but with this understanding will come the memory of having met the same sort of beauty elsewhere in greater intensity. It will be said, rather, that he understands the books than that the books enlighten him. In the culture of the mind, as in the culture of fields, there is a law of diminishing return. If a book reveal to us something of which we were unconscious, it feeds us with its energy; if it reveal to us nothing but the fact that its author knew something which we knew, it draws energy from us.

Now it is inconceivable that any knowledge of Homer, Dante, Chaucer, and Shakespeare could ever diminish our enjoyment of Sappho, or of Villon, or of Heine, or of the "Poema del Cid," or, perhaps, of Leopardi, though we would enjoy him in great part as a commentator, as a friend looking with us toward the classics and seeing, perhaps, into them further than we had seen.

The donative authors, or the real classics, interilluminate each other, and I should define a "classic" as a book our enjoyment of which cannot be diminished by any amount of reading of other books, or even—and this is the fiercer test—by a first-hand knowledge of life.

Any author whose light remains visible in this place where the greater lamps are flashing back and forth upon each other is of no mean importance; of him it can be said without qualification that he has attained his own *virtù*. It is true that the results of Guido Cavalcanti and of Arnaut Daniel are in great measure included in the "Divina Commedia," yet there remains over a portion not quite soluble, and in trying at this late date to reinstate them in our canon, I do nothing that Dante has not done before me; one reads their work, in fact, on his advice ("Purgatorio," XI and XXVI). In each case their virtue is a virtue of precision. In Arnaut, as I have said before, this fineness has its effect in his style, his form, the relation of his words and tune, and in his content.

IX. ON TECHNIQUE

"SKILL IN TECHNIQUE," says Joseph Conrad, "is something more than honesty." And if this is applicable to the racing of yachts it should be no less applicable to the writing of poetry.

We can imagine easily the delight of Ysaye and M. Nickisch on being invited, firstly to dinner and secondly to listen to your fourteen-year-old daughter play Beethoven; or lifting the parallel to more exact preciseness, let us suppose the child, never having taken a music lesson in her life, hears Busoni play Chopin, and on the spur of the moment, thinking to produce similar effect, hires a hall and produces what she thinks sounds somewhat the same. These things are in the realm of music mildly unthinkable; but then the ordinary piano teacher spends more thought on the art of music than does the average "poet" on the art of poetry. No great composer has, so far as I know, boasted an ignorance of musical tradition or thought himself less a musician because he could play Mozart correctly. Yet it is not uncommon to hear practising "poets" speak of "technique" as if it were a thing antipathetic to "poetry." And they mean something that is more or less true. Likewise you will hear people, one set of them, raging against form—by which they mean external symmetry—and another set against free verse. And it is quite certain that none of these people have any exact, effable concept of what they do mean; or if they have a definite dislike of something properly dislikable, they only succeeded in expressing a dislike for something not quite it and not quite not it.

As for the ancients, we say for them it was quite easy. There was then an interest in poetry. Homer had the advantage of writing for an audience each of whom knew something of

First appeared in *The New Age* (London), Jan. 25, 1912.

a ship and of a sword. One could allude to things that all understood.

Let us imagine to-day a contest between Jack Johnson and the surviving "White Hope"; let us imagine Court circles deeply interested; let us imagine Olympia filled half with the "flower of the realm" and half with chieftains from Zlyzmmbaa; let us suppose that everyone had staked their last half-crown, and that the victors were going to rape all the wives and daughters of the vanquished, and there was a divorce scandal inextricably entangled in the affair; and that if the blacks won they were going to burn the National Gallery and the home of Sir Florence Tlallina-Lalina.

It is very hard to reproduce the simplicity of the epic period. Browning does, it is true, get at life almost as "simply" as did Ovid and Catullus; but then he was one "classicist" 'mid a host of Victorians. Even this is not Homer.

Let us return to our hypothetical prize-fight. In an account of the fight what details would we demand? Fine psychological analysis of the combatants? Character study? Or the sort of details that a sporting crowd want from a fight that they have stakes on? Left-lead for the jaw. Counter. If the fight were as important as the one mentioned they might even take it from one who called sacred things by uninitiated names: "an almighty swat in the thorax," "wot-for in the kisser," "a resounding blow upon the optic"—bad, this last. Leave it in the hands of the "descriptive writer." *Qui sono io profano.*

The very existence of the "descriptive writer" shows that the people are not without some vague, indefined hunger for euphues, for the decorated "Elizabethan" speech. And the "descriptive writer" is so rare, I am told, that one "great daily" had to have their "coronation" done by an Italian and translated.

And as for poetry, for verse, and the people,

I remember a series of "poems" in a new form that ran long in the "New York Journal," and with acclaim, one a day. Alas! I can only remember two of them, as follows:—

1. In the days of old Pompei
   Did the people get away?
                          Nay! Nay!

2. In the days of Charlemagne
   Did the people get champagne?
                          Guess again!

Yet even these verses will appeal only to "certain classes," and our prize-fight is a phantom, *Eheu fugaces!* How, then, shall the poet in this dreary day attain universality, how write what will be understood of "the many" and lauded of "the few"?

What interest have all men in common? What forces play upon them all? Money and sex and to-morrow. And we have called money "fate" until that game is played out. And sex? Well, poetry has been erotic, or amative, or something of that sort—at least, a vast deal of it has—ever since it stopped being epic—and this sort of thing interests the inexperienced. And to-morrow? We none of us agree about.

We are nevertheless one humanity, compounded of one mud and of one aether; and every man who does his own job really well has a latent respect for every other man who does *his* own job really well; this is our lasting bond; whether it be a matter of buying up all the little brass farthings in Cuba and selling them at a quarter per cent. advance, or of delivering steam-engines to King Menelek across three rivers and one hundred and four ravines, or of conducting some new crotchety variety of employers' liability insurance, or of punching another man's head, the man who really does the thing well, if he be pleased afterwards to talk about it, gets always his auditors' attention; he gets his audience the moment he says something so intimate that it proves him the expert; he does not, as a rule, sling generalities; he gives the particular case for what it is worth; the truth is the individual.

As for the arts and their technique—tech-nique is the means of conveying an exact impression of exactly what one means in such a way as to exhilarate.

When it comes to poetry, I hold no brief for any particular system of metric. Europe supplies us with three or five or perhaps more systems. The early Greek system of measure by quantity, which becomes the convention of later Greek and of Latin verse; the Provençal system, measure (*a*) by number of syllables, (*b*) by number of stressed syllables, which has become the convention of most European poetry; the Anglo-Saxon system of alliteration; these all concern the scansion. For terminations we have rhyme in various arrangements, blank verse, and the Spanish system of assonance. English is made up of Latin, French, and Anglo-Saxon, and it is probable that all these systems concern us. It is not beyond the pales of possibility that English verse of the future will be a sort of orchestration taking account of all these systems.

When I say above that technique is the means of conveying an exact impression of exactly what one means, I do not by any means mean that poetry is to be stripped of any of its powers of vague suggestion. Our life is, in so far as it is worth living, made up in great part of things indefinite, impalpable; and it is precisely because the arts present us these things that we—humanity—cannot get on without the arts. The picture that suggests indefinite poems, the line of verse that means a gallery of paintings, the modulation that suggests a score of metaphors and is contained in none: it is these things that touch us nearly that "matter."

The artist discriminates, that is, between one kind of indefinability and another, and poetry is a very complex art. Its media are on one hand the simplest, the least interesting, and on the other the most arcane, most fascinating. It is an art of pure sound bound in through an art of arbitrary and conventional symbols. In so far as it is an art of pure sound, it is allied with music, painting, sculpture; in so far as it is an art of arbitrary symbols, it is allied to prose.

A word exists when two or more people agree to mean the same thing by it.

Permit me one more cumbersome simile, for I am trying to say something about the masterly use of words, and it is not easy. Let us imagine that words are like great hollow cones of steel of different dullness and acuteness; I say great because I want them not too easy to move; they must be of different sizes. Let us imagine them charged with a force like electricity, or, rather, radiating a force from their apexes—some radiating, some sucking in. We must have a greater variety of activity than with electricity—not merely positive and negative; but let us say $+$, $-$, $\times$, $\div$, $+a$, $-a$, $\times a$, $\div a$, etc. Some of these kinds of force neutralise each other, some augment; but the only way any two cones can be got to act without waste is for them to be so placed that their apexes and a line of surface meet exactly. When this conjunction occurs let us say their force is not added one's to the other's, but multiplied the one's by the other's; thus three or four words in exact juxtaposition are capable of radiating this energy at a very high potentiality; mind you, the juxtaposition of their vertices must be exact and the angles or "signs" of discharge must augment and not neutralise each other. This peculiar energy which fills the cones is the power of tradition, of centuries of race consciousness, of agreement, of association; and the control of it is the "Technique of Content," which nothing short of genius understands.

There is the slighter "technique of manner," a thing reducible almost to rules, a matter of "j's" and "d's," of order and sequence, a thing attenuable, a thing verging off until it degenerates into rhetoric; and this slighter technique is also a thing of price, notwithstanding that all the qualities which differentiate poetry from prose are things born before syntax; this technique of surface is valuable above its smoother virtues simply because it is technique, and because technique is the only gauge and test of a man's lasting sincerity.

Everyone, or nearly everyone, feels at one time or another poetic, and falls to writing verses; but only that man who cares and believes really in the pint of truth that is in him will work, year in and year out, to find the perfect expression.

If technique is thus the protection of the public, the sign manual by which it distinguishes between the serious artist and the disagreeable young person expressing its haedinus egotism, it is no less a protection to the artist himself during the most crucial period of his development. I speak now of technique seriously studied, of a searching into cause and effect, into the purposes of sound and rhythm as such, not—not by any means—of a conscientious and clever imitation of the master of the moment, of the poet in vogue.

How many have I seen, how many have we all of us known, young, with promising poetic insides, who produce one book and die of it? For in our time, at least, the little public that does read new poetry is not twice bored by the same aspirant, and if a man's first book has not in it some sign of a serious struggle with the bases of the art he has small likelihood of meeting them in a second. But the man who has some standard reasonably high—consider, says Longinus, in what mood Diogenes or Sophocles would have listened to your effusion —does, while he is striving to bring his work within reach of his own conception of it, get rid of the first froth of verse, which is in nearly every case quite like the first verse-froth of everyone else. He emerges decently clean after some reasonable purgation, not nearly a master, but licensed, an initiate, with some chance of conserving his will to speak and of seeing it mature and strengthen with the ripening and strengthening of the mind itself until, by the favour of the gods, he come upon some lasting excellence.

Let the poet who has been not too long ago born make very sure of this, that no one cares to hear, in strained iambics, that he feels sprightly in spring, is uncomfortable when his sexual desires are ungratified, and that he has read about human brotherhood in last year's magazines. But let a man once convince thirty people that he has some faint chance of finding, or that he, at least, is determined and ready to suffer all drudgery in attempting to find, some entanglement of words so subtle, so crafty that they can be read or heard without yawning, after the reading of Pindar and Me-leager, and of "As ye came from the holy land of Walsinghame" and "Tamlin," and of a passage from John Keats—let thirty or a dozen people believe this, and the man of whom they believe it will find friendship where he had little expected it, and delightful things will befall him suddenly and with no other explanation.

Imagism

PROLEGOMENA (1912)

TIME WAS when the poet lay in a green field with his head against a tree and played his diversion on a ha'penny whistle, and Caesar's predecessors conquered the earth, and the predecessors of golden Crassus embezzled, and fashions had their say, and let him alone. And presumably he was fairly content in this circumstance, for I have small doubt that the occasional passer-by, being attracted by curiosity to know why any one should lie under a tree and blow diversion on a ha'penny whistle, came and conversed with him, and that among these passers-by there was on occasion a person of charm or a young lady who had not read *Man and Superman;* and looking back upon this naïve state of affairs we call it the age of gold.

Metastasio, and he should know if any one, assures us that this age endures—even though the modern poet is expected to holloa his verses down a speaking tube to the editors of cheap magazines—S. S. McClure, or some one of that sort—even though hordes of authors

meet in dreariness and drink healths to the "Copyright Bill"; even though these things be, the age of gold pertains. Imperceivably, if you like, but pertains. You meet unkempt Amyclas in a Soho restaurant and chant together of dead and forgotten things—it is a manner of speech among poets to chant of dead, half-forgotten things, there seems no special harm in it; it has always been done—and it's rather better to be a clerk in the Post Office than to look after a lot of stinking, verminous sheep—and at another hour of the day one substitutes the drawing-room for the restaurant and tea is probably more palatable than mead and mare's milk, and little cakes than honey. And in this fashion one survives the resignation of Mr. Balfour, and the iniquities of the American customs-house, *e quel bufera infernal,* the periodical press. And then in the middle of it, there being apparently no other person at once capable and available one is stopped and asked to explain oneself.

I begin on the chord thus querulous, for I would much rather lie on what is left of Catullus' parlour floor and speculate the azure beneath it and the hills off to Salo and Riva with their forgotten gods moving unhindered amongst them, than discuss any processes and theories of art whatsoever. I would rather play tennis. I shall not argue.

CREDO

Rhythm. I believe in an "absolute rhythm," a rhythm, that is, in poetry which corresponds exactly to the emotion or shade of emotion to be expressed. A man's rhythm must be interpretative, it will be, therefore, in the end, his own, uncounterfeiting, uncounterfeitable.

Symbols. I believe that the proper and perfect symbol is the natural object, that if a man use "symbols" he must so use them that their symbolic function does not obtrude; so that *a* sense, and the poetic quality of the passage, is not lost to those who do not understand the symbol as such, to whom, for instance, a hawk is a hawk.

Technique. I believe in technique as the test of a man's sincerity; in law when it is ascertainable; in the trampling down of every convention that impedes or obscures the determination of the law, or the precise rendering of the impulse.

Form. I think there is a "fluid" as well as a "solid" content, that some poems may have form as a tree has form, some as water poured into a vase. That most symmetrical forms have certain uses. That a vast number of subjects cannot be precisely, and therefore not properly rendered in symmetrical forms.

"Thinking that alone worthy wherein the whole art is employed." [1] I think the artist should master all known forms and systems of metric, and I have with some persistence set about doing this, searching particularly into those periods wherein the systems came to birth or attained their maturity. It has been complained, with some justice, that I dump my note-books on the public. I think that only after a long struggle will poetry attain such a degree of development, or, if you will, modernity, that it will vitally concern people who are accustomed, in prose, to Henry James and

[1] Dante, *De Volgari Eloquio.*

Anatole France, in music to Debussy. I am constantly contending that it took two centuries of Provence and one of Tuscany to develop the media of Dante's masterwork, that it took the latinists of the Renaissance, and the Pleiade, and his own age of painted speech to prepare Shakespeare his tools. It is tremendously important that great poetry be written, it makes no jot of difference who writes it. The experimental demonstrations of one man may save the time of many—hence my furore over Arnaut Daniel—if a man's experiments try out one new rime, or dispense conclusively with one iota of currently accepted nonsense, he is merely playing fair with his colleagues when he chalks up his result.

No man ever writes very much poetry that "matters." In bulk, that is, no one produces much that is final, and when a man is not doing this highest thing, this saying the thing once for all and perfectly; when he is not matching Ποικιλόθρον', ἀθάνατ' 'Αφρόδιτα, or "Hist—said Kate the Queen," he had much better be making the sorts of experiment which may be of use to him in his later work, or to his successors.

"The lyf so short, the craft so long to lerne." It is a foolish thing for a man to begin his work on a too narrow foundation, it is a disgraceful thing for a man's work not to show steady growth and increasing fineness from first to last.

As for "adaptations"; one finds that all the old masters of painting recommend to their pupils that they begin by copying masterwork, and proceed to their own composition.

As for "Every man his own poet," the more every man knows about poetry the better. I believe in every one writing poetry who wants to; most do. I believe in every man knowing enough of music to play "God bless our home" on the harmonium, but I do not believe in every man giving concerts and printing his sin.

The mastery of any art is the work of a lifetime. I should not discriminate between the "amateur" and the "professional." Or rather I should discriminate quite often in favour of the amateur, but I should discriminate between the amateur and the expert. It is certain that the present chaos will endure until the Art of poetry has been preached down the amateur gullet, until there is such a general understanding of the fact that poetry is an art and not a pastime; such a knowledge of technique; of technique of surface and technique of content, that the amateurs will cease to try to drown out the masters.

If a certain thing was said once for all in Atlantis or Arcadia, in 450 Before Christ or in 1290 after, it is not for us moderns to go saying it over, or to go obscuring the memory of the dead by saying the same thing with less skill and less conviction.

My pawing over the ancients and semi-ancients has been one struggle to find out what has been done, once for all, better than it can ever be done again, and to find out what remains for us to do, and plenty does remain, for if we still feel the same emotions as those which launched the thousand ships, it is quite certain that we come on these feelings differently, through different nuances, by different intellectual gradations. Each age has its own abounding gifts yet only some ages transmute them into matter of duration. No good poetry is ever written in a manner twenty years old, for to write in such a manner shows conclusively that the writer thinks from books, convention and *cliché*, and not from life, yet a man feeling the divorce of life and his art may naturally try to resurrect a forgotten mode if he finds in that mode some leaven, or if he think he sees in it some element lacking in contemporary art which might unite that art again to its sustenance, life.

In the art of Daniel and Cavalcanti, I have seen that precision which I miss in the Victorians, that explicit rendering, be it of external nature, or of emotion. Their testimony is of the eyewitness, their symptoms are first hand.

As for the nineteenth century, with all respect to its achievements, I think we shall look back upon it as a rather blurry, messy sort of a period, a rather sentimentalistic, mannerish sort of a period. I say this without any self-righteousness, with no self-satisfaction.

As for there being a "movement" or my being of it, the conception of poetry as a "pure art" in the sense in which I use the term, revived with Swinburne. From the puritanical revolt to Swinburne, poetry had been merely the vehicle—yes, definitely, Arthur Symon's scruples and feelings about the word not withholding—the ox-cart and post-chaise for transmitting thoughts poetic or otherwise. And perhaps the "great Victorians," though it is doubtful, and assuredly the "nineties" continued the development of the art, confining their improvements, however, chiefly to sound and to refinements of manner.

Mr Yeats has once and for all stripped English poetry of its perdamnable rhetoric. He has boiled away all that is not poetic—and a good deal that is. He has become a classic in his own lifetime and *nel mezzo del cammin*. He has made our poetic idiom a thing pliable, a speech without inversions.

Robert Bridges, Maurice Hewlett and Frederic Manning are in their different ways seriously concerned with overhauling the metric, in testing the language and its adaptability to certain modes. Ford Hueffer is making some sort of experiments in modernity. The Provost of Oriel continues his translation of the *Divina Commedia*.

As to Twentieth century poetry, and the poetry which I expect to see written during the next decade or so, it will, I think, move against poppy-cock, it will be harder and saner, it will be what Mr Hewlett calls "nearer the bone." It will be as much like granite as it can be, its force will lie in its truth, its interpretative power (of course, poetic force does always rest there); I mean it will not try to seem forcible by rhetorical din, and luxurious riot. We will have fewer painted adjectives impeding the shock and stroke of it. At least for myself, I want it so, austere, direct, free from emotional slither.

A FEW DON'TS (1913)

An "image" is that which presents an intellectual and emotional complex in an instant of time. I use the term "complex" rather in the technical sense employed by the newer psychologists, such as Hart, though we might not agree absolutely in our application.

It is the presentation of such a "complex" instantaneously which gives that sense of sudden liberation; that sense of freedom from time limits and space limits; that sense of sudden growth, which we experience in the presence of the greatest works of art.

It is better to present one Image in a lifetime than to produce voluminous works.

All this, however, some may consider open to debate. The immediate necessity is to tabulate A LIST OF DON'TS for those beginning to write verses. I can not put all of them into Mosaic negative.

To begin with, consider the three propositions (demanding direct treatment, economy of words, and the sequence of the musical phrase), not as dogma—never consider anything as dogma—but as the result of long contemplation, which, even if it is some one else's contemplation, may be worth consideration.

Pay no attention to the criticism of men who have never themselves written a notable work. Consider the discrepancies between the actual writing of the Greek poets and dramatists, and the theories of the Graeco-Roman grammarians, concocted to explain their metres.

LANGUAGE

Use no superfluous word, no adjective which does not reveal something.

Don't use such an expression as "dim lands *of peace.*" It dulls the image. It mixes an abstraction with the concrete. It comes from the writer's not realizing that the natural object is always the *adequate* symbol.

Go in fear of abstractions. Do not retell in mediocre verse what has already been done in good prose. Don't think any intelligent person is going to be deceived when you try to shirk all the difficulties of the unspeakably difficult art of good prose by chopping your composition into line lengths.

What the expert is tired of today the public will be tired of tomorrow.

Don't imagine that the art of poetry is any simpler than the art of music, or that you can please the expert before you have spent at least as much effort on the art of verse as the average piano teacher spends on the art of music.

Be influenced by as many great artists as you can, but have the decency either to acknowledge the debt outright, or to try to conceal it.

Don't allow "influence" to mean merely that you mop up the particular decorative vocabulary of some one or two poets whom you happen to admire. A Turkish war correspondent was recently caught red-handed babbling in his despatches of "dove-grey" hills, or else it was "pearl-pale," I can not remember.

Use either no ornament or good ornament.

RHYTHM AND RHYME

Let the candidate fill his mind with the finest cadences he can discover, preferably in a foreign language,[1] so that the meaning of the words may be less likely to divert his attention from the movement; e.g. Saxon charms, Hebridean Folk Songs, the verse of Dante, and the lyrics of Shakespeare—if he can dissociate the vocabulary from the cadence. Let him dissect the lyrics of Goethe coldly into their component sound values, syllables long and short, stressed and unstressed, into vowels and consonants.

[1] This is for rhythm, his vocabulary must of course be found in his native tongue.

It is not necessary that a poem should rely on its music, but if it does rely on its music that music must be such as will delight the expert.

Let the neophyte know assonance and alliteration, rhyme immediate and delayed, simple and polyphonic, as a musician would expect to know harmony and counterpoint and all the minutiae of his craft. No time is too great to give to these matters or to any one of them, even if the artist seldom have need of them.

Don't imagine that a thing will "go" in verse just because it's too dull to go in prose.

Don't be "viewy"—leave that to the writers of pretty little philosophic essays. Don't be descriptive; remember that the painter can describe a landscape much better than you can, and that he has to know a deal more about it.

When Shakespeare talks of the "Dawn in russet mantle clad" he presents something which the painter does not present. There is in this line of his nothing that one can call description; he presents.

Consider the way of the scientists rather than the way of an advertising agent for a new soap.

The scientist does not expect to be acclaimed as a great scientist until he has *discovered* something. He begins by learning what has been discovered already. He goes from that point onward. He does not bank on being a charming fellow personally. He does not expect his friends to applaud the results of his freshman class work. Freshmen in poetry are unfortunately not confined to a definite and recognizable class room. They are "all over the shop." Is it any wonder "the public is indifferent to poetry"?

Don't chop your stuff into separate *iambs*. Don't make each line stop dead at the end, and then begin every next line with a heave. Let the beginning of the next line catch the rise of the rhythm wave, unless you want a definite longish pause.

In short, behave as a musician, a good musician, when dealing with that phase of your art which has exact parallels in music. The same laws govern, and you are bound by no others.

Naturally, your rhythmic structure should not destroy the shape of your words, or their natural sound, or their meaning. It is improbable that, at the start, you will be able to get a rhythm-structure strong enough to affect them very much, though you may fall a victim to all sorts of false stopping due to line ends and caesurae.

The Musician can rely on pitch and the volume of the orchestra. You can not. The term harmony is misapplied in poetry; it refers to simultaneous sounds of different pitch. There is, however, in the best verse a sort of residue of sound which remains in the ear of the hearer and acts more or less as an organ-base.

A rhyme must have in it some slight element of surprise if it is to give pleasure; it need not be bizarre or curious, but it must be well used if used at all.

Vide further Vildrac and Duhamel's notes on rhyme in *"Technique Poétique."*

That part of your poetry which strikes upon the imaginative *eye* of the reader will lose nothing by translation into a foreign tongue; that which appeals to the ear can reach only those who take it in the original.

Consider the definiteness of Dante's presentation, as compared with Milton's rhetoric. Read as much of Wordsworth as does not seem too unutterably dull.

If you want the gist of the matter go to Sappho, Catullus, Villon, Heine when he is in the vein, Gautier when he is not too frigid; or, if you have not the tongues, seek out the leisurely Chaucer. Good prose will do you no harm, and there is good discipline to be had by trying to write it.

Translation is likewise good training, if you find that your original matter "wobbles" when you try to rewrite it. The meaning of the poem to be translated can not "wobble."

If you are using a symmetrical form, don't put in what you want to say and then fill up the remaining vacuums with slush.

Don't mess up the perception of one sense by trying to define it in terms of another. This is usually only the result of being too lazy to find the exact word. To this clause there are possibly exceptions.

The first three simple prescriptions * will

* In the essay on "Imagisme" by F. S. Flint, printed below. Flint's essay first appeared in conjunction with Pound's "A Few Don'ts" in *Poetry: A Magazine of Verse* (March 1913).

throw out nine-tenths of all the bad poetry now accepted as standard and classic; and will prevent you from many a crime of production.

". . . *Mais d'abord il faut être un poète,*" as MM. Duhamel and Vildrac have said at the end of their little book, "*Notes sur la Technique Poétique.*"

IMAGISME (1913), BY F. S. FLINT

SOME CURIOSITY has been aroused concerning *Imagisme,* and as I was unable to find anything definite about it in print, I sought out an *imagiste,* with intent to discover whether the group itself knew anything about the "movement." I gleaned these facts.

The *imagistes* admitted that they were contemporaries of the Post Impressionists and the Futurists; but they had nothing in common with these schools. They had not published a manifesto. They were not a revolutionary school; their only endeavor was to write in accordance with the best tradition, as they found it in the best writers of all time,—in Sappho, Catullus, Villon. They seemed to be absolutely intolerant of all poetry that was not written in such endeavor, ignorance of the best tradition forming no excuse. They had a few rules, drawn up for their own satisfaction only, and they had not published them. They were:

1. Direct treatment of the "thing," whether subjective or objective.

2. To use absolutely no word that did not contribute to the presentation.

First appeared in *Poetry: A Magazine of Verse.* Copyright March 1913 by The Modern Poetry Association. When this essay was first published, the editor of *Poetry* supplied the following explanation: "In response to many requests for information regarding *Imagism* and the *Imagistes,* we publish this note by Mr. Flint, supplementing it with further exemplification by Mr. Pound. It will be seen from these that *Imagism* is not necessarily associated with Hellenic subjects, or with *vers libre* as a prescribed form."

3. As regarding rhythm: to compose in sequence of the musical phrase, not in sequence of a metronome.

By these standards they judged all poetry, and found most of it wanting. They held also a certain "Doctrine of the Image," which they had not committed to writing; they said that it did not concern the public, and would provoke useless discussion.

The devices whereby they persuaded approaching poetasters to attend their instruction were:

1. They showed him his own thought already splendidly expressed in some classic (and the school musters altogether a most formidable erudition).

2. They re-wrote his verses before his eyes, using about ten words to his fifty.

Even their opponents admit of them—ruefully—"At least they do keep bad poets from writing!"

I found among them an earnestness that is amazing to one accustomed to the usual London air of poetic dilettantism. They consider that Art is all science, all religion, philosophy and metaphysic. It is true that *snobisme* may be urged against them; but it is at least *snobisme* in its most dynamic form, with a great deal of sound sense and energy behind it; and they are stricter with themselves than with any outsider.

AS FOR IMAGISME (1915)

THE TERM "Imagisme" has given rise to a certain amount of discussion. It has been taken by some to mean Hellenism; by others the word is used most carelessly, to designate any sort of poem in vers libre. Having omitted to copyright the word at its birth I cannot prevent its misuse. I can only say what I meant by the word when I made it. Moreover, I cannot guarantee that my thoughts about it will remain absolutely stationary. I spend the greater part of my time meditating the arts, and I should find this very dull if it were not possible for me occasionally to solve some corner of the mystery, or, at least to formulate more clearly my own thoughts as to the nature of some mystery or equation.

In the second article of this series I pointed out that energy creates pattern. I gave examples. I would say further that emotional force gives the image. By this I do not mean that it gives an "explanatory metaphor"; though it might be hard to draw an exact border line between the two. We have left false metaphor, ornamental metaphor to the rhetorician. That lies outside this discussion.

Intense emotion causes pattern to arise in the mind—if the mind is strong enough. Perhaps I should say, not pattern, but pattern-units, or units of design. (I do not say that intense emotion is the sole possible cause of such units. I say simply that they can result from it. They may also result from other sorts of energy.) I am using this term "pattern-unit," because I want to get away from the confusion between "pattern" and "applied decoration." By applied decoration I mean something like the "wall of Troy pattern." The invention was merely the first curley-cue, or the first pair of them. The rest is repetition, is copying.

By pattern-unit or vorticist picture I mean

First appeared in *The New Age* (London), Jan. 28, 1915.

the single jet. The difference between the pattern-unit and the picture is one of complexity. The pattern-unit is so simple that one can bear having it repeated several or many times. When it becomes so complex that repetition would be useless, then it is a picture, an "arrangement of forms."

Not only does emotion create the "pattern-unit" and the "arrangement of forms," it creates also the Image. The Image can be of two sorts. It can arise within the mind. It is then "subjective." External causes play upon the mind, perhaps; if so, they are drawn into the mind, fused, transmitted, and emerge in an Image unlike themselves. Secondly, the Image can be objective. Emotion seizing up some external scene or action carries it intact to the mind; and that vortex purges it of all save the essential or dominant or dramatic qualities, and it emerges like the external original.

In either case the Image is more than an idea. It is a vortex or cluster of fused ideas and is endowed with energy. If it does not fulfil these specifications, it is not what I mean by an Image. It may be a sketch, a vignette, a criticism, an epigram or anything else you like. It may be impressionism, it may even be very good prose. By "direct treatment," one means simply that having got the Image one refrains from hanging it with festoons.

From the Image to Imagisme: Our second contention was that poetry to be good poetry should be at least as well written as good prose. This statement would seem almost too self-evident to need any defence whatsoever. Obviously, if a man has anything to say, the interest will depend on what he has to say, and not on a faculty for saying "exiguous" when he means "narrow," or for putting his words hindside before. Even if his thought be very slight it will not gain by being swathed in sham lace.

Thirdly, one believes that emotion is an organiser of form, not merely of visible forms and colours, but also of audible forms. This basis of music is so familiar that it would seem to need no support. Poetry is a composition or an "organisation" of words set to "music." By "music" here we can scarcely mean much more than rhythm and timbre. The rhythm form is false unless it belongs to the particular creative emotion or energy which it purports to represent. Obviously one does not discard "regular metres" because they are a "difficulty." Any ass can say:

"John Jones stood on the floor. He saw the ceiling" or decasyllabicly,
"John Jones who rang the bell at number eight."

There is no form of platitude which cannot be turned into iambic pentameter without labour. It is not difficult, if one has learned to count up to ten, to begin a new line on each eleventh syllable or to whack each alternate syllable with an ictus.

Emotion also creates patterns of timbre. But one "discards rhyme," not because one is incapable of rhyming neat, fleet, sweet, meet, treat, eat, feet, but because there are certain emotions or energies which are not to be represented by the over-familiar devices or patterns; just as there are certain "arrangements of form" that cannot be worked into dados.

Granted, of course, that there is great freedom in pentameter and that there are a great number of regular and beautifully regular metres fit for a number of things, and quite capable of expressing a wide range of energies or emotions.

The discovery that bad vers libre can be quite as bad as any other sort of bad verse is by no means modern. Over eleven centuries ago Rihaku (Li Po) complained that imitators of Kutsugen (Ch'u Yuan) couldn't get any underlying rhythm into their vers libre, that they got "bubbles not waves."

Yo ba geki tai ha Kai riu to mu giu.
"Yoyu and Shojo stirred up decayed (en-ervated) waves. Open current flows about in bubbles, does not move in wave lengths." If a man has no emotional energy, no impulse, it is of course much easier to make something which looks like "verse" by reason of having a given number of syllables, or even of accents, per line, than for him to invent a music or rhythm-structure. Hence the prevalence of "regular" metric. Hence also bad vers libre. The only advantage of bad vers libre is that it is, possibly, more easy to see how bad it is . . . but even this advantage is doubtful.

By bad verse, whether "regular" or "free," I mean verse which pretends to some emotion which did not assist at its parturition. I mean also verse made by those who have not sufficient skill to make the words move in rhythm of the creative emotion. Where the voltage is so high that it fuses the machinery, one has merely the "emotional man" not the artist. The best artist is the man whose machinery can stand the highest voltage. The better the machinery, the more precise, the stronger; the more exact will be the record of the voltage and of the various currents which have passed through it.

These are bad expressions if they lead you to think of the artist as wholly passive, as a mere receiver of impressions. The good artist is perhaps a good seismograph, but the difference between man and a machine is that man can in some degree "start his machinery going." He can, within limits, not only record but create. At least he can move as a force; he can produce "order-giving vibrations"; by which one may mean merely, he can departmentalise such part of the life-force as flows through him.

To recapitulate, then, the vorticist position; or at least my position at the moment is this:

Energy, or emotion, expresses itself in form. Energy, whose primary manifestation is in pure form, i.e., form as distinct from likeness or association can only be expressed in painting or sculpture. Its expression can vary from a "wall of Troy pattern" to Wyndham Lewis' "Timon of Athens," or a Wadsworth woodblock. Energy expressing itself in pure sound, i.e., sound as distinct from articulate speech, can only be expressed in music. When an energy or emotion "presents an image," this may find adequate expression in words. It is very probably a waste of energy to express it in any more tangible medium. The verbal expression of the image may be reinforced by a suitable or cognate rhythm-form and by timbre-form. By rhythm-form and timbre-form I do not mean something which must of necessity have a "repeat" in it. It is certain that a too obvious "repeat" may be detrimental.

The test of invention lies in the primary pigment, that is to say, in that part of any art which is peculiarly of that art as distinct from "the other arts." The vorticist maintains that the "organising" or creative-inventive faculty is the thing that matters; and that the artist having this faculty is a being infinitely separate from the other type of artist who merely goes on weaving arabesques out of other men's "units of form."

Superficial capability needs no invention whatsoever, but a great energy has, of necessity, its many attendant inventions.

A RETROSPECT (1918)

THERE HAS BEEN so much scribbling about a new fashion in poetry, that I may perhaps be pardoned this brief recapitulation and retrospect.

In the spring or early summer of 1912, "H. D.," Richard Aldington and myself decided that we were agreed upon the three principles following:

1. Direct treatment of the "thing" whether subjective or objective.

2. To use absolutely no word that does not contribute to the presentation.

3. As regarding rhythm: to compose in the sequence of the musical phrase, not in sequence of a metronome.

Upon many points of taste and of predilection we differed, but agreeing upon these three positions we thought we had as much right to a group name, at least as much right, as a number of French "schools" proclaimed by Mr. Flint in the August number of Harold Monro's magazine for 1911.

This school has since been "joined" or "fol-

lowed" by numerous people who, whatever their merits, do not show any signs of agreeing with the second specification. Indeed *vers libre* has become as prolix and as verbose as any of the flaccid varieties that preceded it. It has brought faults of its own. The actual language and phrasing is often as bad as that of our elders without even the excuse that the words are shovelled in to fill a metric pattern or to complete the noise of a rhyme-sound. Whether or no the phrases followed by the followers are musical must be left to the reader's decision. At times I can find a marked metre in "vers libres," as stale and hackneyed as any pseudo-Swinburnian, at times the writers seem to follow no musical structure whatever. But it is, on the whole, good that the field should be ploughed. Perhaps a few good poems have come from the new method, and if so it is justified.

Criticism is not a circumscription or a set of prohibitions. It provides fixed points of departure. It may startle a dull reader into alertness. That little of it which is good is mostly in stray phrases; or if it be an older artist helping a younger it is in great measure but rules of thumb, cautions gained by experience.

From *Modern Art and Its Philosophy* (1914), by *T. E. Hulme*

1. There are two kinds of art, geometrical and vital, absolutely distinct in kind from one another. These two arts are not modifications of one and the same art but pursue different aims and are created for the satisfaction of different necessities of the mind.

2. Each of these arts springs from and corresponds to a certain general attitude towards the world. You get long periods of time in which only one of these arts with its corresponding mental attitudes prevails. The vital art of Greece and the Renaissance corresponded to a certain attitude of mind and the geometrical has always gone with a different general attitude, of greater intensity than this.

And 3—this is really the point I am making for—that the re-emergence of geometrical art may be the precursor of the re-emergence of the corresponding attitude towards the world, and so, of the break-up of the Renaissance humanistic attitude. The fact that this change comes first in art, before it comes in thought, is easily understandable for this reason. So thoroughly are we soaked in the spirit of the period we live in, so strong is its influence over us, that we can only escape from it in an unexpected way, as it were, a side direction like art.

I am emphasising, then, the absolute character of the difference between these two arts, not only because it is important for the understanding of the new art itself, but because it enables me to maintain much wider theses.

That is the logical order in which I present my convictions. I did not naturally arrive at them in that order. I came to believe first of

From *Speculations*, ed. Herbert Read. Reprinted by permission of Humanities Press Inc., New York.

all, for reasons quite unconnected with art, that the Renaissance attitude was coming to an end, and was then confirmed in that by the emergence of this art. I commenced by a change in philosophy and illustrated this by a change in art rather than vice versa. A thesis like my last one is so sweeping that it sounds a little empty. It would be quite ludicrous for me to attempt to state such a position in the space of the half page I intend to devote to it, but perhaps I can make it sound more plausible by saying how I came personally to believe it. You will have to excuse my putting it in autobiographical shape, for, after all, the break-up of a general attitude if it ever occurs will be a collection of autobiographies. First of all comes the conviction that in spite of its apparent extraordinary variety, European philosophy since the Renaissance does form a unity. You can separate philosophy into two parts, the technical and scientific part, that which more properly would be called metaphysics, and another part in which the machinery elaborated in the first is used to express the philosopher's attitude towards the world, what may be called his conclusions. These emerge in the last chapter of the book. In the first chapters the philosopher may be compared to a man in armour; he intimidates you, as a kind of impersonal machine. In the last chapter you perceive him naked, as perfectly human. Every philosopher says the world is other than it seems to be; in the last chapter he tells you what he thinks it is. As he has taken the trouble to prove it, you may assume that he regards the final picture of the world he gives as satisfactory.

Now here is my point. In a certain sense, all

philosophy since the Renaissance is satisfied with a certain conception of the relation of man to the world. Now what is this conception? You get the first hint of it in the beginnings of the Renaissance itself, in a person like Pico Della Mirandola, for example. You get the hint of an idea there of something, which finally culminates in a doctrine which is the opposite of the doctrine of original sin: the belief that man as a part of nature was after all something satisfactory. The change which Copernicus is supposed to have brought about is the exact contrary of the fact. Before Copernicus, man was not the centre of the world; after Copernicus he was. You get a change from a certain profundity and intensity to that flat and insipid optimism which, passing through its first stage of decay in Rousseau, has finally culminated in the state of slush in which we have the misfortune to live. . . .

I come now to the application of the distinction thus elaborately constructed between geometrical and vital art to what is going on at the present moment.

If the argument I have followed is correct, I stand committed to two statements:—

1. . . . that a new geometrical art is emerging which may be considered as different in kind from the art which preceded it, it being much more akin to the geometrical arts of the past, and

2. . . . that this change from a vital to a geometrical art is the product of and will be accompanied by a certain change of sensibility, a certain change of general attitude, and that this new attitude will differ in kind from the humanism which has prevailed from the Renaissance to now, and will have certain analogies to the attitude of which geometrical art was the expression in the past.

Naturally both of these sweeping statements run a good deal ahead of the facts and of my ability to prove them. I must here, therefore, make the same qualification and warning about both of the statements. Though both the new

Weltanschauung and the new geometrical art will have certain analogies with corresponding periods in the past, yet it is not for a moment to be supposed that there is anything more than an analogy here. The new geometrical art will probably in the end not in the least resemble archaic art, nor will the new attitude to the world be very much like the Byzantine, for example. As to what actually they both will culminate in, it would obviously be ludicrous for me to attempt to say. It would be more ludicrous to attempt to do this in the case of the general attitude, than it would in the case of the art itself. For one of my points at the beginning of this paper was that one's mind is so soaked in the thought and language of the period, that one can only perceive the break-up of that period in a region like art which is— when one's mind is focussed on thought itself —a kind of side activity.

One can only make certain guesses at the new attitude by the use of analogy. Take two other attitudes of the past which went with geometrical art: say primitive and Byzantine. There is a certain likeness and a certain unlikeness in relation to man and the outside world. The primitive springs from what we have called a kind of mental space-shyness, which is really an attitude of fear before the world; the Byzantine from what may be called, inaccurately, a kind of contempt for the world. Though these two attitudes differ very much, yet there is a common element in the idea of separation as opposed to the more intimate feeling towards the world in classical and Renaissance thought. In comparison with the flat and insipid optimism of the belief in progress, the new attitude may be in a certain sense inhuman, pessimistic. Yet its pessimism will not be world-rejecting in the sense in which the Byzantine was.

But one is on much surer ground in dealing with the art itself. On what grounds does one base this belief that a new geometrical art is appearing? There is first the more negative proof provided by a change of taste.

You get an extraordinary interest in similar

arts in the past, in Indian sculpture, in Byzantine art, in archaic art generally, and this interest is not as before a merely archaeological one. The things are liked directly, almost as they were liked by the people who made them, as being direct expressions of an attitude which you want to find expressed. I do not think for a moment that this is conscious. I think that under the influence of a false conception of the nature of art, that most people, even when they feel it, falsify their real appreciation by the vocabulary they use—naïve, fresh, charm of the exotic, and so on.

A second and more positive proof is to be found in the actual creation of a new modern geometrical art.

You get at the present moment in Europe a most extraordinary confusion in art, a complete breaking away from tradition. So confusing is it that most people lump it altogether as one movement and are unaware that it is in fact composed of a great many distinct and even contradictory elements, being a complex movement of parts that are merely reactionary, parts that are dead, and with one part only containing the possibility of development. When I speak of a new complex geometrical art then, I am not thinking of the whole movement. I am speaking of one element which seems to be gradually hardening out, and separating itself from the others. I don't want anyone to suppose, for example, that I am speaking of futurism which is, in its logical form, the exact opposite of the art I am describing, being the deification of the flux, the last efflorescence of impressionism. I also exclude a great many things which—as I shall attempt to show later were perhaps necessary preliminaries to this art, but which have now been passed by—most of the work in fact which is included under the term post-impressionism—Gauguin, Maillol, Brancusi.

If space allowed I could explain why I also exclude certain elements of cubism, what I might call analytical cubism—the theories about interpenetration which you get in Metzinger for example.

Vorticism

VORTICISM (1914)

"IT IS NO MORE ridiculous that a person should receive or convey an emotion by means of an arrangement of shapes, or planes, or colours, than that they should receive or convey such emotion by an arrangement of musical notes."

I suppose this proposition is self-evident.

Whistler said as much, some years ago, and Pater proclaimed that "All arts approach the conditions of music."

Whenever I say this I am greeted with a storm of "Yes, but" . . . s. "But why isn't this art futurism?" "Why isn't?" "Why don't?" and above all: "What, in Heaven's name, has it got to do with your Imagiste poetry?"

Let me explain at leisure, and in nice, orderly, old-fashioned prose.

We are all futurists to the extent of believing with Guillaume Appollinaire that "On ne peut pas porter *partout* avec soi le cadavre de son père." But "futurism," when it gets into art, is, for the most part, a descendant of impressionism. It is a sort of accelerated impressionism.

There is another artistic descent *via* Picasso and Kandinsky; *via* cubism and expressionism. One does not complain of neo-impressionism or of accelerated impressionism and "simultaneity," but one is not wholly satisfied by them. One has perhaps other needs.

It is very difficult to make generalities about three arts at once. I shall be, perhaps, more lucid if I give, briefly, the history of the vorticist art with which I am most intimately connected, that is to say, vorticist poetry. Vorticism has been announced as including such and such a painting and sculpture and "Imagisme" in verse. I shall explain "Imagisme," and then proceed to show its inner relation to certain modern paintings and sculpture.

Imagisme, in so far as it has been known at all, has been known chiefly as a stylistic movement, as a movement of criticism rather than of creation. This is natural, for, despite all possible celerity of publication, the public is always, and of necessity, some years behind the artists' actual thought. Nearly anyone is ready to accept "Imagisme" as a department of poetry, just as one accepts "lyricism" as a department of poetry.

There is a sort of poetry where music, sheer melody, seems as if it were just bursting into speech.

There is another sort of poetry where painting or sculpture seems as if it were "just coming over into speech."

The first sort of poetry has long been called "lyric." One is accustomed to distinguish easily between "lyric" and "epic" and "didactic." One is capable of finding the "lyric" passages in a drama or in a long poem not otherwise "lyric." This division is in the grammars and school books, and one has been brought up to it.

The other sort of poetry is as old as the lyric and as honourable, but, until recently, no one had named it. Ibycus and Liu Ch'e presented the "Image." Dante is a great poet by reason of this faculty, and Milton is a wind-bag because of his lack of it. The "image" is the furthest possible remove from rhetoric. Rhetoric is the art of dressing up some unimportant matter so as to fool the audience for the time being. So much for the general category. Even Aristotle distinguishes between rhetoric, "which is persuasion," and the analytical examination of truth. As a "critical" movement, the "Imagisme" of 1912 to '14 set out "to bring poetry up to the level of prose." No one is so quixotic as to believe that contemporary poetry holds any such position. . . . Stendhal formulated the need in his *De L'Amour*:—

"La poésie avec ses comparaisons obligées, sa mythologie que ne croit pas le poète, sa dignité de style à la Louis XIV et tout l'attirail de ses ornements appelés poétique, est bien au dessous de la prose dès qu'il s'agit de donner une idée claire et précise des mouvements de coeur, or dans ce genre on n'émeut que par la clarté."

Flaubert and De Maupassant lifted prose to the rank of a finer art, and one has no patience with contemporary poets who escape from all the difficulties of the infinitely difficult art of good prose by pouring themselves into loose verses.

The tenets of the Imagiste faith were published in March, 1913, as follows:—

1. Direct treatment of the "thing," whether subjective or objective.

2. To use absolutely no word that does not contribute to the presentation.

3. As regarding rhythm: to compose in sequence of the musical phrase, not in sequence of the metronome.

There followed a series of about forty cautions to beginners, which need not concern us here.

The arts have indeed "some sort of common bond, some interrecognition." Yet certain emotions or subjects find their most appropriate expression in some one particular art. The work of art which is most "worth while" is the work which would need a hundred works of any other kind of art to explain it. A fine statue is the core of a hundred poems. A fine poem is a score of symphonies. There is music which would need a hundred paintings to express it. There is no synonym for the *Victory of Samothrace* or for Mr. Epstein's flenites. There is no painting of Villon's *Frères Humains*. Such works are what we call works of the "first intensity."

A given subject or emotion belongs to that artist, or to that sort of artist who must know it most intimately and most intensely before he can render it adequately in his art. A painter must know much more about a sunset than a writer, if he is to put it on canvas. But when the poet speaks of "Dawn in russet mantle clad," he presents something which the painter cannot present.

I said in the preface to my *Guido Cavalcanti* that I believed in an absolute rhythm. I believe that every emotion and every phase of emotion has some toneless phrase, some rhythm-phrase to express it.

(This belief leads to *vers libre* and to experiments in quantitative verse.)

To hold a like belief in a sort of permanent metaphor is, as I understand it, "symbolism" in its profounder sense. It is not necessarily a belief in a permanent world, but it is a belief in that direction.

Imagisme is not symbolism. The symbolists dealt in "association," that is, in a sort of allusion, almost of allegory. They degraded the symbol to the status of a word. They made it a form of metonomy. One can be grossly "symbolic," for example, by using the term "cross" to mean "trial." The symbolist's *symbols* have a fixed value, like numbers in arithmetic, like 1, 2, and 7. The imagiste's images have a variable significance, like the signs *a*, *b*, and *x* in algebra.

Moreover, one does not want to be called a symbolist, because symbolism has usually been associated with mushy technique.

On the other hand, Imagisme is not Impressionism, though one borrows, or could borrow, much from the impressionist method of presentation. But this is only negative definition. If I am to give a psychological or philosophical definition "from the inside," I can only do so autobiographically. The precise statement of such a matter must be based on one's own experience.

In the "search for oneself," in the search for "sincere self-expression," one gropes, one finds some seeming verity. One says "I am" this, that, or the other, and with the words scarcely uttered one ceases to be that thing.

I began this search for the real in a book called *Personae*, casting off, as it were, complete masks of the self in each poem. I continued in long series of translations, which were but more elaborate masks.

Secondly, I made poems like "The Return," which is an objective reality and has a complicated sort of significance, like Mr. Epstein's "Sun God," or Mr. Brzeska's "Boy with a Coney." Thirdly, I have written "Heather," which represents a state of consciousness, or "implies," or "implicates" it.

A Russian correspondent, after having called it a symbolist poem, and having been convinced that it was not symbolism, said slowly: "I see, you wish to give people new eyes, not to make them see some new particular thing."

These two latter sorts of poems are impersonal, and that fact brings us back to what I said about absolute metaphor. They are Imagisme, and in so far as they are Imagisme, they fall in with the new pictures and the new sculpture.

Whistler said somewhere in the *Gentle Art*: "The picture is interesting not because it is Trotty Veg, but because it is an arrangement in colour." The minute you have admitted that, you let in the jungle, you let in nature and truth and abundance and cubism and Kandinsky, and the lot of us. Whistler and Kandinsky and some cubists were set to getting extraneous matter out of their art; they were ousting literary values. The Flaubertians talk a good deal about "constatation." "The 'nineties" saw a movement against rhetoric. I think all these things move together, though they do not, of course, move in step.

The painters realise that what matters is form and colour. Musicians long ago learned that programme music was not the ultimate music. Almost anyone can realize that to use a symbol *with an ascribed or intended meaning* is, usually, to produce very bad art. We all remember crowns, and crosses, and rainbows, and what not in atrociously mumbled colour.

The Image is the poet's pigment.[1] The painter should use his colour because he sees it or feels it. I don't much care whether he is representative or non-representative. He should *depend*, of course, on the creative, not upon the mimetic or representational part in his work. It is the same in writing poems, the author must use his *image* because he sees it or feels it, *not* because he thinks he can use it to back up some creed or some system of ethics or economics.

An *image*, in our sense, is real because we know it directly. If it have an age-old traditional meaning this may serve as proof to the professional student of symbology that we have stood in the deathless light, or that we have walked in some particular arbour of his traditional paradiso, but that is not our affair. It is our affair to render the *image* as we have perceived or conceived it.

Browning's "Sordello" is one of the finest *masks* ever presented. Dante's "Paradiso" is the most wonderful *image*. By that I do not mean that it is a perseveringly imagistic performance. The permanent part is Imagisme, the rest, the discourses with the calendar of saints and the discussions about the nature of the moon, are philology. The form of sphere above sphere, the varying reaches of light, the minutiae of pearls upon foreheads, all these are parts of the Image. The image is the poet's pigment; with that in mind you can go ahead

and apply Kandinsky, you can transpose his chapter on the language of form and colour and apply it to the writing of verse. As I cannot rely on your having read Kandinsky's *Ueber das Geistige in der Kunst*, I must go on with my autobiography.

Three years ago in Paris I got out of a "metro" train at La Concorde, and saw suddenly a beautiful face, and then another and another, and then a beautiful child's face, and then another beautiful woman, and I tried all that day to find words for what this had meant to me, and I could not find any words that seemed to me worthy, or as lovely as that sudden emotion. And that evening, as I went home along the Rue Raynouard, I was still trying and I found, suddenly, the expression. I do not mean that I found words, but there came an equation . . . not in speech, but in little splotches of colour. It was just that—a "pattern," or hardly a pattern, if by "pattern" you mean something with a "repeat" in it. But it was a word, the beginning, for me, of a language in colour. I do not mean that I was unfamiliar with the kindergarten stories about colours being like tones in music. I think that sort of thing is nonsense. If you try to make notes permanently correspond with particular colours, it is like tying narrow meanings to symbols.

That evening, in the Rue Raynouard, I realized quite vividly that if I were a painter, or if I had, often, *that kind* of emotion, or even if I had the energy to get paints and brushes and keep at it, I might found a new school of painting, of "non-representative" painting, a painting that would speak only by arrangements in colour.

And so, when I came to read Kandinsky's chapter on the language of form and colour, I found little that was new to me. I only felt that some one else understood what I understood, and had written it out very clearly. It seems quite natural to me that an artist should have just as much pleasure in an arrangement of planes or in a pattern of figures, as in painting portraits of fine ladies, or in portraying

[1] The image has been defined as "that which presents an intellectual and emotional complex in an instant of time."

the Mother of God as the symbolists bid us.

When I find people ridiculing the new arts, or making fun of the clumsy odd terms that we use in trying to talk of them amongst ourselves; when they laugh at our talking about the "ice-block quality" in Picasso, I think it is only because they do not know what thought is like, and that they are familiar only with argument and gibe and opinion. That is to say, they can only enjoy what they have been brought up to consider enjoyable, or what some essayist has talked about in mellifluous phrases. They think only "the shells of thought," as De Gourmont calls them; the thoughts that have been already thought out by others.

Any mind that is worth calling a mind must have needs beyond the existing categories of language, just as a painter must have pigments or shades more numerous than the existing names of the colours.

Perhaps this is enough to explain the words in my "Vortex" [2]:—

Every concept, every emotion, presents itself to the vivid consciousness in some primary form. It belongs to the art of this form.

That is to say, my experience in Paris should have gone into paint. If instead of colour I had perceived sound or planes in relation, I should have expressed it in music or in sculpture. Colour was, in that instance, the "primary pigment"; I mean that it was the first adequate equation that came into consciousness. The Vorticist uses the "primary pigment." Vorticism is art before it has spread itself into flaccidity, into elaboration and secondary applications.

What I have said of one vorticist art can be transposed for another vorticist art. But let me go on then with my own branch of vorticism, about which I can probably speak with greater clarity. All poetic language is the language of exploration. Since the beginning of bad writing, writers have used images as

ornaments. The point of Imagisme is that it does not use images *as ornaments*. The image is itself the speech. The image is the word beyond formulated language.

I once saw a small child go to an electric light switch and say, "Mamma, can I *open* the light?" She was using the age-old language of exploration, the language of art. It was a sort of metaphor, but she was not using it as ornamentation.

One is tired of ornamentations, they are all a trick, and any sharp person can learn them.

The Japanese have had the sense of exploration. They have understood the beauty of this sort of knowing. A Chinaman said long ago that if a man can't say what he has to say in twelve lines he had better keep quiet. The Japanese have evolved the still shorter form of the *hokku*.

The fallen blossom flies back to its branch:
A butterfly.

That is the substance of a very well-known *hokku*. Victor Plarr tells me that once, when he was walking over snow with a Japanese naval officer, they came to a place where a cat had crossed the path, and the officer said, "Stop, I am making a poem." Which poem was, roughly, as follows:—

The footsteps of the cat upon the snow:
(are like) plum-blossoms.

The words "are like" would not occur in the original, but I add them for clarity.

The "one image poem" is a form of superposition, that is to say, it is one idea set on top of another. I found it useful in getting out of the impasse in which I had been left by my metro emotion. I wrote a thirty-line poem, and destroyed it because it was what we call work "of second intensity." Six months later I made a poem half that length; a year later I made the following *hokku*-like sentence:—

The apparition of these faces in the crowd:
Petals, on a wet, black bough.

[2] Appearing in the July number of *Blast*.

I dare say it is meaningless unless one has drifted into a certain vein of thought.[3] In a poem of this sort one is trying to record the precise instant when a thing outward and objective transforms itself, or darts into a thing inward and subjective.

This particular sort of consciousness has not been identified with impressionist art. I think it is worthy of attention.

The logical end of impressionist art is the cinematograph. The state of mind of the impressionist tends to become cinematographical. Or, to put it another way, the cinematograph does away with the need of a lot of impressionist art.

There are two opposed ways of thinking of a man: firstly, you may think of him as that toward which perception moves, as the toy of circumstance, as the plastic substance *receiving* impressions; secondly, you may think of him as directing a certain fluid force against circumstance, as *conceiving* instead of merely reflecting and observing. One does not claim that one way is better than the other, one notes a diversity of the temperament. The two camps always exist. In the 'eighties there were symbolists opposed to impressionists, now you have vorticism, which is, roughly speaking, expressionism, neo-cubism, and imagism gathered together in one camp and futurism in the other. Futurism is descended from impressionism. It is, in so far as it is an art movement, a kind of accelerated impressionism. It is a spreading, or surface art, as opposed to vorticism, which is intensive.

The vorticist has not this curious tic for destroying past glories. I have no doubt that Italy needed Mr. Marinetti, but he did not set on the egg that hatched me, and as I am wholly opposed to his aesthetic principles I

see no reason why I, and various men who agree with me, should be expected to call ourselves futurists. We do not desire to evade comparison with the past. We prefer that the comparison be made by some intelligent person whose idea of "the tradition" is not limited by the conventional taste of four or five centuries and one continent.

Vorticism is an intensive art. I mean by this, that one is concerned with the relative intensity, or relative significance of different sorts of expression. One desires the most intense, for certain forms of expression *are* "more intense" than others. They are more dynamic. I do not mean they are more emphatic, or that they are yelled louder. I can explain my meaning best by mathematics.

There are four different intensities of mathematical expression known to the ordinarily intelligent undergraduate, namely: the arithmetical, the algebraic, the geometrical, and that of analytical geometry.

For instance, you can write

$$3 \times 3 + 4 \times 4 = 5 \times 5,$$
or, differently, $3^2 + 4^2 = 5^2.$

That is merely conversation or "ordinary common sense." It is a simple statement of one fact, and does not implicate any other.

Secondly, it is true that

$$3^2 + 4^2 = 5^2, \ 6^2 + 8^2 = 10^2,$$
$$9^2 + 12^2 = 15^2, \ 39^2 + 52^2 = 65^2.$$

These are all separate facts, one may wish to mention their underlying similarity; it is a bore to speak about each one in turn. One expresses their "algebraic relation" as

$$a^2 + b^2 = c^2.$$

That is the language of philosophy. It MAKES NO PICTURE. This kind of statement applies to a lot of facts, but it does not grip hold of Heaven.

Thirdly, when one studies Euclid one finds that the relation of $a^2 + b^2 = c^2$ applies to the ratio between the squares on the two sides of a right-angled triangle and the square on the

---

[3] Mr. Flint and Mr. Rodker have made longer poems depending on a similar presentation of matter. So also have Richard Aldington, in his *In Via Sestina*, and "H. D." in her *Oread*, which latter poems express much stronger emotions than that in my lines here given. Mr. Hueffer gives an interesting account of a similar adventure of his own in his review of the Imagiste anthology.

hypotenuse. One still writes it $a^2 + b^2 = c^2$, but one has begun to talk about form. Another property or quality of life has crept into one's matter. Until then one had dealt only with numbers. But even this statement does not *create* form. The picture is given you in the proposition about the square on the hypotenuse of the right-angled triangle being equal to the sum of the squares on the two other sides. Statements in plane or descriptive geometry are like talk about art. They are a criticism of the form. The form is not created by them.

Fourthly, we come to Descartian or "analytical geometry." Space is conceived as separated by two or by three axes (depending on whether one is treating form in one or more planes). One refers points to these axes by a series of co-ordinates. Given the idiom, one is able *actually to create.*

Thus, we learn that the equation $(x - a)^2 + (y - b)^2 = r^2$ governs the circle. It is the circle. It is not a particular circle, it is any circle and all circles. It is nothing that is not a circle. It is the circle free of space and time limits. It is the universal, existing in perfection, in freedom from space and time. Mathematics is dull ditchwater until one reaches analytics. But in analytics we come upon a new way of dealing with form. It is in this way that art handles life. The difference between art and analytical geometry is the difference of subject-matter only. Art is more interesting in proportion as life and the human consciousness are more complex and more interesting than forms and numbers.

This statement does not interfere in the least with "spontaneity" and "intuition," or with their function in art. I passed my last *exam.* in mathematics on sheer intuition. I saw where the line *had* to go, as clearly as I ever saw an image, or felt *caelestem intus vigorem.*

The statements of "analytics" are "lords" over fact. They are the thrones and dominations that rule over form and recurrence. And in like manner are great works of art lords over fact, over race-long recurrent moods, and

over to-morrow.

Great works of art contain this fourth sort of equation. They cause form to come into being. By the "image" I mean such an equation; not an equation of mathematics, not something about a, b, and c, having something to do with form, but about *sea, cliffs, night,* having something to do with mood.

The image is not an idea. It is a radiant node or cluster; it is what I can, and must perforce, call a VORTEX, from which, and through which, and into which, ideas are constantly rushing. In decency one can only call it a VORTEX. And from this necessity came the name "vorticism." *Nomina sunt consequentia rerum,* and never was that statement of Aquinas more true than in the case of the vorticist movement.

It is as true for the painting and the sculpture as it is for the poetry. Mr. Wadsworth and Mr. Lewis are not using words, they are using shape and colour. Mr. Brzeska and Mr. Epstein are using "planes in relation," they are dealing with a relation of planes different from the sort of relation of planes dealt with in geometry, hence what is called "the need of organic forms in sculpture."

I trust I have made clear what I mean by an "intensive art." The vorticist movement is not a movement of mystification, though I dare say many people "of good will" have been considerably bewildered.

The organization of forms is a much more energetic and creative action than the copying or imitating of light on a haystack.

There is undoubtedly a language of form and colour. It is not a symbolical or allegorical language depending on certain meanings having been ascribed, in books, to certain signs and colours.

Certain artists working in different media have managed to understand each other. They know the good and bad in each other's work, which they could not know unless there were a common speech.

As for the excellence of certain contemporary artists, all I can do is to stand up for my own beliefs. I believe that Mr. Wyndham Lewis is a very great master of design; that he has brought into our art new units of design and new manners of organisation. I think that his series "Timon" is a great work. I think he is the most articulate expression of my own decade. If you ask me what his "Timon" means, I can reply by asking you what the old play means. For me his designs are a creation on the same *motif*. That *motif* is the fury of intelligence baffled and shut in by circumjacent stupidity. It is an emotional *motif*. Mr. Lewis's painting is nearly always emotional.

Mr. Wadsworth's work gives me pleasure, sometimes like the pleasure I have received from Chinese and Japanese prints and painting; for example, I derive such pleasure from Mr. Wadsworth's "Khaki." Sometimes his work gives me a pleasure which I can only compare to the pleasure I have in music, in music as it was in Mozart's time. If an outsider wishes swiftly to understand this new work, he can do worse than approach it in the spirit wherein he approaches music.

"Lewis is Bach." No, it is incorrect to say that "Lewis is Bach," but our feeling is that certain works of Picasso and certain works of Lewis have in them something which is to painting what certain qualities of Bach are to music. Music was vorticist in the Bach-Mozart period, before it went off into romance and sentiment and description. A new vorticist music would come from a new computation of the mathematics of harmony, not from a mimetic representation of dead cats in a foghorn, alias noise-tuners.

Mr. Epstein is too well known to need presentation in this article. Mr. Brzeska's sculpture is so generally recognized in all camps that one does not need to bring in a brief concerning it. Mr. Brzeska has defined sculptural feeling as "the appreciation of masses in relation," and sculptural ability as "the defining of these masses by planes." There comes a time when one is more deeply moved by that form of intelligence which can present "masses in relation" than by that combination of patience and trickery which can make marble chains with free links and spin out bronze until it copies the feathers on a general's hat. Mr. Etchells still remains more or less of a mystery. He is on his travels, whence he has sent back a few excellent drawings. It cannot be made too clear that the work of the vorticists and the "feeling of inner need" existed before the general noise about vorticism. We worked separately, we found an underlying agreement, we decided to stand together.

NOTE

I am often asked whether there can be a long imagiste or vorticist poem. The Japanese, who evolved the hokku, evolved also the Noh plays. In the best "Noh" the whole play may consist of one image. I mean it is gathered about one image. Its unity consists in one image, enforced by movement and music. I see nothing against a long vorticist poem.

On the other hand, no artist can possibly get a vortex into every poem or picture he does. One would like to do so, but it is beyond one. Certain things seem to demand metrical expression, or expression in a rhythm more agitated than the rhythms acceptable to prose, and these subjects, though they do not contain a vortex, may have some interest, an interest as "criticism of life" or of art. It is natural to express these things, and a vorticist or imagiste writer may be justified in presenting a certain amount of work which is not vorticism or imagisme, just as he might be justified in printing a purely didactic prose article. Unfinished sketches and drawings have a similar interest; they are trials and attempts toward a vortex.

THE NEW AGE permits one to express beliefs which are in direct opposition to those held by the editing staff. In this, *The New Age* sets a most commendable example to certain other periodicals which not only demand that all writers in their columns shall turn themselves into a weak and puling copy of the editorial board, but even try to damage one's income if one ventures to express contrary beliefs in the columns of other papers.

There is perhaps no more authentic sign of the senility of a certain generation of publicists (now, thank heaven, gradually fading from the world) than their abject terror in the face of motive ideas. An age may be said to be decadent, or a generation may be said to be in a state of prone senility, when its creative minds are dead and when its survivors maintain a mental dignity—to wit, the dignity or stationariness of a corpse in its cerements. Excess or even absinthe is not the sure sign of decadence. If a man is capable of creative, or even of mobile, thought he will not go in terror of other men so endowed. He will not call for an inquisition or even a persecution of other men who happen to think something which he has not yet thought, or of which he may not yet have happened to hear.

The public divides itself into sections according to temper and alertness; it may think with living London, or with moribund London, or with Chicago, or Boston, or even with New Zealand; and behind all these there are possibly people who think on a level with Dublin, antiquarians, of course, and students of the previous age. For example, Sir Hugh Lane tried to give Dublin a collection of pictures, Degas, Corot and Manet, and they called him a charlatan and cried out for real pictures "like the lovely paintings which we

First appeared in *The New Age* (London), Jan. 14, 1915.

see reproduced in our city art shops." I have even seen a paper from Belfast which brands J. M. Synge as a "decadent." Is such a country fit for Home Rule? I ask as the merest outsider having not the slightest interest in the question. I have met here in London two men still believing in Watts, and I suppose anything is possible—any form of atavism that you may be willing to name.

I suppose any new development or even any change in any art has to be pushed down the public throat with a ramrod. The public has always squealed. A public which has gushed over the sentimentalities of Rodin adorns Epstein's work with black butterflies, à cause de pudeur. The wickedest and most dashing publisher of "the nineties," of the "vicious, disreputable nineties," demands that our antiseptic works be submitted to ladylike censorship. And the papers in Trieste rejoice that futurism is a thing of the past, that a new god is come to deliver them. Such is the state of the world at the beginning of A.D. 1915.

The political world is confronted with a great war, a species of insanity. The art world is confronted with a species of quiet and sober sanity called Vorticism, which I am for the third or fourth time called upon to define, quietly, lucidly, with precision.

Vorticism is the use of, or the belief in the use of, *the primary pigment*, straight through all of the arts.

If you are a cubist, or an expressionist, or an imagist, you may believe in one thing for painting and a very different thing for poetry. You may talk about volumes, or about colour that "moves in," or about a certain form of verse, without having a correlated aesthetic which carries you through all of the arts. Vorticism means that one is interested in the creative faculty as opposed to the mimetic. We believe that it is harder to make than to copy. We believe in maximum efficiency, and we go to a work of art not for tallow candles or cheese, but for something which we cannot get anywhere else. We go to a particular art for something which we cannot get in any other art. If we want form and colour we go to a painting, or we make a painting. If we want form without colour and in two dimensions, we want drawing or etching. If we want form in three dimensions, we want sculpture. If we want an image or a procession of images, we want poetry. If we want pure sound, we want music.

These different desires are not one and the same. They are divers desires and they demand divers sorts of satisfaction. The more intense the individual life, the more vivid are the divers desires of that life. The more alive and vital the mind, the less will it be content with dilutations; with diluted forms of satisfaction.

I might put it differently. I might say, "I like a man who goes the whole hog." If he wants one sort of, say, "philosophy," he goes to Spinoza. If he wants another sort of "philosophy," he goes to Swedenborg. But nothing under heaven will induce him to have recourse to the messy sort of author who tries to mix up these two incompatible sorts of thought, and who produces only a muddle. Art deals with certitude. There is no "certitude" about a thing which is pretending to be something else.

A painting is an arrangement of colour patches on a canvas, or on some other substance. It is a good or bad painting according as these colour-patches are well or ill arranged. After that it can be whatever it likes. It can represent the Blessed Virgin, or Jack Johnson, or it need not represent at all, it can be. These things are a matter of taste. A man may follow his whim in these matters without the least harm to his art sense, so long as he remembers that it is merely his whim and that it is not a matter of "art criticism" or of "aesthetics." When a man prefers a Blessed Virgin by Watts to a portrait of a nasty pawnbroker by Rembrandt, one ceases to consider him as a person seriously interested in painting. There is nothing very new about that. When a man begins to be more interested in the "arrangement" than in the dead matter arranged, then he begins "to have an eye for" the difference between the good, the bad and the mediocre in Chinese painting. His remarks on Byzantine, and Japanese, and on ultra-modern painting begin to be interesting and intelligible. You do not demand of a mountain or a tree that it shall be like something; you do not demand that "natural beauty" be limited to mean only a few freaks of nature, cliffs looking like faces, etc. The worst symbolist of my acquaintance—that is to say, the most fervent admirer of Watts' pictures—has said to me more than once, quoting Nietzsche most inadvertently, "The artist is part of nature, therefore he never imitates nature." That text serves very well for my side of the case. Is a man capable of admiring a picture on the same terms as he admires a mountain? The picture will never become the mountain. It will never have the mountain's perpetual variety. The photograph will reproduce the mountain's contour with greater exactitude. Let us say that a few people choose to admire the picture on more or less the same terms as those on which they admire the mountain. Then what do I mean by "forms well organised"?

An organisation of forms expresses a confluence of forces. These forces may be the "love of God," the "life-force," emotions, passions, what you will. For example: if you clap a strong magnet beneath a plateful of iron filings, the energies of the magnet will proceed to organise form. It is only by applying a particular and suitable force that you can bring order and vitality and thence beauty into a plate of iron filings, which are otherwise as "ugly" as anything under heaven. The design in the magnetised iron filings expresses a confluence of energy. It is not "meaningless" or "inexpressive."

There are, of course, various sorts or various subdivisions of energy. They are all capable of expressing themselves in "an organisation of form." I saw, some months since, the "automatic" paintings of Miss Florence Seth. They were quite charming. They were the best automatic paintings I have seen. "Automatic painting" means paintings done by people who begin to paint without preconception, who believe, or at least assert, that the painting is done without volition on their part, that their hands are guided by "spirits," or by some mysterious agency over which they have little or no control. "Will and consciousness are our vortex." The friend who sent me to see Miss Seth's painting did me a favour, but he was very much in the wrong if he thought my interest was aroused because Miss Seth's painting was vorticist.

Miss Seth's painting was quite beautiful. It was indeed much finer than her earlier mimetic work. It had richness of colour, it had the surety of articulation which one finds in leaves and in viscera. There was in it also an unconscious use of certain well-known symbols, often very beautifully disguised with elaborate detail. Often a symbol appeared only in a fragment, wholly unrecognisable in some pictures, but capable of making itself understood by comparison with other fragments of itself appearing in other pictures. Miss Seth had begun with painting obviously Christian symbols, doves, etc. She had gone on to paint less obvious symbols, of which she had no explanation. She had no theories about the work, save that it was in some way mediumistic. In her work, as in other "automatic" paintings which I have seen, the structure was similar to the structure of leaves and viscera. It was, that is to say, exclusively *organic*. It is not surprising that the human mind in a state of lassitude or passivity should take on again the faculties of the unconscious or sub-human energies or minds of nature; that the momentarily dominant atom of personality should, that is to say, retake the pattern-making faculty which lies in the flower-seed or in the grain or in the animal cell.

This is not vorticism. They say that an infant six weeks old is both aquatic and arbo-

real, that it can both swim and hang from a small branch by its fist, and that by the age of six months it has lost these faculties. I do not know whether or no this is true. It is a scientist's report, I have never tried it on a six-weeks-old infant. If it is so, we will say that instinct "revives" or that "memory throws back," or something of that sort. The same phrase would apply to the pattern-making instinct revived in somnolents or in mediumistic persons.

Note especially that their paintings have only organic structures, that their forms are the forms already familiar to us in sub-human nature. Their work is interesting as a psychological problem, not as creation. I give it, however, along with my paragraph on iron filings, as an example of energy expressing itself in pattern.

We do not enjoy an arrangement of "forms and colours" because it is a thing isolated in nature. Nothing is isolated in nature. This organisation of form and colour is "expression"; just as a musical arrangement of notes by Mozart is expression. The vorticist is expressing his complex consciousness. He is not like the iron filings, expressing electrical magnetism; not like the automatist, expressing a state of cell-memory, a vegetable or visceral energy. Not, however, that one despises vegetable energy or wishes to adorn the rose or the cyclamen, which are vegetable energies expressed in form. One, as a human being, cannot pretend fully to express oneself unless one express instinct and intellect together. The softness and the ultimate failure of interest in automatic painting are caused by a complete lack of conscious intellect. Where does this bring us? It brings us to this: Vorticism is a legitimate expression of life.

My personal conviction is as follows: Time was when I began to be interested in "the beauties of nature." According to impressionism I began to see the colour of shadows, etc. It was very interesting. I noted refinements in colour. It was very interesting. Time was when I began to make something of light and shade.

I began to see that if you were representing a man's face you would represent the side on which light shone by very different paint from that whereby you would express the side which rested in shadow. All these things were, and are, interesting. One is more alive for having these swift-passing, departmentalised interests in the flow of life about one. It is by swift apperceptions of this sort that one differentiates oneself from the brute world. To be civilised is to have swift apperception of the complicated life of today; it is to have a subtle and instantaneous perception of it, such as savages and wild animals have of the necessities and dangers of the forest. It is to be no less alive or vital than the savage. It is a different kind of aliveness.

And vorticism, especially that part of vorticism having to do with form—to wit, vorticist painting and sculpture—has brought me a new series of apperceptions. It has not brought them solely to me. I have my new and swift perceptions of forms, of possible form-motifs; I have a double or treble or tenfold set of stimulae in going from my home to Piccadilly. What was a dull row of houses is become a magazine of forms. There are new ways of seeing them. There are ways of seeing the shape of the sky as it juts down between the houses. The tangle of telegraph wires is conceivable not merely as a repetition of lines; one sees the shapes defined by the different branches of wire. The lumber yards, the sidings of railways cease to be dreary.

The musical conception of form, that is to say the understanding that you can use form as a musician uses sound, that you can select motives of form from the forms before you, that you can recombine and recolour them and "organise" them into new form—this conception, this state of mental activity, brings with it a great joy and refreshment. I do not wish to convert anyone. I simply say that a certain sort of pleasure is available to anyone who wants it. It is one of the simple pleasures of those who have no money to spend on joy-rides and on suppers at the Ritz.

This "musical conception of form" is more than post-impressionism. Manet took impressions of colour. They say Cézanne began taking "impressions of form." That is not the same thing as conceiving the forms about one as a source of "form-motifs," which motifs one can use later at one's pleasure in more highly developed compositions.

It is possible that this search for form-motif will lead us to some synthesis of western life comparable to the synthesis of oriental life which we find in Chinese and Japanese painting. This lies with the future. Perhaps there is some adumbration of it in Mr. Wadsworth's "Harbour of Flushing."

At any rate I have put down some of my reasons for believing in the vorticist painters and sculptors. I have at least in part explained why I believe in Mr. Wyndham Lewis; why I think him a more significant artist than Kandinsky (admitting that I have not yet seen enough of Kandinsky's work to use a verb stronger than "think"); why I think that Mr. Lewis' work will contain certain elements not to be found in Picasso, whom I regard as a great artist, but who has not yet expressed all that we mean by vorticism.

Note that I am not trying to destroy anyone's enjoyment of the Quattrocento, nor of the Victory of Samothrace, nor of any work of art which is approximately the best of its kind. I state that there is a new gamut of artistic enjoyments and satisfactions; that vorticist painting is not meaningless; and that anyone who cares to may enjoy it.

The Serious Artist (1913)

IT IS CURIOUS that one should be asked to rewrite Sidney's *Defence of Poesy* in the year of grace 1913. During the intervening centuries, and before them, other centres of civilization had decided that good art was a blessing and that bad art was criminal, and they had spent some time and thought in trying to find means whereby to distinguish the true art from the sham. But in England now, in the age of Gosse as in the age of Gosson we are asked if the arts are moral. We are asked to define the relation of the arts to economics, we are asked what position the arts are to hold in the ideal republic. And it is obviously the opinion of many people less objectionable than the Sydney Webbs that the arts had better not exist at all.

I take no great pleasure in writing prose about aesthetic. I think one work of art is worth forty prefaces and as many apologiae. Nevertheless I have been questioned earnestly and by a person certainly of good will. It is as if one said to me: what is the use of open spaces in this city, what is the use of rose-trees and why do you wish to plant trees and lay out parks and gardens? There are some who do not take delight in these things. The rose springs fairest from some buried Caesar's throat and the dogwood with its flower of four petals (our dogwood, not the tree you call by that name) is grown from the heart of Aucassin, or perhaps this is only fancy. Let us pursue the matter in ethic.

It is obvious that ethics are based on the nature of man, just as it is obvious that civics are based upon the nature of men when living together in groups.

It is obvious that the good of the greatest number cannot be attained until we know in some sort of what that good must consist. In other words we must know what sort of an animal man is, before we can contrive his maximum happiness, or before we can decide what percentage of that happiness he can have without causing too great a percentage of unhappiness to those about him.

The arts, literature, poesy, are a science, just as chemistry is a science. Their subject is man, mankind and the individual. The subject of chemistry is matter considered as to its composition.

The arts give us a great percentage of the lasting and unassailable data regarding the nature of man, of immaterial man, of man considered as a thinking and sentient creature. They begin where the science of medicine leaves off or rather they overlap that science. The borders of the two arts overcross.

From medicine we learn that man thrives best when duly washed, aired and sunned. From the arts we learn that man is whimsical, that one man differs from another. That men differ among themselves as leaves upon trees differ. That they do not resemble each other as do buttons cut by machine.

From the arts also we learn in what ways man resembles and in what way he differs from certain other animals. We learn that certain men are often more akin to certain animals than they are to other men of different composition. We learn that all men do not desire the same things and that it would therefore be inequitable to give to all men two acres and a cow.

It would be manifestly inequitable to treat the ostrich and the polar bear in the same fashion, granted that it is not unjust to have them pent up where you can treat them at all.

An ethic based on a belief that men are different from what they are is manifestly stupid. It is stupid to apply such an ethic as it is to apply laws and morals designed for a nomadic tribe, or for a tribe in the state of barbarism, to a people crowded into the slums of a modern metropolis. Thus in the tribe it is well to beget children, for the more strong male children you have in the tribe the less likely you are to be bashed on the head by males of the neighbouring tribes, and the more female children the more rapidly the tribe will increase. Conversely it is a crime rather worse than murder to beget children in a slum, to beget children for whom no fitting provision is made, either as touching their physical or economic wellbeing. The increase not only afflicts the child born but the increasing number of the poor keeps down the wage. On this count the bishop of London, as an encourager of this sort of increase, is a criminal of a type rather lower and rather more detestable than the souteneur.

I cite this as one example of inequity persisting because of a continued refusal to consider a code devised for one state of society, in its (the code's) relation to a different state of society. It is as if, in physics or engineering, we refused to consider a force designed to affect one mass, in its relation (i.e. the force's) to another mass wholly differing, or in some notable way differing, from the first mass.

As inequities can exist because of refusals to consider the actualities of a law in relation to a social condition, so can inequities exist through refusal to consider the actualities of the composition of the masses, or of the individuals to which they are applied.

If all men desired above everything else two acres and a cow, obviously the perfect state would be that state which gave to each man two acres and a cow.

If any science save the arts were able more precisely to determine what the individual does not actually desire, then that science would be of more use in providing the data for ethics.

In the like manner, if any sciences save medicine and chemistry were more able to determine what things were compatible with physical wellbeing, then those sciences would be of more value for providing the data of hygiene.

This brings us to the immorality of bad art. Bad art is inaccurate art. It is art that makes false reports. If a scientist falsifies a report either deliberately or through negligence we consider him as either a criminal or a bad scientist according to the enormity of his offence, and he is punished or despised accordingly.

If he falsifies the reports of a maternity hospital in order to retain his position and get profit and advancement from the city board, he may escape detection. If he declines to make such falsification he may lose financial rewards, and in either case his baseness or his pluck may pass unknown and unnoticed save by a very few people. Nevertheless one does not have to argue his case. The layman knows soon enough on hearing it whether the physician is to be blamed or praised.

If an artist falsifies his report as to the nature of man, as to his own nature, as to the nature of his ideal of the perfect, as to the nature of his ideal of this, that or the other, of god, if god exist, of the life force, of the nature of good and evil, if good and evil exist, of the force with which he believes or disbelieves this, that or the other, of the degree in which he suffers or is made glad; if the artist falsifies his reports on these matters or on any other matter in order that he may conform to the taste of his time, to the proprieties of a sovereign, to the conveniences of a preconceived code of ethics, then that artist lies. If he lies out of deliberate will to lie, if he lies out of carelessness, out of laziness, out of cowardice, out of any sort of negligence whatsoever, he nevertheless lies and he should be punished or despised in proportion to the seriousness of his offence. His offence is of the same nature as the physician's and according to his position and the nature of his lie he is responsible for future oppressions and for future misconceptions. Albeit his lies are known to only a few, or his truth-telling to only a few. Albeit he may pass without censure for one and without praise for the other. Albeit he can only be punished on the plane of his crime and by nothing save the contempt of those who know of his crime. Perhaps it is caddishness rather than crime. However there is perhaps nothing worse for a man than to know that he is a cur and to know that someone else, if only one person, knows it.

We distinguish very clearly between the physician who is doing his best for a patient, who is using drugs in which he believes, or who is in a wilderness, let us say, where the patient can get no other medical aid. We distinguish, I say, very clearly between the failure of such a physician, and the act of that physician, who ignorant of the patient's disease, being in reach of more skilful physicians, deliberately denies an ignorance of which he is quite conscious, refuses to consult other physicians, tries to prevent the patient's having access to more skilful physicians, or deliberately tortures the patient for his own ends.

One does not need to read black print to learn this ethical fact about physicians. Yet it takes a deal of talking to convince a layman that bad art is "immoral." And that good art however "immoral" it is, is wholly a thing of virtue. Purely and simply that good art can NOT be immoral. By good art I mean art that bears true witness, I mean the art that is most precise. You can be wholly precise in representing a vagueness. You can be wholly a liar in pretending that the particular vagueness was precise in its outline. If you cannot understand this with regard to poetry, consider the matter in terms of painting.

If you have forgotten my statement that the arts bear witness and define for us the inner nature and conditions of man, consider the Victory of Samothrace and the Taj of Agra. The man who carved the one and the man who designed the other may either or both of them have looked like an ape, or like two apes

respectively. They may have looked like other apelike or swinelike men. We have the Victory and the Taj to witness that there was something within them differing from the contents of apes and of the other swinelike men. Thus we learn that humanity is a species or genus of animals capable of a variation that will produce the desire for a Taj or a Victory, and moreover capable of effecting that Taj or Victory in stone. We know from other testimony of the arts and from ourselves that the desire often overshoots the power of efficient presentation; we therefore conclude that other members of the race may have desired to effect a Taj or a Victory. We even suppose that men have desired to effect more beautiful things although few of us are capable of forming any precise mental image of things, in their particular way, more beautiful than this statue or this building. So difficult is this that no one has yet been able to effect a restoration for the missing head of the Victory. At least no one has done so in stone, so far as I know. Doubtless many people have stood opposite the statue and made such heads in their imagination.

As there are in medicine the art of diagnosis and the art of cure, so in the arts, so in the particular arts of poetry and of literature, there is the art of diagnosis and there is the art of cure. They call one the cult of ugliness and the other the cult of beauty.

The cult of beauty is the hygiene, it is sun, air and the sea and the rain and the lake bathing. The cult of ugliness, Villon, Baudelaire, Corbière, Beardsley are diagnosis. Flaubert is diagnosis. Satire, if we are to ride this metaphor to staggers, satire is surgery, insertions and amputations.

Beauty in art reminds one what is worth while. I am not now speaking of shams. I mean beauty, not slither, not sentimentalizing about beauty, not telling people that beauty is the proper and respectable thing. I mean beauty. You don't argue about an April wind, you feel bucked up when you meet it. You feel bucked up when you come on a swift moving thought in Plato or on a fine line in a statue.

Even this pother about gods reminds one that something is worth while. Satire reminds one that certain things are not worth while. It draws one to consider time wasted.

The cult of beauty and the delineation of ugliness are not in mutual opposition.

II

I have said that the arts give us our best data for determining what sort of creature man is. As our treatment of man must be determined by our knowledge or conception of what man is, the arts provide data for ethics.

These data are sound and the data of generalizing psychologists and social theoricians are usually unsound, for the serious artist is scientific and the theorist is usually empiric in the medieval fashion. That is to say a good biologist will make a reasonable number of observations of any given phenomenon before he draws a conclusion, thus we read such phrases as "over 100 cultures from the secretions of the respiratory tracts of over 500 patients and 30 nurses and attendants." The results of each observation must be precise and no single observation must in itself be taken as determining a general law, although, after experiment, certain observations may be held as typical or normal. The serious artist is scientific in that he presents the image of his desire, of his hate, of his indifference as precisely that, as precisely the image of his own desire, hate or indifference. The more precise his record the more lasting and unassailable his work of art.

The theorist, and we see this constantly illustrated by the English writers on sex, the theorist constantly proceeds as if his own case, his own limits and predilections were the typical case, or even as if it were the universal. He is constantly urging someone else to behave as he, the theorist, would like to behave. Now art never asks anybody to do anything, or to think anything, or to be anything. It exists as the trees exist, you can admire, you can sit in the shade, you can pick bananas, you can cut firewood, you can do as you jolly well please.

Also you are a fool to seek the kind of art you don't like. You are a fool to read classics because you are told to and not because you like them. You are a fool to aspire to good taste if you haven't naturally got it. If there is one place where it is idiotic to sham that place is before a work of art. Also you are a fool not to have an open mind, not to be eager to enjoy something you might enjoy but don't know how to. But it is not the artist's place to ask you to learn, or to defend his particular works of art, or to insist on your reading his books. Any artist who wants your particular admiration is, by just so much, the less artist.

The desire to stand on the stage, the desire of plaudits has nothing to do with serious art. The serious artist may like to stand on the stage, he may, apart from his art, be any kind of imbecile you like, but the two things are not connected, at least they are not concentric. Lots of people who don't even pretend to be artists have the same desire to be slobbered over, by people with less brains than they have.

The serious artist is usually, or is often as far from the aegrum vulgus as is the serious scientist. Nobody has heard of the abstract mathematicians who worked out the determinants that Marconi made use of in his computations for the wireless telegraph. The public, the public so dear to the journalistic heart, is far more concerned with the shareholders in the Marconi company.

The permanent property, the property given to the race at large is precisely these data of the serious scientist and of the serious artist; of the scientist as touching the relations of abstract numbers, of molecular energy, of the composition of matter, etc.; of the serious artist, as touching the nature of man, of individuals.

Men have ceased trying to conquer the world [1] and to acquire universal knowledge. Men still try to promote the ideal state. No perfect state will be founded on the theory, or on the working hypothesis that all men are

[1] *Blind Optimism* A.D. 1913.

alike. No science save the arts will give us the requisite data for learning in what ways men differ.

The very fact that many men hate the arts is of value, for we are enabled by finding out what part of the arts they hate, to learn something of their nature. Usually when men say they hate the arts we find that they merely detest quackery and bad artists.

In the case of a man's hating one art and not the others we may learn that he is of defective hearing or of defective intelligence. Thus an intelligent man may hate music or a good musician may detest very excellent authors.

And all these things are very obvious.

Among thinking and sentient people the bad artist is contemned as we would contemn a negligent physician or a sloppy, inaccurate scientist, and the serious artist is left in peace, or even supported and encouraged. In the fog and the outer darkness no measures are taken to distinguish between the serious and the unserious artist. The unserious artist being the commoner brand and greatly outnumbering the serious variety, and it being to the temporary and apparent advantage of the false artist to gain the rewards proper to the serious artist, it is natural that the unserious artist should do all in his power to obfuscate the lines of demarcation.

Whenever one attempts to demonstrate the difference between serious and unserious work, one is told that "it is merely a technical discussion." It has rested at that—in England it has rested at that for more than three hundred years. The people would rather have patent medicines than scientific treatment. They will occasionally be told that art as art is not a violation of God's most holy laws. They will not have a specialist's opinion as to what art is good. They will not consider the "problem of style." They want "The value of art to life" and "Fundamental issues."

As touching fundamental issues: The arts give us our data of psychology, of man as to his interiors, as to the ratio of his thought to his emotions, etc., etc., etc.

The touchstone of an art is its precision. This precision is of various and complicated sorts and only the specialist can determine whether certain works of art possess certain sorts of precision. I don't mean to say that any intelligent person cannot have more or less sound judgement as to whether a certain work of art is good or not. An intelligent person can usually tell whether or not a person is in good health. It is none the less true that it takes a skilful physician to make certain diagnoses or to discern the lurking disease beneath the appearance of vigour.

It is no more possible to give in a few pages full instructions for knowing a masterpiece than it would be to give full instructions for all medical diagnosis.

III

EMOTION AND POESY

Obviously, it is not easy to be a great poet. If it were, many more people would have done so. At no period in history has the world been free of people who have mildly desired to be great poets and not a few have endeavoured conscientiously to be such.

I am aware that adjectives of magnitude are held to savour of barbarism. Still there is no shame in desiring to give great gifts and an enlightened criticism does not draw ignominious comparisons between Villon and Dante. The so-called major poets have most of them given their *own* gift but the peculiar term "major" is rather a gift to them from Chronos. I mean that they have been born upon the stroke of their hour and that it has been given them to heap together and arrange and harmonize the results of many men's labour. This very faculty for amalgamation is a part of their genius and it is, in a way, a sort of modesty, a sort of unselfishness. They have not wished for property.

The men from whom Dante borrowed are remembered as much for the fact that he did borrow as for their own compositions. At the same time he gave of his own, and no mere compiler and classifier of other men's discoveries is given the name of "major poet" for more than a season.

If Dante had not done a deal more than borrow rhymes from Arnaut Daniel and theology from Aquinas he would not be published by Dent in the year of grace 1913.

We might come to believe that the thing that matters in art is a sort of energy, something more or less like electricity or radio-activity, a force transfusing, welding, and unifying. A force rather like water when it spurts up through very bright sand and sets it in swift motion. You may make what image you like.

I do not know that there is much use in composing an answer to the often asked question: What is the difference between poetry and prose?

I believe that poetry is the more highly energized. But these things are relative. Just as we say that a certain temperature is hot and another cold. In the same way we say that a certain prose passage "is poetry" meaning to praise it, and that a certain passage of verse is "only prose" meaning dispraise. And at the same time "Poetry!!!" is used as a synonym for "Bosh! Rott!! Rubbish!!!" The thing that counts is "Good writing."

And "Good writing" is perfect control. And it is quite easy to control a thing that has in it no energy—provided that it be not too heavy and that you do not wish to make it move.

And, as all the words that one would use in writing about these things are the vague words of daily speech, it is nearly impossible to write with scientific preciseness about "prose and verse" unless one writes a complete treatise on the "art of writing," defining each word as one would define the terms in a treatise on chemistry. And on this account all essays about "poetry" are usually not only dull but inaccurate and wholly useless. And on like account if you ask a good painter to tell you what he is trying to do to a canvas he will very probably wave his hands helplessly and murmur that "He—eh—eh—he can't talk about it." And that if you "see anything at all, he is quite—eh—more

or less—eh—satisfied."

Nevertheless it has been held for a shameful thing that a man should not be able to give a reason for his acts and words. And if one does not care about being taken for a mystificateur one may as well try to give approximate answers to questions asked in good faith. It might be better to do the thing thoroughly, in a properly accurate treatise, but one has not always two or three spare years at one's disposal, and one is dealing with very subtle and complicated matter, and even so, the very algebra of logic is itself open to debate.

Roughly then, Good writing is writing that is perfectly controlled, the writer says just what he means. He says it with complete clarity and simplicity. He uses the smallest possible number of words. I do not mean that he skimps paper, or that he screws about like Tacitus to get his thought crowded into the least possible space. But, granting that two sentences are at times easier to understand than one sentence containing the double meaning, the author tries to communicate with the reader with the greatest possible despatch, save where for any one of forty reasons he does not wish to do so.

Also there are various kinds of clarity. There is the clarity of the request: Send me four pounds of ten-penny nails. And there is the syntactical simplicity of the request: Buy me the kind of Rembrandt I like. This last is an utter cryptogram. It presupposes a more complex and intimate understanding of the speaker than most of us ever acquire of anyone. It has as many meanings, almost, as there are persons who might speak it. To a stranger it conveys nothing at all.

It is the almost constant labour of the prose artist to translate this latter kind of clarity into the former; to say "Send me the kind of Rembrandt I like" in the terms of "Send me four pounds of ten-penny nails."

The whole thing is an evolution. In the beginning simple words were enough: Food; water; fire. Both prose and poetry are but an extension of language. Man desires to communicate with his fellows. He desires an ever in-

creasingly complicated communication. Gesture serves up to a point. Symbols may serve.
When you desire something not present to the
eye or when you desire to communicate ideas,
you must have recourse to speech. Gradually
you wish to communicate something less bare
and ambiguous than ideas. You wish to communicate an idea and its modifications, an idea
and a crowd of its effects, atmospheres, contradictions. You wish to question whether a certain formula works in every case, or in what
per cent of cases, etc., etc., etc., you get the
Henry James novel.

You wish to communicate an idea and its
concomitant emotions, or an emotion and its
concomitant ideas, or a sensation and its derivative emotions, or an impression that is emotive, etc., etc., etc. You begin with the yeowl
and the bark, and you develop into the dance
and into music, and into music with words,
and finally into words with music, and finally
into words with a vague adumbration of music, words suggestive of music, words measured,
or words in a rhythm that preserves some accurate trait of the emotive impression, or of the
sheer character of the fostering or parental
emotion.

When this rhythm, or when the vowel and
consonantal melody or sequence seems truly to
bear the trace of emotion which the poem (for
we have come at last to the poem) is intended
to communicate, we say that this part of the
work is good. And "this part of the work" is by
now "technique." That "dry, dull, pedantic"
technique, that all bad artists rail against. It is
only a part of technique, it is rhythm, cadence,
and the arrangement of sounds.

Also the "prose," the words and their sense
must be such as fit the emotion. Or, from the
other side, ideas, or fragments of ideas, the
emotion and concomitant emotions of this
"Intellectual and Emotional Complex" (for
we have come to the intellectual and emotional complex) must be in harmony, they
must form an organism, they must be an oak
sprung from an acorn.

When you have words of a lament set to the
rhythm and tempo of There'll be a Hot Time

in the Old Town to-night you have either an
intentional burlesque or you have rotten art.
Shelley's Sensitive Plant is one of the rottenest
poems ever written, at least one of the worst
ascribable to a recognized author. It jiggles to
the same tune as A little peach in the orchard
grew. Yet Shelley recovered and wrote the fifth
act of the Cenci.

IV

It is occasionally suggested by the wise that
poets should acquire the graces of prose. That
is an extension of what has been said above
anent control. Prose does not need emotion. It
may, but it need not, attempt to portray emotion.

Poetry is a centaur. The thinking, word-ar-
ranging, clarifying faculty must move and leap
with the energizing, sentient, musical faculties.
It is precisely the difficulty of this amphibious
existence that keeps down the census record of
good poets. The accomplished prose author
will tell you that he "can only write poetry
when he has a bellyache" and thence he will
argue that poetry just isn't an art.

I dare say there are very good marksmen who
just can't shoot from a horse.

Likewise if a good marksman only mounted
a few times he might never acquire any proficiency in shooting from the saddle. Or leaving metaphor, I suppose that what, in the long
run, makes the poet is a sort of persistence of
the emotional nature, and, joined with this, a
peculiar sort of control.

The saying that "a lyric poet might as well
die at thirty" is simply saying that the emotional nature seldom survives this age, or that
it becomes, at any rate, subjected and incapable of moving the whole man. Of course this
is a generality, and, as such, inaccurate.

It is true that most people poetize more or
less, between the ages of seventeen and twenty-
three. The emotions are new, and, to their possessor, interesting, and there is not much mind
or personality to be moved. As the man, as his
mind, becomes a heavier and heavier machine,
a constantly more complicated structure, it requires a constantly greater voltage of emotional

energy to set it in harmonious motion. It is certain that the emotions increase in vigour as a vigorous man matures. In the case of Guido we have his strongest work at fifty. Most important poetry has been written by men over thirty.

"En l'an trentiesme de mon eage," begins Villon and considering the nature of his life thirty would have seen him more spent than forty years of more orderly living.

Aristotle will tell you that "The apt use of metaphor, being as it is, the swift perception of relations, is the true hall-mark of genius." That abundance, that readiness of the figure is indeed one of the surest proofs that the mind is upborne upon the emotional surge.

By "apt use," I should say it were well to understand, a swiftness, almost a violence, and certainly a vividness. This does not mean elaboration and complication.

There is another poignancy which I do not care to analyse into component parts, if, indeed, such vivisection is possible. It is not the formal phrasing of Flaubert much as such formality is desirable and noble. It is such phrasing as we find in

> Era gìa l'ora che volge il disio
> Ai naviganti. . . .

Or the opening of the ballata which begins:

> Perch 'io non spero di tornar già mai
> Ballatetta, in Toscana.

Or:

> S'ils n 'ayment fors que pour l'argent,
> On ne les ayme que pour l'heure.

Or, in its context:

> The fire that stirs about her, when she stirs,

or, in its so different setting,

> Ne maeg werigmod wryde withstondan
> ne se hreo hyge helpe gefremman:
> forthon domgeorne dreorigne oft
> in hyra breostcofan bindath faeste.

These things have in them that passionate simplicity which is beyond the precisions of the intellect. Truly they are perfect as fine prose is perfect, but they are in some way different from the clear statements of the observer. They are in some way different from that so masterly ending of the Herodias: "Comme elle était très lourde ils la portaient alternativement" or from the constatation in St. Julian Hospitalier: "Et l'idée lui vient d'employer son existence au service des autres."

The prose author has shown the triumph of his intellect and one knows that such triumph is not without its sufferings by the way, but by the verses one is brought upon the passionate moment. This moment has brought with it nothing that violates the prose simplicities. The intellect has not found it but the intellect has been moved.

There is little but folly in seeking the lines of division, yet if the two arts must be divided we may as well use that line as any other. In the verse something has come upon the intelligence. In the prose the intelligence has found a subject for its observations. The poetic fact pre-exists.

In a different way, of course, the subject of the prose pre-exists. Perhaps the difference is undemonstrable, perhaps it is not even communicable to any save those of good will. Yet I think this orderliness in the greatest poetic passages, this quiet statement that partakes of the nature of prose and is yet floated and tossed in the emotional surges, is perhaps as true a test as that mentioned by the Greek theorician.

v

La poésie, avec ses comparaisons obligées, sa mythologie que ne croit pas le poète, sa dignité de style à la Louis XIV, et tout l'attirail de ses ornements appelés poétiques, est bien audessous de la prose dès qu'il s'agit de donner une idée claire et précise des mouvements du coeur; or, dans ce genre, on n'émeut que par la clarté.
—*Stendhal*

And that is precisely why one employs oneself in seeking precisely the poetry that shall be without this flummery, this fustian *à la Louis XIV*, "*farcie de comme.*" The above critique of Stendhal's does not apply to the

Poema del Cid, nor to the parting of Odysseus and Calypso. In the writers of the duo-cento and early tre-cento we find a precise psychology, embedded in a now almost unintelligible jargon, but there nevertheless. If we cannot get back to these things; if the serious artist cannot attain this precision in verse, then he must either take to prose or give up his claim to being a serious artist.

It is precisely because of this fustian that the Parnassiads and epics of the eighteenth century and most of the present-day works of most of our contemporary versifiers are pests and abominations.

As the most efficient way to say nothing is to keep quiet, and as technique consists precisely in doing the thing that one sets out to do, in the most efficient manner, no man who takes three pages to say nothing can expect to be seriously considered as a technician. To take three pages to say nothing is not style, in the serious sense of that word.

There are several kinds of honest work. There is the thing that will out. There is the conscientious formulation, a thing of infinitely greater labour, for the first is not labour at all, though the efficient doing of it may depend on a deal of labour foregoing.

There is the "labour foregoing," the patient testing of media, the patient experiment which shall avail perhaps the artist himself, but is as likely to avail some successor.

The first sort of work may be poetry.

The second sort, the conscientious formulation, is more than likely to be prose.

The third sort of work savours of the laboratory, it concerns the specialist, and the dilettante, if that word retains any trace of its finer and original sense. A dilettante proper is a person who takes delight in the art, not a person who tries to interpose his inferior productions between masterwork and the public.

I reject the term connoisseurship, for "connoisseurship" is so associated in our minds with a desire for acquisition. The person possessed of connoisseurship is so apt to want to buy the rare at one price and sell it at another. I do not believe that a person with this spirit has ever *seen* a work of art. Let me restore the foppish term dilettante, the synonym for folly, to its place near the word *diletto*.

The dilettante has no axe to grind for himself. If he be artist as well, he will be none the less eager to preserve the best precedent work. He will drag out "sources" that prove him less original than his public would have him.

As for Stendhal's stricture, if we can have a poetry that comes as close as prose, *pour donner une idée claire et précise*, let us have it, "E di venire a ciò io studio quanto posso . . . che la mia vita per alquanti anni duri.". . . And if we cannot attain to such a poetry, noi altri poeti, for God's sake let us shut up. Let us "Give up, go down," etcetera; let us acknowledge that our art, like the art of dancing in armour, is out of date and out of fashion. Or let us go to our ignominious ends knowing that we have strained at the cords, that we have spent our strength in trying to pave the way for a new sort of poetic art—it is not a new sort but an old sort—but let us know that we have tried to make it more nearly possible for our successors to recapture this art. To write a poetry that can be carried as a communication between intelligent men.

To this end *io studio quanto posso*. I have tried to establish a clear demarcation. I have been challenged on my use of the phrase "great art" in an earlier article. It is about as useless to search for a definition of "great art" as it is to search for a scientific definition of life. One knows fairly well what one means. One means something more or less proportionate to one's experience. One means something quite different at different periods of one's life.

It is for some such reason that all criticism should be professedly personal criticism. In the end the critic can only say "I like it," or "I am moved," or something of that sort. When he has shown us himself we are able to understand him.

Thus, in painting, I mean something or other vaguely associated in my mind with work labelled Dürer, and Rembrandt, and Velasquez, etc., and with the painters whom I scarcely know, possibly of T'ang and Sung—though I dare say I've got the wrong labels—and with some Egyptian designs that should probably be thought of as sculpture.

And in poetry I mean something or other associated in my mind with the names of a dozen or more writers.

On closer analysis I find that I mean something like "maximum efficiency of expression"; I mean that the writer has expressed something interesting in such a way that one cannot re-say it more effectively. I also mean something associated with discovery. The artist must have discovered something—either of life itself or of the means of expression.

Great art must of necessity be a part of good art. I attempted to define good art in an earlier chapter. I must bear true witness. Obviously great art must be an exceptional thing. It cannot be the sort of thing anyone can do after a few hours' practice. It must be the result of some exceptional faculty, strength, or perception. It must almost be that strength of perception working with the connivance of fate, or chance, or whatever you choose to call it.

And who is to judge? The critic, the receiver, however stupid or ignorant, must judge for himself. The only really vicious criticism is the academic criticism of those who make the grand abnegation, who refuse to say what they think, if they do think, and who quote accepted opinion; these men are the vermin, their treachery to the great work of the past is as great as that of the false artist to the present. If they do not care enough for the heritage to have a personal conviction then they have no licence to write.

Every critic should give indication of the sources and limits of his knowledge. The criticism of English poetry by men who knew no language but English, or who knew little but English and school-classics, has been a marasmus.

When we know to what extent each sort of expression has been driven, in, say, half a dozen great literatures, we begin to be able to tell whether a given work has the excess of great art. We would not think of letting a man judge pictures if he knew only English pictures, or music if he knew only English music—or only French or German music for that matter.

The stupid or provincial judgment of art bases itself on the belief that great art must be like the art that it has been reared to respect.

The Hard and Soft in French Poetry

(1918)

I APOLOGIZE for using the semetaphorical terms "hard" and "soft" in this essay, but after puzzling over the matter for some time I can see no other way of setting about it. By "hardness" I mean a quality which is in poetry nearly al-

ways a virtue—I can think of no case where it is not. By softness I mean an opposite quality which is not always a fault. Anyone who dislikes these textural terms may lay the blame on Théophile Gautier, who certainly suggests them in *Emaux et Camées*; it is his hardness that I had first in mind. He exhorts us to cut in hard substance, the shell and the Parian.

We may take it that Gautier achieved hardness in *Emaux et Camées*; his earlier work did in France very much what remained for the men of "the nineties" to accomplish in England. An examination of what Gautier wrote in "the thirties" will show a similar beauty, a similar sort of technique. If the Parnassians were following Gautier they fell short of his merit. Heredia is perhaps the best of them. He tries to make his individual statements more "poetic"; his whole, for all this, becomes frigid. Samain follows him and begins to go "soft," there is just a suggestion of muzziness. Heredia is "hard," but there or thereabouts he ends. It is perhaps that Gautier is intent on being "hard"; is intent on conveying a certain verity of feeling, and he ends by being truly poetic. Heredia wants to be poetic *and* hard; the hardness appears to him as a virtue in the poetic. And one tends to conclude that all attempts to be poetic in some manner or other defeat their own end; whereas an intentness on the quality of the emotion to be conveyed makes for poetry.

Another possible corollary is that the subject matter will very nearly make the poem. Subject matter will, of course, not make the poem; e.g., compare Mangan's *Kathleen ni Houlihan*, with Yeats' *Song that Red Hanrahan made about Ireland*, where the content is almost identical.

On the other hand the man who first decides that certain things are poetry has great advantage over all who follow him, and who accede in his opinion. Gautier did decide that certain things were worth making into poems, whereas the Parnassians only acceded in other men's opinions about subject matter, and accepted Gautier's advice to cut, metaphorically, in hard stone, etc.

Gautier is individual and original even in such poems as the *Poem of Woman*, and the *Symphony in White Major*, which seem but variants on old themes. I have found what might be a germ of the *Symphony* in Renaissance Latin, and there is an Elizabethan lyric about *Swan's down ever*. Nevertheless Gautier's way of thinking about these things was at bottom his own.

His originality is not in his form, his hard, close-cut lines and stanzas. Bernard, a poet praised by Voltaire, and at one time Rameau's librettist, wrote French in clear hard little stanzas:

J'ai vu Daphné, Terpsichore légère,
  Sur un tapis de rose et de fougère,
  S'abandonner à des bonds pleins d'appas,
Voler, languir . . .

This is not from a stanza but it shows Bernard's perfectly orderly method.

Gautier writing in opposition to, or in rejection of, the swash of Hugo, De Musset & Co. came undoubtedly as a contrast, but he can scarcely have seemed so "different" to Frenchmen versed in their own earlier poetry as he does to the English reader coming upon him with slight prelude save English.

We have however some hardness in English, and in Landor we have a hardness which is not of necessity "rugged"; as in "Past ruin'd Ilion Helen lives." Indeed, Gautier might well be the logical successor to Landor, were he not in all probability the logical co-heir with Landor of certain traditions.

Landor is, from poem to poem, extremely uneven. Our feeling of him must in part rest on our admiration of his prose. Lionel Johnson had a certain hardness and smoothness, but was more critic than poet, and not a very great poet. There is definite statement in George Herbert, and likewise in Christina Rossetti, but I do not feel that they have much part in this essay. I do not feel that their quality is really the quality I am seeking here to define.

We have in English a certain gamut of styles: we have the good Chaucerian, almost the only style in English where "softness" is tolerable; we have the good Elizabethan; which is not wholly un-Chaucerian: and the bad, or muzzy, Elizabethan; and the Miltonic, which is a bombastic and rhetorical Elizabethan coming from an attempt to write English with Latin syntax. Its other mark is that the rich words have gone: *i.e.*, words like *preluciand*, which have a folk tradition and are, in feeling, germane to all Europe: *Leuchend, luisant, lucente;* these words are absent in Miltonism, and purely pedantic words, like *irriguous*, have succeeded them.

We have Pope, who is really the Elizabethan satiric style, more or less born out of Horace, and a little improved or at least regularized. And we have Landor—that is, Landor at his best. And after that we have "isms" and "eses": the pseudo-Elizabethanism—*i.e.*, bad Keats; the romantics, Swinburnese, Browningese, neo-celticism. And how the devil a poet writing English manages to find or make a language for poems is a mystery.

It is approximately true, or at least it is a formulation worth talking over: that French prose is good in proportion as it reaches a sort of norm; English prose is good in proportion as a man makes it an individual language, one which he alone uses. This statement must not be swallowed whole. And we must also remember that when Italians were writing excellent and clear prose—in the time of Henry VIII—Englishmen could scarcely make a clear prose formulation even in documents of state and instructions to envoys; so backward were things in this island, so rude in prose the language which had been exquisite in the lyrics of Chaucer.[1]

French "clarity" can be talked to death, and there are various kinds of French prose—the Voltaire-Anatole France kind, the Stendhal roughness and directness, the Flaubertian art, and also the "soft" prose. Flaubert and Anatole France are both "softer" than Voltaire and Stendhal. Remy de Gourmont is almost the only writer who seems to me good in a French prose which must, I think, be called "soft." It is with him a peculiar and personal medium.

If this seem an over-long prologue, think how little discussion there is of these things. Only a few professors and their favourite students seem to have read enough to be able to consider a matter of style with any data at their disposal—these and a few poets of the better sort; and professors are not paid to spread heresies and bring uncertainties into accepted opinion; and poets of the worse sort seem seldom to have any reading. So a prologue is needed even for a brief attempt to find out where French verse has got to; or where it had arrived a few years ago, seeing that since the war, *faute de combattants*, no one has had time to go forward, or even to continue the work of 1912–1914—since undigested war is no better for poetry than undigested anything else.

Since Gautier, Corbière has been hard, not with a glaze or parian finish, but hard like weather-bit granite. And Heredia and Samain have been hard decreasingly, giving gradually smoothness for hardness. And Jammes has been "soft," in his earlier poems with a pleasurable softness. And De Regnier seems to verge out of Parnassianism into an undefined sort of poetry. Tailhade is hard in his satire.

Romains, Vildrac, Spire, Arcos, are not hard, any one of them, though Spire can be acid. These men have left the ambitions of Gautier; they have done so deliberately, or at least they have, in the quest of something well worth seeking, made a new kind of French poetry. I first wrote of *Unanimisme* in the *New Age* something over four years ago. Romains is the centre of it. A recent English essay on the subject, trying to point to English *unanimistes*, is pure rubbish, and shows no comprehension on the part of its author. Romains' *unanimisme* is a definite theory, almost a religion. He alone of the better French poets seems to have written at its dictates. The rest of the men of his decade have not written to a theory. Romains has, I think, more intellect than the rest of them, and he is an equally notable poet. He has tried to make, and in places succeeded in making, poetry out of crowd-psychology. Vildrac has been personal and humanitarian. Arcos and Spire have delineated. Romains' portrayal of the collective emotions of a school of little girls

---

[1] Moderate this statement by consideration of Mallory. E.P.

out for the day is the most original poem in our generation's French. His series of "prayers" —to the God-one, the god-couple, the god-house, the god-street, and so on—is extremely interesting. Vildrac's short narrative poems are a progress on the pseudo-Maupassant story, and have parallels in English. Romains has no English parallel. Allowing for personal difference, I should say that Spire and Arcos write "more or less as I do myself." I do not mean to make any comparison of merits, but this comparison is the easiest or simplest way of telling the general reader "what sort of poems" they have written.

I do not think I have copied their work, and they certainly have not copied mine. We are contemporary and as sonnets of a certain sort were once written on both sides of the channel, so these short poems depicting certain phases of contemporary life are now written on both sides of the channel; with, of course, personal differences.

Vildrac has written *Auberge* and *Visite*, and no doubt these poems will be included in any anthology of the period. The thing that puzzles me in attempting to appreciate both Romains and Vildrac is just this question of "hardness," and a wonder how poetry can get on without it—not by any means demanding that it be ubiquitous. For I do not in the least mean that I want their poems rewritten "hard"; any more than I should want Jammes' early poems rewritten "hard." A critic must spend some of his time asking questions— which perhaps no one can answer. It is much more his business to stir up curiosity than to insist on acceptances.

How to Read, Part II (1928-31)

IT IS as important for the purpose of thought to keep language efficient as it is in surgery to keep tetanus bacilli out of one's bandages.

In introducing a person to literature one would do well to have him examine works where language is efficiently used; to devise a system for getting directly and expeditiously at such works, despite the smokescreens erected by half-knowing and half-thinking critics. To get at them, despite the mass of dead matter that these people have heaped up and conserved round about them in the proportion: one barrel of sawdust to each half-bunch of grapes.

Great literature is simply language charged with meaning to the utmost possible degree.

When we set about examining it we find

that this charging has been done by several clearly definable sorts of people, and by a periphery of less determinate sorts.

1. *The inventors*, discoverers of a particular process or of more than one mode and process. Sometimes these people are known, or discoverable; for example, we know, with reasonable certitude, that Arnaut Daniel introduced certain methods of rhyming, and we know that certain finenesses of perception appeared first in such a troubadour or in G. Cavalcanti. We do not know, and are not likely to know, anything definite about the precursors of Homer.

2. *The masters*. This is a very small class, and there are very few real ones. The term is properly applied to inventors who, apart from their own inventions, are able to assimilate and co-ordinate a large number of preceding inventions. I mean to say they either start with a core of their own and accumulate adjuncts, or

they digest a vast mass of subject-matter, apply a number of known modes of expression, and succeed in pervading the whole with some special quality or some special character of their own, and bring the whole to a state of homogeneous fullness.

3. *The diluters*, these who follow either the inventors or the "great writers," and who produce something of lower intensity, some flabbier variant, some diffuseness or tumidity in the wake of the valid.

4. (And this class produces the great bulk of all writing.) The men who do more or less good work in the more or less good style of a period. Of these the delightful anthologies, the song books, are full, and choice among them is the matter of taste, for you prefer Wyatt to Donne, Donne to Herrick, Drummond of Hawthornden to Browne, in response to some purely personal sympathy, these people add but some slight personal flavour, some minor variant of a mode, without affecting the main course of the story.

At their faintest *"Ils n'existent pas, leur ambiance leur confert une existence."* They do not exist: their ambience confers existence upon them. When they are most prolific they produce dubious cases like Virgil and Petrarch, who probably pass, among the less exigeant, for colossi.

5. *Belles Lettres*. Longus, Prévost, Benjamin Constant, who are not exactly "great masters," who can hardly be said to have originated a form, but who have nevertheless brought some mode to a very high development.

6. And there is a supplementary or sixth class of writers, the starters of crazes, the Ossianic McPhersons, the Gongoras [1] whose wave of fashion flows over writing for a few centuries or a few decades, and then subsides, leaving things as they were.

It will be seen that the first two classes are the more sharply defined: that the difficulty of classification for particular lesser authors in-

[1] One should perhaps apologize, or express a doubt as to the origin of Gongorism, or redefine it or start blaming it on some other spaniard.

creases as one descends the list, save for the last class, which is again fairly clear.

The point is, that if a man knows the facts about the first two categories, he can evaluate almost any unfamiliar book at first sight. I mean he can form a just estimate of its worth, and see how and where it belongs in this schema.

As to crazes, the number of possible diseases in literature is perhaps not very great, the same afflictions crop up in widely separated countries without any previous communication. The good physician will recognize a known malady, even if the manifestation be superficially different.

The fact that six different critics will each have a different view concerning what author belongs in which of the categories here given, does not in the least invalidate the categories. When a man knows the facts about the first two categories, the reading of work in the other categories will not greatly change his opinion about those in the first two.

LANGUAGE

Obviously this knowledge cannot be acquired without knowledge of various tongues. The same discoveries have served a number of races. If a man has not time to learn different languages he can at least, and with very little delay, be told what the discoveries were. If he wish to be a good critic he will have to look for himself.

Bad critics have prolonged the use of demoded terminology, usually a terminology originally invented to describe what had been done before 300 B.C., and to describe it in a rather exterior fashion. Writers of second order have often tried to produce works to fit some category or term not yet occupied in their own local literature. If we chuck out the classifications which apply to the outer shape of the work, or to its occasion, and if we look at what actually happens, in, let us say, poetry, we will find that the language is charged or energized in various manners.

That is to say, there are three "kinds of poetry":

MELOPOEIA, wherein the words are charged, over and above their plain meaning, with some musical property, which directs the bearing or trend of that meaning.

PHANOPOEIA, which is a casting of images upon the visual imagination.

LOGOPOEIA, "the dance of the intellect among words," that is to say, it employs words not only for their direct meaning, but it takes count in a special way of habits of usage, of the context we *expect* to find with the word, its usual concomitants, of its known acceptances, and of ironical play. It holds the aesthetic content which is peculiarly the domain of verbal manifestation, and cannot possibly be contained in plastic or in music. It is the latest come, and perhaps most tricky and undependable mode.

The *melopoeia* can be appreciated by a foreigner with a sensitive ear, even though he be ignorant of the language in which the poem is written. It is practically impossible to transfer or translate it from one language to another, save perhaps by divine accident, and for half a line at a time.

Phanopoeia can, on the other hand, be translated almost, or wholly, intact. When it is good enough, it is practically impossible for the translator to destroy it save by very crass bungling, and the neglect of perfectly well-known and formulative rules.

Logopoeia does not translate; though the attitude of mind it expresses may pass through a paraphrase. Or one might say, you can *not* translate it "locally," but having determined the original author's state of mind, you may or may not be able to find a derivative or an equivalent.

PROSE

The language of prose is much less highly charged, that is perhaps the only availing distinction between prose and poesy. Prose permits greater factual presentation, explicitness, but a much greater amount of language is needed. During the last century or century and a half, prose has, perhaps for the first time, perhaps for the second or third time, arisen to challenge the poetic pre-eminence. That is to say, *Coeur Simple*, by Flaubert, is probably more important than Théophile Gautier's *Carmen*, etc.

The total charge in certain nineteenth-century prose works possibly surpasses the total charge found in individual poems of that period; but that merely indicates that the author has been able to get his effect cumulatively, by a greater heaping up of factual data; imagined fact, if you will, but nevertheless expressed in factual manner.

By using several hundred pages of prose, Flaubert, by force of architectonics, manages to attain an intensity comparable to that in Villon's *Heaulmière*, or his prayer for his mother. This does not invalidate my dissociation of the two terms: poetry, prose.

In *phanopoeia* we find the greatest drive toward utter precision of word; this art exists almost exclusively by it.

In *melopoeia* we find a contrary current, a force tending often to lull, or to distract the reader from the exact sense of the language. It is poetry on the borders of music and music is perhaps the bridge between consciousness and the unthinking sentient or even insentient universe.

All writing is built up of these three elements, plus "architectonics" or "the form of the whole," and to know anything about the relative efficiency of various works one must have some knowledge of the maximum already attained by various authors, irrespective of where and when.[2]

It is not enough to know that the Greeks attained to the greatest skill in melopoeia, or even that the Provençaux added certain diverse developments and that some quite minor, nineteenth-century Frenchmen achieved certain elaborations.

It is not quite enough to have the general idea that the Chinese (more particularly Ri-

[2] Lacuna at this point to be corrected in criticism of Hindemith's "Schwanendreher." E.P. Sept. 1938.

haku and Omakitsu) attained the known maximum of *phanopoeia*, due perhaps to the nature of their written ideograph, or to wonder whether Rimbaud is, at rare moments, their equal. One wants one's knowledge in more definite terms.

It is an error to think that vast reading will automatically produce any such knowledge or understanding. Neither Chaucer with his forty books, nor Shakespeare with perhaps half a dozen, in folio, can be considered illiterate. A man can learn more music by working on a Bach fugue until he can take it apart and put it together, than by playing through ten dozen heterogeneous albums.

You may say that for twenty-seven years I have thought consciously about this particular matter, and read or read at a great many books, and that with the subject never really out of my mind, I don't yet know half there is to know about *melopoeia*.

There are, on the other hand, a few books that I still keep on my desk, and a great number that I shall never open again. But the books that a man needs to know in order to "get his bearings," in order to have a sound judgement of any bit of writing that may come before him, are very few. The list is so short, indeed, that one wonders that people, professional writers in particular, are willing to leave them ignored and to continue dangling in mid-chaos emitting the most imbecile estimates, and often vitiating their whole lifetime's production.

Limiting ourselves to the authors who actually invented something, or who are the "first known examples" of the process in working order, we find:

OF THE GREEKS: Homer, Sappho. (The "great dramatists" decline from Homer, and depend immensely on him for their effects; their "charge," at its highest potential, depends so often, and so greatly on their being able to count on their audience's knowledge of the *Iliad*. Even Aeschylus is rhetorical.) [3]

[3] E.P.'s later and unpublished notes revise all this in so far as they demand much greater recognition of Sophokles.

OF THE ROMANS: As we have lost Philetas, and most of Callimachus, we may suppose that the Romans added a certain sophistication; at any rate, Catullus, Ovid, Propertius, all give us something we cannot find now in Greek authors.

A specialist may read Horace if he is interested in learning the precise demarcation between what can be learned about writing, and what cannot. I mean that Horace is the perfect example of a man who acquired all that is acquirable, without having the root. I beg the reader to observe that I am being exceedingly iconoclastic, that I am omitting thirty established names for every two I include. I am chucking out Pindar, and Virgil, without the slightest compunction. I do not suggest a "course" in Greek or Latin literature, I name a few isolated writers; five or six pages of Sappho. One can throw out at least one-third of Ovid. That is to say, I am omitting the authors who can teach us no new or no more effective method of "charging words."

OF THE MIDDLE AGES: The Anglo-Saxon *Seafarer*, and some more cursory notice of some medieval narrative, it does not so greatly matter what narrative, possibly the *Beowulf*, the *Poema del Cid*, and the sagas of *Grettir* and *Burnt Nial*. And then, in contrast, troubadours, perhaps thirty poems in Provençal, and for comparison with them a few songs by Von Morungen, or Wolfram von Essenbach, and von der Vogelweide; and then Bion's *Death of Adonis*.

From which mixture, taken in this order, the reader will get his bearings on the art of poetry made to be sung; for there are three kinds of *melopoeia*: (1) that made to be sung to a tune; (2) that made to be intoned or sung to a sort of chant; and (3) that made to be spoken; and the art of joining words in each of these kinds is different, and cannot be clearly understood until the reader knows that there are three different objectives.

OF THE ITALIANS: Guido Cavalcanti and Dante; perhaps a dozen and a half poems of Guido's, and a dozen poems by his contemporaries, and the *Divina Commedia*.

In Italy, around the year 1300, there were new values established, things said that had not been said in Greece, or in Rome or elsewhere.

VILLON: After Villon and for several centuries, poetry can be considered as *fioritura*, as an efflorescence, almost an effervescence, and without any new roots. Chaucer is an enrichment, one might say a more creamy version of the "matter of France," and he in some measure preceded the verbal richness of the classic revival, but beginning with the Italians after Dante, coming through the Latin writers of the Renaissance, French, Spanish, English, Tasso, Ariosto, etc., the Italians always a little in the lead, the whole is elaboration, medieval basis, and wash after wash of Roman or Hellenic influence. I mean one need not read any particular part of it for purpose of learning one's comparative values.

If one were studying history and not poetry, one might discover the medieval mind more directly in the opening of Mussato's *Ecerinus* than even in Dante. The culture of Chaucer is the same as that which went contemporaneously into Ferrara, with the tongue called *"francoveneto."*

One must emphasize one's contrasts in the quattrocento. One can take Villon as pivot for understanding them. After Villon, and having begun before his time, we find this *fioritura*, and for centuries we find little else, even in Marlowe and Shakespeare there is this embroidery of language, this talk about the matter, rather than presentation. I doubt if anyone ever acquired discrimination in studying "The Elizabethans." You have grace, richness of language, abundance, but you have probably nothing that isn't replaceable by something else, no ornament that wouldn't have done just as well in some other connection, or for which some other figure of rhetoric couldn't have served, or which couldn't have been distilled from literary antecedents.

The "language" had not been heard on the London stage, but it had been heard in the Italian law courts, etc.; there were local attempts, all over Europe, to teach the public (in Spain, Italy, England) Latin diction. "Poetry" was considered to be (as it still is considered by a great number of drivelling imbeciles) synonymous with "lofty and flowery language."

One Elizabethan specialist has suggested that Shakespeare, disgusted with his efforts, or at least despairing of success, as a poet, took to the stage. The drama is a mixed art; it does not rely on the charge that can be put into the word, but calls on gesture and mimicry and "impersonation" for assistance. The actor must do a good half of the work. One does no favour to drama by muddling the two sets of problems.

Apologists for the drama are continually telling us in one way or another that drama either cannot use at all, or can make but a very limited use of words charged to their highest potential. This is perfectly true. Let us try to keep our minds on the problem we started with, i.e., the art of writing, the art of "charging" language with meaning.

After 1450 we have the age of *fioritura*; after Marlowe and Shakespeare came what was called a "classic" movement, a movement that restrained without inventing. Anything that happens to mind in England has usually happened somewhere else first. Someone invents something, then someone develops, or some dozens develop a frothy or at any rate creamy enthusiasm or over-abundance, then someone tries to tidy things up. For example, the estimable Pleiad emasculating the French tongue, and the French classicists, and the English classicists, etc., all of which things should be relegated to the subsidiary zone: period interest, historical interest, bric-à-brac for museums.

At this point someone says: "O, but the ballads." All right, I will allow the voracious peruser a half-hour for ballads (English and Spanish, or Scottish, Border, and Spanish). There is nothing easier than to be distracted from one's point, or from the main drive of one's subject by a desire for utterly flawless equity and omniscience.

Let us say, but directly in parenthesis, that there was a very limited sort of *logopoeia* in seventeenth- and eighteenth-century satire.

And that Rochester and Dorset may have introduced a new note, or more probably re-introduced an old one, that reappears later in Heine.

Let us also cut loose from minor details and minor exceptions: the main fact is that we "have come" or that "humanity came" to a point where verse-writing can or could no longer be clearly understood without the study of prose-writing.

Say, for the sake of argument, that after the slump of the Middle Ages, prose "came to" again in Machiavelli; admit that various sorts of prose had existed, in fact nearly all sorts had existed. Herodotus wrote history that is litera-ture. Thucydides was a journalist. (It is a mod-ern folly to suppose that vulgarity and cheap-ness have the merit of novelty; they have always existed, and are of no interest in them-selves.)

There have been bombast, oratory, legal speech, balanced sentences, Ciceronian impres-siveness; Petronius had written a satiric novel, Longus had written a delicate nouvelle. The prose of the Renaissance leaves us Rabelais, Brantôme, Montaigne. A determined specialist can dig interesting passages, or sumptuous pas-sages, or even subtle passages out of Pico, the medieval mystics, scholastics, platonists, none of which will be the least use to a man trying to learn the art of "charging language."

I mean to say that from the beginning of literature up to A.D. 1750 poetry was the su-perior art, and was so considered to be, and if we read books written before that date we find the number of interesting books in verse at least equal to the number of prose books still readable; and the poetry contains the quintes-sence. When we want to know what people were like before 1750, when we want to know that they had blood and bones like ourselves, we go to the poetry of the period.

But, as I have said, the *"fioritura* business" set in. And one morning Monsieur Stendhal, not thinking of Homer, or Villon, or Catullus, but having a very keen sense of actuality, no-ticed that "poetry," *la poésie,* as the term was then understood, the stuff written by his French contemporaries, or sonorously rolled at him from the French stage, was a damn nui-sance. And he remarked that poetry, with its bagwigs and its bobwigs, and its padded calves and its periwigs, its "fustian à la Louis XIV," was greatly inferior to prose for conveying a clear idea of the diverse states of our conscious-ness ("les mouvements du coeur").

And at that moment the serious art of writ-ing "went over to prose," and for some time the important developments of language as means of expression were the developments of prose. And a man cannot clearly understand or justly judge the value of verse, modern verse, any verse, unless he has grasped this.

From Date Line (1934)

CRITICISM HAS at least the following categories, differing greatly in the volume of their verbal manifestation, and not equally zoned.

1. Criticism by discussion, extending from mere yatter, logic-chopping, and description of

tendencies up to the clearly defined record of procedures and an attempt to formulate more or less general principles.

Aristotle being neither poet nor complete imbecile contented himself with trying to for-mulate some of the general interior and exte-rior relations of work already extant.

He has presumably the largest bastard family of any philosopher. Ninkus, Pinkus and Swinky all try to say what the next writer must do.

Dante who was capable of executing the work and of holding general ideas, set down a partial record of procedures.

2. Criticism by translation.

3. Criticism by exercise in the style of a given period.

As you would not seriously consider a man's knowledge of tennis until he either could make or had made some sort of show in a tournament, so we can assume that until a man can actually control a given set of procedures there must be many elements in them of which he has but an imperfect knowledge.

This introduces almost a personal note, or at least a long-delayed reply to carpers who objected to my spending three days in translating Fontenelle on the grounds that I should have been "doing original work and not wasting my energies in translation." They took the *Divagation* as a proof that I was merely gathering daisies.

4. Criticism via music, meaning definitely the setting of a poet's words; e.g. in *Le Testament*, Villon's words, and in *Cavalcanti*, I have set Guido's and Sordello's. In the famous caricature of Edward and Alfonso, seated on a bench in the Bois, the elder monarch remarks to the younger: "A vôtre âge j'étais seulement Prince de Galles, c'est le seul moyen de bien connaître Paris."

This is the most intense form of criticism save:

5. Criticism in new composition.

For example the criticism of Seneca in Mr. Eliot's *Agon* is infinitely more alive, more vigorous than in his essay on Seneca.

Years ago I made the mistake of publishing a volume (*Instigations*) without blatantly telling the reader that the book had a design.

Coming after an era of gross confusion and irrelevance, wherein malicious camouflage is infinitely more general than any sort of coherence whatsoever, such violent rupture with the general public habit is perfectly useless, and may, for all I know, be unfair to those readers who inhabit a middle zone between effulgent intellect and *les cuistres*.

There would have been no point in asking indulgence as long as the appearances were so greatly against one, I mean so long as the appearance of mere haphazard gave ground for argument, and the reader of ill-will had ample basis for hostile demonstration.

Criticism so far as I have discovered has two functions:

1. Theoretically it tries to forerun composition, to serve as gunsight, though there is, I believe, no recorded instance of the foresight having EVER been of the slightest use save to actual composers. I mean the man who formulates any forward reach of co-ordinating principle is the man who produces the demonstration.

The others who use the principle learn usually from the example, and in most cases merely dim and dilute it.

I think it will usually be found that the work outruns the formulated or at any rate the published equation, or at most they proceed as two feet of one biped.

2. Excernment. The general ordering and weeding out of what has actually been performed. The elimination of repetitions. The work analogous to that which a good hanging committee or a curator would perform in a National Gallery or in a biological museum;

The ordering of knowledge so that the next man (or generation) can most readily find the live part of it, and waste the least possible time among obsolete issues. . . .

T. S. ELIOT

Introduction

The best of my *literary* criticism—apart from a few notorious phrases which have had a truly embarrassing success in the world—consists of essays on poets and poetic dramatists who had influenced me. It is a by-product of my private poetry work-shop; or a prolongation of the thinking that went into the formation of my own verse. In retrospect, I see that I wrote best about poets whose work had influenced my own . . . My criticism has this in common with that of Ezra Pound, that its merits and its limitations can be fully appreciated only when it is considered in relation to the poetry I have written myself.

("The Frontiers of Criticism," 1956)

IN THIS PASSAGE from one of his later essays Eliot clearly marks out his affinities with Pound's critical method. Largely under the influence of Pound's example, Eliot developed early in his career the belief that the poet-critic is an indispensable figure who, although "always trying to defend the kind of poetry he is writing," is responsible for the general health of the literary tradition. Eliot's essays collected in *The Sacred Wood* (1920) are riddled with debts to Pound's critical practice, and many of his most "notorious" critical phrases—such as the "objective correlative"—can be traced to a clear source in Pound's writings. In the end Eliot became the more important critic, probably the most important critic since Matthew Arnold (whom he resembles in so many ways), but he was—in Pound's terms—a "master" rather than an "inventor," synthesizing and extending the leading critical ideas of his age but not exercising a formative influence on any literary movement. His early essays and poems may be regarded as consolidations of the gains made through Pound's more erratic and tendentious journalism, just as *The Waste Land* may be seen, in Pound's own words, as "the justification of the 'movement,' of our modern experiment, since 1900." Ultimately Eliot was to build up a body of criticism far more judicious and "normative" than that of Pound, a critical canon which is of equal use to the artist and the literary scholar; but it is well to remember that in his early years his critical writings were prompted by the same concerns as Pound's. While Pound was "blasting and bombardiering" in the pages of the little magazines, Eliot was recording similar ideas in the measured and soothing prose of the *Times Literary Supplement.*

As Eliot suggests by the italicizing of "*literary* criticism," much of his writing was of a larger scope, dealing with social, religious, and cultural problems. It is convenient to divide his career as a critic into two parts, with the uneasy dividing line established by his 1928 declaration that he was a classicist in literature, an Anglo-Catholic in religion, and a royalist in politics (Preface to *For Lancelot Andrewes*). Of course the transition was not clear-cut: many of the later essays remind us of the author of *The Sacred Wood* and *Homage to John Dryden,* and the criticism produced between 1925 and 1935 is as hard to categorize as the verse of that period, which bridges the gap between "The Hollow Men" and the first of the *Four Quartets.* Still, if one compares the essays of *Homage to John Dryden* (1924) with a product of ten years later, *After Strange Gods* (subtitled *A Primer of Modern Heresy*), the difference is absolutely plain. Eliot has moved away from a preoccupation with literary problems and technical analysis toward a larger Arnoldian concern with moral and political ideas. Unfortunately, Eliot's later comments on the cultural tradition and the social responsibilities of literature were, unlike Arnold's, alarmingly out of touch with the temper of his age. His conservative ideals and elitist principles spoke only to those who were already convinced; and although the later canon is filled with impressive documents of literary and cultural criticism, his special position as arbiter of the times had long since disappeared. The best measure of the difference between the early and late essays is not the obvious variance in subject matter but the changes in style of attack. In the early essays Eliot's prose is precise and economical, and his selection of illustrative quotations is marvelously effective. Following the method of Arnold's "touchstones," those revealing passages which lay bare a style or attitude, Eliot filled his early essays with quotations which have all the intensity and clarity of a Joycean epiphany. In fact, one might claim that the essays are organized around these "epiphanies." Most of the famous quotations in the early essays appear also in the poetry, the two contexts reinforcing each other and providing that double validation which is the hallmark of the great poet-critic. For example, the echoes from seventeenth-century drama in "Gerontion" and *The Waste Land* are best glossed from Eliot's essays on Elizabethan and Jacobean drama, while the passage from Lancelot Andrewes' Nativity sermon which is central to both "Gerontion" and "The Journey of the Magi" ("A cold coming they had of it . . . The Word, and not be able to speak a word?") is given in full and with detailed commentary in Eliot's essay on Andrewes. Some of the epigraphs to Eliot's early poems, which invariably derive from his critical activity, became slogans for the age (the quotation from *The Jew of Malta* which heads "Portrait of a Lady" seems to have obsessed Hemingway, who used it at least three times in his works).

It is this special talent for precise and comparative literary analysis, with a particular text always in view, that we miss in Eliot's later essays. Already in the Charles Eliot Norton lectures of 1932–33 (published as *The Use of Poetry and the Use of Criticism*) we feel a slackening in his style, accompanied by a growing movement away from the problems of contemporary literature. Whereas the earlier essays on sixteenth- and seventeenth-century figures had made them seem contemporaries, the leisurely essays of *The Use of Poetry and the Use of Criticism* make us feel that the subjects—Dryden, Wordsworth, Coleridge, Keats, Shelley, even Arnold—are separated from us in time and attitude. The penultimate chapter on "The Modern Mind" (reprinted in this section) is truly of the present day, enlivened as it is by the debate with I. A. Richards, but here once more we have a sense that the focus of Eliot's criticism has become less sharp. This shift in style may be accounted for in part by the fact that many of his later essays, beginning with *The Use of Poetry and the Use of Criticism*, were first delivered as lectures and retained the looser form; but even this circumstance is indicative of a change in Eliot's conception of his literary career. The man who closed *The Criterion* in 1939 was a different personality from the young critic who had founded the journal in 1922. Readers will always return to Eliot's later criticism for insights into his own creative process, and for shrewd commentary on literary and cultural history, but Eliot's role as the most influential poet-critic of his own or any other age came to an end with his work on the *Four Quartets*. They are the last examples of his great criticism, and perhaps the most subtle. The concluding parts of each *Quartet*, where the poet moves easily from the incarnation of language to the Incarnation of the Christian faith, provide a fitting coda to Eliot's achievement as a major critic, and point up the affinities between his religious and literary ideals far more successfully than the discursive essays of his later decades.

> Words strain,
> Crack and sometimes break, under the burden,
> Under the tension, slip, slide, perish,
> Decay with imprecision, will not stay in place,
> Will not stay still. Shrieking voices
> Scolding, mocking, or merely chattering,
> Always assail them. The Word in the desert

Is most attacked by voices of temptation,
The crying shadow in the funeral dance,
The loud lament of the disconsolate chimera.
(*Burnt Norton*, 1935)

Eliot's later criticism is characterized by a persistent tension between vestiges of his earlier critical theories and the overriding demands of his social and religious beliefs (see the curious paragraph on "Religion and Literature," reprinted in this section, where the identification of "literature" is relegated to the methods of literary criticism, while the assessment of its "greatness" is referred to extraliterary standards). A different tension, however, pervades the earlier essays, a tension between the pragmatic strategies of the poet-critic and the more systematic demands of literary theory. Eliot moves uneasily between the role of the theoretical critic, determined to examine the artistic process and the bases for literary judgments, and the role of the instigator-critic as exemplified by Ezra Pound. Like Arnold in his 1853 Preface, or T. E. Hulme in "Modern Art and Its Philosophy," Eliot strove for a classic objectivity in his critical theory, an escape from "personality"; yet few poets of his age wrote verse which was more personal in its origins and references. At the same time as Eliot's criticism persuades us that the artist should efface himself from his work, fusing "emotions" and "feelings" into an impersonal form (see Part II of "Tradition and the Individual Talent"), his own personality is constantly breaking through the austere surface of his verse, whetting our interest in biographical data and personal associations. The paradox in Eliot's poetry is that of an objective structure or narrative form which contains a highly personal orchestration of tone and images; but the paradox in his early criticism strikes equally deep, and is worth examining for a moment.

The total argument of "Tradition and the Individual Talent," which Eliot refers to as an "Impersonal theory of poetry," divides itself into two parts: a theory of literary tradition and historical consciousness, which will be touched on later, and a theory of literary creation which sees the making of a poem as an "escape from personality," not an "expression of personality." It is in the second half of the argument that the ambiguity occurs. Eliot contends that the process of turning personal emotions into universal emotions or "feelings" is an objective process, and he bolsters this claim for objectivity by making his language as "scientific" as possible:

There remains to define this process of depersonalization and its relation to the sense of tradition. It is in this depersonalization that art may be said to approach the condition of science. I, therefore, invite you to consider, as a suggestive analogy, the action which takes place when a bit of finely filiated platinum is introduced into a chamber containing oxygen and sulphur dioxide.

We are reminded of the pseudo-scientific element in Eliot's coinage of the term "objective correlative" to describe "a set of objects, a situation, a chain of events which shall be the formula of that *particular* emotion" the artist wishes to express (there is an obvious debt here to Pound's comment, in *The Spirit of Romance,* that "poetry is a sort of inspired mathematics, which gives us equations . . . for the human emotions"). Just as in his early poetry Eliot uses the ironic contrast between "scientific" imagery and sentimental emotion as a means of protecting his personality, so in his early criticism he calls on scientific metaphors to give the coloration of "impersonality."

But in spite of the mathematical and scientific metaphors, Eliot's view of the creative process is essentially Romantic-Symbolist, while his view of tradition and convention is truly Classical. He often said that the origins of a work of art, the intentions of the author, have "no relation to the poem," and behind most of his comments on the creative process lies the post-Romantic assumption that the work of art is autonomous, an independent organism with its own laws of existence and its own life. "We can only say that a poem, in some sense, has its own life; that its parts form something quite different from a body of neatly ordered biographical data; that the feeling, or emotion, or vision, resulting from the poem is something different from the feeling or emotion or vision in the mind of the poet" (Preface to *The Sacred Wood,* 1928). A corollary to this would be that "a poem may appear to mean very different things to different readers, and all of these meanings may be different from what the author thought he meant. . . . The different interpretations may all be partial formulations of one thing; the ambiguities may be due to the fact that the poem means more, not less, than ordinary speech can communicate" ("The Music of Poetry," 1942).

So Eliot seems to espouse a theory of the autonomous work of art, while at the same time he insists that the nature of the work is determined by a delicate interaction between tradition and the individual talent. The two claims are not irreconcilable by any means, but Eliot's vagueness in the handling of theoretical language and his unwillingness to formulate a theoretical system make the reconciliation difficult. Any group of Eliot's critical essays, if reduced to the theoretical structures favored by aestheticians and systematic critics, will prove to be hopelessly ambiguous. A Classical theory of objectivity is at war with a number of post-Romantic assumptions, while a view of the art-work as an independent organism is compromised at every turn by a sensible recognition of the many ways in which art is dependent on our extra-literary activities. The well-known passage from the 1928 Preface to *The Sacred Wood* which describes the poem as having "its own life" (quoted above) is followed immediately by a qualification: "On the other hand, poetry as certainly has something to do with morals, and with religion, and even with politics perhaps, though we cannot say what." At every turn Eliot is saved from the restrictions of formula and theory by his own lively sensibility, and by his awareness of the radical imperfections which limit any work of art and the interpretations based upon it. The difference between his comments on "tradition" and those on the "impersonality" of the creative process is that the former are the natural outgrowth of sensitive reading and his own practice, while the latter are (like Poe's literary theories) rationales after the fact.

Eliot's personal view of the literary tradition began with his own creative needs, and was then shaped to fit the needs of contemporary literature in a manner which left intact the authority of received literary opinion. It is Pound's view with the eccentricities and glaring omissions smoothed away, an accommodation between the demands of the present and the restraining "order" of inherited judgments. While Pound was revolutionary in his refashioning of the tradition, Eliot displayed the classical impulse to make something fresh and new and relevant with the least possible displacement of existing values. Throughout his essays we are reminded that he began his career as a scholar, and always retained that sense of "fact" and historical context which is the essential counterbalance for the impulse to "make it new." Eliot's criticism is scholarly because, in Wallace Stevens' phrase, it displays "an ancient aspect touching a new mind," and because it does justice to both the instinct for conservation and the instinct for change.

In his Introduction to Pound's *Selected Poems* (1928) Eliot remarks that "the form in which I began to write, in 1908 or 1909, was directly drawn from the study of Laforgue together with the later Elizabethan drama; and I do not know anyone who started from exactly that point." This crossing of two disparate literary strains, so important to the formation of his early verse, was to remain the center of Eliot's idea of tradition, the point upon which the entire axis of the past revolved. Elsewhere Eliot made the conjunction more precise: "Jules Laforgue, and Tristan Corbière in many of his poems, are nearer to the 'school of Donne' than any modern English poet" ("The Metaphysical Poets," 1921). This perception of deep affinities between the French poets of the late nineteenth century and the literature of early seventeenth-century England is so central to both Eliot's poetry and criticism that we should explore its implications further, and the best starting-point is the famous passage on "dissociation of sensibility."

Eliot's theory that the development of seventeenth-century literature was marked by a "dissociation of sensibility," with Milton and Dryden the chief culprits, and that this "dissociation" still plagues our culture, can and has been challenged on historical grounds. The important point, however, is not the general historical truth of the assumption but what it reveals about Eliot's view of the early seventeenth century, a period which was crucial to his entire sense of the literary past. The following quotation, which opens the passage reprinted in this section, attempts to explain that "mechanism of sensibility" which Eliot admired, and which he found strangely reincarnated in certain French poets of the immediate past.

A thought to Donne was an experience; it modified his sensibility. When a poet's mind is perfectly equipped for its work, it is constantly amalgamating disparate experience; the ordinary man's experience is chaotic, irregular, fragmentary. The latter falls in love, or reads Spinoza, and these two experiences have nothing to do with each other, or with the noise of the typewriter or the smell of cooking; in the mind of the poet these experiences are always forming new wholes.

In Eliot's view the hallmark of poetic greatness is the ability to hold a complex of feelings and emotions in a single thought, and to express this complex as a unified experience. Hence the "wit" of the Metaphysical poets and the irony of Laforgue, qualities which Eliot sought to emulate in his own verse, became, touchstones to the best in the literary tradition. The figures which stand highest in Eliot's judgment—Dante, the Metaphysicals and the Elizabethan dramatists, Dryden in certain moods, the nineteenth-century French masters of irony and wit—are those who display this fusion of thought and experience; while the poets of whom he is most critical, such as Milton and Shelley, are those artists of immense power who nonetheless lack a unified sensibility.

This argument would have no force whatever if it were not substantiated throughout Eliot's early essays by scrupulous attention to the analysis of individual passages, and by unobtrusive references to the heritage of English criticism. The description of the poet's esemplastic mind quoted above convinces us partly because of its appeal to experience, and partly because it echoes Coleridge's famous exposition of the powers of the Imagination near the end of Chapter XIV of *Biographia Literaria*:

The poet, described in *ideal* perfection, brings the whole soul of man into activity . . . He diffuses a tone and spirit of unity, that blends, and (as it were) *fuses*, each into each, by that synthetic and magical power, to which we have exclusively appropriated the name of imagination. This power . . . reveals itself in the balance or reconciliation of opposite or discordant qualities: of sameness, with difference; of the general, with the concrete; the idea, with the image; the individual, with the representative; the sense of novelty and freshness, with old and familiar objects . . .

Eliot's essays are resonant with echoes from the critical tradition, and these add subtly but effectively to the power of his argument. In the essay on "Andrew Marvell," for example, Eliot quotes one of Marvell's more bizarre images and refers us to Samuel Johnson's *Life of Cowley*, meanwhile commenting that the images of Marvell's *To His Coy Mistress*, by way of contrast, "are not only witty, but satisfy the elucidation of Imagination given by Coleridge" in Chapter XIV of *Biographia Literaria*. The condensation and range of reference in these few lines are astonishing. To the reader familiar with the history of English criticism they reveal Eliot's acute awareness of the way in which his subject was treated by his great predecessors, and show that he considered the Coleridgean Imagination one solution to the critical problems raised in Johnson's essay: Johnson had described the "wit" of the Metaphysical poets as "a kind of *discordia concors*; a combination of dissimilar images, or discovery of occult resemblances in things apparently unlike," but Eliot clearly feels that Johnson's description, uttered in a tone of disapproval, can be turned to the highest praise if we place it in the context of Coleridge's poetic theory. All of Eliot's best essays are rich in this sort of historical reference, which can range from explicit citations to faint but significant echoes of tone and phrasing (note the rhythms of Coleridge's passage on the Imagination in Eliot's description of the "Auditory Imagination"). In the long run, Eliot's essays are more satisfactory than those of Pound because they not only realign the past and order the present but display a constant awareness of their own place in the history of literary criticism.

When we turn to the practical test of Eliot's idea of tradition, his ability to judge and explain and assimilate the best literature of his own generation, no better example presents itself than Joyce's *Ulysses*. When *Ulysses* appeared in 1922 it was hailed as a triumph of the revolutionary spirit, a radical departure from all the standards and forms of English literature. But Eliot, who had first read the novel in serial form several years before, was already prepared to treat it as the perfect example of "the new (the really new) work of art" which enters the established order of literary works and alters our view of them; moreover, he could see that Joyce's use of the past, in the form of parallels with the *Odyssey*, supported his own proposition in "Tradition and the Individual Talent" that "the past should be altered by the present as much as the present is directed by the past."

In using the myth, in manipulating a continuous parallel between contemporaneity and antiquity, Mr. Joyce is pursuing a method which others must pursue after him. They will not be imitators, any more than the scientist who uses the discoveries of an Einstein in pursuing his own, independent, further investigations. It is simply a way of controlling, of ordering, of giving a shape and a significance to the immense panorama of futility and anarchy which is contemporary history. . . . It is a method for which the horoscope is auspicious. Psychology (such as it is, and whether our reaction to it be comic or serious), ethnology, and *The Golden Bough* have concurred to make possible what was impossible even a few years ago. Instead of narrative method we may now use the mythical method. It is, I seriously believe, a step toward making the modern world possible for art . . .

("*Ulysses*, Order, and Myth," 1923)

Ulysses was published at a climactic moment in Eliot's career as poet-critic, when work on *The Waste Land* and his most important early essays had just been completed, and his response to it displays all that is best in his criticism: a deep respect for fact, cosmopolitan standards of judgment, equal attention to the foreground and background of the literary tradition. It is revealing of the two men and their different but related approaches that Pound should have concentrated on the radical properties of *Ulysses* and its immediate impact, while Eliot was intent upon placing the work in the widest possible context.

A Note on Sources

The early essays of T. S. Eliot (1888–1965), which altered the direction of English literary criticism, were first collected in *The Sacred Wood* (1920). Most of the important essays from *The Sacred Wood*, as well as a selection of criticism from the 1920's and 1930's, may be found in *Selected Essays* (1932, 1950). The Charles Eliot Norton lectures, delivered at Harvard in 1932–33, were published as *The Use of Poetry and the Use of Criticism* (1933); while the Page-Barbour lectures given at the University of Virginia in 1933 were gathered as *After Strange Gods* (1934). Most of Eliot's critical essays of 1936–56, including the two Milton essays, may be found in *On Poetry and Poets* (1957); while *To Criticize the Critic* (1965) reprints other important later essays, as well as "Ezra Pound: His Metric and Poetry" (1917) and "Reflections on 'Vers Libre'" (1917). Eliot's essays on culture and religion not collected in the above volumes may be found in *Thoughts After Lambeth* (1931), *The Idea of a Christian Society* (1939), and *Notes Towards the Definition of Culture* (1948). Important uncollected essays are "*Ulysses*, Order, and Myth" (1923; reprinted in *James Joyce: Two Decades of Criticism*, ed. Seon Givens) and the Preface to Ezra Pound's *Selected Poems* (1928; still in print). For a full listing of Eliot's critical writings see Donald Gallup, *T. S. Eliot: A Bibliography* (1970).

In addition to the comments on Eliot's criticism in general studies of his poetry, the following deal exclusively with his criticism: R. P. Blackmur, "In the Hope of Straightening Things Out" (1951), in *The Lion and the Honeycomb* (1955); M. C. Bradbrook, "Eliot's Critical Method," in *T. S. Eliot: A Study of His Writings by Several Hands*, ed. B. Rajan (1949); Victor Brombert, *The Criticism of T. S. Eliot: Problems of an 'Impersonal Theory' of Poetry* (1949); Stanley Edgar Hyman, "T. S. Eliot and Tradition in Criticism," in *The Armed Vision* (1948); Fei-Pai Lu, *T. S. Eliot: The Dialectical Structure of His Theory of Poetry* (1966); René Wellek, "The Criticism of T. S. Eliot," *Sewanee Review*, LXIV (1956).

Less sympathetic views of Eliot's criticism may be found in Yvor Winters, "T. S. Eliot, or the Illusion of Reaction," in *In Defense of Reason* (1947), and Eliseo Vivas, "The Objective Correlative of T. S. Eliot" (1944), in *Creation and Discovery* (1955).

Reflections on Vers Libre (1917)

*Ceux qui possèdent leur vers libre y tiennent: on
n'abandonne que le vers libre.*
Duhamel et Vildrac.

A lady, renowned in her small circle for the accuracy of her stop-press information of literature, complains to me of a growing pococurantism. "Since the Russians came in I can read nothing else. I have finished Dostoevski, and I do not know what to do." I suggested that the great Russian was an admirer of Dickens, and that she also might find that author readable. "But Dickens is a sentimentalist; Dostoevski is a realist." I reflected on the amours of Sonia and Rashkolnikov, but forbore to press the point, and I proposed *It Is Never too Late to Mend.* "But one cannot read the Victorians at all!" While I was extracting the virtues of the proposition that Dostoevski is a Christian, while Charles Reade is merely pious, she added that she could no longer read any verse but *vers libre.*

It is assumed that *vers libre* exists. It is assumed that *vers libre* is a school; that it consists of certain theories; that its group or groups of theorists will either revolutionize or demoralize poetry if their attack upon the iambic pentameter meets with any success. *Vers libre* does not exist, and it is time that this preposterous fiction followed the *élan vital* and the eighty thousand Russians into oblivion.

When a theory of art passes it is usually

found that a groat's worth of art has been bought with a million of advertisement. The theory which sold the wares may be quite false, or it may be confused and incapable of elucidation, or it may never have existed. A mythical revolution will have taken place and produced a few works of art which perhaps would be even better if still less of the revolutionary theories clung to them. In modern society such revolutions are almost inevitable. An artist happens upon a method, perhaps quite unreflectingly, which is new in the sense that it is essentially different from that of the second-rate people about him, and different in everything but essentials from that of any of his great predecessors. The novelty meets with neglect; neglect provokes attack; and attack demands a theory. In an ideal state of society one might imagine the good New growing naturally out of the good Old, without the need for polemic and theory; this would be a society with a living tradition. In a sluggish society, as actual societies are, tradition is ever lapsing into superstition, and the violent stimulus of novelty is required. This is bad for the artist and his school, who may become circumscribed by their theory and narrowed by their polemic; but the artist can always console himself for his errors in his old age by considering that if he had not fought nothing would have been accomplished.

Vers libre has not even the excuse of a polemic; it is a battle-cry of freedom, and there is no freedom in art. And as the so-called *vers libre* which is good is anything but "free," it can better be defended under some other label. Particular types of *vers libre* may be supported on the choice of content, or on the method of handling the content. I am aware that many writers of *vers libre* have introduced such innovations, and that the novelty of their choice and manipulation of material is confused—if not in their own minds, in the minds of many of their readers—with the novelty of the form. But I am not here concerned with imagism, which is a theory about the use of material; I am only concerned with the theory of the verse-form in which imagism is cast. If *vers libre* is a genuine verse-form it will have a positive definition. And I can define it only in negatives: (1) absence of pattern, (2) absence of rhyme, (3) absence of metre.

The third of these qualities is easily disposed of. What sort of a line that would be which would not scan at all I cannot say. Even in the popular American magazines, whose verse columns are now largely given over to *vers libre,* the lines are usually explicable in terms of prosody. Any line can be divided into feet and accents. The simpler metres are a repetition of one combination, perhaps a long and a short, or a short and a long syllable, five times repeated. There is, however, no reason why, within the single line, there should be any repetition; why there should not be lines (as there are) divisible only into feet of different types. How can the grammatical exercise of scansion make a line of this sort more intelligible? Only by isolating elements which occur in other lines, and the sole purpose of doing this is the production of a similar effect elsewhere. But repetition of effect is a question of pattern.

Scansion tells us very little. It is probable that there is not much to be gained by an elaborate system of prosody, by the erudite complexities of Swinburnian metre. With Swinburne, once the trick is perceived and the scholarship appreciated, the effect is somewhat

diminished. When the unexpectedness, due to the unfamiliarity of the metres to English ears, wears off and is understood, one ceases to look for what one does not find in Swinburne; the inexplicable line with the music which can never be recaptured in other words. Swinburne mastered his technique, which is a great deal, but he did not master it to the extent of being able to take liberties with it, which is everything. If anything promising for English poetry is hidden in the metres of Swinburne, it probably lies far beyond the point to which Swinburne has developed them. But the most interesting verse which has yet been written in our language has been done either by taking a very simple form, like the iambic pentameter, and constantly withdrawing from it, or taking no form at all, and constantly approximating to a very simple one. It is this contrast between fixity and flux, this unperceived evasion of monotony, which is the very life of verse.

I have in mind two passages of contemporary verse which would be called *vers libre.* Both of them I quote because of their beauty:

Once, in finesse of fiddles found I ecstasy,
In the flash of gold heels on the hard pavement.
Now see I
That warmth's the very stuff of poesy.
Oh, God, make small
The old star-eaten blanket of the sky,
That I may fold it round me and in comfort lie.

This is a complete poem. The other is part of a much longer poem:

There shut up in his castle, Tairiran's,
She who had nor ears nor tongue save in her
      hands,
Gone—ah, gone—untouched, unreachable!
She who could never live save through one
      person,
She who could never speak save to one
      person,
And all the rest of her a shifting change,
A broken bundle of mirrors . . . !

It is obvious that the charm of these lines could not be, without the constant suggestion and the skilful evasion of iambic pentameter.

At the beginning of the seventeenth century, and especially in the verse of John Webster, who was in some ways a more cunning technician than Shakespeare, one finds the same constant evasion and recognition of regularity. Webster is much freer than Shakespeare, and that his fault is not negligence is evidenced by the fact that his verse acquires this freedom. That there is also carelessness I do not deny, but the irregularity of carelessness can be at once detected from the irregularity of deliberation. (In *The White Devil* Brachiano dying, and Cornelia mad, deliberately rupture the bonds of pentameter.)

> I recover, like a spent taper, for a flash
> and instantly go out.

> Cover her face; mine eyes dazzle; she died
> young.

> You have cause to love me, I did enter you
> in my heart
> Before you would vouchsafe to call for the
> keys.

> This is a vain poetry: but I pray you tell me
> If there were proposed me, wisdom, riches,
> and beauty,
> In three several young men, which should
> I choose?

These are not lines of carelessness. The irregularity is further enhanced by the use of short lines and the breaking up of lines in dialogue, which alters the quantities. And there are many lines in the drama of this time which are spoilt by regular accentuation.

> I loved this woman in spite of my heart.
> (*The Changeling*)

> I would have these herbs grow up in his grave.
> (*The White Devil*)

> Whether the spirit of greatness or of
> woman . . .   (*The Duchess of Malfi*)

The general charge of decadence cannot be preferred. Tourneur and Shirley, who I think will be conceded to have touched nearly the bottom of the decline of tragedy, are much more regular than Webster or Middleton. Tourneur will polish off a fair line of iambics even at the cost of amputating a preposition from its substantive, and in the *Atheist's Tragedy* he has a final "of" in two lines out of five together.

We may therefore formulate as follows: the ghost of some simple metre should lurk behind the arras in even the "freest" verse; to advance menacingly as we doze, and withdraw as we rouse. Or, freedom is only truly freedom when it appears against the background of an artificial limitation.

Not to have perceived the simple truth that *some* artificial limitation is necessary except in moments of the first intensity is, I believe, a capital error of even so distinguished a talent as that of Mr. E. L. Masters. The *Spoon River Anthology* is not material of the first intensity; it is reflective, not immediate; its author is a moralist, rather than an observer. His material is so near to the material of Crabbe that one wonders why he should have used a different form. Crabbe is, on the whole, the more intense of the two; he is keen, direct, and unsparing. His material is prosaic, not in the sense that it would have been better done in prose, but in the sense of requiring a simple and rather rigid verse-form, and this Crabbe has given it. Mr. Masters requires a more rigid verse-form than either of the two contemporary poets quoted above, and his epitaphs suffer from the lack of it.

So much for metre. There is no escape from metre; there is only mastery. But while there obviously is escape from rhyme, the *vers librists* are by no means the first out of the cave.

> The boughs of the trees
> Are twisted
> By many bafflings;
> Twisted are
> The small-leafed boughs.
> But the shadow of them
> Is not the shadow of the mast head
> Nor of the torn sails.

When the white dawn first
Through the rough fir-planks
Of my hut, by the chestnuts,
Up at the valley-head,
Came breaking, Goddess,
I sprang up, I threw round me
My dappled fawn-skin . . .

Except for the more human touch in the second of these extracts a hasty observer would hardly realize that the first is by a contemporary, and the second by Matthew Arnold.

I do not minimize the services of modern poets in exploiting the possibilities of rhymeless verse. They prove the strength of a Movement, the utility of a Theory. What neither Blake nor Arnold could do alone is being done in our time. "Blank verse" is the only accepted rhymeless verse in English—the inevitable iambic pentameter. The English ear is (or was) more sensitive to the music of the verse and less dependent upon the recurrence of identical sounds in this metre than in any other. There is no campaign against rhyme. But it is possible that excessive devotion to rhyme has thickened the modern ear. The rejection of rhyme is not a leap at facility; on the contrary, it imposes a much severer strain upon the language. When the comforting echo of rhyme is removed, success or failure in the choice of words, in the sentence structure, in the order, is at once more apparent. Rhyme removed, the poet is at once held up to the standards of prose. Rhyme removed, much ethereal music leaps up from the word, music which has

hitherto chirped unnoticed in the expanse of prose. Any rhyme forbidden, many Shagpats were unwigged.

And this liberation from rhyme might be as well a liberation *of* rhyme. Freed from its exacting task of supporting lame verse, it could be applied with greater effect where it is most needed. There are often passages in an unrhymed poem where rhyme is wanted for some special effect, for a sudden tightening-up, for a cumulative insistence, or for an abrupt change of mood. But formal rhymed verse will certainly not lose its place. We only need the coming of a Satirist—no man of genius is rarer—to prove that the heroic couplet has lost none of its edge since Dryden and Pope laid it down. As for the sonnet I am not so sure. But the decay of intricate formal patterns has nothing to do with the advent of *vers libre*. It had set in long before. Only in a closely-knit and homogeneous society, where many men are at work on the same problems, such a society as those which produced the Greek chorus, the Elizabethan lyric, and the Troubadour canzone, will the development of such forms ever be carried to perfection. And as for *vers libre*, we conclude that it is not defined by absence of pattern or absence of rhyme, for other verse is without these; that it is not defined by nonexistence of metre, since even the *worst* verse can be scanned; and we conclude that the division between Conservative Verse and *vers libre* does not exist, for there is only good verse, bad verse, and chaos.

Tradition and the Individual Talent (1919)

In English writing we seldom speak of tradition, though we occasionally apply its name in deploring its absence. We cannot refer to "the tradition" or to "a tradition"; at most, we employ the adjective in saying that the poetry of So-and-so is "traditional" or even "too traditional." Seldom, perhaps, does the word appear except in a phrase of censure. If otherwise, it is vaguely approbative, with the implication, as to the work approved, of some pleasing archaeological reconstruction. You can hardly make the word agreeable to English ears without this comfortable reference to the reassuring science of archaeology.

Certainly the word is not likely to appear in our appreciations of living or dead writers. Every nation, every race, has not only its own creative, but its own critical turn of mind; and is even more oblivious of the shortcomings and limitations of its critical habits than of those of its creative genius. We know, or think we know, from the enormous mass of critical writing that has appeared in the French language the critical method or habit of the French; we only conclude (we are such unconscious people) that the French are "more critical" than we, and sometimes even plume ourselves a little with the fact, as if the French were the less spontaneous. Perhaps they are; but we might remind ourselves that criticism is as inevitable as breathing, and that we should be none the worse for articulating what passes in our minds when we read a book and feel an emotion about it, for criticizing our own minds in their work of criticism. One of the facts that might come to light in this process is our

From *Selected Essays*, New Edition, by T. S. Eliot, copyright, 1932, 1936, 1950, by Harcourt Brace Jovanovich, Inc.; copyright, 1960, 1964, by T. S. Eliot. Reprinted by permission of the publisher.

tendency to insist, when we praise a poet, upon those aspects of his work in which he least resembles any one else. In these aspects or parts of his work we pretend to find what is individual, what is the peculiar essence of the man. We dwell with satisfaction upon the poet's difference from his predecessors, especially his immediate predecessors; we endeavour to find something that can be isolated in order to be enjoyed. Whereas if we approach a poet without this prejudice we shall often find that not only the best, but the most individual parts of his work may be those in which the dead poets, his ancestors, assert their immortality most vigorously. And I do not mean the impressionable period of adolescence, but the period of full maturity.

Yet if the only form of tradition, of handing down, consisted in following the ways of the immediate generation before us in a blind or timid adherence to its successes, "tradition" should positively be discouraged. We have seen many such simple currents soon lost in the sand; and novelty is better than repetition. Tradition is a matter of much wider significance. It cannot be inherited, and if you want it you must obtain it by great labour. It involves, in the first place, the historical sense, which we may call nearly indispensable to any one who would continue to be a poet beyond his twenty-fifth year; and the historical sense involves a perception, not only of the pastness of the past, but of its presence; the historical sense compels a man to write not merely with his own generation in his bones, but with a feeling that the whole of the literature of Europe from Homer and within it the whole of the literature of his own country has a simultaneous existence and composes a simultaneous order. This historical sense, which is a sense of the timeless as well as of the temporal and of the timeless and of the temporal together, is what makes a writer traditional. And it is at the same time what makes a writer most acutely conscious of his place in time, of his own contemporaneity.

No poet, no artist of any art, has his complete meaning alone. His significance, his appreciation is the appreciation of his relation to the dead poets and artists. You cannot value him alone; you must set him, for contrast and comparison, among the dead. I mean this as a principle of aesthetic, not merely historical, criticism. The necessity that he shall conform, that he shall cohere, is not onesided; what happens when a new work of art is created is something that happens simultaneously to all the works of art which preceded it. The existing monuments form an ideal order among themselves, which is modified by the introduction of the new (the really new) work of art among them. The existing order is complete before the new work arrives; for order to persist after the supervention of novelty, the *whole* existing order must be, if ever so slightly, altered; and so the relations, proportions, values of each work of art toward the whole are readjusted; and this is conformity between the old and the new. Whoever has approved this idea of order, of the form of European, of English literature will not find it preposterous that the past should be altered by the present as much as the present is directed by the past. And the poet who is aware of this will be aware of great difficulties and responsibilities.

In a peculiar sense he will be aware also that he must inevitably be judged by the standards of the past. I say judged, not amputated, by them; not judged to be as good as, or worse or better than, the dead; and certainly not judged by the canons of dead critics. It is a judgment, a comparison, in which two things are measured by each other. To conform merely would be for the new work not really to conform at all; it would not be new, and would therefore not be a work of art. And

we do not quite say that the new is more valuable because it fits in; but its fitting in is a test of its value—a test, it is true, which can only be slowly and cautiously applied, for we are none of us infallible judges of conformity. We say: it appears to conform, and is perhaps individual, or it appears individual, and many conform; but we are hardly likely to find that it is one and not the other.

To proceed to a more intelligible exposition of the relation of the poet to the past: he can neither take the past as a lump, an indiscriminate bolus, nor can he form himself wholly on one or two private admirations, nor can he form himself wholly upon one preferred period. The first course is inadmissible, the second is an important experience of youth, and the third is a pleasant and highly desirable supplement. The poet must be very conscious of the main current, which does not at all flow invariably through the most distinguished reputations. He must be quite aware of the obvious fact that art never improves, but that the material of art is never quite the same. He must be aware that the mind of Europe—the mind of his own country—a mind which he learns in time to be much more important than his own private mind—is a mind which changes, and that this change is a development which abandons nothing *en route*, which does not superannuate either Shakespeare, or Homer, or the rock drawing of the Magdalenian draughtsmen. That this development, refinement perhaps, complication certainly, is not, from the point of view of the artist, any improvement. Perhaps not even an improvement from the point of view of the psychologist or not to the extent which we imagine; perhaps only in the end based upon a complication in economics and machinery. But the difference between the present and the past is that the conscious present is an awareness of the past in a way and to an extent which the past's awareness of itself cannot show.

Some one said: "The dead writers are remote from us because we *know* so much more than they did." Precisely, and they are that which we know.

I am alive to a usual objection to what is clearly part of my programme for the *métier* of poetry. The objection is that the doctrine requires a ridiculous amount of erudition (pedantry), a claim which can be rejected by appeal to the lives of poets in any pantheon. It will even be affirmed that much learning deadens or perverts poetic sensibility. While, however, we persist in believing that a poet ought to know as much as will not encroach upon his necessary receptivity and necessary laziness, it is not desirable to confine knowledge to whatever can be put into a useful shape for examinations, drawing-rooms, or the still more pretentious modes of publicity. Some can absorb knowledge, the more tardy must sweat for it. Shakespeare acquired more essential history from Plutarch than most men could from the whole British Museum. What is to be insisted upon is that the poet must develop or procure the consciousness of the past and that he should continue to develop this consciousness throughout his career.

What happens is a continual surrender of himself as he is at the moment to something which is more valuable. The progress of an artist is a continual self-sacrifice, a continual extinction of personality.

There remains to define this process of depersonalization and its relation to the sense of tradition. It is in this depersonalization that art may be said to approach the condition of science. I, therefore, invite you to consider, as a suggestive analogy, the action which takes place when a bit of finely filiated platinum is introduced into a chamber containing oxygen and sulphur dioxide.

II

Honest criticism and sensitive appreciation are directed not upon the poet but upon the poetry. If we attend to the confused cries of the newspaper critics and the *susurrus* of popular repetition that follows, we shall hear the names of poets in great numbers; if we seek not Blue-book knowledge but the enjoyment of poetry, and ask for a poem, we shall seldom find it. I have tried to point out the importance of the relation of the poem to other poems by other authors, and suggested the conception of poetry as a living whole of all the poetry that has ever been written. The other aspect of this Impersonal theory of poetry is the relation of the poem to its author. And I hinted, by an analogy, that the mind of the mature poet differs from that of the immature one not precisely in any valuation of "personality," not being necessarily more interesting, or having "more to say," but rather by being a more finely perfected medium in which special, or very varied, feelings are at liberty to enter into new combinations.

The analogy was that of the catalyst. When the two gases previously mentioned are mixed in the presence of a filament of platinum, they form sulphurous acid. This combination takes place only if the platinum is present; nevertheless the newly formed acid contains no trace of platinum, and the platinum itself is apparently unaffected; has remained inert, neutral, and unchanged. The mind of the poet is the shred of platinum. It may partly or exclusively operate upon the experience of the man himself; but, the more perfect the artist, the more completely separate in him will be the man who suffers and the mind which creates; the more perfectly will the mind digest and transmute the passions which are its material.

The experience, you will notice, the elements which enter the presence of the transforming catalyst, are of two kinds: emotions and feelings. The effect of a work of art upon the person who enjoys it is an experience different in kind from any experience not of art. It may be formed out of one emotion, or may be a combination of several; and various feelings, inhering for the writer in particular words or phrases or images, may be added to compose the final result. Or great poetry may be made without the direct use of any emotion whatever: composed out of feelings solely. Canto XV of the *Inferno* (Brunetto Latini) is a working up of the emotion evident in the situation; but the effect, though single as that of any work of art, is obtained by considerable complexity of detail. The last quatrain gives an image, a feeling attaching to an image, which "came," which did not develop simply out of what precedes, but which was probably in suspension in the poet's mind until the proper combination arrived for it to add itself to. The poet's mind is in fact a receptacle for seizing and storing up numberless feelings, phrases, images, which remain there until all the particles which can unite to form a new compound are present together.

If you compare several representative passages of the greatest poetry you see how great is the variety of types of combination, and also how completely any semi-ethical criterion of "sublimity" misses the mark. For it is not the "greatness," the intensity, of the emotions, the components, but the intensity of the artistic process, the pressure, so to speak, under which the fusion takes place, that counts. The episode of Paolo and Francesca employs a definite emotion, but the intensity of the poetry is something quite different from whatever intensity in the supposed experience it may give the impression of. It is no more intense, furthermore, than Canto XXVI, the voyage of Ulysses, which has not the direct dependence upon an emotion. Great variety is possible in the process of transmutation of emotion: the murder of Agamemnon, or the agony of Othello, gives an artistic effect apparently closer to a possible original than the scenes from Dante. In the *Agamemnon*, the artistic emotion approximates to the emotion of an actual spectator; in *Othello* to the emotion of the protagonist himself. But the difference between art and the event is always absolute; the combination which is the murder of Agamemnon is probably as complex as that which is the voyage of Ulysses. In either case there has been a fusion of elements. The ode of Keats contains a number of feelings which have nothing particular to do with the nightingale, but which the nightingale, partly, perhaps, because of its attractive name, and partly because of its reputation, served to bring together.

The point of view which I am struggling to attack is perhaps related to the metaphysical theory of the substantial unity of the soul: for my meaning is, that the poet has, not a "personality" to express, but a particular medium, which is only a medium and not a personality, in which impressions and experiences combine in peculiar and unexpected ways. Impressions and experiences which are important for the man may take no place in the poetry, and those which become important in the poetry may play quite a negligible part in the man, the personality.

I will quote a passage which is unfamiliar enough to be regarded with fresh attention in the light—or darkness—of these observations:

> And now methinks I could e'en chide myself
> For doating on her beauty, though her death
> Shall be revenged after no common action.
> Does the silkworm expend her yellow labours
> For thee? For thee does she undo herself?
> Are lordships sold to maintain ladyships
> For the poor benefit of a bewildering minute?
> Why does yon fellow falsify highways,
> And put his life between the judge's lips,
> To refine such a thing—keeps horse and men
> To beat their valours for her? . . .

In this passage (as is evident if it is taken in its context) there is a combination of positive and negative emotions: an intensely strong attraction toward beauty and an equally intense fascination by the ugliness which is contrasted with it and which destroys it. This balance of contrasted emotion is in the dramatic situation to which the speech is pertinent, but that situation alone is inadequate to it. This is, so to speak, the structural emotion, provided by the drama. But the whole effect, the dominant tone, is due to the fact that a number of floating feelings, having an affinity to this emotion by no means superficially evident, have combined with it to give us a new art emotion.

It is not in his personal emotions, the emotions provoked by particular events in his life, that the poet is in any way remarkable or interesting. His particular emotions may be simple, or crude, or flat. The emotion in his poetry will be a very complex thing, but not with the complexity of the emotions of people who have very complex or unusual emotions in life. One error, in fact, of eccentricity in poetry is to seek for new human emotions to express; and in this search for novelty in the wrong place it discovers the perverse. The business of the poet is not to find new emotions, but to use the ordinary ones and, in working them up into poetry, to express feelings which are not in actual emotions at all. And emotions which he has never experienced will serve his turn as well as those familiar to him. Consequently, we must believe that "emotion recollected in tranquillity" is an inexact formula. For it is neither emotion, nor recollection, nor, without distortion of meaning, tranquillity. It is a concentration, and a new thing resulting from the concentration, of a very great number of experiences which to the practical and active person would not seem to be experiences at all; it is a concentration which does not happen consciously or of deliberation. These experiences are not "recollected," and they finally unite in an atmosphere which is "tranquil" only in that it is a passive attending upon the event. Of course this is not quite the whole story. There is a great deal, in the writing of poetry, which must be conscious and deliberate. In fact, the bad poet is usually unconscious where he ought to be conscious, and conscious where he ought to be unconscious.

Both errors tend to make him "personal." Poetry is not a turning loose of emotion, but an escape from emotion; it is not the expression of personality, but an escape from personality. But, of course, only those who have personality and emotions know what it means to want to escape from these things.

III

δ δὲ νοῦς ἴσως Θειότερόν τι χαὶ ἀπαθές ἐστιν.

This essay proposes to halt at the frontier of metaphysics or mysticism, and confine itself to such practical conclusions as can be applied by the responsible person interested in poetry. To divert interest from the poet to the poetry is a laudable aim: for it would conduce to a juster estimation of actual poetry, good and bad. There are many people who appreciate the expression of sincere emotion in verse, and there is a smaller number of people who can appreciate technical excellence. But very few know when there is an expression of *significant* emotion, emotion which has its life in the poem and not in the history of the poet. The emotion of art is impersonal. And the poet cannot reach this impersonality without surrendering himself wholly to the work to be done. And he is not likely to know what is to be done unless he lives in what is not merely the present, but the present moment of the past, unless he is conscious, not of what is dead, but of what is already living.

The Perfect Critic (1920)

*Eriger en lois ses impressions personnelles, c'est le grand
effort d'un homme s'il est sincère.*
LETTRES À L'AMAZONE.

COLERIDGE was perhaps the greatest of English
critics, and in a sense the last. After Coleridge
we have Matthew Arnold; but Arnold—I think
it will be conceded—was rather a propagandist
for criticism than a critic, a popularizer rather
than a creator of ideas. So long as this island
remains an island (and we are no nearer the
Continent than were Arnold's contemporaries) the work of Arnold will be important; it
is still a bridge across the Channel, and it will
always have been good sense. Since Arnold's
attempt to correct his countrymen, English
criticism has followed two directions. When a
distinguished critic observed recently, in a
newspaper article, that "poetry is the most
highly organized form of intellectual activity,"
we were conscious that we were reading neither
Coleridge nor Arnold. Not only have the words
"organized" and "activity," occurring together
in this phrase, that familiar vague suggestion
of the scientific vocabulary which is characteristic of modern writing, but one asked questions which Coleridge and Arnold would not
have permitted one to ask. How is it, for instance, that poetry is more "highly organized"
than astronomy, physics, or pure mathematics,
which we imagine to be, in relation to the
scientist who practises them, "intellectual activity" of a pretty highly organized type?
"Mere strings of words," our critic continues
with felicity and truth, "flung like dabs of
paint across a blank canvas, may awaken surprise . . . but have no significance whatever

From *The Sacred Wood*. Reprinted by permission
of Methuen & Co. Ltd., London.

in the history of literature." The phrases by
which Arnold is best known may be inadequate, they may assemble more doubts than
they dispel, but they usually have some meaning. And if a phrase like "the most highly
organized form of intellectual activity" is the
highest organization of thought of which contemporary criticism, in a distinguished representative, is capable, then, we conclude, modern criticism is degenerate.

The verbal disease above noticed may be
reserved for diagnosis by and by. It is not a
disease from which Mr. Arthur Symons (for
the quotation was, of course, not from Mr.
Symons) notably suffers. Mr. Symons represents the other tendency; he is a representative
of what is always called "aesthetic criticism"
or "impressionistic criticism." And it is this
form of criticism which I propose to examine
at once. Mr. Symons, the critical successor of
Pater, and partly of Swinburne (I fancy that
the phrase "sick or sorry" is the common property of all three), *is* the "impressionistic critic."
He, if anyone, would be said to expose a
sensitive and cultivated mind—cultivated, that
is, by the accumulation of a considerable variety of impressions from all the arts and several languages—before an "object"; and his
criticism, if anyone's, would be said to exhibit
to us, like the plate, the faithful record of the
impressions, more numerous or more refined
than our own, upon a mind more sensitive
than our own. A record, we observe, which is
also an interpretation, a translation; for it must
itself impose impressions upon us, and these
impressions are as much created as transmitted

by the criticism. I do not say at once that this
is Mr. Symons; but it is the "impressionistic"
critic, and the impressionistic critic is supposed
to be Mr. Symons.

At hand is a volume which we may test.[1]
Ten of these thirteen essays deal with single
plays of Shakespeare, and it is therefore fair
to take one of these ten as a specimen of the
book:

> Antony and Cleopatra is the most wonderful,
> I think, of all Shakespeare's plays . . .

and Mr. Symons reflects that Cleopatra is the
most wonderful of all women:

> The queen who ends the dynasty of the Ptol-
> emies has been the star of poets, a malign star
> shedding baleful light, from Horace and Proper-
> tius down to Victor Hugo; and it is not to poets
> only . . .

What, we ask, is this for? as a page on Cleopatra, and on her possible origin in the dark
lady of the Sonnets, unfolds itself. And we
find, gradually, that this is not an essay on a
work of art or a work of intellect; but that Mr.
Symons is living through the play as one might
live it through in the theatre; recounting, commenting:

> In her last days Cleopatra touches a certain
> elevation . . . she would die a thousand times,
> rather than live to be a mockery and a scorn in
> men's mouths . . . she is a woman to the last
> . . . so she dies . . . the play ends with a touch
> of grave pity . . .

Presented in this rather unfair way, torn
apart like the leaves of an artichoke, the impressions of Mr. Symons come to resemble a
common type of popular literary lecture, in
which the stories of plays or novels are retold,
the motives of the characters set forth, and the
work of art therefore made easier for the beginner. But this is not Mr. Symons' reason for
writing. The reason why we find a similarity
between his essay and this form of education
is that Antony and Cleopatra is a play with

[1] *Studies in Elizabethan Drama.* By Arthur Symons.

which we are pretty well acquainted, and of
which we have, therefore, our own impressions.
We can please ourselves with our own impressions of the characters and their emotions; and
we do not find the impressions of another
person, however sensitive, very significant. But
if we can recall the time when we were ignorant of the French symbolists, and met with
The Symbolist Movement in Literature, we
remember that book as an introduction to
wholly new feelings, as a revelation. After we
have read Verlaine and Laforgue and Rimbaud
and return to Mr. Symons' book, we may find
that our own impressions dissent from his.
The book has not, perhaps, a permanent value
for the one reader, but it has led to results of
permanent importance for him.

The question is not whether Mr. Symons'
impressions are "true" or "false." So far as you
can isolate the "impression," the pure feeling,
it is, of course, neither true nor false. The
point is that you never rest at the pure feeling;
you react in one of two ways, or, as I believe
Mr. Symons does, in a mixture of the two
ways. The moment you try to put the impressions into words, you either begin to analyse and construct, to "ériger en lois," or you
begin to create something else. It is significant
that Swinburne, by whose poetry Mr. Symons
may at one time have been influenced, is one
man in his poetry and a different man in his
criticism; to this extent and in this respect
only, that he is satisfying a different impulse;
he is criticizing, expounding, arranging. You
may say this is not the criticism of a critic,
that it is emotional, not intellectual—though
of this there are two opinions, but it is in the
direction of analysis and construction, a beginning to "ériger en lois," and not in the direction of creation. So I infer that Swinburne
found an adequate outlet for the creative impulse in his poetry; and none of it was forced
back and out through his critical prose. The
style of the latter is essentially a prose style;
and Mr. Symons' prose is much more like
Swinburne's poetry than it is like his prose. I
imagine—though here one's thought is moving

in almost complete darkness—that Mr. Symons is far more disturbed, far more profoundly affected, by his reading than was Swinburne, who responded rather by a violent and immediate and comprehensive burst of admiration which may have left him internally unchanged. The disturbance in Mr. Symons is almost, but not quite, to the point of creating; the reading sometimes fecundates his emotions to produce something new which is not criticism, but is not the expulsion, the ejection, the birth of creativeness.

The type is not uncommon, although Mr. Symons is far superior to most of the type. Some writers are essentially of the type that reacts in excess of the stimulus, making something new out of the impressions, but suffers from a defect of vitality or an obscure obstruction which prevents nature from taking its course. Their sensibility alters the object, but never transforms it. Their reaction is that of the ordinary emotional person developed to an exceptional degree. For this ordinary emotional person, experiencing a work of art, has a mixed critical and creative reaction. It is made up of comment and opinion, and also new emotions which are vaguely applied to his own life. The sentimental person, in whom a work of art arouses all sorts of emotions which have nothing to do with that work of art whatever, but are accidents of personal association, is an incomplete artist. For in an artist these suggestions made by a work of art, which are purely personal, become fused with a multitude of other suggestions from multitudinous experience, and result in the production of a new object which is no longer purely personal, because it is a work of art itself.

It would be rash to speculate, and is perhaps impossible to determine, what is unfulfilled in Mr. Symons' charming verse that overflows into his critical prose. Certainly we may say that in Swinburne's verse the circuit of impression and expression is complete; and Swinburne was therefore able, in his criticism, to be more a critic than Mr. Symons. This gives us an intimation why the artist is—each within his own limitations—oftenest to be depended upon as a critic; his criticism will be criticism, and not the satisfaction of a suppressed creative wish—which, in most other persons, is apt to interfere fatally.

Before considering what the proper critical reaction of artistic sensibility is, how far criticism is "feeling" and how far "thought," and what sort of "thought" is permitted, it may be instructive to prod a little into that other temperament, so different from Mr. Symons', which issues in generalities such as that quoted near the beginning of this article.

II

L'écrivain de style abstrait est presque toujours un sentimental, du moins un sensitif. L'écrivain artiste n'est presque jamais un sentimental, et très rarement un sensitif.
LE PROBLÈME DU STYLE.

THE STATEMENT already quoted, that "poetry is the most highly organized form of intellectual activity," may be taken as a specimen of the abstract style in criticism. The confused distinction which exists in most heads between "abstract" and "concrete" is due not so much to a manifest fact of the existence of two types of mind, an abstract and a concrete, as to the existence of another type of mind, the verbal, or philosophic. I, of course, do not imply any general condemnation of philosophy; I am, for the moment, using the word "philosophic" to cover the unscientific ingredients of philosophy; to cover, in fact, the greater part of the philosophic output of the last hundred years. There are two ways in which a word may be "abstract." It may have (the word "activity," for example) a meaning which cannot be grasped by appeal to any of the senses; its apprehension may require a deliberate suppression of analogies of visual or muscular experience, which is none the less an effort of imagination. "Activity" will mean for the trained scientist, if he employ the term, either nothing at all or something still more exact than anything it suggests to us. If we are allowed to accept certain remarks of Pascal and Mr. Bertrand Russell about mathematics, we believe that the mathematician deals with objects—if he will permit us to call them objects—which directly affect his sensibility. And during a good part of history the philosopher endeavoured to deal with objects which he believed to be of the same exactness as the mathematician's. Finally Hegel arrived, and if not perhaps the first, he was certainly the most prodigious exponent of emotional systematization, dealing with his emotions as if they were definite objects which had aroused those emotions. His followers have as a rule taken for granted that words have definite meanings, overlooking the tendency of words to become indefinite emotions. (No one who had not witnessed the event could imagine the conviction in the tone of Professor Eucken as he pounded the table and exclaimed *Was ist Geist? Geist ist* . . .) If verbalism were confined to professional philosophers, no harm would be done. But their corruption has extended very far. Compare a mediaeval theologian or mystic, compare a seventeenth-century preacher, with any "liberal" sermon since Schleiermacher, and you will observe that words have changed their meanings. What they have lost is definite, and what they have gained is indefinite.

The vast accumulations of knowledge—or at least of information—deposited by the nineteenth century have been responsible for an equally vast ignorance. When there is so much to be known, when there are so many fields of knowledge in which the same words are used with different meanings, when every one knows a little about a great many things, it becomes increasingly difficult for anyone to know whether he knows what he is talking about or not. And when we do not know, or when we do not know enough, we tend always to substitute emotions for thoughts. The sentence so frequently quoted in this essay will serve for an example of this process as well as any, and may be profitably contrasted with the opening phrases of the *Posterior Analytics*. Not only all knowledge, but all feeling, is in perception. The inventor of poetry as the most highly organized form of intellectual activity was not engaged in perceiving when he composed this definition; he had nothing to be aware of except his own emotion about "poetry." He was, in fact, absorbed in a very different "activity" not only from that of Mr. Symons, but from that of Aristotle.

Aristotle is a person who has suffered from the adherence of persons who must be regarded less as his disciples than as his sectaries. One must be firmly distrustful of accepting Aristotle in a canonical spirit; this is to lose the whole living force of him. He was primarily a man of not only remarkable but universal intelligence; and universal intelligence means that he could apply his intelligence to anything. The ordinary intelligence is good only for certain classes of objects; a brilliant man of science, if he is interested in poetry at all, may conceive grotesque judgments: like one poet because he reminds him of himself, or another because he expresses emotions which he admires; he may use art, in fact, as the outlet for the egotism which is suppressed in his own speciality. But Aristotle had none of these impure desires to satisfy; in whatever sphere of interest, he looked solely and steadfastly at the object; in his short and broken treatise he provides an eternal example—not of laws, or even of method, for there is no method except to be very intelligent, but of intelligence itself swiftly operating the analysis of sensation to the point of principle and definition.

It is far less Aristotle than Horace who has been the model for criticism up to the nineteenth century. A precept, such as Horace or Boileau gives us, is merely an unfinished analysis. It appears as a law, a rule, because it does not appear in its most general form; it is empirical. When we understand necessity, as Spinoza knew, we are free because we assent. The dogmatic critic, who lays down a rule, who affirms a value, has left his labour incomplete. Such statements may often be justifiable as a saving of time; but in matters of great importance the critic must not coerce, and he must not make judgments of worse and better. He must simply elucidate: the reader will form the correct judgment for himself.

And again, the purely 'technical" critic—the critic, that is, who writes to expound some novelty or impart some lesson to practitioners of an art—can be called a critic only in a narrow sense. He may be analysing perceptions and the means for arousing perceptions, but his aim is limited and is not the disinterested exercise of intelligence. The narrowness of the aim makes easier the detection of the merit or feebleness of the work; even of these writers there are very few—so that their "criticism" is of great importance within its limits. So much suffices for Campion. Dryden is far more disinterested; he displays much free intelligence; and yet even Dryden—or any *literary* critic of the seventeenth century—is not quite a free mind, compared, for instance, with such a mind as Rochefoucauld's. There is always a tendency to legislate rather than to inquire, to revise accepted laws, even to overturn, but to reconstruct out of the same material. And the free intelligence is that which is wholly devoted to inquiry.

Coleridge, again, whose natural abilities, and some of whose performances, are probably more remarkable than those of any other modern critic, cannot be estimated as an intelligence completely free. The nature of the restraint in his case is quite different from that which limited the seventeenth-century critics, and is much more personal. Coleridge's metaphysical interest was quite genuine, and was, like most metaphysical interest, an affair of his emotions. But a literary critic should have no emotions except those immediately provoked by a work of art—and these (as I have already hinted) are, when valid, perhaps not to be called emotions at all. Coleridge is apt to take leave of the data of criticism, and arouse the suspicion that he has been diverted into a metaphysical hare-and-hounds. His end does not always appear to be the return to the work of art with improved perception and intensified, because more conscious, enjoyment; his centre of interest changes, his feelings are impure. In the derogatory sense he is more "philosophic" than Aristotle. For everything that Aristotle says illuminates the literature which is the occasion for saying it; but Coleridge only now and then. It is one more instance of the pernicious effect of emotion.

Aristotle had what is called the scientific mind—a mind which, as it is rarely found among scientists except in fragments, might better be called the intelligent mind. For there is no other intelligence than this, and so far as artists and men of letters are intelligent (we may doubt whether the level of intelligence among men of letters is as high as among men of science) their intelligence is of this kind. Sainte-Beuve was a physiologist by training; but it is probable that his mind, like that of the ordinary scientific specialist, was limited in its interest, and that this was not, primarily, an interest in art. If he was a critic, there is no doubt that he was a very good one; but we may conclude that he earned some other name. Of all modern critics, perhaps Remy de Gourmont had most of the general intelligence of Aristotle. An amateur, though an excessively able amateur, in physiology, he combined to a remarkable degree sensitiveness, erudition, sense of fact and sense of history, and generalizing power.

We assume the gift of a superior sensibility. And for sensibility wide and profound reading does not mean merely a more extended pasture. There is not merely an increase of understanding, leaving the original acute impression unchanged. The new impressions modify the impressions received from the objects already known. An impression needs to be constantly refreshed by new impressions in order that it may persist at all; it needs to take its place in a system of impressions. And this system tends to become articulate in a generalized statement of literary beauty.

There are, for instance, many scattered lines and tercets in the *Divine Comedy* which are capable of transporting even a quite uninitiated reader, just sufficiently acquainted with the roots of the language to decipher the meaning, to an impression of over-powering beauty. This impression may be so deep that no subsequent study and understanding will intensify it. But at this point the impression is emotional; the reader in the ignorance which we postulate is unable to distinguish the poetry from an emotional state aroused in himself by the poetry, a state which may be merely an indulgence of his own emotions. The poetry may be an accidental stimulus. The end of the enjoyment of poetry is a pure contemplation from which all the accidents of personal emotion are removed; thus we aim to see the object as it really is and find a meaning for the words of Arnold. And without a labour which is largely a labour of the intelligence, we are unable to attain that stage of vision *amor intellectualis Dei.*

Such considerations, cast in this general form, may appear commonplaces. But I believe that it is always opportune to call attention to the torpid superstition that appreciation is one thing, and "intellectual" criticism something else. Appreciation in popular psychology is one faculty, and criticism another,

an arid cleverness building theoretical scaffolds upon one's own perceptions or those of others. On the contrary, the true generalization is not something superposed upon an accumulation of perceptions; the perceptions do not, in a really appreciative mind, accumulate as a mass, but form themselves as a structure; and criticism is the statement in language of this structure; it is a development of sensibility. The bad criticism, on the other hand, is that which is nothing but an expression of emotion. And emotional people—such as stockbrokers, politicians, men of science—and a few people who pride themselves on being unemotional—detest or applaud great writers such as Spinoza or Stendhal because of their "frigidity."

The writer of the present essay once committed himself to the statement that "The poetic critic is criticizing poetry in order to create poetry." He is now inclined to believe that the "historical" and the "philosophical" critics had better be called historians and philosophers quite simply. As for the rest, there are merely various degrees of intelligence. It is fatuous to say that criticism is for the sake of "creation" or creation for the sake of criticism. It is also fatuous to assume that there are ages of criticism and ages of creativeness, as if by plunging ourselves into intellectual darkness we were in better hopes of finding spiritual light. The two directions of sensibility are complementary; and as sensibility is rare, unpopular, and desirable, it is to be expected that the critic and the creative artist should frequently be the same person.

Andrew Marvell (1921)

THE TERCENTENARY of the former member for Hull deserves not only the celebration proposed by that favoured borough, but a little serious reflection upon his writing. That is an act of piety, which is very different from the resurrection of a deceased reputation. Marvell has stood high for some years; his best poems are not very many, and not only must be well known, from the *Golden Treasury* and the *Oxford Book of English Verse,* but must also have been enjoyed by numerous readers. His grave needs neither rose nor rue nor laurel; there is no imaginary justice to be done; we may think about him, if there be need for thinking, for our own benefit, not his. To bring the poet back to life—the great, the perennial, task of criticism—is in this case to squeeze the drops of the essence of two or three poems; even confining ourselves to these, we may find some precious liquor unknown to the present age. Not to determine rank, but to isolate this quality, is the critical labour. The fact that of all Marvell's verse, which is itself not a great quantity, the really valuable part consists of a very few poems indicates that the unknown quality of which we speak is probably a literary rather than a personal quality; or, more truly, that it is a quality of a civilization, of a traditional habit of life. A poet like Donne, or like Baudelaire or Laforgue, may almost be considered the inventor of an attitude, a system of feeling or of morals. Donne is difficult to analyse: what appears at one time a curious personal point of view may at another time appear rather the precise concentration of a kind of feeling diffused in the air about him. Donne and his shroud, the shroud and his motive for

wearing it, are inseparable, but they are not the same thing. The seventeenth century sometimes seems for more than a moment to gather up and to digest into its art all the experience of the human mind which (from the same point of view) the later centuries seem to have been partly engaged in repudiating. But Donne would have been an individual at any time and place; Marvell's best verse is the product of European, that is to say Latin, culture.

Out of that high style developed from Marlowe through Jonson (for Shakespeare does not lend himself to these genealogies) the seventeenth century separated two qualities: wit and magniloquence. Neither is as simple or as apprehensible as its name seems to imply, and the two are not in practice antithetical; both are conscious and cultivated, and the mind which cultivates one may cultivate the other. The actual poetry, of Marvell, of Cowley, of Milton, and of others, is a blend in varying proportions. And we must be on guard not to employ the terms with too wide a comprehension; for like the other fluid terms with which literary criticism deals, the meaning alters with the age, and for precision we must rely to some degree upon the literacy and good taste of the reader. The wit of the Caroline poets is not the wit of Shakespeare, and it is not the wit of Dryden, the great master of contempt, or of Pope, the great master of hatred, or of Swift, the great master of disgust. What is meant is some quality which is common to the songs in *Comus* and Cowley's Anacreontics and Marvell's Horatian Ode. It is more than a technical accomplishment, or the vocabulary and syntax of an epoch; it is, what we have designated tentatively as wit, a tough reasonableness beneath the slight lyric grace. You cannot find it in Shelley or Keats or

Wordsworth; you cannot find more than an echo of it in Landor; still less in Tennyson or Browning; and among contemporaries Mr. Yeats is an Irishman and Mr. Hardy is a modern Englishman—that is to say, Mr. Hardy is without it and Mr. Yeats is outside of the tradition altogether. On the other hand, as it certainly exists in Lafontaine, there is a large part of it in Gautier. And of the magniloquence, the deliberate exploitation of the possibilities of magnificence in language which Milton used and abused, there is also use and even abuse in the poetry of Baudelaire.

Wit is not a quality that we are accustomed to associate with "Puritan" literature, with Milton or with Marvell. But if so, we are at fault partly in our conception of wit and partly in our generalizations about the Puritans. And if the wit of Dryden or of Pope is not the only kind of wit in the language, the rest is not merely a little merriment or a little levity or a little impropriety or a little epigram. And, on the other hand, the sense in which a man like Marvell is a "Puritan" is restricted. The persons who opposed Charles I and the persons who supported the Commonwealth were not all of the flock of Zeal-of-the-land Busy or the United Grand Junction Ebenezer Temperance Association. Many of them were gentlemen of the time who merely believed, with considerable show of reason, that government by a Parliament of gentlemen was better than government by a Stuart; though they were, to that extent, Liberal Practitioners, they could hardly foresee the tea-meeting and the Dissidence of Dissent. Being men of education and culture, even of travel, some of them were exposed to that spirit of the age which was coming to be the French spirit of the age. This spirit, curiously enough, was quite opposed to the tendencies latent or the forces active in Puritanism; the contest does great damage to the poetry of Milton; Marvell, an active servant of the public, but a lukewarm partisan, and a poet on a smaller scale, is far less injured by it. His line on the statue of Charles II, "It is such a King as no chisel can mend," may be set off against

his criticism of the Great Rebellion: "Men . . . ought and might have trusted the King." Marvell, therefore, more a man of the century than a Puritan, speaks more clearly and unequivocally with the voice of his literary age than does Milton.

This voice speaks out uncommonly strong in the *Coy Mistress*. The theme is one of the great traditional commonplaces of European literature. It is the theme of *O mistress mine*, of *Gather ye rosebuds*, of *Go, lovely rose*; it is in the savage austerity of Lucretius and the intense levity of Catullus. Where the wit of Marvell renews the theme is in the variety and order of the images. In the first of the three paragraphs Marvell plays with a fancy which begins by pleasing and leads to astonishment.

> Had we but world enough and time,
> This coyness, lady, were no crime,
>   . . . I would
> Love you ten years before the Flood,
> And you should, if you please, refuse
> Till the conversion of the Jews;
> My vegetable love should grow
> Vaster than empires and more slow. . . .

We notice the high speed, the succession of concentrated images, each magnifying the original fancy. When this process has been carried to the end and summed up, the poem turns suddenly with that surprise which has been one of the most important means of poetic effect since Homer:

> But at my back I always hear
> Time's wingèd chariot hurrying **near**,
> And yonder all before us lie
> Deserts of vast eternity.

A whole civilization resides in these lines:

> Pallida Mors aequo pulsat pede pauperum
>   tabernas,
> Regumque turris. . . .

And not only Horace but Catullus himself:

> Nobis, cum semel occidit brevis lux,
> Nox est perpetua una dormienda.

The verse of Marvell has not the grand reverberation of Catullus's Latin; but the image of

Marvell is certainly more comprehensive and penetrates greater depths than Horace's.

A modern poet, had he reached the height, would very likely have closed on this moral reflection. But the three strophes of Marvell's poem have something like a syllogistic relation to each other. After a close approach to the mood of Donne,

> then worms shall try
> That long-preserved virginity . . .
> The grave's a fine and private place,
> But none, I think, do there embrace,

the conclusion,

> Let us roll all our strength and all
> Our sweetness up into one ball,
> And tear our pleasures with rough strife,
> Thorough the iron gates of life.

It will hardly be denied that this poem contains wit; but it may not be evident that this wit forms the crescendo and diminuendo of a scale of great imaginative power. The wit is not only combined with, but fused into, the imagination. We can easily recognize a witty fancy in the successive images ("my *vegetable* love," "till the conversion of the Jews"), but this fancy is not indulged, as it sometimes is by Cowley or Cleveland, for its own sake. It is structural decoration of a serious idea. In this it is superior to the fancy of *L'Allegro, Il Penseroso,* or the lighter and less successful poems of Keats. In fact, this alliance of levity and seriousness (by which the seriousness is intensified) is a characteristic of the sort of wit we are trying to identify. It is found in

> Le squelette était invisible
> Au temps heureux de l'art païen!

of Gautier, and in the *dandysme* of Baudelaire and Laforgue. It is in the poem of Catullus which has been quoted, and in the variation by Ben Jonson:

> Cannot we deceive the eyes
> Of a few poor household spies?
> 'Tis no sin love's fruits to steal,
> But that sweet sin to reveal,
> To be taken, to be seen,
> These have sins accounted been.

It is in Propertius and Ovid. It is a quality of a sophisticated literature; a quality which expands in English literature just at the moment before the English mind altered; it is not a quality which we should expect Puritanism to encourage. When we come to Gray and Collins, the sophistication remains only in the language, and has disappeared from the feeling. Gray and Collins were masters, but they had lost that hold on human values, that firm grasp of human experience, which is a formidable achievement of the Elizabethan and Jacobean poets. This wisdom, cynical perhaps but untired (in Shakespeare, a terrifying clairvoyance), leads toward, and is only completed by, the religious comprehension; it leads to the point of the *Ainsi tout leur a craqué dans la main* of Bouvard and Pécuchet.

The difference between imagination and fancy, in view of this poetry of wit, is a very narrow one. Obviously, an image which is immediately and unintentionally ridiculous is merely a fancy. In the poem *Upon Appleton House,* Marvell falls in with one of these undesirable images, describing the attitude of the house toward its master:

> Yet thus the leaden house does sweat,
> And scarce endures the master great;
> But, where he comes, the swelling hall
> Stirs, and the square grows spherical;

which, whatever its intention, is more absurd than it was intended to be. Marvell also falls into the even commoner error of images which are over-developed or distracting; which support nothing but their own misshapen bodies:

> And now the salmon-fishers moist
> Their leathern boats begin to hoist;
> And, like Antipodes in shoes,
> Have shod their heads in their canoes.

Of this sort of image a choice collection may be found in Johnson's *Life of Cowley.* But the images in the *Coy Mistress* are not only witty, but satisfy the elucidation of Imagination given by Coleridge:

This power . . . reveals itself in the balance or reconcilement of opposite or discordant qualities: of sameness, with difference; of the general, with the concrete; the idea with the image; the individual with the representative; the sense of novelty and freshness with old and familiar objects; a more than usual state of emotion with more than usual order; judgment ever awake and steady self-possession with enthusiasm and feeling profound or vehement. . . .

Coleridge's statement applies also to the following verses, which are selected because of their similarity, and because they illustrate the marked caesura which Marvell often introduces in a short line:

> The tawny mowers enter next,
> Who seem like Israelites to be
> Walking on foot through a green sea . . .

> And now the meadows fresher dyed,
> Whose grass, with moister colour dashed,
> Seems as green silks but newly washed . . .

> He hangs in shades the orange bright,
> Like golden lamps in a green night . . .

> Annihilating all that's made
> To a green thought in a green shade . . .

> Had it lived long, it would have been
> Lilies without, roses within.

The whole poem, from which the last of these quotations is drawn (*The Nymph and the Fawn*), is built upon a very slight foundation, and we can imagine what some of our modern practitioners of slight themes would have made of it. But we need not descend to an invidious contemporaneity to point the difference. Here are six lines from *The Nymph and the Fawn*:

> I have a garden of my own,
> But so with roses overgrown
> And lilies, that you would it guess
> To be a little wilderness;
> And all the spring-time of the year
> It only lovèd to be there.

And here are five lines from *The Nymph's Song to Hylas* in the *Life and Death of Jason*, by William Morris:

> I know a little garden close
> Set thick with lily and red rose.

> Where I would wander if I might
> From dewy dawn to dewy night,
> And have one with me wandering.

So far the resemblance is more striking than the difference, although we might just notice the vagueness of allusion in the last line to some indefinite person, form, or phantom, compared with the more explicit reference of emotion to object which we should expect from Marvell. But in the latter part of the poem Morris divaricates widely:

> Yet tottering as I am, and weak,
> Still have I left a little breath
> To seek within the jaws of death
> An entrance to that happy place;
> To seek the unforgotten face
> Once seen, once kissed, once reft from me
> Anigh the murmuring of the sea.

Here the resemblance, if there is any, is to the latter part of *The Coy Mistress*. As for the difference, it could not be more pronounced. The effect of Morris's charming poem depends upon the mistiness of the feeling and the vagueness of its object; the effect of Marvell's upon its bright, hard precision. And this precision is not due to the fact that Marvell is concerned with cruder or simpler or more carnal emotions. The emotion of Morris is not more refined or more spiritual; it is merely more vague: if any one doubts whether the more refined or spiritual emotion can be precise, he should study the treatment of the varieties of discarnate emotion in the *Paradiso*. A curious result of the comparison of Morris's poem with Marvell's is that the former, though it appears to be more serious, is found to be slighter; and Marvell's *Nymph and the Fawn*, appearing more slight, is the more serious.

> So weeps the wounded balsam; so
> The holy frankincense doth flow;
> The brotherless Heliades
> Melt in such amber tears as these.

These verses have the suggestiveness of true poetry; and the verses of Morris, which are nothing if not an attempt to suggest, really suggest nothing; and we are inclined to infer that the suggestiveness is the aura around a bright clear centre, that you cannot have the aura alone. The day-dreamy feeling of Morris is essentially a slight thing; Marvell takes a slight affair, the feeling of a girl for her pet, and gives it a connexion with that inexhaustible and terrible nebula of emotion which surrounds all our exact and practical passions and mingles with them. Again, Marvell does this in a poem which, because of its formal pastoral machinery, may appear a trifling object:

CLORINDA.　Near this, a fountain's liquid bell
　　　　　　Tinkles within the concave shell.

DAMON.　　Might a soul bathe there and be
　　　　　　clean,
　　　　　　Or slake its drought?

where we find that a metaphor has suddenly rapt us to the image of spiritual purgation. There is here the element of *surprise*, as when Villon says:

　　Necessité faict gens mesprendre
　　Et faim saillir le loup des boys,

the surprise which Poe considered of the highest importance, and also the restraint and quietness of tone which make the surprise possible. And in the verses of Marvell which have been quoted there is the making the familiar strange, and the strange familiar, which Coleridge attributed to good poetry.

The effort to construct a dream-world, which alters English poetry so greatly in the nineteenth century, a dream-world utterly different from the visionary realties of the *Vita Nuova* or of the poetry of Dante's contemporaries, is a problem of which various explanations may no doubt be found; in any case, the result makes a poet of the nineteenth century, of the same size as Marvell, a more trivial and less serious figure. Marvell is no greater personality than William Morris, but he had something much more solid behind him: he had the vast and penetrating influence of Ben Jonson. Jonson never wrote anything purer than Marvell's *Horatian Ode*; this ode has that same quality of

wit which was diffused over the whole Elizabethan product and concentrated in the work of Jonson. And, as was said before, this wit which pervades the poetry of Marvell is more Latin, more refined, than anything that succeeded it. The great danger, as well as the great interest and excitement, of English prose and verse, compared with French, is that it permits and justifies an exaggeration of particular qualities to the exclusion of others. Dryden was great in wit, as Milton in magniloquence; but the former, by isolating this quality and making it by itself into great poetry, and the latter, by coming to dispense with it altogether, may perhaps have injured the language. In Dryden wit becomes almost fun, and thereby loses some contact with reality; becomes pure fun, which French wit almost never is.

The midwife placed her hand on his thick skull,
With this prophetic blessing: Be thou dull . . .

A numerous host of dreaming saints succeed,
Of the true old enthusiastic breed.

This is audacious and splendid; it belongs to satire besides which Marvell's Satires are random babbling, but it is perhaps as exaggerated as:

Oft he seems to hide his face,
But unexpectedly returns,
And to his faithful champion hath in place
Bore witness gloriously; whence Gaza mourns
And all that band them to resist
His uncontrollable intent.

How oddly the sharp Dantesque phrase "whence Gaza mourns" springs out from the brilliant contortions of Milton's sentence!

Who from his private gardens, where
He lived reservèd and austere,
　(As if his highest plot
　To plant the bergamot)

Could by industrious valour climb
To ruin the great work of Time,
　And cast the kingdoms old
　Into another mold;

　　·　·　·　·　·　·

The Pict no shelter now shall find
Within his parti-coloured mind,
But, from this valour sad,
Shrink underneath the plaid:

There is here an equipoise, a balance and proportion of tones, which, while it cannot raise
Marvell to the level of Dryden or Milton, ex-
torts an approval which these poets do not receive from us, and bestows a pleasure at least
different in kind from any they can often give.
It is what makes Marvell a classic; or classic in
a sense in which Gray and Collins are not; for
the latter, with all their accredited purity, are
comparatively poor in shades of feeling to contrast and unite.

We are baffled in the attempt to translate
the quality indicated by the dim and anti-
quated term wit into the equally unsatisfactory
nomenclature of our own time. Even Cowley is
only able to define it by negatives:

Comely in thousand shapes appears;
Yonder we saw it plain; and here 'tis now,
Like spirits in a place, we know not how.

It has passed out of our critical coinage altogether, and no new term has been struck to replace it; the quality seldom exists, and is never
recognized.

In a true piece of Wit all things must be
Yet all things there agree;
As in the Ark, join'd without force or strife,
All creatures dwelt, all creatures that had life.
Or as the primitive forms of all
(If we compare great things with small)
Which, without discord or confusion, lie
In that strange mirror of the Deity.

So far Cowley has spoken well. But if we are
to attempt even no more than Cowley, we,
placed in a retrospective attitude, must risk
much more than anxious generalizations. With
our eye still on Marvell, we can say that wit is
not erudition; it is sometimes stifled by erudition, as in much of Milton. It is not cynicism,
though it has a kind of toughness which may
be confused with cynicism by the tender-

minded. It is confused with erudition because
it belongs to an educated mind, rich in generations of experience; and it is confused with
cynicism because it implies a constant inspection and criticism of experience. It involves,
probably, a recognition, implicit in the expression of every experience, of other kinds of experience which are possible, which we find as
clearly in the greatest as in poets like Marvell.
Such a general statement may seem to take us
a long way from *The Nymph and the Fawn*, or
even from the *Horatian Ode*; but it is perhaps
justified by the desire to account for that precise taste of Marvell's which finds for him the
proper degree of seriousness for every subject
which he treats. His errors of taste, when he
trespasses, are not sins against this virtue; they
are conceits, distended metaphors and similes,
but they never consist in taking a subject too
seriously or too lightly. This virtue of wit is not
a peculiar quality of minor poets, or of the
minor poets of one age or of one school; it is
an intellectual quality which perhaps only becomes noticeable by itself, in the work of lesser
poets. Furthermore, it is absent from the work
of Wordsworth, Shelley, and Keats, on whose
poetry nineteenth-century criticism has unconsciously been based. To the best of their poetry
wit is irrelevant:

Art thou pale for weariness
Of climbing heaven and gazing on the earth,
Wandering companionless
Among the stars that have a different birth,
And ever changing, like a joyless eye,
That finds no object worth its constancy?

We should find it difficult to draw any useful
comparison between these lines of Shelley and
anything by Marvell. But later poets, who
would have been the better for Marvell's quality, were without it; even Browning seems
oddly immature, in some way, beside Marvell.
And nowadays we find occasionally good irony,
or satire, which lack wit's internal equilibrium,
because their voices are essentially protests
against some outside sentimentality or stupidity; or we find serious poets who are afraid of

acquiring wit, lest they lose intensity. The quality which Marvell had, this modest and certainly impersonal virtue—whether we call it wit or reason, or even urbanity—we have patently failed to define. By whatever name we call it, and however we define that name, it is something precious and needed and apparently extinct; it is what should preserve the reputation of Marvell. *C'était une belle âme, comme on ne fait plus à Londres.*

Four Definitions

"THE OBJECTIVE CORRELATIVE" (1919)

THE ONLY WAY of expressing emotion in the form of art is by finding an "objective correlative"; in other words, a set of objects, a situation, a chain of events which shall be the formula of that *particular* emotion; such that when the external facts, which must terminate in sensory experience, are given, the emotion is immediately evoked. If you examine any of Shakespeare's more successful tragedies, you will find this exact equivalence; you will find that the state of mind of Lady Macbeth walking in her sleep has been communicated to you by a skilful accumulation of imagined sensory impressions; the words of Macbeth on hearing of his wife's death strike us as if, given the sequence of events, these words were automatically released by the last event in the series. The artistic "inevitability" lies in this complete adequacy of the external to the emotion; and this is precisely what is deficient in *Hamlet*. Hamlet (the man) is dominated by an emo-

From "Hamlet and His Problems" in *Selected Essays,* New Edition, by T. S. Eliot, copyright, 1932, 1936, 1950, by Harcourt Brace Jovanovich, Inc.; copyright, 1960, 1964, by T. S. Eliot. Reprinted by permission of the publisher.

tion which is inexpressible, because it is in *excess* of the facts as they appear. And the supposed identity of Hamlet with his author is genuine to this point: that Hamlet's bafflement at the absence of objective equivalent to his feelings is a prolongation of the bafflement of his creator in the face of his artistic problem. Hamlet is up against the difficulty that his disgust is occasioned by his mother, but that his mother is not an adequate equivalent for it; his disgust envelops and exceeds her. It is thus a feeling which he cannot understand; he cannot objectify it, and it therefore remains to poison life and obstruct action. None of the possible actions can satisfy it; and nothing that Shakespeare can do with the plot can express Hamlet for him. And it must be noticed that the very nature of the *données* of the problem precludes objective equivalence. To have heightened the criminality of Gertrude would have been to provide the formula for a totally different emotion in Hamlet; it is just *because* her character is so negative and insignificant that she arouses in Hamlet the feeling which she is incapable of representing.

"DISSOCIATION OF SENSIBILITY" (1921)

THE DIFFERENCE is not a simple difference of degree between poets. It is something which had happened to the mind of England between the time of Donne or Lord Herbert of Cherbury and the time of Tennyson and Browning; it is the difference between the intellectual poet and the reflective poet. Tennyson and Browning are poets, and they think; but they do not feel their thought as immediately as the odour of a rose. A thought to Donne was an experience; it modified his sensibility. When a poet's mind is perfectly equipped for its work, it is constantly amalgamating disparate experience; the ordinary man's experience is chaotic, irregular, fragmentary. The latter falls in love, or reads Spinoza, and these two experiences have nothing to do with each other, or with the noise of the typewriter or the smell of cooking; in the mind of the poet these experiences are always forming new wholes.

We may express the difference by the following theory: The poets of the seventeenth century, the successors of the dramatists of the sixteenth, possessed a mechanism of sensibility which could devour any kind of experience. They are simple, artificial, difficult, or fantastic, as their predecessors were; no less nor

more than Dante, Guido Cavalcanti, Guinizelli, or Cino. In the seventeenth century a dissociation of sensibility set in, from which we have never recovered; and this dissociation, as is natural, was aggravated by the influence of the two most powerful poets of the century, Milton and Dryden. Each of these men performed certain poetic functions so magnificently well that the magnitude of the effect concealed the absence of others. The language went on and in some respects improved; the best verse of Collins, Gray, Johnson, and even Goldsmith satisfies some of our fastidious demands better than that of Donne or Marvell or King. But while the language became more refined, the feeling became more crude. The feeling, the sensibility, expressed in the *Country Churchyard* (to say nothing of Tennyson and Browning) is cruder than that in the *Coy Mistress*.

The second effect of the influence of Milton and Dryden followed from the first, and was therefore slow in manifestation. The sentimental age began early in the eighteenth century, and continued. The poets revolted against the ratiocinative, the descriptive; they thought and felt by fits, unbalanced; they reflected. In one or two passages of Shelley's *Triumph of Life*, in the second *Hyperion*, there are traces of a struggle toward unification of sensibility. But Keats and Shelley died, and Tennyson and Browning ruminated.

"THE AUDITORY IMAGINATION" (1932)

WHAT I CALL the "auditory imagination" is the feeling for syllable and rhythm, penetrating far

below the conscious levels of thought and feeling, invigorating every word; sinking to the most primitive and forgotten, returning to the origin and bringing something back, seeking the beginning and the end. It works through meanings, certainly, or not without meanings in the ordinary sense, and fuses the old and obliterated and the trite, the current, and the new and surprising, the most ancient and the most civilized mentality.

"RELIGION AND LITERATURE" (1935)

WHAT I have to say is largely in support of the following propositions: Literary criticism should be completed by criticism from a definite ethical and theological standpoint. In so far as in any age there is common agreement on ethical and theological matters, so far can literary criticism be substantive. In ages like our own, in which there is no such common agreement, it is the more necessary for Christian readers to scrutinize their reading, especially of works of imagination, with explicit ethical and theological standards. The "greatness" of literature cannot be determined solely by literary standards; though we must remember that whether it is literature or not can be determined only by literary standards.

Arnold and Pater (1930)

ALTHOUGH Pater is as appropriate to the 'seventies as to the 'eighties, because of the appearance of *Studies in the History of the Renaissance* in 1873, I have chosen to discuss him in this volume [1] because of the date 1885, the middle of the decade, which marks the publication of *Marius the Epicurean*. The first may certainly be counted the more "influential" book; but *Marius* illustrates another but related aspect of Pater's work. His writing of course extended well into the 'nineties; but I doubt whether any one would consider the later books and essays of anything like the importance, in social history or in literary history, of the two I have mentioned.

The purpose of the present paper is to indicate a direction from Arnold, through Pater, to the 'nineties, with, of course, the solitary figure of Newman in the background.

It is necessary first of all to estimate the aesthetic and religious views of Arnold: in each of which, to borrow his own phrase against him, there is an element of *literature* and an element of *dogma*. As Mr. J. M. Robertson has well pointed out in his *Modern Humanists Reconsidered*, Arnold had little gift for consistency or for definition. Nor had he the power of connected reasoning at any length: his flights are either short flights or circular flights. Nothing in his prose work, therefore, will stand very close analysis, and we may well feel that the positive content of many words is very small. Culture and Conduct are the first things, we are told; but what Culture and Conduct are, I feel that I know less well on every reading. Yet Arnold does still hold us, at least with *Culture and Anarchy* and *Friendship's Garland*. To my generation, I am sure, he was

[1] A volume entitled *The Eighteen-Eighties*. Edited by Walter de la Mare for the Royal Society of Literature.

a more sympathetic prose writer than Carlyle or Ruskin; yet he holds his position and achieves his effects exactly on the same plane, by the power of his rhetoric and by representing a point of view which is particular though it cannot be wholly defined.

But the revival of interest in Arnold in our time—and I believe he is admired and read not only more than Carlyle and Ruskin, but than Pater—is a very different thing from the influence he exerted in his own time. We go to him for refreshment and for the companionship of a kindred point of view to our own, but not as disciples. And therefore it is the two books I have mentioned that are most readable. Even the *Essays in Criticism* cannot be read very often; *Literature and Dogma, God and the Bible,* and *Last Essays on Church and Religion,* have served their turn and can hardly be read through. In these books he attempts something which must be austerely impersonal; in them reasoning power matters, and it fails him; furthermore, we have now our modern solvers of the same problem Arnold there set himself, and they, or some of them, are more accomplished and ingenious in this sort of rationalizing than Arnold was. Accordingly, and this is my first point, his Culture survives better than his Conduct, because it can better survive vagueness of definition. But both Culture and Conduct were important for his own time.

Culture has three aspects, according as we look at it in *Culture and Anarchy,* in *Essays in Criticism,* or in the abstract. It is in the first of these two books that Culture shows to best advantage. And the reason is clear: Culture there stands out against a background to which it is contrasted, a background of definite items of ignorance, vulgarity and prejudice. As an invective against the crudities of the industrialism of his time, the book is perfect of its kind. Compared with Carlyle, it looks like clear thinking, and is certainly clearer expression; and compared with Arnold, Ruskin often appears long-winded and peevish. Arnold taught English expository and critical prose a restraint and urbanity it needed. And hardly, in this

book, do we question the meaning of Culture; for the good reason that we do not need to. Even when we read that Culture "is a study of perfection," we do not at that point raise an eyebrow to admire how much Culture appears to have arrogated from Religion. For we have shortly before been hearing something about "the will of God," or of a joint firm called "reason and the will of God"; and soon after we are presented with Mr. Bright and Mr. Frederic Harrison as foils to Culture; and appearing in this way between the will of God and Mr. Bright, Culture is here sufficiently outlined to be recognizable. *Culture and Anarchy* is on the same side as *Past and Present* or *Unto this Last.* Its ideas are really no clearer;—one reason why Arnold, Carlyle and Ruskin were so influential, for precision and completeness of thought do not always make for influence. (Arnold, it is true, gave something else: he produced a kind of illusion of precision and clarity; that is, maintained these qualities as ideals of style.)

Certainly, the prophets of the period just before that of which I am supposed to be writing excelled in denunciation (each in his own way) rather than in construction; and each in his own fashion lays himself open to the charge of tedious querulousness. And an idea, such as that of Culture, is apt to lead to consequences which its author cannot foresee and probably will not like. Already, in the *Essays,* Culture begins to seem a little more priggish—I do not say "begins" in a chronological sense—and a little more anaemic. Where Sir Charles Adderley and Mr. Roebuck appear, there is more life than in the more literary criticism. Arnold is in the end, I believe, at his best in satire and in apologetics for literature, in his defence and enunciation of a needed attitude.

To us, as I have said, Arnold is rather a friend than a leader. He was a champion of "ideas" most of whose ideas we no longer take seriously. His Culture is powerless to aid or to harm. But he is at least a forerunner of what is now called Humanism, of which I must here say something, if only to contrast it and com-

pare it with the Aestheticism of Pater. How far
Arnold is responsible for the birth of Humanism would be difficult to say; we can at least
say that it issues very naturally from his doctrine, that Charles Eliot Norton is largely responsible for its American form, and that
therefore Arnold is another likely ancestor. But
the resemblances are too patent to be ignored.
The difference is that Arnold could father
something apparently quite different—the view
of life of Walter Pater. The resemblance is
that literature, or Culture, tended with Arnold
to usurp the place of Religion. From one point
of view, Arnold's theory of Art and his theory
of Religion are quite harmonious, and Humanism is merely the more coherent structure.
Arnold's prose writings fall into two parts;
those on Culture and those on Religion; and
the books about Christianity seem only to say
again and again—merely that the Christian
faith is of course impossible to the man of culture. They are tediously negative. But they are
negative in a peculiar fashion: their aim is to
affirm that the emotions of Christianity can
and must be preserved without the belief.
From this proposition two different types of
man can extract two different types of conclusion: (1) that Religion is Morals, (2) that Religion is Art. The effect of Arnold's religious
campaign is to divorce Religion from thought.

In Arnold himself there was a powerful element of Puritan morality, as in most of his
contemporaries, however diverse. And the
strength of his moral feeling—we might add its
blindness also—prevented him from seeing
how very odd might look the fragments of the
fabric which he knocked about so recklessly.
"The power of Christianity has been in the immense emotion which it has excited," he says;
not realizing at all that this is a counsel to get
all the emotional kick out of Christianity one
can, without the bother of believing it; without
reading the future to foresee *Marius the Epi-*
curean, and finally *De Profundis.* Furthermore,
in his books dealing with Christianity he seems
bent upon illustrating in himself the provin-
cialisms which he rebuked in others. "M. de

Lavelaye," he says in the preface to *God and*
the Bible, with as deferential a manner as if he
were citing M. Renan himself, "is struck, as
any judicious Catholic may well be struck, with
the superior freedom, order, stability, and religious earnestness, of the Protestant Nations as
compared with the Catholic." He goes on complacently, "Their religion has made them what
they are." I am not here concerned with the
genuine differences between Catholic and Protestant; only with the tone which Arnold adopts
in this preface and throughout this book; and
which is in no wise more liberal than that of
Sir Charles Adderley or Mr. Roebuck or "Mr.
Tennyson's great broad-shouldered Englishman." He girds at (apparently) Herbert Spencer for substituting *Unknowable* for *God;* quite
unaware that his own Eternal not ourselves
comes to exactly the same thing as the Unknowable. And when we read Arnold's discourses on Religion, we return to scrutinize his
Culture with some suspicion.

For Arnold's Culture, at first sight so enlightened, moderate and reasonable, walks so
decorously in the company of the will of God,
that we may overlook the fact that it tends to
develop its own stringent rules and restrictions.

Certainly, culture will never make us think it
an essential of religion whether we have in our
Church discipline "a popular authority of elders," as Hooker calls it, or whether we have Epis-
copal jurisdiction.

Certainly, "culture" in itself can never make us
think so, any more than it can make us think
that the quantum theory is an essential of
physical science: but such people as are interested in this question at all, however cultured
they be, hold one or the other opinion pretty
strongly; and Arnold is really affirming that to
Culture all theological and ecclesiastical differences are indifferent. But this is a rather positive dogma for Culture to hold. When we take
Culture and Anarchy in one hand, and *Litera-*
ture and Dogma in the other, our minds are
gradually darkened by the suspicion that Arnold's objection to Dissenters is partly that

they do hold strongly to that which they believe, and partly that they are not Masters of
Arts of Oxford. Arnold, as Master of Arts,
should have had some scruple about the use of
words. But in the very preface to the second
edition of *Literature and Dogma* he says:

The *Guardian* proclaims "the miracle of the
incarnation" to be the "fundamental truth" for
Christians. How strange that on me should de-
volve the office of instructing the *Guardian* that
the fundamental thing for Christians is not the
Incarnation but the imitation of Christ!

While wondering whether Arnold's own "imitation" is even a good piece of mimicry, we notice that he employs *truth* and *thing* as interchangeable: and a very slight knowledge of the
field in which he was skirmishing should have
told him that a "fundamental truth" in theology and a "fundamental thing" in his own
loose jargon have nothing comparable about
them. The total effect of Arnold's philosophy
is to set up Culture in the place of Religion,
and to leave Religion to be laid waste by the
anarchy of feeling. And Culture is a term
which each man not only may interpret as he
pleases, but must indeed interpret as he can. So
the gospel of Pater follows naturally upon the
prophecy of Arnold.

Even before the 'seventies began Pater seems
to have written, though not published, the
words:

The theory, or idea, or system, which requires
of us the sacrifice of any part of this experience,
in consideration of some interest into which we
cannot enter, or some abstract morality we have
not identified with ourselves, or what is only conventional, has no real claim upon us.[2]

Although more outspoken in repudiating any
measure than man for all things, Pater is not
really uttering anything more subversive than
the following words of Arnold:

Culture, disinterestedly seeking in its aim at
perfection to see things as they really are, shows
us how worthy and divine a thing is the religious

[2] In quoting from *The Renaissance* I use the first
edition throughout.

side in man, though it is not the whole of man.
But while recognizing the grandeur of the religious side in man, culture yet makes us eschew
an inadequate conception of man's totality.

Religion, accordingly, is merely a " 'side' in
(*sic*) man"; a side which so to speak must be
kept in its place. But when we go to Arnold to
enquire what is "man's totality," that we may
ourselves aim at so attractive a consummation,
we learn nothing; any more than we learn
about the "secret" of Jesus of which he has
so much to say.

The degradation of philosophy and religion,
skilfully initiated by Arnold, is competently
continued by Pater. "The service of philosophy, and of religion and culture as well, to the
human spirit," he says in the 1873 conclusion
to *The Renaissance*, "is to startle it into a
sharp and eager observation." "We shall
hardly have time," he says, "to make theories
about the things we see and touch." Yet we
have to be "curiously testing new opinions"; so
it must be—if opinions have anything to do
with theories, and unless wholly capricious and
unreasoning they must have—that the opinions
we test can only be those provided for our enjoyment by an inferior sort of drudges who are
incapable of enjoying our own free life, because all their time is spent (and "*we* hardly
have time") in making theories. And this again
is only a development of the intellectual Epi-
cureanism of Arnold.

Had Pater not had one gift denied to Arnold, his permutation of Arnold's view of life
would have little interest. He had a taste for
painting and the plastic arts, and particularly
for Italian painting, a subject to which Ruskin
had introduced the nation. He had a visual
imagination; he had also come into contact
with another generation of French writers than
that which Arnold knew; the zealous Puritanism of Arnold was in him considerably mitigated, but the zeal for culture was equally viru-
lent. So his peculiar appropriation of religion
into culture was from another side: that of
emotion, and indeed of sensation; but in making this appropriation, he was only doing what

Arnold had given license to do.

Marius the Epicurean marks indeed one of the phases of the fluctuating relations between religion and culture in England since the Reformation; and for this reason the year 1885 is an important one. Newman, in leaving the Anglican Church, had turned his back upon Oxford. Ruskin, with a genuine sensibility for certain types of art and architecture, succeeded in satisfying his nature by translating everything immediately into terms of morals. The vague religious vapourings of Carlyle, and the sharper, more literate social fury of Ruskin yield before the persuasive sweetness of Arnold. Pater is a new variation.

We are liable to confusion if we call this new variation the "aesthete." Pater was, like the other writers I have just mentioned (except Newman), a moralist. If, as the *Oxford Dictionary* tells us, an aesthete is a "professed appreciator of the beautiful," then there are at least two varieties: those whose profession is most vocal, and those whose appreciation is most professional. If we wish to understand painting, we do not go to Oscar Wilde for help. We have specialists, such as Mr. Berenson, or Mr. Roger Fry. Even in that part of his work which can only be called literary criticism, Pater is always primarily the moralist. In his essay on Wordsworth he says:

To treat life in the spirit of art, is to make life a thing in which means and ends are identified: to encourage such treatment, the true moral significance of art and poetry.

That was his notion: to find the "true moral significance of art and poetry." Certainly, a writer may be none the less classified as a moralist, if his moralising is suspect or perverse. We have today a witness in the person of M. André Gide. As always in his imaginary portraits, so frequently in his choice of other writers as the subjects of critical studies, Pater is inclined to emphasize whatever is morbid or associated with physical malady. His admirable study of Coleridge is charged with this attraction.

More than Childe Harold (he says of Coleridge), more than Werther, more than René himself, Coleridge, by what he did, what he was, and what he failed to do, represents that inexhaustible discontent, languor, and homesickness, that endless regret, the chords of which ring all through our modern literature.

Thus again in Pascal he emphasizes the malady, with its consequences upon the thought; but we feel that somehow what is important about Pascal has been missed. But it is not that he treats philosophers "in the spirit of art," exactly; for when we read him on Leonardo or Giorgione, we feel that there is the same preoccupation, coming between him and the object as it really is. He is, in his own fashion, moralizing upon Leonardo or Giorgione, on Greek art or on modern poetry. His famous dictum: "Of this wisdom, the poetic passion, the desire of beauty, the love of art for art's sake has most; for art comes to you professing frankly to give nothing but the highest quality to your moments as they pass, and simply for those moments' sake," is itself a theory of ethics; it is concerned not with art but with life. The second half of the sentence is of course demonstrably untrue, or else being true of everything else besides art is meaningless; but it is a serious statement of morals. And the disapproval which greeted this first version of the Conclusion to *The Renaissance* is implicitly a just recognition of that fact. "Art for art's sake" is the offspring of Arnold's Culture; and we can hardly venture to say that it is even a perversion of Arnold's doctrine, considering how very vague and ambiguous that doctrine is.

When religion is in a flourishing state, when the whole mind of society is moderately healthy and in order, there is an easy and natural association between religion and art. Only when religion has been partly retired and confined, when an Arnold can sternly remind us that Culture is wider than Religion, do we get "religious art" and in due course "aesthetic religion." Pater undoubtedly had from childhood a religious bent, naturally to all that was liturgical and ceremonious. Certainly this is a real and important part of religion; and Pater cannot thereby be accused of insincerity and "aestheticism." His attitude must be considered both in relation to his own mental powers and to his moment of time. There were other men like him, but without his gift of style, and such men were among his friends. In the pages of Thomas Wright, Pater, more than most of his devout friends, appears a little absurd. His High Churchmanship is undoubtedly very different from that of Newman, Pusey and the Tractarians, who, passionate about dogmatic essentials, were singularly indifferent to the sensuous expressions of orthodoxy. It was also dissimilar to that of the priest working in a slum parish. He was "naturally Christian"— but within very narrow limitations: the rest of him was just the cultivated Oxford don and disciple of Arnold, for whom religion was a matter of feeling, and metaphysics not much more. Being incapable of sustained reasoning, he could not take philosophy or theology seriously; just as being primarily a moralist, he was incapable of seeing any work of art simply as it is.

Marius the Epicurean represents the point of English history at which the repudiation of revealed religion by men of culture and intellectual leadership coincides with a renewed interest in the visual arts. It is Pater's most arduous attempt at a work of literature; for *Plato and Platonism* can be almost dissolved into a series of essays. *Marius* itself is incoherent; its method is a number of fresh starts; its content is a hodge-podge of the learning of the classical don, the impressions of the sensitive holiday visitor to Italy, and a prolonged flirtation with the liturgy. Even A. C. Benson, who makes as much of the book as any one can, observes in a passage of excellent criticism:

But the weakness of the case is, that instead of emphasizing the power of sympathy, the Christian conception of Love, which differentiates Christianity from all other religious systems, Marius is after all converted, or brought near to the threshold of the faith, more by its sensuous appeal, its liturgical solemnities; the element,

that is to say, which Christianity has in common with all religions, and which is essentially human in character. And more than that, even the very peace which Marius discerns in Christianity is the old philosophical peace over again.

This is sound criticism. But—a point with which Dr. Benson was not there concerned— it is surely a merit, on the part of Pater, and one which deserves recognition, to have clarified the issues. Matthew Arnold's religion is the more confused, because he conceals, under the smoke of strong and irrational moral prejudice, just the same, or no better, Stoicism and Cyrenaicism of the amateur classical scholar. Arnold Hellenizes and Hebraicizes in turns; it is something to Pater's credit to have Hellenized purely.

Of the essence of the Christian faith, as Dr. Benson frankly admits, Pater knew almost nothing. One might say also that his intellect was not powerful enough to grasp—I mean, to grasp as firmly as many classical scholars whose names will never be so renowned as that of Pater—the essence of Platonism or Aristotelianism or Neo-Platonism. He therefore, or his Marius, moves quite unconcerned with the intellectual activity which was then amalgamating Greek metaphysics with the tradition of Christ; just as he is equally unconcerned with the realities of Roman life as we catch a glimpse of them in Petronius, or even in such a book as Dill's on the reign of Marcus Aurelius. Marius merely *drifts* towards the Christian Church, if he can be said to have any motion at all; nor does he or his author seem to have any realization of the chasm to be leapt between the meditations of Aurelius and the Gospel. To the end, Marius remains only a half-awakened soul. Even at his death, in the midst of the ceremonies of which he is given the benefit, his author reflects "often had he fancied of old that not to die on a dark or rainy day might itself have a little alleviating grace or favour about it," recalling to our minds the "springing of violets from the grave" in the Conclusion to *The Renaissance*, and the death of Flavian.

I have spoken of the book as of some importance. I do not mean that its importance is due to any influence it may have exerted. I do not believe that Pater, in this book, has influenced a single first-rate mind of a later generation. His view of art, as expressed in *The Renaissance*, impressed itself upon a number of writers in the 'nineties, and propagated some confusion between life and art which is not wholly irresponsible for some untidy lives. The theory (if it can be called a theory) of "art for art's sake" is still valid in so far as it can be taken as an exhortation to the artist to stick to his job; it never was and never can be valid for the spectator, reader or auditor. How far *Marius the Epicurean* may have assisted a few "conversions" in the following decade I do not know: I only feel sure that with the direct current of religious development it has had nothing to do at all. So far as that current—or one important current—is concerned, *Marius* is much nearer to being merely due to Pater's contact—a contact no more intimate than that of Marius himself—with something which was happening and would have happened without him.

The true importance of the book, I think, is as a document of one moment in the history of thought and sensibility in the nineteenth century. The dissolution of thought in that age, the isolation of art, philosophy, religion, ethics and literature, is interrupted by various chimerical attempts to effect imperfect syntheses. Religion became morals, religion became art, religion became science or philosophy; various blundering attempts were made at alliances between various branches of thought. Each half-prophet believed that he had the whole truth. The alliances were as detrimental all round as the separations. The right practice of "art for art's sake" was the devotion of Flaubert or Henry James; Pater is not with these men, but rather with Carlyle and Ruskin and Arnold, if some distance below them. *Marius* is significant chiefly as a reminder that the religion of Carlyle or that of Ruskin or that of Arnold or that of Tennyson or that of Browning, is not enough. It represents, and Pater represents more positively than Coleridge of whom he wrote the words, "that inexhaustible discontent, languor, and homesickness . . . the chords of which ring all through our modern literature."

The Modern Mind (1933)

THERE IS a sentence in Maritain's *Art and Scholasticism* which occurs to me in this context: "Work such as Picasso's," he says, "shows a fearful progress in self-consciousness on the part of painting."

So far I have drawn a few light sketches to indicate the changes in the self-consciousness of poets thinking about poetry. A thorough history of this "progress in self-consciousness" in

Reprinted by permission of the publishers from T. S. Eliot, *The Use of Poetry and the Use of Criticism*. Cambridge, Mass.: Harvard University Press, Copyright, 1933, by the President and Fellows of Harvard College; 1961 by Thomas Stearns Eliot.

poetry and the criticism of poetry would have kinds of criticism to consider which do not fall within the narrow scope of these lectures: the history of Shakespeare criticism alone, in which, for instance, Morgann's essay on the character of Falstaff, and Coleridge's *Lectures on Shakespeare* would be representative moments, would have to be considered in some detail. But we have observed the notable development in self-consciousness in Dryden's Prefaces, and in the first serious attempt, which he made, at a valuation of the English poets. We have seen his work in one direction continued, and a method perfected, by Johnson in his careful estimation of a number of poets, an estimate arrived at by the application of what are on the whole admirably consistent standards. We have found a deeper insight into the nature of the poetic activity in remarks scattered through the writings of Coleridge and in the *Preface* of Wordsworth and in the Letters of Keats; and a perception, still immature, of the need to elucidate the social function of poetry in Wordsworth's *Preface* and in Shelley's *Defence*. In the criticism of Arnold we find a continuation of the work of the Romantic poets with a new appraisal of the poetry of the past by a method which, lacking the precision of Johnson's, gropes towards wider and deeper connexions. I have not wished to exhibit this "progress in self-consciousness" as being necessarily *progress* with an association of higher value. For one thing, it cannot be wholly abstracted from the general changes in the human mind in history; and that these changes have any teleological significance is not one of my assumptions.

Arnold's insistence upon order in poetry according to a moral valuation was, for better or worse, of the first importance for his age. When he is not at his best he obviously falls between two stools. Just as his poetry is too reflective, too ruminative, to rise ever to the first rank, so also is his criticism. He is not, on the one hand, quite a pure enough poet to have the sudden illuminations which we find in the criticism of Wordsworth, Coleridge and Keats; and on the other hand he lacked the mental discipline, the passion for exactness in the use of words and for consistency and continuity of reasoning, which distinguishes the philosopher. He sometimes confuses words and meanings: neither as poet nor as philosopher should he have been satisfied with such an utterance as that "poetry is at bottom a criticism of life." A more profound insight into poetry and a more exact use of language than Arnold's are required. The critical method of Arnold, the assumptions of Arnold, remained valid for the rest of his century. In quite diverse developments, it is the criticism of Arnold that sets the

tone: Walter Pater, Arthur Symons, Addington Symonds, Leslie Stephen, F. W. H. Myers, George Saintsbury—all the more eminent critical names of the time bear witness to it.

Whether we agree or not with any or all of his conclusions, whether we admit or deny that his method is adequate, we must admit that the work of Mr. I. A. Richards will have been of cardinal importance in the history of literary criticism. Even if his criticism proves to be entirely on the wrong track, even if this modern "self-consciousness" turns out to be only a blind alley, Mr. Richards will have done something in accelerating the exhaustion of the possibilities. He will have helped indirectly to discredit the criticism of persons qualified neither by sensibility nor by knowledge of poetry, from which we suffer daily. There is some hope of greater clarity; we should begin to learn to distinguish the appreciation of poetry from theorising about poetry, and to know when we are not talking about poetry but about something else suggested by it. There are two elements in Richards's scheme, both of considerable importance for its ultimate standing, of which I have the gravest doubts but with which I am not here concerned: his theory of Value and his theory of Education (or rather the theory of Education assumed in or implied by his attitude in *Practical Criticism*). As for psychology and linguistics, that is his field and not mine. I am more concerned here with what seem to me to be a few unexamined assumptions that he has made. I do not know whether he still adheres to certain assertions made in his early essay *Science and Poetry*; but I do not understand that he has yet made any public modification of them. Here is one that is in my mind:

The most dangerous of the sciences is only now beginning to come into action. I am thinking less of Psychoanalysis or of Behaviourism than of the whole subject which includes them. It is very probable that the Hindenburg Line to which the defence of our traditions retired as a result of the onslaughts of the last century will be blown up in the near future. If this should happen a mental chaos such as man has never experienced may be expected. We shall then be thrown back, as Matthew Arnold foresaw, upon poetry. Poetry is capable of saving us. . . .

I should have felt completely at a loss in this passage, had not Matthew Arnold turned up; and then it seemed to me that I knew a little better what was what. I should say that an affirmation like this was highly characteristic of one type of modern mind. For one of the things that one can say about the modern mind is that it comprehends every extreme and degree of opinion. Here, from the essay, *Art and Scholasticism*, which I have already quoted, is Mr. Maritain: "It is a deadly error to expect poetry to provide the supersubstantial nourishment of man."

Mr. Maritain is a theologian as well as philosopher, and you may be sure that when he says "deadly error" he is in deadly earnest. But if the author of *Anti-Moderne* is hardly to be considered a "modern" man, we can find other varieties of opinion. In a book called *The Human Parrot*, Mr. Montgomery Belgion has two essays, one called *Art and Mr. Maritain* and the other *What is Criticism*, from which you will learn that neither Maritain nor Richards knows what he is talking about. Mr. Richards further maintains that the experience of poetry is not a mystical revelation, and the Abbé Henri Brémond,[1] in *Prayer and Poetry*, is concerned with telling us in what kind and degree it is. On this point Mr. Belgion is apparently in accord with Mr. Richards. And we may be wise to keep in mind a remark of Mr. Herbert Read in *Form in Modern Poetry*: "If a literary critic happens to be also a poet . . . he is liable to suffer from dilemmas which do not trouble the philosophic calm of his more prosaic colleagues."

Beyond a belief that poetry does something of importance, or has something of importance to do, there does not seem to be much agree-

[1] While preparing this book for press I learn with great regret of the Abbé Brémond's untimely death. It is a great pity that he could not have lived to complete the *Histoire du sentiment religieux en France*.

ment. It is interesting that in our time, which has not produced any vast number of important poets, so many people—and there are many more—should be asking questions about poetry. These problems are not those which properly concern poets as poets at all; if poets plunge into the discussion, it is probably because they have interests and curiosities outside of writing poetry. We need not summon those who call themselves Humanists (for they have for the most part not been primarily occupied with the nature and function of poetry) to bear witness that we have here the problem of religious faith and its substitutes. Not all contemporary critics, of course, but at least a number who appear to have little else in common, seem to consider that art, specifically poetry, has something to do with religion, though they disagree as to what this something may be. The relationship is not always envisaged so moralistically as it was by Arnold, nor so generally as in the statement by Mr. Richards which I quoted. For Mr. Belgion, for instance,

An outstanding example of poetic allegory is in the final canto of the *Paradiso*, where the poet seeks to give an allegorical account of the Beatific Vision, and then declares his efforts vain. We may read this over and over again, and in the end we shall no more have had a revelation of the nature of the Vision than we had before ever we had heard of either it or Dante.

Mr. Belgion seems to have taken Dante at his word. But what we experience as readers is never exactly what the poet experienced, nor would there be any point in its being, though certainly it has some relation to the poet's experience. What the poet experienced is not poetry but poetic material; the writing of the poetry is a fresh "experience" for him, and the reading of it, by the author or anyone else, is another thing still. Mr. Belgion, in denying a theory which he attributes to Mr. Maritain, seems to me to make his own mistakes; but it is a religion-analogy which is in question. Mr. Richards is much occupied with the religious problem simply in the attempt to avoid it. In an appendix to the second edition of *Principles of Literary Criticism* he has a note on my own verse, which, being as favourable as I could desire, seems to me very acute. But he observes that Canto XXVI of the *Purgatorio* illuminates my "persistent concern with sex, the problem of our generation, as religion was the problem of the last." I readily admit the importance of Canto XXVI, and it was shrewd of Mr. Richards to notice it; but in his contrast of sex and religion he makes a distinction which is too subtle for me to grasp. One might think that sex and religion were "problems" like Free Trade and Imperial Preference; it seems odd that the human race should have gone on for so many thousands of years before it suddenly realised that religion and sex, one right after the other, presented problems.

It has been my view throughout—and it is only a commonplace after all—that the development and change of poetry and of the criticism of it is due to elements which enter from outside. I tried to draw attention not so much to the importance of Dryden's "contribution" to literary criticism, as if he were merely adding to a store of quantity, as to the importance of the fact that he should *want* to articulate and expound his views on drama and translation and on the English poetry of the past; and, when we came to Johnson, to call attention to the further development of an historical consciousness which made Johnson *want* to estimate, in more detail, the English poets of his own age and of previous ages;[2] and it seemed to me that Wordsworth's theories about poetry drew their aliment from social sources. To Matthew Arnold we owe the credit of bringing the religious issue explicitly into the discussion of literature and poetry; and with due respect to Mr. Richards, and with Mr. Richards himself as a witness, it does not seem to me that this "issue" has been wholly put aside and replaced by that of "sex." My contemporaries seem to me still to be occupied with it, whether they call themselves churchmen, or agnostics,

[2] The fact that Johnson was working largely to order only indicates that this historical consciousness was already developed.

or rationalists, or social revolutionists. The contrast between the doubts that our contemporaries express, and the questions that they ask and the problems they put themselves, and the attitude of at least a part of the past, was well put by Jacques Rivière in two sentences:

If in the seventeenth century Molière or Racine had been asked why he wrote, no doubt he would have been able to find but one answer; that he wrote "for the entertainment of decent people" (*pour distraire les honnêtes gens*). It is only with the advent of Romanticism that the literary act came to be conceived as a sort of raid on the absolute and its result as a revelation.

Rivière's form of expression is not, to my mind, altogether happy. One might suppose that all that had happened was that a wilful perversity had taken possession of literary men, a new literary disease called Romanticism. That is one of the dangers of expressing one's meaning in terms of "Romanticism": it is a term which is constantly changing in different contexts, and which is now limited to what appear to be purely literary and purely local problems, now expanding to cover almost the whole of the life of a time and of nearly the whole world. It has perhaps not been observed that in its more comprehensive significance "Romanticism" comes to include nearly everything that distinguishes the last two hundred and fifty years or so from their predecessors, and includes so much that it ceases to bring with it any praise or blame. The change to which Rivière alludes is not a contrast between Molière and Racine on the one hand and more modern French writers on the other; it neither reflects credit upon the former nor implies inferiority in the latter. In the interest of clarity and simplicity I wish myself to avoid employing the terms Romanticism and Classicism, terms which inflame political passions, and tend to prejudice our conclusions. I am only concerned with my contention that the notion of what poetry is for, of what is its function to do, does change, and therefore I quoted Rivière; I am concerned further with criticism as evidence of the conception of the use of poetry in the critic's time, and assert that in order to compare the work of different critics we must investigate their assumptions as to what poetry does and ought to do. Examination of the criticism of our time leads me to believe that we are still in the Arnold period.

I speak of Mr. Richards's views with some diffidence. Some of the problems he discusses are themselves very difficult, and only those are qualified to criticise who have applied themselves to the same specialised studies and have acquired proficiency in this kind of thinking. But here I limit myself to passages in which he does not seem to be speaking as a specialist, and in which I have no advantage of special knowledge either. There are two reasons why the writer of poetry must not be thought to have any great advantage. One is that a discussion of poetry such as this takes us far outside the limits within which a poet may speak with authority; the other is that the poet does many things upon instinct, for which he can give no better account than anybody else. A poet can try, of course, to give an honest report of the way in which he himself writes: the result may, if he is a good observer, be illuminating. And in one sense, but a very limited one, he knows better what his poems "mean" than can anyone else; he may know the history of their composition, the material which has gone in and come out in an unrecognisable form, and he knows what he was trying to do and what he was meaning to mean. But what a poem means is as much what it means to others as what it means to the author; and indeed, in the course of time a poet may become merely a reader in respect to his own works, forgetting his original meaning—or without forgetting, merely changing. So that, when Mr. Richards asserts that *The Waste Land* effects "a complete severance between poetry and *all* beliefs" I am no better qualified to say No! than is any other reader. I will admit that I think that either Mr. Richards is wrong, or I do not understand his meaning. The statement might mean that it was the first poetry to do what all poetry in the past would

have been the better for doing: I can hardly think that he intended to pay me such an unmerited compliment. It might also mean that the present situation is radically different from any in which poetry has been produced in the past: namely, that now there is nothing in which to believe, that Belief itself is dead; and that therefore my poem is the first to respond properly to the modern situation and not call upon Make-Believe. And it is in this connexion, apparently, that Mr. Richards observes that "poetry is capable of saving us."

A discussion of Mr. Richards's theories of knowledge, value and meaning would be by no means irrelevant to this assertion, but it would take us far afield, and I am not the person to undertake it. We cannot of course refute the statement "poetry is capable of saving us" without knowing which one of the multiple definitions of salvation Mr. Richards has in mind.[3] (A good many people behave as if they thought so too: otherwise their interest in poetry is difficult to explain.) I am sure, from the differences of environment, of period, and of mental furniture, that salvation by poetry is not quite the same thing for Mr. Richards as it was for Arnold; but so far as I am concerned these are merely different shades of blue. In *Practical Criticism* Mr. Richards provides a recipe which I think throws some light upon his theological ideas. He says:

Something like a technique or ritual for heightening sincerity might well be worked out. When our response to a poem after our best efforts remains uncertain, when we are unsure whether the feelings it excites come from a deep source in our experience, whether our liking or disliking is genuine, is *ours*, or an accident of fashion, a response to surface details or to essentials, we may perhaps help ourselves by considering it in a frame of feelings whose sincerity is beyond our questioning. Sit by the fire (with eyes shut and fingers pressed firmly upon the

[3] See his *Mencius on the Mind*. There is of course a locution in which we say of someone "he is not one of *us*"; it is possible that the "us" of Mr. Richards's statement represents an equally limited and select number.

eyeballs) and consider with as full "realisation" as possible—

five points which follow, and which I shall comment upon one by one. We may observe, in passing, the intense religious seriousness of Mr. Richards's attitude towards poetry.[4] What he proposes—for he hints in the passage above that his sketch might be elaborated—is nothing less than a regimen of Spiritual Exercises. Now for the points.

I. *Man's loneliness (the isolation of the human situation)*.

Loneliness is known as a frequent attitude in romantic poetry, and in the form of "lonesomeness" (as I need not remind American readers) is a frequent attitude in contemporary lyrics known as "the blues." But in what sense is Man in general isolated, and from what? What *is* the "human situation"? I can understand the isolation of the human situation as Plato's Diotima expounds it, or in the Christian sense of the separation of Man from God; but not an isolation which is not a separation from anything in particular.

II. *The facts of birth and of death, in their inexplicable oddity.*

I cannot see why the facts of birth and of death should appear odd in themselves, unless we have a conception of some other way of coming into the world and of leaving it, which strikes us as more natural.

III. *The inconceivable immensity of the Universe.*

It was not, we remember, the "immense spaces" themselves but their *eternal silence* that terrified Pascal. With a definite religious background this is intelligible. But the effect of popular astronomy books (like Sir James

[4] This passage is introduced by a long and important discussion of Confucius' conception of "sincerity," which should be read attentively. In passing, it is worthy of remark that Mr. Richards shares his interest in Chinese philosophy with Mr. Ezra Pound and with the late Irving Babbitt. An investigation of an interest common to three apparently quite different thinkers would, I believe, repay the labour. It seems to indicate, at least, a deracination from the Christian tradition. The thought of these three men seems to me to have an interesting similarity.

Jeans's) upon me is only of the insignificance of vast space.

IV. *Man's place in the perspective of time.*

I confess that I do not find this especially edifying either, or stimulating to the imagination, unless I bring to its contemplation some belief that there is a sense and a meaning in the place of human history in the history of the world. I fear that in many people this subject of meditation can only stimulate the idle wonder and greed for facts which are satisfied by Mr. Wells's compendia.

V. *The enormity (sc. enormousness) of man's ignorance.*

Here again, I must ask, ignorance of what? I am acutely aware, for instance, of my own ignorance of specific subjects on which I want to know more; but Mr. Richards does not, surely, mean the ignorance of any individual man, but of *Man*. But "ignorance" must be relative to the sense in which we take the term "knowledge"; and in *Mencius on the Mind* Mr. Richards has given us a useful analysis of the numerous meanings of "knowledge." Mr. Richards, who has engaged in what I believe will be most fruitful investigations of controversy as systematised misunderstanding, may justly be able to accuse me of perverting his meanings. But his modern substitute for the *Exercises* of St. Ignatius is an appeal to our feelings, and I am only trying to set down how they affect mine. To me Mr. Richards's five points only express a modern emotional attitude which I cannot share, and which finds its most sentimental expression in *A Free Man's Worship*. And as the contemplation of Man's place in the Universe has led Lord Russell to write such bad prose, we may wonder whether it will lead the ordinary aspirant to understanding of good poetry. It is just as likely, I suspect, to confirm him in his taste for the second-rate.

I am willing to admit that such an approach to poetry may help some people: my point is that Mr. Richards speaks as though it were good for everybody. I am perfectly ready to concede the existence of people who feel, think and believe as Mr. Richards does in these matters, if he will only concede that there are some people who do not. He told us in *Science and Poetry*:

> For centuries . . . countless pseudo-statements—about God, about the universe, about human nature, the relations of mind to mind, about the soul, its rank and destiny . . . have been believed; now they are gone, irrecoverably; and the knowledge which has killed them is not of a kind upon which an equally fine organisation of the mind can be based.

I submit that this is itself a pseudo-statement, if there is such a thing. But these things are indeed gone, so far as Mr. Richards is concerned, if they are no longer believed by people whose minds Mr. Richards respects: we have no ground for controversy there. I only assert again that what he is trying to do is essentially the same as what Arnold wanted to do: to preserve emotions without the beliefs with which their history has been involved. It would seem that Mr. Richards, on his own showing, is engaged in a rear-guard religious action.[5]

Mr. Maritain, with an equally strong conviction that poetry will *not* save us, is equally despondent about the world of to-day. "Could any weakness," he asks, "be greater than the weakness of our contemporaries?" It is no more, as I have said before, the particular business of the poet as poet to concern himself with Maritain's attempt to determine the position of poetry in a Christian world than it is to concern himself with Richards's attempt to determine the position of poetry in a pagan world: but these various ambient ideas get in through the pores, and produce an unsettled state of mind. Trotsky, whose *Literature and Revolution* is the most sensible statement of a Communist attitude that I have seen,[6] is pretty

clear on the relation of the poet to his environment. He observes:

> Artistic creation is always a complicated turning inside out of old forms, under the influence of new stimuli which originate outside of art. In this large sense of the word, art is a handmaiden. It is not a disembodied element feeding on itself, but a function of social man indissolubly tied to his life and environment."

There is a striking contrast between this conception of art as a handmaiden, and that which we have just observed of art as a saviour. But perhaps the two notions are not so opposed as they appear. Trotsky seems, in any case, to draw the commonsense distinction between art and propaganda, and to be dimly aware that the material of the artist is not his beliefs as *held*, but his beliefs as *felt* (so far as his beliefs are part of his material at all); and he is sensible enough to see that a period of revolution is not favourable to art, since it puts pressure upon the poet, both direct and indirect, to make him overconscious of his beliefs as *held*. He would not limit Communist poetry to the writing of panegyrics upon the Russian State, any more than I should limit Christian poetry to the composition of hymns; the poetry of Villon is just as "Christian" in this way as that of Prudentius or Adam of St. Victor—though I think it would be a long time before Soviet society could afford to approve a Villon, if one arose.[7] It is probable, however, that Russian literature will become increasingly unintelligible, increasingly meaningless, to the peoples of Western Europe unless they develop in the same direction as Russia. Even as things are, in the present chaos of opinion and belief, we may expect to find quite different literatures

---

[5] Somewhat in the spirit of "religion without revelation," of which a greater exponent than Mr. Julian Huxley was Emmanuel Kant. On Kant's attempt (which deeply influenced later German theology) see an illuminating passage in A. E. Taylor's *The Faith of a Moralist*, vol. ii, chap. ii.

[6] There were also some interesting articles in *The New Republic* by Mr. Edmund Wilson, in controversy (if I remember correctly) with Mr. Michael

Gold. I regret that I cannot give the exact reference. The major part of Trotsky's book is not very interesting for those who are unacquainted with the modern Russian authors: one suspects that most of Trotsky's swans are geese.

[7] The Roman and Communist idea of an index of prohibited books seems to me perfectly sound in principle. It is a question (*a*) of the goodness and universality of the cause, (*b*) of the intelligence that goes to the application.

existing in the same language and the same country. "The unconcealed and palpable influence of the devil on an important part of contemporary literature," says Mr. Maritain, "is one of the significant phenomena of the history of our time." I can hardly expect most of my readers to take this remark seriously;[8] those who do will have very different criteria of criticism from those who do not. Another observation of Mr. Maritain's may be less unacceptable:

> By showing us where moral truth and the genuine supernatural are situate, religion saves poetry from the absurdity of believing itself destined to transform ethics and life: saves it from overweening arrogance.

This seems to me to be putting the finger on the great weakness of much poetry and criticism of the nineteenth and twentieth centuries. But between the motive which Rivière attributed to Molière and Racine[9] and the motive of Matthew Arnold bearing on shoulders immense what he thought to be the orb of the poet's fate, there is a serious *via media*.

As the doctrine of the moral and educational value of poetry has been elaborated in different forms by Arnold and Mr. Richards, so the Abbé Brémond presented a modern equivalent for the theory of divine inspiration. The task of *Prayer and Poetry* is to establish the likeness, and the difference of kind and degree, between poetry and mysticism. In his attempt to demonstrate this relation he safeguards himself by just qualifications, and makes many penetrating remarks about the nature of poetry. I will confine myself to two pieces of caution. My first qualm is over the assertion that "the more of a poet any particular poet is, the more he is tormented by the need of commu-

nicating his experience." This is a downright sort of statement which is very easy to accept without examination; but the matter is not so simple as all that. I should say that the poet is tormented primarily by the need to write a poem—and so, I regret to find, are a legion of people who are not poets: so that the line between "need" to write and "desire" to write is by no means easy to draw. And what is the experience that the poet is so bursting to communicate? By the time it has settled down into a poem it may be so different from the original experience as to be hardly recognisable. The "experience" in question may be the result of a fusion of feelings so numerous, and ultimately so obscure in their origins, that even if there be communication of them, the poet may hardly be aware of what he is communicating; and what is there to be communicated was not in existence before the poem was completed. "Communication" will not explain poetry. I will not say that there is not always some varying degree of communication in poetry, or that poetry could exist without any communication taking place. There is room for very great individual variation in the motives of equally good individual poets; and we have the assurance of Coleridge, with the approval of Mr. Housman, that "poetry gives most pleasure when only generally and not perfectly understood." And I think that my first objection to Brémond's theory is related to the second, in which also the question of motive and intention enters. Any theory which relates poetry very closely to a religious or a social scheme of things aims, probably, to *explain* poetry by discovering its natural laws; but it is in danger of *binding* poetry by legislation to be observed—and poetry can recognise no such laws. When the critic falls into this error he has probably done what we all do: when we generalise about poetry, as I have said before, we are generalising from the poetry which we best know and best like; not from all poetry, or even all of the poetry which we have read. What is "all poetry"? Everything written in verse which a sufficient number of the best minds have consid-

---

[8] With the influence of the devil on contemporary literature I shall be concerned in more detail in another book.

[9] Which does not seem to me to cover the case. Let us say that it was the primary motive (even in *Athalie*). An exact statement would need much space; for we cannot concern ourselves only with what went on inside the poet's head, but with the general state of society.

ered to be poetry. By a sufficient number, I mean enough persons of different types, at different times and places, over a space of time, and including foreigners as well as those to whom the language is native, to cancel every personal bias and eccentricity of taste (for we must all be slightly eccentric in taste to have any taste at all). Now when an account like the Abbé Brémond's is tested by being made itself a test, it tends to reveal some narrowness and exclusiveness; at any rate, a good deal of poetry that I like would be excluded, or given some other name than poetry; just as other writers who like to include much prose as being essentially "poetry" create confusion by including too much. That there is a relation (not necessarily poetic, perhaps merely psychological) between mysticism and some kinds of poetry, or some of the kinds of state in which poetry is produced, I make no doubt. But I prefer not to define, or to test, poetry by means of speculations about its origins; you cannot find a sure test for poetry, a test by which you may distinguish between poetry and mere good verse, by reference to its putative antecedents in the mind of the poet. Brémond seems to me to introduce extra-poetic laws for poetry: such laws as have been frequently made, and constantly violated.

There is another danger in the association of poetry with mysticism besides that which I have just mentioned, and that of leading the reader to look in poetry for religious satisfactions. These were dangers for the critic and the reader; there is also a danger for the poet. No one can read Mr. Yeats's *Autobiographies* and his earlier poetry without feeling that the author was trying to get as a poet something like the exaltation to be obtained, I believe, from hashisch or nitrous oxide. He was very much fascinated by self-induced trance states, calculated symbolism, mediums, theosophy, crystal-gazing, folklore and hobgoblins. Golden apples, archers, black pigs and such paraphernalia abounded. Often the verse has an hypnotic charm: but you cannot take heaven by magic, especially if you are, like Mr. Yeats, a very sane

person. Then, by a great triumph of development, Mr. Yeats began to write and is still writing some of the most beautiful poetry in the language, some of the clearest, simplest, most direct.[10]

The number of people capable of appreciating "all poetry" is probably very small, if not merely a theoretical limit; but the number of people who can get *some* pleasure and benefit from some poetry is, I believe, very large. A perfectly satisfactory theory which applied to all poetry would do so only at the cost of being voided of all content; the more usual reason for the unsatisfactoriness of our theories and general statements about poetry is that while professing to apply to all poetry, they are really theories about, or generalisations from, a limited range of poetry. Even when two persons of taste like the same poetry, this poetry will be arranged in their minds in slightly different patterns; our individual taste in poetry bears the indelible traces of our individual lives with all their experience pleasurable and painful. We are apt either to shape a theory to cover the poetry that we find most moving, or—what is less excusable—to choose the poetry which illustrates the theory we want to hold. You do not find Matthew Arnold quoting Rochester or Sedley. And it is not merely a matter of individual caprice. Each age demands different things from poetry, though its demands are modified, from time to time, by what some new poet has given. So our criticism, from age to age, will reflect the things that the age demands; and the criticism of no one man and of no one age can be expected to embrace the whole nature of poetry or exhaust all of its uses. Our contemporary critics, like their predecessors, are making particular responses to particular situations. No two readers, perhaps, will go to poetry with quite the same demands. Amongst all these demands from poetry and responses to it there is always some permanent

[10] The best analysis of the weakness of Mr. Yeats's poetry that I know is in Mr. Richards's *Science and Poetry*. But I do not think that Mr. Richards quite appreciated Mr. Yeats's later work.

element in common, just as there are standards of good and bad writing independent of what any one of us happens to like and dislike; but every effort to formulate the common element is limited by the limitations of particular men in particular places and at particular times; and these limitations become manifest in the perspective of history.

From Poe to Valéry (1948)

WHAT I attempt here is not a judicial estimate of Edgar Allan Poe; I am not trying to decide his rank as a poet or to isolate his essential originality. Poe is indeed a stumbling block for the judicial critic. If we examine his work in detail, we seem to find in it nothing but slipshod writing, puerile thinking unsupported by wide reading or profound scholarship, haphazard experiments in various types of writing, chiefly under pressure of financial need, without perfection in any detail. This would not be just. But if, instead of regarding his work analytically, we take a distant view of it as a whole, we see a mass of unique shape and impressive size to which the eye constantly returns. Poe's influence is equally puzzling. In France the influence of his poetry and of his poetic theories has been immense. In England and America it seems almost negligible. Can we point to any poet whose style appears to have been formed by a study of Poe? The only one whose name immediately suggests itself is—Edward Lear. And yet one cannot be sure that one's own writing has *not* been influenced by Poe. I can name positively certain poets whose work has influenced me, I can name others whose work, I am sure, has not; there may be still others of whose influence I am unaware, but whose influence I might be brought to acknowledge; but about Poe I shall never be sure. He wrote very few poems, and of those few only half a dozen have had a great success: but those few are as

well known to as large a number of people, are as well remembered by everybody, as any poems ever written. And some of his tales have had an important influence upon authors, and in types of writing where such influence would hardly be expected.

I shall here make no attempt to explain the enigma. At most, this is a contribution to the study of his influence; and an elucidation, partial as it may be, of one cause of Poe's importance in the light of that influence. I am trying to look at him, for a moment, as nearly as I can, through the eyes of three French poets, Baudelaire, Mallarmé and especially Paul Valéry. The sequence is itself important. These three French poets represent the beginning, the middle and the end of a particular tradition in poetry. Mallarmé once told a friend of mine that he came to Paris because he wanted to know Baudelaire; that he had once seen him at a bookstall on a quai, but had not had the courage to accost him. As for Valéry, we know from the first letter to Mallarmé, written when he was hardly more than a boy, of his discipleship of the elder poet; and we know of his devotion to Mallarmé until Mallarmé's death. Here are three literary generations, representing almost exactly a century of French poetry. Of course, these are poets very different from each other; of course, the literary progeny of Baudelaire was numerous and important, and there are other lines of descent from him. But I think we can trace the development and descent of one particular theory of the nature of poetry through these three poets and it is a theory which takes its origin in the theory, still more than in the practice, of Edgar Poe. And the impression we get of the influence of Poe is the more impressive, because of the fact that Mallarmé, and Valéry in turn, did not merely derive from Poe through Baudelaire: each of them subjected himself to that influence directly, and has left convincing evidence of the value which he attached to the theory and practice of Poe himself. Now, we all of us like to believe that we understand our own poets better than any foreigner can do; but I think we should be prepared to entertain the possibility that these Frenchmen have seen something in Poe that English-speaking readers have missed.

My subject, then, is not simply Poe but Poe's effect upon three French poets, representing three successive generations; and my purpose is also to approach an understanding of a peculiar attitude towards poetry, by the poets themselves, which is perhaps the most interesting, possibly the most characteristic, and certainly the most original development of the aesthetic of verse made in that period as a whole. It is all the more worthy of examination if, as I incline to believe, this attitude towards poetry represents a phase which has come to an end with the death of Valéry. For our study of it should help towards the understanding of whatever it may be that our generation and the next will find to take its place.

Before concerning myself with Poe as he appeared in the eyes of these French poets, I think it as well to present my own impression of his status among American and English readers and critics; for, if I am wrong, you may have to criticize what I say of his influence in France with my errors in mind. It does not seem to me unfair to say that Poe has been regarded as a minor, or secondary, follower of the Romantic Movement: a successor to the so-called "Gothic" novelists in his fiction, and a follower of Byron and Shelley in his verse. This however is to place him in the English tradition; and there certainly he does not belong. English readers sometimes account for that in Poe which is outside of any English tradition, by saying that it is American; but this does not seem to me wholly true either, especially when we consider the other American writers of his own and an earlier generation. There is a certain flavour of provinciality about his work, in a sense in which Whitman is not in the least provincial: it is the provinciality of the person who is not at home where he belongs, but cannot get to anywhere else. Poe is a kind of displaced European; he is attracted to Paris, to Italy and to Spain, to places which he could endow with romantic gloom and grandeur. Although his ambit of movement hardly extended beyond the limits of Richmond and Boston longitudinally, and neither east nor west of these centres, he seems a wanderer with no fixed abode. There can be few authors of such eminence who have drawn so little from their own roots, who have been so isolated from any surroundings.

I believe the view of Poe taken by the ordinary cultivated English or American reader is something like this: Poe is the author of a few, a very few short poems which enchanted him for a time when he was a boy, and which do somehow stick in the memory. I do not think that he re-reads these poems, unless he turns to them in the pages of an anthology; his enjoyment of them is rather the memory of an enjoyment which he may for a moment recapture. They seem to him to belong to a particular period when his interest in poetry had just awakened. Certain images, and still more certain rhythms, abide with him. This reader also remembers certain of the tales—not very many —and holds the opinion that *The Gold Bug* was quite good for its times, but that detective fiction has made great strides since then. And he may sometimes contrast him with Whitman, having frequently re-read Whitman, but not Poe.

As for the prose, it is recognized that Poe's tales had great influence upon some types of popular fiction. So far as detective fiction is concerned, nearly everything can be traced to two authors: Poe and Wilkie Collins. The two influences sometimes concur, but are also responsible for two different types of detective. The efficient professional policeman originates with Collins, the brilliant and eccentric amateur with Poe. Conan Doyle owes much to Poe, and not merely to Monsieur Dupin of *The Murders in the Rue Morgue.* Sherlock Holmes was deceiving Watson when he told him that he had bought his Stradivarius violin for a few shillings at a second-hand shop in the Tottenham Court Road. He found that violin in the ruins of the house of Usher. There is a close similarity between the musical exercises of Holmes and those of Roderick Usher: those wild and irregular improvisations which, although on one occasion they sent Watson off to sleep, must have been excruciating to any ear trained to music. It seems to me probable that the romances of improbable and incredible adventure of Rider Haggard found their inspiration in Poe—and Haggard himself had imitators enough. I think it equally likely that H. G. Wells, in his early romances of scientific exploration and invention, owed much to the stimulus of some of Poe's narratives—*Gordon Pym,* or *A Descent into the Maelstrom* for example, or *The Facts in the Case of Monsieur Valdemar.* The compilation of evidence I leave to those who are interested to pursue the inquiry. But I fear that nowadays too few readers open *She* or *The War of the Worlds* or *The Time Machine*: fewer still are capable of being thrilled by their predecessors.

What strikes me first, as a general difference between the way in which the French poets whom I have cited took Poe, and the way of American and English critics of equivalent authority, is the attitude of the former towards Poe's *œuvre,* towards his work as a whole. Anglo-Saxon critics are, I think, more inclined to make separate judgments of the different parts of an author's work. We regard Poe as a man who dabbled in verse and in kinds of prose, without settling down to make a thoroughly good job of any one *genre.* These French readers were impressed by the variety of form of expression, because they found, or

thought they found, an essential unity; while admitting, if necessary, that much of the work is fragmentary or occasional, owing to circumstances of poverty, frailty and vicissitude, they nevertheless take him as an author of such seriousness that his work must be grasped as a whole. This represents partly a difference between two kinds of critical mind; but we must claim, for our own view, that it is supported by our awareness of the blemishes and imperfections of Poe's actual writing. It is worth while to illustrate these faults, as they strike an English-speaking reader.

Poe had, to an exceptional degree, the feeling for the incantatory element in poetry, of that which may, in the most nearly literal sense, be called "the magic of verse." His versification is not, like that of the greatest masters of prosody, of the kind which yields a richer melody, through study and long habituation, to the maturing sensibility of the reader returning to it at times throughout his life. Its effect is immediate and undeveloping; it is probably much the same for the sensitive schoolboy and for the ripe mind and cultivated ear. In this unchanging immediacy, it partakes perhaps more of the character of very good *verse* than of poetry—but that is to start a hare which I have no intention of following here, for it is, I am sure, "poetry" and not "verse." It has the effect of an incantation which, because of its very crudity, stirs the feelings at a deep and almost primitive level. But, in his choice of the word which has the right *sound,* Poe is by no means careful that it should have also the right *sense.* I will give one comparison of uses of the same word by Poe and by Tennyson—who, of all English poets since Milton, had probably the most accurate and fastidious appreciation of the sound of syllables. In Poe's *Ulalume*— to my mind one of his most successful, as well as typical, poems—we find the lines

> It was night, in the lonesome October
> Of my most immemorial year.

Immemorial, according to the Oxford Dictionary, means: "that is beyond memory or out of mind; ancient beyond memory or record: extremely old." None of these meanings seems applicable to this use of the word by Poe. The year was not beyond memory—the speaker remembers one incident in it very well; at the conclusion he even remembers a funeral in the same place just a year earlier. The line of Tennyson, equally well known, and justly admired because the sound of the line responds so well to the sound which the poet wishes to evoke, may already have come to mind:

The moan of doves in immemorial elms.

Here *immemorial*, besides having the most felicitous sound value, is exactly the word for trees so old that no one knows just how old they are.

Poetry, of different kinds, may be said to range from that in which the attention of the reader is directed primarily to the sound, to that in which it is directed primarily to the sense. With the former kind, the sense may be apprehended almost unconsciously; with the latter kind—at these two extremes—it is the sound, of the operation of which upon us we are unconscious. But, with either type, sound and sense must cooperate; in even the most purely incantatory poem, the dictionary meaning of words cannot be disregarded with impunity.

An irresponsibility towards the meaning of words is not infrequent with Poe. *The Raven* is, I think, far from being Poe's best poem; though, partly because of the analysis which the author gives in *The Philosophy of Composition*, it is the best known.

In there stepped a stately Raven of the saintly days of yore,

Since there is nothing particularly saintly about the raven, if indeed the ominous bird is not wholly the reverse, there can be no point in referring his origin to a period of saintliness, even if such a period can be assumed to have existed. We have just heard the raven described as *stately*; but we are told presently that he is *ungainly*, an attribute hardly to be reconciled,

without a good deal of explanation, with *stateliness*. Several words in the poem seem to be inserted either merely to fill out the line to the required measure, or for the sake of a rhyme. The bird is addressed as "no craven" quite needlessly, except for the pressing need of a rhyme to "raven"—a surrender to the exigencies of rhyme with which I am sure Malherbe would have had no patience. And there is not always even such schoolboy justification as this: to say that the lamplight "gloated o'er" the sofa cushions is a freak of fancy which, even were it relevant to have a little gloating going on somewhere, would appear forced.

Imperfections in *The Raven* such as these —and one could give others—may serve to explain why *The Philosophy of Composition*, the essay in which Poe professes to reveal his method in composing *The Raven*—has not been taken so seriously in England or America as in France. It is difficult for us to read that essay without reflecting, that if Poe plotted out his poem with such calculation, he might have taken a little more pains over it: the result hardly does credit to the method. Therefore we are likely to draw the conclusion that Poe in analysing his poem was practising either a hoax, or a piece of self-deception in setting down the way in which he wanted to think that he had written it. Hence the essay has not been taken so seriously as it deserves.

Poe's other essays in poetic aesthetic deserve consideration also. No poet, when he writes his own *art poétique*, should hope to do much more than explain, rationalize, defend or prepare the way for his own practice: that is, for writing his own kind of poetry. He may think that he is establishing laws for all poetry; but what he has to say that is worth saying has its immediate relation to the way in which he himself writes or wants to write: though it may well be equally valid to his immediate juniors, and extremely helpful to them. We are only safe in finding, in his writing about poetry, principles valid for any poetry, so long as we check what he says by the kind of poetry he writes. Poe has a remarkable passage about the impossibility of writing a long poem—for a long poem, he holds, is at best a series of short poems strung together. What we have to bear in mind is that he himself was incapable of writing a long poem. He could conceive only a poem which was a single simple effect: for him, the whole of a poem had to be in one mood. Yet it is only in a poem of some length that a variety of moods can be expressed; for a variety of moods requires a number of different themes or subjects, related either in themselves or in the mind of the poet. These parts can form a whole which is more than the sum of the parts; a whole such that the pleasure we derive from the reading of any part is enhanced by our grasp of the whole. It follows also that in a long poem some parts may be deliberately planned to be less "poetic" than others: these passages may show no lustre when extracted, but may be intended to elicit, by contrast, the significance of other parts, and to unite them into a whole more significant than any of the parts. A long poem may gain by the widest possible variations of intensity. But Poe wanted a poem to be of the first intensity throughout: it is questionable whether he could have appreciated the more philosophical passages in Dante's *Purgatorio*. What Poe had said has proved in the past of great comfort to other poets equally incapable of the long poem; and we must recognize that the question of the possibility of writing a long poem is not simply that of the strength and staying power of the individual poet, but may have to do with the conditions of the age in which he finds himself. And what Poe has to say on the subject is illuminating, in helping us to understand the point of view of poets for whom the long poem is impossible.

The fact that for Poe a poem had to be the expression of a single mood—it would here be too long an excursis to try to demonstrate that *The Bells*, as a deliberate exercise in several moods, is as much a poem of one mood as any of Poe's—this fact can better be understood as a manifestation of a more fundamental weakness. Here, what I have to say I put forward only tentatively: but it is a view which I should like to launch in order to see what becomes of it. My account may go to explain, also, why the work of Poe has for many readers appealed at a particular phase of their growth, at the period of life when they were just emerging from childhood. That Poe had a powerful intellect is undeniable: but it seems to me the intellect of a highly gifted young person before puberty. The forms which his lively curiosity takes are those in which a pre-adolescent mentality delights: wonders of nature and of mechanics and of the supernatural, cryptograms and cyphers, puzzles and labyrinths, mechanical chess-players and wild flights of speculation. The variety and ardour of his curiosity delight and dazzle; yet in the end the eccentricity and lack of coherence of his interests tire. There is just that lacking which gives dignity to the mature man: a consistent view of life. An attitude can be mature and consistent, and yet be highly sceptical: but Poe was no sceptic. He appears to yield himself completely to the idea of the moment: the effect is, that all of his ideas seem to be *entertained* rather than believed. What is lacking is not brain power, but that maturity of intellect which comes only with the maturing of the man as a whole, the development and coordination of his various emotions. I am not concerned with any possible psychological or pathological explanation: it is enough for my purpose to record that the work of Poe is such as I should expect of a man of very exceptional mind and sensibility, whose emotional development has been in some respect arrested at an early age. His most vivid imaginative realizations are the realization of a dream: significantly, the ladies in his poems and tales are always ladies lost, or ladies vanishing before they can be embraced. Even in *The Haunted Palace*, where the subject appears to be his own weakness of alcoholism, the disaster has no moral significance; it is treated impersonally as an isolated phenomenon; it has not behind it the terrific force of such lines as those of François Villon when he speaks of his own fallen state.

*   *   *

Having said as much as this about Poe, I must proceed to inquire what it was that three great French poets found in his work to admire, which we have not found. We must first take account of the fact that none of these poets knew the English language very well. Baudelaire must have read a certain amount of English and American poetry: he certainly borrows from Gray, and apparently from Emerson. He was never familiar with England, and there is no reason to believe that he spoke the language at all well. As for Mallarmé, he taught English and there is convincing evidence of his imperfect knowledge, for he committed himself to writing a kind of guide to the use of the language. An examination of this curious treatise, and the strange phrases which he gives under the impression that they are familiar English proverbs, should dispel any rumour of Mallarmé's English scholarship. As for Valéry, I never heard him speak a word of English, even in England. I do not know what he had read in our language: Valéry's second language, the influence of which is perceptible in some of his verse, was Italian.

It is certainly possible, in reading something in a language imperfectly understood, for the reader to find what is not there; and when the reader is himself a man of genius, the foreign poem read may, by a happy accident, elicit something important from the depths of his own mind, which he attributes to what he reads. And it is true that in translating Poe's prose into French, Baudelaire effected a striking improvement: he transformed what is often a slipshod and a shoddy English prose into admirable French. Mallarmé, who translated a number of Poe's poems into French prose, effected a similar improvement: but on the other hand, the rhythms, in which we find so much of the originality of Poe, are lost. The evidence that the French overrated Poe because of their imperfect knowledge of English remains accordingly purely negative: we can venture no farther than saying that they were not disturbed by weaknesses of which we are very much aware. It does not account for their high opinion of Poe's *thought*, for the value which they attach to his philosophical and critical exercises. To understand that we must look elsewhere.

We must, at this point, avoid the error of assuming that Baudelaire, Mallarmé and Valéry all responded to Poe in exactly the same way. They are great poets, and they are each very different from the other; furthermore, they represent, as I have reminded you, three different generations. It is with Valéry that I am here chiefly concerned. I therefore say only that Baudelaire, to judge by his introduction to his translation of the tales and essays, was the most concerned with the personality of the man. With the accuracy of his portrait I am not concerned: the point is that in Poe, in his life, his isolation and his worldly failure, Baudelaire found the prototype of *le poète maudit*, the poet as the outcast of society—the type which was to realize itself, in different ways, in Verlaine and Rimbaud, the type of which Baudelaire saw himself as a distinguished example. This nineteenth-century archetype, *le poète maudit*, the rebel against society and against middle-class morality (a rebel who descends of course from the continental myth of the figure of Byron) corresponds to a particular social situation. But, in the course of an introduction which is primarily a sketch of the man Poe and his biography, Baudelaire lets fall one remark indicative of an aesthetic that brings us to Valéry:

"He believed [says Baudelaire], true poet that he was, that the goal of poetry is of the same nature as its principle, and that it should have nothing in view but itself."

"A poem does not say something—it *is* something": that doctrine has been held in more recent times.

The interest for Mallarmé is rather in the technique of verse, though Poe's is, as Mallarmé recognizes, a kind of versification which does not lend itself to use in the French language. But when we come to Valéry, it is neither the man nor the poetry, but the *theory* of poetry, that engages his attention. In a very early letter to Mallarmé, written when he was a very young man, introducing himself to the elder poet, he says: "I prize the theories of Poe, so profound and so insidiously learned; I believe in the omnipotence of rhythm, and especially in the suggestive phrase." But I base my opinion, not primarily upon this credo of a very young man, but upon Valéry's subsequent theory and practice. In the same way that Valéry's poetry, and his essays on the act of poetry, are two aspects of the same interest of his mind and complement each other, so for Valéry the poetry of Poe is inseparable from Poe's poetic theories.

This brings me to the point of considering the meaning of the term "la poésie pure": the French phrase has a connotation of discussion and argument which is not altogether rendered by the term "pure poetry."

All poetry may be said to start from the emotions experienced by human beings in their relations to themselves, to each other, to divine beings, and to the world about them; it is therefore concerned also with thought and action, which emotion brings about, and out of which emotion arises. But, at however primitive a stage of expression and appreciation, the function of poetry can never be simply to arouse these same emotions in the audience of the poet. You remember the account of Alexander's feast in the famous ode of Dryden. If the conqueror of Asia was actually transported with the violent emotions which the bard Timotheus, by skilfully varying his music, is said to have aroused in him, then the great Alexander was at the moment suffering from automatism induced by alcohol poisoning, and was in that state completely incapable of appreciating musical or poetic art. In the earliest poetry, or in the most rudimentary enjoyment of poetry, the attention of the listener is directed upon the subject matter; the effect of the poetic art is felt, without the listener being wholly conscious of this art. With the development of the consciousness of language, there is

another stage, at which the auditor, who may by that time have become the reader, is aware of a double interest in a story for its own sake, and in the way in which it is told: that is to say, he becomes aware of style. Then we may take a delight in discrimination between the ways in which different poets will handle the same subject; an appreciation not merely of better or worse, but of differences between styles which are equally admired. At a third stage of development, the subject may recede to the background: instead of being the purpose of the poem, it becomes simply a necessary means for the realization of the poem. At this stage the reader or listener may become as nearly indifferent to the subject matter as the primitive listener was to the style. A complete unconsciousness or indifference to the style at the beginning, or to the subject matter at the end, would however take us outside of poetry altogether: for a complete unconsciousness of anything but subject matter would mean that for that listener poetry had not yet appeared; a complete unconsciousness of anything but style would mean that poetry had vanished.

This process of increasing self-consciousness —or, we may say, of increasing consciousness of language—has as its theoretical goal what we may call *la poésie pure*. I believe it to be a goal that can never be reached, because I think that poetry is only poetry so long as it preserves some "impurity" in this sense: that is to say, so long as the subject matter is valued for its own sake. The Abbé Brémond, if I have understood him, maintains that while the element of *la poésie pure* is necessary to make a poem a poem, no poem can consist of *la poésie pure* solely. But what has happened in the case of Valéry is a change of attitude toward the subject matter. We must be careful to avoid saying that the subject matter becomes "less important." It has rather a different kind of importance: it is important as *means*: the *end* is the poem. The subject exists for the poem, not the poem for the subject. A poem may employ several subjects, combining them in a particular way; and it may be meaningless to ask

"What is the subject of the poem?" From the union of several subjects there appears, not another subject, but the poem.

Here I should like to point out the difference between a theory of poetry propounded by a student of aesthetics, and the same theory as held by a poet. It is one thing when it is simply an account of how the poet writes, without knowing it, and another thing when the poet himself writes consciously according to that theory. In affecting writing, the theory becomes a different thing from what it was merely as an explanation of how the poet writes. And Valéry was a poet who wrote very consciously and deliberately indeed: perhaps, at his best, not wholly under the guidance of theory; but his theorizing certainly affected the kind of poetry that he wrote. He was the most self-conscious of all poets.

To the extreme self-consciousness of Valéry must be added another trait: his extreme scepticism. It might be thought that such a man, without belief in anything which could be the subject of poetry, would find refuge in a doctrine of "art for art's sake." But Valéry was much too sceptical to believe even in art. It is significant, the number of times that he describes something he has written as an *ébauche* —a rough draft. He had ceased to believe in *ends*, and was only interested in *processes*. It often seems as if he had continued to write poetry, simply because he was interested in the introspective observation of himself engaged in writing it: one has only to read the several essays—sometimes indeed more exciting than his verse, because one suspects that he was more excited in writing them—in which he records his observations. There is a revealing remark in *Variété V*, the last of his books of collected papers: "As for myself, who am, I confess, much more concerned with the formation or the fabrication of works [of art] than with the works themselves," and, a little later in the same volume: "In my opinion the most authentic philosophy is not in the objects of reflection, so much as in the very act of thought and its manipulation."

Here we have, brought to their culmination by Valéry, two notions which can be traced back to Poe. There is first the doctrine, elicited from Poe by Baudelaire, which I have already quoted: "A poem should have nothing in view but itself"; second the notion that the composition of a poem should be as conscious and deliberate as possible, that the poet should observe himself in the act of composition—and this, in a mind as sceptical as Valéry's, leads to the conclusion, so paradoxically inconsistent with the other, that the act of composition is more interesting than the poem which results from it.

First, there is the "purity" of Poe's poetry. In the sense in which we speak of "purity of language" Poe's poetry is very far from pure, for I have commented upon Poe's carelessness and unscrupulousness in the use of words. But in the sense of *la poésie pure*, that kind of purity came easily to Poe. The subject is little, the treatment is everything. He did not have to achieve purity by a process of purification, for his material was already tenuous. Second, there is that defect in Poe to which I alluded when I said that he did not appear to believe, but rather to entertain, theories. And here again, with Poe and Valéry, extremes meet, the immature mind playing with ideas because it had not developed to the point of convictions, and the very adult mind playing with ideas because it was too sceptical to hold convictions. It is by this contrast, I think, that we can account for Valéry's admiration for *Eureka*—that cosmological fantasy which makes no deep impression upon most of us, because we are aware of Poe's lack of qualification in philosophy, theology or natural science, but which Valéry, after Baudelaire, esteemed highly as a "prose poem." Finally, there is the astonishing result of Poe's analysis of the composition of *The Raven*. It does not matter whether *The Philosophy of Composition* is a hoax, or a piece of self-deception, or a more or less accurate record of Poe's calculations in writing the poem; what matters is that it suggested to Valéry a method and an occupation—that of observing himself write.

Of course, a greater than Poe had already studied the poetic process. In the *Biographia Literaria* Coleridge is concerned primarily, of course, with the poetry of Wordsworth; and he did not pursue his philosophical enquiries concurrently with the writing of his poetry; but he does anticipate the question which fascinated Valéry: "What am I doing when I write a poem?" Yet Poe's *Philosophy of Composition* is a *mise au point* of the question which gives it capital importance in relation to this process which ends with Valéry. For the penetration of the poetic by the introspective critical activity is carried to the limit by Valéry, the limit at which the latter begins to destroy the former. M. Louis Bolle, in his admirable study of this poet, observes pertinently: "This intellectual narcissism is not alien to the poet, even though he does not explain the whole of his work: 'why not conceive as a work of art the production of a work of art?'"

Now, as I think I have already hinted, I believe that the *art poétique* of which we find the germ in Poe, and which bore fruit in the work of Valéry, has gone as far as it can go. I do not believe that this aesthetic can be of any help to later poets. What will take its place I do not know. An aesthetic which merely contradicted it would not do. To insist on the all-importance of subject-matter, to insist that the poet should be spontaneous and irreflective, that he should depend upon inspiration and neglect technique, would be a lapse from what is in any case a highly civilized attitude to a barbarous one. We should have to have an aesthetic which somehow comprehended and transcended that of Poe and Valéry. This question does not greatly exercise my mind, since I think that the poet's theories should arise out of his practice rather than his practice out of his theories. But I recognize first that within this tradition from Poe to Valéry are some of those modern poems which I most admire and enjoy; second, I think that the tradition itself represents the most interesting development of poetic consciousness anywhere in that same hundred years; and finally I value this exploration of certain poetic possibilities for its own sake, as we believe that all possibilities should be explored. And I find that by trying to look at Poe through the eyes of Baudelaire, Mallarmé and most of all Valéry, I become more thoroughly convinced of his importance, of the importance of his *work* as a whole. And, as for the future: it is a tenable hypothesis that this advance of self-consciousness, the extreme awareness of and concern for language which we find in Valéry, is something which must ultimately break down, owing to an increasing strain against which the human mind and nerves will rebel; just as, it may be maintained, the indefinite elaboration of scientific discovery and invention, and of political and social machinery, may reach a point at which there will be an irresistible revulsion of humanity and a readiness to accept the most primitive hardships rather than carry any longer the burden of modern civilization. Upon that I hold no fixed opinion: I leave it to your consideration.

Poetry and Drama, Part I (1951)

REVIEWING my critical output for the last thirty-odd years, I am surprised to find how constantly I have returned to the drama, whether by examining the work of the contemporaries of Shakespeare, or by reflecting on the possibilities of the future. It may even be that people are weary of hearing me on this subject. But, while I find that I have been composing variations on this theme all my life, my views have been continually modified and renewed by increasing experience; so that I am impelled to take stock of the situation afresh at every stage of my own experimentation.

As I have gradually learned more about the problems of poetic drama, and the conditions which it must fulfil if it is to justify itself, I have made a little clearer to myself, not only my own reasons for wanting to write in this form, but the more general reasons for wanting to see it restored to its place. And I think that if I say something about these problems and conditions, it should make clearer to other people whether and if so why poetic drama has anything potentially to offer the playgoer, that prose drama cannot. For I start with the assumption that if poetry is merely a decoration, an added embellishment, if it merely gives people of literary tastes the pleasure of listening to poetry at the same time that they are witnessing a play, then it is superfluous. It must justify itself dramatically, and not merely be fine poetry shaped into a dramatic form. From this it follows that no play should be written in verse for which prose is *dramatically* adequate. And from this it follows, again, that the audience, its attention held by the dramatic action, its emotions stirred by the situation between the

characters, should be too intent upon the play to be wholly conscious of the medium.

Whether we use prose or verse on the stage, they are both but means to an end. The difference, from one point of view, is not so great as we might think. In those prose plays which survive, which are read and produced on the stage by later generations, the prose in which the characters speak is as remote, for the best part, from the vocabulary, syntax, and rhythm of our ordinary speech—with its fumbling for words, its constant recourse to approximation, its disorder, and its unfinished sentences—as verse is. Like verse, it has been written, and rewritten. Our two greatest prose stylists in the drama—apart from Shakespeare and the other Elizabethans who mixed prose and verse in the same play—are, I believe, Congreve and Bernard Shaw. A speech by a character of Congreve or of Shaw has—however clearly the characters may be differentiated—that unmistakable personal rhythm which is the mark of a prose style, and of which only the most accomplished conversationalists—who are for that matter usually monologuists—show any trace in their talk. We have all heard (too often!) of Molière's character who expressed surprise when told that he spoke prose. But it was M. Jourdain who was right, and not his mentor or his creator: he did not speak prose—he only talked. For I mean to draw a triple distinction: between prose, and verse, and our ordinary speech which is mostly below the level of either verse or prose. So if you look at it in this way, it will appear that prose, on the stage, is as artificial as verse: or alternatively, that verse can be as natural as prose.

But while the sensitive member of the audience will appreciate, when he hears fine prose spoken in a play, that this is something better than ordinary conversation, he does not regard it as a wholly different language from that which he himself speaks, for that would interpose a barrier between himself and the imaginary characters on the stage. Too many people, on the other hand, approach a play which they know to be in verse, with the consciousness of the difference. It is unfortunate when they are repelled by verse, but can also be deplorable when they are attracted by it—if that means that they are prepared to enjoy the play and the language of the play as two separate things. The chief effect of style and rhythm in dramatic speech, whether in prose or verse, should be unconscious.

From this it follows that a mixture of prose and verse in the same play is generally to be avoided: each transition makes the auditor aware, with a jolt, of the medium. It is, we may say, justifiable when the author wishes to produce this jolt: when, that is, he wishes to transport the audience violently from one plane of reality to another. I suspect that this kind of transition was easily acceptable to an Elizabethan audience, to whose ears both prose and verse came naturally; who liked highfalutin and low comedy in the same play; and to whom it seemed perhaps proper that the more humble and rustic characters should speak in a homely language, and that those of more exalted rank should rant in verse. But even in the plays of Shakespeare some of the prose passages seem to be designed for an effect of contrast which, when achieved, is something that can never become old-fashioned. The knocking at the gate in *Macbeth* is an example that comes to everyone's mind; but it has long seemed to me that the alternation of scenes in prose with scenes in verse in *Henry IV* points an ironic contrast between the world of high politics and the world of common life. The audience probably thought they were getting their accustomed chronicle play garnished with amusing scenes of low life; yet the prose scenes of both Part I and Part II provide a sardonic comment upon the bustling ambitions of the chiefs of the parties in the insurrection of the Percys.

To-day, however, because of the handicap under which verse drama suffers, I believe that prose should be used very sparingly indeed; that we should aim at a form of verse in which everything can be said that has to be said; and that when we find some situation which is intractable in verse, it is merely that our form of verse is inelastic. And if there prove to be scenes which we cannot put in verse, we must either develop our verse, or avoid having to introduce such scenes. For we have to accustom our audiences to verse to the point at which they will cease to be conscious of it; and to introduce prose dialogue, would only be to distract their attention from the play itself to the medium of its expression. But if our verse is to have so wide a range that it can say anything that has to be said, it follows that it will not be "poetry" all the time. It will only be "poetry" when the dramatic situation has reached such a point of intensity that poetry becomes the natural utterance, because then it is the only language in which the emotions can be expressed at all.

It is indeed necessary for any long poem, if it is to escape monotony, to be able to say homely things without bathos, as well as to take the highest flights without sounding exaggerated. And it is still more important in a play, especially if it is concerned with contemporary life. The reason for writing even the more pedestrian parts of a verse play in verse instead of prose is, however, not only to avoid calling the audience's attention to the fact that it is at other moments listening to poetry. It is also that the verse rhythm should have its effect upon the hearers, without their being conscious of it. A brief analysis of one scene of Shakespeare's may illustrate this point. The opening scene of *Hamlet*—as well constructed an opening scene as that of any play ever written— has the advantage of being one that everybody knows.

What we do not notice, when we witness this scene in the theatre, is the great variation of style. Nothing is superfluous, and there is no line of poetry which is not justified by its dramatic value. The first twenty-two lines are built

of the simplest words in the most homely idiom. Shakespeare had worked for a long time in
the theatre, and written a good many plays, before reaching the point at which he could write
those twenty-two lines. There is nothing quite
so simplified and sure in his previous work. He
first developed conversational, colloquial verse
in the monologue of the character part—
Faulconbridge in *King John,* and later the
Nurse in *Romeo and Juliet.* It was a much further step to carry it unobtrusively into the dialogue of brief replies. No poet has begun to
master dramatic verse until he can write lines
which, like these in *Hamlet,* are *transparent.*
You are consciously attending, not to the poetry, but to the meaning of the poetry. If you
were hearing *Hamlet* for the first time, without
knowing anything about the play, I do not
think that it would occur to you to ask whether
the speakers were speaking in verse or prose.
The verse is having a different effect upon us
from prose; but at the moment, what we are
aware of is the frosty night, the officers keeping
watch on the battlements, and the foreboding
of an ominous action. I do not say that there is
no place for the situation in which part of one's
pleasure will be the enjoyment of hearing beautiful poetry—providing that the author gives it,
in that place, dramatic inevitability. And of
course, when we have both seen a play several
times and read it between performances, we begin to analyse the means by which the author
has produced his effects. But in the immediate
impact of this scene we are unconscious of the
medium of its expression.

From the short, brusque ejaculations at the
beginning, suitable to the situation and to the
character of the guards—but not expressing
more character than is required for their function in the play—the verse glides into a slower
movement with the appearance of the courtiers
Horatio and Marcellus.

> Horatio says 'tis but our fantasy, . . .

and the movement changes again on the appearance of Royalty, the ghost of the King, into
the solemn and sonorous

> What art thou, that usurp'st this time of
> night, . . .

(and note, by the way, this anticipation of the
plot conveyed by the use of the verb *usurp*);
and majesty is suggested in a reference reminding us whose ghost this is:

> So frown'd he once, when, in an angry parle,
> He smote the sledded Polacks on the ice.

There is an abrupt change to staccato in Horatio's words to the Ghost on its second appearance; this rhythm changes again with the words

> We do it wrong, being so majestical,
> To offer it the show of violence;
> For it is, as the air, invulnerable,
> And our vain blows malicious mockery.

The scene reaches a resolution with the words
of Marcellus:

> It faded on the crowing of the cock.
> Some say that ever 'gainst that season comes
> Wherein our Saviour's birth is celebrated,
> The bird of dawning singeth all night long . . .

and Horatio's answer:

> So have I heard and do in part believe it.
> But, look, the morn, in russet mantle clad,
> Walks o'er the dew of yon high eastern hill.
> Break we our watch up.

This is great poetry, and it is dramatic; but besides being poetic and dramatic, it is something
more. There emerges, when we analyse it, a
kind of musical design also which reinforces
and is one with the dramatic movement. It has
checked and accelerated the pulse of our emotion without our knowing it. Note that in these
last words of Marcellus there is a deliberate
brief emergence of the poetic into consciousness. When we hear the lines

> But, look, the morn, in russet mantle clad,
> Walks o'er the dew of yon high eastern hill,

we are lifted for a moment beyond character,
but with no sense of unfitness of the words
coming, and at this moment, from the lips of
Horatio. The transitions in the scene obey laws
of the music of dramatic poetry. Note that the

two lines of Horatio which I have quoted twice are preceded by a line of the simplest speech which might be either verse or prose:

So have I heard and do in part believe it,

and that he follows them abruptly with a half line which is hardly more than a stage direction:

Break we our watch up.

It would be interesting to pursue, by a similar analysis, this problem of the double pattern in great poetic drama—the pattern which may be examined from the point of view of stagecraft or from that of the music. But I think that the examination of this one scene is enough to show us that verse is not merely a formalization, or an added decoration, but that it intensifies the drama. It should indicate also the importance of the unconscious effect of the verse upon us. And lastly, I do not think that this effect is felt only by those members of an audience who "like poetry" but also by those who go for the play alone. By the people who do not like poetry, I mean those who cannot sit down with a book of poetry and enjoy reading it: these people also, when they go to a play in verse, should be affected by the poetry. And these are the audiences whom the writer of such a play ought to keep in mind.

At this point I might say a word about those plays which we call *poetic*, though they are written in prose. The plays of John Millington Synge form rather a special case, because they are based upon the idiom of a rural people whose speech is naturally poetic, both in imagery and in rhythm. I believe that he even incorporated phrases which he had heard from these country people of Ireland. The language of Synge is not available except for plays set among that same people. We can draw more general conclusions from the plays in prose, so much admired in my youth, and now hardly even read, by Maeterlinck. These plays are in a different way restricted in their subject matter; and to say that the characterization in them is dim is an understatement. I do not deny that they have some poetic quality. But in order to be poetic in prose, a dramatist has to be so consistently poetic that his scope is very limited. Synge wrote plays about characters whose originals in life talked poetically, so he could make them talk poetry and remain real people. The poetic prose dramatist who has not this advantage, has to be too poetic. The poetic drama in prose is more limited by poetic convention or by our conventions as to what subject matter is poetic, than is the poetic drama in verse. A really dramatic verse can be employed, as Shakespeare employed it, to say the most matter-of-fact things.

Yeats is a very different case from Maeterlinck or Synge. A study of his development as a dramatist would show, I think, the great distance he went, and the triumph of his last plays. In his first period, he wrote plays in verse about subjects conventionally accepted as suitable for verse, in a metric which—though even at that early stage having the personal Yeats rhythm —is not really a form of speech quite suitable for anybody except mythical kings and queens. His middle-period *Plays for Dancers* are very beautiful, but they do not solve any problem for the dramatist in verse: they are poetic prose plays with important interludes in verse. It was only in his last play *Purgatory* that he solved his problem of speech in verse, and laid all his successors under obligation to him.

I. A. RICHARDS

Introduction

THE FIRST CHAPTER of I. A. Richards' *Principles of Literary Criticism* is entitled "The Chaos of Critical Theories." Here, at the beginning of his first major critical statement, Richards surveys all previous criticism, and finds it virtually useless. "A few conjectures, a supply of admonitions, many acute isolated observations, some brilliant guesses, much oratory and applied poetry, inexhaustible confusion, a sufficiency of dogma, no small stock of prejudices, whimsies and crotchets, a profusion of mysticism, a little genuine speculation, sundry stray inspirations, pregnant hints and random *aperçus*; of such as these, it may be said without exaggeration, is extant critical theory composed." After such an opening we can expect only one message: literary criticism must be reformed. Brilliantly and ruthlessly, Richards sets out to replace the chaos of critical theories with a practical, scientific criticism that ordinary men can put to use.

Many other modern critics have begun their work by insisting that the whole direction of critical thought must be changed. But of Richards alone can it be said that against all odds he succeeded; modern literary criticism has been remade according to his suggestions. Moreover, the techniques of close reading he developed have affected not only critical theory but the ways that most of us read poetry. Richards' insights color almost every course in literature, almost every book of critical analysis, almost every critic's personal stock of assumptions. For better or worse, he did set in motion the reform for which he had called.

What is the nature of that reform? To begin with, Richards asks a set of questions which hardly concerned earlier critics; above all, the question "What gives the experience of reading a certain poem its value?" The words "experience" and "value," along with the word "communication," dominate much of *Principles of Literary Criticism.* They are words that refer not so much to aesthetics as to mental processes, or psychology; and the first principle of Richards' criticism is to recast aesthetic questions in psychological terms. In place of a criticism that seeks to define the forms of works of art or to compare poetry to the world it imitates, Richards sets a criticism that seeks to describe the workings of the mind. "Few competent persons are nowadays so deluded as actually to hold the mystical view that there is a quality Beauty which inheres or attaches to external objects, yet throughout all the discussion of works of art the drag exercised by language towards this view can be felt. . . . Whether we are discussing music, poetry, painting, sculpture or architecture, we are forced to speak as though certain physical objects—vibrations of strings and of columns of air, marks printed on paper, canvases and pigments, masses of marble, fabrics of freestone, are what we are talking about. And yet the remarks we make as critics do not apply to such objects but to states of mind, to experiences." The honest critic, according to this view, will demystify his language by ceasing to talk about abstract entities he can never know, and by speaking instead about something he knows very well: the effects of art upon the mind.

Such an emphasis upon mental processes, and upon the ways they are expressed through language, had been characteristic of Richards' work from the start. Born in 1893, he read Moral Sciences at Magdalene College, Cambridge (A.B., 1915), at a time when Cambridge philosophers like G. E. Moore, Bertrand Russell, and Ludwig Wittgenstein were redirecting philosophy toward an empirical study of the operations of language. The conjunction of modern linguistics with modern psychology convinced Richards and many of his contemporaries that, like the philosophers, they had hold of a magnificent new instrument of analysis: a way of tracing all ideas to their roots in mental experience. Psychology was the field, and linguistic analysis the method, through which age-old questions might finally be resolved. Thus Richards' first book, *The Foundations of Aesthetics* (1922), written in collaboration with C. K. Ogden and James Wood, considers an ancient mystery, What is Beauty?, and gives a decisive modern answer: "synaesthesis," a harmonious state of feeling. His next book, *The Meaning of Meaning* (1923), also written with Ogden, takes the next logical step, and tries to describe the whole set of experiences we call "meaning." Like Wittgenstein (or Charles Sanders Peirce, the American pragmatist much admired by Richards), Richards seeks meaning not so much in the absolute significations of words as in the way words "behave," the way they are used by people for symbolic or emotive effect. Words have no life of their own, though primitive people may believe in such "word magic." Rather, "a language transaction or a communication may be defined as a use of symbols in such a way that acts of reference occur in a hearer which are similar in all relevant respects to those which are symbolised by them in the speaker" (*The Meaning of Meaning*, p. 333). Similarly, the meaning of a work of art can only be understood in terms of the responses it induces in an attentive audience.

The Meaning of Meaning is a powerful book, because of the promise it carries: a solution to the problems of misunderstanding and illogic that blight daily life. Ogden and Richards tell us again and again that modern science has at last made possible a fruitful and accurate view of language. "A new Science, the Science of Symbolism, is now ready to emerge, and with it will come a new educational technique." Behind their work lies a profound faith in scientific method; they are therapists, doctors engaged in curing language from its sickness. Indeed, unsympathetic critics have objected that Richards' attitude toward poetry as well as language is basically clinical. Most of his interpretations (according to R. S. Crane) depend on the model of a stimulus-response experiment, like Pavlov's training of dogs, in which a reader gradually learns to align his responses with the signals given by the experimenter (or the poet). The stimulus of a poem challenges the reader to find an appropriate meaning, and to accommodate the signs transmitted by the text to his own understanding and feelings. By watching this process in turn, the critic will come to recognize the likely sources of confusion, to diagnose reading errors, and eventually to suggest possible cures. Finally, as a result of many such experiments, a whole new science may come to light, Richards' Science of Symbolism.

Whatever the merits of this theory, applied most fully in *Principles of Literary Criticism* (1924), its practical repercussions turned out to be revolutionary. A clinical analysis of reading, unlike other kinds of literary theory, can be put to the test. In 1929 Richards published the results of such tests in his most influential book, *Practical Criticism: A Study of Literary Judgment*. The book is based upon a very simple idea. Over a period of years Richards distributed printed sheets of poems, without identifying their authors, to groups of Cambridge undergraduates, who were invited to read them carefully, comment on them freely, and return their written comments (anonymously) at the end of the week. The heart of *Practical Criticism* consists of those comments, selected and annotated by Richards, along with his estimate of what they reveal about the way most of us read. Much care was taken to preserve an air of scientific objectivity; for instance, the comments are called "protocols." At any rate, few readers of the book would deny that the experiment worked. *Practical Criticism* exposes the actual and alarming truth of how people respond when confronted with a naked poem.

The truth is, most of us read badly. Our own preconceptions, our own expectations condition our ability to respond, and we force them into the words of the poem. Randall Jarrell once wrote that a good reader approaches a poem as he would approach a person, with curiosity and respect; but few readers exhibit so much good will. The protocols prickle with animus and defenses built against the poem, with a fatal lack of curiosity. Thus a reader of Hopkins' "Spring and Fall: to a young child" ("Margaret, are you grieving/ Over Goldengrove unleaving?") writes, "The thought is worthless, and hopelessly muddled. A nonsensical conglomeration of words. Expressed in jerky, disconnected phrases, without rhythm," condemning a thought he seems not to have taken the trouble to understand and a rhythm he has not bothered to analyze. Similarly, many readers are made nervous by poetic sentiment. "The Poet has used his technical perfection to express a common human failing to which he is subject, in veiled language; he is ashamed of it and only wishes to be understood by fellow sufferers (or cowards)." As Richards comments adroitly, "the reader's own revulsion at his own devious excesses is counted against the poet." The poems most approved by Richards' students tend to be those (like J. D. C. Pellew's "The Temple") that appeal to stock responses without making any demands; poems that demand a more complicated or ironic response (like D. H. Lawrence's "Piano" or Longfellow's "In the Churchyard at Cambridge") tend to be heartily disliked. Nor can one trust the mass of readers to construe the plain sense of even the most transparent poem.

What accounts for such bad reading? Richards himself supplies some shrewd psychological explanations, most famously in a chapter of *Practical Criticism* called "Irrelevant Associations and Stock Responses." The thrust of his argument is that reading occurs not in the poem but in ourselves, and that few people possess the flexibility and harmony of mind that will open them to the poem rather than close them in their own narcissistic and obstinate set of ideas. Given Longfellow's poem about a lady who lies in a churchyard, for instance, many readers expect a kind of sermon, and either recoil from the platitudes they insist on finding, or blame the poet for having frustrated them by composing something unexpectedly light and urbane. Every one of us, if he is honest, will confess to similar errors. In a certain frame of mind, we all project our own train of thought or emotion onto a work of art and then, like as not, criticize it for our own distortions. Indeed, *Practical Criticism* seems to prove that poems criticize *us*; each of our flaws of character, each of our quirks of mind, stands out in critical commentary as vividly as if thrown upon a screen. A poem, like a Rorschach test, mirrors the mind of the beholder, and because poems demand far more sensitive and sincere responses than ink blots, the cracks they reveal are far more graphic.

Lest we despair entirely of readers, however, we should notice an argument often urged against Richards' experiment: "unhistorical readings are bad readings." By deliberately suppressing such vital information as the author of the poem, the time when it was written, even the title, *Practical Criticism* sets up conditions that almost guarantee its poor results. A few facts—a poem about "the king of all our hearts" is called "For the Eightieth Birthday of George Meredith"—would clear up many of the worst blunders. A similar argument is often made against the experiments of behaviorist psychologists. Rats are forced to run mazes, for instance, rather than to steal cheese, because they are so much worse at the former than the latter. Thus the psychologist can control his experiment thoroughly, chart dramatic changes in the capacity of his subjects as they improve, and record those extreme responses that make for an impressive learning curve. In the same way, Richards provokes extremes of misreading by creating a situation in which people are too ignorant to read well. Richards is not immune to this argument. He is not above tampering with a poem (for example, dropping the third and fourth lines of "Spring and Fall") to lure his readers into more instructive mistakes. In an experiment with "Fifteen Lines from Landor" reported in *Speculative Instruments* (1955), he concludes by quoting the opening three lines of the poem, "omitted by me in this experiment to heighten the difficulty," and remarks that "I do not think that their presence would have made much difference to the comments." But such a remark clearly begs the question; the experiment loses its scientific validity as soon as it contrives its methods to arrange a desired result. Richards' methods may help to make bad readers as well as to find them.

Nevertheless, the lessons of *Practical Criticism* can hardly be ignored. Every college class in literature supplies a laboratory for testing Richards' results, and on the whole teachers who have repeated his experiment (like the editors of this book) have witnessed that their own students read just as badly. Nor would many critics be justified in complacency about their own performance. Evidently the whole process of reading a poem, simple as it may seem, is extraordinarily difficult. It requires a sacrifice of self, a relaxation of the will, of which few men are capable, as well as a vast reserve of experience and information. Richards himself, attempting to describe an ideal reader, pictures a kind of secular saint, modeled on Confucian doctrines of sincerity: the self-complete man, harmonious and ordered, whose mind, "being more at one within itself . . . thereby becomes more appropriately responsive to the outer world." But self-complete men, like ideal readers, are rare.

Just because poetry so powerfully exposes the limitations of readers, however, it can go far to heal them. Richards uses his experiment to suggest that poetry has a unique civilizing virtue. Poems evoke and master an immense complication of human response, and they force their readers to extend their own responses. By reading a poem again and again, by subjecting ourselves to the discipline of critical analysis, we gradually refine ourselves; we become at last "sincere." Thus the humanities offer men a method of organizing and concentrating their experiences. In *Science and Poetry* (1926; reissued as *Poetries and Sciences*, 1970), a popularization of *Principles of Literary Criticism*, Richards mounts an eloquent defense of poetry as a source of value. Scientific statements, he argues, are justified only by their truth; they deal with existent objects and certifiable facts—with fixities and definites, as the mentor of Richards' most searching book, *Coleridge on Imagination* (1934), might say. Poetic statements, on the other hand, are not obliged to be true or false. Rather, the strength of poetry is what Richards calls, in a somewhat unfortunate phrase, the pseudo-statement, "a form of words which is justified entirely by its effect in releasing or organizing our impulses and attitudes." Most conversation falls into a similar category; we speak to elicit a response, not to point at an object. Indeed, as Wittgenstein pointed out, even the arguments of philosophers are basically *sprachspiele*, "language-games," not significations of things. Pseudo-statement is the means by which human emotions interact and develop. Far from being inferior to scientific description, it is more vital to the way men function as biological organisms, or adapt themselves to cope with the world.

In training people to be more sincere (in Richards' sense of "harmonious"), poetry above all other sorts of pseudo-statement has two distinct advantages: its disinterestedness and its profundity. Unlike advertising, politics, or other attempts to organize our impulses, poems make no special claim upon us; the profit, if we respond to Milton or Keats, is ours, not the poet's. Poetry is liberating because it does not *use* us. Moreover, it asks for a tremendous depth of response. To interpret the best poems, we need to draw on every resource at our command, our keenest intelligence, our most sensitive feelings. Reading poetry, therefore, and learning to read it better, can give students practice at becoming more attentive and more harmoniously functioning human beings. Poetry, Richards has written, "is capable of saving us, or since some have found a scandal in this word, of preserving us or rescuing us from confusion and frustration" (*Science and Poetry*, 1935).

The scope of such a claim for the effects of poetry is intentionally daring and extravagant. Richards associates his position with words of Matthew Arnold—"The future of poetry is immense"—but in fact Richards goes far beyond Arnold, since he implies that the experience of reading poetry can substitute for culture. The study of poems, for Richards, furnishes each of us a personal alternative to the broad norms of culture, by allowing each man a "pseudo-culture" of his own, a personal method for harmonizing his responses. The humanities are to be justified by psychology, not by tradition. In "The Modern Mind" (reprinted above), T. S. Eliot replies that Richards has put poetry in the place of religion, thus "leading the reader to look in poetry for religious satisfactions." Yet to charge Richards with an elementary confusion of poetry and religion would be unfair. More than with poetry itself, he is concerned with human potential, and he champions poetry not because it offers final truths but because it induces men to realize their potentials. Richards promulgates no dogma, no doctrine; he hopes only to teach men to teach themselves. He is primarily, in other words, an educator.

That emphasis on education led Richards to many strange byways in his later career—to China and Harvard, where during the 1930's and 1940's he set up programs in Basic English; to Walt Disney studios, where in 1943 he devised a film to teach English to beginners. The logic of this development has been clear. Having discovered in his early studies how badly people read, Richards took the alternative to despair, and set out to improve reading techniques both by simplifying the difficulty of language and by improving methods of interpretation. Basic English, a streamlined language invented by C. K. Ogden, Richards' collaborator, was designed to enable illiterates and foreign students to master the essentials they need for understanding. But Richards' ambitions for education are far greater. More and more it has seemed to him that the flaws of interpretation displayed by his students account for the greater misunderstandings between people and nations that plague our world. Although Richards has never entirely abandoned literary criticism, he has increasingly devoted himself to more basic problems of interpretation. One of his most recent books, *Design for Escape: World Education through Modern Media* (1968), advocates using all our contemporary resources for one essential purpose: teaching people, through language, how to use their minds. Poetry too must be an instrument of that purpose. "The quality of our living—not only of our thinking, but of our feeling, desiring, willing, and the rest—is most intimately mixed up with the state of order-disorder within our lexical-structural would-be system. And Poetry, as I have been saying, is our exemplar of that would-be system at its most entire—being most itself" ("The Future of Poetry," *So Much Nearer*, 1968, p. 176).

Perhaps Richards' major influence, however, has been in a more narrow field, the close analysis of literary texts. Once again, the experiments that led to *Practical Criticism* played a major role. The varying interpretations that students apply to a poem may be seen as the result of their mistakes, but often it is obvious that the poem itself justifies many kinds of reading. Many coherent responses, many contradictory possibilities of interpretation, seem to lurk within a single poetic text or word. Thus Richards points out that in Hopkins' line, "And yet you will weep and know why," a great change in meaning can be induced by removing the accent from "will." "Then the accents may fall on 'weep' and on 'and'; the sense being that in the future she will know the reason for a sorrow that is now only a blind grief. When 'will' is accentuated it ceases to be an auxiliary verb and becomes the present tense of the verb 'to will.' She persists in weeping and in demanding the reason for the falling of the leaves, and perhaps also for her grief. The rhythmical difference made by the change of sense is immense. Both the sense and the movement rejected by the poet are very good, however, and doubtless some readers will privately retain them." The implications of the last sentence are far-reaching. Evidently readers may be justified in retaining meanings that the poet may not have intended, or even consciously rejected. Richards makes room for multiple responses to a text, and suggests that nothing can confer authority on a particular interpretation but the sincerity or profundity of the response itself.

In 1927, as Richards was conducting his experiments, Robert Graves and Laura Riding published A *Survey of Modernist Poetry,* which demonstrated that the original, lightly punctuated version of Shakespeare's sonnet 129, "Th' expense of spirit in a waste of shame," plays with a fascinating wealth of equivocal meanings—"had," for instance, "may mean the swallowing of the bait by the taker, or the catching of the taker by the bait, or 'lust had,' or 'had by lust.' " The same year a twenty-one-year-old student of Richards went off for two weeks to draft a 30,000 word manuscript. The student was William Empson; the manuscript became *Seven Types of Ambiguity* (1930). In this seminal work, stimulated both by Richards and by the Graves-Riding analysis, Empson brilliantly applies the lessons of his master. Text after text is scrutinized with a freedom of response and an alertness to alternative possibilities that turn lines of poetry into a web of interwoven meanings, as fascinating, as changeable, as lovely, as difficult to fix, as Keats's Lamia. Empson does not attempt to arrive at an interpretation of a poem but to show that even the simplest poem resists simple interpretation: the multiplicity is all. The formal categories of ambiguity he constructs are less impressive than the example of his own lively and protean responses at work. Commenting on Richards' analysis of "And yet you will weep and know why," for instance, he demonstrates that the ambiguities, which Richards seems to have thought more or less accidental, can be read into the very fabric of the poem; the contrast between two sorts of weeping (willful present or sorrowful future) or two sorts of knowledge (intuitive and intellectual) may point the poem toward a type of ambiguity "when two or more meanings of a statement do not agree among themselves, but combine to make clear a more complicated state of mind in the author." Whatever we may think of such readings, the complicated state of mind they display in the critic is infectious. Few readers, after Empson, have been able to believe that interpreting a poem requires no art. Henry James's criticism of fiction put an end to the "comfortable, good-humored feeling abroad that a novel is a novel, as a pudding is a pudding, and that our only business with it could be to swallow it"; Empson's criticism of poetry helped put an end to readers who swallow poems.

Richards' own criticism, however, tends to concentrate less upon ambiguity of meaning than upon the way that many meanings can be synthesized by a poetic structure. For him the fascination of poetry resides in its power of mastering and organizing the complications it calls forth. It was almost inevitable, therefore, that he should be haunted by the poet and critic who above all others sought to describe an organic ideal of poetry: Samuel Taylor Coleridge. In *Coleridge on Imagination,* Richards argues that Coleridge refuses—like Richards himself—to separate his theory of value from his psychology, and thus constructs a theory of Imagination that does justice to the unity of mental process. No less than "the whole soul of man in activity," or a language that, like Coleridge's wind harp, constantly adjusts the trembling balance between the world and the mind, can satisfy a critic who looks to poetry to heal the divided consciousness of the mass of men.

The practical result of Richards' search for synthesis is his emphasis upon the syntheses made by poems. Following Coleridge, Richards creates a poetics based on tensions and balances—as Shakespeare's genius, according to both critics, perfectly assimilates both art and nature, blending the two into one. A successful poem, on this theory, may be known by the quantity and complication of impulses it is able to unify. A poor poem will fail through winning its unity too cheaply, by appealing to a limited stock of responses; a good poem will risk such complex responses that it wins its balance against the odds. Hence Richards, unlike the great majority of critics, actually commits himself to a theory of poetic value, and insists that valid principles of literary criticism will be able to distinguish good work from bad. Several corollaries follow from this notion. Since sentiment pleads for one particular feeling at the expense of all others, it imposes a radical limitation on possible responses; sentimental poetry, therefore, can never attain to the highest value. Ironic poetry, on the other hand, refrains from directing our impulses into too narrow a channel; therefore, when a rich irony is compatible with a high degree of organization, a poem may accumulate value through reading after reading.

Here Richards' theory builds a foundation for the movement we still know (now rather nostalgically) as the New Criticism. A poetics of tensions, elimination of contexts outside the poem, close linguistic analysis of images and metaphors, a love of irony, all became absorbed into the practice of the next generation of critics, particularly in America. John Crowe Ransom's important study, *The New Criticism* (1941), begins with a full-length essay on Richards, and in spite of some tactful objections to Richards' psychological bias Ransom obviously believes that criticism has entered a new and better era; *Seven Types of Ambiguity*, he says, "is the most imaginative account of readings ever printed, and Empson the closest and most resourceful reader that poetry has yet publicly had." A similar influence underlies the anthology *Understanding Poetry* (1938), by Cleanth Brooks and Robert Penn Warren, which for another generation trained college students in techniques of reading. Nor has the influence faded even now. Today the school of New Critics seems to have passed into history, but their methods of close reading can be discerned not far below the surface of most serious analysis of poetry.

Nevertheless, Richards' own literary criticism does not follow the line of his influence on others; he is no more a New Critic than Marx was a Marxist. In spite of his enormous effect on techniques of close reading, he has published few analyses of poems. Some critics have gone so far as to maintain that he will survive primarily as a theorist or apologist for poetry, who lacks the literary sensitivity to write practical criticism of any special merit. Surely this argument is wrong. Many students exposed to Richards as a teacher will testify that he responds to poems with a vigor and subtlety of judgment that few critics can match. More-

over, his own occasional comments in print, for instance on Donne's
First Anniversary in "The Interactions of Words" (*The Language of
Poetry*, ed. Allen Tate, 1942), bear witness to a reader extraordinary for
his relish and insight. It is this reader who gives life to *Practical Criticism*; he sits tactfully behind the scenes, yet comes forward in glimpses
to correct a mistake, point to a superficial interpretation, deepen the
meaning of a phrase, establish the emotional climate suitable to a line,
suggest a more sincere response, clarify an idea—until we realize that,
with the unobtrusiveness that only the best teachers achieve, he has
taught us by example a whole new method of reading.

Why then has Richards given us so few instances of his own practical criticism? Perhaps a part of the answer is that he refuses to believe
that interpretation of a poem can be definitive. Much of the most impressive New Criticism has been predicated (intentionally or not) upon
the assumption that a poem is a sort of puzzle that an alert reader can
solve. By reaching the point of analysis at which the poem's form and
content are seen to be inextricable, such critics arrive at elegant interpretative solutions. But Richards tends to believe that poems are problems *without* solutions. In a recent essay, suggestively titled "How Does
a Poem Know When It Is Finished?" (1963), he describes poems as
"living, feeling, knowing *beings* in their own right; the so-called metaphor that treats a poem as organic is not a metaphor, but a literal description. A poem is an activity, seeking to become itself." It follows
that even the best critical examination of a poem will fix it in an artificial posture that distorts its living reality. "The examining eye—the descriptive instrument or screen by which [the poem] is held stable for
observation and appraisal—can and frequently does reform it. The
proper moral to draw might be: *Let us not lose the poem in our account
of it.*" Richards' own criticism seldom makes the mistake of trying to
substitute its own formulations for the poem. Typically, his lively intellect dances around a poem, throwing out clues and inklings, without
pretending to achieve a conclusive judgment.

Indeed, it is the experimental, playful quality of Richards' criticism
that teaches us most about his response to poetry. So far from dogmatic,
he can be an unpredictable critic, leaping from point to point as he
shares the excitement of a new experience. The lines "To and fro/
Across the fretted snow/ Figures, footprints, shadows go," for instance,
from his own poem "Harvard Yard in April: April in Harvard Yard,"
spur him to this comment on "fretted": "The illuminating Dictionary
adds a comment on *gnaw at* which pleased me when I saw it. It says,
'Now only of small animals.' A mouse, I suppose, can fret a bit of
cheese (as a fret saw does plywood); but when a grizzly bear chaws up
a man, that isn't fretting. I liked that; it seemed to offer my line a spice
of meaning I had not been aware of. It turned the people who had been
leaving all those tracks on the snow into only small animals after all and
gave a diminishing-glass sharpness to the scene" (*Goodbye Earth*,
1958). The sense of discovery is strong in such passages. Each time

Richards reads a poem, he seems to react with freshly minted feelings, and to conduct "experiments in multiple definition" (the subtitle of *Mencius on the Mind*, 1932). Poetry does not furnish him with occasions for displaying an analytical technique; it serves to make his world new.

A similar willingness to experiment helps account for Richards' provocative and controversial style. From the first that style has offended men of letters. Brash, assertive, enormously confident, it seems to announce a ruthless scientific bias that will sweep away the tactful niceties of literary discourse. Thus the diagram that accompanies "The Analysis of a Poem" (reprinted below) reduces an object of art to a psychological "hieroglyph." Even the style of Richards' later criticism, which is notably more qualified and tentative, can bristle with scientific jargon dismaying to a literary ear. Yet the positive air with which Richards sometimes tells us he has settled the major questions of aesthetics should not deceive us. He evokes science not to diminish works of art but to bring to them "the celebrated open-mindedness, the suspension of judgment, and the hypothetical procedure that figure in so many accounts of scientific inquiry." His style, like his experimental method, is intended to free poems from the prettified automatic responses with which critics have encrusted them. And Richards' effect on literary criticism, even on those critics who disapprove of his manner, has been liberating.

Moreover, all Richards' quirks of style tend toward an incisive purpose: he shocks his readers into the future. No other critic so regularly appeals to the future rather than the past to justify his arguments. In *Speculative Instruments* (1955) Richards coined a word he has come to use often: "feed-forward." A complement to "feedback," especially as used in cybernetics, "feed-forward" represents the purposive activity that points us toward discoveries, on the principle that "We do not *find* anything unless we *know* what we are looking for." Richards maintains that his major professional preoccupations, criticism and pedagogy, "constitute two fairly high-level feed-forward systems"; and in relation to his own work, at least, the claim can hardly be denied. He has always experimented with designs for a better criticism; he has always tried to feed the future of poetry.

Such devotion to the future gives Richards' career a rare consistency. *Principles of Literary Criticism*, his earliest "machine to think with," is charged with the excitement of an explorer; the new psychology, the new aesthetics, will transform all our theories of value. "The controversies which the world has known in the past are as nothing to those which are ahead. I would wish this book to be regarded as a contribution towards these choices of the future." Forty-six years later, in his review of "Jakobson's Shakespeare," he is just as excited: "Those who take poetry, and what it might do for man, seriously may think, indeed, of these new revelations of order as a powerful helping hand offered to us in this time of frightened and bewildered disaffection." Returning to

the same sonnet whose ambiguities Graves and Riding had once analyzed, he still looks forward; he continues to search for a more precise
critical statement and for values men can use.

A Note on Sources

The literary criticism of Ivor Armstrong Richards (1893–   ) is expressed most fully by three books: *Principles of Literary Criticism*
(1924), a theoretical "machine to think with"; *Practical Criticism*
(1929), "a study of literary judgment"; and *Coleridge on Imagination*
(1934), a search for an organic understanding of language and poetry.
Each of these volumes has a companion: *Science and Poetry* (1926)
spells out the implications of *Principles, Interpretation in Teaching*
(1938) experiments with practical criticism of prose, and *The Philosophy of Rhetoric* (1936) applies Coleridge's conceptions of imaginative
growth to language. *Speculative Instruments* (1955) and *So Much
Nearer* (1968) include a few essays in literary criticism. Several of Richards' other books also touch on criticism, among them *The Foundations
of Aesthetics* (with C. K. Ogden and James Wood, 1922), *The Meaning of Meaning* (with Ogden, 1923), *Mencius on the Mind* (1932),
How to Read a Page (1942), and *Design for Escape* (1968). His poems
are collected in *Goodbye Earth* (1958) and *The Screens* (1960). Among
the rare examples of Richards' practical criticism, "Gerard Hopkins,"
The Dial (1926), and "The Interactions of Words," in *The Language
of Poetry*, ed. Allen Tate (1942), are notable. A convenient way to follow the development of his thought is through comparison of the original *Science and Poetry* (1926) with the revised versions of 1935 and
1970—the last, entitled *Poetries and Sciences*, includes an important
commentary.

More has been written on Richards' theory than on that of any other
modern literary critic. Historically important are T. S. Eliot, "The
Modern Mind" (1933; reprinted above); R. P. Blackmur, "A Critic's
Job of Work," *The Double Agent* (1935); F. R. Leavis, "Dr. Richards,
Bentham and Coleridge," *Scrutiny* (1935); John Crowe Ransom, "I. A.
Richards: the Psychological Critic," *The New Criticism* (1941); and
Stanley Edgar Hyman, "I. A. Richards and the Criticism of Interpretation," *The Armed Vision* (1948). Two full-length studies have appeared recently: W. H. N. Hotopf, *Language, Thought and Comprehension: A Case Study of the Writings of I. A. Richards* (1965), a long
and unfriendly analysis of Richards' linguistic theories; and Jerome P.
Schiller, *I. A. Richards' Theory of Literature* (1969), a sympathetic
attempt to define and improve Richards' critical position. Schiller includes a useful bibliography.

From *Principles of Literary Criticism*

(1924)

XVI. THE ANALYSIS OF A POEM

*Toutes choses sont dites déjà, mais comme personne
n'écoute il faut toujours recommencer.*
ANDRÉ GIDE.

THE QUALIFICATIONS of a good critic are three. He must be an adept at experiencing, without eccentricities, the state of mind relevant to the work of art he is judging. Secondly, he must be able to distinguish experiences from one another as regards their less superficial features. Thirdly, he must be a sound judge of values.

Upon all these matters psychology, even in its present conjectural state, has a direct bearing. The critic is, throughout, judging of experiences, of states of mind; but too often he is needlessly ignorant of the general psychological form of the experiences with which he is concerned. He has no clear ideas as to the elements present or as to their relative importance. Thus, an outline or schema of the mental events which make up the experience of "looking at" a picture or "reading" a poem, can be of great assistance. At the very least an understanding of the probable structures of these experiences can remove certain miscon-

From *The Principles of Literary Criticism* by I. A. Richards. Reprinted by permission of Harcourt Brace Jovanovich, Inc.

ceptions which tend to make the opinions of individuals of less service to other individuals than need be.

Two instances will show this. There are certain broad features in which all agree a poem of Swinburne is unlike a poem of Hardy. The use of words by the two poets is different. Their methods are dissimilar, and the proper approach for a reader differs correspondingly. An attempt to read them in the same way is unfair to one of the poets, or to both, and leads inevitably to defects in criticism which a little reflection would remove. It is absurd to read Pope as though he were Shelley, but the essential differences cannot be clearly marked out unless such an outline of the general form of a poetic experience, as is here attempted, has been provided. The psychological means employed by these poets are demonstrably different. Whether the effects are also dissimilar is a further question for which the same kind of analysis is equally required.

This separation inside the poetic experience of certain parts which are means from certain other parts which are the ends upon which the poetic value of the experience depends, leads up to our other instance. It is unquestionable that the actual experiences, which even good critics undergo when reading, as we say, *the same poem*, differ very widely. In spite of certain conventions, which endeavour to conceal these inevitable discrepancies for social purposes, there can be no doubt that the experiences of readers in connection with particular poems are rarely similar. This is unavoidable. Some differences are, however, much more important than others. Provided the ends, in which the value of the poem lies, are attained, differences in the means need not prevent critics from agreement or from mutual service. Those discrepancies alone are fatal which affect the fundamental features of experiences, the features upon which their *value* depends. But enough is now known of the ways in which minds work for superficial and fundamental parts of experiences to be distinguished. One of the greatest living critics praises the line:

The fringed curtain of thine eyes advance,

for the "ravishing beauty" of the visual images excited. This common mistake of exaggerating personal accidents in the means by which a poem attains its end into the chief value of the poem is due to excessive trust in the commonplaces [1] of psychology.

In the analysis of the experience of reading a poem, a diagram, or hieroglyph, is convenient, provided that its limitations are clearly recognised. The spatial relations of the parts of the diagram, for instance, are not intended to stand for spatial relations between parts of what is represented; it is not a picture of the nervous system. Nor are temporal relations

[1] The description of images belongs to the first steps in psychology, and it is often possible to judge the rank and standing of a psychologist by the degree of importance which he attaches to their peculiarities. On theoretical grounds it seems probable that they are luxury products (cf. *The Meaning of Meaning*, pp. 148–151) peculiarly connected with the reproduction of emotion. For a discussion of some experimental investigations into their utility, Spearman, *The Nature of Intelligence*, Ch. XII, may be consulted.

intended. Spatial metaphors, whether drawn as diagrams or merely imagined, are dangers only to the unwary. The essential service which pictures can give in abstract matters, namely, the simultaneous and compact representation of states of affairs which otherwise tend to remain indistinct and confused, is worth the slight risk of misunderstanding which they entail.

We may begin then with a diagrammatic representation of the events which take place when we read a poem. Other literary experiences will only differ from this in their greater simplicity.

The eye is depicted as reading a succession of printed words. As a result there follows a stream of reaction in which six distinct kinds of events may be distinguished.

I. The visual sensations of the printed words.

II. Images very closely associated with these sensations.

III. Images relatively free.

IV. References to, or "thinkings of," various things.

V. Emotions.

VI. Affective-volitional attitudes.

Each of these kinds of occurrences requires some brief description and explanation.

Upon the visual sensations of the printed words all the rest depends (in the case of a reader not previously acquainted with the poem); but with most readers they have in themselves no great importance. The individual shapes of the letters, their size and spacing, have only a minor effect upon the whole reaction. No doubt readers differ greatly in this respect; with some, familiarity plays a great part. They find it unpleasant and disturbing to read a poem in any but the edition in which they first became acquainted with it. But the majority of readers are less exigent. Provided that the print is clear and legible, and allows the habitual eye-movements of reading to be easily performed, the full response arises equally well from widely differing sensations. Those for whom this is true have, in

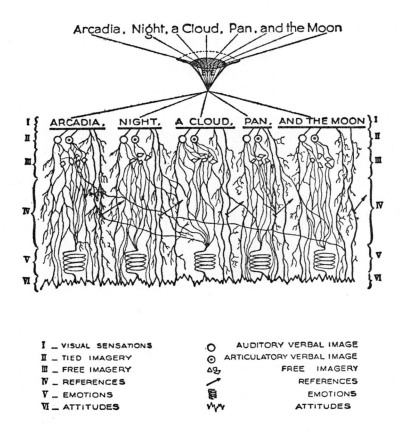

Arcadia, Night, a Cloud, Pan, and the Moon

ARCADIA, NIGHT, A CLOUD, PAN, AND THE MOON

I — VISUAL SENSATIONS
II — TIED IMAGERY
III — FREE IMAGERY
IV — REFERENCES
V — EMOTIONS
VI — ATTITUDES

○ AUDITORY VERBAL IMAGE
⊙ ARTICULATORY VERBAL IMAGE
Δ☊ FREE IMAGERY
⟋ REFERENCES
 EMOTIONS
ᾙᾙᾙ ATTITUDES

the present state of economic organisation, a decided advantage over the more fastidious. This does not show that good printing is a negligible consideration; and the primary place of calligraphy in the Chinese arts is an indication to the contrary. It shows merely that printing belongs to another branch of the arts. In the poetic experience words take effect through their associated images, and through what we are, as a rule, content to call their meaning. What meaning is and how it enters into the experience we shall consider.

TIED IMAGES

Visual sensations of words do not commonly occur by themselves. They have certain regular companions so closely tied to them as to be only with difficulty disconnected. The chief of these are the auditory image—the sound of the words in the mind's ear—and the image of articulation—the feel in the lips, mouth, and throat, of what the words would be like to speak.

Auditory images of words are among the most obvious of mental happenings. Any line of verse or prose slowly read, will, for most people, sound mutely in the imagination somewhat as it would if read aloud. But the degree of correspondence between the image-sounds, and the actual sounds that the reader would produce, varies enormously. Many people are able to imagine word-sounds with greater delicacy and discrimination than they can utter them. But the reverse case is also found. What importance then is to be attached to clear, rich and delicate sound imagery in silent reading? How far must people who differ in their capacity to produce such images differ in their total reactions to poems? And what are the advantages of reading aloud? Here we reach one of the practical problems of criticism for which this analysis is required. A discussion is best postponed until the whole analysis has been given. The principal confusion which prevents a clear understanding of the point at issue does, however, concern images and may be dealt with here. It is of great importance in connection with the topic of the following section.

The sensory qualities of images, their vivacity, clearness, fullness of detail and so on, do not bear any constant relation to their effects. Images differing in these respects may have closely similar consequences. Too much importance has always been attached to the sensory qualities of images. What gives an image efficacy is less its vividness as an image than its character as a mental event peculiarly connected with sensation. It is, in a way which no one yet knows how to explain, a relict of sensation and our intellectual and emotional response to it depends far more upon its being, through this fact, a representative of a sensation, than upon its sensory resemblance to one. An image may lose almost all its sensory nature to the point of becoming scarcely an image at all, a mere skeleton, and yet represent a sensation quite as adequately as if it were flaring with hallucinatory vividity. In other words, what matters is not the sensory *resemblance* of an image to the sensation which is its prototype, but some other relation, at present hidden from us in the jungles of neurology.

Care then should be taken to avoid the natural tendency to suppose that the more clear and vivid an image the greater will be its efficacy. There are trustworthy people who, according to their accounts, never experience

any imagery at all. If certain views commonly expressed about the arts are true, by which vivid imagery is an all-important part of the experience, then these people are incapable of art experiences, a conclusion which is contrary to the facts. The views in question are overlooking the fact that *something* takes the place of vivid images in these people, and that, provided the image-substitute is efficacious, their lack of mimetic imagery is of no consequence. The efficacy required must, of course, include control over emotional as well as intellectual reactions. Needless perhaps to add that with persons of the image-producing types an increase in delicacy and vivacity in their imagery will probably be accompanied by increased subtlety in effects. Thus it is not surprising that certain great poets and critics have been remarkable for the vigour of their imagery, and dependent upon it. No one would deny the usefulness of imagery to some people; the mistake is to suppose that it is indispensable to all.

Articulatory imagery is less noticeable; yet the quality of silent speech is perhaps even more dependent upon these images than upon sound-images. Collocations of syllables which are awkward or unpleasant to utter are rarely delightful to the ear. As a rule the two sets of images are so intimately connected that it is difficult to decide which is the offender. In "Heaven, which man's generation draws," the sound doubtless is as harsh as the movements required are cramping to the lips.

The extent to which interference with one set of images will change the other may be well seen by a simple experiment. Most people, if they attempt a silent recitation while opening the mouth to its fullest stretch or holding the tongue firmly between the teeth, will notice curious transformations in the auditory images. How the experiment should be interpreted is uncertain, but it is of use in making the presence of both kinds of verbal imagery evident to those who may have overlooked them hitherto. Images of articulation should not, however, be confused with those minimal actual movements which for some people (for all, as behaviourists maintain) accompany the silent rehearsing of words.

These two forms of tied imagery might also be called verbal images, and supply the elements of what is called the "formal structure" of poetry. They differ from those to which we now proceed in being images of words, not of things words stand for, and in their very close connection with the visual sensations of printed words.

FREE IMAGERY

Free images, or rather one form of these, visual images, pictures in the mind's eye, occupy a prominent place in the literature of criticism, to the neglect somewhat of other forms of imagery, since, as was remarked in a preceding chapter, for every possible kind of sensation there is a corresponding possible image.

The assumption, natural before investigation, that all attentive and sensitive readers will experience the same images, vitiates most of the historical discussions from that of Longinus to that of Lessing. Even in the present day, when there is no excuse for such ignorance, the mistake still thrives, and an altogether too crude, too hasty, and too superficial form of criticism is allowed to pass unchallenged. It cannot be too clearly recognised that individuals differ not only in the type of imagery which they employ, but still more in the particular images which they produce. In their whole reactions to a poem, or to a single line of it, their free images are the point at which two readings are most likely to differ, and the fact that they differ may very well be quite immaterial. Fifty different readers will experience not one common picture but fifty different pictures. If the value of the poem derived from the value *qua* picture of the visual image excited then criticism might well despair. Those who would stress this part of the poetic reaction can have but crude views on pictures.

But if the value of the visual image in the experience is not pictorial, if the image is not to be judged as a picture, how is it to be judged? It is improbable that the many critics, some of them peculiarly well qualified in the visual arts, who have insisted upon the importance of imagery, have been entirely wasting their time. It ought to be possible to give an account of the place of free imagery in the whole poetic experience which will explain this insistence. What is required will be found if we turn our attention from the sensory qualities of the imagery to the more fundamental qualities upon which its efficacy in modifying the rest of the experience depends. It has been urged above that images which are different in their sensory qualities may have the same effects. If this were not the case the absence of glaring differences between people of different image-type would be astonishing. But since images may represent sensations without resembling them, and represent them in the sense of replacing them, as far as effects in directing thought and arousing emotion go, differences in their mimetic capacity become of minor importance. As we have seen, it is natural for those whose imagery is vivid, to suppose that vivacity and clearness go together with power over thought and feeling. It is the power of an image over these that is as a rule being praised when an intelligent and sensitive critic appears merely to be praising the picture floating before his mind's eye. To judge the image as a picture is judged, would, as we have seen, be absurd; and what is sought in poetry by those painters and others whose interest in the world is primarily visual is not pictures but records of observation, or stimuli of emotion.

Thus, provided the images (or image-substitutes for the imageless) have the due effects, deficiencies in their sensory aspect do not matter. But the proviso is important. In all forms of imagery sensory deficiencies are for many people signs and accompaniments of defective efficacy, and the habit of reading so as to allow the fullest development to imagery in its sensory aspect is likely to encourage the full development of this more essential feature, its efficacy, if the freaks and accidents of the sensory side are not taken too seriously.

Some exceptions to this general recommendation will occur to the reader. Instances in plenty may be found in which a full development of the sensory aspect of images is damaging to their effects. Meredith is a master of this peculiar kind of imagery:

> Thus piteously Love closed what he begat
> The union of this ever diverse pair!
> These two were rapid falcons in a snare,
> Condemned to do the flitting of the bat.

The emotional as well as the intellectual effects of the various images here suggested are much impaired if we produce them vividly and distinctly.

IMPULSES AND REFERENCES

We have now to consider those more fundamental effects upon which stress has been laid above as the true places of the values of the experience. It will be well at this point to reconsult the diagram. The vertical lines which run capriciously downwards from the visual sensations of the words, through their tied imagery and onward to the bottom of the diagram, are intended to represent, schematically, streams of impulses flowing through in the mind.

They start in the visual sensations, but the depiction of the tied imagery is intended to show how much of their further course is due to it. The placing of the free imagery in the third division is intended to suggest that while some free images may arise from visual words alone, they take their character in a large part as a consequence of the tied imagery. Thus the great importance of the tied imagery, of the formal elements, is emphasised in the diagram.

These impulses are the weft of the experience, the warp being the pre-existing systematic structure of the mind, that organised system of possible impulses. The metaphor is of course inexact, since weft and warp here are not independent. Where these impulses run, and how they develop, depends entirely upon

the condition of the mind, and this depends upon the impulses which have previously been active in it. It will be seen then that impulses —their direction, their strength, how they modify one another—are the essential and fundamental things in any experience. All else, whether intellectual or emotional, arises as a consequence of their activity. The thin trickle of stimulation which comes in through the eye finds an immense hierarchy of systems of tendencies poised in the most delicate stability. It is strong enough and rightly enough directed to disturb some of these without assistance. The literal sense of a word can be grasped on the prompting of the mere sight of it, without hearing it or mentally pronouncing it. But the effects of this stimulation are immensely increased and widened when it is reinforced by fresh stimulation from tied images, and it is through these that most of the emotional effects are produced. As the agitation proceeds new reinforcement comes with every fresh system which is excited. Thus, the paradoxical fact that so trifling an irritation as the sight of marks on paper is able to arouse the whole energies of the mind becomes explicable.

To turn now to references, the only mental happenings which are as closely connected with visual words as their tied images are those mysterious events which are usually called thoughts. Thus the arrow symbol in the hieroglyph should perhaps properly be placed near the visual impression of the word. The mere sight of any familiar word is normally followed by a thought of whatever the word may stand for. This thought is sometimes said to be the "meaning," the literal or prose "meaning" of the word. It is wise, however, to avoid the use of "meaning" as a symbol altogether. The terms "thought" and "idea" are less subtle in their ambiguities, and when defined may perhaps be used without confusion.

What is essential in thought is its direction or reference to things. What is this direction or reference? How does a thought come to be "of" one thing rather than another? What is the link between a thought and what it is "of"? . . . Without a fairly clear, although, of course, incomplete view, it is impossible to avoid confusion and obscurity in discussing such topics as truth in art, the intellect-*versus*-emotion *imbroglio*, the scope of science, the nature of religion and many others with which criticism must deal.

The facts upon which speculations as to the relations between thoughts and the things which they are "of" have been based, have as a rule been taken from introspection. But the facts which introspection yields are notoriously uncertain, and the special position of the observer may well preclude success. Introspection is competent, in some cases, to discover the relations between events which take place within the mind, but cannot by itself give information as to the relations of these events with the external world, and it is precisely this which we are inquiring into when we ask, What connection is there between a thought and that which it is a thought of? For an answer to this question we must look further.

There is no doubt that causal relations hold between events in the mind and events outside it. Sometimes these relations are fairly simple. The striking of a clock is the cause of our thinking of its striking. In such a case the external thing is linked with the thought "of" it in a fairly direct fashion, and the view here taken is that to be a thought "of" the striking is to be merely a thought caused in this fashion by the striking. A thought of the striking is nothing else and nothing more than a thought caused by it.

But most thoughts are "of" things which are not present and not producing direct effects in the mind. This is so when we read. What is directly affecting the mind is words on paper, but the thoughts aroused are not thoughts "of" the words, but of other things which the words *stand for*. How, then, can a causal theory of thinking explain the relation between these remote things and the thoughts which are "of" them? To answer this we must look at the way in which we learn what words stand for. Without a process of learning we should only think of the words.

The process of learning to use words is not difficult to analyse. On a number of occasions the word is heard in connection with objects of a certain kind. Later the word is heard in the absence of any such object. In accordance with one of the few fundamental laws known about mental process, something then happens in the mind which is like what would happen if such an object were actually present and engaging the attention. The word has become a *sign* of an object of that kind. The word which formerly was a part of the cause of a certain effect in the mind is now followed by a similar effect in the absence of the rest of the previous cause, namely, an object of the kind in question. This kind of causation appears to be peculiar to living tissue. The relation now between the thought and what it is "of" is more indirect, the thought is "of" something which formerly was part cause, together with the sign, of similar thoughts. It is "of" the missing part of the sign, or more strictly "of" anything which would complete the sign as a cause.

Thoughts by this account are general, they are of anything *like* such and such things, except when the object thought of and the thought are connected by direct causal relations, as, for instance, when we think of a word we are hearing. Only when these direct relations hold can we succeed in thinking simply of "That." We have to think instead of "something of a kind." By various means, however, we can contrive that there shall only be one thing of the kind, and so the need for particularity in our thoughts is satisfied. The commonest way in which we do this is by thoughts which make the kind spatial and temporal. A thought of "mosquito" becomes a thought of "mosquito there now" by combining a thought of "thing of mosquito kind" with a thought of "thing of there kind" and a thought of "thing of now kind." The awkwardness of these phrases, it may be mentioned, is irrelevant. Combined thoughts of this sort, we may notice, are capable of truth and falsity, whereas a simple thought—of "whatever is now" for instance—can only be true. Whether a thought is true or false depends simply upon whether there is anything of the kind referred to, and there must be something now. It is by no means certain that there must be anything there always. And most probably no mosquito is where we thought it was then.

The natural generality and vagueness of all reference which is not made specific by the aid of space and time is of great importance for the understanding of the senses in which poetry may be said to be true.

In the reading of poetry the thought due simply to the words, their *sense* it may be called, comes first; but other thoughts are not of less importance. These may be due to the auditory verbal imagery, and we have onomatopoeia,[2] but this is rarely independent of the sense. More important are the further thoughts caused by the sense, the network of interpretation and conjecture which arises therefrom, with its opportunities for aberrations and misunderstanding. Poems, however, differ fundamentally in the extent to which such further interpretation is necessary. The mere sense without any further reflection is very often sufficient thought, in Swinburne, for instance, for the full response—

There glowing ghosts of flowers
Draw down, draw nigh;
And wings of swift spent hours
  Take flight and fly;
She sees by formless gleams
She hears across cold streams
  Dead mouths of many dreams that sing and
  sigh.

Little beyond vague thoughts of the things the words stand for is here required. They do not have to be brought into intelligible connection with one another. On the other hand, Hardy would rarely reach his full effect through sound and sense alone—

"Who's in the next room?—who?
    I seemed to see
Somebody in the dawning passing through
    Unknown to me."
"Nay: you saw nought. He passed invisibly."

Between these and even more extreme cases, every degree of variation in the relative importance of sound, sense, and further interpretation, between form and content in short, can be found. A temptation to which few do not succumb is to suppose that there is some "proper relation" for these different parts of the experience, so that a poem whose parts are in this relation must thereby be a greater or better poem than another whose parts are differently disposed. This is another instance of the commonest of critical mistakes, the confusion of means with ends, of technique with value. There is no more a "proper place" for sound or for sense in poetry than there is one and only one "proper shape" for an animal. A dog is not a defective kind of cat, nor is Swinburne a defective kind of Hardy. But this sort of criticism is extraordinarily prevalent. The objection to Swinburne on the ground of a lack of thought is a popular specimen.

Within certain types, needless to say, some structures are more likely to be successful than others. Given some definite kind of effect as the goal, or some definite structure already being used, a good deal can of course be said as to the most probable means, or as to what may or may not be added. Lyric cannot dispense with tied imagery, it is clear, nor can we neglect the character of this imagery in reading it. A prose composition has to be longer than a lyric to produce an equal definiteness of developed effect. Poems in which there is much turmoil of emotion are likely to be strongly rhythmical and to be in metre, as we shall see when we come to discuss rhythm and metre. Drama can hardly dispense with a great deal of conjecture and further interpretation which

[2] Two kinds of onomatopoeia should be distinguished. In one the sound of the words (actual or imaginal) is like some natural sound (the buzzing of bees, galloping horses, and so forth). In the other it is not like any such sound but such as merely to call up free auditory images of the sounds in question. The second case is by far the more common.

in most forms of the novel is replaced by analysis and explanation, and in narrative poetry is commonly omitted altogether; and so on.

But no general prescription that in great poetry there *must* always be this or that,—deep thought, superb sound or vivid imagery—is more than a piece of ignorant dogmatism. Poetry may be almost devoid even of mere sense, let alone thought, or *almost* without sensory (or formal) structure, and yet reach the point than which no poem goes further. The second case, however, is very rare. Almost always, what seems structureless proves to have still a loose and tenuous (it may be an intermittent) structure. But we can for example shift the words about very often in Walt Whitman without loss, even when he is almost at his best.

It is difficult to represent diagrammatically what takes place in thought in any satisfactory fashion. The impulse coming in from the visual stimulus of the printed word must be imagined as reaching some system in the brain in which effects take place not due merely to this present stimulus, but also to past occasions on which it has been combined with other stimulations. These effects are thoughts; and they in their groupings act as signs for yet other thoughts. The little arrows are intended to symbolise these references to things outside the mind.

EMOTIONS AND ATTITUDES

Feeling or emotion is not, we have insisted above, another and a rival mode of apprehending nature. So far as a feeling or an emotion does refer to anything, it refers in the way described, through its origin. Feelings, in fact, are commonly signs, and the differences between those who "see" things by intuition, or "feel" them, and those who reason them out, is commonly only a difference between users of signs and users of symbols. Both signs and symbols are means by which our past experience assists our present responses. The advantages of symbols, due to the ease with which they are controlled and communicated, their

public nature, as it were, are obvious. Their disadvantages as compared with such relatively private signs as emotions or organic sensations are perhaps less evident. Words, when used symbolically or scientifically, not figuratively and emotively, are only capable of directing thought to a comparatively few features of the more common situations. But feeling is sometimes a more subtle way of referring, more dangerous also, because more difficult to corroborate and to control, and more liable to confusion. There is no inherent superiority, however, in feeling as opposed to thought, there is merely a difference in applicability; nor is there any opposition or clash between them except for those who are mistaken either in their thinking or in their feeling, or in both. . . .

As regards emotions and attitudes little need be added to what has already been said. Emotions are primarily signs of attitudes and owe their great prominence in the theory of art to this. For it is the attitudes evoked which are the all-important part of any experience. Upon the texture and form of the attitudes involved its value depends. It is not the intensity of the conscious experience, its thrill, its pleasure or its poignancy which gives it value, but the organisation of its impulses for freedom and fullness of life. There are plenty of ecstatic instants which are valueless; the character of consciousness at any moment is no certain sign of the excellence of the impulses from which it arises. It is the most convenient sign that is available, but it is very ambiguous and may be very misleading. A more reliable but less accessible set of signs can be found in the readiness for this or that kind of behaviour in which we find ourselves after the experience. Too great insistence upon the quality of the momentary *consciousness* which the arts occasion has in recent times been a prevalent critical blunder. The Epilogue to Pater's *Renaissance* is the *locus classicus*. The after-effects, the permanent modifications in the structure of the mind, which works of art can produce, have been overlooked. No one is ever quite the same again after any experience; his possibilities have altered in some degree. And among all the agents by which "the widening of the sphere of human sensibility" may be brought about, the arts are the most powerful, since it is through them that men may most co-operate and in these experiences that the mind most easily and with least interference organises itself.

XXV. BADNESS IN POETRY

Il faut dissiper un malentendu: nous sommes pourris d'art!
L<small>E</small> C<small>ORBUSIER</small>-S<small>AUGNIER</small>.

T<small>HE</small> T<small>HEORY</small> O<small>F</small> badness in poetry has never received the study which it deserves, partly on account of its difficulty. For with bad art even more than with good unless we are careful to distinguish the communicative from the value aspects, even when these are connected, we shall find the issues obscured. Sometimes art is bad because communication is defective, the vehicle inoperative; sometimes because the experience communicated is worthless; sometimes for both reasons. It would perhaps be best to restrict the term bad art to cases in which genuine communication does to a considerable degree take place, what is communicated being worthless, and to call the other cases defective art. But this is not the usual practice of critics, any work which produces an experience displeasing to the critic being commonly called bad, whether or not this experience is like that responsible for the work.

Let us begin by considering an instance of defective communication; choosing an example in which it is likely that the original experience had some value.

THE POOL

Are you alive?
I touch you.

From *The Principles of Literary Criticism* by I. A. Richards. Reprinted by permission of Harcourt Brace Jovanovich, Inc.

You quiver like a sea-fish.
I cover you with my net.
What are you—banded one?

I take a complete work to avoid possible unfairness. Here we have the whole of the link which is to mediate between the experiences of the author and of the reader. Aristotle, in a different connection, it is true, and for different reasons, affirmed that a work of art must possess a certain magnitude, and we can adapt his remark here. Not the brevity only of the vehicle, but its simplicity, makes it ineffective. The sacrifice of metre in free verse needs, in almost all cases, to be compensated by length. The loss of so much of the formal structure leads otherwise to tenuousness and ambiguity. Even when, as here, the original experience is presumably slight, tenuous and fleeting, the mere correspondence of matter to form is insufficient. The experience evoked in the reader is not sufficiently specific. A poet may, it is true, make an unlimited demand upon his reader, and the greatest poets make the greatest claim, but the demand made must be proportional to the poet's own contribution. The reader here supplies too much of the poem. Had the poet said only, "I went and poked about for rocklings and caught the pool itself," the reader, who converts what is printed above into a poem, would still have been able to construct an experience of equal value; for what results is almost independent of the author.

To pass to a case in which communication is successful, where the objection lies to what is communicated:

After the fierce midsummer all ablaze
  Has burned itself to ashes and expires
  In the intensity of its own fires,
Then come the mellow, mild, St Martin days
Crowned with the calm of peace, but sad with
    haze.
  So after Love has led us, till he tires
  Of his own throes and torments, and desires,
Comes large-eyed Friendship: with a restful gaze
He beckons us to follow, and across
  Cool, verdant vales we wander free from care.
  Is it a touch of frost lies in the air?
Why are we haunted with a sense of loss?
  We do not wish the pain back, or the heat;
  And yet, and yet, these days are incomplete.

As to the success of the communication there can be no question. Both the popularity of the author, Ella Wheeler Wilcox, of whose work this is a favourable specimen, and records of the response made by well-educated persons, who read it without being aware of the authorship, leave this beyond doubt. It reproduces the state of mind of the writer very exactly. With a very numerous class of readers pleasure and admiration ensue. The explanation is, probably, in the soothing effect of aligning the very active Love-Friendship groups of impulses with so settled yet rich a group as the Summer-Autumn simile brings in. The mind finds for a moment an attitude in which to contemplate a pair of situations (Love and Friendship) together, situations which are for many minds particularly difficult to see together. The heavy regular rhythm, the dead stamp of the rimes, the obviousness of the descriptions ("mellow, mild, St Martin"; "cool verdant vales") their alliteration, the triteness of the close, all these accentuate the impression of conclusiveness. The restless spirit is appeased, one of its chief problems is made to seem as if, regarded from a lofty, all-embracing standpoint, it is no problem but a process of nature.

* * *

This reconciliation, this appeasement, is common to much good and to much bad poetry alike. But the value of it depends upon the level of organisation at which it takes place, upon whether the reconciled impulses are adequate or inadequate. In this case those who have adequate impulses as regards *any* of the four main systems involved, Summer, Autumn, Love, Friendship, are not appeased. Only for those who make certain conventional, stereotyped maladjustments instead, does the magic work.

The nature and source of these stock conventional attitudes is of great interest. Suggestion is very largely responsible for them. The normal child under the age of ten is probably free from them, or at least with him they have no fixity or privileged standing. But as general reflection develops the place of the free direct play of experience is taken by the deliberate organisation of attitudes, a clumsy and crude substitute. "Ideas," as they are commonly called, arise. A boy's "Idea" of Friendship or of Summer or of his Country is not, though the name would seem to imply it, primarily an intellectual affair. It is rather an attitude, or set of attitudes, of tendencies to act in certain fashions rather than others. Now reflection, unless very prolonged and very arduous, tends to fix the attitude by making us dwell in it, by *removing us from experience*. In the development of any attitude there are stages, points of rest, of relatively greater stability. These, as we dwell in them, become more and more difficult to pass, and it is not surprising that most people remain all their lives in various halfway houses.

These stages or levels of emotional adjustment seem, for the most part, to be fixed not by any special suitability to circumstances, certainly not to present circumstances, but much more by social suggestion and by accidents which withdraw us from actual experience, the one force which might push us further. At present bad literature, bad art, the cinema, etc., are an influence of the first importance in fixing immature and actually inapplicable attitudes to most things. Even the decision as to what constitutes a pretty girl or a handsome young man, an affair apparently natural and personal enough, is largely determined by magazine covers and movie stars. The quite common opinion that the arts have after all very little effect upon the community shows only that too little attention is being paid to the effects of bad art.

The losses incurred by these artificial fixations of attitudes are evident. Through them the average adult is worse, not better adjusted to the possibilities of his existence than the child. He is even in the most important things functionally unable to face facts: do what he will he is only able to face fictions, fictions projected by his own stock responses.

Against these stock responses the artist's internal and external conflicts are fought, and with them the popular writer's triumphs are made. Any combination of these general Ideas, hit at the right level or halting point of development, is, if suitably advertised, certain of success. Best-sellers in all the arts, exemplifying as they do the most general levels of attitude development, are worthy of very close study. No theory of criticism is satisfactory which is not able to explain their wide appeal and to give clear reasons why those who disdain them are not necessarily snobs.

The critic and the Sales Manager are not ordinarily regarded as of the same craft, nor are the poet and the advertising agent. It is true that some serious artists are occasionally tempted into poster designing. It is, however, doubtful whether their work pays. But the written appeals which have the soundest financial prospects as estimated by the most able American advertisers are such that no critic can safely ignore them. For they do undoubtedly represent the literary ideals present and future of the people to whom they are addressed.[1] They are tested in a way which few

---

[1] A specimen: "The thoughtful man, the man on business bent, wends his way to Wembley with definite purpose. He seeketh knowledge, desireth increase of commerce or willeth to study new epoch-making inventions."—*Official Advertisement.*

other forms of literature are tested, their effects are watched by adepts whose livelihood depends upon the accuracy of their judgment, and they are among the best indices available of what is happening to taste. Criticism will justify itself as an applied science when it is able to indicate how an advertisement may be profitable without necessarily being crass. We shall see later under what conditions popularity and possible high value are compatible.

The strongest objection to, let us say, the sonnet we have quoted, is that a person who enjoys it, through the very organisation of his responses which enables him to enjoy it, is debarred from appreciating many things which, if he could appreciate them, he would prefer. . . . Even a good critic at a sufficiently low ebb of neural potency might mistake such a sonnet for one of Shakespeare's or with more ease for one of Rossetti's. But when vigilance was restored he would see, or at least feel, the differences. The point is that a reader who, at a high degree of vigilance, thoroughly enters into and enjoys this class of verse, is necessarily so organised that he will fail to respond to poetry. Time and much varied experience might change him sufficiently, but by then he would no longer be able to enjoy such verse, he would no longer be the same person.

A general statement such as this about the incompatibility of inexpressibly complex adjustments must naturally be incapable of strict proof. Individuals with alternating personalities and subject to fugues would have to be considered. So would the phenomena of "mutations of regime" unaccompanied by change of vigilance if such occur. None the less very much evidence substantiates the statement. The experience of all those who have passed through the stages in the development of attitudes presupposed by great poetry is probably conclusive.

Even though the intricacies of the nervous system should be capable of getting round this objection, there remain sufficient other reasons why indulgence in verse of this character should be condemned. There can be no doubt whatever that the value of the experience which results from it is small. On a pleasure theory of value there might well be doubt, since those who do enjoy it certainly appear to enjoy it in a high degree. But on the theory here maintained, the fact that those who have passed through the stage of enjoying the *Poems of Passion* to that of enjoying the bulk of the contents of the *Golden Treasury*, for example, do not return, settles the matter. We must bear in mind, of course, the conditions which have to be satisfied before this test is conclusive. That a man who has passed through the stage of drinking nothing but beer to the stage of drinking nothing but brandy rarely returns, does not prove that brandy is the better drink. It merely proves that it is the more efficient intoxicant. We have to ask in applying the test what the responses in question are, and in the case of poetry they are so varied, so representative of all the activities of life, that actual universal preference on the part of those who have tried both kinds fairly is the same (on our view) as superiority in value of the one over the other. Keats, by universal qualified opinion, is a more efficient poet than Wilcox, and that is the same thing as saying that his works are more valuable.

XXX. THE DEFINITION OF A POEM

Men take the words they find in use among their neighbours, and that they may not seem ignorant what they stand for use them confidently without much troubling their heads about a certain fixed meaning. . . . it being all one to draw these men out of their mistakes, who have no settled notions, as to dispossess a Vagrant of his habitation, who has no settled abode. This I guess to be so; and every one may observe in himself or others whether it be so or not.

LOCKE.

It MAY BE useful to collect here some of the results of the foregoing sections and consider them from the point of view of the practising critic. The most salient perhaps is the desirability of distinguishing clearly between the communicative and the value aspects of a work of art. We may praise or condemn a work on either ground or upon both, but if it fails entirely as a vehicle of communication we are, to say the least, not well placed for denying its value.

From *The Principles of Literary Criticism* by I. A. Richards. Reprinted by permission of Harcourt Brace Jovanovich, Inc.

But, it may be said, it will then have no value for *us* and its value or disvalue for us is all that we as critics pretend or should pretend to judge. To make such a reply, however, is to abdicate as a critic. At the least a critic is concerned with the value of things for himself and for people like him. Otherwise his criticism is mere autobiography. And any critic worth attention makes a further claim, a claim to sanity. His judgment is only of general interest in so far as it is representative and reflects what happens in a mind of a certain kind, developed in a certain fashion. The services of bad critics are sometimes not less than those of good critics, but that is only because we can divine from their responses what other people's responses are likely to be.

We must distinguish between standard or normal criticism and erratic or eccentric criticism. As critics Lamb or Coleridge are very far from normal; none the less they are of extraordinary fertility in suggestion. Their responses are often erratic even when of most revelatory character. In such cases we do not take them as standards to which we endeavour to approximate, we do not attempt to see eye to eye with them. Instead we use them as means by which to make quite different approaches ourselves to the works which they have characteristically but eccentrically interpreted.

The distinction between a personal or idiosyncratic judgment and a normative is sometimes overlooked. A critic should often be in a position to say, "I don't like this but I know it is good," or "I like this and condemn it," or "This is the effect which it produces upon me, and this quite different effect is the one it should produce." For obvious reasons he rarely makes any such statements. But many people would regard praise of a work which is actually disliked by the praiser as immoral. This is a confusion of ideas. Any honest reader knows fairly well the points at which his sensibility is distorted, at which he fails as a normal critic and in what ways. It is his duty to take these into consideration in passing judgment upon the value of a work. His rank as a critic depends at least as much upon his ability to discount these personal peculiarities as upon any hypothetical impeccability of his actual responses.

So far we have been considering those cases in which the vehicle is sufficiently adequate and the critic sufficiently representative and careful for the response to be a good index of the value of the poem. But these cases are comparatively rare. The superstition which any language not intolerably prolix and uncouth encourages that there is something actual, *the poem*, which all readers have access to and

upon which they pass judgment, misleads us. We naturally talk about poems (and pictures, etc.) in a way which makes it impossible for anybody to discover what it is we are talking about. Most critical discussion, in other words, is primarily emotive with only a very loose and fourfold equivocal reference. We may be talking about the artist's experience, such of it as is relevant, or about the experience of a qualified reader who made no mistakes, or about an ideal and perfect reader's possible experience, or about our own actual experience. All four in most cases will be qualitatively different. Communication is perhaps never perfect, so the first and the last will differ. The second and third differ also, from the others and from one another, the third being what we ought unrestrictedly to experience, or the best experience we could possibly undergo, whereas the second is merely what we ought to experience as things are, or the best experience that we can expect.

Which of these possible definitions of a poem shall we adopt? The question is one of convenience merely; but it is by no means easy to decide. The most usual practice is to mean by *the poem* either the first or the last; or, by forgetting what communication is, to mean both confusedly together. The last involves the personal judgment to which exception was taken on the previous page, and has the further disadvantage that there would be for every sonnet as many poems as readers. A and B, discussing *Westminster Bridge* as they thought, would unwittingly be discussing two different things. For some purposes, for the disentanglement of some misunderstandings, it is convenient to define a poem temporarily in this manner.

To define the poem as the artist's experience is a better solution. But it will not do as it stands since nobody but the artist has that experience. We must be more ingenious. We cannot take any single experience as the poem; we must have a class of more or less similar experiences instead. Let us mean by *Westminster Bridge* not the actual experience which led Wordsworth on a certain morning about a century ago to write what he did, but the class composed of all actual experiences, occasioned by the words, which do not differ within certain limits from that experience. Then anyone who has had one of the experiences comprised in the class can be said to have read the poem. The permissible ranges of variation in the class need (of course) very careful scrutiny. To work them out fully and draw up a neat formal definition of a poem would be an amusing and useful occupation for any literary logician with a knowledge of psychology. The experiences must evidently include the reading of the words with fairly close correspondence in rhythm and tune. Pitch difference would not matter, provided that pitch relations were preserved. Imagery might be allowed to vary indefinitely in its sensory aspect but would be narrowly restricted otherwise. If the reader will run over the diagram of a poetic experience given in Chapter XVI and consider in what respects his and his friends' experiences must agree if they are to be able to refer to them indifferently as though they were one and the same without confusion or misunderstanding, he will see what kind of thing a detailed definition of a poem would be.

This, although it may seem odd and complicated, is by far the most convenient, in fact it is the only workable way of defining a poem; namely, as a class of experiences which do not differ in any character more than a certain amount, varying for each character, from a standard experience. We may take as this standard experience the relevant experience of the poet when contemplating the completed composition.[1]

Anyone whose experience approximates in this degree to the standard experience will be able to judge the poem and his remarks about it will be about some experience which is included in the class. Thus we have what we want, a sense, namely, in which a critic can be said to have not read the poem or to have misread it. In this sense unrecognised failures are extremely common.

The justification for this outbreak of pedantry, as it may appear, is that it brings into prominence one of the reasons for the backwardness of critical theory. If the definition of a poem is a matter of so much difficulty and complexity, the discussion of the principles by which poetry should be judged may be expected to be confused. Critics have as yet hardly begun to ask themselves what they are doing or under what conditions they work. It is true that a recognition of the critic's predicament need not be explicit in order to be effective, but few with much experience of literary debate will underestimate the extent to which it is disregarded or the consequences which ensue from this neglect. The discussions in the foregoing chapters are intended as no more than examples of the problems which an explicit recognition of the situation will admit and of the ways in which they will be solved.

---

[1] Difficulties even here arise, e.g. the poet may be dissatisfied without reason. Coleridge thought *Kubla Khan* merely "a psychological curiosity" without poetic merits, and may have been justified in some degree. If he was not, it is his dream experience which we should presumably have to take as our standard.

From Science and Poetry (1926)

II. THE POETIC EXPERIENCE

EXTRAORDINARY claims have often been made for poetry . . . claims which very many people are inclined to view with astonishment or with the smile which tolerance gives to the enthusiast. Indeed a more representative modern view would be that the future of poetry is *nil*. Peacock's conclusion in his *The Four Ages of Poetry* finds a more general acceptance. "A poet in our times is a semi-barbarian in a civilized community. He lives in the days that are past. . . . In whatever degree poetry is cultivated, it must necessarily be to the neglect of some branch of useful study: and it is a lamentable thing to see minds, capable of better things, running to seed in the specious indolence of these empty aimless mockeries of intellectual exertion. Poetry was the mental rattle that awakened the attention of intellect in the infancy of civil society: but for the maturity of mind to make a serious business of the playthings of its childhood, is as absurd as for a grown man to rub his gums with coral, and cry to be charmed asleep by the jingle of silver bells." And with more regret many others— Keats was among them—have thought that the inevitable effect of the advance of science would be to destroy the possibility of poetry.

What is the truth in this matter? How is our estimate of poetry going to be affected by science? And how will poetry itself be influenced? The extreme importance which has in the past been assigned to poetry is a fact which must be

accounted for whether we conclude that it was rightly assigned or not, and whether we consider that poetry will continue to be held in such esteem or not. It indicates that the case for poetry, whether right or wrong, is one which turns on momentous issues. We shall not have dealt adequately with it unless we have raised questions of great significance.

Very much toil has gone to the endeavour to explain the high place of poetry in human affairs, with, on the whole, few satisfactory or convincing results. This is not surprising. For in order to show how poetry is important it is first necessary to discover to some extent what it is. Until recently this preliminary task could only be very incompletely carried out; the psychology of instinct and emotion was too little advanced; and, moreover, the wild speculations natural in pre-scientific enquiry definitely stood in the way. Neither the professional psychologist, whose interest in poetry is frequently not intense, nor the man of letters, who as a rule has no adequate ideas of the mind as a whole, has been equipped for the investigation. Both a passionate knowledge of poetry and a capacity for dispassionate psychological analysis are required if it is to be satisfactorily prosecuted.

It will be best to begin by asking, "What *kind of a thing*, in the widest sense, is poetry?" When we have answered this we shall be ready to ask, "How can we use and misuse it?" and "What reasons are there for thinking it valuable?"

Let us take an experience, ten minutes of a person's life, and describe it in broad outline. It is now possible to indicate its general structure, to point out what is important in it, what trivial and accessory, which features depend upon which, how it has arisen, and how it is probably going to influence his future experience. There are, of course, wide gaps in this description, none the less it *is* at last possible to understand in general how the mind works in an experience, and what sort of stream of events the experience is.

A poem, let us say Wordsworth's *Westminster Bridge* sonnet, is such an experience, it is the experience the right kind of reader has when he peruses the verses. And the first step to an understanding of the place and future of poetry in human affairs is to see what the general structure of such an experience is. Let us begin by reading it very slowly, preferably aloud, giving every syllable time to make its full effect upon us. And let us read it experimentally, repeating it, varying our tone of voice until we are satisfied that we have caught its rhythm as well as we are able, and—whether our reading is such as to please other people or not—we ourselves at least are certain how it should "go."

Earth has not anything to show more fair:
Dull would he be of soul who could pass by
A sight so touching in its majesty:
This City now doth like a garment wear
The beauty of the morning: silent, bare,
Ships, towers, domes, theatres and temples lie
Open to the fields, and to the sky;
All bright and glittering in the smokeless air.
Never did sun more beautifully steep
In his first splendour valley, rock or hill;
Ne'er saw I, never felt, a calm so deep!
The river glideth at its own sweet will:
Dear God! the very houses seem asleep
And all that mighty heart is lying still!

We may best make our analysis of the experience that arises through reading these lines from the surface inwards, to speak metaphorically. The surface is the impression of the printed words on the retina. This sets up an agitation which we must follow as it goes deeper and deeper.

The first things to occur (if they do not, the rest of the experience will be gravely inadequate) are the sound of the words "in the mind's ear" and the feel of the words imaginarily spoken.[1] These together give the *full body*, as it were, to the words, and it is with the full bodies of words that the poet works, not with their printed signs. But many people lose nearly everything in poetry through these indispensable parts escaping them.

Next arise various pictures "in the mind's eye"; not of words but of things for which the words stand; perhaps of ships, perhaps of hills; and together with them, it may be, other images of various sorts. Images of what it feels like to stand leaning on the parapet of Westminster Bridge. Perhaps that odd thing an image of "silence." But, unlike the image-bodies of the words themselves, those other images of things are not vitally important. Those who have them may very well think them indispensable, and *for them* they may be necessary; but other people may not require them at all. This is a point at which differences between individual minds are very marked.

Thence onwards the agitation which is the experience divides into a major and a minor branch, though the two streams have innumerable interconnections and influence one another intimately. Indeed it is only as an expositor's artifice that we may speak of them as two streams.

The minor branch we may call the intellectual stream; the other, which we may call the active, or emotional, stream, is made up of the play of our interests.

The intellectual stream is fairly easy to follow; it follows itself, so to speak; but it is the less important of the two. In poetry it matters only *as a means*; it directs and excites the active stream. It is made up of thoughts, which are not static little entities that bob up into

[1] The view of the mind-body problem assumed here is defended and maintained with references to the contemporary authorities who hold it, in *The Meaning of Psychology* by C. K. Ogden, Chapter II. (London, Kegan, Paul; New York, Harpers; 1926.)

consciousness and down again out of it, but fluent happenings, events, which reflect or point to the things the thoughts are of. Exactly how they do this is a matter which is still much disputed.

This pointing to or reflecting things is all that thoughts do. They appear to do much more; which is our chief illusion. The realm of thought is never a sovereign state. Our thoughts are the servants of our interests, and even when they seem to rebel it is usually our interests that are in disorder. Our thoughts are pointers and it is the other, the active, stream which deals with the things which thoughts reflect or point to.

Some people who read verse (they do not often read much of it) are so constituted that very little more happens than this intellectual stream of thoughts. It is perhaps superfluous to point out that they miss the real poem. To exaggerate this part of the experience, and give it too much importance on its own account, is a notable current tendency, and for many people explains why they do not read poetry.

The active branch is what really matters; for from it all the energy of the whole agitation comes. The thinking which goes on is somewhat like the play of an ingenious and invaluable "governor" run by, but controlling, the main machine. Every experience is essentially some interest or group of interests swinging back to rest.

To understand what an interest is we should picture the mind as a system of very delicately poised balances, a system which so long as we are in health is constantly growing. Every situation we come into disturbs some of these balances to some degree. The ways in which they swing back to a new equipoise are the impulses with which we respond to the situation. And the chief balances in the system are our chief interests.

Suppose that we carry a magnetic compass about in the neighbourhood of powerful magnets. The needle waggles as we move and comes to rest pointing in a new direction whenever we stand still in a new position. Suppose that instead of a single compass we carry an arrangement of many magnetic needles, large and small, swung so that they influence one another, some able only to swing horizontally, others vertically, others hung freely. As we move, the perturbations in this system will be very complicated. But for every position in which we place it there will be a final position of rest for all the needles into which they will in the end settle down, a general poise for the whole system. But even a slight displacement may set the whole assemblage of needles busily readjusting themselves.

One further complication. Suppose that while all the needles influence one another, some of them respond only to some of the outer magnets among which the system is moving. The reader can easily draw a diagram if his imagination needs a visual support.

The mind is not unlike such a system if we imagine it to be incredibly complex. The needles are our interests, varying in their importance, that is in the degree to which any movement they make involves movement in the other needles. Each new disequilibrium, which a shift of position, a fresh situation, entails, corresponds to a need; and the wagglings which ensue as the system rearranges itself are our responses, the impulses through which we seek to meet the need. Often the new poise is not found until long after the original disturbance. Thus states of strain can arise which last for years.

The child comes into the world as a comparatively simple arrangement. Few things affect him comparatively speaking, and his responses also are few and simple, but he very quickly becomes more complicated. His recurrent needs for food and for various attentions are constantly setting all his needles swinging. Little by little separate needs become departmentalized as it were, sub-systems are formed; hunger causes one set of responses, the sight of his toys another, loud noises yet another, and so on. But the sub-systems never become quite independent. So he grows up, becoming susceptible to ever more numerous and more delicate influences.

He grows more discriminating in some respects, he is thrown out of equilibrium by slighter differences in his situation. In other respects he becomes more stable. From time to time, through growth, fresh interests develop; sex is the outstanding example. His needs increase, he becomes capable of being upset by quite new causes, he becomes responsive to quite new aspects of the situation.

This development takes a very indirect course. It would be still more erratic if society did not mould and remould him at every stage, reorganising him incompletely two or three times over before he grows up. He reaches maturity in the form of a vast assemblage of major and minor interests, partly a chaos, partly a system, with some tracts of his personality fully developed and free to respond, others tangled and jammed in all kinds of accidental ways. It is this incredibly complex assemblage of interests to which the printed poem has to appeal. Sometimes the poem is itself the influence which disturbs us, sometimes it is merely the means by which an already existing disturbance can right itself. More usually perhaps it is both at once.

We must picture then the stream of the poetic experience as the swinging back into equilibrium of these disturbed interests. We are reading the poem in the first place only because we are in some way interested in doing so, only because some interest is attempting to regain its poise thereby. And whatever happens as we read happens only for a similar reason. We understand the words (the intellectual branch of the stream goes on its way successfully) only because an interest is reacting through that means, and all the rest of the experience is equally but more evidently our adaptation working itself out.

The rest of the experience is made up of emotions and attitudes. Emotions are what the reaction, with its reverberations in bodily changes, feels like. Attitudes are the impulses towards one kind of behaviour or another which are set ready by the response. They are,

as it were, its outward going part.[2] Sometimes, as here in *Westminster Bridge*, they are very easily overlooked. But consider a simpler case— a fit of laughter which it is absolutely essential to conceal, in Church or during a solemn interview, for example. You contrive not to laugh; but there is no doubt about the activity of the impulses in their restricted form. The much more subtle and elaborate impulses which a poem excites are not different in principle. They do not show themselves as a rule, they do not come out into the open, largely because they are so complex. When they have adjusted themselves to one another and become organized into a coherent whole, the needs concerned may be satisfied. *In a fully developed man a state of readiness for action will take the place of action when the full appropriate situation for action is not present.* The essential peculiarity of poetry as of all the arts is that the full appropriate situation is *not* present. It is an *actor* we are seeing upon the stage, not Hamlet. So readiness for action takes the place of actual behaviour.

This is the main plan then of the experience. Signs on the retina, taken up by sets of needs (remember how many other impressions all day long remain entirely *unnoticed* because no interest responds to them); thence an elaborate agitation of impulses, one branch of which is *thoughts* of what the words mean, the other an emotional response leading to the development of *attitudes*, preparations, that is, for action which may or may not take place; the two branches being in intimate connection.

We must look now a little more closely at these connections. It may seem odd that we do not more definitely make the thoughts the rulers and causes of the rest of the response. To do just this has been in fact the grand error of traditional psychology. Man prefers to stress the features which distinguish him from monkey, and chief among these are his intellectual capacities. Important though they are, he has given them a rank to which they are not en-

---

[2] For a further discussion of attitudes see the author's *Principles of Literary Criticism*, Chapter XV.

titled. Intellect is an adjunct to the interests, a means by which they adjust themselves more successfully. Man is not in any sense primarily an intelligence; he is a system of interests. Intelligence helps man but does not run him.

Partly through this natural mistake, and partly because intellectual operations are so much easier to study, the whole traditional analysis of the working of the mind has been turned upside down. It is largely as a remedy from the difficulties which this mistake involves that poetry may have so much importance in the future. But let us look again more closely at the poetic experience.

In the first place, why is it essential in reading poetry to give the words their full imagined sound and body? What is meant by saying that the poet works with this sound and body? The answer is that even before the words have been intellectually understood and the thoughts they occasion formed and followed, the movement and sound of the words is playing deeply and intimately upon the interests. How this happens is a matter which has yet to be successfully investigated, but that it happens no sensitive reader of poetry doubts. A good deal of poetry and even some great poetry exists (*e.g.*, some of Shakespeare's Songs and, in a different way, much of the best of Swinburne) in which the sense of the words can be *almost* entirely missed or neglected without loss. Never perhaps entirely without effort, however; though sometimes with advantage. But the plain fact that the relative importance of grasping the sense of the words may vary (compare Browning's *Before* with his *After*) is enough for our purpose here.

In nearly all poetry the sound and feel of the words, what is often called the *form* of the poem in opposition to its *content*, get to work first, and the sense in which the words are taken is subtly influenced by this fact. Most words are ambiguous as regards their plain sense, especially in poetry. We can take them as we please in a variety of senses. The sense we are pleased to choose is the one which most suits the impulses already stirred through the form of the verse. The same thing can be noticed in conversation. Not the strict logical sense of what is said, but the tone of voice and the occasion are the primary factors by which we interpret. Science, it is worth noting, endeavours with increasing success to bar out these factors. We believe a scientist because he can substantiate his remarks, not because he is eloquent or forcible in his enunciation. In fact, we distrust him when he seems to be influencing us by his manner.

In its use of words poetry is just the reverse of science. Very definite thoughts do occur, but not because the words are so chosen as logically to bar out all possibilities but one. No. But because the manner, the tone of voice, the cadence and the rhythm play upon our interests and make *them* pick out from among an indefinite number of possibilities the precise particular thought which they need. This is why poetical descriptions often seem so much more accurate than prose descriptions. Language logically and scientifically used cannot describe a landscape or a face. To do so it would need a prodigious apparatus of names for shades and nuances, for precise particular qualities. These names do not exist, so other means have to be used. The poet, even when, like Ruskin or De Quincey, he writes in prose, makes the reader pick out the precise particular sense required from an indefinite number of possible senses which a word, phrase or sentence may carry. The means by which he does this are many and varied. Some of them have been mentioned above, but the way in which he uses them is the poet's own secret, something which cannot be taught. He knows how to do it, but he does not himself know how it is done.

Misunderstanding and under-estimation of poetry is mainly due to over-estimation of the thought in it. We can see still more clearly that thought is not the prime factor if we consider for a moment not the experience of the reader but that of the poet. Why does the poet use these words and no others? Not because they stand for a series of thoughts which in themselves are what he is concerned to communicate. It is never what a poem *says* which matters, but what it *is*. The poet is not writing as a scientist. He uses these words because the interests which the situation calls into play combine to bring them, just in this form, into his consciousness *as a means of ordering, controlling and consolidating* the whole experience. The experience itself, the tide of impulses sweeping through the mind, is the source and the sanction of the words. They represent this experience itself, not any set of perceptions or reflections, though often to a reader who approaches the poem wrongly they will seem to be only a series of remarks about other things. But to a suitable reader the words—if they actually spring from experience and are not due to verbal habits, to the desire to be effective, to factitious excogitation, to imitation, to irrelevant contrivances, or to any other of the failings which prevent most people from writing poetry—the words will reproduce in his mind a similar play of interests putting him for the while into a similar situation and leading to the same response.

Why this should happen is still somewhat of a mystery. An extraordinarily intricate concourse of impulses brings the words together. Then in another mind the affair in part reverses itself, the words bring into being a similar concourse of impulses. The words which seem to be the effect of the experience in the first instance, seem to become the cause of a similar experience in the second. A very odd thing to happen, not exactly paralleled outside communication. But this description is not quite accurate. The words, as we have seen, are not simply the effect in one case, nor the cause in the other. In both cases they are the part of the experience which binds it together, which gives it a definite structure and keeps it from being a mere welter of disconnected impulses. They are *the key*, to borrow a useful metaphor from McDougall, for this particular combination of impulses. So regarded, it is less strange that what the poet wrote should reproduce his experience in the mind of the reader.

VI. POETRY AND BELIEFS

THE BUSINESS of the poet, as we have seen, is to give order and coherence, and so freedom, to a body of experience. To do so through words which act as its skeleton, as a structure by which the impulses which make up the experience are adjusted to one another and act together. The means by which words do this are many and varied. To work them out is a problem for psychology. A beginning has been indicated above, but only a beginning. What little can be done shows already that most critical dogmas of the past are either false or nonsense. A little knowledge is not here a danger, but clears the air in a remarkable way.

Roughly and inadequately, even in the light of our present knowledge, we can say that words work in the poem in two main fashions. As sensory stimuli and as (in the *widest* sense) symbols. We must refrain from considering the sensory side of the poem, remarking only that it is *not* in the least independent of the other side, and that it has for definite reasons prior importance in most poetry. We must confine ourselves to the other function of words in the poem, or rather, omitting much that is of secondary relevance, to one form of that function, let me call it *pseudo-statement*.

It will be admitted—by those who distinguish between scientific statement, where truth is ultimately a matter of verification as this is understood in the laboratory, and emotive utterance, where "truth" is primarily acceptability *by* some attitude, and more remotely is the acceptability *of* this attitude itself—that it is *not* the poet's business to make true statements. Yet poetry has constantly the air of making statements, and important ones; which is one reason why some mathematicians cannot read it. They find the alleged statements to be *false*. It will be agreed that their approach to poetry and their expectations from it are mistaken. But what exactly is the other, the right, the poetic, approach and how does it differ from the mathematical?

The poetic approach evidently limits the framework of possible consequences into which the pseudo-statement is taken. For the scientific approach this framework is unlimited. Any and every consequence is relevant. If any of the consequences of a statement conflicts with acknowledged fact then so much the worse for the statement. Not so with the pseudo-statement when poetically approached. The problem is—just how does the limitation work? The usual account is in terms of a supposed universe of discourse, a world of make-believe, of imagination, of recognised fictions common to the poet and his readers. A pseudo-statement which fits into this system of assumptions would be regarded as "poetically true"; one which does not, as "poetically false." This attempt to treat "poetic truth" on the model of general "coherence theories" is very natural for certain schools of logicians; but is inadequate, on the wrong lines from the outset. To mention two objections out of many; there is no means of discovering what the "universe of discourse" is on any occasion, and the kind of coherence which must hold within it, supposing it to be discoverable, is not an affair of logical relations. Attempt to define the system of propositions into which

"O Rose, thou art sick!"

must fit, and the logical relations which must hold between them if it is to be "poetically true"; the absurdity of the theory becomes evident.

We must look further. In the poetic ap-

proach the relevant consequences are not logical or to be arrived at by a partial relaxation of logic. Except occasionally and by accident logic does not enter at all. They are the consequences which arise through our emotional organisation. The acceptance which a pseudo-statement receives is entirely governed by its effects upon our feelings and attitudes. Logic only comes in, if at all, in subordination, as a servant to our emotional response. It is an unruly servant, however, as poets and readers are constantly discovering. A pseudo-statement is "true" if it suits and serves some attitude or links together attitudes which on other grounds are desirable. This kind of truth is so opposed to scientific truth that it is a pity to use so similar a word, but at present it is difficult to avoid the malpractice.[1]

This brief analysis may be sufficient to indicate the fundamental disparity and opposition between pseudo-statements as they occur in poetry and statements as they occur in science. A pseudo-statement is a form of words which is justified entirely by its effect in releasing or organising our impulses and attitudes (due regard being had for the better or worse organisations of these *inter se*); a statement, on the other hand, is justified by its truth, *i.e.* its correspondence, in a highly technical sense, with the fact to which it points.

Statements true and false alike do of course constantly touch off attitudes and action. Our daily practical existence is largely guided by them. On the whole true statements are of more service to us than false ones. None the less we do not and, at present, cannot order our emotions and attitudes by true statements alone. Nor is there any probability that we ever shall contrive to do so. This is one of the great new dangers to which civilisation is exposed. Countless pseudo-statements—about God, about the universe, about human nature, the relations of mind to mind, about the soul, its

[1] For an account of the various senses of truth and of the ways in which they may be distinguished in discussion cf. *The Meaning of Meaning*, by C. K. Ogden and the author, Chapters VII and X.

rank and destiny—pseudo-statements which are pivotal points in the organisation of the mind, vital to its well-being, have suddenly become, for sincere, honest and informal minds, impossible to believe. For centuries they have been believed; now they are gone, irrecoverably; and the knowledge which has killed them is not of a kind upon which an equally fine organisation of the mind can be based.

This is the contemporary situation. The remedy, since there is no prospect of our gaining adequate knowledge, and since indeed it is fairly clear that genuine knowledge cannot serve us here and can only increase our practical control of Nature, is to cut our pseudo-statements free from belief, and yet retain them, in this released state, as the main instruments by which we order our attitudes to one another and to the world. Not so desperate a remedy as may appear, for poetry conclusively shows that even the most important among our attitudes can be aroused and maintained without any belief entering in at all. Those of Tragedy, for example. We need no beliefs, and indeed we must have none, if we are to read *King Lear*. Pseudo-statements to which we attach no belief and statements proper such as science provides cannot conflict. It is only when we introduce illicit beliefs into poetry that danger arises. To do so is from this point of view a profanation of poetry.

Yet an important branch of criticism which has attracted the best talents from prehistoric times until to-day consists of the endeavour to persuade men that the functions of science and poetry are identical, or that the one is a "higher form" of the other, or that they conflict and we must choose between them.

The root of this persistent endeavour has still to be mentioned; it is the same as that from which the Magical View of the world arose. If we give to a pseudo-statement the kind of unqualified acceptance which belongs by right only to certified scientific statements, if we can contrive to do this, the impulses and attitudes with which we respond to it gain a notable stability and vigour. Briefly, if we can contrive

to believe poetry, then the world *seems*, while we do so, to be transfigured. It used to be comparatively easy to do this, and the habit has become well established. With the extension of science and the neutralisation of nature it has become difficult as well as dangerous. Yet it is still alluring; it has many analogies with drug-taking. Hence the endeavours of the critics referred to. Various subterfuges have been devised along the lines of regarding Poetic Truth as figurative, symbolic; or as more immediate, as a truth of Intuition, not of reason; or as a higher form of the same truth as reason yields. Such attempts to use poetry as a denial or as a corrective of science are very common. One point can be made against them all: they are never worked out in detail. There is no equivalent to Mill's *Logic* expounding any such view. The language in which they are framed is usually a blend of obsolete psychology and emotive exclamations.

The long-established and much-encouraged habit of giving to emotive utterances—whether pseudo-statements simple, or looser and larger wholes taken as saying something figuratively —the kind of assent which we give to established facts, has for most people debilitated a wide range of their responses. A few scientists, caught young and brought up in the laboratory, are free from it; but then, as a rule, they pay no *serious* attention to poetry. For most men the recognition of the neutrality of nature brings about—through this habit—a divorce from poetry. They are so used to having their responses propped up by beliefs, however vague, that when these shadowy supports are removed they are no longer able to respond. Their attitudes to so many things have been forced in the past, over-encouraged. And when the world-picture ceases to assist there is a collapse. Over whole tracts of natural emotional response we are to-day like a bed of dahlias whose sticks have been removed. And this effect of the neutralisation of nature is only in its beginnings. Consider the probable effects upon love-poetry in the near future of the kind of enquiry into basic human constitution exemplified by psycho-analysis.

A sense of desolation, of uncertainty, of futility, of the groundlessness of aspirations, of the vanity of endeavour, and a thirst for a life-giving water which seems suddenly to have failed, are the signs in consciousness of this necessary reorganisation of our lives.[2] Our attitudes and impulses are being compelled to become self-supporting; they are being driven back upon their biological justification, made once again sufficient to themselves. And the only impulses which seem strong enough to continue unflagging are commonly so crude that, to more finely developed individuals, they hardly seem worth having. Such people cannot live by warmth, food, fighting, drink, and sex alone. Those who are least affected by the change are those who are emotionally least removed from the animals. As we shall see at the close of this essay, even a considerable poet [D. H. Lawrence] may attempt to find relief by a reversion to primitive mentality.

It is important to diagnose the disease correctly and to put the blame in the right quarter. Usually it is some alleged "materialism" of science which is denounced. This mistake is due partly to clumsy thinking, but chiefly to relics of the Magical View. For even if the Universe were "spiritual" all through (whatever that assertion might mean; all such assertions are probably nonsense), that would not make it any more accordant to human attitudes. It is

[2] To those familiar with Mr. Eliot's *The Waste Land,* my indebtedness to it at this point will be evident. He seems to me by this poem, to have performed two considerable services for this generation. He has given a perfect emotive description of a state of mind which is probably inevitable for a while to all meditative people. Secondly, by effecting a complete severance between his poetry and *all* beliefs, and this without any weakening of the poetry, he has realised what might otherwise have remained largely a speculative possibility, and has shown the way to the only solution of these difficulties. "In the destructive element immerse. That is the way."

not what the universe is made of but how it works, the law it follows, which makes knowledge of it incapable of spurring on our emotional responses, and further the nature of knowledge itself makes it inadequate. The contact with things which we therein establish is too sketchy and indirect to help us. We are beginning to know too much about the bond which unites the mind to its object in knowledge for that old dream of a perfect knowledge which would guarantee perfect life to retain its sanction. What was thought to be pure knowledge, we see now to have been shot through with hope and desire with fear and wonder, and these intrusive elements indeed gave it all its power to support our lives. In knowledge, in the "How?" of events, we can find hints by which to take advantage of circumstances in our favour and avoid mischances. But we cannot get from it a *raison d'être* or a justification of more than a relatively lowly kind of life.

The justification, or the reverse, of any attitude lies, not in the object, but in itself, in its serviceableness to the whole personality. Upon its place in the whole system of attitudes, which is the personality, all its worth depends. This is true equally for the subtle, finely compounded attitudes of the civilised individual as for the simpler attitudes of the child.

In brief, experience is its own justification; and this fact must be faced, although sometimes—by a lover, for example—it may be very difficult to accept. Once it is faced, it is apparent that all the attitudes to other human beings and to the world in all its aspects, which have been serviceable to humanity, remain as they were, as valuable as ever. Hesitation felt in admitting this is a measure of the strength of the evil habit we have described. But many of these attitudes, valuable as ever, are, now that they are being set free, more difficult to maintain, because we still hunger after a basis in belief.

From Practical Criticism (1929)

[THE CHIEF DIFFICULTIES OF CRITICISM]

A. First must come the difficulty of *making out the plain sense* of poetry. The most disturbing and impressive fact brought out by this experiment is that a large proportion of average-to-good (and in some cases, certainly, devoted) readers of poetry frequently and repeatedly *fail to understand it*, both as a statement and as an expression. They fail to make out its prose sense, its plain, overt meaning, as a set of ordinary, intelligible, English sentences, taken quite apart from any further poetic significance. And equally, they misapprehend its feeling, its tone, and its intention. They would travesty it in a paraphrase. They fail to construe it just as a schoolboy fails to construe a piece of Caesar. How serious in its effects in different instances this failure may be, we shall have to consider with care. It is not confined to one class of readers; not only those whom we would suspect fall victims. Nor is it only the most abstruse poetry which so betrays us. In fact, to set down, for once, the brutal truth, no immunity is possessed on any occasion, not by the most reputable scholar, from this or any other of these critical dangers.

B. Parallel to, and not unconnected with, these difficulties of interpreting the meaning are the difficulties of *sensuous apprehension*. Words in sequence have a form to the mind's ear and the mind's tongue

From *Practical Criticism* by I. A. Richards. Reprinted by permission of Harcourt Brace Jovanovich, Inc.

and larynx, even when silently read. They have a movement and may have a rhythm. The gulf is wide between a reader who naturally and immediately perceives this form and movement (by a conjunction of sensory, intellectual and emotional sagacity) and another reader, who either ignores it or has to build it up laboriously with finger-counting, table-tapping and the rest; and this difference has most far-reaching effects.

C. Next may come those difficulties that are connected with the place of *imagery*, principally visual imagery, in poetic reading. They arise in part from the incurable fact that we differ immensely in our capacity to visualise, and to produce imagery of the other senses. Also the importance of our imagery as a whole, as well as of some pet particular type of image, in our mental lives varies surprisingly. Some minds can do nothing and get nowhere without images; others seem to be able to do everything and get anywhere, reach any and every state of thought and feeling without making use of them. Poets on the whole (though by no means all poets always) may be suspected of exceptional imaging capacity, and some readers are constitutionally prone to stress the place of imagery in reading, to pay great attention to it, and even to judge the value of the poetry by the images it excites in them. But images are erratic things; lively images aroused in one mind need have no similarity to the equally lively images stirred by the same line of poetry in another, and neither set need have anything to do with any images which may have existed in the poet's mind. Here is a troublesome source of critical deviations.

D. Thirdly, more obviously, we have to note the powerful very pervasive influence of *mnemonic irrelevances*. These are misleading effects of the reader's being reminded of some personal scene or adventure, erratic associations, the interference of emotional reverberations from a past which may have nothing to do with the poem. Relevance is not an easy notion to define or to apply, though some instances of irrelevant intrusions are among the simplest of all accidents to diagnose.

E. More puzzling and more interesting are the critical traps that surround what may be called *Stock Responses*. These have their opportunity whenever a poem seems to, or does, involve views and emotions already fully prepared in the reader's mind, so that what happens appears to be more of the reader's doing than the poet's. The button is pressed, and then the author's work is done, for immediately the record starts playing in quasi- (or total) independence of the poem which is supposed to be its origin or instrument.

Whenever this lamentable redistribution of the poet's and reader's share in the labour of poetry occurs, or is in danger of occurring, we require to be especially on our guard. Every kind of injustice may be committed as well by those who just escape as by those who are caught.

F. *Sentimentality* is a peril that needs less comment here. It is a question of the due measure of response. This over-facility in certain emotional directions is the Scylla whose Charybdis is—

G. *Inhibition.* This, as much as Sentimentality, is a positive phenomenon, though less studied until recent years and somewhat masked under the title of Hardness of Heart. But neither can well be considered in isolation.

H. *Doctrinal adhesions* present another troublesome problem. Very much poetry—religious poetry may be instanced—seems to contain or imply views and beliefs, true or false, about the world. If this be so, what bearing has the truth-value of the views upon the worth of the poetry? Even if it be not so, if the beliefs are not really contained or implied, but only seem so to a non-poetical reading, what should be the bearing of the reader's conviction, if any, upon his estimate of the poetry? Has poetry anything to say; if not, why not, and if so, how? Difficulties at this point are a fertile source of confusion and erratic judgment.

I. Passing now to a different order of difficulties, the effects of *technical presuppositions* have to be noted. When something has once been well done in a certain fashion we tend to expect similar things to be done in the future in the same fashion, and are disappointed or do not recognise them if they are done differently. Conversely, a technique which has shown its ineptitude for one purpose tends to become discredited for all. Both are cases of mistaking means for ends. Whenever we attempt to judge poetry from outside by technical details we are putting means before ends, and—such is our ignorance of cause and effect in poetry—we shall be lucky if we do not make even worse blunders. We have to try to avoid judging pianists by their hair.

J. Finally, *general critical preconceptions* (prior demands made upon poetry as a result of theories—conscious or unconscious —about its nature and value), intervene endlessly, as the history of criticism shows only too well, between the reader and the poem. Like an unlucky dietetic formula they may cut him off from what he is starving for, even when it is at his very lips.

From the Conclusion of
Coleridge on Imagination (1934)

[TOWARD A POETIC ORDER]

THE WANING OF any one mode of order—a traditional morality, or a religious sanction or symbolization for it—is not the loss of all possibilities of order. The traditional schemas by which man gave an account of himself and the world in which he lived were made by him, and though they have lost their power to help him as they formerly helped him, he has not lost his power to make new ones. It is easy to represent what has been occurring as a course of error, as due to the pernicious influence of arrogant science, or of Cartesianism or of Rousseau; as an infection of the mind by "heresies," or as departure from a norm to which, if man is to become again a noble animal, he must return. Dramas in which the proper balance of our faculties has been destroyed by exorbitant claims from one or other of them, in which science displaces religious belief, or sentiment ousts reason, or dreams cloud Reality,

> What will be forever
> What was from of old,

—by corruption from which disasters we now wander, a lost generation, in a wrecked universe —are not hard to invent.

> It was man did it, man
> Who imagined imagination;
> And he did what man can
> He uncreated creation

as Mr. R. G. Eberhart exclaimed. But these

dramatic pictures of our predicament are utterances of distress. Though they may sometimes pretend to be diagnoses, they are myths reflecting our unease. What they profess to describe is too vast a matter to be handled by that other system of myths (those of Science and History) to which diagnoses belong, and in which verification is possible. And as philosophic myths they are not of the kind which contribute directly to a new order. For the concepts they use belong to the order which has passed, and they are disqualified by the movement they describe. It is better, as an alternative philosophic myth, to suppose that the great drift is not due merely to internal conflicts between sub-orders of our mythology but rather to an inevitable growth of human awareness— inevitable because Man goes on and he retains, in recent centuries, increasing touch with his past.

To put the burden of constituting an order for our minds on the poet may seem unfair. It is not the philosopher, however, or the moralist who puts it on him, but birth. And it is only another aspect of the drift by which knowledge in all its varieties—scientific, moral, religious —has come to seem a vast mythology with its sub-orders divided according to their different pragmatic sanctions, that the poet should thus seem to increase so inordinately in importance. (There is a figure of speech here, of course, for the burden is not on individual poets but upon the poetic function. With Homer, Dante and Shakespeare in mind, however, the importance of the single poet is not to be under-estimated.)

For while any part of the world-picture is regarded as not of mythopoeic origin, poetry—
earlier recognized as mythopoeic—could not
but be given a second place. If philosophic
contemplation, or religious experience, or science gave us Reality, then poetry gave us something of less consequence, at best some sort of
shadow. If we grant that all is myth, poetry, as
the myth-making which most brings "the whole
soul of man into activity," [1] and as working
with words, "parts and germinations of the
plant" and, through them, in "the medium by
which spirits communicate with one another" [2]
becomes the necessary channel for the recon-
stitution of order.

But this last phrase is tainted also with a
picturesque mock-desperate dramatization of
our situation. The mind has never been in order. There is no vanished perfection of balance
to be restored. The great ages of poetry have
mostly been times torn by savage and stupid
dissension, intolerant, unreasonable, and confused in other aspects of human endeavour.

Allas, allas! now may men wepe and cryel
For in our dayes nis but covetyse
And doublenesse, and tresoun and envye,
Poysoun, manslauhtre, and mordre in sondry
    wyse.

In all this our own age may be preparing to
emulate them; but that is no more a reason to
anticipate a new great age for poetry than the
new possibility of a material paradise now offered by science is a reason for thinking that the
day of poetry is over. Eras that produced no
poetry that is remembered have been as disordered as ours. There are better reasons, in
the work of modern poets, to hope that a creative movement is beginning and that poetry,
freed from a mistaken conception of its limitations and read more discerningly than hereto-
fore, will remake our minds and with them our
world. Such an estimate of the power of poetry
may seem extravagant; but it was Milton's no
less than Shelley's, Blake's or Wordsworth's.

[1] Coleridge's *Biographia Literaria*, ed. J. Shawcross
(1907), II, 12.
[2] *Ibid.*, I, 168.

It has been the opinion of many with whom we
need not be ashamed to agree: "The study of
poetry (if we will trust Aristotle) offers to mankind a certain rule, and pattern, of living well
and happily; disposing us to all civil offices of
society. If we will believe Tully, it nourisheth
and instructeth our youth; delights our age;
adorns our prosperity; comforts our adversity;
entertains us at home . . . insomuch as the
wisest and best learned have thought her the
absolute mistress of manners, and nearest of
kin to virtue." Ben Jonson here may merely be
repeating commonplaces from antiquity; he
may be writing a set piece without concern for
what he is saying—but this is unlikely; he may
not have been aware of the reasons for such
opinions; they were left for Coleridge to display; but he was certainly well placed to judge
whether they were creditable opinions or not.
Neither the authorities he cites, nor "this robust, surly, and observing dramatist" himself,
may be thought insufficiently acquainted with
ordinary lives, or with the forces that may
amend them.

Poetry may have these powers and yet, for
removable and preventable causes, the study of
poetry be of no great use to us. A candid witness must declare, I fear, that its benefits are
often unobtrusive where we would most expect
them. But the study of poetry, for those born
in this age, is more arduous than we suppose.
It is therefore rare. Many other things pass by
its name and are encouraged to its detriment.

To free it from distracting trivialities, from
literary chit-chat, from discussion of form
which does not ask what has the form, from
flattening rationalization, from the clouds of
unchecked sensibility and unexamined interpretations is a minor duty of criticism. But there is
a more positive task: to recall that poetry is the
supreme use of language, man's chief co-
ordinating instrument, in the service of the
most integral purposes of life; and to explore,
with thoroughness, the intricacies of the modes
of language as working modes of the mind.

The sage may teach a doctrine without

words; but, if so, it is a doctrine about another world than ours and for another life. Our world and our life have grown and taken what order they have for us through separated meanings which we can only hold together or keep apart through words. The sage may avoid words because our power of controlling certain kinds of meaning through them is too slight; but without the use of words in the past he would have had no doctrine to teach. The meanings sufficient for the dumb creatures are not enough for man.

Because all objects which we can name or otherwise single out—the simplest objects of the senses and the most recondite entities that speculation can conjecture, the most abstract constructions of the intellect and the most concrete aims of passion alike—are projections of man's interests; because the Universe as it is known to us is a fabric whose forms, as we can alone know them, have arisen in and through reflection; and because that reflection, whether made by the intellect in science or by "the whole soul of man" in poetry, has developed through language—and, apart from language, can neither be continued nor maintained—the study of the modes of language becomes, as it attempts to be thorough, the most fundamental and extensive of all inquiries. It is no preliminary or preparation for other profounder studies, which though they use language more or less trustfully, may be supposed to be autonomous, uninfluenced by verbal processes. The very formation of the objects which these studies propose to examine takes place through the processes (of which imagination and fancy are modes) by which the words they use acquire their meanings.

Criticism is the science of these meanings and the meanings which larger groups of words may carry. It is no mere account of what men have written or how they have written it, taken as questions to be judged by borrowed standards or to be asked without inquiry into the little that we can yet surmise about the growth of the mind and therewith the expansion of our outlook on the world.

Thus the more traditional subjects of criticism, Coleridge's differentiation of imagination from fancy, and his still abstruser ponderings on objectification and the living word, unite with the analysis of the ambiguities and confusions that are overt or latent in all cases of metaphor, transference or projection to form one study. It is embryonic still, through which its possibilities are the less restricted. It offers little intellectual rest or satisfaction; but should we look for satisfaction here where all the problems meet? What it does offer is an immense opportunity for improving our technique of understanding.

With Coleridge we step across the threshold of a general theoretical study of language capable of opening to us new powers over our minds comparable to those which systematic physical inquiries are giving us over our environment. The step across was of the same type as that which took Galileo into the modern world. It requires the shift from a preoccupation with the What and Why to the How of language. The problems of Poetry became for Coleridge, sometimes, interesting as problems with a structure of their own. They ceased to be mere voids waiting to be filled. The interest shifted from the answers to the questions; and, with that, a new era for criticism began. Beyond the old tasks of reaffirming ancient conclusions and defending them from foolish interpretations, an illimitable field of work has become accessible.

The change would have been delayed if Coleridge had not been a philosopher as well as a critic. And it has this consequence, that critics in the future must have a theoretical equipment of a kind which has not been felt to be necessary in the past. (So physicists may at times sigh for the days in which less mathematics was required by them.) But the critical equipment will not be *primarily* philosophical. It will be rather a command of the methods of comparing our meanings. As the theory of Poetry develops, what is needed will be disengaged from philosophy much as the methodology of physics has been disengaged.

From *The Philosophy of Rhetoric* (1936)

V. METAPHOR

It was Aristotle, no lesser man, who said, in *The Poetics*, "The greatest thing by far is to have a command of metaphor." But he went on to say, "This alone cannot be imparted to another: it is the mark of genius, for to make good metaphors implies an eye for resemblances." I do not know how much influence this remark has had: or whether it is at all responsible for our feeling that what it says is common-sense. But question it for a moment and we can discover in it, if we will to be malicious, here at the very beginning of the subject, the evil presence of three of the assumptions which have ever since prevented the study of this "greatest thing by far" from taking the place it deserves among our studies and from advancing, as theory and practice, in the ways open to it.

One assumption is that "an eye for resemblances" is a gift that some men have but others have not. But we all live, and speak, only through our eye for resemblances. Without it we should perish early. Though some may have better eyes than others, the differences between them are in degree only and may be remedied, certainly in some measure, as other differences are, by the right kinds of teaching and study. The second assumption denies this and holds that, though everything else may be taught, "This alone cannot be imparted to another." I cannot guess how seriously Aristotle meant this or what other subjects of teaching he had in mind as he spoke. But, if we con-

sider how we all of us attain what limited measure of a command of metaphor we possess, we shall see that no such contrast is valid. As individuals we gain our command of metaphor just as we learn whatever else makes us distinctively human. It is all imparted to us from others, with and through the language we learn, language which is utterly unable to aid us except through the command of metaphor which it gives. And that brings up the third and worst assumption—that metaphor is something special and exceptional in the use of language, a deviation from its normal mode of working, instead of the omnipresent principle of all its free action.

Throughout the history of Rhetoric, metaphor has been treated as a sort of happy extra trick with words, an opportunity to exploit the accidents of their versatility, something in place occasionally but requiring unusual skill and caution. In brief, a grace or ornament or *added* power of language, not its constitutive form. Sometimes, it is true, a writer will venture on speculations that go deeper. I have just been echoing Shelley's observation that "Language is vitally metaphorical; that is, it marks the before unapprehended relations of things and perpetuates their apprehension, until words, which represent them, become, through time, signs for portions or classes of thought instead of pictures of integral thoughts: and then, if no new poets should arise to create afresh the associations which have been thus disorganised, language will be dead to all the nobler purposes of human intercourse." But that is an exceptional utterance and its implications have not yet been taken account of by rhetoricians. Nor have philosophers, as a body, done much better, though historians of language have long taught that we can find no word or description for any of the intellectual operations which, if its history is known, is not seen to have been taken, by metaphor, from a description of some physical happening. Only Jeremy Bentham, as successor to Bacon and Hobbes, insisted—with his technique of archetypation and phraseoplerosis—upon one inference that might be drawn; namely, that the mind and all its doings are fictions. He left it to Coleridge, F. H. Bradley and Vaihinger to point to the further inference; namely, that matter and its adventures, and all the derivative objects of contemplation, are fictions too, of varied rank because of varied service.

I have glanced for a moment at these deep waters into which a serious study of metaphor may plunge us, because possibly fear of them may be one cause why the study has so often not been enterprising and why Rhetoric traditionally has limited its inquiry to relatively superficial problems. But we shall not advance in even these surface problems unless we are ready to explore, as best we can, the depths of verbal interaction which give rise to them.

That metaphor is the omnipresent principle of language can be shown by mere observation. We cannot get through three sentences of ordinary fluid discourse without it, as you will be noticing throughout this lecture. Even in the rigid language of the settled sciences we do not eliminate or prevent it without great difficulty. In the semi-technicalised subjects, in aesthetics, politics, sociology, ethics, psychology, theory of language and so on, our constant chief difficulty is to discover how we are using it and how our supposedly fixed words are shifting their senses. In philosophy, above all, we can take no step safely without an unrelaxing awareness of the metaphors we, and our audience, may be employing; and though we may pretend to eschew them, we can attempt to do so only by detecting them. And this is the more true, the more severe and abstract the philosophy is. As it grows more abstract we think in-

creasingly by means of metaphors that we profess *not* to be relying on. The metaphors we are avoiding steer our thought as much as those we accept. So it must be with any utterance for which it is less easy to know what we are saying than what we are not saying. And in philosophy, of which this is almost a definition, I would hold with Bradley that our pretence to do without metaphor is never more than a bluff waiting to be called. But if that is a truth, it is easier to utter than to accept with its consequences or to remember.

The view that metaphor is omnipresent in speech can be recommended theoretically. If you recall the context theorem of meaning; meaning as the delegated efficacy of signs by which they bring together into new unities the abstracts, or aspects, which are the missing parts of their various contexts, you will recollect some insistence that a word is normally a substitute for (or means) not one discrete past impression but a combination of general aspects. Now that is itself a summary account of the principle of metaphor. In the simplest formulation, when we use a metaphor we have two thoughts of different things active together and supported by a single word, or phrase, whose meaning is a resultant of their interaction.

"As to metaphorical expression," said Dr. Johnson, "that is a great excellence in style, when it is used with propriety, for it gives you two ideas for one." He is keeping, you see, to the limited traditional view of metaphor. As to the excellence of a style that gives you two ideas for one, that depends on what the two ideas do to one another, or conjointly do for us. We find, of course, when we look closer that there is an immense variety in these modes of interaction between co-present thoughts, as I will call them, or, in terms of the context theorem, between different missing parts or aspects of the different contexts of a word's meaning. In practice, we distinguish with marvellous skill between these modes of interaction, though our skill varies. The Elizabethans, for example, were far more widely skilled in the use of metaphor—both in utterance and in interpretation—than we are. A fact which made Shakespeare possible. The 18th Century narrowed its skill down, defensively, to certain modes only. The early 19th Century revolted against this and specialized in other modes. The later 19th Century and my generation have been recovering from these two specializations. That, I suggest, is a way of reformulating the Classic-Romantic antithesis which it would be interesting to try out.

But it could not be tried out without a better developed theory of metaphor than is yet available. The traditional theory noticed only a few of the modes of metaphor; and limited its application of the term *metaphor* to a few of them only. And thereby it made metaphor seem to be a verbal matter, a shifting and displacement of words, whereas fundamentally it is a borrowing between and intercourse of *thoughts*, a transaction between contexts. *Thought* is metaphoric, and proceeds by comparison, and the metaphors of language derive therefrom. To improve the theory of metaphor we must remember this. And the method is to take more note of the skill in thought which we possess and are intermittently aware of already. We must translate more of our skill into discussable science. Reflect better upon what we do already so cleverly. Raise our implicit recognitions into explicit distinctions.

As we do so we find that all the questions that matter in literary history and criticism take on a new interest and a wider relevance to human needs. In asking how language works we ask about how thought and feeling and all the other modes of the mind's activity proceed, about how we are to learn to live and how that "greatest thing of all," a command of metaphor—which is great only because it is a command of life—may best, in spite of Aristotle, "be imparted to another." But to profit we must remember, with Hobbes, that "the scope of all speculation is the performance of some action or thing to be done" and, with Kant, that—"We can by no means require of the pure practical reason to be subordinated to

the speculative, and thus to reverse the order, since every interest is at last practical, and even that of the speculative reason is but conditional, and is complete only in its practical use." Our theory, as it has its roots in practice, must also have its fruit in improved skill. "I am the child," says the Sufi mystic, "whose father is his son, and the wine whose vine is its jar," summing up so the whole process of that meditation which does not forget what it is really about.

This much has been an introduction or preparation to put the theory of metaphor in a more important place than it has enjoyed in traditional Rhetoric. It is time to come down from these high speculations to consider some simple steps in analysis which may make the translation of our skill with metaphor into explicit science easier. A first step is to introduce two technical terms to assist us in distinguishing from one another what Dr. Johnson called the two ideas that any metaphor, at its simplest, gives us. Let me call them the tenor and the vehicle. One of the oddest of the many odd things about the whole topic is that we have no agreed distinguishing terms for these two halves of a metaphor—in spite of the immense convenience, almost the necessity, of such terms if we are to make any analyses without confusion. For the whole task is to compare the different relations which, in different cases, these two members of a metaphor hold to one another, and we are confused at the start if we do not know which of the two we are talking about. At present we have only some clumsy descriptive phrases with which to separate them. "The original idea" and "the borrowed one"; "what is really being said or thought of" and "what it is compared to"; "the underlying idea" and "the imagined nature"; "the principal subject" and "what it resembles" or, still more confusing, simply "the meaning" and "the metaphor" or "the idea" and "its image."

How confusing these must be is easily seen, and experience with the analysis of metaphors fully confirms the worst expectations. We need the word "metaphor" for the whole double unit, and to use it sometimes for one of the two components in separation from the other is as injudicious as that other trick by which we use "the meaning" here sometimes for the work that the whole double unit does and sometimes for the other component—the tenor, as I am calling it—the underlying idea or principal subject which the vehicle or figure means. It is not surprising that the detailed analysis of metaphors, if we attempt it with such slippery terms as these, sometimes feels like extracting cube-roots in the head. Or, to make a more exact comparison, what would the most elementary arithmetic feel like, if we used the word *twelve* (12) sometimes for the number one (1), sometimes for the number two (2) and sometimes for the number twenty-one (21) as well, and had somehow to remember, or see, unassisted by our notation, which uses we were making of it at different places in our calculations? All these words, *meaning, expression, metaphor, comparison, subject, figure, image*, behave so, and when we recognize this we need look no further for a part, at least, of the explanation of the backward state of the study. Why rhetoricians have not long ago remedied this defect of language for their purpose, would perhaps be a profitable matter for reflection. I do not know a satisfactory answer. As the best teacher I ever knew, G. E. Moore, once remarked, "Why we should use the same form of verbal expression to convey such different meanings is more than I can say. It seems to me very curious that language should have grown up as if it were expressly designed to mislead philosophers; and I do not know why it should have."

The words "figure" and "image" are especially and additionally misleading here. They both sometimes stand for the whole double unit and sometimes for one member of it, the vehicle, as opposed to the other. But in addition they bring in a confusion with the sense in which an image is a copy or revival of a sense-perception of some sort, and so have made rhetoricians think that a figure of speech,

an image, or imaginative comparison, must have something to do with the presence of images, in this other sense, in the mind's eye or the mind's ear. But, of course, it need not. No images of this sort need come in at any point. We had one instance of the vicious influence of this red-herring in my first lecture—Lord Kames' antic with the mental picture he supposed we must form of Shakespeare's peacock-feather. Whole schools of rhetoric and criticism have gone astray after it. Lessing's discussion of the relations of the arts, for example, is grievously spoilt by it. We cannot too firmly recognize that how a figure of speech works has nothing necessarily to do with how any images, as copies or duplicates of sense perceptions, may, for reader or writer, be backing up his words. In special cases for certain readers they may come in—there is a long chapter of individual psychology which is relevant here. But the words can do almost anything without them, and we must put no assumption about their necessary presence into our general theory.

I can illustrate both the convenience of such technical terms as *tenor* and *vehicle* and the evil influence of the imagery assumption, with another citation from Lord Kames, from Chapter 20, paragraph 6, of his *Elements of Criticism*. You will see from the very difficulty of making out just what he is saying, how much we need rigid technicalities here. His point is, I think, evidently mistaken; but before we can be satisfied that it is mistaken, we have to be certain what it is; and what I want first to direct your attention upon is the clumsy and distracting language in which he has to state it. He is preparing to set up a rule to be observed by writers in "constructing a metaphor." He says, "In the fourth place, the comparison . . . being in a metaphor sunk by imagining the principal subject to be that very thing which it only resembles; an opportunity is furnished to describe it (i.e., the principal subject) in terms taken strictly or literally with respect to its imagined nature."

To use my proposed terms—we can describe

or qualify the tenor by describing the vehicle. He goes on, "This suggests another rule: That in constructing a metaphor, the writer ought to make use of such words only as are applicable literally to the imagined nature of his subject." That is, he must not use any further metaphor in describing the vehicle. "Figurative words," he says, "ought carefully to be avoided; for such complicated figures, instead of setting the principal subject in a strong light, involve it in a cloud; and it is well if the reader, without rejecting by the lump, endeavour patiently to gather the plain meaning, regardless of the figures."

Let me invite you to consider what is being done here very carefully, for it illustrates, I believe, most of the things which have made the traditional studies of metaphor not very profitable. And notice first how it shows the 18th Century assumptions that figures are a mere embellishment or added beauty and that the plain meaning, the tenor, is what alone really matters and is something that, "regardless of the figures," might be gathered by the patient reader.

A modern theory would object, first, that in many of the most important uses of metaphor, the copresence of the vehicle and tenor results in a meaning (to be clearly distinguished from the tenor) which is not attainable without their interaction. That the vehicle is not normally a mere embellishment of a tenor which is otherwise unchanged by it but that vehicle and tenor in co-operation give a meaning of more varied powers than can be ascribed to either. And a modern theory would go on to point out that with different metaphors the relative importance of the contributions of vehicle and tenor to this resultant meaning varies immensely. At one extreme the vehicle may become almost a mere decoration or coloring of the tenor, at the other extreme, the tenor may become almost a mere excuse for the introduction of the vehicle, and so no longer be "the principal subject." And the degree to which the tenor is imagined "to be that very thing which it only resembles" also varies immensely. . . .

Let us study Lord Kames a little longer: How about this suggested rule that we should carefully avoid mounting metaphor upon metaphor? What would be the effect of taking it seriously? It would, if we accepted and observed it, make havoc of most writing and speech. It is disregarding—under cover of the convenient excuse that they are dead—the most regular sustaining metaphors of all speech. It would make, I think, Shakespeare the faultiest writer who ever held a pen; and it turns an obstinately blind eye upon one of the most obvious features of current practice in every minute of our speech. Look, for example, at Lord Kames' own sentence. "Such complicated figures, instead of setting the principal subject in a strong light, involve it in a cloud." What about that "strong" light? The light is a vehicle and is described—without anyone experiencing the least difficulty—by a secondary metaphor, a figurative word. But you may say, "No! *Strong* is no longer a figurative word as applied to light. It is as literally descriptive of light as it is of a man or a horse. It carries not two ideas but one only. It has become 'adequated,' or is dead, and is no longer a metaphor." But however stone dead such metaphors seem, we can easily wake them up, and, if Kames were right, to wake them up would be to risk involving the tenor in a cloud, and nothing of the sort happens. This favourite old distinction between dead and living metaphors (itself a two-fold metaphor) is, indeed, a device which is very often a hindrance to the play of sagacity and discernment throughout the subject. For serious purposes it needs a drastic re-examination.

We are in fact immeasurably more adroit in handling complicated metaphors than Kames will allow us to be. He gives an example of a breach of his rule which is worth examining if only to show how easily a theory can paralyse normal aptitude in such things. He takes these two lines

A stubborn and unconquerable flame
Creeps in his veins and drinks the streams of life.

"Let us analyse this expression," he says. "That a fever may be imagined a flame, I admit; though more than one step is necessary to come at the resemblance." I, for my part, would have supposed, on the contrary, that we could hardly find a simpler transference, since both a fever and a flame are instances of a rise in temperature! But he goes on to detail these steps. "A fever by heating the body, resembles fire; and it is no stretch to imagine a fever to be a fire. Again, by a figure of speech, flame may be put for fire, because they are commonly conjoined; and therefore a fever may be termed a flame. But now, admitting a fever to be a flame, its effects ought to be explained in words that agree literally to a flame. This rule is not observed here; for a flame drinks figuratively only, not properly."

Well and good! But who, for all that, has any difficulty in understanding the lines? The interactions of tenor and vehicle are not in the least hampered by the secondary vehicle.

I have taken this instance of vain pedantry chiefly to accustom you to my use of these technical terms, but partly too to support the contention that the best part of the traditional discussion of metaphor is hardly more than a set of cautionary hints to overenthusiastic schoolboys, hints masquerading as fundamental theory of language. Lord Kames is not exceptionally limited in his treatment or abnormally obtuse. You will find similar things in Johnson when he discusses Cowley and Donne for example, in Monboddoe, and Harris and Withers, and Campbell, in all the chief 18th Century Rhetoricians.

Not until Coleridge do we get any adequate setting of these chief problems of language. But Coleridge's thought has not even yet come into its own. And, after Coleridge, in spite of the possibilities which he opened, there was a regrettable slackening of interest in the questions. The 18th Century was mistaken in the way it put them and in the technique it attempted to use, but it at least knew that they were important questions and that there is unlimited work to be done upon them. And so Lord Kames' *Elements of Criticism*, though I

may seem to have been making fun of it in places, and though it is so full of similar things as to be most absorbing reading, is still a very valuable and instructive book offering a model not only of misconceptions to be avoided but of problems to be taken up, reframed and carried forward. Turning his pages you will again and again find points raised, which, if his treatment of them is unsatisfactory, are none the less points that no serious study of language should neglect. One such will serve me as a peg for a pair of warnings or morals of which any ambitious attempt to analyse metaphors is constantly in need of.

Kames quotes from *Othello* the single line

> Steep'd me in poverty to the very lips

and comments, "The resemblance is too faint to be agreeable—Poverty must here be conceived to be a fluid which it resembles not in any manner." Let us look at Othello's whole speech. We shall find that it is not an easy matter to explain or justify that "steep'd." It comes, you will recall, when Othello first openly charges Desdemona with unfaithfulness,

> Had it pleas'd heaven
> To try me with affliction, had he rain'd
> All kinds of sores, and shames, on my bare head,
> Steep'd me in poverty to the very lips,
> Given to captivity me and my utmost hopes,
> I should have found in some part of my soul
> A drop of patience; but alas! to make me
> The fixed figure for the time of scorn
> To point his slow and moving finger at;
> Yet could I bear that too; well, very well.
> But there, where I have garner'd up my heart,
> Where either I must live or bear no life,
> The fountain from the which my current runs,
> Or else dries up; to be discarded thence!
> Or keep it as a cistern for foul toads
> To knot and gender in!

What are we to say of that word *steep*, how answer Kames? He is indeed too mild, in saying "the resemblance is too faint to be agreeable." It's not a case of a lack of resemblance but of too much diversity, too much sheer oppositeness. For Poverty, the tenor, is a state of deprivation, of desiccation; but the vehicle—the sea or vat in which Othello is to be steeped—gives an instance of superfluity. In poverty all is outgoing, without income; were we "steeped to the very lips" it would be the incomings that we would have to fight against.[1] You will have noticed that the whole speech returns again and again to these liquid images: "had they rained," "a drop of patience," "The fountain from the which my current runs, Or else dries up." None of these helps *steep* out, and one of them "a drop of patience" makes the confused, disordered effect of *steep* seem much worse. I do not myself find any defence of the word except this, which seems indeed quite sufficient —as dramatic necessities commonly are—that Othello is himself horribly disordered, that the utterance is part of "the storm of horrour and outrage" with which he is assailing Desdemona and that a momentarily deranged mind speaks so and *is* obsessed with images regardless of their fittingness. Othello, we might say, is drowning in this storm (Cf. Act II, i, 212–21), and knows it.

The morals I would point with this instance are: First, that not to see how a word *can* work is never by itself sufficient proof that it will not work. Second, conversely, that to see how it ought to work will not prove that it does. Any detailed examination of metaphor brings us into such risk of pedantry and self-persuasion, that these morals seem worth stress. Yet a critical examination of metaphor, with these morals in mind, is just now what literary criticism chiefly needs.

To come back to Kames, his objection that "the resemblance is too faint to be agreeable" (notice the amusing assumption that a writer must of course always aim to be agreeable!)— assumed that tenor and vehicle must be linked by their resemblance and that their interaction comes about through their resemblance one to another. And yet Kames himself elsewhere takes some pride, and justifiably, in pointing

out a type of figure which does not depend upon resemblance but upon other relations between tenor and vehicle. He says that it has been overlooked by former writers, and that it must be distinguished from other figures as depending on a different principle.

"*Giddy brink, jovial wine, daring wound* are examples of this figure. Here are adjectives that cannot be made to signify any quality of the substantives to which they are joined: a *brink*, for example, cannot be termed *giddy* in a sense, either proper or figurative, that can signify any of its qualities or attributes. When we examine attentively the expression, we discover that a *brink* is termed *giddy* from producing that effect in those who stand on it. . . . How," he asks, "are we to account for this figure, which we see lies in the thought [I am not sure what *lies* means here. I think he means "has its ground or explanation in the thought" not "utters falsehood."] and to what principle shall we refer it? Have the poets a privilege to alter the nature of things, and at pleasure to bestow attributes upon a subject to which they do not belong?" Most moderns would say "Of course, they have!" But Kames does not take that way out. He appeals instead to a principle of contiguous association. "We have had often occasion to inculcate, that the mind passeth easily and sweetly along a train of connected objects, and, when the objects are intimately connected, that it is disposed to carry along the good or bad properties of one to another, especially when it is in any degree inflamed with these properties." He then lists eight varieties of these contiguous inflammations— without, I think, at all clearly realizing what an immense extension of the theory of possibilities of metaphoric interaction he has made with this new principle. Once we begin "to examine attentively" interactions which do not work through *resemblances* between tenor and vehicle, but depend upon other relations between them including *disparities*, some of our most prevalent, over-simple, ruling assumptions about metaphors as comparisons are soon exposed.

[1] In the partly parallel "And steep my senses in forgetfulness" (*Henry IV*, P. II, III, i) Lethe, by complicating the metaphor, removes the difficulty.

But let us take one more glance at this *giddy brink* first. Is Kames right in saying that a *brink* cannot be termed *giddy* in a sense that can signify any of its qualities or attributes? Is he right in turning *giddy* into *giddy-making* —"a brink is termed giddy from producing that effect in those who stand on it"? Is it not the case that at the moment of giddiness the brink itself is perceived as swimming? As the man totters in vertigo, the world spins too and the brink becomes not merely giddy-making but actually vertiginous, seems itself to stagger with a dizziness and to whirl with a bewildering rapidity. The eyes nystagmically rolling give away their motion to the world—including the brink. Thus the brink as perceived, which is the brink that the poet is speaking of, actually itself acquires a giddiness. If so, we may doubt for a moment whether there is a metaphor here at all—until we notice how this whirling that infects the world as we grow giddy comes to it by a process which is itself radically metaphoric. Our eyes twitch, but it is the world which seems to spin. So it is with a large part, perhaps, in the final account, with *all* our perceptions. Our world is a projected world, shot through with characters lent to it from our own life. "We receive but what we give." The processes of metaphor in language, the exchanges between the meanings of words which we study in explicit verbal metaphors, are super-imposed upon a perceived world which is itself a product of earlier or unwitting metaphor, and we shall not deal with them justly if we forget that this is so. That is why, if we are to take the theory of metaphor further than the 18th Century took it, we must have some general theorem of meaning. And since it was Coleridge who saw most deeply and clearly into this necessity, and, with his theory of the imagination, has done most to supply it, I may fittingly close this Lecture with a passage from Appendix C of *The Statesman's Manual*, in which Coleridge is stating that theory symbolically.

A symbol, for him, is a translucent instance, which "while it enunciates the whole, abides itself as a living part of that unity of which it is the representative." So here he takes the vegetable kingdom, or any plant, as an object of meditation through and in which to see the universal mode of imagination—of those metaphoric exchanges by which the individual life and its world grow together. If we can follow the meditation we are led, I believe, to Coleridge's conception of imaginative growth more easily and safely than by any other road. For, as the plant here is a symbol, in his sense, of all growth, so the passage too is itself a symbol, a translucent instance, of imagination.

He has been speaking of the book of Nature that "has been the music of gentle and pious minds in all ages, it is the poetry of all human nature, to read it likewise in a figurative sense, and to find therein correspondences and symbols of the spiritual world.

"I have at this moment before me, in the flowery meadow, on which my eye is now reposing, one of its most soothing chapters, in which there is no lamenting word, no one character of guilt or anguish. For never can I look and meditate on the vegetable creation, without a feeling similar to that with which we gaze at a beautiful infant that has fed itself asleep at its mother's bosom, and smiles in its strange dream of obscure yet happy sensations. The same tender and genial pleasure takes possession of me, and this pleasure is checked and drawn inward by the like aching melancholy, by the same whispered remonstrance, and made restless by a similar impulse of aspiration. It seems as if the soul said to herself: From this state hast *thou* fallen! Such shouldst thou still become, thy Self all permeable to a holier power! thy self at once hidden and glorified by its own transparency, as the accidental and dividuous in this quiet and harmonious object is subjected to the life and light of nature which shines in it, even as the transmitted power, love and wisdom, of God over all, fills and shines through nature! But what the plant is, by an act not its own and unconsciously— that must thou make thyself to become! must by prayer and by a watchful and unresisting

spirit, join at least with the preventive and as-
sisting grace to make thyself, in that light of
conscience which inflameth not, and with that
knowledge which puffeth not up!

"But further . . . I seem to myself to behold in the quiet objects on which I am gazing, more than an arbitrary illustration, more
than a mere simile, the work of my own fancy.
I feel an awe, as if there were before my eyes
the same power as that of the reason—the same
power in a lower dignity, and therefore a symbol established in the truth of things. I feel it
alike, whether I contemplate a single tree or
flower, or meditate on vegetation throughout
the world, as one of the great organs of the life
of nature. Lo!—with the rising sun it com-
mences its outward life and enters into open
communion with all the elements at once assimilating them to itself and to each other. At
the same moment it strikes its roots and unfolds its leaves, absorbs and respires, steams

forth its cooling vapour and finer fragrance,
and breathes a repairing spirit, at once the food
and tone of the atmosphere, into the atmosphere that feeds *it*. Lo!—at the touch of light
how it returns an air akin to light, and yet with
the same pulse effectuates its own secret
growth, still contracting to fix what expanding
it had refined. Lo!—how upholding the cease-
less plastic motion of the parts in the profoundest rest of the whole, it becomes the
visible *organismus* of the whole silent or elementary life of nature and therefore, in incor-
porating the one extreme becomes the symbol
of the other; the natural symbol of that higher
life of reason."

What Coleridge has here said of this "open
communion" is true also of the word—in the
free metaphoric discursive sentence. "Are not
words," he had asked nineteen years before,
"Are not words parts and germinations of the
plant?"

[THE USES OF RHETORIC]

It is an old dream that in time psychology
might be able to tell us so much about our
minds that we would at last become able to discover with some certainty what we mean by our
words and how we mean it. An opposite or
complementary dream is that with enough improvement in Rhetoric we may in time learn so
much about words that they will tell us how
our minds work. It seems modest and reasonable to combine these dreams and hope that a
patient persistence with the problems of Rhetoric may, while exposing the causes and modes

From the *Philosophy of Rhetoric* by I. A. Richards.
Copyright 1936 by Oxford University Press, Inc. Renewed 1964 by I. A. Richards. Reprinted by permission.

of the misinterpretation of words, also throw
light upon and suggest a remedial discipline
for deeper and more grievous disorders; that,
as the small and local errors in our everyday
misunderstandings with language are models in
miniature of the greater errors which disturb
the development of our personalities, their
study may also show us more about how these
large scale disasters may be avoided. That at
least was Plato's hope, as it was Spinoza's belief that there is but one end for the sciences.
"Above all things, a method must be thought
out of healing the understanding and purifying it at the beginning, that it may with the
greatest success understand things correctly."

Jakobson's Shakespeare: The Subliminal Structures of a Sonnet (1970)

WHAT MAY very likely prove a landmark in the long-awaited approach of descriptive linguistics to the account of poetry is now appearing in the studies of many kinds of poems in many different languages that Roman Jakobson is issuing and about to issue. For the general reader of English the most decisive of these will probably be the analysis of Shakespeare's sonnet 129, "Th' expence of Spirit. . . ." (recently published as a pamphlet: *Shakespeare's Verbal Art in Th' expence of Spirit*, The Hague: Mouton). This candidate for topmost rank among sonnets is now shown to have a degree of exactly describable structural order which—could it have been pointed out to them in such precise unchallengeable detail—would cer-

tainly have thrown Shakespeare himself along with his most intent and admiring readers into deeply wondering astonishment. Just what the consequences of these demonstrations—for readers, critics and poets—will be (or should be) is a topic deserving of as much concern as outcomes of, say, recent discoveries in genetics (with which there may be traceable linkages) or those of space exploration or those of man's ever-mounting capacity to destroy himself. Those who take poetry, and what it might do for man, seriously may think, indeed, of these new revelations of order as a powerful helping hand offered to us in this time of frightened and bewildered disaffection. Throughout history, and long before it, poetry has been among

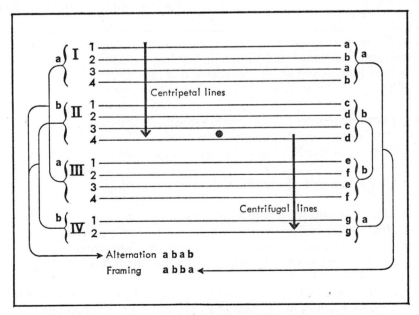

Reproduced from *The Times Literary Supplement*, May 28, 1970, by permission.

man's chief sustainers. A big general increase in his understanding of how it works may well be a practical aid towards saner policies.

Before presenting detail let us look at some of the key ideas, instruments of the demonstration. Most of these are familiar and all are highly intelligible. What is new is that Jakobson and his co-worker Lawrence Jones have applied them in a manner as impressive in its scope as in its scale.

Below is the sonnet with its four strophes and the binary oppositions of its rimes and some other structural features indicated.

The first key ideas are of ODD and EVEN. In each quatrain the odd lines rime. So do the even, and so do the two lines of the couplet. Now apply odd and even to the strophes: I, III odd: II, IV even. The next key idea is that of BINARY CORRESPONDENCE: presence or absence, at a place, of a character, e.g., being a noun, as opposed to not being a noun.

In terms of binary correspondences we can now, with the distinctions developed in linguistics, display precisely for a four-strophe poem:

(1) how far the odd pair (I and III), how far the even pair (II and IV), and how far the two pairs correspond;

(2) how far the outer strophes (I and IV), how far the inner strophes (II and III), and how far inner and outer correspond;

(3) how far the first pair I and II, how far the last pair III and IV, and how far the two pairs correspond.

We will be concerned with correspondences (agreements and oppositions in specific respects) at all levels: from sound-character up, through grammatic and sentence form to utterance aim—between the four strophes taken in these groupings and not omitting relations between the couplet and the rest.

The next key idea is that of CENTER of the poem. In this sonnet the central distich (II 3, 4) is this center and more narrowly the point marked •.

Now we are ready to consider Jakobson's indications of the breaks in its lines, the binary oppositions of its rime pattern and the repetitions of its rime words.

Note first that the position of the breaks and, with that, the movement of the poem, changes at the center after the word *layd*. Until that point the break in each line comes in the middle of the middle foot. After it, the breaks come either at the beginning or at the

---

I 1 Th' expence of Spirit | in a waste of shame [gram.
   2 Is *lust* in action, | and till action, *lust* [n-gr. noun
   3 Is perjurd, murdrous, | blouddy full of blame, [gram.
   4 Savage, *extreame*, rude, | cruel, not to trust, [non-noun

II 1 Injoyd no sooner | but dispised straight, [not-noun
   2 Past reason hunted, | and no sooner *had*
   3 Past reason hated | as a swollowed bayt, [noun
                   •
   4 On purpose layd | to make | the taker *mad.*

III 1 *Mad*⟨e⟩ In pursut | and in possession so, [not-noun
   2 *Had*, having, and in quest, | to have *extreame*, [not-noun
   3 A blisse in proofe | and provd | a⟨nd⟩ very wo, [noun
   4 Before a joy proposd | behind | a dreame, [noun

IV 1 All this the world | *well* knowes | yet none knowes *well* [not-noun
   2 To shun the heaven | that leads | men to this hell. [noun

end of the third foot or at both points. With the centrifugal lines the placing of the breaks and the degree of dominance allotted them are more optional than with the centripetal lines.

Take now the repetitions of rime words. The second rime word of each quatrain is repeated and so is the rime word of the couplet. In the first and last instances the repetition occurs in the same line: I, 2 *lust*, IV, 1 *well*. Moreover, around and framing the central distich—

> Past reason hated as a swollowed bayt,
> On purpose layd to make the taker mad

—*had* (II, 2) is repeated in III, 2 as an initial rime to *Mad⟨e⟩* (III, 1), which is itself an instance of Puttenham's figure: *redouble* (last word of one line = first word of next). Note further the accord between *On purpose* and *In pursut*: the nasals of *On* and *In*, the common prefixes of *purpose* and *Pursut*. A very remarkable frame is thus built up around *make the taker mad/Mad⟨e⟩*.

This will be the moment to consider these angle-bracketed ⟨ ⟩ 'misprints': *a⟨nd⟩*, we will grant, should be *a*; but *Mad⟨e⟩ In*? Is that as certain? It is with an agreeable sense of relaxation that one realizes that he need not always agree with Jakobson, who points out (citing Kökeritz) that the plays can spell *mad*, *made* and *made*, *mad* and that Shakespeare could pun on these two words, yet concludes, "the adjective *mad* and not the participle *made* is evidently meant." Why not *Made* with a supplied *mad* and a merely auditory full stop following it? The added emphasis by double echo of *make* and *mad* to the key line of the poem—

> On purpose layd to make the taker mad

—is worth weighing; and the capital *I* of *In pursut* could be so explained. It is one thing to become mad; it is another to have been deliberately *made mad*, with the preceding line so driving the point home.

As Jakobson remarks, Puttenham's figure, *translacer* (repetition of the same root with different affixes), is very evident throughout the inner strophes: *Injoyd* (II, 1)—*joy* (III, 4),

had—*having*—*to have* (III, 2), *in proofe*—*provd* (III, 3), as well as *On purpose* (II, 4) —*In pursut* (III, 1)—*proposd* (III, 4), are the instances. And a complementary figure (repetition of the same qualifiers with different root), is as evident: *Past reason hunted*—*Past reason hated* (II, 2, 3). Reflections, all these, perhaps, of what happens when a taker is made mad and undergoes those pervasive changes.

Look now at the conduct of the rimes. The first rime, but none of the others, is grammatical. That is, *of shame* and *of blame* can be put into the same grammatical pigeonhole. The second rime is non-grammatical, the riming words *lust* and *trust* belong to different word-classes; the first is a noun, the second is not. In II, *straight*, *bayt* invert this noun–non-noun order, as do all the remaining pairs except the crucial central rimes, *had-mad*, final and initial, commented upon above.

Is the reader by this time beginning to think that such a degree of order and design in a poem is somewhat preternatural? Jakobson is in a position to reply that it is the reader's notions as to what is natural that need to be extended.

SALIENCE OF THE CENTRAL THEME

What do all these evidences of order (and many more) amount to? To an immense concentration and convergence on giving clarity and salience to the central theme of the poem embodied in the central distich (II, 3–4). As Jakobson brings out, these two lines are different in vital respects from the six lines preceding and from the six lines following them. In these other lines there are striking grammatical parallelisms between features of their hemistiches:

I, 1 of Spirit—of shame;
I, 2 in action—till action;
I, 3 murdrous—blouddy;
I, 4 Savage—cruel;
II, 1 injoyd—dispised;
II, 2 hunted—had;
III, 1 In pursut—in possession;
III, 2 having—to have;

III, 3 A blisse—a . . . wo;
III, 4 a joy—a dreame;
IV, 1 well knowes—knowes well;
IV, 2 heaven—hell.

In the middle two lines there is none of this. But there is a simile, the only simile in the poem: II, 3 *as a swollowed bayt*. And more: there is a construction with subordinates dependent step by step: A) *hated* B) *as a swollowed bayt* C) *on purpose layd* D) *to make* E) *the taker* F) *mad*. Significantly, an analogous construction appears in the other even strophe, the couplet: A) *none knowes well* B) *to shun* C) *the heaven* D) *that leads* E) *men* F) *to this hell*. Between these there is another sort of parallelism: C) *on purpose layd=heaven* D) *to make=that leads* E) *the taker =men* (the only two animates in the poem) and F) *mad=to this hell*. And through this parallelism the only simile: *as a . . . bayt*, prepares for the only metaphor: *the heaven . . . this hell*.

Not a few deeply challenging questions arise if we try now to explore the implications—for the reader, the critic and the poet—of the presence of so much relatively unnoticed order in a poem. Jakobson, in his "Subliminal Verbal Patterning in Poetry" (*Studies in General and Oriental Linguistics*, Tokyo, 1970, which he and Shigeo Kawamoto have edited), after enshrining the central problem in the first word of his title alludes pertinently to the widespread occurrence, in highly diverse fields, of orderings which "cannot be viewed as negligible accidentals governed by the rule of chance." Leaves and shells show amazingly systematic structure which the plants and molluscs cannot be supposed to know anything of. We do not with these appeal to any subliminal awareness though recent advances in genetics—as acutely discussed by Jakobson in his *Rapport: Actes du X⁰ Congrès International des Linguistes*. Bucarest, 28 Août–2 Septembre, 1967—seem almost ready to suggest effective substitutes. But with the poet the variations both in his knowledge of what he is doing and of how he does it,

do suggest that Herbart's notion of a variable threshold, a *limen* below which he is not aware and above which he may to some degree be aware, has its services to offer. Most readers, perhaps, after some immersion in Jakobson's demonstrations, may agree that their thresholds as regards noting what lines of verse are doing have been somewhat lowered. Our knowledge of how we put our sentences together can be highly variable. Sometimes we speak with much conscious control and insight; sometimes with so little that we may be deeply surprised by what we have been doing. This last has been a good joke against poets since Socrates, who remarks in the *Apology*: "They are like oracles in that."

But Socrates took oracles seriously too. That a poet may know hardly anything about his compositions entails nothing as to their value or as to his knowing how to compose. Plainly we have two senses of *know* at work here: almost the two that Shakespeare has opposed in the last line but one of his sonnet:

All this the world well knowes yet none knowes well.

Just as "the adverb *well* when preposed and postposed displays two distinct semantic nuances: 'widely knows' in the former case and 'knows enough' in the final position" (p. 23), so the two *knowes* do distinct work; the first= "is cognizant of"; the second="is able to." *Knowledge about* and *know how* are being contrasted.

OUTCOMES OF JAKOBSON'S ANALYTICS

For reader, critic and poet it seems highly important that these two sorts of 'knowing' be not confused. Both have their variable thresholds. We fluctuate in our knowledge about anything (with degree of fatigue, for example) and also in our ability to perform. But the two do not necessarily vary together. Raising "knowledge about" need not raise ability to perform. Unfortunately, there are obdurate institutionalized pedagogic prepossessions which cling to beliefs that it will. In practice and general opinion these two sorts of knowing are misleadingly entwined. The typical instance arises with Grammar as a school subject. Being able to pass a hard paper in Grammar and being able to write effectively need not go together. The abilities required are different. Which brings us back to the possible outcomes of Jakobsonian analytics in the teaching and discussion of poetry.

There are bound to be dangers; all new powers bring them. One is that teachers and discussants will substitute busy-work with the descriptions for concern with the poetry. They may become too preoccupied with marking the items for the items to take other effect. There is little profit in noting that strophes I and II here present nine diphthongs /ai/ (with only the nearby doubtful *Mad⟨e⟩* in the rest) if the words in which they occur don't transfix the reader.

Another risk is that critics may develop a presupposition that poetry which doesn't lend itself so well to such investigations, or reward them so richly, *must* somehow be inferior. Critics are fond of doing that. They pick on something as a merit: say, metaphor or sensory imagery. Then any poem not crowded with tropes or vivid with presentations they look down on. We have to recall Coleridge: "Let us not pass an act of Uniformity against poets." The business of any good poem is to be itself, not anything else.

As to the poet, writing is not the only pursuit in which means can get in the way of ends. Consciously crafty composition may distract from and quite occult poetic aim and outcome. But that is hardly a new hazard.

There are subtler considerations than these which more need exploration. Let us assume that many at least of the structural relations Jakobson displays so perspicuously are among the necessary means by which the poem works. Then any good reader (any in whom the poem has worked) will have been worked on by them. In *that* sense he will have noticed them, i.e., *responded to them.* On the other hand most readers, I believe, will admit that they had not themselves noticed all or much of

what has now been pointed to conclusively, in sonnet 129. None the less they may have responded to it. Thus we have, here, too, two senses of *notice* corresponding to "be conscious of" (="be able to give an account of") and "respond to" (="know how to take").

Keeping these as clearly distinct as we can, we may observe:

1. That probably only some, not all, of the features consciously discerned and included in the *account* will be actually operative in shaping the *response.* The machinery of distinctions used in the account has developed to meet general linguistic needs and purposes. It has only in part been devised primarily and expressly for the description of poetic structure. It may therefore distort, may invite attention to features not essential to the poetic process.

2. That the separation of essential features from others (for which conscious notice may be distractive or obstructive) is inevitably a very tricky undertaking. It is not easily paralleled in simpler tasks of analysis. Changing the consciously noted features, adding or removing features, opening up or shutting down what is consciously attended to, may very likely not leave the other features unchanged—as regards their participation in the work of the poem. (In chemistry it may be otherwise.) So how can we *experiment* and compare in the matter?

3. And yet we do. Any writer weighing one word as against another, any reader wondering which of two interpretations to prefer, is experimenting. But neither (ordinarily) is, in his comparings, recognizing the phonological or grammatical characters of selected items in the Jakobsonian way. He is only trying out one *response* as against another. What sways and guides him then (ordinarily) as he chooses between them is something in many respects *other than* (and working through different compromises from) the phono-grammatic-semantic interplay that Jakobson so adroitly and discerningly puts on exhibit. That fine, multi-dimensional network of distinctions and relations traces, catches and places—more and more justly every year—what it has been pain-

stakingly and resourcefully devised to display: essential aspects of the characters and relations of words, the conditions of their cooperations toward what they jointly are doing. But there is still *much more* to be in some way taken account of before a fully satisfying description of how a poem works can be given.

We may recall that rather similar reflections to these have accompanied many stages of the attempt throughout history to say a little more about how the human being works. And poems are but specific examples of the working of human beings.

That *much more*, of course, is what we label as the semantic, thematic structure, whose exact and systematic description still must (and for long will) elude linguistics. It is, however, that for which the phonologic and grammatic achievements (mostly of recent decades and many due to Jakobson) are indispensable preparation. What they have prepared us to expect is that—in due time and after prodigious labour—it will be possible to present distinctions and relations between components of meanings of utterances (in all their dimensions) much on the model of the ancillary studies: phonology and grammar. The semantic-thematic network needed for describing at all exactly how words, sentences, utterances, discourse . . . build up meanings may well be more complex still; but, as an intellectual instrument, it is likely to rely on analogous combinations of opposition and requirement. There is much indeed here waiting to be done, in remedy of current muddle. As Jakobson has remarked with his characteristic candour and sense of reality: "We stand before a nearly unexplored question of inter-relation between message and context." (*Parts and Wholes*, edited by Daniel Lerner, New York, 1963, p. 159.)

TOWARDS THE DEEP STRUCTURE

Meanwhile, though no *systematic* technique for the analysis and description of meanings is as yet available, there is no lack of paraphrastic *literary* means of indicating them. The techni-

cal and the literary means cooperate, while they contrast most interestingly. Here in Jakobson's treatment is an example of technical description:

All this the world well knowes yet none knowes well,
To shun the heaven that leads men to this hell.

The sound texture of the couplet is particularly dense: in initial position we observe five instances of /th/ three of /w/ (against two /th/ and two /w/ throughout the twelve lines of the quatrains). In stressed words initial and final /n/ occur seven times and /l/ five times (whereas the twelve lines of the first three strophes show no /n/ and a mere total of three /l/ in the same position). Among the vowels the six /ɛ/ of the couplet (3 + 3) are the most apparent. The sequence of three monosyllables with an internal /ɛ/, *heaven*/h ɛ vn/—*men*/m ɛ n/—*hell*/h ɛ l/, follows the vertical iconographic disposition and developmental order of the story; the affinity of the first noun with the second is underlined by the final /n/ and with the third one by the initial /h/. [pp. 27–8]

With this technical account we may compare:

If the first centrifugal line of the sonnet introduces the hero, *the taker*, however, still not as an agent but as a victim, the final centrifugal line brings the exposure of the malevolent culprit, *the heaven that leads men to this hell*, and thus discloses by what perjurer the joy was proposed and the lure laid. [p. 18]

and

Both personal nouns of the poem (II *taker* and IV *men*) characterize human beings as passive goals of extrinsic non-human and inhuman actions. [p. 20]

and

The final line seems to refer to the ultimate persona, the celestial condemner of mankind. [p. 27]

In a much used and often misleading term of current linguistics, these explications seem indeed to be reaching toward the "deep structure" of the poem. The interpreter seems to be placing Shakespeare at a viewpoint not too far removed from that of the author of *Milton's God.*

Many readers, many minds. These elucidations can perhaps prepare us for what will be, I suspect, for more than a few of today's readers an overriding and truly a revolutionary question: What about the position which sonnet 129 is so intricately, so miraculously, designed to define, to display and to sanction? If, in Shelley's phrasing, poets are indeed "the hierophants of an unapprehended inspiration . . . the trumpets that sing to battle . . . the influence that is moved not, but moves . . . the unacknowledged legislators of the world," what poem more than this could better confront such terms? To put "today's question" in appropriately frank and simplicist fashion: "Is not Shakespeare's view of lust now out of date? Does not a re-spelling of that old four-letter word with three letters instead, as *sex*, make all the difference in the world?" This way of putting it may suggest that today's questioners seem to be mistaking a poem—radically dramatic in genre as it may be—for a preachment, a hortatory discourse. This would be a mistake which linguistic analysis as impressive as this might conceivably encourage. Guardedly taken they will not.

With due caution, however, the reply that other readers may be inclined to offer—basing it, they will believe, on a more comprehensive experience and a sharper awareness of human behaviour, not omitting today's figures for crimes of violence—could be something like this: "Much though we might like to think so, we doubt whether that would be wise." Obviously an immensely complex profit and loss budget has here to be heeded. And what alert reflective mind, able to look into and attempt to weigh more than one position for living, more than one view of what matters more than what, will lightly decide? May it not be wiser to compare a variety of positions—including, say, that of Donne who, in Shakespeare's time,

was the first man, they say, to use the word *sex* in its presently dominant sense.

> We see by this, it was not sexe;
> We see, we saw not what did move.

(Both Donne and Shelley above are echoing Aristotle on the "unmoved mover" and Aristotle was echoing Plato.) It is mutually illumining to put a stanza of *The Exstasie* beside sonnet 129:

> So must pure lovers' soules descend
> T'affections, and to faculties,
> That sense may reach and apprehend;
> Else a great Prince in prison lies.

The affections and faculties are here those sentiments and loyalties (structures of feelings and will) which can mediate between reason and lust and restore the deposed rule of order. And beside *The Exstasie* we might put that strangest of poems *The Phoenix and the Turtle* which so resembles *The Exstasie*, being in its central theme another "dialogue of one."

> Property was thus appalled,
> That the self was not the same;
> Single nature's double name
> Neither two nor one was called.

Those venturing such a reply would not perhaps suppose that it would be of effect. They might as readily wonder whether they will not see Shakespeare, and this sonnet 129 in particular, put on tomorrow's Index as especially corrupting to the innocent mind. This controversy is as much a matter of choice as of evidence; the eye of the soul, as *Republic* (518C) has it, is not so readily turned round. I find I wrote (forty-six years ago) at the end of the preface to my first book: "The controversies which the world has known in the past are as nothing to those that are ahead." I wish I could now feel that I was mistaken or that Man's incredibly increasing powers were about to yield greater protection than peril. The ability to read better, more discerningly and justly, which Jakobson's demonstrations could promote, may, we should hope, be a help.

NORTHROP FRYE

Introduction

MANY OF THE CURRENTS of modern literary criticism converge in the work of Northrop Frye. Frye has given new meaning to Ezra Pound's claims for the purity and autonomy of poetry; he has written a sympathetic book on T. S. Eliot (1963); and he shares I. A. Richards' faith in the power of poetry to expand human vision—it is Frye, not Richards, who has said that "the attempt of genuine criticism is to bring literature to 'life' by annihilating stock responses." Moreover, most of the other critics and critical schools represented in this book are also related to Frye. More than any other modern critic he stands at the center of critical activity; he brings things together.

The relation of Frye to other critics is not an accident. First and last, he has attempted to build a theoretical structure of criticism with room for everyone, a house where critics of different persuasions can live. The *Anatomy of Criticism* (1957), above all, is such a house. It implies that literary scholars and critics are taking part, whether they know it or not, in a single community, whose unity derives from the fundamental knowledge of literature that each contributes to. The house is large, of course, and so many critical languages are spoken there that it constantly threatens to become a Tower of Babel. But Frye serves the community by interpreting for it. He tries to show that in criticism, as Eliot said of literature, the existing monuments "form an ideal order among themselves, and are not simply collections of the writings of individuals." And the effort to define such an ideal order has been Frye's great, and unique, contribution to critical theory.

It is on this effort that Frye's reputation rests; he is known as a "systematic thinker," a critic who makes systems. Actually, he himself prefers the word "schematic," since he offers not so much a program or method of criticism as an exploration of the patterns into which it falls. The *Anatomy* "attempts to provide an outline of a schema which . . . I hoped would serve as a guide to practical criticism." Thus Frye constantly arranges the literary universe into structures like "The Four Forms of Prose Fiction" or the seasonal "Archetypes of Literature" articulated below. In *Anatomy of Criticism*, the schema receives its fullest elaboration. Criticism itself is divided into four kinds: historical (theory of modes); ethical (theory of symbols); archetypal (theory of myths); and rhetorical (theory of genres). Each kind, in turn, contains several subdivisions; ethical criticism, for instance, breaks into four phases: literal or descriptive, formal, mythical, and anagogic. While the symmetry of the *Anatomy* is not perfect, the book does construct regular and shapely patterns, largely organized around groups of four, with some of the precise beauty of a spider web or a primitive work of art.

That regularity has been the cause of some suspicion. Does Frye's schema reflect criticism itself, or his own ingenious fabrication of patterns? His definition of the four forms of prose fiction, for instance, invokes a rule of symmetry. One form, the novel, is extroverted and personal; a second, the romance, introverted and personal; a third, the confession, introverted and intellectual. Therefore, Frye concludes, "our next step is evidently to discover a fourth form of fiction which is extroverted and intellectual." The pattern itself, it seems, demands a fourth form. The inductive methods of science, Frye's critics would charge, cannot be ruled by such patterns; scientists must accept what they find rather than fit links into their own chain of ideas.

One answer to this charge, Frye's own answer, would be to insist that his method *is* inductive, that he finds schemata because the nature of poetic thinking is schematic. All men, especially all poets, impose order on the world; it was not Frye, after all, who decreed that men should parcel the year into four seasons. Another sufficient answer might begin with that fourth form of fiction, defined by Frye as the *anatomy*: "A form of prose fiction, traditionally known as the Menippean or Varronian satire and represented by Burton's *Anatomy of Melancholy*, characterized by a great variety of subject-matter and a strong interest in ideas." By calling his own work an *Anatomy*, Frye wittily calls attention to its enormous variety, its richness of ideas. In any case, the test must be how much Frye's schemata make clear, how much they can be put to use. The number of critics who, over the past few decades, have found them helpful offers impressive testimony to their value.

Beyond "systematic" or "schematic," however, another word for Frye's mode of criticism might be "visionary." Many critics base their theories on one poet above all, like Coleridge on Wordsworth, or Valéry on himself. The central figure in Frye's theory, as the selections below demonstrate, is William Blake. Indeed, the way that Frye was forced to develop an entire theory of literature in order to do justice to Blake's meaning is one of the most remarkable consequences in the history of literary criticism. In retrospect, like many unpredictable discoveries, it looks entirely logical. Studying Blake's major poems, Frye "was puzzled and annoyed by a schematic quality in these prophecies that refused to dissolve into what I then regarded as properly literary forms. . . . This problem began to solve itself as soon as I realized that poetic thought is inherently and necessarily schematic. . . . I finished my book in the full conviction that learning to read Blake was a step, and for me a necessary step, in learning to read poetry, and to write criticism. For if poetic thought is inherently schematic, criticism must be so too. . . . I am suggesting that no one can read Blake seriously and sympathetically without feeling that the keys to poetic thought are in him . . ." ("The Keys to the Gates," *Some British Romantics*, 1966). What Frye learned most from Blake was vision, a way of looking at the world as if it were contained in a human mind or a human body: "the poetic activity is fundamentally one of identifying the human with the non-human world. This identity is what the poetic metaphor expresses, and the end of the poetic vision is the humanization of reality" ("The Road of Excess"). The book which expresses that understanding, *Fearful Symmetry* (1947), holds the keys to Frye's thought. From it, and the imagination that informs it, flows the rest of his work.

What is the fabric of that vision? First, it predicates the autonomy of poetry and the poetic imagination, their essential independence from nature. Like Blake, Frye refuses to accept restraints on the poet's freedom to construct worlds of his own; he holds "a conception of literature as a body of hypothetical creations which is not necessarily involved in the worlds of truth and fact, nor necessarily withdrawn from them, but which may enter into any kind of relationship to them." Literature, in such a view, resembles mathematics, since it "proceeds hypothetically and by internal consistency, not descriptively and by outward fidelity to nature." Thus the critic, like the mathematician, thinks of his field as a universe complete in itself, composed not of numbers but of verbal relationships. Literature is nothing more or less than the sum total of such relations. And the world of things, within the poet's universe, dances to his tune.

Moreover, the autonomous world of poetry need not, cannot, obey any laws but its own. As poems are made of words, so poetry is made of poems. When we study Milton's "Lycidas," for instance, we must look to other poems to find the forms and contexts on which it draws. Literary forms and literary significances do not exist outside literature. "Milton is not writing an obituary: he does not start with Edward King and his life and times, but with the conventions and archetypes that poetry requires for such a theme" ("Literature as Context: Milton's *Lycidas*," 1959, *Fables of Identity*). Poems make a society among themselves, where they imitate and reflect each other; Milton makes "Lycidas" out of the form of pastoral elegy, conventional ideas and images, the store of English poetic language, the structure of the Adonis myth. Nor does this analysis suggest that he is "unoriginal": where but in the world of literature can literature be born? "Because works of literature form a verbal society, and because the forms of literature can only be derived from other literary forms, literature is allusive, not externally or incidentally allusive, but substantially and integrally so." The chain of allusions, if we follow it, will lead us back to Homer, or forward to the last poet's last word. Nor has the chain an end. In the poetic universe, in the critic's vision, the total form of literature is perfect and self-enclosed.

No aspect of Frye's critical theory has been more controversial than his claims for literary autonomy. The relation of literature to life, the dependency of the imagination upon the reality that it "spurns and craves," have long been accepted as basic tenets of Western thought. Indeed, many critics have argued that the dialogue or tension between nature and art constitutes the major theme of poetry, and have spent their lives explicating such tensions. Frye suggests that their efforts, if not wrong, are only partial: the struggle between art and nature might itself be viewed as an artistic myth. Consider, for instance, Yeats's famous, exhaustively analyzed "Sailing to Byzantium." The movement of the poem is clear: the speaker, an old man, quits the sensual country of the young and sails to the holy city of Byzantium, where he prays to be taken out of nature and become a timeless artifact. On a first reading, we might suppose the poem to be a perfect illustration of Frye's theory, as the artist abandons the world of nature and takes a form composed of art itself. Then details begin to intrude: we notice that the form of the golden bird on its golden bough mirrors "birds in the trees," and that the world of art, perfect as it is, is nothing but a transformation of the natural. At this point, a critic may want to return to the title of the poem, and remind us that it speaks of "sailing," not of arriving; the old man longs for the purity of Byzantium, but his poem exists in the moment between sensual life and pure form, in the tension of the journey itself. Thus the center of the poem may be viewed as the poet's desperate, never totally satisfied longing to be consumed, to purge himself of mortality. If we accept this reading, we may say that it demonstrates the impossibility of an autonomous art. Yet Frye might reply that the opposite is true, that the desire of the poet for a more than worldly perfection, impossible in life, is precisely what the poem satisfies and achieves. The sensual world, the golden world, the feelings of the poet are all absorbed into the form of the poem itself, which realizes them by transfiguring them into a single mythic structure. If "Sailing to Byzantium" describes an interplay between art and nature, nevertheless the total form of its words constructs an autonomous world of poetry.

As we look further into that world, moreover, we may begin to discern how many images it shares with other poems. From a great many such encounters, derived especially from his reading of Blake, Frye draws another essential part of his theory, the notion of the archetype: "a symbol, usually an image, which recurs often enough in literature to be recognizable as an element of one's literary experience as a whole." Repeated again and again in art throughout history, archetypes, rather than nature, seem to be the materials of which poetry is made. Thus "Sailing to Byzantium" constructs its world, not by simulating a trip from Ireland to Turkey but by gathering together images that form an archetype of the comic vision: "the city, the tree, the bird, the community of sages, the geometrical gyre and the detachment from the cyclic world." Such images are not in themselves good or bad—they recur in comic strips as well as Shakespeare—but essential; they constitute every artist's stock in trade. Each poet arranges them according to the dictates of his own vision, each critic tries to find a schema that will include them. Nor, according to Frye, do archetypes require any mystical explanation; they are as concrete and practical in literature as rhythms in music or patterns in painting.

Once we begin to recognize archetypes, however, we may want to know their origins. Do they actually *inhere* in literature, or do we only imagine them? A paradigm of this line of questioning may be taken from Shaw's *Saint Joan:* "JOAN. I hear voices telling me what to do. They come from God./ ROBERT. They come from your imagination./ JOAN. Of course. That is how the messages of God come to us." With regard to poetry, we must understand, Joan's answer is not an equivocation. The archetypal voices heard by poets do come from the imagination, because only there does the poetic universe exist. Once again, Blake above all other poets teaches this lesson to the critic: "the true Man is the source, he being the Poetic Genius." But the universality of archetypes suggests that they belong to a single human imagination shared by all men. "As all men are alike in outward form," says Blake, "So (and with the same infinite variety) all are alike in the Poetic Genius" (*All Religions Are One*). Insofar as he dares to trust his imagination and become a poet, every man has access to archetypes, and to the poetic universe where vision holds sway. Finding archetypes accommodated to his own mind, furthermore, he will be prepared for another recognition: all archetypes together form part of the total dream of man. In this phase, which Frye calls the anagogic, the imagination assumes complete authority. "The study of literature takes us toward seeing poetry as the imitation of infinite social action and infinite human thought, the mind of a man who is all men, the universal creative word which is all words" (*Anatomy of Criticism*, p. 125).

At its highest level, therefore, Frye's criticism takes on an enormous project: a map of the imagination. Its archetypes and myths, its charts and schema, sketch a poetic universe where man can know himself and fulfill himself as an imaginative being. In that universe, theoretically, criticism becomes identical with vision itself. "On the higher limit is criticism triumphant, the inner possession of literature as an imaginative force to which all study of literature leads, and which is criticism at once glorified and invisible" ("Criticism, Visible and Invisible," *College English*, 1964).

Can such a theory, impressive as it is, be put into practice? The answer is that it can be and has been. Visionary criticism sheds light most of all on that body of poetry called "apocalyptic," like Blake's prophecies or the Book of Revelations, where the categories of reality assume the forms of human desire, and metaphor becomes "pure and potentially total identification, without regard to plausibility or ordinary experience." But perhaps even more significant, since the *Anatomy of Criticism*, has been the revelation of how many other kinds of work can be illuminated by Frye's map of imagination. Shakespeare's late comic romances, for instance, perfectly illustrate the archetypes of comic vision; and Wordsworth is coming to be seen less as a nature poet than a visionary. Indeed, the appreciation of apocalyptic poetry may even rearrange the hierarchy of literary genres. Critics who regard literature as an imitation of nature have often preferred those forms which seem more "real": tragedy, which reminds us of our human predicament in a world that brings suffering and death; irony, or "realism," which reminds us of human ignorance and powerlessness. But Frye's criticism emphasizes that in the world of art and the imagination all visions are equally real. Comedy and romance, no less than tragedy and irony, draw upon universal archetypes; they live in a world of art where death may yield to resurrection and human helplessness be saved by a magical mastery over nature. Moreover, as champions of the ideal, they perfectly conform to the desires of the creative imagination. Tragedy and comedy, in Frye's view, only represent different seasons of the human spirit; if winter comes, can spring be far behind? In books like *A Natural Perspective: The Development of Shakespearean Comedy and Romance* (1965) and *Fools of Time: Studies in Shakespearean Tragedy* (1967) he has set the balance right by demonstrating that each form has its own appropriate criticism, its own rules of imagination.

What Frye refuses to do is to judge which form or play is "better." Value judgments, he has said again and again, play no necessary part in criticism. Perhaps none of his positions has been more questioned, or more misunderstood. Yet to some degree what he says is obviously true: criticism can never *establish* values. The most superficial acquaintance with the history of criticism will teach us how much the rise and fall of tastes influences even the best of judges. A modern reader who thought his critical sense superior to Samuel Johnson's would probably be a fool; but a modern reader who repeated Johnson's opinions on "Lycidas" or Henry Fielding would doubtless be *called* a fool. Criticism reflects our knowledge, but evaluation reflects our time and our state of mind. "The sense of value is an individual, unpredictable, variable, incommunicable, indemonstrable, and mainly intuitive reaction to knowledge. In knowledge the context of the work of literature is literature; in value-judgement, the context of the work of literature is the reader's experience" ("On Value-Judgements," *Contemporary Literature*, 1968). To conceive of criticism as the pursuit of values, Frye argues, bespeaks a kind of anti-intellectualism, an exaltation of the reader and his feelings over the poem. Such feelings may be very important, of course, to the reader himself; but with the genuine activity of criticism they have little to do.

If Frye's indifference to value judgments distresses his critics, the reason may be their involvement in another elementary confusion—the equation of criticism with direct experience of literature. It is a simple truth, but a truth easy to forget, that reading a poem and criticizing it are two separate kinds of activity. Criticism, R. P. Blackmur has said, is the formal discourse of an amateur. A good reader ought to be an amateur in the best sense of the word, the sense that includes "lover"; but as a critic he engages in formal discourse, the careful weighing of words and facts and theories; and no formal discourse can ever recreate the unique and complicated experience of reading. The confusion between reading and criticism could only arise at a time when readers and critics have felt guilty about what they do: readers, because their enjoyment seems less serious than the intense analysis of literature they are told about in books and college courses; critics, because as teachers they often doubt that their students enjoy reading at all, and they want their analysis to touch life and readers directly. Such guilt, sometimes healthy in the classroom, can also be destructive, by promoting stilted reading and vulgar criticism. Hence Frye's warning in the *Anatomy*: "archetypal criticism, which can do nothing but abstract and typify and reduce to convention, has only a 'subconscious' role in the direct experience of literature, where uniqueness is everything" (p. 361). Such a separation between criticism and direct experience, properly understood, should not be confining but liberating. Freed from value judgments and direct responses, the critic can explore the autonomous world of poetry wherever it may lead him; freed from justifying his tastes by critical arguments, the reader can cultivate his own most personal experiences.

Indeed, Frye's ideas have had this sort of liberating effect on many minds. As a teacher, he aims to break the barriers of prejudice and ignorance that hold the imagination in prison. Geoffrey Hartman has spoken of Frye's "criticism without walls"; and the comparison implied by this image is worth exploring. In the *Psychology of Art* (1949), André Malraux coined a famous phrase, "Le Musée imaginaire," first translated as the "Museum without Walls." Thanks to modern photography, Malraux maintains, works of art have been "cut loose from their cultural environment." In picture books, the scale of art objects is falsified, they lose their position in time and space, their relations with each other become reconstituted; African, Asian, American art are mixed together; statues of gods, once sacred, are reduced to the role of secular curiosities. Thus each of us, in modern times, can construct his own order of art, a new "Imaginary Art Museum." Such a museum, existing in the vision, is: 1) democratic (since available to anyone with access to a library); 2) international (as well as intertemporal); 3) related to works of art only synthetically (since the context of the object, and even its form in three dimensions, have been removed). Whatever losses may be entailed by this process of abstraction, nevertheless "ours is the first culture in history to have completely broken down the barriers between conflicting stylistic traditions and to have achieved the possibility of making contact with the entire range of mankind's artistic creations as a totality" (Joseph Frank, "Malraux's Metaphysics of Art," *The Widening Gyre,* 1963).

The *Anatomy of Criticism,* like the art criticism of Malraux, confronts the whole order of literary creation and seeks to encompass it in an articulated museum of the mind. Similarly, Frye's museum is : 1) democratic (literature does not belong to an elite); 2) international and intertemporal (every time and place contributes works to the total literary order); 3) related to specific works only synthetically (criticism, like literature itself, or like science, must be autonomous, and not dependent on any single work within its field). Frye holds to these principles with a rare consistency. His belief in democracy, for instance, goes so far as to suggest a startling test for any coherent literary theory: Can it be taught to an intelligent schoolboy? (Blake's piper, we may recall, wrote songs that "Every child may joy to hear.") Frye rejects the notion that poetry is a mystery known to few, or an ornament of life, or a luxury: "It is essential for the teacher of literature, at every level, to remember that in a modern democracy a citizen participates in society mainly through his imagination" ("Elementary Teaching and Elementary Scholarship," *PMLA,* 1964). Thus every citizen should be encouraged to develop his own imaginary museum, and to participate in the universal human vision that all of us share. The end of such an education will be knowledge: knowledge of the full human achievement that lives in poetry, and therefore of our own humanity as imaginative beings.

Ultimately, then, Frye's criticism aims at a perception of harmony: "reforging the broken links between creation and knowledge, art and science, myth and concept, is what I envisage for criticism." Such harmony cannot be imposed from outside. Rather, like Blake's Jerusalem, it is a way of seeing that every man must build within himself. The literary critic has no quarrel with other men's ideas, or with the world. At his best, as Frye says at the end of *The Well-Tempered Critic* (1963), he holds the keys to a larger world, "the world that man exists and participates in through his imagination. It is the world in which our imaginations move and have their being while we are also living in the 'real' world, where our imaginations find the ideals that they try to pass on to belief and action, where they find the vision which is the source of both the dignity and the joy of life." In modern literary criticism, Northrop Frye is the spokesman for that world.

Every selection from Northrop Frye's literary criticism begins with two great problems and one small advantage. The problems are, first, that he is so prolific—no selection can do justice to the full range of his work—and, second, that he is so schematic—*Anatomy of Criticism* is a coherent whole that should not be cut into pieces. The advantage is that he is so consistent. Wherever we pick up his work, like Blake's, we shall find clues that, followed, can lead us to the whole. This selection tries to emphasize that consistency, by tracing the development of Frye's critical theory from its early stages to its full formulation. In so doing, we have concentrated upon the steps to the *Anatomy*, and some applications of the *Anatomy*, rather than the *Anatomy* itself. A fuller selection from Frye would include a greater variety of his practical criticism, as well as more examples of his construction of a schema. But we believe that our own selection fairly represents his principal concerns. For a student who wants to know Frye better, there is no alternative to reading all the *Anatomy of Criticism*.

A Note on Sources

Northrop Frye (1912–   ) came late to professional literary studies, having first been ordained in the United Church of Canada (1936). Many of his early essays, including the important "Music in Poetry," *University of Toronto Quarterly* (1941), and the three reprinted below, were incorporated into *Anatomy of Criticism* (1957). His first book, in which many of his critical ideas appear already developed, is *Fearful Symmetry: A Study of William Blake* (1947). He has since published studies of *T. S. Eliot* (1963); Milton, *The Return of Eden* (1965); and *A Study of English Romanticism* (1968); as well as highly influential books on Shakespearean comedy and romance, *A Natural Perspective* (1965), and Shakespearean tragedy, *Fools of Time* (1967). Frye's most elegant short statement of his critical theory is *The Educated Imagination* (1963); like *The Well-Tempered Critic* (1963) and *The Critical Path* (1971), two other graceful summaries of principles, it originated as a series of lectures. Other lectures, *The Modern Century* (1967), discuss the heritage of Canadian culture. There have been two excellent collections of Frye's essays: *Fables of Identity: Studies in Poetic Mythology* (1963) reveals the range of his critical interests; and *The Stubborn Structure: Essays on Criticism and Society* (1970) shows an increasing concern with humanistic education.

The most useful study of Frye to date is *Northrop Frye in Modern Criticism*, ed. Murray Krieger (1966). Its papers, originally delivered at the English Institute, include favorable essays by Angus Fletcher and Geoffrey Hartman, a dissent by W. K. Wimsatt, and Frye's own commentary; Krieger contributes an introduction, and John Grant a fine bibliography. For discerning criticism of Frye, see Frank Kermode, *Puzzles and Epiphanies* (1962), and Andrew Von Hendy, "A Poetics for Demogorgon," *Criticism* (1966).

From *Fearful Symmetry* (1947)

FROM THE WORD WITHIN THE WORD

WHEN we perceive, or rather reflect on, the general, we perceive as an ego: when we perceive as a mental form, or rather create, we perceive as part of a universal Creator or Perceiver, who is ultimately Jesus. Jesus is the Logos or Word of God, the totality of creative power, the universal visionary in whose mind we perceive the particular. But the phrase "Word of God" is obviously appropriate also to all works of art which reveal the same perspective, these latter being recreations of the divine vision which is Jesus. The archetypal Word of God, so to speak, sees this world of time and space as a single creature in eternity and infinity, fallen and redeemed. This is the vision of God (subjective genitive: the vision which God in us has). In this world the Word of God is the aggregate of works of inspired art, the Scripture written by the Holy Spirit which spoke by the prophets. Properly interpreted, all works of art are phases of that archetypal vision. The vision of the Last Judgment, said Blake, "is seen by the Imaginative Eye of Every one according to the situation he holds." And the greater the work of art, the more completely it reveals the gigantic myth which is the vision of this world as God sees it, the outlines of that vision being creation, fall, redemption and apocalypse.

The Bible is the world's greatest work of art and therefore has primary claim to the title of God's Word. It takes in, in one immense sweep, the entire world of experience from the creation to the final vision of the City of God, embracing heroic saga, prophetic vision, legend, symbolism, the Gospel of Jesus, poetry and oratory on the way. It bridges the gap between a lost Golden Age and the time that the Word became flesh and dwelt among us, and it alone gives us the vision of the life of Jesus in this world. For some reason or other the Jews managed to preserve an imaginative tradition which the Greeks and others lost sight of, and possessed only in disguised and allegorical forms. The Classical poets, says Blake:

Assert that Jupiter usurped the Throne of his Father, Saturn, & brought on an Iron Age & Begat on Mnemosyne, or Memory, The Greek Muses, which are not Inspiration as the Bible is. Reality was Forgot, & the Vanities of Time & Space only Remember'd & call'd Reality. Such is the Mighty difference between Allegoric Fable & Spiritual Mystery. Let it here be Noted that the Greek Fables originated in Spiritual Mystery & Real Visions, which are lost & clouded in Fable & Allegory, while the Hebrew Bible & the Greek Gospel are Genuine, Preserv'd by the Saviour's Mercy. The Nature of my Work is Visionary or Imaginative; it is an Endeavour to Restore what the Ancients call'd the Golden Age.

We shall come to this distinction between allegory and vision in a moment. There are two obvious inferences from the passage: first, that Blake's poetry is all related to a central myth; and secondly, that the primary basis of this myth is the Bible, so that if we know how Blake read the Bible "in its infernal or diabolical sense" we shall have little difficulty with his symbolism. The central principle of this diabolic interpretation is that the Bible is one

From *Fearful Symmetry: A Study of William Blake* by Northrop Frye (copyright 1947 by Princeton University Press); pp. 108–111. Reprinted by permission of the author and Princeton University Press.

poem, completely consistent in imagery and symbolism. Blake cared nothing about questions of authorship or historical accuracy: no one expects poetry, legend and saga to be reliable history or to come down to us ascribed to the right authors:

I cannot concieve the Divinity of the books in the Bible to consist either in who they were written by, or at what time, or in the historical evidence which may be all false in the eyes of one man & true in the eyes of another, but in the Sentiments & Examples, which, whether true or Parabolic, are Equally useful. . . .

Nor did he care, in spite of the somewhat un-Blakean sound of "Sentiments & Examples," that Jehovah often urges a ferocious cruelty extremely repugnant to a civilized mind: if one gives up the attempt to extract a unified moral code out of the Bible this becomes a profoundly true vision of a false god. So Blake was ready to give a tolerant and sympathetic reading either to Swedenborg's *True Christian Religion* or to Paine's *Age of Reason*. His own ideas of the Bible were unaffected by Paine's iconoclasm, but he considered that the latter might be useful in breaking up a good deal of stupid orthodoxy: in doing that Paine was working for Christianity, and against only the socially accepted perversion of it, or Antichrist.

The Bible is therefore the archetype of Western culture, and the Bible, with its derivatives, provides the basis for most of our major art: for Dante, Milton, Michelangelo, Raphael, Bach, the great cathedrals, and so on. The most complete form of art is a cyclic vision, which, like the Bible, sees the world between the two poles of fall and redemption. In Western art this is most clearly represented in the miracle-play sequences and encyclopedic symbolism of the Gothic cathedrals, which often cover the entire imaginative field from creation to the Last Judgment, and always fit integrally into some important aspect of it.

However, while "The Old & New Testaments are the Great Code of Art," to regard them as forming a peculiar and exclusive Word of God is a sectarian error, the same one that the Jews made and that proved such a disaster to them. All myths and rituals hint darkly and allegorically at the same visions that we find in the Bible, which is why they have such a strong resemblance to Christian myths and rituals, a resemblance explained by early Church Fathers as diabolic parodies or Bibles of Hell, as Blake calls his own prophecies. There are many great visions outside the range of the Bible, such as the Icelandic Eddas and the *Bhagavadgita*, almost equally faithful to the central form of the Word of God, and the Bible no less than Classical legends comes from older and more authentic sources. For when Blake speaks of "the Stolen and Perverted Writings of Homer & Ovid," "set up by artifice against the Sublime of the Bible," he is not only implying the old Philonic doctrine that Plato and Ovid got their creation myths from Moses: he is also hinting at older Scriptures still from which the Bible itself has been derived:

The antiquities of every Nation under Heaven, is no less sacred than that of the Jews. . . . How other antiquities came to be neglected and disbelieved, while those of the Jews are collected and arranged, is an enquiry worthy both of the Antiquarian and the Divine.

This feeling that the Bible does not exhaust the Word of God accounts for the phenomenon of what we may call contrapuntal symbolism, that is, the use of un-Christian mythology, usually Classical, to supplement and round out a Christian poem.

The cyclic vision in poetry is the true epic, whether based on the Bible, as in Dante and Milton, or outside its direct influence. The Classical epic represented by Homer and Virgil, which makes a rule of beginning in the middle, Blake thought comparatively formless: much closer to his ideas are the more easy-going epics like Ovid's *Metamorphoses*, which starts at the creation and works down; or, in fact, even the philosophical epics which also deal with cosmological themes, like *De Rerum Natura*. So are the Gnostic systems, which are intolerably dull and puzzling considered as abstract theologies, but might have more interest if read as epic poems. The *Légendes des Siècles* indicate that the drawing-up of huge cyclic schemes did not perish with Blake, though perhaps only in *Back to Methuselah* has English literature a contemporary example of a complete cyclic form.

The meaning of history, like the meaning of art, is to be found in its relation to the same great archetype of human existence. The inner form of history is not the same thing as the progress of time: a linear chronicle is a wild fairy tale in which the fate of an empire hangs on the shape of a beauty's nose, or the murder of a noble moron touches off a world war. And no poet concerned with human beings ever bothers to draw an individual as such: he is concerned with selecting the significant aspects of him. Significant in relation to what?

In relation to the unity of his conception. But what makes that conception worth conceiving in the first place? Its relation, Blake would say, to the primary Word of God. We say that there is something universal in Quixote, Falstaff, Hamlet, Milton's Satan. But "something universal" is rather vague: just what is universal about them? As soon as we attempt to answer this, we begin in spite of ourselves to elaborate our own versions of the archetypal myth. The true epic is a cyclic vision of life, and the true drama, including narrative and heroic poetry, is an episode of that cyclic vision, just as Greek tragedies were slices from the Homeric banquet. Great art, therefore, is more conventional than most people realize, and if Chaucer and Shakespeare are read in their "infernal or diabolic sense" we shall find in them the same imaginative conceptions that we find in the cyclic visions.

[FROM THE CONCLUSION]

It is clear that the argument over whether art is complete in itself or suggests something beyond itself, whether it is pure form or a guide to better living, amoral delight or ornamental instruction, is dealt with by Blake as he deals with all questions that are cracked down the middle by a cloven fiction. According to Blake, no such dilemma exists: if it were possible to delight without instruction, there could be no qualitative difference between painting the Sistine ceiling and cutting out paper dolls; if it were possible to instruct without delighting, art would be merely the kindergarten class of philosophy and science. There is nothing to be said for the shivering virgin theory of art, according to which art is a fragile evocation of pure beauty surrounded by rough disciplines

From *Fearful Symmetry: A Study of William Blake* by Northrop Frye (copyright 1947 by Princeton University Press); pp. 418–428. Reprinted by permission of the author and Princeton University Press.

such as theology and morals, and in constant danger of being polluted by them. There is nothing to be said either for the thus-we-see theory which finds the meaning of art in a set of moral generalizations inferred from it. The work of art suggests something beyond itself most obviously when it is most complete in itself: its integrity is an image or form of the universal integration which is the body of a divine Man. All Blake's own art, therefore, is at the same time an attempt to achieve absolute clarity of vision and a beginner's guide to the understanding of an archetypal vision of which it forms part. We cannot understand Blake without understanding how to read the Bible, Milton, Ovid and the Prose Edda at least as he read them, on the assumption that an archetypal vision, which all great art without exception shows forth to us, really does exist. If he is wrong, we have merely distorted the meaning of these other works of prophecy;

if he is right, the ability we gain by deciphering him is transferable, and the value of studying him extends far beyond our personal interest in Blake himself.

Any student of Blake may come to feel that he insists too much on revelation, that his lights are too intense and glaring, that he does not sufficiently sympathize with a reader's tendency to feel let down when a tantalizing mystery is fully explained. Surely the deliberate illusion of the magician has a place in art as well as mental enlightenment. This is more or less the feeling already referred to that the Prophecies are too diagrammatic to have the poetic impact of great art, or even to be consistent with Blake's own condemnation of arid and "spectral" rationalism. We tried to explain this, however, in terms of Blake's historical context. It is all very well for Socrates to point out that the poet's inspiration is one thing and his conscious understanding of what he is saying another. The Greek dramatists contemporary with Socrates could make mythological figures humanly credible because a great deal of their work was done for them: they were interpreting religious and historical traditions to which their audiences were already prepared to attach an archetypal significance. The same is true of Milton's Satan: it is even true, though less obviously so, of many of Shakespeare's characters. It is, for instance, impossible to understand the significance of Shylock, the Jew who represents a humor of revenge and a confidence in a bond and a law and a just judgment, without a fairly comprehensive grasp of the argument of the Christian Bible; and however the Puritan preacher around the corner might thunder against the godless playhouse, he would sooner or later, if he knew his job of expounding Scripture, educate his hearers in the understanding of Shylock.

The audience of a Greek or Christian poet would find it difficult to understand barbarian or heathen symbolism unless it were first translated into the terms familiar to them. That fact does not affect the poet, or limit his universal significance; it relates solely to the audience. In Christian times most of Virgil's readers assumed that his fourth eclogue was a prophecy of the Christian Messiah. That has the great advantage of seeing an archetypal pattern in the poem, and is far ahead of the merely incompetent criticism which sees nothing in it but extravagant flattery. Insofar as such readers conceived of the truth of Christianity as rational rather than visionary, it has the disadvantage of distorting Virgil's meaning. That is a serious but by no means fatal defect; interpreting Virgil's symbolism in Christian terms is translation, and translation may be legitimate even though it always has to ignore many aspects of the poet's original achievement. It is better to read Virgil in the original symbolism as well as the original language, but the one, like the other, must have a meaning communicable to us. Every poet, including Blake, must first be studied in connection with his own age, but there comes a point at which the value of this study becomes exhausted and the conception of "anachronism" is rendered meaningless. What makes the poet worth studying at all is his ability to communicate beyond his context in time and space: we therefore are the present custodians of his meaning, and the profundity of his appeal is relative to our own outlook.

It is here that Blake comes in with his doctrine that "all had originally one language, and one religion." If we follow his own method, and interpret this in imaginative instead of historical terms, we have the doctrine that all symbolism in all art and all religion is mutually intelligible among all men, and that there is such a thing as an iconography of the imagination. Blake suggests to the student of English literature that to recognize the existence of a total form of vision would not be a new discovery, but a return to essential critical principles that should never have been lost sight of. If we look back at Elizabethan scholars, with their rhetorical textbooks and mythological handbooks, their commentaries on Plutarch and Ovid and their allegorical interpretations of Homer and Virgil, we may see that when Chapman spoke of "not onely all learning, gouernment, and wisedome being deduc't as from a bottomlesse fountaine from him [Homer], but all wit, elegancie, disposition, and iudgement," he meant exactly what he said. It is merely an attempt to complete the humanist revolution, then, to point out that the conception of the Classical in art and the conception of the scriptural or canonical in religion have always tended to approximate one another; that the closer the approximation, the healthier it is for both religion and art; that on this approximation the authority of humane letters has always rested, and that the sooner they are identified with each other the better. Such a cultural revolution would absorb not only the Classical but all other cultures into a single visionary synthesis, deepen and broaden the public response to art, deliver the artist from the bondage of a dingy and nervous naturalism called, in a term which is a little masterpiece of question-begging, "realism," and restore to him the catholicity of outlook that Montaigne and Shakespeare possessed. And though the one religion would be, as far as Blake is concerned, Christianity, it would be a Christianity equated with the broadest possible vision of life, so that it would simply be reading Virgil with the maximum instead of the minimum of imaginative power to see once again the form of the Prince of Peace in Pollio's baby, and unite the Roman poet's "*occidet et serpens*" with the tempter of Eve and Midgard.

The great value of Blake is that he insists so urgently on this question of an imaginative iconography, and forces us to learn so much of its grammar in reading him. He differs from other poets only in the degree to which he compels us to do this. The disadvantage of demonstrating a total form of vision from Homer or Shakespeare is that they give so much for so little effort, and it is easy for their commentators to incur the charge of needless over-subtlety. The advantage of demonstrating it from Blake's Prophecies is that without it,

except to the rare and lucky possessor of a set of the original engravings, they give almost nothing. Homer and Shakespeare are not superficial, but they do possess a surface, and reward superficial reading more than it deserves. The reason for Blake's uniqueness is that in his day certain conditions which he blamed, perhaps with some reason, on Locke and the Deists, had brought about a great decline both in mythopoeic art and in the public ability to respond to it. With the exaggeration natural to one in his position, he thought of his age as much less mythopoeic than it actually was; but still he was essentially right in his feeling that archetypal symbolism in his day, if not exactly, in his own words, drawn into one man's loins, was still rare enough for a very explicit treatment of it to be poetically justifiable.

Mythopoeic art revived in the Romantic period, but under the influence of a metaphysic that tended to think of the world of appearance as the object of knowledge and the world of reality within it as unknowable, or, at best, revealed only in flashes of intuition. Hence the importance of suggestive evocation in Romantic art, with its implication that the comprehension of symbolic meanings is a haphazard and fitful process. Our art has passed beyond Romanticism, but our criticism is still largely in it. It is still generally felt that the mythopoeic faculty in art is subconscious, and that if one wishes to produce effective symbolism one must, as Johnson said of Ossian, abandon one's mind to it. Poets are still studied in terms of the Romantic psychological myth of a subliminal real self conflicting with a censorious rational consciousness. Great Christian poems from *Beowulf* to *The Faerie Queene* and beyond have been explained as glossing an instinctive paganism by a perfunctory Christianity, and great tragedies have been interpreted as more or less disguised expressions of philosophical pessimism, of the kind fashionable in the Romantic period. And though we should not get far in science or mathematics without a feeling of pleasurable excitement in solving puzzles, the complicated pattern is felt to be somehow vulgar in poetry. We are encouraged not to rack the arts to search their profundities, but to respond to them with a sensitive receptivity, a relaxed awareness of "appreciation" which, whatever may be said for it, is clearly not what Dante and Spenser expected from their readers. And now that poets have become, in Shelley's phrase, unacknowledged legislators, critics, with one great exception, have largely forgotten their own language, like Kingsley's gorilla. Ruskin spoke that language in a diffuse splutter with a thick moral accent, but he did speak it, and illuminated four or five arts with his knowledge of it. But this part of his work attracted few disciples, and the present response to symbolism in art seems to be content with a state of amiable confusion.

The allegorical approach to literature is often, therefore, spoken of as a fantastic freak of pedantry, though it lasted for centuries, and probably millennia, whereas our modern neglect of it is an ignorant parvenu of two centuries and a half. Surely if the word "pedantry" means anything, it means that kind of contact with culture which consists in belittling the size and scope of the conceptions of genius, the "nothing but" principle of reading everything on the minimum imaginative level. It is of course true that one may read too much into a poem, but as Blake says, "If the fool would persist in his folly he would become wise," and oversubtlety is an example of the sort of folly he had in mind. Imaginative intensity applied to a wrong or inadequate object can be corrected; a deficiency in intensity never can be. Of course those who are incapable of distinguishing between a recognition of archetypes and a Procrustean methodology which forces everything into a prefabricated scheme would be well advised to leave the whole question alone. But it is with symbolism as with etymology: the true course is neither to accept all resemblances as proving common descent from a single ancestor, nor reject them all as coincidence, but to establish the laws by which

the real relationships may be recognized. If such laws exist, it will be quite possible to develop an imaginative accuracy in reading the arts which is not, like the accuracy of pedantry, founded purely on inhibitions.

The Romantic tradition has one thing in it of great value: it encourages the poet to find his symbols in his own way, and does not impose *a priori* patterns on his imagination. Blake could have told Baudelaire that if he pursued his vision of evil far enough, it would eventually take the form of a gigantic, cruel, elusive and shadowy whore, drunk with the blood of poets and part of the indifference of the order of nature, whom Blake himself calls Rahab. And it was perhaps an advantage to Baudelaire not to be told that. But the advantage of having a large public able instantly to recognize his giantess would far outweigh the very remote possibility that he would not have had sense enough to realize, as Blake did, that he should create his own symbolic system and not be enslaved by another man's. It is with criticism as with so many other aspects of contemporary life: for better or worse the reign of *laissez faire* is over, and the problem of achieving order without regimentation is before us.

It is fortunate that art does not have to wait for critical theory to keep pace with it. The age that has produced the hell of Rimbaud and the angels of Rilke, Kafka's castle and James's ivory tower, the spirals of Yeats and the hermaphrodites of Proust, the intricate dying-god symbolism attached to Christ in Eliot and the exhaustive treatment of Old Testament myths in Mann's study of Joseph, is once again a great mythopoeic age. In *Finnegans Wake*, apparently, we are being told once more that the form of reality is either that of a gigantic human body or of an unending series of cycles, and that the artist's function is to achieve an epiphany of the former out of the chaos of nature and history. Here again is a work of art in which every letter as well as every word has been studied and put into its fit place, which is a puzzle to the intellectual powers and utter gibberish to the corporeal understanding. To all the symbols mentioned above there are many suggestive analogues in Blake, and a theory of symbolism broad enough to develop the critical and appreciative side of contemporary culture will almost have to draw heavily on him.

Blake's doctrine of a single original language and religion implies that the similarities in ritual, myth and doctrine among all religions are more significant than their differences. It implies that a study of comparative religion, a morphology of myths, rituals and theologies, will lead us to a single visionary conception which the mind of man is trying to express, a vision of a created and fallen world which has been redeemed by a divine sacrifice and is proceeding to regeneration. In our day psychology and anthropology have worked great changes in our study of literature strongly suggestive of a development in this direction, and many of the symbols studied in the subconscious, the primitive and the hieratic minds are expanding into patterns of great comprehensiveness, the relevance of which to literary symbolism is not open to question. Anthropology tells us that the primitive imaginative gropings which take the forms of ceremonies and of myths invented to explain them show striking similarities all over the world. Psychology tells us that these ritual patterns have their counterpart in dreams elaborated by the subconscious. And whether we accept Blake's conclusion or not, a less far-reaching inference is almost irresistible.

Neither the study of ritual nor of mythopoeic dreams takes us above a subconscious mental level, nor does such study, except in rare cases, attempt to suggest anything more than a subconscious unity among men. But if we can find such impressive archetypal forms emerging from sleeping or savage minds, it is surely possible that they would emerge more clearly from the concentrated visions of genius. These myths and dreams are crude art-forms, blurred and dim visions, rough drafts of the more accurate work of the artist. In time the communal myth precedes the individual one, but the latter focuses and clarifies the former,

and when a work of art deals with a primitive myth, the essential meaning of that myth is not disguised, or sublimated, or refined, but revealed. A comparative study of dreams and rituals can lead us only to a vague and intuitive sense of the unity of the human mind; a comparative study of works of art should demonstrate it beyond conjecture. In the meantime, Blake's Orc may help us to understand that a connection between sex and fire does not exist only in the fact that incendiarists are often sexual perverts, and Blake's ghost of a flea may illustrate the fact that an identification of the character of an animal with the character of a human being does not exist only in totemism.

It is conceivable that such a study—the study of anagogy, if a name is wanted—would supply us with the missing piece in contemporary thought which, when supplied, will unite its whole pattern. Twentieth century culture has produced a large number of theories which seem to demand some kind of fitting together, and we have found a good many analogues to them in Blake. There are theories of history as a sequence of cultural organisms passing through certain stages of growth to a declining metropolitan phase which we are in now, as the Roman Empire was in it before us, which may remind us of Blake's Orc cycle. There are at the same time theories of history as a sequence of revolutionary struggles proceeding toward a society completely free of both exploiters and their victims, which may remind us of Blake's Seven Eyes. There are metaphysical theories of time, and of the divine as the concretion of a form in time, which may remind us of Blake's Los. There are psychological theories of contending forces within the soul which may remind us of Blake's Four Zoas. There are anthropological theories of a universal diffusion throughout primitive society of archetypal myths and rituals underlying all religion and art and connected chiefly with the cult of a dying and reviving god, which may remind us of Blake's Druidism. There are scientific theories of the relativity of the physical world to its human perceivers, and of the mystery of the universe as the analytic aspect of its reality, which may remind us of Blake's vision of Golgonooza. There are new formulations of the Christian conceptions of visionary understanding and of the recreation of the Word of God, new occult conceptions of creative imagination, and new cults with new historical and theological traditions, which have a resemblance to something in our poet. Besides all this, we now have certain facts about the social developments of "Deism" over a century which confirms a good deal of Blake's analysis of them.

The combination of ignorance and lack of space has caused all this to be expressed very baldly, but it would not be honest to omit all mention of the obvious contemporary references of Blake's thought, and in any case the professional caution of a lawyer is not for Blake's interpreters. Now of course the critic's task is to stimulate the understanding of his poet, not belief in what he says, and one naturally resents being told that Blake has "a message for our time." That, however, is the precise opposite of the point we are trying to make. Blake once drew a "Visionary Head" of someone he called his "spiritual preceptor," a vaguely Oriental-looking creature with an expression of baffling inscrutability; and any student of Blake may feel that he too is something of a "preceptor," an oracular revealer of mysteries. But if the reader is left with the impression that there is, or that the writer thinks that there is, something uncanny about Blake's insight, the whole purpose of this book, which is to establish Blake as a typical poet and his thinking as typically poetic thinking, will be overthrown. Anyone who accepts Blake as a preceptor will find his first precept to be that any poet whose work is on a big enough scale will yield an equal harvest of thought if we will take the trouble to learn something about the synthetic and concrete processes of the poetic mind.

The modern reader of Blake may amuse himself, as suggested above, by finding in Blake the germs of ideas later developed by so many of the most important thinkers of our day. In each case the propriety of comparing an exhaustive research into a subject with a few suggestive hints about it may be doubted: it is the poetic articulation, the imaginative unity, of Blake's ideas that is important. Now Blake says that "Real Poets" have no competition: the primary impression which the real poet makes on the reader is not that of comparative greatness, but of positive goodness or genuineness. And this sense of genuineness is the unity of the positive impressions we receive. We are back at Blake's doctrine that "Every Poem must necessarily be a perfect Unity," with which we began. When we try to express the "quality" of a poem we usually refer to one of its attributes. Blake teaches us that a poem's quality is its *whatness*, the unified pattern of its words and images.

A novelist can say "he ran like a rabbit" without involving the rabbit in a larger pattern of symbolism; but if he does indicate a central symbol, a scarlet letter, a white whale or a golden bowl, he forces us to consider his story as an imaginative unity. And at a certain pitch of concentration peripheral and random images begin to disappear: it has been shown by several critics of Shakespeare that there are very few images in the later plays without some thematic significance. And here the framework of archetypal symbolism provided by Blake may be of some value in trying to unify in our minds the symbolism of another poet. The student of Blake, reading Keats's *Endymion*, may see in the pattern of its symbols, the moon, love, silver, water, sleep, night, dew, "eternal spring," triple rhythms, and its drowsy, relaxed and rather feminine charm, a vision of the state of existence which Blake calls Beulah. He will be able to see how the themes of the elusive virgin, the young shepherd poet, the kingdom under the ocean, the "fabric crystalline" presided over by Circe, the escape from a watery world by exploring the "symbol-essences" of all forms and substances, and so on, fit together. He will be able to see the relation of the world of *Endymion* to Spenser's Gardens of Adonis and Bower of Bliss, and so understand how Keats interpreted and made use of Spenser. The meaning of a poem by Keats is not in Blake, it is in Keats: but it *is* in Keats, and a knowledge of Blake may make it easier to see it there. And after we have met an archetypal symbol employed by Blake, Keats and Spenser in a few more poets, a far bigger problem in interpretation begins to take shape, and here again we may find Blake of unique value as a vademecum.

Behind the pattern of images in poetry, however, is a pattern of words. In poetry the word is a complex of ideas and images, ambiguous and associative in meaning, synthetically apprehended. In ordinary speech the word is something much more blurred and commonplace. Even Blake's favorite words "imagination" and "vision" are now rather tarnished, because so long used for the sentimental vagueness associated with them by vague and sentimental people. The point of view which Blake associates with Locke will attach still other meanings to them. But as the poet must use recognized words, his literary tact can go only so far: he cannot overcome a confirmed habit of responding only to words in their commonplace meanings. One can see this very clearly in translation. It is impossible that a Greek tragedian can have meant by *ananke* what the average English reader means by "necessity." But the translator must use some word, and the real difficulty lies in the reader's inability to recreate the word "necessity" into a conception with the associative richness of *ananke*. It has been said of Boehme that his books are like a picnic to which the author brings the words and the reader the meaning. The remark may have been intended as a sneer at Boehme, but it is an exact description of all works of literary art without exception.

Where are we to find the meanings of words? Sophocles is dead, and eke his language, and both at once are buried in dictionaries which give only the translator's equivalent. The meaning of *ananke* must be sought in the meaning of the poetic form in which it is found, in the *raison d'être* of Greek tragedy. Here a knowledge of the historical origin and context of Greek tragedy is necessary, but we have explained why we must eventually move beyond this. Just as we must find the meaning of *ananke* in its relation to its context in Greek tragedy, so we must find the meaning of Greek tragedy in its relation to the context of all tragedy, the great drama of death and redemption of which it forms a crucial episode. Thus in pursuing the meaning of a word in poetry we follow the course of the meaning of the word "word" itself, which signifies the unit of meaning, the Scripture, and the Son of God and Man.

We have seen that in his relation to English literature Blake attaches himself to a certain unity of ideas held in the English Renaissance, most clearly illustrated in the first book of *The Faerie Queene* and *Areopagitica*. We traced this unity of ideas [in the sixth chapter], and are now in a position to sum it up more briefly as the unity of the meanings belonging to "word" in the above paragraph. In its Renaissance context it was a combination of certain Protestant and humanist tendencies, of new ideas about the Word of God combined with new ideas about the words of man. If we understand that to Blake there are no puns or ambiguities or accidents in the range of the meaning of "word," but a single and comprehensible form, we have wound up all of his golden string and are standing in front of his gate. But gates are to be opened, and there is still much to be seen by the light of the vision Blake saw—perhaps the same light that broke in on the dying Falstaff when he babbled of green fields and played with flowers, and on his hostess when she told how he had gone into "Arthur's" bosom, and how he had talked, of the Whore of Babylon.

Three Essays Toward
Anatomy of Criticism (1957)

THE FUNCTION OF CRITICISM AT
THE PRESENT TIME (1949)

THE SUBJECT-MATTER of literary criticism is an art, and criticism is presumably an art too. This sounds as though criticism were a parasitic form of literary expression, an art based on pre-existing art, a second-hand imitation of creative power. The conception of the critic as a creator *manqué* is very popular, especially among artists. Yet the critic has specific jobs to do which the experience of literature has proved to be less ignoble. One obvious function of criticism is to mediate between the artist and his public. Art that tries to do without criticism is apt to get involved in either of two fallacies. One is the attempt to reach the public directly through "popular" art, the assumption being that criticism is artificial and public taste natural. Below this is a further assumption about natural taste which goes back to Rousseau. The opposite fallacy is the conception of art as a mystery, an initiation into an esoteric community. Here criticism is restricted to masonic signs of occult understanding, to significant exclamations and gestures and oblique cryptic comments. This fallacy is like the other one in assuming a rough correlation between the merit of art and the degree of public response to it, though the correlation it assumes is inverse. But art of this kind is cut off from society as a whole, not so

Reprinted from *University of Toronto Quarterly*, October 1949, by permission of the author and of the publisher, University of Toronto Press.

much because it retreats from life—the usual charge against it—as because it rejects criticism.

On the other hand, a public that attempts to do without criticism, and asserts that it knows what it likes, brutalizes the arts. Rejection of criticism from the point of view of the public, or its guardians, is involved in all forms of censorship. Art is a continuously emancipating factor in society, and the critic, whose job it is to get as many people in contact with the best that has been and is being thought and said, is, at least ideally, the pioneer of education and the shaper of cultural tradition. There is no immediate correlation either way between the merits of art and its general reception. Shakespeare was more popular than Webster, but not because he was a greater dramatist; W. H. Auden is less popular than Edgar Guest, but not because he is a better poet. But after the critic has been at work for a while, some positive correlation may begin to take shape. Most of Shakespeare's current popularity is due to critical publicity.

Why does criticism have to exist? The best and shortest answer is that it can talk, and all the arts are dumb. In painting, sculpture, or music it is easy enough to see that the art shows forth, and cannot *say* anything. And, though it sounds like a frantic paradox to say that the poet is inarticulate or speechless, literary works also are, for the critic, mute complexes of facts, like the data of science. Poetry is a *disinterested* use of words: it does not address a reader directly. When it does so, we feel that the poet has a certain distrust in the capacity of readers and critics to interpret his meaning without assistance, and has therefore stopped creating a poem and begun to talk. It is not merely tradition that impels a poet to invoke a Muse and protest that his utterance is involuntary. Nor is it mere paradox that causes Mr. MacLeish, in his famous "Ars Poetica," to apply the words "mute," "dumb," and "wordless" to a poem. The poet, as Mill saw in a wonderful flash of critical insight, is not heard, but overheard. The first assumption of criticism, and the assumption on which the autonomy of criticism rests, is not that the poet does not know what he is talking about, but that he cannot talk about what he knows, any more than the painter or composer can.

The poet may of course have some critical ability of his own, and so interpret his own work; but the Dante who writes a commentary on the first canto of the *Paradiso* is merely one more of Dante's critics. What he says has a peculiar interest, but not a peculiar authority. Poets are too often the most unreliable judges of the value or even the meaning of what they have written. When Ibsen maintains that *Emperor and Galilean* is his greatest play and that certain episodes in *Peer Gynt* are not allegorical, one can only say that Ibsen is an indifferent critic of Ibsen. Wordsworth's Preface to the *Lyrical Ballads* is a remarkable document, but as a piece of Wordsworthian criticism nobody would give it more than about a B plus. Critics of Shakespeare are often supposed to be ridiculed by the assertion that if Shakespeare were to come back from the dead he would not be able to understand their criticism and would accuse them of reading far more meaning into his work than he intended. This, though pure hypothesis, is likely enough: we have very little evidence of Shakespeare's interest in criticism, either of himself or of anyone else. But all that this means is that Shakespeare, though a great dramatist, was not also the greatest of Shakespearean critics. Why should he be?

The notion that the poet is necessarily his own best interpreter is indissolubly linked with the conception of the critic as a parasite or jackal of literature. Once we admit that he has a specific field of activity, and that he has autonomy within that field, we are forced to concede that criticism deals with literature in terms of a specific conceptual framework. This framework is not that of literature itself, for this is the parasite theory again, but neither is it something outside literature, for in that case the autonomy of criticism would again disappear, and the whole subject would be assimilated to something else.

Here, however, we have arrived at another conception of criticism which is different from the one we started with. This autonomous organizing of literature may be criticism, but it is not the activity of mediating between the artist and his public which we at first ascribed to criticism. There is one kind of critic, evidently, who faces the public and another who is still as completely involved in literary values as the poet himself. We may call this latter type the critic proper, and the former the critical reader. It may sound like quibbling to imply such a distinction, but actually the whole question of whether the critic has a real function, independent both of the artist at his most explicit and of the public at its most discriminating, is involved in it.

Our present-day critical traditions are rooted in the age of Hazlitt and Arnold and Sainte-Beuve, who were, in terms of our distinction, critical readers. They represented, not another conceptual framework within literature, but the reading public at its most expert and judicious. They conceived it to be the task of a critic to exemplify how a man of taste uses and evaluates literature, and thus how literature is to be absorbed into society. The nineteenth century has bequeathed to us the conception of the *causerie*, the man of taste's reflections on works of literature, as the normal form of critical expression. I give one example of the difference between a critic and a critical reader which amounts to a head-on collision. In one of his curious, brilliant, scatter-brained footnotes to *Munera Pulveris*, John Ruskin says:

Of Shakespeare's names I will afterwards speak at more length; they are curiously—often barbarously—mixed out of various traditions and languages. Three of the clearest in meaning have been already noticed. Desdemona—"δυσδαιμονία," *miserable fortune*—is also plain enough. Othello is, I believe, "the careful"; all the calamity of the tragedy arising from the single flaw and error in his magnificently collected strength. Ophelia, "serviceableness," the true, lost wife of Hamlet, is marked as having a Greek name by that of her brother, Laertes; and its signification is once exquisitely alluded to in that brother's last word of her, where her gentle preciousness is opposed to the uselessness of the churlish clergy:—"A *ministering* angel shall my sister be, when thou liest howling."

On this passage Matthew Arnold comments as follows:

Now, really, what a piece of extravagance all that is! I will not say that the meaning of Shakspeare's names (I put aside the question as to the correctness of Mr. Ruskin's etymologies) has no effect at all, may be entirely lost sight of; but to give it that degree of prominence is to throw the reins to one's whim, to forget all moderation and proportion, to lose the balance of one's mind altogether. It is to show in one's criticism, to the highest excess, the note of provinciality.

Ruskin is a critic, perhaps the only important one that the Victorian age produced, and, whether he is right or wrong, what he is attempting is genuine criticism. He is trying to interpret Shakespeare in terms of a conceptual framework which belongs to the critic alone, and yet relates itself to the plays alone. Arnold is perfectly right in feeling that this is not the sort of material that the public critic can directly use. But he does not suspect the existence of criticism as we have defined it above. Here it is Arnold who is the provincial. Ruskin has learned his trade from the great iconologi-

cal tradition which comes down through classical and biblical scholarship into Dante and Spenser, both of whom he knew how to read, and which is incorporated in the medieval cathedrals he had pored over in such detail. Arnold is assuming, as a universal law of nature, certain "plain sense" critical assumptions which were hardly heard of before Dryden's time and which can assuredly not survive the age of Freud and Jung and Frazer and Cassirer. What emerges from this is that the critic and critical reader are each better off when they know of one another's existence, and perhaps best off when their work forms different aspects of the same thing.

However, the *causerie* does not, or at least need not, involve any fallacy in the theory of criticism itself. The same cannot be said of the reaction against the *causerie* which has produced the leading twentieth-century substitute for criticism. This is the integrated system of religious, philosophical, and political ideas which takes in, as a matter of course, a critical attitude to literature. Thus Mr. Eliot defines his outlook as classical in literature, royalist in politics, anglo-catholic in religion; and it is clear that the third of these has been the spark-plug, the motivating power that drives the other two. Mr. Allen Tate describes his own critical attitude as "reactionary" in a sense intended to include political and philosophical overtones, and the same is true of Hulme's *Speculations*, which are primarily political speculations. Mr. Yvor Winters collects his criticism under the title "In Defence of Reason." What earthly business, one may inquire, has a literary critic to defend reason? He might as well be defending virtue. And so we could go through the list of Marxist, Thomist, Kierkegaardian, Freudian, Jungian, Spenglerian, or existential critics, all determined to substitute a critical attitude for criticism, all proposing, not to find a conceptual framework for criticism within literature, but to attach criticism to one of a miscellany of frameworks outside it.

The axioms and postulates of criticism have

to grow out of the art that the critic is dealing with. The first thing that the literary critic has to do is to read literature, to make an inductive survey of his own field and let his critical principles shape themselves solely out of his knowledge of that field. Critical principles cannot be taken over ready-made from theology, philosophy, politics, science, or any combination of these. Further, an inductive survey of his own field is equally essential for the critic of painting or of music, and so each art has its own criticism. Aesthetics, or the consideration of art as a whole, is not a form of criticism but a branch of philosophy. I state all this as dogma, but I think the experience of literature bears me out. To subordinate criticism to a critical attitude is to stereotype certain values in literature which can be related to the extra-literary source of the value-judgment. Mr. Eliot does not mean to say that Dante is a greater poet than Shakespeare or perhaps even Milton; yet he imposes on literature an extra-literary schematism, a sort of religio-political colour-filter, which makes Dante leap into prominence, shows Milton up as dark and faulty, and largely obliterates the outlines of Shakespeare. All that the genuine critic can do with this colour-filter is to murmur politely that it shows things in a new light and is indeed a most stimulating contribution to criticism.

If it is insisted that we cannot criticize literature until we have acquired a coherent philosophy of criticism with its centre of gravity in something else, the existence of criticism as a separate subject is still being denied. But there is one possibility further. If criticism exists, it must be, we have said, an examination of literature in terms of a conceptual framework derivable from an inductive survey of the literary field. The word "inductive" suggests some sort of scientific procedure. What if criticism is a science as well as an art? The writing of history is an art, but no one doubts that scientific principles are involved in the historian's treatment of evidence, and that the presence of this scientific element is what distinguishes history from legend. Is it also a scientific element in criticism which distinguishes it from *causerie* on the one hand, and the superimposed critical attitude on the other? For just as the presence of science changes the character of a subject from the casual to the causal, from the random and intuitive to the systematic, so it also safeguards the integrity of a subject from external invasions. So we may find in science a means of strengthening the fences of criticism against enclosure movements coming not only from religion and philosophy, but from the other sciences as well.

If criticism is a science, it is clearly a social science, which means that it should waste no time in trying to assimilate its methods to those of the natural sciences. Like psychology, it is directly concerned with the human mind, and will only confuse itself with statistical methodologies. I understand that there is a Ph.D. thesis somewhere that displays a list of Hardy's novels in the order of the percentages of gloom that they contain, but one does not feel that that sort of procedure should be encouraged. Yet as the field is narrowed to the social sciences the distinctions must be kept equally sharp. Thus there can be no such thing as a sociological "approach" to literature. There is no reason why a sociologist should not work exclusively on literary material, but if he does he should pay no attention to literary values. In his field Horatio Alger and the writer of the Elsie books are more important than Hawthorne or Melville, and a single issue of the *Ladies' Home Journal* is worth all of Henry James. The literary critic using sociological data is similarly under no obligation to respect sociological values.

It seems absurd to say that there *may* be a scientific element in criticism when there are dozens of learned journals based on the assumption that there is, and thousands of scholars engaged in a scientific procedure related to literary criticism. Either literary criticism is a science, or all these highly trained and intelligent people are wasting their time on a pseudo-science, one to be ranked with phrenology and election forecasting. Yet one is forced to wonder whether scholars as a whole are consciously aware that the assumptions on which their work is based are scientific ones. In the growing complication of secondary sources which constitutes literary scholarship, one misses, for the most part, that sense of systematic progressive consolidation which belongs to a science. Research begins in what is known as "background," and one would expect it, as it goes on, to organize the foreground as well. The digging up of relevant information about a poet should lead to a steady consolidating progress in the criticism of his poetry. One feels a certain failure of nerve in coming out of the background into the foreground, and research seems to prefer to become centrifugal, moving away from the works of art into more and more research projects. I have noticed this particularly in two fields in which I am interested, Blake and Spenser. For every critic of Spenser who is interested in knowing what, say, the fourth book of *The Faerie Queene* actually means as a whole, there are dozens who are interested primarily in how Spenser used Chaucer, Malory, and Ariosto in putting it together. So far as I know there is no book devoted to an analysis of the argument of *The Faerie Queene* itself, though there are any number on its sources, and, of course, background. As for Blake, I have read a whole shelf of books on his poetry by critics who did not know what any of his major poems meant. The better ones were distinguishable only by the fact that they did not boast of their ignorance.

The reason for this is that research is ancillary to criticism, but the critic to whom the researcher should entrust his materials hardly exists. What passes for criticism is mainly the work of critical readers or spokesmen of various critical attitudes, and these make, in general, a random and haphazard use of scholarship. Such criticism is therefore often regarded by the researcher as a subjective and regressive dilettantism, interesting in its place, but not real work. On the other hand, the critical reader is apt to treat the researcher as Hamlet did the grave-digger, ignoring everything he throws out except an odd skull that he can pick up and moralize about. Yet unless research consolidates into a criticism which preserves the scientific and systematic element in research, the literary scholar will be debarred by his choice of profession from ever making an immediately significant contribution to culture. The absence of direction in research is, naturally, clearest on the very lowest levels of all, where it is only a spasmodic laying of unfertilized eggs in order to avoid an administrative axe. Here the research is characterized by a kind of desperate tentativeness, an implied hope that some synthesizing critical Messiah of the future will find it useful. A philologist can show the relationship of even the most minute study of dialect to his subject as a whole, because philology is a properly organized science. But the researcher who collects all a poet's references to the sea or God or beautiful women does not know who will find this useful or in what ways it could be used, because he has no theory of imagery.

I am not, obviously, saying that literary scholarship at present is doing the wrong thing or should be doing something else: I am saying that it should be possible to get a clearer and more systematic comprehension of what it is doing. Most literary scholarship could be described as prior criticism (the so-called "lower" criticism of biblical scholarship), the editing of texts and the collecting of relevant facts. Of the posterior (or "higher") criticism that is obviously the final cause of this work we have as yet no theory, no tradition, and above all no systematic organization. We have, of course, a good deal of the thing itself. There is even some good posterior criticism of Spenser, though most of it was written in the eighteenth century. And in every age the great scholar will do the right thing by the instinct of genius. But genius is rare, and scholarship is not.

Sciences normally begin in a state of naïve induction: they come immediately in contact with phenomena and take the things to be explained as their immediate data. Thus physics began by taking the immediate sensations of experience, classified as hot, cold, moist, and dry, as fundamental principles. Eventually physics turned inside out, and discovered that its real function was to explain what heat and moisture were. History began as chronicle; but the difference between the old chronicler and the modern historian is that to the chronicler the events he recorded were also the structure of history, whereas the historian sees these events as historical phenomena, to be explained in terms of a conceptual framework different in shape from them. Similarly each modern science has had to take what Bacon calls (though in another context) an inductive leap, occupying a new vantage ground from which it could see its former principles as new things to be explained. As long as astronomers regarded the movements of heavenly bodies as the *structure* of astronomy, they were compelled to regard their own point of view as fixed. Once they thought of movement as itself an explainable phenomenon, a mathematical theory of movement became the conceptual framework, and so the way was cleared for the heliocentric solar system and the law of gravitation. As long as biology thought of animal and vegetable forms of life as constituting its subject, the different branches of biology were largely efforts of cataloguing. As soon as it was the existence of forms of life themselves that had to be explained, the theory of evolution and the conceptions of protoplasm and the cell poured into biology and completely revitalized it.

It occurs to me that literary criticism is now in such a state of naïve induction as we find in a primitive science. Its materials, the masterpieces of literature, are not yet regarded as phenomena to be explained in terms of a conceptual framework which criticism alone possesses. They are still regarded as somehow constituting the framework or form of criticism as well. I suggest that it is time for criticism to leap to a new ground from which it can discover what the organizing or containing forms of its conceptual framework are. And no one can examine the present containing forms of criticism without being depressed by an overwhelming sense of unreality. Let me give one example.

In confronting any work of literature, one obvious containing form is the genre to which it belongs. And criticism, incredible as it may seem, has as yet no coherent conception of genres. The very word sticks out in an English sentence as the unpronounceable and alien thing it is. In poetry, the common-sense Greek division by methods of performance, which distinguishes poetry as lyric, epic, or dramatic according to whether it is sung, spoken, or shown forth, survives vestigially. On the whole it does not fit the facts of Western poetry, though in Joyce's *Portrait* there is an interesting and suggestive attempt made to re-define the terms. So, apart from a drama which belongs equally to prose, a handful of epics recognizable as such only because they are classical imitations, and a number of long poems also called epics because they are long, we are reduced to the ignoble and slovenly practice of calling almost the whole of poetry "lyric" because the Greeks had no other word for it. The Greeks did not need to develop a classification of prose forms: we do, but have never done so. The circulating-library distinction between fiction and non-fiction, between books which are about things admitted not to be true and books which are about everything else, is apparently satisfactory to us. Asked what the forms of prose fiction are, the literary critic can only say, "well, er—the novel." Asked what form of prose fiction *Gulliver's Travels*, which is clearly not a novel, belongs to, there is not one critic in a hundred who could give a definite answer, and not one in a thousand who would regard the answer (which happens to be "Menippean satire") as essential to the critical treatment of the book. Asked what he is working on, the critic will invariably say that he is working on Donne, or Shelley's thought, or the period from 1640 to 1660, or give some other answer which implies that history, or philosophy, or literature itself, constitutes the structural basis of criticism. It would never occur to any critic to say, for instance, "I am working on the theory of genres." If he actually were interested in this, he would say that he was working on a "general" topic; and the work he would do would probably show the marks of naïve induction: that is, it would be an effort to classify and pigeonhole instead of clarifying the tradition of the genre.

If we do not know how to handle even the genre, the most obvious of all critical conceptions, it is hardly likely that subtler instruments will be better understood. In any work of literature the characteristics of the language it is written in form an essential critical conception. To the philologist, literature is a function of language, its works linguistic documents, and to the philologist the phrase "English literature" makes sense. It ought not to make any sense at all to a literary critic. For while the philologist sees English literature as illustrating the organic growth of the English language, the literary critic can only see it as the miscellaneous pile of literary works that happened to get written in English. (I say in English, not in England, for the part of "English literature" that was written in Latin or Norman French has a way of dropping unobtrusively into other departments.) Language is an important secondary aspect of literature, but when magnified into a primary basis of classification it becomes absurdly arbitrary.

Critics, of course, maintain that they know this, and that they keep the linguistic categories only for convenience. But theoretical fictions have a way of becoming practical assumptions, and in no time the meaningless convenience of "English literature" expands into the meaningless inconvenience of the "history of English literature." Now, again, the historian must necessarily regard literature as an historical product and its works as historical documents. It is also quite true that the time a work was written in forms an essential critical conception. But again, to the literary critic, as such, the phrase "history of English literature"

ought to mean nothing at all. If he doubts this, let him try writing one, and he will find himself confronted by an insoluble problem of form, or rather by an indissoluble amorphousness. The "history" part of his project is an abstract history, a bald chronicle of names and dates and works and influences, deprived of all the real historical interest that a real historian would give it, however much enlivened with discussions of "background." This chronicle is periodically interrupted by conventional judgments of value lugged in from another world, which confuse the history and yet are nothing by themselves. The *form* of literary history has not been discovered, and probably does not exist, and every successful one has been either a textbook or a *tour de force*. Linear time is not an exact enough category to catch literature, and all writers whatever are subtly belittled by a purely historical treatment.

Biography, a branch of history, presents a similar fallacy to the critic, for the biographer turns to a different job and a different kind of book when he turns to criticism. Again, the man who wrote the poem is one of the legitimate containing forms of criticism. But here we have to distinguish the poet *qua* poet, whose work is a single imaginative body, from the poet as man, who is something else altogether. The latter involves us in what is known as the personal heresy, or rather the heroic fallacy. For a biographer, poetry is an emanation of a personality; for the literary critic it is not, and the problem is to detach it from the personality and consider it on impersonal merits. The no man's land between biography and criticism, the process by which a poet's impressions of his environment are transmuted into poetry, has to be viewed by biographer and critic from opposite points of view. The process is too complex ever to be completely unified, Lowes's *Road to Xanadu* being the kind of exception that goes a long way to prove the rule. In Johnson's *Lives of the Poets* a biographical narrative is followed by a critical analysis, and the break between them is so sharp that it is represented in the text by a space.

In all these cases, the same principle recurs. The critic is surrounded by biography, history, philosophy, and language. No one doubts that he has to familiarize himself with these subjects. But is his job only to be the jackal of the historian, the philologist, and the biographer, or can he use these subjects in his own way? If he is not to sell out to all his neighbours in turn, what is distinctive about his approach to the poet's life, the time when he lived, and the language he wrote? To ask this is to raise one of the problems involved in the whole question of what the containing forms of literature are as they take their place in the conceptual framework of criticism. This confronts me with the challenge to make my criticism of criticism constructive. All I have space to do is to outline what I think the first major steps should be.

We have to see what literature is, and try to distinguish the category of literature among all the books there are in the world. I do not know that criticism has made any serious effort to determine what literature is. Next, as discussed above, we should examine the containing forms of criticism, including the poet's life, his historical context, his language, and his thought, to see whether the critic can impose a unified critical form on these things, without giving place to or turning into a biographer, an historian, a philologist, or a philosopher. Next, we should establish the broad distinctions, such as that between prose and poetry, which are preparatory to working out a comprehensive theory of genres. I do not know that critics have clearly explained what the difference between prose and poetry, for instance, really is. Then we should try to see whether the critic, like his neighbours the historian and the philosopher, lives in his own universe. To the historian there is nothing that cannot be considered historically; to the philosopher nothing that cannot be considered philosophically. Does the critic aspire to contain all things in criticism, and so swallow history and philosophy in his own synthesis, or must he be forever the historian's and philosopher's

pupil? If I have shown up Arnold in a poor light, I should say that he is the only one I know who suggests that criticism can be, like history and philosophy, a total attitude to experience. And finally, since criticism may obviously deal with anything in a poem from its superficial texture to its ultimate significance, the question arises whether there are different levels of meaning in literature, and, if so, whether they can be defined and classified.

It follows that arriving at value-judgments is not, as it is so often said to be, part of the immediate tactic of criticism. Criticism is not well enough organized as yet to know what the factors of value in a critical judgment are. For instance, as was indicated above in connection with Blake and Spenser, the question of the quality of a poet's thinking as revealed in the integration of his argument is an essential factor in a value-judgment, but many poets are exhaustively discussed in terms of value without this factor being considered. Contemporary judgments of value come mainly from either the critical reader or from the spokesman of a critical attitude. That is, they must be on the whole either unorganized and tentative, or over-organized and irrelevant. For no one can jump directly from research to a value-judgment. I give one melancholy instance. I recently read a study of the sources of mythological allusions in some of the romantic poets, which showed that for the second part of *Faust* Goethe had used a miscellany of cribs, some of dubious authenticity. "I have now, I hope," said the author triumphantly at the end of his investigation, "given sufficient proof that the second part of *Faust* is not a great work of art." I do not deny the ultimate importance of the value-judgment. I would even consider the suggestion that the value-judgment is precisely what distinguishes the social from the natural science. But the more important it is, the more careful we should be about getting it solidly established.

What literature is may perhaps best be understood by an analogy. We shall have to labour the analogy, but that is due mainly to the novelty of the idea here presented. Mathematics appears to begin in the counting and measuring of objects, as a numerical commentary on the world. But the mathematician does not think of his subject as the counting and measuring of physical objects at all. For him it is an autonomous language, and there is a point at which it becomes in a measure independent of that common field of experience which we think of as the physical world, or as existence, or as reality, according to our mood. Many of its terms, such as irrational numbers, have no direct connection with the common field of experience, but depend for their meaning solely on the interrelations of the subject itself. Irrational numbers in mathematics may be compared to prepositions in verbal languages, which, unlike nouns and verbs, have no external symbolic reference. When we distinguish pure from applied mathematics, we are thinking of the former as a disinterested conception of numerical relationships, concerned more and more with its inner integrity, and less and less with its reference to external criteria.

Where, in that case, is pure mathematics going? We may gain a hint from the final chapter of Sir James Jeans' *Mysterious Universe*, which I choose because it shows some of the characteristics of the imaginative leap to a new conceptual framework already mentioned. There, the author speaks of the failure of physical cosmology in the nineteenth century to conceive of the universe as ultimately mechanical, and suggests that a mathematical approach to it may have better luck. The universe cannot be a machine, but it may be an interlocking set of mathematical formulas. What this means is surely that pure mathematics exists in a mathematical universe which is no longer a commentary on an "outside" world, but contains that world within itself. Mathematics is at first a form of understanding an objective world regarded as its content, but in the end it conceives of the content as being itself mathematical in form, so that when the conception of the mathematical universe is reached, form and content become the same thing.

Jeans was a mathematician, and thought of his mathematical universe as *the* universe. Doubtless it is, but it does not follow that the only way of conceiving it is mathematical. For we think also of literature at first as a commentary on an external "life" or "reality." But just as in mathematics we have to go from three apples to three, and from a square field to a square, so in reading Jane Austen we have to go from the faithful reflection of English society to the novel, and pass from literature as symbol to literature as an autonomous language. And just as mathematics exists in a mathematical universe which is at the circumference of the common field of experience, so literature exists in a verbal universe, which is not a commentary on life or reality, but contains life and reality in a system of verbal relationships. This conception of a verbal universe, in which life and reality are inside literature, and not outside it and being described or represented or approached or symbolized by it, seems to me the first postulate of a properly organized criticism.

It is vulgar for the critic to think of literature as a tiny palace of art looking out upon an inconceivably gigantic "life." "Life" should be for the critic only the seed-plot of literature, a vast mass of potential literary forms, only a few of which will grow up into the greater world of the verbal universe. Similar universes exist for all the arts. "We make to ourselves pictures of facts," says Wittgenstein, but by pictures he means representative illustrations, which are not pictures. Pictures as pictures are themselves facts, and exist only in a pictorial universe. It is easy enough to say that while the stars in their courses may form the subject of a poem, they will still remain the stars in their courses, forever outside poetry. But this is pure regression to the common field of experience, and nothing more; for the more strenuously we try to conceive the stars in their courses in nonliterary ways, the more assuredly we shall fall into the idioms and conventions of some other mental universe. The conception of a constant external reality acts as a kind of censor principle in the arts. Painting has been much bedevilled by it, and much of the freakishness of modern painting is clearly due to the energy of its revolt against the representational fallacy. Music on the other hand has remained fairly free of it: at least no one, as far as I know, insists that it is flying in the face of common sense for music to do anything but reproduce the sounds heard in external nature. In literature the chief function of representationalism is to neutralize its opposing fallacy of an "inner" or subjective reality.

These different universes are presumably different ways of conceiving the same universe. What we call the common field of experience is a provisional means of unifying them on the level of sense-perception, and it is natural to infer a higher unity, a sort of beatification of common sense. But it is not easy to find any human language capable of reaching such exalted heights. If it is true, as is being increasingly asserted, that metaphysics is a system of verbal constructions with no direct reference to external criteria by means of which its truth or falsehood may be tested, it follows that metaphysics forms part of the verbal universe. Theology postulates an ultimate reality in God, but it does not assume that man is capable of describing it in his own terms, nor does it claim to be itself such a description. In any case, if we assert this final unity too quickly we may injure the integrity of the different means of approaching it. It does not help a poet much to tell him that the function of literature is to empty itself into an ocean of super-verbal significance, when the nature of that significance is unknown.

Pure mathematics, we have said, does not relate itself directly to the common field of experience, but indirectly, not to avoid it, but with the ultimate design of swallowing it. It thus presents the appearance of a series of hypothetical possibilities. It by-passes the confirmation from without which is the goal of applied mathematics, and seeks it only from within: its conclusions are related primarily to its own premises. Literature also proceeds by hypothetical possibilities. The poet, said Sidney, never affirmeth. He never says "this is so"; he says "let there be such a situation," and poetic truth, the validity of his conclusion, is to be tested primarily by its coherence with his original postulate. Of course, there is applied literature, just as there is applied mathematics, which we test historically, by its lifelikeness, or philosophically, by the cogency of its propositions. Literature, like mathematics, is constantly useful, a word which means having a continuing relationship to the common field of experience. But pure literature, like pure mathematics, is disinterested, or useless: it contains its own meaning. Any attempt to determine the category of literature must start with a distinction between the verbal form which is primarily itself and the verbal form which is primarily related to something else. The former is a complex verbal fact, the latter a complex of verbal symbols.

We have to use the mathematical analogy once more before we leave it. Literature is, of course, dependent on the haphazard and unpredictable appearance of creative genius. So actually is mathematics, but we hardly notice this because in mathematics a steady consolidating process goes on, and the work of its geniuses is absorbed in the evolving and expanding pattern of the mathematical universe. Literature being as yet unorganized by criticism, it still appears as a huge aggregate or miscellaneous pile of creative efforts. The only organizing principle so far discovered in it is chronology, and when we see the miscellaneous pile strung out along a chronological line, some coherence is given to it by the linear factors in tradition. We can trace an epic tradition by virtue of the fact that Virgil succeeded Homer, Dante Virgil, and Milton Dante. But, as already suggested, this is very far from being the best we can do. Criticism has still to develop a theory of literature which will see this aggregate within a verbal universe, as forms integrated within a total form. An epic, besides occurring at a certain point in time, is also something of a definitive statement of the poet's imaginative experience, whereas a lyric is usually a more fragmentary one. This suggests the image of a kind of radiating circle of literary experience in which the lyric is nearer to a periphery and the epic nearer to a centre. It is only an image, but the notion that literature, like any other form of knowledge, possesses a centre and a circumference seems reasonable enough.

If so, then literature is a single body, a vast organically growing form, and, though of course works of art do not improve, yet it may be possible for criticism to see literature as showing a progressive evolution in time, of a kind rather like what Newman postulates for Catholic dogma. One could collect remarks by the dozen from various critics, many of them quite misleading, to show that they are dimly aware, on some level of consciousness, of the possibility of a critical progress toward a total comprehension of literature which no critical history gives any hint of. When Mr. Eliot says that the whole tradition of Western poetry from Homer down ought to exist simultaneously in the poet's mind, the adverb suggests a transcending by criticism of the tyranny of historical categories. I even think that the consolidation of literature by criticism into the verbal universe was one of the things that Matthew Arnold meant by culture. To begin this process seems to me the function of criticism at the present time.

THE FOUR FORMS OF PROSE FICTION (1950)

THERE SEEMS TO BE no rational classification of prose forms. We are still struggling with the circulating-library conception of fiction as the opposite of "non-fiction," fiction dealing with subjects admitted not to be true, and non-fiction with everything else. The basis for this distinction seems to be a hazy idea that the real meaning of fiction is falsehood or unreality. Thus an autobiography would be classified as non-fiction if the librarian believed the author, and as fiction if she thought he was lying. It is difficult to see what use this can be to a literary critic. Surely the word fiction, which, like poetry, means etymologically something made for its own sake, ought to be applied in criticism to any work of art in prose. Or, if that is too much to ask, at least some protest can be entered against the sloppy habit of identifying fiction with the one genuine form of fiction which we know as the novel.

Let us look at a few of the unclassified books lying on the boundary of "non-fiction" and "literature." Is *Tristram Shandy* a novel? Nearly everyone would say yes, in spite of its easygoing disregard of "story values." Is *Gulliver's Travels* a novel? Here most would demur, including the Dewey decimal system, which puts it under "Satire and Humor." But surely everyone would call it fiction, and if it is fiction, a distinction appears between fiction as a genus and the novel as a species of that genus. Shifting the ground to fiction, then, is *Sartor Resartus* fiction? If not, why not? If it is, is *The Anatomy of Melancholy* fiction? If not, what is its place in English literature? The usual answer is that, though its subject matter is non-fiction, it is written with "style," the presence of which always makes any book literary. Not many critics would want to explore the conception of style involved in this proposition. Is Borrow's *Lavengro* fiction? Everyman's Library says yes; the World's Classics puts it under "Travel and Topography."

The literary historian who identifies fiction with the novel is greatly embarrassed by the length of time that the world managed to get along without the novel, and until he reaches his great deliverance in Defoe, his perspective is intolerably cramped. He is compelled to reduce Tudor fiction to a series of tentative essays in the novel form, which works well enough for Deloney but makes nonsense of Sidney. He postulates a great fictional gap in the seventeenth century which exactly covers the golden age of English prose. He finally discovers that the word novel, which up to about 1900 was still the name of a more or less recognizable form, has since expanded into a catch-all term which can be applied to practically any book that is not "on" something. Clearly, this novel-centered view of prose fiction is a Ptolemaic perspective which is now too complicated to be any longer workable, and some more relative and Copernican view must take its place.

When we start to think seriously about the novel, not as fiction, but as a form of fiction, we feel that its characteristics, whatever they are, are such as make, say, Defoe, Fielding, Austen, and James central in its tradition, and Borrow, Peacock, Melville, and Emily Brontë somehow peripheral. This is not an estimate of merit: we may easily prefer *Moby Dick* to *The Egoist* and yet feel that Meredith's book is closer to being a typical novel. Fielding's conception of the novel as a comic epic in prose seems fundamental to the tradition he did so much to establish. In novels that we think of as typical, like those of Jane Austen, plot and dialogue are closely linked to the conventions of the comedy of manners. The conventions of *Wuthering Heights* are linked rather with the tale and the ballad. They seem to have more affinity with tragedy, and the tragic emotions of passion and fury, which would shatter the balance of tone in Jane Austen, can be safely accommodated here. So can the supernatural, or the suggestion of it, which is difficult to get into a novel. The shape of the plot is different: instead of maneuvering around a central situation, as Jane Austen does, Emily Brontë tells her story with linear accents, and she seems to need the help of a narrator, who would be absurdly out of place in Jane Austen. Conven-

tions so different justify us in regarding *Wuthering Heights* as a different form of prose fiction from the novel, a form which we shall here call the romance.

The essential difference between novel and romance lies in the conception of characterization. The romancer does not attempt to create "real people," for his major characters at least, but stylized figures which expand into psychological archetypes. It is to the romance that the student of Jung would go to find his "libido," his "anima," and his "shadow" reflected in the hero, heroine, and villain respectively. That is why the romance so often radiates a glow of subjective intensity that the novel lacks, and why a suggestion of allegory is constantly creeping in around its fringes. Certain elements of character are released in the romance which make it naturally a more revolutionary form than the novel. The novelist deals with personality, with characters wearing their *personae* or social masks. He needs the framework of a stable society, and many of our best novelists have been conventional to the verge of fussiness. The romancer deals with individuality, with characters *in vacuo* idealized by revery, and, however conservative he may be, something nihilistic and untamable is likely to keep breaking out of his pages.

The prose romance, then, is an independent form of fiction to be distinguished from the novel and extracted from the miscellaneous heap of prose works now covered by that term. Even in the other heap known as "short stories" one can isolate the tale form used by Poe, which bears the same relation to the full-length romance that the short stories of Chekhov or Mansfield do to the novel. We must admit, however, that "pure" examples of either form can never be found; there is hardly any modern romance that could not be made out to be a novel, and *vice versa*. The forms of prose fiction are mixed, like racial strains in human beings, not separable like the sexes. In fact the popular demand in fiction is always for a mixed form, a romantic novel just romance enough for the reader to project his "libido" on the hero and his "anima" on the heroine, and just novel enough to keep these projections in a reassuringly familiar world. It may be asked, therefore, what is the use of making the above distinction, especially when, though undeveloped in criticism, it is by no means unrealized. It is no surprise to hear that Trollope wrote novels and William Morris romances.

The reason is that a great romancer should be examined in terms of the conventions he chose. William Morris should not be left on the side lines of prose fiction merely because the critic has not learned to take the romance form seriously. Nor, in view of what has been said about the revolutionary nature of the romance, should his choice of that form be regarded as an "escape" from his social attitude. If Scott has any claims to be a romancer, it is not good criticism to deal only with his defects as a novelist. The romantic qualities of *The Pilgrim's Progress* too, its archetypal characterization and its revolutionary approach to religious experience, make it a well-rounded example of a literary form: it is not merely a book swallowed by English literature to get some religious bulk in its diet. Finally, when Hawthorne, in the preface to *The House of the Seven Gables*, insists that his story should be read as romance and not as novel, it is possible that he meant what he said, even though he indicates that the prestige of the rival form has induced the romancer to apologize for not using it.

Romance is older than the novel, a fact which has developed the historical illusion that it is something to be outgrown, a juvenile and undeveloped form. The social affinities of the romance, with its grave idealizing of heroism and purity, are with the aristocracy, and it revived in the period we call Romantic as part of the Romantic tendency to archaic feudalism and a cult of the hero, or idealized libido. In England the romances of Scott and, in less degree, the Brontës, are part of a mysterious Northumbrian renaissance, a Romantic reaction against the new industrialism in the Midlands, which also produced the poetry of

Wordsworth and Burns and the philosophy of Carlyle. It is not surprising, therefore, that an important theme in the more bourgeois novel should be the parody of the romance and its ideals. The tradition established by *Don Quixote* continues in a type of novel which looks at a romantic situation from its own point of view, so that the conventions of the two forms make up an ironic compound instead of a sentimental mixture. This subspecies ranges from the spoofing of *Northanger Abbey* to the clinical analyses of *Madame Bovary* and *Lord Jim*.

We have spoken of the tendency to allegory in the romance, arising from the vaguely intensified significance which it gives to human activity. Sexual symbolism is close to the surface of most romance. One thinks of the very Freudian current of water which separates hero from heroine in Morris' *The Sundering Flood*, and of even balder statements of sexual mythopoeia in Poe. On this level too appear the Jungian archetypes already mentioned. Symbolism of this sort may be largely involuntary on the author's part, but conscious allegory belongs to the same tradition. One reason is that the romance, which deals with heroes, is intermediate between the novel, which deals with men, and the myth, which deals with gods. Prose romance first appears as a late development of Classical mythology, and the prose Sagas of Iceland follow close on the mythical Eddas. We see the recrudescence of myth whenever a romancer makes his allegory explicit, as Christian mythical patterns reappear in *The Pilgrim's Progress*, and even more primitive ones in Hawthorne.

The novel does not have this affinity with the myth. It tends rather to expand into a fictional approach to history. The soundness of Fielding's instinct in calling *Tom Jones* a history is confirmed by the general rule that the larger the scheme of a novel becomes, the more obviously its historical nature appears. As it is creative history, however, the novelist usually prefers his material in a plastic, or roughly contemporary state, and feels cramped by a fixed historical pattern. The so-called historical novel is generally a romance presenting some kind of historicized myth. It is perhaps this link with history and a sense of temporal context that has confined the novel, in striking contrast to the worldwide romance, to the alliance of time and Western man.

II

Autobiography is another form which merges with the novel by a series of insensible gradations. By itself it can hardly be called prose fiction at all; but most autobiographies are inspired by a creative, and therefore fictional, impulse to select only those events and experiences in the writer's life that go to build up an integrated pattern. This pattern may be something larger than himself with which he has come to identify himself, or simply the coherence of his character and attitudes. We may call this very important form of prose fiction the confession form, following St. Augustine, who appears to have invented it, and Rousseau, who established a modern type of it. The earlier tradition gave *Religio Medici, Grace Abounding*, and Newman's *Apologia* to English literature, besides the related but subtly different type of confession favored by the mystics.

Here again, as with the romance, there is some value in recognizing a distinct prose form in the confession. It gives several of our best prose works a definable place in fiction instead of keeping them in a vague limbo of books which are not quite literature because they are "thought," and not quite religion or philosophy because they are Examples of Prose Style. The confession, too, like the novel and the romance, has its own short form, the familiar essay, and Montaigne's *livre de bonne foy* is a confession made up of essays in which only the continuous narrative of the longer form is missing. Montaigne's scheme is to the confession what a work of fiction made up of short stories, such as Joyce's *Dubliners* or Boccaccio's *Decameron*, is to the novel or romance.

After Rousseau—in fact in Rousseau—the confession flows into the novel, and the mixture produces the fictional autobiography, the *Künstler-roman*, and kindred types. There is no literary reason why the subject of a confession should always be the author himself, and dramatic confessions have been used in the novel at least since *Moll Flanders*. The "stream of consciousness" technique permits of a much more concentrated fusion of the two forms.

When the confession is combined with the novel, however, the characteristics peculiar to the former show up clearly. Nearly always some theoretical and intellectual interest in religion, politics, or art plays a leading role in the confession. It is his success in integrating his mind on such subjects that makes the author of a confession feel that his life is worth writing about. But this interest in ideas and theoretical statements is alien to the genius of the novel proper, where the technical problem is to dissolve all theory into personal relationships. In Jane Austen, to take a familiar instance, church, state and culture are never examined except as social data, and Henry James has been described as having a mind so fine that no idea could violate it. The novelist who cannot get along without ideas, or has not the patience to digest them in the way that James did, instinctively resorts to what Mill calls a "mental history" of a single character. And when we find that a technical discussion of a theory of aesthetics forms the climax of Joyce's *Portrait*, we realize that what makes this possible is the presence in that novel of another tradition of prose fiction.

The novel tends to be extroverted and personal; its chief interest is in human character as it manifests itself in society. The romance tends to be introverted and personal: it also deals with characters, but in a more subjective way. (Subjective here refers to treatment, not subject matter. The characters of romance are heroic and therefore inscrutable; the novelist is freer to enter his characters' minds because he is more objective.) The confession is also introverted, but intellectualized in content. Our next step is evidently to discover a fourth form of fiction which is extroverted and intellectual.

III

We remarked earlier that most people would call *Gulliver's Travels* fiction but not a novel. It must then be another form of fiction, as it certainly has a form, and we feel that we are turning from the novel to this form, whatever it is, when we turn from Rousseau's *Emile* to Voltaire's *Candide,* or from Butler's *The Way of All Flesh* to the Erewhon books, or from Huxley's *Point Counterpoint* to *Brave New World.* The form thus has its own traditions, and, as the examples of Butler and Huxley show, has preserved some integrity even under the ascendancy of the novel. Its existence is easy enough to demonstrate, and no one will challenge the statement that the literary ancestry of *Gulliver's Travels* and *Candide* runs through Rabelais and Erasmus to Lucian. But while much has been said about the style and thought of Rabelais, Swift, and Voltaire, very little has been made of them as craftsmen working in a specific medium, a point no one dealing with a novelist would ignore. Another great writer in this tradition, Huxley's master Peacock, has fared even worse, for, his form not being understood, a general impression has grown up that his status in the development of prose fiction is that of a slapdash eccentric. Actually, he is as exquisite and precise an artist in his medium as Jane Austen is in hers.

The form used by these authors is the Menippean satire, also more rarely called the Varronian satire, allegedly invented by a Greek cynic named Menippus. His works are lost, but he had two great disciples, the Greek Lucian and the Roman Varro, and the tradition of Varro, who has not survived either except in fragments, was carried on by Petronius and Apuleius. The Menippean satire appears to have developed out of verse satire through the practice of adding prose interludes, but we know it only as a prose form, though one of its recurrent features (seen in Peacock) is the use of incidental verse.

The Menippean satire deals less with people as such than with mental attitudes. Pedants, bigots, cranks, parvenus, virtuosi, enthusiasts, rapacious and incompetent professional men of all kinds, are handled in terms of their "humor" or ruling passion, their occupational approach to life as distinct from their social behavior. The Menippean satire thus resembles the confession in its ability to handle abstract ideas and theories, and differs from the novel in its characterization, which is stylized rather than naturalistic, and presents people as mouthpieces of the ideas they represent. Here again no sharp boundary lines can or should be drawn, but if we compare a character in Jane Austen with a similar character in Peacock we can immediately feel the difference between the two forms. Squire Western belongs to the novel, but Thwackum and Square have Menippean blood in them. A constant theme in the tradition is the ridicule of the *philosophus gloriosus.* Lucian ridicules the Greek philosophers, Rabelais and Erasmus the scholastics, Swift the Cartesians and the Royal Society, Voltaire the Leibnitzians, Peacock the Romantics, Samuel Butler the Darwinians, Huxley the behaviorists. The reason for this is that, while the novelist sees evil and folly as social diseases, the Menippean satirist sees them as diseases of the intellect, as a kind of maddened pedantry which the *philosophus gloriosus* at once symbolizes and defines.

Petronius, Apuleius, Rabelais, Swift, and Voltaire all use a loose-jointed narrative form often confused with the romance. It differs from the romance, however (though there is a strong admixture of romance in Rabelais), as it is not primarily concerned with the exploits of heroes, but relies on the free play of intellectual fancy and the kind of humorous observation that produces caricature. It differs also from the picaresque form, which has the novel's interest in the actual structure of society. At its most concentrated the Menippean satire presents us with a vision of the world in terms of a single intellectual pattern. This it often attains by giving it a logical and self-consistent shift of perspective, presenting it as Lilliputian or Brobdingnagian, or from the point of view of an ass, a savage, or a drunk. Or it will take the form of a "marvelous journey" and present a caricature of a familiar society as the logical structure of an imaginary one. *Erewhon* and *Brave New World* are modern examples. Such a distorting mirror produces at least the unity of its frame: without it, the Menippean satirist inclines to a disorderliness which in *A Tale of a Tub* reaches the point of including a digression in praise of digressions. The intellectual structure he builds up from his story makes for violent dislocations in the customary logic of narrative, though the appearance of carelessness that results reflects only the carelessness of the reader.

The word "satire," in Roman and Renaissance times, meant either of two specific literary forms of that name, one (this one) prose and the other verse. Now it means a tone or attitude which may be found in any form of art whether literary or not. In the Menippean satires we have been discussing, the name of the form also applies to the attitude. As the name of an attitude, satire seems to be a combination of fantasy and morality, bounded on one side by the play of fancy which has no moral sting, and on the other by an invective which has no spontaneous humor. But as the name of a form, the term satire, though confined to literature, is more flexible, and can be either entirely fantastic or entirely moral. The Menippean adventure story may thus be pure fantasy, as it is in the literary fairy tale. The Alice books are perfect Menippean satires, and so is *The Water-Babies*, which has been influenced by Rabelais. The purely moral type is a serious vision of society as a single intellectual pattern, in other words a Utopia.

The short form of the Menippean satire is usually a dialogue or colloquy, in which the dramatic interest is in a conflict of ideas rather than of character. This is the favorite form of Erasmus, and is common in Voltaire. Here again the form is not invariably satiric in attitude, but shades off into more purely fanci-

ful or moral discussions, like the *Imaginary Conversations* of Landor or the "dialogue of the dead." Sometimes this form expands to full length, and more than two speakers are used: the setting then is usually a *cena* or symposium, like the one that looms so large in Petronius. Plato, though much earlier in the field than Menippus, is a strong influence on this type, which stretches in an unbroken tradition down through those urbane and leisurely conversations which define the ideal courtier in Castiglione or the doctrine and discipline of angling in Walton. A modern development produces the country-house weekends in Peacock and Huxley in which the opinions and ideas and cultural interests expressed are as important as the love-making.

The novelist shows his exuberance either by an exhaustive analysis of human relationships, as in Henry James, or of social phenomena, as in Tolstoy. The Menippean satirist, dealing with intellectual themes and attitudes, shows his exuberance in intellectual ways, by piling up an enormous mass of erudition about his theme or in overwhelming his pedantic targets with an avalanche of their own jargon. The tendency of the form to expand into an encyclopedic farrago is most clearly marked, as we should expect, in Rabelais, notably in the great catalogues of torcheculs and epithets of codpieces and methods of divination. The encyclopedic compilations produced in the line of duty by Erasmus and Voltaire suggest that a magpie instinct to collect facts is not unrelated to the type of ability that has made them famous as artists.

This creative treatment of exhaustive erudition is the organizing principle of the greatest Menippean satire in English before Swift, Burton's *Anatomy of Melancholy*. Here human society is studied in terms of the intellectual pattern provided by the conception of melancholy, a symposium of books replaces dialogue, and the result is the most comprehensive survey of human life in one book that English literature had seen since Chaucer, one of Burton's favorite authors. We may note in passing the Utopia in his introduction and his "digressions," which when examined turn out to be scholarly distillations of Menippean forms: the digression of air, of the marvelous journey; the digression of spirits, of the ironic use of erudition; the digression of the miseries of scholars, of the satire on the *philosophus gloriosus*. The word "anatomy" in Burton's title means a dissection or analysis, and expresses very accurately the intellectualized approach of his form. We may as well adopt it as a convenient name to replace the cumbersome and in modern times rather misleading "Menippean satire."

The anatomy of course eventually begins to merge with the novel, producing various hybrids including the *roman à thèse* and novels in which the characters are symbols of social or other ideas, like the proletarian novels of the last decade. It was Sterne, however, the disciple of Burton and Rabelais, who combined them with greatest success. *Tristram Shandy* may be, as was said at the beginning, a novel, but the digressing narrative, the catalogues, the stylizing of character along "humor" lines, the marvelous journey of the great nose, the symposium discussions and the constant ridicule of philosophers and pedantic critics are all features that belong to the anatomy.

IV

To sum up, then: when we examine fiction from the point of view of form, we can see four chief strands binding it together, novel, confession, anatomy, and romance. The six possible combinations of these forms all exist, and we have shown how the novel has combined with each of the other three. Exclusive concentration on one form is rare: the early novels of George Eliot, for instance, are influenced by the romance, and the later ones by the anatomy. The romance-confession hybrid is found, naturally, in the autobiography of a romantic temperament, and is represented in English by George Borrow. The romance-anatomy one we have noticed in Rabelais: a fine modern example is *Moby Dick*, where the romantic theme of the wild hunt expands into an encyclopedic

anatomy of the whale. Confession and anatomy are united in *Sartor Resartus*. More comprehensive fictional schemes usually employ at least three forms: we can see strains of novel, romance, and confession in *Pamela*, of novel, romance, and anatomy in *Don Quixote*, of novel, confession, and anatomy in Proust, and of romance, confession, and anatomy in Apuleius.

I deliberately make this sound schematic in order to suggest the advantage of having a simple and logical explanation for the form of, say, *Moby Dick* or *Tristram Shandy*. The usual critical approach to the *form* of such works resembles that of the doctors in Brobdingnag, who after great wrangling finally pronounced Gulliver a *lusus naturae*. It is the anatomy in particular that has baffled critics, and there is hardly any fiction writer deeply influenced by it who has not been accused of disorderly conduct. As for the question which so many feel it necessary to ask at this point, whether Melville or Sterne "knew" that they were combining an anatomy form with a romance or a novel, the answer is, as usual, yes and no. They knew what they were doing, but they knew as creators know, not as critics explain.

The reader may be reminded here of Joyce, for describing his books as monstrous has become a nervous tic. I find "demogorgon," "behemoth," and "white elephant" in good critics; the bad ones could probably do much better. The care that Joyce took to organize *Ulysses* and *Finnegans Wake* amounted nearly to obsession, but as they are not organized on familiar principles of prose fiction, the impression of shapelessness remains. Let us try our formulas on him.

If a reader were asked to set down a list of the things that had most impressed him about *Ulysses*, it might reasonably be somewhat as follows. First, the clarity with which the sights and sounds and smells of Dublin come to life, the rotundity of the character-drawing and the naturalness of the dialogue. Second, the elaborate way that the story and characters are parodied by being set against archetypal heroic patterns, notably the one provided by the Odyssey. Third, the revelation of character and incident through the searching use of the stream-of-consciousness technique. Fourth, the constant tendency to be encyclopedic and exhaustive both in technique and in subject matter, and to see both in highly intellectualized terms. It should not be too hard for us by now to see that these four points describe elements in the book which relate to the novel, romance, confession, and anatomy respectively. *Ulysses*, then, is a complete prose epic with all four forms employed in it, all of practically equal importance, and all essential to one another, so that the book is a unity and not an aggregate.

This unity is built up from an intricate scheme of parallel contrasts. The romantic archetypes of Hamlet and Ulysses are like remote stars in a literary heaven looking down quizzically on the shabby creatures of Dublin obediently intertwining themselves in the patterns set by their influences. In the "Cyclops" and "Circe" episodes particularly there is a continuous parody of realistic patterns by romantic ones which reminds us, though the irony leans in the opposite direction, of *Madame Bovary*. The relation of novel and confession techniques is similar: the author jumps into his characters' minds to follow their stream of consciousness, and out again to describe them externally. In the novel-anatomy combination, too, found in the "Ithaca" chapter, the sense of lurking antagonism between the personal and intellectual aspects of the scene accounts for much of its pathos. The same principle of parallel contrast holds good for the other three combinations: of romance and confession in "Nausicaa" and "Penelope," of confession and anatomy in "Proteus" and "The Lotos-Eaters," of romance and anatomy (a rare and fitful combination) in "Sirens" and parts of "Circe."

In *Finnegans Wake* the unity of design goes far beyond this. The dingy story of the sodden HCE and his pinched wife is not contrasted with the archetypes of Tristram and the divine king: HCE is himself Tristram and the divine king. As the setting is a dream, no contrast is possible between confession and novel, between a stream of consciousness inside the mind and the appearances of other people outside it. Nor is the existential world of the novel to be separated from the intelligible world of the anatomy. The forms we have been isolating in fiction, and which depend for their existence on the common-sense dichotomies of the day-light consciousness, vanish in *Finnegans Wake* into a fifth and quintessential form.

All that we have space to say of this fifth form is that it is the one traditionally associated with scriptures and sacred books, and treats life in terms of the fall and awakening of the human soul and the creation and apocalypse of nature. The Bible is of course the definitive example of it: the Egyptian Book of the Dead and the Icelandic Prose Edda, both of which have left deep imprints on *Finnegans Wake*, also belong to it. Perhaps we could see tendencies to this form in Joyce's masters, "stern swift and jolly roger" (Rabelais), if we were to read them as Joyce did. To go further would exceed our present objective, which is merely to give an explanation of some literary phenomena that appear to need it.

THE ARCHETYPES OF LITERATURE (1951)

EVERY ORGANIZED body of knowledge can be learned progressively; and experience shows

Reprinted by permission of the author and *The Kenyon Review* (Winter 1951).

that there is also something progressive about the learning of literature. Our opening sentence has already got us into a semantic difficulty. Physics is an organized body of knowledge about nature, and a student of it says that he is learning physics, not that he is learning nature. Art, like nature, is the subject of a systematic study, and has to be distinguished from the study itself, which is criticism. It is therefore impossible to "learn literature": one learns about it in a certain way, but what one learns, transitively, is the criticism of literature. Similarly, the difficulty often felt in "teaching literature" arises from the fact that it cannot be done: the criticism of literature is all that can be directly taught. So while no one expects literature itself to behave like a science, there is surely no reason why criticism, as a systematic and organized study, should not be, at least partly, a science. Not a "pure" or "exact" science, perhaps, but these phrases form part of a 19th Century cosmology which is no longer with us. Criticism deals with the arts and may well be something of an art itself, but it does not follow that it must be unsystematic. If it is to be related to the sciences too, it does not follow that it must be deprived of the graces of culture.

Certainly criticism as we find it in learned journals and scholarly monographs has every characteristic of a science. Evidence is examined scientifically; previous authorities are used scientifically; fields are investigated scientifically; texts are edited scientifically. Prosody is scientific in structure; so is phonetics; so is philology. And yet in studying this kind of critical science the student becomes aware of a centrifugal movement carrying him away from literature. He finds that literature is the central division of the "humanities," flanked on one side by history and on the other by philosophy. Criticism so far ranks only as a subdivision of literature; and hence, for the systematic mental organization of the subject, the student has to turn to the conceptual framework of the historian for events, and to that of the philosopher for ideas. Even the more centrally placed critical sciences, such as textual editing, seem to be part of a "background" that recedes into history or some other non-literary field. The thought suggests itself that the ancillary critical disciplines may be related to a central expanding pattern of systematic comprehension which has not yet been established, but which, if it were established, would prevent them from being centrifugal. If such a pattern exists, then criticism would be to art what philosophy is to wisdom and history to action.

Most of the central area of criticism is at present, and doubtless always will be, the area of commentary. But the commentators have little sense, unlike the researchers, of being contained within some sort of scientific discipline: they are chiefly engaged, in the words of the gospel hymn, in brightening the corner where they are. If we attempt to get a more comprehensive idea of what criticism is about, we find ourselves wandering over quaking bogs of generalities, judicious pronouncements of value, reflective comments, perorations to works of research, and other consequences of taking the large view. But this part of the critical field is so full of pseudo-propositions, sonorous nonsense that contains no truth and no falsehood, that it obviously exists only because criticism, like nature, prefers a waste space to an empty one.

The term "pseudo-proposition" may imply some sort of logical positivist attitude on my own part. But I would not confuse the significant proposition with the factual one; nor should I consider it advisable to muddle the study of literature with a schizophrenic dichotomy between subjective-emotional and objective-descriptive aspects of meaning, considering that in order to produce any literary meaning at all one has to ignore this dichotomy. I say only that the principles by which one can distinguish a significant from a meaningless statement in criticism are not clearly defined. Our first step, therefore, is to recognize and get rid of meaningless criticism: that is, talking about literature in a way that cannot help to build up a systematic structure of knowledge. Casual value-judgments belong not to criticism but to the history of taste, and reflect, at best, only the social and psychological compulsions which prompted their utterance.

All judgments in which the values are not based on literary experience but are sentimental or derived from religious or political prejudice may be regarded as casual. Sentimental judgments are usually based either on nonexistent categories or antitheses ("Shakespeare studied life, Milton books") or on a visceral reaction to the writer's personality. The literary chit-chat which makes the reputations of poets boom and crash in an imaginary stock exchange is pseudo-criticism. That wealthy investor Mr. Eliot, after dumping Milton on the market, is now buying him again; Donne has probably reached his peak and will begin to taper off; Tennyson may be in for a slight flutter but the Shelley stocks are still bearish. This sort of thing cannot be part of any systematic study, for a systematic study can only progress: whatever dithers or vacillates or reacts is merely leisure-class conversation.

We next meet a more serious group of critics who say: the foreground of criticism is the impact of literature on the reader. Let us, then, keep the study of literature centripetal, and base the learning process on a structural analysis of the literary work itself. The texture of any great work of art is complex and ambiguous, and in unravelling the complexities we may take in as much history and philosophy as we please, if the subject of our study remains at the center. If it does not, we may find that in our anxiety to write about literature we have forgotten how to read it.

The only weakness in this approach is that it is conceived primarily as the antithesis of centrifugal or "background" criticism, and so lands us in a somewhat unreal dilemma, like the conflict of internal and external relations in philosophy. Antitheses are usually resolved, not by picking one side and refuting the other, or by making eclectic choices between them, but by trying to get past the antithetical way of stating the problem. It is right that the first critical apprehension should take the form of a rhetorical or structural analysis of a work of art. But a purely structural approach has the same limitation in criticism that it has in biology. In itself it is simply a discrete series of analyses based on the mere existence of the literary structure, without developing any explanation of how the structure came to be what it was and what its nearest relatives are. Structural analysis brings rhetoric back to criticism, but we need a new poetics as well, and the attempt to construct a new poetics out of rhetoric alone can hardly avoid a mere complication of rhetorical terms into a sterile jargon. I suggest that what is at present missing from literary criticism is a co-ordinating principle, a central hypothesis which, like the theory of evolution in biology, will see the phenomena it deals with as parts of a whole. Such a principle, though it would retain the centripetal perspective of structural analysis, would try to give the same perspective to other kinds of criticism too.

The first postulate of this hypothesis is the same as that of any science: the assumption of total coherence. The assumption refers to the science, not to what it deals with. A belief in an order of nature is an inference from the intelligibility of the natural sciences; and if the natural sciences ever completely demonstrated the order of nature they would presumably exhaust their subject. Criticism, as a science, is totally intelligible; literature, as the subject of a science, is, so far as we know, an inexhaustible source of new critical discoveries, and would be even if new works of literature ceased to be written. If so, then the search for a limiting principle in literature in order to discourage the development of criticism is mistaken. The assertion that the critic should not look for more in a poem than the poet may safely be assumed to have been conscious of putting there is a common form of what may be called the fallacy of premature teleology. It corresponds to the assertion that a natural phenomenon is as it is because Providence in its inscrutable wisdom made it so.

Simple as the assumption appears, it takes a long time for a science to discover that it is in fact a totally intelligible body of knowledge. Until it makes this discovery it has not been born as an individual science, but remains an embryo within the body of some other subject. The birth of physics from "natural philosophy" and of sociology from "moral philosophy" will illustrate the process. It is also very approximately true that the modern sciences have developed in the order of their closeness to mathematics. Thus physics and astronomy assumed their modern form in the Renaissance, chemistry in the 18th Century, biology in the 19th, and the social sciences in the 20th. If systematic criticism, then, is developing only in our day, the fact is at least not an anachronism.

We are now looking for classifying principles lying in an area between two points that we have fixed. The first of these is the preliminary effort of criticism, the structural analysis of the work of art. The second is the assumption that there is such a subject as criticism, and that it makes, or could make, complete sense. We may next proceed inductively from structural analysis, associating the data we collect and trying to see larger patterns in them. Or we may proceed deductively, with the consequences that follow from postulating the unity of criticism. It is clear, of course, that neither procedure will work indefinitely without correction from the other. Pure induction will get us lost in haphazard guessing; pure deduction will lead to inflexible and over-simplified pigeon-holing. Let us now attempt a few tentative steps in each direction, beginning with the inductive one.

II

The unity of a work of art, the basis of structural analysis, has not been produced solely by the unconditioned will of the artist, for the artist is only its efficient cause: it has form, and consequently a formal cause. The fact that revision is possible, that the poet makes changes not because he likes them better but because they are better, means that poems, like poets, are born and not made. The poet's task is to deliver the poem in as uninjured a state as possible, and if the poem is alive, it is equally anxious to be rid of him, and screams to be cut loose from his private memories and associa-

tions, his desire for self-expression, and all the other navel-strings and feeding tubes of his ego. The critic takes over where the poet leaves off, and criticism can hardly do without a kind of literary psychology connecting the poet with the poem. Part of this may be a psychological study of the poet, though this is useful chiefly in analysing the failures in his expression, the things in him which are still attached to his work. More important is the fact that every poet has his private mythology, his own spectroscopic band or peculiar formation of symbols, of much of which he is quite unconscious. In works with characters of their own, such as dramas and novels, the same psychological analysis may be extended to the interplay of characters, though of course literary psychology would analyse the behavior of such characters only in relation to literary convention.

There is still before us the problem of the formal cause of the poem, a problem deeply involved with the question of genres. We cannot say much about genres, for criticism does not know much about them. A good many critical efforts to grapple with such words as "novel" or "epic" are chiefly interesting as examples of the psychology of rumor. Two conceptions of the genre, however, are obviously fallacious, and as they are opposite extremes, the truth must lie somewhere between them. One is the pseudo-Platonic conception of genres as existing prior to and independently of creation, which confuses them with mere conventions of form like the sonnet. The other is that pseudo-biological conception of them as evolving species which turns up in so many surveys of the "development" of this or that form.

We next inquire for the origin of the genre, and turn first of all to the social conditions and cultural demands which produced it—in other words to the material cause of the work of art. This leads us into literary history, which differs from ordinary history in that its containing categories, "Gothic," "Baroque," "Romantic," and the like are cultural categories, of little use to the ordinary historian. Most literary history does not get as far as these categories, but even so we know more about it than about most kinds of critical scholarship. The historian treats literature and philosophy historically; the philosopher treats history and literature philosophically; and the so-called "history of ideas" approach marks the beginning of an attempt to treat history and philosophy from the point of view of an autonomous criticism.

But still we feel that there is something missing. We say that every poet has his own peculiar formation of images. But when so many poets use so many of the same images, surely there are much bigger critical problems involved than biographical ones. As Mr. Auden's brilliant essay *The Enchafèd Flood* shows, an important symbol like the sea cannot remain within the poetry of Shelley or Keats or Coleridge: it is bound to expand over many poets into an archetypal symbol of literature. And if the genre has a historical origin, why does the genre of drama emerge from medieval religion in a way so strikingly similar to the way it emerged from Greek religion centuries before? This is a problem of structure rather than origin, and suggests that there may be archetypes of genres as well as of images.

It is clear that criticism cannot be systematic unless there is a quality in literature which enables it to be so, an order of words corresponding to the order of nature in the natural sciences. An archetype should be not only a unifying category of criticism, but itself a part of a total form, and it leads us at once to the question of what sort of total form criticism can see in literature. Our survey of critical techniques has taken us as far as literary history. Total literary history moves from the primitive to the sophisticated, and here we glimpse the possibility of seeing literature as a complication of a relatively restricted and simple group of formulas that can be studied in primitive culture. If so, then the search for archetypes is a kind of literary anthropology, concerned with the way that literature is informed by pre-literary categories such as ritual, myth and folk tale. We next realize that the relation between these categories and literature is by no means purely

one of descent, as we find them reappearing in the greatest classics—in fact there seems to be a general tendency on the part of great classics to revert to them. This coincides with a feeling that we have all had: that the study of mediocre works of art, however energetic, obstinately remains a random and peripheral form of critical experience, whereas the profound masterpiece seems to draw us to a point at which we can see an enormous number of converging patterns of significance. Here we begin to wonder if we cannot see literature, not only as complicating itself in time, but as spread out in conceptual space from some unseen center.

This inductive movement towards the archetype is a process of backing up, as it were, from structural analysis, as we back up from a painting if we want to see composition instead of brushwork. In the foreground of the grave-digger scene in *Hamlet,* for instance, is an intricate verbal texture, ranging from the puns of the first clown to the *danse macabre* of the Yorick soliloquy, which we study in the printed text. One step back, and we are in the Wilson Knight and Spurgeon group of critics, listening to the steady rain of images of corruption and decay. Here too, as the sense of the place of this scene in the whole play begins to dawn on us, we are in the network of psychological relationships which were the main interest of Bradley. But after all, we say, we are forgetting the genre: *Hamlet* is a play, and an Elizabethan play. So we take another step back into the Stoll and Shaw group and see the scene conventionally as part of its dramatic context. One step more, and we can begin to glimpse the archetype of the scene, as the hero's *Liebestod* and first unequivocal declaration of his love, his struggle with Laertes and the sealing of his own fate, and the sudden sobering of his mood that marks the transition to the final scene, all take shape around a leap into and return from the grave that has so weirdly yawned open on the stage.

At each stage of understanding this scene we are dependent on a certain kind of scholarly organization. We need first an editor to clean up the text for us, then the rhetorician and philologist, then the literary psychologist. We cannot study the genre without the help of the literary social historian, the literary philosopher and the student of the "history of ideas," and for the archetype we need a literary anthropologist. But now that we have got our central pattern of criticism established, all these interests are seen as converging on literary criticism instead of receding from it into psychology and history and the rest. In particular, the literary anthropologist who chases the source of the Hamlet legend from the pre-Shakespeare play to Saxo, and from Saxo to nature-myths, is not running away from Shakespeare: he is drawing closer to the archetypal form which Shakespeare recreated. A minor result of our new perspective is that contradictions among critics, and assertions that this and not that critical approach is the right one, show a remarkable tendency to dissolve into unreality. Let us now see what we can get from the deductive end.

III

Some arts move in time, like music; others are presented in space, like painting. In both cases the organizing principle is recurrence, which is called rhythm when it is temporal and pattern when it is spatial. Thus we speak of the rhythm of music and the pattern of painting; but later, to show off our sophistication, we may begin to speak of the rhythm of painting and the pattern of music. In other words, all arts may be conceived both temporally and spatially. The score of a musical composition may be studied all at once; a picture may be seen as the track of an intricate dance of the eye. Literature seems to be intermediate between music and painting: its words form rhythms which approach a musical sequence of sounds at one of its boundaries, and form patterns which approach the hieroglyphic or pictorial image at the other. The attempts to get as near to these boundaries as possible form the main body of what is called experimental writing. We may call the rhythm of literature the narrative, and the pattern, the simultaneous mental grasp of the verbal structure, the meaning or significance. We hear or listen to a narrative, but when we grasp a writer's total pattern we "see" what he means.

The criticism of literature is much more hampered by the representational fallacy than even the criticism of painting. That is why we are apt to think of narrative as a sequential representation of events in an outside "life," and of meaning as a reflection of some external "idea." Properly used as critical terms, an author's narrative is his linear movement; his meaning is the integrity of his completed form. Similarly an image is not merely a verbal replica of an external object, but any unit of a verbal structure seen as part of a total pattern or rhythm. Even the letters an author spells his words with form part of his imagery, though only in special cases (such as alliteration) would they call for critical notice. Narrative and meaning thus become respectively, to borrow musical terms, the melodic and harmonic contexts of the imagery.

Rhythm, or recurrent movement, is deeply founded on the natural cycle, and everything in nature that we think of as having some analogy with works of art, like the flower or the bird's song, grows out of a profound synchronization between an organism and the rhythms of its environment, especially that of the solar year. With animals some expressions of synchronization, like the mating dances of birds, could almost be called rituals. But in human life a ritual seems to be something of a voluntary effort (hence the magical element in it) to recapture a lost rapport with the natural cycle. A farmer must harvest his crop at a certain time of year, but because this is involuntary, harvesting itself is not precisely a ritual. It is the deliberate expression of a will to synchronize human and natural energies at that time which produces the harvest songs, harvest sacrifices and harvest folk customs that we call rituals. In ritual, then, we may find the origin of narrative, a ritual being a temporal sequence of acts in which the conscious meaning or significance is latent: it can be seen by an observer, but is largely concealed from the participators themselves. The pull of ritual is toward pure narrative, which, if there could be such a thing, would be automatic and unconscious repetition. We should notice too the regular tendency of ritual to become encyclopedic. All the important recurrences in nature, the day, the phases of the moon, the seasons and solstices of the year, the crises of existence from birth to death, get rituals attached to them, and most of the higher religions are equipped with a definitive total body of rituals suggestive, if we may put it so, of the entire range of potentially significant actions in human life.

Patterns of imagery, on the other hand, or fragments of significance, are oracular in origin, and derive from the epiphanic moment, the flash of instantaneous comprehension with no direct reference to time, the importance of which is indicated by Cassirer in *Myth and Language*. By the time we get them, in the form of proverbs, riddles, commandments and etiological folk tales, there is already a considerable element of narrative in them. They too are encyclopedic in tendency, building up a total structure of significance, or doctrine, from random and empiric fragments. And just as pure narrative would be unconscious act, so pure significance would be an incommunicable state of consciousness, for communication begins by constructing narrative.

The myth is the central informing power that gives archetypal significance to the ritual and archetypal narrative to the oracle. Hence the myth *is* the archetype, though it might be convenient to say myth only when referring to narrative, and archetype when speaking of significance. In the solar cycle of the day, the seasonal cycle of the year, and the organic cycle of human life, there is a single pattern of significance, out of which myth constructs a central narrative around a figure who is partly the sun, partly vegetative fertility and partly a god or archetypal human being. The crucial importance of this myth has been forced on literary critics by Jung and Frazer in particular, but the several books now available on it are not always systematic in their approach, for which reason I supply the following table of its phases:

1. The dawn, spring and birth phase. Myths of the birth of the hero, of revival and resurrection, of creation and (because the four phases are a cycle) of the defeat of the powers of darkness, winter and death. Subordinate characters: the father and the mother. The archetype of romance and of most dithyrambic and rhapsodic poetry.

2. The zenith, summer, and marriage or triumph phase. Myths of apotheosis, of the sacred marriage, and of entering into Paradise. Subordinate characters: the companion and the bride. The archetype of comedy, pastoral and idyll.

3. The sunset, autumn and death phase. Myths of fall, of the dying god, of violent death and sacrifice and of the isolation of the hero. Subordinate characters: the traitor and the siren. The archetype of tragedy and elegy.

4. The darkness, winter and dissolution phase. Myths of the triumph of these powers; myths of floods and the return of chaos, of the defeat of the hero, and Götterdämmerung myths. Subordinate characters: the ogre and the witch. The archetype of satire (see, for instance, the conclusion of *The Dunciad*).

The quest of the hero also tends to assimilate the oracular and random verbal structures, as we can see when we watch the chaos of local legends that results from prophetic epiphanies consolidating into a narrative mythology of departmental gods. In most of the higher religions this in turn has become the same central quest-myth that emerges from ritual, as the Messiah myth became the narrative structure of the oracles of Judaism. A local flood may beget a folk tale by accident, but a comparison of flood stories will show how quickly such tales become examples of the myth of dissolution. Finally, the tendency of both ritual and epiphany to become encyclopedic is realized in the definitive body of myth which constitutes the sacred scriptures of religions. These sacred scriptures are consequently the first documents that the literary critic has to study to gain a comprehensive view of his subject. After he has understood their structure, then he can descend from archetypes to genres, and see how the drama emerges from the ritual side of myth and lyric from the epiphanic or fragmented side, while the epic carries on the central encyclopedic structure.

Some words of caution and encouragement are necessary before literary criticism has clearly staked out its boundaries in these fields. It is part of the critic's business to show how all literary genres are derived from the quest-myth, but the derivation is a logical one within the science of criticism: the quest-myth will constitute the first chapter of whatever future handbooks of criticism may be written that will be based on enough organized critical knowledge to call themselves "introductions" or "outlines" and still be able to live up to their titles. It is only when we try to expound the derivation chronologically that we find ourselves writing pseudo-prehistorical fictions and theories of mythological contract. Again, because psychology and anthropology are more highly developed sciences, the critic who deals with this kind of material is bound to appear, for some time, a dilettante of those subjects. These two phases of criticism are largely undeveloped in comparison with literary history and rhetoric, the reason being the later development of the sciences they are related to. But the fascination which *The Golden Bough* and Jung's book on libido symbols have for literary critics is not based on dilettantism, but on the fact that these books are primarily studies in literary criticism, and very important ones.

In any case the critic who is studying the principles of literary form has a quite different interest from the psychologist's concern with states of mind or the anthropologist's with social institutions. For instance: the mental response to narrative is mainly passive; to significance mainly active. From this fact Ruth Benedict's *Patterns of Culture* develops a distinction between "Apollonian" cultures based on obedience to ritual and "Dionysiac" ones based on a tense exposure of the prophetic mind to epiphany. The critic would tend rather to note how popular literature which appeals to the inertia of the untrained mind puts a heavy emphasis on narrative values, whereas a sophisticated attempt to disrupt the connection between the poet and his environment produces the Rimbaud type of *illumination*, Joyce's solitary epiphanies, and Baudelaire's conception of nature as a source of oracles. Also how literature, as it develops from the primitive to the self-conscious, shows a gradual shift of the poet's attention from narrative to significant values, this shift of attention being the basis of Schiller's distinction between naive and sentimental poetry.

The relation of criticism to religion, when they deal with the same documents, is more complicated. In criticism, as in history, the divine is always treated as a human artifact. God for the critic, whether he finds him in *Paradise Lost* or the Bible, is a character in a human story; and for the critic all epiphanies are explained, not in terms of the riddle of a possessing god or devil, but as mental phenomena closely associated in their origin with dreams. This once established, it is then necessary to say that nothing in criticism or art compels the critic to take the attitude of ordinary waking consciousness towards the dream or the god. Art deals not with the real but with the conceivable; and criticism, though it will eventually have to have some theory of conceivability, can never be justified in trying to develop, much less assume, any theory of actuality. It is necessary to understand this before our next and final point can be made.

We have identified the central myth of literature, in its narrative aspect, with the quest-myth. Now if we wish to see this central myth as a pattern of meaning also, we have to start with the workings of the subconscious where the epiphany originates, in other words in the dream. The human cycle of waking and dreaming corresponds closely to the natural cycle of light and darkness, and it is perhaps in this correspondence that all imaginative life begins. The correspondence is largely an antithesis: it is in daylight that man is really in the power of darkness, a prey to frustration and weakness; it is in the darkness of nature that the "libido" or conquering heroic self awakes. Hence art, which Plato called a dream for awakened minds, seems to have as its final cause the resolution of the antithesis, the mingling of the sun and the hero, the realizing of a world in which the inner desire and the outward circumstance coincide. This is the same goal, of course, that the attempt to combine human and natural power in ritual has. The social function of the arts, therefore, seems to be closely connected with visualizing the goal of work in human life. So in terms of significance, the central myth of art must be the vision of the end of social effort, the innocent world of fulfilled desires, the free human society. Once this is understood, the integral place of criticism among the other social sciences, in interpreting and systematizing the vision of the artist, will be easier to see. It is at this point that we can see how religious conceptions of the final cause of human effort are as relevant as any others to criticism.

The importance of the god or hero in the myth lies in the fact that such characters, who are conceived in human likeness and yet have more power over nature, gradually build up the vision of an omnipotent personal community beyond an indifferent nature. It is this community which the hero regularly enters in his apotheosis. The world of this apotheosis thus begins to pull away from the rotary cycle of the quest in which all triumph is temporary. Hence if we look at the quest-myth as a pattern of imagery, we see the hero's quest first of all in terms of its fulfillment. This gives us our central pattern of archetypal images, the vision of innocence which sees the world in terms of total human intelligibility. It corresponds to, and is usually found in the form of, the vision of the unfallen world or heaven in religion. We may call it the comic vision of life, in contrast to the tragic vision, which sees the quest only in the form of its ordained cycle.

We conclude with a second table of contents, in which we shall attempt to set forth the central pattern of the comic and tragic visions. One essential principle of archetypal criticism is that the individual and the universal forms of an image are identical, the reasons being too complicated for us just now. We proceed according to the general plan of the game of Twenty Questions, or, if we prefer, of the Great Chain of Being:

1. In the comic vision the *human* world is a community, or a hero who represents the wish-fulfillment of the reader. The archetype of images of symposium, communion, order, friendship and love. In the tragic vision the human world is a tyranny or anarchy, or an individual or isolated man, the leader with his back to his followers, the bullying giant of romance, the deserted or betrayed hero. Marriage or some equivalent consummation belongs to the comic vision; the harlot, witch and other varieties of Jung's "terrible mother" belong to the tragic one. All divine, heroic, angelic or other superhuman communities follow the human pattern.

2. In the comic vision the *animal* world is a community of domesticated animals, usually a flock of sheep, or a lamb, or one of the gentler birds, usually a dove. The archetype of pastoral images. In the tragic vision the animal world is seen in terms of beasts and birds of prey, wolves, vultures, serpents, dragons and the like.

3. In the comic vision the *vegetable* world is a garden, grove or park, or a tree of life, or a rose or lotus. The archetype of Arcadian images, such as that of Marvell's green world or of Shakespeare's forest comedies. In the tragic vision it is a sinister forest like the one in *Comus* or at the opening of the *Inferno*, or a heath or wilderness, or a tree of death.

4. In the comic vision the *mineral* world is a city, or one building or temple, or one stone, normally a glowing precious stone—in fact the whole comic series, especially the tree, can be conceived as luminous or fiery. The archetype of geometrical images: the "starlit dome" belongs here. In the tragic vision the mineral world is seen in terms of deserts, rocks and ruins, or of sinister geometrical images like the cross.

5. In the comic vision the *unformed* world is a river, traditionally fourfold, which influenced the Renaissance image of the temperate

body with its four humors. In the tragic vision this world usually becomes the sea, as the narrative myth of dissolution is so often a flood myth. The combination of the sea and beast images gives us the leviathan and similar water-monsters.

Obvious as this table looks, a great variety of poetic images and forms will be found to fit it. Yeats's "Sailing to Byzantium," to take a famous example of the comic vision at random, has the city, the tree, the bird, the community of sages, the geometrical gyre and the detachment from the cyclic world. It is, of course, only the general comic or tragic context that determines the interpretation of any symbol: this is obvious with relatively neutral archetypes like the island, which may be Prospero's island or Circe's.

Our tables are, of course, not only elementary but grossly over-simplified, just as our inductive approach to the archetype was a mere hunch. The important point is not the deficiencies of either procedure, taken by itself, but the fact that, somewhere and somehow, the two are clearly going to meet in the middle. And if they do meet, the ground plan of a systematic and comprehensive development of criticism has been established.

Nature and Homer (1958)

IN THE FIRST PART of the *Essay on Criticism* Pope deals with a critical principle and a group of critical facts. The principle is that a work of art is an imitation of nature. The facts are dealt with by being reduced to the principle. The method of arguing is typically youthful, even granting that Pope was an incredibly precocious youth. It is a fact that a poet observes certain literary conventions, but these are really nature methodized. It is a fact that a poet works with a specific mental quality which Pope calls wit, but then wit is really nature to advantage dressed. Above all, it is a fact that a poem is an imitation of other poems. It is possible that Virgil imitated nature; it is certain that he imitated Homer. This obtrusively stubborn fact has to be hammered down a little before it is on a level with the principle:

When first young Maro in his youthful mind
A work t' outlast immortal Rome designed,
Perhaps he seemed above the critic's law,

And but from Nature's fountains scorned to draw:
But when t' examine ev'ry part he came,
Nature and Homer were, he found, the same.

The traditional view of the relation of art to nature, as enunciated by Aristotle, broadened by the late Classical rhetoricians, and developed by Christianity, preserves a distinction that is much less clear in Pope. In this view there are two levels of nature. The lower one is the ordinary physical world, which is theologically "fallen"; the upper is a divinely sanctioned order, existing in Eden before the Fall, and mirrored in the Classical and Boethian myth of the Golden Age. To this upper world we may attain by means of education, obedience to law, and the habit of virtue; or, as the Elizabethans said, by adding nurture to nature. The upper world is the world of "art," and though art may be represented by a bewildering variety of things, such as magic in *The Tempest* or the grafting of a tree in *The Winter's Tale*, still it usually includes what we mean by art, and poetry, for all its Renaissance defenders, is one of the most important of the educational and regenerative agents that lead us up to the world of art. When Sidney says: "(Nature's) world is brazen; the poets only deliver a golden," he means by nature the ordinary or fallen world. When he says that art "doth grow in effect a second nature" he is saying that the upper level is also within the natural order. As Burke was to say later, "art is man's nature." The educated and virtuous man is as natural as the animal, but he lives in a world of specifically human nature, where moral goodness is natural. Thus in *Comus* the Lady brushes off Comus's argument that her chastity is unnatural by saying that nature "Means her provision only to the good." This conception of art as not "artificial" in the modern sense but as identical with nature conceived as a morally intelligible order is the basis of Pope's reductive argument—the art itself is nature, as Polixenes says in *The Winter's Tale*.

The two levels are further subdivided into four. The lower level has in its basement the world of sin and moral corruption, which is strictly speaking unnatural, though it often appears to be an intensification of ordinary nature, as it does in *Comus*. The ordinary physical world above it, the nature of animals and plants, is morally neutral, and hence not a resting place for man. Man is in this nature but not of it; he must either go downward into sin or upward into his proper human world. The upper level has above it a supernatural order, which operates in this one as the economy of grace, providence, and salvation. The supernatural world is often associated, as in the *Nativity Ode*, with the world above the moon, the starry spheres that suffer no change or decay. Of course even this is still nature, and its relation to the world of God's actual presence symbolic only, but the symbolizing of the higher by the lower "heaven" has been traditional throughout the Christian period. The last stanza of Spenser's *Mutabilitie Cantoes* is a familiar English example.

The four words may also be thought of as concentric, as they are in Dante, where hell is at the centre of the earth, paradise is in the surrounding world of the planets, and purgatory, the world of moral education in which we move upward to our original unfallen nature in Eden, fills a space between the ordinary world and paradise. Thus, in its medieval and Renaissance formulation, art, including poetry, belongs in a world of its own, a world which is, from one point of view at least, *bigger* than ordinary nature, and contains and comprehends it on all sides. Bigger is a physical metaphor, and it was certainly easier to conceive the metaphor when the Ptolemaic universe provided the physical analogies for it that Dante's poem affords. In Pope's anxiety to reduce everything to nature we can see the later tendency to think of art as a specialized development or by-product of nature, sitting precariously in the middle of nature and trying to draw support from its surroundings. As it seems even more self-evident to us than it did to Pope that nature is "bigger" than the world of art, we must return to the fundamental distinction on which all literary criticism has, at least historically, been founded.

In Plato's *Republic* there are four levels too, of a different though significantly related kind. There are two major divisions, the ideal or intelligible world and the physical or objective world. On the upper level of the intelligible world, there is *nous*, the knowledge of reality in which the subjective form, or human soul, is united with the objective form or idea. Below it is *dianoia*, knowledge *about* reality, of the kind given us by mathematics. Below this, in the upper level of the lower division, is *pistis*, or knowledge *of* the physical world, the knowledge of bodies which the human body is equipped to receive, and at the bottom is *eikasia*, or opinion, knowledge *about* the physical world, whose relation to *pistis* corresponds to the relation of *dianoia* to *nous*. The first three levels correspond roughly to the analogy between reason, will, and appetite in the mind and the ruler, guard, and artisan in the just state on which the whole scheme of the *Republic* turns. *Eikasia* corresponds to the work of the artist who imitates the physical world, and, though not necessarily erroneous in itself, it is a potential source of error, and is unnecessary in a just state.

The equation of art and *eikasia* is implicit only in the *Republic*, as Socrates evidently intends his argument about poets to be tentative, or perhaps paradoxical. Let the poets and their defenders, he says, refute it if they can, and we shall listen to them with respect. Plato himself, in other dialogues, gives the art he approves of a much higher rating, and Plato's influence has been strongest on such critics as Shelley who have claimed the maximum for their art. But the art Plato approves of is hardly, in his terms, an imitation of nature at all, and if we are to keep the conception of imitation the only answer to the argument in the *Republic* is the one that Aristotle's *Poetics* first made possible. The relation of art to nature is not an external relation of reproduction to model, but an internal relation of form to content. Art does not reflect nature; it contains nature, for the essence of content is to be contained. Hence art, no less than mathematics, is, in Plato's terminology, a mode of (at least) *dianoia*, not of *eikasia*. Of course nature is the environment as well as the content of art, and in that respect will always be external to it. That is why the figure of the mirror has been so frequently employed to illustrate the relationship. But the indispensable axiom that, as long as we are talking about art, nature is inside art as its content, not outside it as its model, was written once for all into the critic's handbook by Longinus when he identified the "sublime," not with size, but with the mental capacity that appreciates the vastness of nature and, in the stock but expressive phrase, "takes it in." Thus art is, unlike Alice, as natural as life, but twice as large:

What is it they saw, those godlike writers who in their work aim at what is greatest and overlook precision in every detail? This, among other things: that nature judged man to be no lowly or ignoble creature when she brought us into this life and into the whole universe as into a great celebration, to be spectators of her whole performance and most ambitious actors. She implanted at once into our souls an invincible love for all that is great and more divine than ourselves. That is why the whole universe gives insufficient scope to man's power of contemplation and reflection, but his thoughts often pass beyond the boundaries of the surrounding world. (tr. G. M. A. Grube, Library of Liberal Arts, p. 47)

We are not concerned here with the later versions of the relation of art to nature, but only with the critical confusions caused by the notion that art is somehow formed by its content. The terms nature, life, reality, experience, are all interchangeable in the primitive language of criticism: they are all synonyms for content. Hence life or experience cannot be the formal cause of art; the impulse to give a literary shape to something can only come from previous contact with literature. The forms of literature cannot exist outside literature, and a writer's technical ability, his power to construct a literary form, depends more on his literary scholarship than on any other factor—a point of some importance for universities that teach writing courses. Of course experience may turn up something with an accidental resemblance to literary form—in fact literary criticism badly needs a term corresponding to "picturesque," such as the "literatesque" suggested by Bagehot. Failing such a term, we express the idea very vaguely: if a man is killed in the street by a car, it is a horrifying experience to see, but it is not a "tragedy" any more than it is a novel or an epic. Every writer is constantly on the lookout for experiences that seem to have a story or poem in them, but the story or poem is not in them; it is in the writer's grasp of the literary tradition and his power of assimilating experience to it.

When Henry James was asked about the part played by experience in writing, he could only say that one should be the kind of writer on whom no experience is "lost," that is, a writer with enough technical knowledge of literature to be constantly absorbing his experience into literary forms and conventions. Such a maxim hardly sounds controversial, yet much bewilderment has been caused by using terms of content as metaphors for form. If we are examining the sketch books of two artists and find that B appeals to us much more than A, we may say: A is dead and lifeless; B's drawings are full of life: or, A is dull and uninspired; B has the fire of imagination in him: or, A thinks only of his drawing; B is looking at the subject. But all these are secondary and rationalized ways of saying "B draws better." If he draws better, his command of drawing is the primary fact, not his relation to life or imagination, or nature, all of which are haphazard guesses about him.

Critics who stress the imitation of nature usually have a strong respect for tradition: critics who stress the "original," like Edward Young, usually prefer to speak of the poet as inspired or creative. But no matter how we think of the poetic process, its end is to produce a new member of a class of things called poems or novels or plays which is already in existence. The parents of a new baby are proud of its novelty; they may even speak of it as unique; but the source of their pride is the fact that it is a recognizable human being, and conforms to a prescribed convention. The same principle holds when a new work of art is called "original." In literature, as in life, the unconventionally new is a monstrosity, as critics from Horace onward have constantly insisted. Such terms as original and inspired are value-judgments, and as my position on the role of value-judgments has been a good deal discussed and often misunderstood, I may summarize it here in four points. (1) Every value-judgment contains within it an antecedent categorical judgment, as we obviously cannot tell how good a thing is until we know what it is. (2) Inadequate value-judgments nearly always owe their inadequacy to an insufficient knowledge of what the categories of literature are. (3) Categorical judgments are based on a knowledge that can be learned and which should constantly increase; value-judgments are based on a skill derived only from such knowledge as we already have. (4) Therefore, knowledge, or

scholarship, has priority to value-judgments, constantly corrects their perspective, and always has the power of veto over them, whereas subordinating knowledge to value-judgments leads to impossible pedantries. Rymer's value-judgment of *Othello* as nothing but a bloody farce is not bad criticism; it is logical criticism based on narrow scholarship.

It seems to be difficult for the modern mind to take in the conception of a formal cause which follows most of its effects. The efficient cause of a poem may be the poet; its material cause may be nature, life, reality, experience, or whatever is being shaped. But its formal cause, the literary shape itself, is inside poetry, poetry being, not a simple aggregate of poems, but a body of forms and categories to which every new poem attaches itself somewhere. The difficulty in understanding this is, of course, increased by the law of copyright and the false analogy it suggests between writing and other forms of marketing. In Young's *Conjectures on Original Composition*, already glanced at, we can see a hazy mercantile analogy taking shape between the original writer and the entrepreneur, and between the plagiary and the mere worker. When Young comes to the unshakable fact of the imitation of earlier poems by poets, he draws a distinction (of rhetorical origin, going back to Longinus) between the poem and its author: the true original, he says, imitates not the *Iliad* but Homer, the poem being assumed to be the by-product of a personality. But a poet's personality is either unconnected with his work or part of its convention. Two Romantic poets with very remarkable personalities were Byron and Landor. Landor's personality is not integral with his poetry: it is so different as to have suggested Yeats's theory of the mask, or the poetic personality as the *opposite* of the actual one, and his personality has consequently survived only as a biographical curiosity. With Byron the personality is, so to speak, built in to the poetry, which means that Byron's personality has poetic importance because it conforms to a literary convention. This coincidence of a poetic personality with a fictional archetype is as old as Homer (for the legendary blind bard comes apparently from Homer's own Demodocus) and new enough to account for the cult of Scott Fitzgerald in our day.

Another form of the confusion between literary and personal experience is easier to recognize, though its sources are harder to identify: the confusion between literary and personal sincerity. If a poet is really in love, his Muse may well desert him; if he is a Courtly Love poet writing sonnets to an aging and irascible duchess informing her that he is her devoted slave for life, that her eyes have struck him irremediably with Cupid's dart, that he must die unless she accords him grace—all of which means, in terms of personal sincerity, that he wants a job tutoring her children—he may break out into passionate eloquence. It is not the experience of love but practice in writing love sonnets that releases the floods of poetic emotion. Ever so often Shakespeare criticism is invaded by eager amateurs proving that Shakespeare must have been a lawyer or soldier to speak with such authority about law or soldiering: there are probably books somewhere proving that he must have been a murderer to have written *Macbeth*, or that he must have gone to Italy incognito and spent years as a Renaissance prince to understand so well the psychology of royalty. Here again what is in itself an elementary fallacy often operates under cover in more sophisticated criticism.

For instance: one of the main sources of the confusion is the fact that the *profession* of personal sincerity is itself a literary convention. A Courtly Love poet may be as second-hand in inspiration as you please, but the one thing he is sure to transcribe from his sources is the statement that while most of his predecessors have got their emotions out of books, he really means what he says. The first sonnet of *Astrophel and Stella* ends with the famous line: "Fool, said my Muse to me, look in thy heart and write," which means, as a biographical fact, that Sidney has been looking into Petrarch. In the fifteenth sonnet Sidney ridicules his inferiors thus:

You that poor Petrarch's deceased woes
With new-born sighs and den'zened wit do sing:
You take wrong ways . . .

But he is in a position to say this, not because he is doing something different, but because he is doing the same thing better. All this we may readily concede, as Courtly Love conventions are remote enough from us to be recognized as conventions. But when Wordsworth informs us in the prefaces and poems of the *Lyrical Ballads* that he is letting nature and experience be his teacher he is using precisely the same convention of professing personal sincerity that Sidney is using. He may have believed it himself; so may Sidney; there is no reason why so much higher a proportion of his readers should have believed *him*. Personal sincerity in the poet is like virtue in Machiavelli's prince: the reality of it is of no consequence; the appearance of it may be.

Because works of literature form a verbal society, and because the forms of literature can only be derived from other literary forms, literature is allusive, not externally or incidentally allusive, but substantially and integrally so. To start with a simple example: G. K. Chesterton's poem *The Donkey*, after describing the grotesque appearance and miserable life of the animal, ends with the quatrain:

Fools! For I also had my hour,
One far fierce hour and sweet:
There was a shouting round my ears,
And palms before my feet.

The allusion to the first Palm Sunday is not incidental to the poem: it is the whole point of the poem: it is, once again, its formal cause. The Bible is, of course, central to many things in our experience besides literature, but a purely literary allusion may play an informing role equally well, as an allusion to Agamemnon does at the end of Eliot's *Sweeney among the Nightingales* or in Yeats's *Leda*. Agamemnon is one of the founding fathers of our literary society: that is why an allusion to him has the tremendous evocative authority of our whole literary tradition behind it. It is possible to carry the same principle a step further. When Byron writes:

> The mountain looks on Marathon,
> And Marathon looks on the sea

we are reminded of Longinus and his comment on a speech of Demosthenes, that the orator "turns what is essentially an argument into a supremely great and passionate passage" by a reference to Marathon. It is true that both Demosthenes and Byron are talking about the freedom of Greece; but Marathon carries this evocative ring *to us* because it is a battle of literary importance. As events become history, they disappear into books, and are absorbed into the conventions of books. As time goes on, and historical tradition becomes more tenuous, only the events with conventional poetic associations can carry the thrilling magic of a great name. When Lincoln said of the heroes of Gettysburg: "The world will little note nor long remember what we say here, but it can never forget what they did here," he was using one of the oldest literary conventions in the business, the so-called tapas of modesty, which is even older than the profession of sincerity. He was rhetorically right in using it, and yet what he said is not really true: it is almost impossible to remember the name and dates of battles unless there is some literary reason for doing so, and if the name "Gettysburg" evokes strong feelings when it is as far away from us as we are from Marathon, it will do so only because of whatever literary tradition may have begun with Lincoln's speech.

I do not deny the reality of the sense of the unexpected, the shocking or radically novel, about the original writer, but the difference between the original and the derivative writer does need restating, on the basis of the fact that the original writer is derivative at a deeper level. There are many aspects to the subject of originality in literature, but I have space to deal with only one.

There are no primitives today, and no way of tracing the origin of the impulse to put things into literary form. Everyone, however, lives in continuous contact with words. Much

of this contact is with words used descriptively, i.e., to convey information, or what passes as such. But there is a residual contact with words used for entertainment in the broadest sense. For literary people a good deal or most of this contact is with literature, in the conventional modes of books and plays. For people with no consistent literary taste it takes various sub-literary forms: reading the comics, watching television, staying up with detective stories, listening to funny stories, gossiping, and the like. And however thickly covered up with commercial formulas such experience may be today, it is continuous with the popular literary experience of the past. By popular literature I mean roughly the imaginative verbal experience of those with no specifically literary training or interest. The popular in this sense is the contemporary primitive, and it tends to become primitive with the passing of time. Much of it is rubbish, though occasionally a very good work of literature may become popular in the sense of affording a key to imaginative experience for the untrained: *Huckleberry Finn* and some of Dickens's novels are nineteenth-century examples. In simpler societies popular literature consists largely of ballads, myths, folk tales, and similar forms which persist in recognizable disguises to our own day, especially in the nursery rhymes and fairy tales of childhood.

Literature often becomes superficially or inorganically conventional. This usually happens when it follows the narrowing dialectic of a cultural elite belonging to a class which is culturally ascendant but is losing its social effectiveness. The drama of the late Caroline private theatre tended to narrow its appeal in this way, until a social revolution that seemed oddly to coincide with an inner collapse of vitality swept it out in 1642. The original writer in such a situation is likely to do something that will be decried by this elite as vulgar, and hailed by a later generation as turning from literary convention to experience. Thus at the end of the eighteenth century, with so many poets ringing the changes on what Cowper calls Philomela's "mechanick" woe, Blake's *Songs of Innocence* and Wordsworth's *Lyrical Ballads* are a breath of fresh air. Hence our readiness to accept Wordsworth's statement that he is ignoring bookish models and making a direct contact with life. As usual, this account is oversimplified. What Blake and Wordsworth also did was to set up a new series of literary echoes: keepsake poems, broadside ballads, moralizing tales for children, were suddenly shown to have an undreamed-of potentiality in their trite formulas.

It is difficult to think of any new and startling development in literature that has not bestowed glass slippers and pumpkin coaches on some subliterary Cinderella. The most obvious example is Elizabethan popular drama, the flower and fruit of what ran to seed with Carlell and Glapthorne. However great the difference in value between *King Lear* and *King Cambyses*, it is hardly likely that Shakespeare would have got as far as *King Lear* if he had not been shrewd enough to see literary possibilities in *King Cambyses* that more highbrow contemporaries did not see. The same practical shrewdness is evident in his exploiting of the formula of primitive romance and *commedia dell' arte* improvisations in his last period.

The same principle affects many aspects of modern literature. I am not thinking so much of, say, Yeats's interest in the legends and superstitions of the Irish peasantry, which is a usual enough type of interest in popular literary experience: I am thinking rather of the exploiting of a squalid lower-middle-class subculture in *Ulysses*, of Yeats's own use of an equally dingy type of occult literature, of the newspaper verse idioms in Auden, of the way in which experimental drama has been affected by primitive and archaic types of popular drama from *Sweeney Agonistes* to *Waiting for Godot*, the latter being of course a frozen vaudeville act. Graham Greene has spoken with great contempt of "books to read while you wait for the bus," but such "entertainments" as *Brighton Rock* and *The Ministry of Fear* are literary developments of precisely the formulas of such books. Wherever we turn in literature it is the same story: every fresh contact with "life" involves also a reshaping of literary con-

vention. Wordsworth's attempt "to choose incidents and situations from common life . . . as far as was possible in a selection of language really used by men" echoes the similar attempt with which Spenser in the *Shepheards Calender* revitalized Tudor poetry, described by E. K. as bringing "great grace, and, as one would say, auctoritie to the verse." Let us compare two passages from representative poems of the turn of this century, one from a lyric in *A Shropshire Lad* and the other from John Davidson's *Thirty Bob a Week*:

> "Rest you so from trouble sore,
> Fear the heat o' the sun no more,
> Nor the snowing winter wild,
> Now you labour not with child.
>
> "Empty vessel, garment cast,
> We that wore you long shall last.
> —Another night, another day."
> So my bones within me say.

I step into my heart and there I meet
    A god-almighty devil singing small,
Who would like to shout and whistle in the
    street,
    And squelch the passers flat against the wall;
If the whole world was a cake he had the power
    to take,
    He would take it, ask for more, and eat it all.

And I meet a sort of simpleton beside,
    The kind that life is always giving beans;
With thirty bob a week to keep a bride
    He fell in love and married in his teens:
At thirty bob he stuck; but he knows it isn't
    luck:
    He knows the seas are deeper than tureens.

The first reaction of a student coming upon these two poems might well be to say that the Housman poem was exquisite and the Davidson one noisy and sentimental doggerel. His second reaction might well be to swing to the opposite extreme and say that one is mere literature and the other a transcription from life, so shattering in its impact as to make it impossible for us to think of Housman as a serious poet at all by comparison. His next duty is to get the assumptions behind these value-judgments sorted out in his mind. Housman's poetry is steeped in conventions that are themselves deeply absorbed in the literary tradition, conventions ranging from the ballad to the sentimental nineteenth-century lyric, and including a deliberate echo of Shakespeare. The Davidson poem uses the idiom and rhythm of a music-hall song to express the kind of life that the music hall indirectly reflects. Housman is deliberately erudite in his use of convention; Davidson deliberately the reverse; but they are equally conventional. By that time, the student will be experienced enough in criticism to have stopped wanting to make comparative value-judgments.

There is no question of finding a primitive or popular core of literary experience in every work of literature: I am dealing here only with the special case in which literature may give, to a hasty observer, the illusion of turning away from books to "life." In our age, as in every age of literature, there are certain assumptions held by our cultural elite that need to be examined with detachment and catholicity of taste. In the Renaissance it was assumed that epic and tragedy were the aristocrats of literary forms, and that major poets would normally devote themselves to these genres. The assumption produced many dull epics and pedantic tragedies, but it also encouraged the genius of Spenser and Milton, of Marlowe and not impossibly of Shakespeare. At the same time we keep a sharp eye out for such diversifiers of literary experience as Donne and Marvell, or, to go further afield, as Deloney, Dorothy Osborne, or Samuel Pepys. In our day it is assumed that the "creative" writer devotes himself to poetry, fiction, and drama, and a great deal of the creative energy of our writing will undoubtedly run through these genres. To press the assumption too far, to assume not only that all "creative" writers would work in these genres but that all who do work in them are creative people, would be ascribing an inherently creative quality to the genres themselves, which is clearly non-

sense. It is possible that a substantial proportion of our genuinely "creative" writers may work in such peripheral genres as journalism, popular science, criticism, comic strips, or biography. If so, they will not be turning from literature to life, but exploring different literary conventions.

The opposite extreme from elite standards is the anti-intellectual fallacy of sentimentalizing sub-literary experience in itself. All of us, even the most highbrow, spend much time in the sub-literary world; all of us derive many surreptitious pleasures from it; but this world is, from the point of view of actual literature, mainly a babbling chaos, waiting for the creative word to brood over it and bring it to literary life. In itself it is made up of the most rigidly stylized conventions: the primitive, like the decadent, is inorganically conventional, and what it suggests to the artist is not new content, but new possibilities in the treatment of convention. In short, it is not the world of ordinary life or raw experience, but a suburban literary world.

The critic, once he understands this, may derive much pleasure and profit from attempting to unify his literary experience on all levels, without confusing his value-judgments. If he has a passion for detective stories, he may study the way in which the readability of this genre is increased by the rigidity of its conventions: it is almost a literary development of an important genre of sub-literary experience, the word-puzzle. If he has a special fondness for P. G. Wodehouse, he may discover not only that Wodehouse is the most conventionalized of modern comic writers, but that the conventions used are identical with those of Plautus. If he is moved in spite of himself by a sentimental movie or magazine story, he may recognize the same devices that move him on a different level in *Pericles* or *The Winter's Tale*. Wherever he goes in his imaginative verbal experience, the conventions of literature contain the experience; their formal laws hold everywhere; and from this point of view there is no difference between the scholarly and the popular in the world of words. Nature and Homer are, we find, the same.

The Road of Excess (1963)

It will be easiest for me to begin with a personal reference. My first sustained effort in scholarship was an attempt to work out a unified commentary on the prophetic books of Blake. These poems are mythical in shape: I had to learn something about myth to write about them, and so I discovered, after the book was published, that I was a member of a school of "myth criticism" of which I had not previously heard. My second effort, completed ten years later, was an attempt to work out a unified commentary on the theory of literary criticism, in which again myth had a prominent place. To me, the progress from one interest to the other was inevitable, and it was obvious to anyone who read both books that my critical ideas had been derived from Blake. How completely the second book was contained in embryo in the first, however, was something I did not realize myself until I recently read through *Fearful Symmetry*, for the first time in fifteen years, in order to write a preface to a new paperback edition. It seems perhaps worth while to examine what has been so far a mere assumption, the actual connecting links between my study of Blake and my study of the theory of criticism. At least the question is interesting to me, and so provides the only genuine motive yet discovered for undertaking any research.

Blake is one of the poets who believe that, as Wallace Stevens says, the only subject of poetry is poetry itself, and that the writing of a poem is itself a theory of poetry. He interests a critic because he removes the barriers between poetry and criticism. He defines the greatest poetry as "allegory addressed to the intellectual powers," and defends the practice of not being too explicit on the ground that it

Reprinted from *Myth and Symbol*, ed. B. Slote, 1963, by permission of University of Nebraska Press.

"rouzes the faculties to act." His language in his later prophecies is almost deliberately colloquial and "unpoetic," as though he intended his poetry to be also a work of criticism, just as he expected the critic's response to be also a creative one. He understood, in his own way, the principle later stated by Arnold that poetry is a criticism of life, and it was an uncompromising way. For him, the artist demonstrates a certain way of life: his aim is not to be appreciated or admired, but to transfer to others the imaginative habit and energy of his mind. The main work of criticism is teaching, and teaching for Blake cannot be separated from creation.

Blake's statements about art are extreme enough to make it clear that he is demanding some kind of mental adjustment to take them in. One of the Laocoon Aphorisms reads: "A Poet, a Painter, a Musician, an Architect: the Man Or Woman who is not one of these is not a Christian." If we respond to this in terms of what we ordinarily associate with the words used, the aphorism will sound, as Blake intended it to sound, like someone in the last stages of paranoia. Blake has an unusual faculty for putting his central beliefs in this mock-paranoid form, and in consequence has deliberately misled all readers who would rather believe that he was mad than that their own use of language could be inadequate. Thus when a Devil says in *The Marriage of Heaven and Hell*: "those who envy or calumniate great men hate God; for there is no other God," our habitual understanding of the phrase "great men" turns the remark into something that makes Carlyle at his worst sound by comparison like a wise and prudent thinker. When we read in the *Descriptive Catalogue*, however, that Chaucer's Parson is "according to Christ's definition, the greatest of his age," we begin to wonder if this paradoxical Devil has really so sulphurous a smell. Similarly, Blake's equating of the arts with Christianity implies, first, that his conception of art includes much more than we usually associate with it, and, second, that it excludes most of what we do associate with it. Blake is calling a work of art what a more conventional terminology would call a charitable act, while at the same time the painting of, say, Reynolds is for him not bad painting but anti-painting. Whether we agree or sympathize with Blake's attitude, what he says does involve a whole theory of criticism, and this theory we should examine.

One feature of Blake's prophecies which strikes every reader is the gradual elimination, especially in the two later poems *Milton* and *Jerusalem* that form the climax of this part of his work, of anything resembling narrative movement. The following passage occurs in Plate 71 of *Jerusalem*:

What is Above is Within, for every-thing in Eternity is translucent:
The Circumference is Within, Without is formed the Selfish Center,
And the Circumference still expands going forward to Eternity,
And the Center has Eternal States; these States we now explore.

I still have the copy of Blake that I used as an undergraduate, and I see that in the margin beside this passage I have written the words "Something moves, anyhow." But even that was more of an expression of hope than of considered critical judgement. This plotless type of writing has been discussed a good deal by other critics, notably Hugh Kenner and Marshall McLuhan, who call it "mental landscape," and ascribe its invention to the French *symbolistes*. But in Blake we not only have the technique already complete, but an even more thoroughgoing way of presenting it.

If we read *Milton* and *Jerusalem* as Blake intended them to be read, we are not reading them in any conventional sense at all: we are staring at a sequence of plates, most of them

with designs. We can see, of course, that a sequence of illustrated plates would be an intolerably cumbersome and inappropriate method of presenting a long poem in which narrative was the main interest. The long poems of other poets that Blake illustrated, such as Young's *Night Thoughts* and Blair's *Grave*, are meditative poems where, even without Blake's assistance, the reader's attention is expected to drop out of the text every so often and soar, or plunge, whichever metaphor is appropriate, although perhaps wander is even more accurate. No doubt the development of Blake's engraving technique had much to do with the plotlessness of the engraved poems. We notice that the three poems of Blake in which the sense of narrative movement is strongest—*Tiriel*, *The French Revolution*, *The Four Zoas*—were never engraved. We notice too that the illustration on a plate often does not illustrate the text on the same plate, and that in one copy of *Jerusalem* the sequence of plates in Part Two is slightly different. The elimination of narrative movement is clearly central to the structure of these poems, and the device of a sequence of plates is consistent with the whole scheme, not a mere accident.

The theme of *Milton* is an instant of illumination in the mind of the poet, an instant which, like the moments of recognition in Proust, links him with a series of previous moments stretching back to the creation of the world. Proust was led to see men as giants in time, but for Blake there is only one giant, Albion, whose dream is time. For Blake in *Milton*, as for Eliot in *Little Gidding*, history is a pattern of timeless moments. What is said, so to speak, in the text of *Milton* is designed to present the context of the illuminated moment as a single simultaneous pattern of apprehension. Hence it does not form a narrative, but recedes spatially, as it were, from that moment. *Jerusalem* is conceived like a painting of the Last Judgement, stretching from heaven to hell and crowded with figures and allusions. Again, everything said in the text is intended to fit somewhere into this simultaneous conceptual pattern, not to form a linear narrative. If I ever get a big enough office, I shall have the hundred plates of my *Jerusalem* reproduction framed and hung around the walls, so that the frontispiece will have the second plate on one side and the last plate on the other. This will be *Jerusalem* presented as Blake thought of it, symbolizing the state of mind in which the poet himself could say: "I see the Past, Present & Future existing all at once Before me." In the still later Job engravings the technique of placing the words within a pictorial unit is of course much more obvious.

Many forms of literature, including the drama, fiction, and epic and narrative poetry, depend on narrative movement in a specific way. That is, they depend for their appeal on the participation of the reader or listener in the narrative as it moves along in time. It is continuity that keeps us turning the pages of a novel, or sitting in a theatre. But there is always something of a summoned-up illusion about such continuity. We may keep reading a novel or attending to a play "to see how it turns out." But once we know how it turns out, and the spell ceases to bind us, we tend to forget the continuity, the very element in the play or novel that enabled us to participate in it. Remembering the plot of anything seems to be unusually difficult. Every member of this audience is familiar with many literary narratives, could even lecture on them with very little notice, and yet could not give a consecutive account of what happened in them, just as all the evangelical zeal of the hero of *The Way of All Flesh* was not equal to remembering the story of the resurrection of Christ in the Gospel of John. Nor does this seem particularly regrettable. Just as the pun is the lowest form of wit, so it is generally agreed, among knowledgeable people like ourselves, that summarizing a plot is the lowest form of criticism.

I have dealt with this question elsewhere, and can only give the main point here. Narrative in literature may also be seen as theme, and theme *is* narrative, but narrative seen as a simultaneous unity. At a certain point in the narrative, the point which Aristotle calls *anagnorisis* or recognition, the sense of linear continuity or participation in the action changes perspective, and what we now see is a total design or unifying structure in the narrative. In detective stories, when we find out who done it, or in certain types of comedy or romance that depend on what are now called "gimmicks," such as Jonson's *Epicoene*, the point of *anagnorisis* is the revelation of something which has previously been a mystery. In such works Aristotle's word *anagnorisis* is best translated "discovery." But in most serious works of literature, and more particularly in epics and tragedies, the better translation is "recognition." The reader already knows what is going to happen, but wishes to see, or rather to participate in, the completion of the design.

Thus the end of reading or listening is the beginning of critical understanding, and nothing that we call criticism can begin until the whole of what it is striving to comprehend has been presented to it. Participation in the continuity of narrative leads to the discovery or recognition of the theme, which *is* the narrative seen as total design. This theme is what, as we say, the story has been all about, the point of telling it. What we reach at the end of participation becomes the center of our critical attention. The elements in the narrative thereupon regroup themselves in a new way. Certain unusually vivid bits of characterization or scenes of exceptional intensity move up near the center of our memory. This reconstructing and regrouping of elements in our critical response to a narrative goes on more or less unconsciously, but the fact that it goes on is what makes remembering plot so difficult.

Thus there are two kinds of response to a work of literature, especially one that tells a story. The first kind is a participating response in time, moving in measure like a dancer with the rhythm of continuity. It is typically an uncritical, or more accurately a pre-critical response. We cannot begin criticism, strictly speaking, until we have heard the author out, unless he is a bore, when the critical response starts prematurely and, as we say, we can't get into the book. The second kind of response is thematic, detached, fully conscious, and one which sees and is capable of examining the work as a simultaneous whole. It may be an act of understanding, or it may be a value-judgement, or it may be both. Naturally these two types of response overlap more in practice than I suggest here, but the distinction between them is clear enough, and fundamental in the theory of criticism. Some critics, including Professors Wimsatt and Beardsley in *The Verbal Icon,* stress the deficiencies of "holism" as a critical theory; but we should distinguish between "holism" as a critical theory and as a heuristic principle.

There are of course great differences of emphasis within literature itself, according to which kind of response the author is more interested in. At one pole of fiction we have the pure storyteller, whose sole interest is in suspense and the pacing of narrative, and who could not care less what the larger meaning of his story was, or what a critic would find in it afterwards. The attitude of such a storyteller is expressed in the well-known preface to *Huckleberry Finn:* "Persons attempting to find a motive in this narrative will be prosecuted; persons attempting to find a moral in it will be banished; persons attempting to find a plot in it will be shot." Motive and moral and plot certainly are in *Huckleberry Finn,* but the author, or so he says, doesn't want to hear about them. All the storyteller wants to do is to keep the attention of his audience to the end: once the end is reached, he has no further interest in his audience. He may even be hostile to criticism or anti-intellectual in his attitude to literature, afraid that criticism will spoil the simple entertainment that he designed. The lyrical poet concerned with expressing certain feelings or emotions in the lyrical conventions of his day often takes a similar attitude, because it is natural for him to identify his conventional literary emotions with his "real" personal emotions. He therefore feels that if the critic finds any meaning or significance in his work beyond the intensity of those emotions, it must be only what the critic wants to say instead. Anticritical statements are usually designed only to keep the critic in his place, but the attitude they represent, when genuine, is objective, thrown outward into the designing of the continuity. It is the attitude that Schiller, in his essay on *Naive and Sentimental Poetry,* means by naive, and which includes what we mean in English by naive. Naive writers' *obiter dicta* are often repeated, for consolation, by the kind of critic who is beginning to suspect that literary criticism is a more difficult discipline than he realized when he entered into it. But it is not possible for any reader today to respond to a work of literature with complete or genuine naivete. Response is what Schiller calls sentimental by its very nature, and is hence to some degree involved with criticism.

If we compare, let us say, Malory with Spenser, we can see that Malory's chief interest is in telling the stories in the "French book" he is using. He seems to know that some of them, especially the Grail stories, have overtones in them that the reader will linger with long after he has finished reading. But Malory makes no explicit reference to this, nor does one feel that Malory himself, preoccupied as he was with a nervous habit of robbing churches, would have been much interested in a purely critical reaction to this book. But for Spenser it is clear that the romance form, the quest of the knight journeying into a dark forest in search of some sinister villain who can be forced to release some suppliant female, is merely a projection of what Spenser really wants to say. When he says at the end of Book II of *The Faerie Queene:*

> Now gins this goodly frame of Temperaunce
> Fayrely to rise

it is clear that his interest is thematic, in the emergence of a fully articulated view of the virtue of Temperance which the reader can contemplate, as it were, like a statue, seeing all of its parts at once. This simultaneous vision extends over the entire poem, for Temperance is

only one of the virtues surrounding the ideal
Prince, and the emergence of the total form of
that Prince is the thematic mould into which
the enormous narrative is finally poured. The
stanza in Spenser, especially the final alexan-
drine, has a role rather similar to the engraved
design in Blake: it deliberately arrests the narrative and forces the reader to concentrate on
something else.

In our day the prevailing attitude to fiction
is overwhelmingly thematic. Even as early as
Dickens we often feel that the plot, when it is a
matter of unplausible mysteries unconvincingly
revealed, is something superimposed on the
real narrative, which is more like a procession
of characters. In our day the born storyteller
is even rather peripheral to fiction, at best a
borderline case like Somerset Maugham, and
the serious novelist is as a rule the novelist who
writes not because he has a story to tell but
because he has a theme to illustrate. One reason for this present preference of the thematic
is that the ironic tone is central to modern literature. It is the function of irony, typically in
Greek tragedy, to give the audience a clearer
view of the total design than the actors themselves are aware of. Irony thus sets up a thematic detachment as soon as possible in the
work, and provides an additional clue to the
total meaning.

There may be, then, and there usually is, a
kind of empathic communion set up in the
reader or audience of a work of literature,
which follows the work continuously to the
end. The sense of empathy may be established
by a story, where we read on to see what happens. Or by a pulsating rhythm, such as the
dactylic hexameter in Homer, which has a
surge and sweep that can carry us through even
the longueurs referred to by Horace. We notice
the effectiveness of rhythm in continuity more
clearly in music, and most clearly in fast movements. I recall a cartoon of a tired man at a
concert consulting his program and saying:
"Well, the next movement is *prestissimo molto
ed appassionato*, thank God." Or by the fluctuating intensity of a mood or emotion, again

most clearly in music and in lyrical poetry. Or
by a continuous sense of lifelikeness in realistic
fiction, a sense which can extend itself even to
realistic painting, as the eye darts from one detail to another. All these empathic responses
are "naive," or essentially pre-critical.

Certain forms of art are also designed to give
us the strongest possible emphasis on the continuous process of creation. The sketch, for example, is often more prized than the finished
painting because of the greater sense of process
in it. *Tachisme* and action-painting, spontaneous improvisation in swing, jazz, or more recently electronic music, and the kind of action-
poetry, often read to jazz, which evokes the
ghosts of those primeval jam-sessions postulated by early critics of the ballad, are more
complete examples. All forms of art which lay
great stress on continuous spontaneity seem to
have a good deal of resistance to criticism, even
to the education which is the natural context of
criticism. We are told in Professor Lord's
Singer of Tales that the most continuous form
of poetry ever devised, the formulaic epic, demands illiteracy for success on the part of the
poet, and there seems to be an inevitable affinity between the continuous and the unreflect-
ing.

It is this continuity which is particularly
Aristotle's imitation of an action. One's attention is completely absorbed in it: no other work
of art is demanding attention at the same time,
hence one has the sense of a unique and novel
experience, at least as an ideal (for of course
one may be rereading a book or seeing a familiar play). But, as in the world of action itself,
one cannot participate and be a spectator at
the same time. At best one is what Wyndham
Lewis calls a "dithyrambic spectator." Lewis's
disapproval of the dithyrambic spectator indicates an opposed emphasis on the detached
contemplation of the entire work of art, and
one so extreme that it talks of eliminating the
sense of linear participating movement in the
arts altogether. It would not clarify our argument to examine Lewis's very muddled polemics at this point, but they have some interest

as documents in a tradition which strongly emphasized a visual and contemplative approach to art. Blake's plotless prophecies are, somewhat unexpectedly, in a similar (though by no means identical) tradition.

Just as the sense of participation in the movement of literature is absorbed, unique and novel, isolated from everything else, so the contemplative sense of its simultaneous wholeness tends to put the work of literature in some kind of framework or context. There are several such contexts, some of them indicated already. One of them is the allegorical context, where the total meaning or significance of the literary work is seen in relation to other forms of significance, such as moral ideas or historical events. A few works of literature, such as *The Pilgrim's Progress*, are technically allegories, which means that this explicit relation to external meaning is also a part of its continuity. Most literary works are not allegorical in this technical sense, but they bear a relation to historical events and moral ideas which is brought out in the kind of criticism usually called commentary. As I have explained elsewhere, commentary allegorizes the works it comments on.

We notice that Blake is somewhat ambiguous in his use of the term "allegory." He says in a letter to Butts, "Allegory addressed to the Intellectual powers . . . is My Definition of the Most Sublime Poetry." But in commenting on one of his paintings of the Last Judgement, he says: "The Last Judgment is not Fable or Allegory, but Vision. Fable or Allegory are a totally distinct & inferior kind of Poetry." The first use of the term recognizes the fact that "the most sublime poetry," including his own prophecies, will demand commentary. The second use indicates that his own poems and pictures are not allegorical in the Spenserian or continuous sense, nor are they allegorical in a much more obvious and central way. They do not subordinate their literary qualities to the ideas they convey, on the assumption that the latter are more important. In the second passage quoted above Blake goes on to say with great precision: "Fable is allegory, but what Critics call

The Fable, is Vision itself." Fable is here taken in its eighteenth-century critical sense of fiction or literary structure. Aristotle's word for intellectual content, *dianoia*, "thought," can be understood in two ways, as a moral attached to a fable, or as the structure of the fable itself. The latter, according to Blake, contains its own moral significances by implication, and it destroys its imaginative quality to assume that some external moral attached to it can be a definitive translation of its "thought."

We touch here on a central dilemma of literature. If literature is didactic, it tends to injure its own integrity; if it ceases wholly to be didactic, it tends to injure its own seriousness. "Didactic poetry is my abhorrence," said Shelley, but it is clear that if the main body of Shelley's work had not been directly concerned with social, moral, religious, philosophical, political issues he would have lost most of his self-respect as a poet. Nobody wants to be an ineffectual angel, and Bernard Shaw, one of Shelley's most direct descendants in English literature, insisted that art should never be anything but didactic. This dilemma is partly solved by giving an ironic resolution to a work of fiction. The ironic resolution is the negative pole of the allegorical one. Irony presents a human conflict which, unlike a comedy, a romance, or even a tragedy, is unsatisfactory and incomplete unless we see in it a significance beyond itself, something typical of the human situation as a whole. What that significance is, irony does not say: it leaves that question up to the reader or audience. Irony preserves the seriousness of literature by demanding an expanded perspective on the action it presents, but it preserves the integrity of literature by not limiting or prescribing for that perspective.

Blake is clearly not an ironic writer, however, any more than he is an allegorist, and we must look for some other element in his thematic emphasis. A third context to which the theme of a literary work may be attached is its context in literature itself, or what we may call its archetypal framework. Just as continuous empathy is naive and absorbed in a unique and

novel experience, so the contemplation of a
unified work is self-conscious, educated, and
one which tends to classify its object. We cannot in practice study a literary work without
remembering that we have encountered many
similar ones previously. Hence after following a
narrative through to the end, our critical response includes the establishing of its categories, which are chiefly its convention and its
genre. In this perspective the particular story is
seen as a *projection* of the theme, as one of an
infinite number of possible ways of getting to
the theme. What we have just experienced we
now see to be a comedy, a tragedy, a courtly
love lyrical complaint, or one of innumerable
treatments of the Tristan or Endymion or
Faust story.

Further, just as some works of literature are
explicitly or continuously allegorical, so some
works are continuously, or at least explicitly,
allusive, calling the reader's attention to their
relation to previous works. If we try to consider
Lycidas in isolation from the tradition of the
pastoral elegy established by Theocritus and
Virgil, or *Ash Wednesday* in isolation from its
relation to Dante's *Purgatorio*, we are simply
reading these works out of context, which is as
bad a critical procedure as quoting a passage
out of context. If we read an Elizabethan sonnet sequence without taking account of the
conventional nature of every feature in it, including the poet's protests that he is not following convention and is really in love with a real
person, we shall merely substitute the wrong
context for the right one. That is, the sonnet
sequence will become a biographical allegory,
as the sonnets of Shakespeare do when, with
Oscar Wilde, we reach the conclusion that the
profoundest understanding of these sonnets,
the deepest appreciation of all their eloquence
and passion and power, comes when we identify the "man in hue" of Sonnet 20 with an unknown Elizabethan pansy named Willie
Hughes.

Blake's prophecies are intensely allusive,
though nine-tenths of the allusions are to the
Bible. "The Old & New Testaments are the
Great Code of Art," Blake says, and he thinks
of the framework of the Bible, stretching from
Creation to Last Judgement and surveying the
whole of human history in between, as indicating the framework of the whole of literary experience, and establishing the ultimate context
for all works of literature whatever. If the Bible
did not exist, at least as a form, it would be
necessary for literary critics to invent the same
kind of total and definitive verbal structure out
of the fragmentary myths and legends and folk
tales we have outside it. Such a structure is the
first and most indispensable of critical conceptions, the embodiment of the whole of literature as an order of words, as a potentially unified imaginative experience. But although its
relation to the Bible takes us well on toward a
solution of the thematic emphasis in Blake's
illuminated poetry, it does not in itself fully
explain that emphasis. If it did, the prophecies
would simply be, in the last analysis, Biblical
commentaries, and this they are far from being.

Blake's uniqueness as a poet has much to do
with his ability to sense the historical significance of his own time. Up to that time, literature and the arts had much the same educational and cultural value that they have now,
but they competed with religion, philosophy,
and law on what were at best equal and more
usually subordinate terms. Consequently when,
for example, Renaissance critics spoke of the
profundity of poetry, they tended to locate that
profundity in its allegorical meaning, the relations that could be established between poetry
and ideas, more particularly moral and religious
ideas. In the Romantic period, on the other
hand, many poets and critics were ready to
claim an authority and importance for poetry
and the imaginative arts prior to that of other
disciplines. When Shelley quotes Tasso on the
similarity of the creative work of the poet to
the creative work of God, he carries the idea a
great deal further than Tasso did. The fact of
this change in the Romantic period is familiar,
but the trends that made it possible are still not
identified with assurance.

My own guess is that the change had something to do with a growing feeling that the origin of human civilization was human too. In traditional Christianity it was not: God planted the garden of Eden and suggested the models for the law, rituals, even the architecture of human civilization. Hence a rational understanding of "nature," which included the understanding of the divine as well as the physical origin of human nature, took precedence over the poetic imagination and supplied a criterion for it. The essential moral ideas fitted into a divine scheme for the redemption of man; we understand the revelation of this scheme rationally; literature forms a series of more indirect parables or emblems of it. Thus poetry could be the companion of camps, as Sidney says: it could kindle an enthusiasm for virtue by providing examples for precepts. The sense of excitement in participating in the action of the heroic narrative of, say, the *Iliad* was heightened by thinking of the theme or total meaning of the *Iliad* as an allegory of heroism. Thus, paradoxically, the Renaissance insistence on the allegorical nature of major poetry preserved the naivete of the participating response. We see this principle at work wherever poet and audience are completely in agreement about the moral implications of a poetic theme, as they are, at least theoretically, in a hiss-the-villain melodrama.

Blake was the first and the most radical of the Romantics who identified the creative imagination of the poet with the creative power of God. For Blake God was not a superhuman lawgiver or the mathematical architect of the stars; God was the inspired suffering humanity of Jesus. Everything we call "nature," the physical world around us, is sub-moral, subhuman, sub-imaginative; every act worth performing has as its object the redeeming of this nature into something with a genuinely human, and therefore divine, shape. Hence Blake's poetry is not allegorical but mythopoeic, not obliquely related to a rational understanding of the human situation, the resolution of which is out of human hands, but a product of the creative energy that alone can redeem that situation.

Blake forces the reader to concentrate on the meaning of his work, but not didactically in the ordinary sense, because his meaning is his theme, the total simultaneous shape of his poem. The context into which the theme or meaning of the individual poem fits is not the received ideas of our cultural tradition, of which it is or should be an allegory. It is not, or not only, the entire structure of literature as an order of words, as represented by the Bible. It is rather the expanded vision that he calls apocalypse or Last Judgement: the vision of the end and goal of human civilization as the entire universe in the form that human desire wants to see it, as a heaven eternally separated from a hell. What Blake did was closely related to the Romantic movement, and Shelley and Keats at least are mythopoeic poets for reasons not far removed from Blake's.

Since the Romantic movement, there has been a more conservative tendency to deprecate the central place it gave to the creative imagination and to return, or attempt to return, to the older hierarchy. T. S. Eliot is both a familiar and a coherent exponent of this tendency, and he has been followed by Auden, with his Kierkegaardian reinforcements. According to Eliot, it is the function of art, by imposing an order on life, to give us the sense of an order in life, and so to lead us into a state of serenity and reconciliation preparatory to another and superior kind of experience, where "that guide" can lead us no further. The implication is that there is a spiritually existential world above that of art, a world of action and behavior, of which the most direct imitation in this world is not art but the sacramental act. This latter is a form of uncritical or pre-critical religious participation that leads to a genuinely religious contemplation, which for Eliot is a state of heightened consciousness with strong affinities to mysticism. Mysticism is a word which has been applied both to Blake and to St. John of the Cross: in other words it has been rather loosely applied, because these two poets have little in common. It is clear that Eliot's mystical affinities are of the St. John of the Cross type. The function of art, for Eliot, is again of the subordinated or allegorical kind. Its order represents a higher existential order, hence its greatest ambition should be to get beyond itself, pointing to its superior reality with such urgency and clarity that it disappears in that reality. This, however, only happens either in the greatest or most explicitly religious art: nine-tenths of our literary experience is on the subordinate plane where we are seeing an order in life without worrying too much about the significance of that order. On this plane the naive pre-critical direct experience of participation can still be maintained, as it is in Renaissance critical theory. The Romantics, according to this view, spoil both the form and the fun of poetry by insisting so much on the profundity of the imaginative experience as to make it a kind of portentous *ersatz* religion.

This leads us back to the aphorism of Blake with which we began, where the artist is identified with the Christian. Elsewhere he speaks of "Religion, or Civilized Life such as it is in the Christian Church," and says that poetry, painting and music are "the three Powers in Man of conversing with Paradise, which the flood did not Sweep away." For Blake art is not a substitute for religion, though a great deal of religion as ordinarily conceived is a substitute for art, in that it abuses the mythopoeic faculty by creating fantasies about another world or rationalizing the evils of this one instead of working toward genuine human life. If we describe Blake's conception of art independently of the traditional myth of fall and apocalypse that embodies it, we may say that the poetic activity is fundamentally one of identifying the

human with the nonhuman world. This identity is what the poetic metaphor expresses, and the end of the poetic vision is the humanization of reality, "All Human Forms identified," as Blake says at the end of *Jerusalem*. Here we have the basis for a critical theory which puts such central conceptions as myth and metaphor into their proper central place. So far from usurping the function of religion, it keeps literature in the context of human civilization, yet without limiting the infinite variety and range of the poetic imagination. The criteria it suggests are not moral ones, nor are they collections of imposing abstractions like Unity, but the interests, in the widest sense, of mankind itself, or himself, as Blake would prefer to say.

In this conception of art the productive or creative effort is inseparable from the awareness of what it is doing. It is this unity of energy and consciousness that Blake attempts to express by the word "vision." In Blake there is no either-or dialectic where one must be either a detached spectator or a preoccupied actor. Hence there is no division, though there may be a distinction, between the creative power of shaping the form and the critical power of seeing the world it belongs to. Any division instantly makes art barbaric and the knowledge of it pedantic—a bound Orc and a bewildered Urizen, to use Blake's symbols. The vision inspires the act, and the act realizes the vision. This is the most thoroughgoing view of the partnership of creation and criticism in literature I know, but for me, though other views may seem more reasonable and more plausible for a time, it is in the long run the only one that will hold.

From A Natural Perspective (1965)

THE RETURN FROM THE SEA

COMEDY, like all forms of art that are presented in time, is primarily an impetus toward completing a certain kind of movement. We have been trying to characterize the nature of the comic drive, and have called it a drive toward identity. This is essentially a social identity, which emerges when the ascendant society of the early part of the play, with its irrational laws, lusts, and tyrannical whims, is dissolved and a new society crystallizes around the marriage of the central characters. It has also an individual form, an awakening to self-knowledge, which is typically a release from a humor or a mechanical form of repetitive behavior.

Shakespearean romantic comedy presents the full or completed form of this movement; ironic comedy presents incomplete or divergent forms of it. As a rule irony is intelligible only as a frustration of a completed movement which is presented in romance: thus we need to have the normal or romantic design at least unconsciously in our minds to understand the parodies of it that irony supplies. We may often think of the happy ending as perfunctory, and sometimes it may seem that, but even in the most sardonic comedies we should not assume that Shakespeare had a different kind of ending in mind that he could have provided for a more highbrow audience. The more highbrow audience might be more ironically minded, more bored with the conventional romantic ending, more inclined to be flattered at being asked to settle for some new variant of it. But Shakespeare, like Shylock, insists on carrying out his

From *A Natural Perspective* (1965). Reprinted by permission of Columbia University Press.

contract to the letter. His festive conclusions with their multiple marriages are not concessions: they are conventions built into the structure of the play from the beginning.

The mythical or primitive basis of comedy is a movement toward the rebirth and renewal of the powers of nature, this aspect of literary comedy being expressed in the imagery more directly than in the structure. The mythical backbone of all literature is the cycle of nature, which rolls from birth to death and back again to rebirth. The first half of this cycle, the movement from birth to death, spring to winter, dawn to dark, is the basis of the great alliance of nature and reason, the sense of nature as a rational order in which all movement is toward the increasingly predictable. Such a conception of nature was of course deeply rooted in the Elizabethan mind: it extends even to the tendency to call anything natural that the writer is accustomed to, as when Sidney expresses horror at the custom of wearing rings in the nose instead of in "the fit and natural places of the ears." In drama, tragedy, the history play (always very close to tragedy) and pure irony (*e.g.* *Troilus and Cressida*) are centered on this first half. There may be many surprises in the last act of a Shakespearean tragedy, but the pervading feeling is of something inevitable working itself out. The histories deal similarly with a kind of "karma" or continuous force of evil action which produces its own inevitable consequences. In the *Henry VI* plays the original sin of the House of Lancaster in deposing Richard and pushing Edmund Mortimer out of the way releases a flood of such "karma" which isolates and overwhelms Talbot in Part One,

Duke Humphrey in Part Two, and the gentle and ineffectual Henry VI himself in Part Three. The organizing conception of the history play is the wheel of fortune, which, according to Chaucer's monk, started turning with the fall of Lucifer, and is repeated in the fall of every great man, who discovers with Wolsey that

> When he falls, he falls like Lucifer,
> Never to hope again.

The wheel of fortune is a tragic conception: it is never genuinely a comic one, though a history play may achieve a technically comic conclusion by stopping the wheel turning halfway. Thus *Henry V* ends with triumphant conquest and a royal marriage, though, as the epilogue reminds us, King Henry died almost immediately and sixty years of unbroken disaster followed. In *Henry VIII* there are three great falls, those of Buckingham, Wolsey, and Queen Catherine, and three corresponding rises, those of Cromwell, Cranmer, and Anne Boleyn. The play ends with the triumph of the last three, leaving the audience to remember that the wheel went on turning and brought them down too. Being a strong king, Henry VIII turns the wheel himself, and is not turned by it, like Richard II, but history never can end as a comedy does, except for the polite fiction, found in Cranmer's prophecy at the end of the play, that the reigning monarch is a Messianic ruler.

Comedy, however, is based on the second half of the great cycle, moving from death to rebirth, decadence to renewal, winter to spring, darkness to a new dawn. We notice that three comedies, *The Winter's Tale, Twelfth Night,* and *A Midsummer Night's Dream,* have solstitial titles: perhaps it is *The Winter's Tale* that expresses the cyclical imagery of comedy most clearly. The "winter's tale," properly speaking, begins with Leontes' guards coming to seize Hermione at the moment when Mamillius is about to whisper his tale into his mother's ear, and it ends in a tremendous storm in which Antigonus perishes and the infant Perdita is exposed. Sixteen years pass, and a new dramatic action begins with a new generation, an action of irresistibly pushing life, heralded by Autolycus' song of the daffodils, and growing to a climax in the great sheepshearing festival scene, where the power of life in nature over the whole year is symbolized by a dance of twelve satyrs. The reviving force pushes on, brings Florizel and Perdita together despite the most frantic parental opposition, discloses the secret of Perdita's birth, brings Hermione to life from a statue, and finally renews life in Leontes.

The same symbolism is presented negatively in *Love's Labour's Lost,* where the audience is cheated of the comic conclusion. The courtiers present themselves to their ladies, first as Russians (Russia to an Elizabethan audience meant primarily cold winters), then as themselves. But the four Jacks panting for their Jills are disappointed; the ladies go away, and the breakup of the comic mood is symbolized by the two lovely songs of spring and winter, in which winter has the last word. Similar imagery comes occasionally into many comedies, as in this oracular speech of Helena in *All's Well:*

> But with the word the time will bring on summer,
> When briars shall have leaves as well as thorns,
> And be as sweet as sharp. We must away;
> Our waggon is prepared, and time revives us.
> All's well that ends well: still the fine's the crown.

This movement from sterility to renewed life is as natural as the tragic movement, because it happens. But though natural it is somehow irrational: the sense of the alliance of nature with reason and predictable order is no longer present. We can see that death is the inevitable result of birth, but new life is not the inevitable result of death. It is hoped for, even expected, but at its core is something unpredictable and mysterious, something that belongs to the imaginative equivalents of faith, hope, and love, not to the rational virtues. The conception of the *same* form of life passing through death to rebirth of course goes outside the order of nature altogether. Yet this conception is so central in Shakespearean romance, as Thaisa revives from a "block" and Hermione from a statue, that perhaps what really emerges in the recognition scenes of these romances is the primitive feeling, which is incorporated in Christianity, that it is *death* that is somehow unnatural, even though it always happens.

We live in an ironic age, and we tend to think, in Freudian terms, of "wish fulfillment" as confined to dreams, a helpless and shadowy counterpart of a "reality principle." In watching tragedy we are impressed by the reality of the illusion: we feel that, for instance, the blinding of Gloucester, though not really happening, is the kind of thing that can and does happen. In watching romantic comedy we are impressed by the illusion of the reality: we feel that, for instance, the conversion of Oliver and Duke Frederick at the end of *As You Like It* is the kind of thing that can't happen, yet we see it happening. In the action of a Shakespearean comedy, however, the kind of force associated with "wish fulfillment" is not helpless or purely a matter of dreams. It is, in the first place, a power as deeply rooted in nature and reality as its opponent; in the second place, it is a power that we see, as the comedy proceeds, taking over and informing the predictable world.

Yet there is a residually irrational element in such comedy, which expresses itself in a great variety of unlikely incidents: unexpected turns in the plot, gratuitous coincidences, unforeseen changes of heart in certain characters, arbitrary interference with the action by fairies or gods or characters who do not enter the play at all. We have already seen how Shakespeare deliberately chooses incredible plots and emphasizes the unlikelihood of his conclusions. The drive toward a comic conclusion is so powerful that it breaks all the chains of probability in the plot, of habit in the characters, even of expectation in the audience; and what emerges at the end is not a logical consequence of the preceding action, as in tragedy, but something more like a metamorphosis.

I have spoken of the readiness with which dramatic assumptions can be translated into propositions or axioms of belief. Tragic assumptions usually turn out to be propositions about a metaphysical fate or about the moral fatality of characteristic acts. The sense of fatality can seldom be far away from tragedy and is usually expressed there, as it is when Romeo speaks of "inauspicious stars," or Gloucester of the indifference and carelessness of the gods. In the nineteenth century it was fashionable to quote such passages to show that Shakespeare was a nineteenth-century pessimist. Those who wished to save him for free will and moral responsibility, on the other hand, could point to the fact that fatality usually cooperates with character: the witches in *Macbeth* may be, as Holinshed says, goddesses of destiny, but it is clear that Macbeth has made a subconscious pact with them before the play begins. In comedy, where there is a sense of violent manipulation of plot, of characters leaping into new roles, or events driving toward a renewing transformation in the teeth of all probability, it is easy to arrive at moral axioms about a divine providence.

. . . It is the wedding masque [in *The Tempest*] in which the dialectic of Shakespearean romance is most fully and completely stated. What the wedding masque presents is the meeting of earth and heaven under the rainbow, the symbol of Noah's new-washed world, after the tempest and flood had receded, and when it was promised that springtime and harvest would not cease. There is in fact a definite recall of the biblical scene:

> Spring come to you at the farthest
> In the very end of the harvest.

But these lines say more: they say that out of the cycle of time in ordinary nature we have reached a paradise (Ferdinand's word), where there is a *ver perpetuum*, where spring and autumn exist together. It is not a timeless world, but it is a world in which time has a quite different relation to experience from ordinary time. Milton says of his Eden that there "spring and autumn/Danced hand in hand," and he may have been thinking of Shakespeare's masque, which ends in a dance of spring nymphs and autumn reapers. And because a new heaven and a new earth is a world of chastity and a recovery of innocence, Venus is expressly excluded from the masque. For Venus belongs to the cycle of life and death below this world, and wherever she is, "dusky Dis" is also.

With the vision of this world, the world of ordinary experience disappears, for the separation has finally been made between reality and illusion, the created and the objective. The world of what Pericles calls "a tempest,/A birth, and death," being finally expelled, becomes the world of nonbeing: we have only, in the words of *The Winter's Tale*, a world ransomed and a world destroyed. In the world of the masque time has become the rhythm of existence, the recovery by man of the energy of nature. In the nonexistent world below, time is the universal devourer that has finally nothing to swallow but itself. Prospero's great speech at the end of the masque tells us that everything we perceive disappears in this time. That is, the world of the spectator is ultimately abolished. What is presented to us must be possessed by us, as Prospero tells us in the Epilogue. We are told that the characters, as usual, will adjourn to hear more about themselves, but we need not follow them, for it is our own identity that we are interested in now. If anything is to make sense of this play, no less than of Peter Quince's play, it must be, as Hippolyta says, our imagination and not theirs. When Prospero's work is done, and there is nothing left to see, the vision of the brave new world becomes the world itself, and the dance of vanishing spirits a revel that has no end.

From *Letter to the English Institute* (1965)

EVERY CRITIC TRIES to be coherent and consistent, and to avoid contradicting himself. Thus he develops his insight into literature out of a systematic framework of ideas about it. But some are better at concealing this framework than others, especially those who are unconscious of it, and so conceal it from themselves. I have been quite unable to conceal it, hence the question of the systematic nature of criticism itself bulks prominently in my writing. On the first page of the *Anatomy* I tried to explain that the system was there for the sake of the insights it contained: the insights were not there for the sake of the system. I put this on the first page because I thought that that page was more likely to be read than others. In spite of this, I am often regarded as a critic

From *Northrop Frye in Modern Criticism*, edited by M. Krieger (1965). Reprinted by permission of Columbia University Press.

equipped with a *summa critica* who approaches all his readers much as Jonah's whale approached Jonah. Actually I am grateful to be read on any terms, but the role of system and schema in my work has another kind of importance. Whatever the light it throws on literature, it throws a good deal of light on me in the act of criticizing. It is the schematic thinker, not the introspective thinker, who most fully reveals his mind in process, and so most clearly illustrates how he arrives at his conclusions.

I think that criticism as a whole is a systematic subject. But I do not think that the criticism of the future will all be contained within the critical system set out in my books. Still less do I think that it will be contained in an eclectic system, a tutti-frutti collection of the best ideas of the best critics. One of the most accurately drawn characters in drama is Reuben the Reconciler, who is listed in the *dramatis personae* of Ben Jonson's *Sad Shepherd,* and whose role was apparently to set everybody right at the end. Jonson never finished the play, so he never appeared. I wish we could throw away the notion of "reconciling," and use instead some such conception as "interpenetration." Literature itself is not a field of conflicting arguments but of interpenetrating visions. I suspect that this is true even of philosophy, where the place of argument seems more functional. The irrefutable philosopher is not the one who cannot be refuted, but the one who is still there after he has been refuted. This is the principle on which I base my view of value-judgments in criticism. I have never said that there were no literary values or that critics should never make value-judgments: what I have said is that literary values are not *established* by critical value-judgments. Every work of literature establishes its own value; in the past, much critical energy has been wasted in trying to reject or minimize these values. But all genuine literature, including Shakespeare, kept turning up, like the neurotic return of a ghost, to haunt and perplex the criticism that rejected it. I think criticism becomes more sensible when it realizes that it has nothing to do with rejection, only with recognition. To recognize is of the gods, as Euripides says. In criticism, as in philosophy, argument is functional, and there is bound to be disagreement. But disagreement is one thing, rejection is another, and critics have no more business rejecting each other than they have rejecting literature. The genuine critic works out his own views of literature while realizing that there are also a great number of other views, actual and possible, which are neither reconcilable nor irreconcilable with his own. They interpenetrate with him, and he with them, each a monad as full of windows as a Park Avenue building.

PART II

Modern Criticism:
Problems and Methods

INTRODUCTION

THE ACHIEVEMENT OF a major critic always defies neat classification. Just as the leading assumptions of a literary age are clearest
in the works of its minor artists, so the outlines of a critical movement
are most evident in the accomplishments of those who are not in-
novators. The principal categories found in any history of twentieth-
century criticism—the "New Criticism," neo-Aristotelianism, Marxist
criticism, and the like—are best illustrated through the practice of work-
aday critics and scholars. R. P. Blackmur may rightfully be thought of,
for example, as an important instigator of the "New Criticism," but for
some normative definition of that term one looks to the essays of his followers: the men whom Ezra Pound called "the diluters," or craftsmen
in a particular genre. One sign of the importance of the seven critics included in this section is their resistance to pigeonholing.

The essays in this section have been chosen with two ends in view:
first, to illustrate the styles and methods of a number of influential modern critics; second, and more important, to indicate some of the major
cross-currents which made the period 1930–1950 the heyday of modern
criticism. Never before in English or American literary history had the
critics of a period loomed so large in relation to the entire cultural scene,
and never before had literature been so closely tied to prevailing critical
theories. Of the seven critics represented here, five turned their hand to
poetry or fiction. These five (the exceptions are F. R. Leavis and R. S.
Crane) may be characterized as distinguished minor artists who wrote
major criticism: and it was this close alliance of criticism and creativity,

with the balance thrown toward criticism, that gave a special quality to the literary life of England and America in the years bracketing the Second World War.

The essays by Edmund Wilson and Lionel Trilling are grouped under the rubric "History and Criticism" because both writers are, in a sense, the heirs of Sainte-Beuve and Taine, preoccupied with that dynamic interchange between culture and personality which produces the representative work of art. Trained in the methods of nineteenth-century historical scholarship, Wilson brought to modern literature an "idea of what literary criticism ought to be—a history of man's ideas and imaginings in the setting of the conditions which have shaped them." In similar fashion, Trilling's early study of Matthew Arnold led him to a concern with the cultural setting of the literary work, that reciprocal relationship which always exists between art and society. Both Wilson and Trilling are activists in the sense that they are interested in the energy which flows from a work of art into society, not just the social forces which determine form and meaning. Both reacted against the factual determinism of old-fashioned historical scholarship, but both wished to preserve the best in this historical method. In all their essays they display the "historical sense" described by T. S. Eliot in "Tradition and the Individual Talent," which "involves a perception, not only of the pastness of the past, but of its presence." They know that we can never fully recapture the life of another age, that something essential in a culture—its vibrant detail, its unstated assumptions—must be forever lost in time. We can never recapture the full sense of Shakespeare that the Elizabethan audience had, but neither can Shakespeare be made wholly our contemporary unless we have a taste for farce and caricature. The historical imagination is a pragmatic accommodation between past and present, a compromise that Wilson and Trilling know must be made. They have one major characteristic in common: they have always shied away from the notion of the autonomous work of art, and from the kind of criticism that is concerned only with formal relationships. Like Arnold, they cannot conceive of a method of literary analysis which does not involve the moral, social, and historical implications of the work of art.

Of all the important modern critics, Edmund Wilson is the most difficult to represent through a selection of essays. Any one essay by Wilson tends to leave the reader with a sense of incompleteness, a feeling that there are loose ends to be gathered, that the critical process has not been rounded off. Such a feeling is the inevitable result of Wilson's method; as our most complete "man of letters" he has spread his attention over an incredible range of literary and cultural topics, and the unity in his critical approach comes not from a fixed critical practice but from the constant presence of a rich literary sensibility. To appreciate Wilson one must read his essays against one another, balancing the more formal analysis of *Axel's Castle* against the psychological and sociological approaches found in *The Triple Thinkers* and *The Wound and the Bow;*

for Wilson has always been a pragmatist, responding to the leading ideas of his time and processing them into his critical approach. The hallmark of his writing is flexibility, a recognition that the "degrees of success attained by the products of the various periods and various personalities" must be relative to time, place, and individual intention.

One sign of Wilson's flexibility is his ability to exploit the insights of both Marxist and Freudian theory. Although antipathetic on the theoretical plane, Marxism and Freudianism enjoyed a twin vogue in the 1930's, since both seemed to promise release from oppression: in the one case social oppression, in the other psychic oppression. As the decade progressed Wilson moved further away from the "symbolist" tradition examined in *Axel's Castle* (1931), and sought out the psychic and economic "wounds" which shape the artist's vision and style. It is instructive to compare his famous reading of Henry James's *The Turn of the Screw* (in *The Triple Thinkers*) with the more doctrinaire "psychoanalytic" studies of James's fiction. The difference is that the typical exponent of Freudian method practices a centrifugal criticism, using the literary evidence as an avenue into the author's psyche; while Wilson's method is centripetal, constantly bringing the insights of psychoanalysis to bear on the motives and symbols of the work itself.

Wilson's essay on "Marxism and Literature" displays the same blend of sympathy and detachment found in *To the Finland Station* (1940), his intellectual history of European socialism. It is interesting to compare this essay with Trilling's "Freud and Literature," which attempts the same kind of balanced assessment of literature's debt to psychoanalysis (the moral would seem to be that Freudian theory owes more to literature than it can ever repay). Trilling's essay is more closely argued, more focused, an example of his critical style at its best: implicit throughout is the Arnoldian belief that literature is a liberating moral and cultural activity. With characteristic precision Trilling lays bare the inadequacies in Freud's theory of the artist and the artistic process, only to affirm the immense value of "his whole conception of the mind . . . which makes poetry indigenous to the very constitution of the mind." The same distinction between immediate applications and general theory is made by Wilson in "Marxism and Literature," where Marxism is rejected as a touchstone to quality ("Marxism by itself can tell us nothing whatever about the goodness or badness of a work of art") but retained for its descriptive value ("What Marxism *can* do, however, is throw a great deal of light on the origins and social significance of works of art"). Wilson's style is more diffuse than Trilling's, his argument less systematic: but both he and Trilling finally convince us because they are unwilling to sacrifice the diversity and complexity of literature to any special theory or easy argument. It is this *openness* which makes the reading of their criticism a liberating experience.

In contrast to the flexibility of Trilling and Wilson, F. R. Leavis and Yvor Winters make their impact through exclusion and rigorous discrimination. In Leavis's most important criticism we find the clear imprint of his twin masters, Arnold and Eliot. Like Arnold, Leavis feels that the sanity of a culture is dependent on the "high seriousness" of its literature; and like Eliot he is committed to the view that the critic is a custodian of tradition, constantly judging the works of the present and reordering those of the past. In the 1930's Leavis applied these convictions to the current English literary scene, and produced his most important and stimulating work. In his principal works of that time, *New Bearings in English Poetry* (1932) and *Revaluation* (1936), and in the pages of his influential literary journal *Scrutiny*, he sought to combine "criticism of literature with criticism of extra-literary values," taking it as axiomatic that "concern for standards of living implies concern for standards in the arts" (*Scrutiny*: A Manifesto, 1932). Fighting against academic complacency and the generally low level of popular literary journalism, Leavis succeeded in placing his stamp on a whole generation of English students and writers. His influence on education was particularly strong: believing that the discipline of literary study was central to the idea of a university, since it is simultaneously a discipline of thought and "a discipline in scrupulous sensitiveness of response to delicate organizations of feeling" (compare Eliot on "dissociation of sensibility"), Leavis set about the task of processing the best modern writers into the literary tradition and purifying that tradition of all he thought imprecise or meretricious. Like Eliot, he took English literature of the early seventeenth century as the key to his idea of tradition, exalting the complexity and moral awareness of Shakespeare and the Metaphysical poets at the expense of Milton's reputation.

The force of Leavis's criticism in the 1930's came from his sense of dedication, which virtually made of literature a secular religion, and from the precision of his literary analysis. The essay on Shelley reprinted in this section is a case in point. Leavis's objections to Shelley may be felt to have their deepest roots in "extra-literary" matters, but his argument is based on a close and rigorous examination of the text. In the Introduction to *Revaluation* Leavis had declared that "in dealing with individual poets the rule of the critic is, or should (I think) be, to work as much as possible in terms of particular analysis—analysis of poems or passages, and to say nothing that cannot be related immediately to judgements about producible texts"; and his examination of Shelley's "Ode to the West Wind" is a perfect example of this method. The analysis leads finally to general questions about the health of Shelley's art, but only by way of detailed attention to imagery, metaphor, and rhythm. The essays on "Shelley" and "The Irony of Swift" are powerful examples of a critical method and tone which rescued much of English literary analysis from the vagueness of "appreciation" and impressionistic criticism.

However, as Leavis's career moved into the 1940's and 1950's the limitations and eccentricities of his approach became more obtrusive. Northrop Frye has said that most critical errors are errors of exclusion, and even in his early work Leavis had shown an alarming narrowness of taste.

It was as if his method could only live through blood sacrifice—Lawrence exalted at the expense of Joyce, Shakespeare at the expense of Milton. The "standards" which had been used to attack Yeats (one of Leavis's notorious blindspots) were eventually applied to the later Eliot, and the idea of "tradition" was gradually reduced from Eliot's dynamic hierarchy to a select gathering of those authors whose "sense of life" jibed with Leavis's own. By the time of *The Great Tradition* (1948), Leavis's study of the English novel, his vision had narrowed to the point where only Jane Austen, George Eliot, Henry James, Joseph Conrad, and Lawrence could be seriously considered. To paraphrase Dr. Johnson, if Dickens be not a great novelist, then where are great novels to be found? Leavis's preoccupation with D. H. Lawrence's work as a touchstone to serious artistic commitment became more and more pronounced as time passed, until some of the later essays almost seem parodies of the earlier method. It is probably fair to say that the Leavis of post-1948 belongs mainly to his disciples, while the Leavis of the 1930's belongs to the mainstream of modern criticism. Certainly his accomplishments of that decade seem secure, firmly embedded as they are in the discipline of literature as it is taught on both sides of the Atlantic. As Lionel Trilling once said, "It is possible to disagree with half the critical statements Dr. Leavis may make, and yet know him to be a critic of the first importance."

In his iconoclastic attitudes, his insistence on rigorous discrimination, and his emphasis on moral judgments, Yvor Winters was the American counterpart to F. R. Leavis. His most influential critical essays were written in the 1930's, and from a point of view totally at odds with the developing "New Criticism" of that time. Like Irving Babbitt, the American critic whom he most closely resembles, Winters regarded Romanticism as a distorting force in modern literature. He rejected the notion of aesthetic autonomy, the belief that a work of art has its own internal order which can be examined in isolation from some external reality; he deplored the reliance of many modern poets on a logic of images or moods rather than on rational plot; he rejected the primitivistic belief in the value of spontaneous feeling which he detected at the heart of most modern works; he distinguished sharply between traditional irony, which is a means for defining emotion, and "Romantic" irony, which he took to be a mask for indecision or sentimentality. In contrast to most of his contemporaries, who found a positive artistic value in the ironic balancing of opposite or discordant feelings, Winters argued for the primacy of rational, paraphrasable statement.

According to my view, the artistic process is one of moral evaluation of human experience, by means of a technique which renders possible an evaluation more precise than any other. The poet tries to understand his experience in rational terms, to state his understanding, and simultaneously to state, by means of the feelings which we attach to words, the kind and degree of emotion that should properly be motivated by this understanding. . . . The 'intensity' of the work of art, which is different from the intensity of the crude experience, lies in this: that what we call intensity in a work of art is a combination of the importance of the original subject and the precision of the judgment; whereas that which we call intensity in life is most often the confused and therefore frightening emotion resulting from a situation which we have not yet had time to meet and understand, and our feeling toward which, as it approaches clarity and control, approaches, though from a considerable distance, the condition of art.

This passage comes from an essay on T. S. Eliot, and Winters' fundamental critical stance is most evident in his opposition to both Eliot's critical theory and poetic practice. Seizing upon several key passages in Eliot's criticism, especially his remarks on the "objective correlative" and "dissociation of sensibility," Winters claims that they exclude the precise judgment of emotion from Eliot's view of art. The result, in a poem such as *The Waste Land,* is a form which reflects the intensity and confusion of experience without bringing it under control. According to Winters, Eliot's verse is a perfect example of "the fallacy of expressive, or imitative, form; the procedure in which the form succumbs to the raw material of the poem."

Eliot need not be defended against Winters' charges, since his entire literary achievement belies Winters' narrow interpretation. But Winters' attack on Eliot, like Leavis's on Joyce, is instructive: it reveals both the great strength of his criticism (a consistent theory applied with unswerving honesty) and its great weakness (a view of the morality of art which constantly slides into didacticism or moralistic judgments). In the opinion of many, Winters' major contribution to modern criticism stemmed directly from the narrowness and consistency of his vision. As a powerful and aggressive opponent of the major tendencies in modern literary criticism, he forced other critics to reexamine their theories and sharpen their statements. Many of his contemporaries would join with R. P. Blackmur in praising Winters as the most valuable member of the "loyal opposition."

The selections from Winters in this section were chosen to give a sense of his fundamental critical position, and are largely theoretical. For this reason they fail to do justice to his great skill as a practical critic, a skill which is most in evidence in his treatment of the English lyric. When faced with a short poem that met his exacting standards of coherence and moral precision, Winters could be a formidable practitioner of "close reading," analyzing sound and imagery in a way which often led to a new understanding of a familiar poet. For the sake of balance and completeness, the interested reader should turn to Winters' analyses of the poetry of Ben Jonson and George Herbert in *Forms of Discovery* (1967). Here the qualities of restrained sympathy and austere perception which inform Winters' own best poems are clearly evident.

The lengthy selection from R. S. Crane's *The Languages of Criticism and the Structure of Poetry* is a comprehensive statement of his major aims and methods. The chief exponent of the so-called "neo-Aristotelian" critical movement which developed at the University of Chicago during the 1940's, Crane came to his work on critical theory after years of exacting literary scholarship. The leading ideas of the "neo-Aristotelians" (as well as their diversities of opinion) may best be found in the collection *Critics and Criticism: Ancient and Modern* (1952), edited by Crane himself. Although the "neo-Aristotelians" are often thought of as opponents of the "New Critics," enlisting scholarly methods in a war on those who would treat the poem as a timeless artifact without historical context, such a view is too limited and too partisan: Crane's ideas might best be seen as complementary to those of such critics as William Empson, Cleanth Brooks, and R. P. Blackmur. In contrast to the "monism" of many of his contemporaries, Crane saw himself as a "pluralist," trying to recognize the virtues of different critical systems and their appropriateness (or inappropriateness) to the literary object in view. As a result, his own views shifted from time to time, providing significant counter-statements to whatever critical fashion threatened to dominate the literary scene. And his lasting influence may well have fallen as heavily on those he opposed as on those, such as Wayne Booth, who are his logical heirs (Booth's *The Rhetoric of Fiction* is in many ways an extension and refinement of Crane's approach to prose fiction).

Crane's most famous essay, "The Concept of Plot and the Plot of *Tom Jones*" (reprinted in *Critics and Criticism*), is a fine example of his "Aristotelianism" in action. Following Aristotle's emphasis on "plot" as the primary element of a drama, subsuming all other qualities, Crane defines "plot" as "the particular temporal synthesis effected by the writer of the elements of action, character, and thought." There are various kinds or degrees of "plot," depending upon which element is dominant, and *Tom Jones* exemplifies the "plot of action." Using this "concept of plot" as a guide, Crane then gives a detailed reading of the novel which emphasizes those qualities of action and structure that might be overlooked by a reader more interested in symbolism or the local effects of language. The problem in this essay, as in so many of Crane's, is the disjuncture between the method and the detailed critical conclusions. One feels that many of the insights could have been gained without recourse to the theoretical apparatus, and indeed Crane confesses at the end of the essay that his method is, like all critical methods, partial and incomplete: Other methods would have yielded other results, valid and revealing. It was this candid "pluralism," along with his emphasis on those qualities of a work of art neglected by the critical fashions of his time, that made Crane an important and appealing figure in an era rich with major critics.

Kenneth Burke might also be classified as a "neo-Aristotelian," in the sense that he is most concerned with literature as dramatic or symbolic action; and he might also be termed "pluralistic," in the sense that he has been eager to assimilate the methods and terminologies of a wide variety of critical approaches. A *Grammar of Motives* (1945), probably his most satisfactory work, is marked by a curious and personal eclecticism, a willingness to wrench linguistic and psychological terms from their traditional contexts and put them to a highly individual use. It would be a grave mistake to try to place Burke in the framework of any "system" or tradition; rather he should be viewed as a typically American individualist, a "do-it-yourself" craftsman who will use any materials at hand for the expression of his personal perceptions. No modern critic has been more open to experience and change, and no critic has been more interested in the *process* by which language dramatizes our common experience. Behind his polysyllabic prose lies a great fund of common sense. If we remember to treat Burke's criticism as a rich fund of suggestion and insight, not the definitive system it appears to be, then most of the difficulties commonly associated with his method fall away. This would seem to be the burden of R. P. Blackmur's comments on Burke in "A Critic's Job of Work":

The real harvest that we barn from Mr. Burke's writings is his presentation of the types of ways the mind works in the written word. He is more interested in the psychological means of the meaning, and how it might mean (and often really does) something else, than in the meaning itself. Like Mr. Richards, but for another purpose, he is engaged largely in the meaning of meaning, and is therefore much bound up with considerations of language, but on the plane of emotional and intellectual patterns rather than on the emotional plane; which is why his essays deal with literature (or other writings) as it dramatizes or unfolds character (a character is a pattern of emotions and notions) rather than with lyric or meditative poetry which is Mr. Richards' field. So we find language containing felt character as well as felt co-ordination. The representation of character, and of aspiration and symbol, must always be rhetorical; and therefore we find that for Mr. Burke the rightly rhetorical is the profoundly hortatory. Thus literature may be seen as an inexhaustible reservoir of moral or character philosophies in action.

It is the technique of such philosophies that Mr. Burke explores, as he pursues it through curiosities of development and conversion and duplicity; it is the technique of the notions that may be put into or taken out of literature, but it is only a part of the technique of literature itself. The final reference is to the psychological and moral possibilities of the mind, and these certainly do not exhaust the technique or the reality of literature. The reality in literature is an object of contemplation and of feeling, like the reality of a picture or a cathedral, not a route of speculation. If we remember this and make the appropriate reductions here as elsewhere, Mr. Burke's essays become as pertinent to literary criticism as they are to the general ethical play of the mind. Otherwise they become too much a methodology for its own sake on the one hand, and too much a philosophy at one remove on the other. A man writes as he can; but those who use his writings have the further responsibility of re-defining their scope, an operation (of which Mr. Burke is a master) which alone uses them to the full.*

Blackmur himself was in many ways the most satisfactory literary critic of his generation. Having come to maturity in the *anni mirabiles*

---

* From *Language as Gesture*, copyright, 1952, by Richard P. Blackmur. Reprinted by permission of Harcourt Brace Jovanovich, Inc.

of modernism, 1921–25, he was instinctively in touch with the best in contemporary literature, and his position as an editor of the *Hound and Horn* (1928–30) drew him to the center of the American literary scene. Blackmur began to write criticism at precisely the time when "close reading" became the dominant mode of literary analysis, and his essays of 1930–34 (collected in *The Double Agent: Essays in Craft and Elucidation*) are models of the genre. His early critical method may be seen as a fusion of three influences: (1) T. S. Eliot's practice of never generalizing without a text at hand; (2) Henry James's gift for delicate moral and aesthetic discriminations; and (3) William Empson's demonstration (in *Seven Types of Ambiguity*, 1930) that the theories of I. A. Richards could be transformed into an intricate procedure for linguistic analysis in which every shading of tone or attitude is related to the poem's general intent. In fact, one might say that Blackmur was uniquely equipped to handle the poets of his age, since his critical sensibility had been shaped by the same forces which determined their techniques, and it is not surprising that his criticism of the 1930's contains the definitive early statements on the art of Yeats, Eliot, Stevens, Cummings, and Marianne Moore. In each case Blackmur's analysis is based upon detailed research and an admirable grasp of the writer's distinctive style or attitude. His form of critical attack varies from author to author, emphasizing linguistic effects in the case of Stevens and Cummings, the use of myth and magic in the case of Yeats, the problem of poetry and belief in the case of Eliot. In each instance Blackmur strikes so close to the essential qualities of the author that his early essays remain authoritative and exciting after nearly forty years; it is safe to say that no critic of the 1930's, save Eliot and Pound, has worn so well.

After the early 1940's, when Blackmur's career as an interpreter of form and language reached its apex in his essays on Henry James, his criticism gradually moved into more speculative realms. Like the later Eliot, he became more interested in the general problems of literature and culture, although without any of the doctrinal aspects that one finds in Eliot's essays. If the two essays reprinted in this section, written twenty years apart, are read against each other, they provide a clear indication of the route Blackmur traveled between 1940 and 1960. Together they chart the direction of his theoretical interests but leave the nature of his earlier analytic work undocumented. His masterful essay of 1935, "A Critic's Job of Work," would be a better representative of his most influential criticism were it not shot through with references to books and critical controversies that have long since faded into literary history; but the ending to that essay remains completely valid, perhaps the finest statement of Blackmur's subtle and complex method, and it seems only fitting to use it as conclusion.

My own approach, such as it is, and if it can be named, does not tell the whole story either; the reader is conscientiously left with the poem with the real work yet to do; and I wish to advance it—as indeed I have been advancing it *seriatim*—only in connection with the reduced and compensated approaches I have laid out; and I expect, too, that if my approach is used at all it will require its own reduction as well as its compensations. Which is why this essay has taken its present form, preferring for once, in the realm of theory and apologetics, the implicit to the explicit statement. It is, I suppose, an approach to literary criticism—to the discourse of an amateur—primarily through the technique, in the widest sense of that word, of the examples handled; technique on the plane of words and even of linguistics in Mr. Richards' sense, but also technique on the plane of intellectual and emotional patterns in Mr. Burke's sense, and technique, too, in that there is a technique of securing and arranging and representing a fundamental view of life. The advantage of the technical approach is I think double. It readily admits other approaches and is anxious to be complemented by them. Furthermore, in a sense, it is able to incorporate the technical aspect, which always exists, of what is secured by other approaches—as I have argued elsewhere that so unpromising a matter as T. S. Eliot's religious convictions may be profitably considered as a dominant element in his technique of revealing the actual. The second advantage of the technical approach is a consequence of the first; it treats of nothing in literature except in its capacity of reduction to literary fact, which is where it resembles scholarship, only passing beyond it in that its facts are usually further into the heart of the literature than the facts of most scholarship. Aristotle, curiously, is here the type and master; as the *Poetics* is nothing but a collection and explanation of the facts of Greek poetry, it is the factual aspect that is invariably produced. The rest of the labor is in the effort to find understandable terms to fit the composition of the facts. After all, it is only the facts about a poem, a play, a novel, that can be reduced to tractable form, talked about, and examined; the rest is the product of the facts, from the technical point of view, and not a product but the thing itself from its own point of view. The rest, whatever it is, can only be known, not talked about.

But facts are not simple or easy to come at; not all the facts will appear to one mind, and the same facts appear differently in the light of different minds. No attention is undivided, no single approach sufficient, no predilection guaranteed, when facts or what their arrangements create are in question. In short, for the arts, *mere* technical scrutiny of any order is not enough without the direct apprehension—which may come first or last—to which all scrutinies that show facts contribute.

It may be that there are principles that cover both the direct apprehension and the labor of providing modes for the understanding of the expressive arts. If so, they are Socratic and found within, and subject to the fundamental skepticism as in Montaigne. There must be seeds, let us say—seeds, germs, beginning forms upon which I can rely and to which I resort. When I use a word, an image, a notion, there must be in its small nodular apparent form, as in the peas I am testing on my desk, at least prophetically, the whole future growth, the whole harvested life; and not rhetorically nor in a formula, but stubbornly, pervasively, heart-hidden, materially, in both the anterior and the eventual prospect as well as in the small handled form of the nub. What is it, what are they, these seeds of understanding? And if I know, are they logical? Do they take the processional form of the words I use? Or do they take a form like that of the silver backing a glass, a dark that enholds all brightness? Is every metaphor—and the assertion of understanding is our great metaphor—mixed by the necessity of its intention? What is the mixture of a word, an image, a notion?

The mixture, if I may start a hare so late, the mixture, even in the fresh use of an old word, is made in the pre-conscious, and is by hypothesis unascertainable. But let us not use hypotheses, let us not desire to ascertain. By intuition we adventure in the preconscious; and there, where the adventure is, there is no need or suspicion of certainty or meaning; there is the living, expanding, *prescient* substance without the tags and handles of conscious form. Art is the looking-glass of the preconscious, and when it is deepest seems to participate in it sensibly. Or, better, for purposes of criticism, our sensibility resumes the division of the senses and faculties at the same time that it preens itself into conscious form. Criticism may have as an object the establishment and evaluation (comparison and analysis) of the modes of making the preconscious *consciously* available.

But this emphasis upon the preconscious need not be insisted on; once recognized it may be tacitly assumed, and the effort of the mind will be, as it were, restored to its own plane—only a little sensitive to the tap-roots below. On its own plane—that is the plane where almost everything is taken for granted in order to assume adequate implementation in handling what is taken for granted by others; where because you can list the items of your bewilderment and can move from one to another you assert that the achievement of motion is the experience of order;—where, therefore, you must adopt always an attitude of provisional skepticism; where, imperatively, you must scrutinize and scrutinize until you have revealed, if it is there, the inscrutable divination, or, if it is not, the void of personal ambition; where, finally, you must stop short only when you have, with all the facts you can muster, indicated, surrounded, detached, somehow found the way demonstrably to get at, in pretty conscious terms which others may use, the substance of your chosen case.*

A Note on Sources

Edmund Wilson (1895–   ), American novelist and critic, has been the leading "man of letters" of his age. He first came to the forefront of American criticism with the publication of *Axel's Castle* (1931), a comprehensive survey of the "symbolist" writers of 1870–1930. During the 1930's Wilson's interest in the relationship between literature and society led to the essays of *The Triple Thinkers* (1938), while his equally compelling interest in psychological criticism produced the studies collected as *The Wound and the Bow* (1941). *To the Finland Station* (1940), Wilson's study of the historical cross-currents which produced the Russian revolution, is his outstanding work of political-cultural analysis; while *The Shock of Recognition* (an original anthology of American literature) and *Patriotic Gore* (a study of Civil War literature) testify to Wilson's lifelong preoccupation with the American scene. His occasional literary criticism of the 1930's and 1940's has been

* From *Language as Gesture*, copyright, 1952, by Richard P. Blackmur. Reprinted by permission of Harcourt Brace Jovanovich, Inc.

collected in *Classics and Commercials* (1950) and *The Shores of Light* (1952).

Lionel Trilling (1905–   ) began his career with *Matthew Arnold* (1939), an intensive study of Arnold and his age. Trilling's later essays on literature and society, collected as *The Liberal Imagination* (1950) and *The Opposing Self* (1955), clearly reflect Arnold's concern with culture and the public imagination. Trilling's more recent essays on literature and education have been published under the title *Beyond Culture* (1965).

F. R. Leavis (1895–   ), the most important English academic critic of his age, has devoted his long career to a redefinition of the English literary tradition. As chief editor of *Scrutiny* (1932–53), Leavis exercised a decisive influence on the teaching and study of literature in England (see *A Selection from "Scrutiny,"* ed. F. R. Leavis, 1968). Leavis's chief essays of the 1930's and 1940's were collected in *New Bearings in English Poetry* (1932), *Revaluation* (1936), and *The Common Pursuit* (1952). His highly selective view of the tradition of the English novel is embodied in *The Great Tradition* (1948), while the special role of D. H. Lawrence as moral and literary touchstone is examined in *D. H. Lawrence, Novelist* (1955). More recently Leavis has published *Anna Karenina and Other Essays* (1967).

Yvor Winters (1900–1968), poet and critic, spent most of his career as professor of English at Stanford University. His early essays on American experimental poetry (*Primitivism and Decadence*, 1937) and classic American writers (*Maule's Curse*, 1938) were collected in 1947 under the title *In Defense of Reason*. Winters' last major work, an historical survey of the short poem in English, was published in 1967 as *Forms of Discovery*.

Kenneth Burke (1897–   ), poet, music critic, and literary theorist, is the author of *Counter-Statement* (1931), *Permanence and Change* (1935), *The Philosophy of Literary Form* (1941), *A Grammar of Motives* (1945), and *A Rhetoric of Motives* (1950). In 1964 the late Stanley Edgar Hyman collected Burke's essays under two titles, *Perspectives by Incongruity* and *Terms for Order*.

R. P. Blackmur (1904–1965), a master of close reading and formal analysis, published his early essays under the titles *The Double Agent* (1935) and *The Expense of Greatness* (1940). The best of his early criticism was collected in 1952 in *Language as Gesture* (published in an abridged version as *Form and Value in Modern Poetry*). Blackmur's later criticism may be found in *The Lion and the Honeycomb* (1955), *Eleven Essays in the European Novel* (1964), and *A Primer of Ignorance* (ed. Joseph Frank, 1967). The latter volume includes Blackmur's 1956 Library of Congress lectures, *Anni Mirabiles, 1921–1925: Reason in the Madness of Letters*.

R. S. Crane (1886–1967) became the chief spokesman for the "Chicago Critics," a group of scholars and critics whose interest in *genre* and convention has been described as "neo-Aristotelian." Their range of investigation is best represented in Crane's edition of their essays, *Critics and Criticism, Ancient and Modern* (1952). Crane's lectures and essays not included in this volume may be found in *The Languages of Criticism and the Structure of Poetry* (1953) and *The Idea of the Humanities* (1967).

HISTORY AND CRITICISM

Edmund Wilson

MARXISM AND LITERATURE (1938)

1. Let us begin with Marx and Engels. What was the role assigned to literature and art in the system of Dialectical Materialism? This role was much less cut-and-dried than is nowadays often supposed. Marx and Engels conceived the forms of human society in any given country and epoch as growing out of the methods of production which prevailed at that place and time; and out of the relations involved in the social forms arose a "super-structure" of higher activities such as politics, law, religion, philosophy, literature and art. These activities were not, as is sometimes assumed, wholly explicable in terms of economics. They showed the mold, in ways direct or indirect, of the social configuration below them, but each was working to get away from its roots in the social classes and to constitute a professional group, with its own discipline and its own standards of value, which cut across class lines. These departments "all react upon one another and upon the economic

From *The Triple Thinkers*, Oxford University Press. Reprinted by permission of Edmund Wilson.

base. It is not the case that the economic situation is the sole active cause and everything else only a passive effect. But there is a reciprocal interaction within a fundamental economic necessity, which in the last instance always asserts itself" (Engels to Hans Starkenburg, January 25, 1894). So that the art of a great artistic period may reach a point of vitality and vision where it can influence the life of the period down to its very economic foundations. Simply, it must cease to flourish with the social system which made it possible by providing the artist with training and leisure, even though the artist may have been working for the destruction of that system.

2. Marx and Engels, unlike some of their followers, never attempted to furnish social-economic formulas by which the validity of works of art might be tested. They had grown up in the sunset of Goethe before the great age of German literature was over, and they had both set out in their youth to be poets; they responded to imaginative work, first of all, on its artistic merits. They could ridicule a

trashy writer like Eugène Sue for what they regarded as his *petit bourgeois* remedies for the miseries of contemporary society (*The Holy Family*); they could become bitter about Ferdinand Freiligrath, who had deserted the Communist League and turned nationalist in 1870 (Marx to Engels, August 22, 1870). And Marx could even make similar jibes at Heine when he thought that the latter had stooped to truckling to the authorities or when he read the expressions of piety in his will (Marx to Engels, December 21, 1866 and May 8, 1856). But Marx's daughter tells us that her father loved Heine "as much as his work and was very indulgent of his political shortcomings. He used to say that the poets were originals, who must be allowed to go their own way, and that one shouldn't apply to them the same standards as to ordinary people." It was not characteristic of Marx and Engels to judge literature—that is, literature of power and distinction—in terms of its purely political tendencies. In fact, Engels always warned the socialist novelists against the dangers of *Tendenz-Literatur* (Engels to Minna Kautsky, November 26, 1885; and to Margaret Harkness, April 1888). In writing to Minna Kautsky about one of her novels, he tells her that the personalities of her hero and heroine have been dissolved in the principles they represent. "(You evidently," he says, "felt the need of publicly taking sides in this book, of proclaiming your opinions to the world . . . But I believe that the tendency should arise from the situation and the action themselves without being explicitly formulated, and that the poet is not under the obligation to furnish the reader with a ready-made historical solution for the future of the conflict which he describes.)" When Ferdinand Lassalle sent Marx and Engels his poetic tragedy, *Franz von Sickingen*, and invited them to criticize it, Marx replied that, "setting aside any purely critical attitude toward the work," it had on a first reading affected him powerfully—characteristically adding that upon persons of a more emotional nature it would doubtless produce an even

stronger effect; and Engels wrote that he had read it twice and had been moved by it so profoundly that he had been obliged to lay it aside in order to arrive at any critical perspective. It was only after pulling themselves together and making some purely literary observations that they were able to proceed to discuss, from their special historical point of view, the period with which the drama dealt and to show how Lassalle's own political position had led him to mistake the role of his hero. Aeschylus Marx loved for his grandeur and for the defiance of Zeus by Prometheus; Goethe they both immensely admired: Engels wrote of him as a "colossal" and "universal" genius whose career had been marred by an admixture in his character of the philistine and the courtier (*German Socialism in Verse and Prose*); Shakespeare Marx knew by heart and was extremely fond of quoting, but never—despite the long, learned and ridiculous essays which have appeared in the Soviet magazine, *International Literature*—attempted to draw from his plays any general social moral. So far, indeed, was Marx from having worked out a systematic explanation of the relation of art to social arrangements that he could assert, apropos of Greek art, in his *Introduction to the Critique of Political Economy*, that "certain periods of highest development of art stand in no direct connection with the general development of society, nor with the material basis and the skeleton structure of its organization."

3. With Marx and Engels there is not yet any tendency to specialize art as a "weapon." They were both too much under the influence of the ideal of the many-sided man of the Renaissance, of the "complete" man, who, like Leonardo, had been painter, mathematician and engineer, or, like Machiavelli, poet, historian and strategist, before the division of labor had had the effect of splitting up human nature and limiting everyone to some single function (Engels' preface to his *Dialectic and Nature*). But with Lenin we come to a Marxist who is specialized himself as an organizer and fighter. Like most Russians, Lenin was

sensitive to music; but Gorky tells us that on one occasion, after listening to Beethoven's Appassionata Sonata and exclaiming that he "would like to listen to it every day: it is marvelous superhuman music—I always think with pride . . . what marvelous things human beings can do," he screwed up his eyes and smiled sadly and added: "But I can't listen to music too often. It affects your nerves, makes you want to say stupid, nice things, and stroke the heads of people who could create such beauty while living in this vile hell. And now you mustn't stroke anyone's head—you might get your hand bitten off." Yet he was fond of fiction, poetry and the theater, and by no means doctrinaire in his tastes. Krupskaya tells how, on a visit to a Youth Commune, he asked the young people, "What do you read? Do you read Pushkin?" " 'Oh, no!' someone blurted out. 'He was a bourgeois. Mayakovsky for us.' Ilyitch smiled. 'I think Pushkin is better.' " Gorky says that one day he found Lenin with *War and Peace* lying on the table: " 'Yes, Tolstoy. I wanted to read over the scene of the hunt, then remembered that I had to write a comrade. Absolutely no time for reading.' . . . Smiling and screwing up his eyes, he stretched himself deliciously in his armchair and, lowering his voice, added quickly, 'What a colossus, eh? What a marvelously developed brain! Here's an artist for you, sir. And do you know something still more amazing? You couldn't find a genuine *muzhik* in literature till this count came upon the scene.' " In his very acute essays on Tolstoy, he deals with him much as Engels deals with Goethe—with tremendous admiration for Tolstoy's genius, but with an analysis of his non-resistance and mysticism in terms not, it is interesting to note, of the psychology of the landed nobility, but of the patriarchal peasantry with whom Tolstoy had identified himself. And Lenin's attitude toward Gorky was much like that of Marx toward Heine. He suggests in one of his letters that Gorky would be helpful as a journalist on the side of the Bolsheviks, but adds that he mustn't be bothered if he is busy writing a book.

4. Trotsky is a literary man as Lenin never was, and he published in 1924 a most remarkable little study called *Literature and Revolution*. In this book he tried to illuminate the problems which were arising for Russian writers with the new society of the Revolution. And he was obliged to come to grips with a question with which Marx and Engels had not been much concerned—the question of what Mr. James T. Farrell in his book, *A Note on Literary Criticism*, one of the few sensible recent writings on this subject, calls "the carry-over value" of literature. Marx had assumed the value of Shakespeare and the Greeks and more or less left it at that. But what, the writers in Russia were now asking, was to be the value of the literature and art of the ages of barbarism and oppression in the dawn of socialist freedom? What in particular was to be the status of the culture of that bourgeois society from which socialism had just emerged and of which it still bore the unforgotten scars? Would there be a new proletarian literature, with new language, new style, new form, to give expression to the emotions and ideas of the new proletarian dictatorship? There had been in Russia a group called the Proletcult, which aimed at monopolizing the control of Soviet literature; but Lenin had discouraged and opposed it, insisting that proletarian culture was not something which could be produced synthetically and by official dictation of policy, but only by natural evolution as a "development of those reserves of knowledge which society worked for under the oppression of capitalism, of the landlords, of the officials." Now, in *Literature and Revolution*, Trotsky asserted that "such terms as 'proletarian literature' and 'proletarian culture' are dangerous, because they erroneously compress the culture of the future into the narrow limits of the present day." In a position to observe from his Marxist point of view the effects on a national literature of the dispossession of a dominant class, he was able to see the unexpected ways in which the presentments of life of the novel-

ists, the feelings and images of the poets, the standards themselves of the critics, were turning out to be determined by their attitudes toward the social-economic crisis. But he did not believe in a proletarian culture which would displace the bourgeois one. The bourgeois literature of the French Revolution had ripened under the old regime; but the illiterate proletariat and peasantry of Russia had had no chance to produce a culture, nor would there be time for them to do so in the future, because the proletarian dictatorship was not to last: it was to be only a transition phase and to lead the way to "a culture which is above classes and which will be the first truly human culture." In the meantime, the new socialist literature would grow directly out of that which had already been produced during the domination of the bourgeoisie. Communism, Trotsky said, had as yet no artistic culture; it had only a political culture.

5. All this seems to us reasonable enough. But, reasonable and cultured as Trotsky is, ready as he is to admit that "one cannot always go by the principles of Marxism in deciding whether to accept or reject a work of art," that such a work "should be judged in the first place by its own law—that is, by the law of art," there is none the less in the whole situation something which is alien to us. We are not accustomed, in our quarter of the world, either to having the government attempt to control literature and art or to having literary and artistic movements try to identify themselves with the government. Yet Russia, since the Revolution, has had a whole series of cultural groups which have attempted to dominate literature either with or without the authority of the government; and Trotsky himself, in his official position, even in combating these tendencies, cannot avoid passing censure and pinning ribbons. Sympathizers with the Soviet regime used to assume that this state of affairs was inseparable from the realization of socialism: that its evils would be easily outgrown and that in any case it was a great thing to have the government take so lively an

interest in culture. I believe that this view was mistaken. Under the Tsar, imaginative literature in Russia played a role which was probably different from any role it had ever played in the life of any other nation. Political and social criticism, pursued and driven underground by the censorship, was forced to incorporate itself in the dramatic imagery of fiction. This was certainly one of the principal reasons for the greatness during the nineteenth century of the Russian theater and novel, for the mastery by the Russian writers—from Pushkin's time to Tolstoy's—of the art of implication. In the fifties and sixties, the stories of Turgenev, which seem mild enough to us today, were capable of exciting the most passionate controversies—and even, in the case of *A Sportsman's Sketches*, causing the dismissal of the censor who had passed it—because each was regarded as a political message. Ever since the Revolution, literature and politics in Russia have remained inextricable. But after the Revolution the intelligentsia themselves were in power; and it became plain that in the altered situation the identification of literature with politics was liable to terrible abuses. Lenin and Trotsky, Lunacharsky and Gorky, worked sincerely to keep literature free; but they had at the same time, from the years of the Tsardom, a keen sense of the possibility of art as an instrument of propaganda. Lenin took a special interest in the moving pictures from the propaganda point of view; and the first Soviet films, by Eisenstein and Pudovkin, were masterpieces of implication, as the old novels and plays had been. But Lenin died; Trotsky was exiled; Lunacharsky died. The administration of Stalin, unliterary and uncultivated himself, slipped into depending more and more on literature as a means of manipulating a people of whom, before the Revolution, 70 or 80 per cent had been illiterate and who could hardly be expected to be critical of what they read. Gorky seems to have exerted what influence he could in the direction of liberalism: to him was due, no doubt, the liquidation of RAPP, the latest device for the monopoly of culture, and the opening of the Soviet canon to the best contemporary foreign writing and the classics. But though this made possible more freedom of form and a wider range of reading, it could not, under the dictatorship of Stalin, either stimulate or release a living literature. Where no political opposition was possible, there was possible no political criticism; and in Russia political questions involve vitally the fate of society. What reality can there be for the Russians, the most socially-minded writers on earth, in a freedom purely "esthetic"? Even the fine melodramatic themes of the post-revolutionary cinema and theater, with their real emotion and moral conviction, have been replaced by simple trash not very far removed from Hollywood, or by dramatized exemplifications of the latest "directive" of Stalin which open the night after the speech that has announced the directive. The recent damning of the music of Shostakovich on the ground that the commissars were unable to hum it seems a withdrawal from the liberal position. And it is probable that the death of Gorky, as well as the imprisonment of Bukharin and Radek, have removed the last brakes from a precipitate descent, in the artistic as well as the political field, into a nightmare of informing and repression. The practice of deliberate falsification of social and political history which began at the time of the Stalin-Trotsky crisis and which has now attained proportions so fantastic that the government does not seem to hesitate to pass the sponge every month or so over everything that the people have previously been told and to present them with a new and contradictory version of their history, their duty, and the characters and careers of their leaders—this practice cannot fail in the end to corrupt every department of intellectual life, till the serious, the humane, the clear-seeing must simply, if they can, remain silent.

6. Thus Marxism in Russia for the moment has run itself into a blind alley—or rather, it has been put down a well. The Soviets seem hardly at the present time to have retained even the Marxist political culture, even in its

cruder forms—so that we are relieved from the authority of Russia as we are deprived of her inspiration. To what conclusions shall we come, then, at this time of day about Marxism and literature—basing our views not even necessarily upon texts from the Marxist Fathers, but upon ordinary commonsense? Well, first of all, that we can go even further than Trotsky in one of the dicta I have quoted above and declare that Marxism by itself can tell us nothing whatever about the goodness or badness of a work of art. A man may be an excellent Marxist, but if he lacks imagination and taste he will be unable to make the choice between a good and an inferior book both of which are ideologically unexceptionable. What Marxism *can* do, however, is throw a great deal of light on the origins and social significance of works of art. The study of literature in its relation to society is as old as Herder—and even Vico. Coleridge had flashes of insight into the connection between literary and social phenomena, as when he saw the Greek state in the Greek sentence and the individualism of the English in the short separate statements of Chaucer's Prologue. But the great bourgeois master of this kind of criticism was Taine, with his *race* and *moment* and *milieu*; yet Taine, for all his scientific professions, responded artistically to literary art, and responded so vividly that his summings-up of writers and re-creations of periods sometimes rival or surpass their subjects. Marx and Engels further deepened this study of literature in relation to its social background by demonstrating for the first time inescapably the importance of economic systems. But if Marx and Engels and Lenin and Trotsky are worth listening to on the subject of books, it is not merely because they created Marxism, but also because they were capable of literary appreciation.

7. Yet the man who tries to apply Marxist principles without real understanding of literature is liable to go horribly wrong. For one thing, it is usually true in works of the highest order that the purport is not a simple message,

but a complex vision of things, which itself is not explicit but implicit; and the reader who does not grasp them artistically, but is merely looking for simple social morals, is certain to be hopelessly confused. Especially will he be confused if the author *does* draw an explicit moral which is the opposite of or has nothing to do with his real purport. Friedrich Engels, in the letter to Margaret Harkness already referred to above, in warning her that the more the novelist allows his political ideas to "remain hidden, the better it is for the work of art," says that Balzac, with his reactionary opinions, is worth a thousand of Zola, with all his democratic ones. (Balzac was one of the great literary admirations of both Engels and Marx, the latter of whom had planned to write a book on him.) Engels points out that Balzac himself was, or believed himself to be, a legitimist engaged in deploring the decline of high society; but that actually "his irony is never more bitter, his satire never more trenchant, than when he is showing us these aristocrats . . . for whom he felt so profound a sympathy," and that "the only men of whom he speaks with undissimulated admiration are his most determined political adversaries, the republican heroes of the Cloître-Saint-Merri, the men who at that period (1830–1836) truly represented the popular masses." Nor does it matter necessarily in a work of art whether the characters are shown engaged in a conflict which illustrates the larger conflicts of society or in one which from that point of view is trivial. In art—it is quite obvious in music, but it is also true in literature—a sort of law of moral interchangeability prevails: we may transpose the actions and the sentiments that move us into terms of whatever we do or are ourselves. Real genius of moral insight is a motor which will start any engine. When Proust, in his wonderful chapter on the death of the novelist Bergotte, speaks of those moral obligations which impose themselves in spite of everything and which seem to come through to humanity from some source outside its wretched self (obligations "invisible only to

fools—and are they really to them?"), he is describing a kind of duty which he felt only in connection with the literary work which he performed in his dark and fetid room; yet he speaks for every moral, esthetic or intellectual passion which holds the expediencies of the world in contempt. And the hero of Thornton Wilder's *Heaven's My Destination*, the traveling salesman who tries to save souls in the smoking car and writes Bible texts on hotel blotters, is something more than a symptom of Thornton Wilder's religious tendencies: he is the type of all saints who begin absurdly; and Wilder's story would be as true of the socialist Upton Sinclair as of the Christian George Brush. Nor does it necessarily matter, for the moral effect of a work of literature, whether the forces of bravery or virtue with which we identify ourselves are victorious or vanquished in the end. In Hemingway's story *The Undefeated*, the old bull-fighter who figures as the hero is actually humiliated and killed, but his courage has itself been a victory. It is true, as I. Kashkin, the Soviet critic, has said, that Hemingway has written much about decadence, but in order to write tellingly about death you have to have the principle of life, and those that have it will make it felt in spite of everything.

8. The Leftist critic with no literary competence is always trying to measure works of literature by tests which have no validity in that field. And one of his favorite occupations is giving specific directions and working out diagrams for the construction of ideal Marxist books. Such formulas are of course perfectly futile. The rules observed in any given school of art become apparent, not before but after, the actual works of art have been produced. As we were reminded by Burton Rascoe at the time of the Humanist controversy, the esthetic laws involved in Greek tragedy were not formulated by Aristotle until at least half a century after Euripides and Sophocles were dead. And the behavior of the Marxist critics has been precisely like that of the Humanists. The Humanists knew down to the last comma

what they wanted a work of literature to be, but they never—with the possible exception, when pressed, of *The Bridge of San Luis Rey*, about which they had, however, hesitations—were able to find any contemporary work which fitted their specifications. The Marxists did just the same thing. In an article called *The Crisis in Criticism* in the *New Masses* of February 1933, Granville Hicks drew up a list of requirements which the ideal Marxist work of literature must meet. The primary function of such a work, he asserted, must be to "lead the proletarian reader to recognize his role in the class struggle"—and it must therefore (1) "directly or indirectly show the effects of the class struggle"; (2) "the author must be able to make the reader feel that he is participating in the lives described"; and, finally, (3) the author's point of view must "be that of the vanguard of the proletariat; he should be, or should try to make himself, a member of the proletariat." This formula, he says, "gives us . . . a standard by which to recognize the perfect Marxian novel"—and adds "no novel as yet written perfectly conforms to our demands." But the doctrine of "socialist realism" promulgated at the Soviet Writers' Congress of August 1934 was only an attempt on a larger scale to legislate masterpieces into existence—a kind of attempt which always indicates sterility on the part of those who engage in it, and which always actually works, if it has any effect at all, to legislate existing good literature *out of* existence and to discourage the production of any more. The prescribers for the literature of the future usually cherish some great figure of the past whom they regard as having fulfilled their conditions and whom they are always bringing forward to demonstrate the inferiority of the literature of the present. As there has never existed a great writer who really had anything in common with these critics' conception of literature, they are obliged to provide imaginary versions of what their ideal great writers are like. The Humanists had Sophocles and Shakespeare; the socialist realists had Tolstoy. Yet it is certain that if

Tolstoy had had to live up to the objectives and prohibitions which the socialist realists proposed he could never have written a chapter; and that if Babbitt and More had been able to enforce against Shakespeare their moral and esthetic injunctions he would never have written a line. The misrepresentation of Sophocles, which has involved even a tampering with his text in the interests not merely of Humanism but of academic classicism in general, has been one of the scandalous absurdities of scholarship. The Communist critical movement in America, which had for its chief spokesman Mr. Hicks, tended to identify their ideal with the work of John Dos Passos. In order to make this possible, it was necessary to invent an imaginary Dos Passos. This ideal Dos Passos was a Communist, who wrote stories about the proletariat, at a time when the real Dos Passos was engaged in bringing out a long novel about the effects of the capitalist system on the American middle class and had announced himself—in the *New Republic* in 1930—politically a "middle-class liberal." The ideal Dos Passos was something like Gorky without the mustache—Gorky, in the meantime, having himself undergone some transmogrification at the hands of Soviet publicity—and this myth was maintained until the Communist critics were finally compelled to repudiate it, not because they had acquired new light on Dos Passos, the novelist and dramatist, but because of his attitude toward events in Russia.

9. The object of these formulas for the future, as may be seen from the above quotations from Mr. Hicks, is to make of art an effective instrument in the class struggle. And we must deal with the dogma that "art is a weapon." It is true that art may be a weapon; but in the case of some of the greatest works of art, some of those which have the longest carry-over value, it is difficult to see that any important part of this value is due to their direct functioning as weapons. The *Divine Comedy*, in its political aspect, is a weapon for Henry of Luxemburg, whom Dante—with his medie-

val internationalism and his lack of sympathy for the nationalistic instincts which were impelling the Italians of his time to get away from their Austrian emperors—was so passionately eager to impose on his countrymen. Today we may say with Carducci that we would as soon see the crown of his "good Frederick" rolling in Olona vale: "Jove perishes; the poet's hymn remains." And, though Shakespeare's *Henry IV* and *Henry V* are weapons for Elizabethan imperialism, their real center is not Prince Hal but Falstaff; and Falstaff is the father of *Hamlet* and of all Shakespeare's tragic heroes, who, if they illustrate any social moral—the moral, perhaps, that Renaissance princes, supreme in their little worlds, may go to pieces in all kinds of terrible ways for lack of a larger social organism to restrain them—do so evidently without Shakespeare's being aware of it. If these works may be spoken of as weapons at all, they are weapons in the more general struggle of modern European man emerging from the Middle Ages and striving to understand his world and himself—a function for which "weapon" is hardly the right word. The truth is that there is short-range and long-range literature. Long-range literature attempts to sum up wide areas and long periods of human experience, or to extract from them general laws; short-range literature preaches and pamphleteers with the view to an immediate effect. A good deal of the recent confusion of our writers in the Leftist camp has been due to their not understanding, or being unable to make up their minds, whether they are aiming at long-range or short-range writing.

10. This brings us to the question of what sort of periods are most favorable for works of art. One finds an assumption on the Left that revolutionary or pre-revolutionary periods are apt to produce new and vital forms of literature. This, of course, is very far from the truth in the case of periods of actual revolution. The more highly developed forms of literature require leisure and a certain amount of stability; and during a period of revolution the writer is usually deprived of both. The literature of the French Revolution consisted of the orations of Danton, the journalism of Camille Desmoulins and the few political poems that André Chenier had a chance to write before he was guillotined. The literature of the Russian Revolution was the political writing of Lenin and Trotsky, and Alexander Blok's poem, *The Twelve*, almost the last fruit of his genius before it was nipped by the wind of the storm. As for pre-revolutionary periods in which the new forces are fermenting, they *may* be great periods for literature—as the eighteenth century was in France and the nineteenth century in Russia (though here there was a decadence after 1905). But the conditions that make possible the masterpieces are apparently not produced by the impending revolutions, but by the phenomenon of literary technique, already highly developed, in the hands of a writer who has had the support of long-enduring institutions. He may reflect an age of transition, but it will not necessarily be true that his face is set squarely in the direction of the future. The germs of the Renaissance are in Dante and the longing for a better world in Virgil, but neither Dante nor Virgil can in any real sense be described as a revolutionary writer: they sum up or write elegies for ages that are passing. The social organisms that give structure to their thought—the Roman Empire and the Catholic Church—are already showing signs of decay. It is impossible, therefore, to identify the highest creative work in art with the most active moments of creative social change. The writer who is seriously intent on producing long-range works of literature should, from the point of view of his own special personal interests, thank his stars if there is no violent revolution going on in his own country in his time. He may disapprove of the society he is writing about, but if it were disrupted by an actual upheaval he would probably not be able to write.

11. But what about "proletarian literature" as an accompaniment of the social revolution? In the earlier days of the Communist regime

in Russia, one used to hear about Russian authors who, in the effort to eliminate from their writings any vestige of the bourgeois point of view, had reduced their vocabulary and syntax to what they regarded as an A B C of essentials —with the result of becoming more unintelligible to the proletarian audience at whom they were aiming than if they had been Symbolist poets. (Indeed, the futurist poet Mayakovsky has since that time become a part of the Soviet canon.) Later on, as I have said, Soviet culture followed the road that Trotsky recommended: it began building again on the classics and on the bourgeois culture of other countries and on able revolutionary Russian writers who had learned their trade before the Revolution. "Soviet publishers"—I quote from the Russian edition of *International Literature,* issue 2 of 1936—"are bringing out Hemingway and Proust not merely in order to demonstrate 'bourgeois decay.' Every genuine work of art —and such are the productions of Hemingway and Proust—enriches the writer's knowledge of life and heightens his esthetic sensibility and his emotional culture—in a word, it figures, in the broad sense, as a factor of educational value. Liberated socialist humanity inherits all that is beautiful, elevating and sustaining in the culture of previous ages." The truth is that the talk in Soviet Russia about proletarian literature and art has resulted from the persistence of the same situation which led Tolstoy under the old regime to put on the muzhik's blouse and to go in for carpentry, cobbling and plowing: the difficulty experienced by an educated minority, who were only about 20 per cent of the people, in getting in touch with the illiterate majority. In America the situation is quite different. The percentage of illiterates in this country is only something like 4 per cent; and there is relatively little difficulty of communication between different social groups. Our development away from England, and from the old world generally, in this respect—in the direction of the democratization of our idiom—is demonstrated clearly in H. L. Mencken's *The American Language;*

and if it is a question of either the use for high literature of the language of the people or the expression of the dignity and importance of the ordinary man, the country which has produced *Leaves of Grass* and *Huckleberry Finn* has certainly nothing to learn from Russia. We had created during our pioneering period a literature of the common man's escape, not only from feudal Europe, but also from bourgeois society, many years before the Russian masses were beginning to write their names. There has been a section of our recent American literature of the last fifteen years or so— the period of the boom and the depression— which has dealt with our industrial and rural life from the point of view of the factory hand and the poor farmer under conditions which were forcing him to fight for his life, and this has been called proletarian literature; but it has been accompanied by books on the white-collar worker, the storekeeper, the well-to-do merchant, the scientist and the millionaire in situations equally disastrous or degrading. And this whole movement of critical and imaginative writing—though with some stimulus, certainly, from Russia—had come quite naturally out of our literature of the past. It is curious to observe that one of the best of the recent strike novels, *The Land of Plenty* by Robert Cantwell, himself a Westerner and a former mill worker, owes a good deal to Henry James.

12. Yet when all these things have been said, all the questions have not been answered. All that has been said has been said of the past; and Marxism is something new in the world: it is a philosophical system which leads directly to programs of action. Has there ever appeared before in literature such a phenomenon as M. André Malraux, who alternates between attempts, sometimes brilliant, to write long-range fiction on revolutionary themes, and exploits of aviation for the cause of revolution in Spain? Here creative political action and the more complex kind of imaginative writing have united at least to the extent that they have arisen from the same vision of history and have been included in the career of one

man. The Marxist vision of Lenin—Vincent Sheean has said it first—has in its completeness and its compelling force a good deal in common with the vision of Dante; but, partly realized by Lenin during his lifetime and still potent for some years after his death, it was a creation, not of literary art, but of actual social engineering. It is society itself, says Trotsky, which under communism becomes the work of art. The first attempts at this art will be inexpert and they will have refractory material to work with; and the philosophy of the Marxist dialectic involves idealistic and mythological elements which have led too often to social religion rather than to social art. Yet the human imagination has already come to conceive the possibility of re-creating human society; and how can we doubt that, as it acquires the power, it must emerge from what will seem by comparison the revolutionary "underground" of art as we have always known it up to now and deal with the materials of actual life in ways which we cannot now even foresee? This is to speak in terms of centuries, of ages; but, in practicing and prizing literature, we must not be unaware of the first efforts of the human spirit to transcend literature itself.

THE HISTORICAL INTERPRETATION
OF LITERATURE (1940)

I WANT to talk about the historical interpretation of literature—that is, about the interpretation of literature in its social, economic and political aspects.

To begin with, it will be worth while to say something about the kind of criticism which seems to be furthest removed from this. There is a kind of comparative criticism which tends to be non-historical. The essays of T. S. Eliot, which have had such an immense influence in our time, are, for example, fundamentally non-historical. Eliot sees, or tries to see, the whole of literature, so far as he is acquainted with it, spread out before him under the aspect of eternity. He then compares the work of different periods and countries, and tries to draw from it general conclusions about what literature ought to be. He understands, of course, that our point of view in connection with literature changes, and he has what seems to me a very sound conception of the whole body of writing of the past as something to which new works are continually being added, and which is not thereby merely increased in bulk

From *The Triple Thinkers*, Oxford University Press. Reprinted by permission of Edmund Wilson.

but modified as a whole—so that Sophocles is no longer precisely what he was for Aristotle, or Shakespeare what he was for Ben Jonson or for Dryden or for Dr. Johnson, on account of all the later literature that has intervened between them and us. Yet at every point of this continual accretion, the whole field may be surveyed, as it were, spread out before the critic. The critic tries to see it as God might; he calls the books to a Day of Judgment. And, looking at things in this way, he may arrive at interesting and valuable conclusions which could hardly be reached by approaching them in any other way. Eliot was able to see, for example—what I believe had never been noticed before—that the French Symbolist poetry of the nineteenth century had certain fundamental resemblances to the English poetry of the age of Donne. Another kind of critic would draw certain historical conclusions from these purely esthetic findings, as the Russian D. S. Mirsky did; but Eliot does not draw them.

Another example of this kind of non-historical criticism, in a somewhat different way and on a somewhat different plane, is the work of the late George Saintsbury. Saintsbury was a connoisseur of wines; he wrote an entertaining book on the subject. And his attitude toward literature, too, was that of the connoisseur. He tastes the authors and tells you about the vintages; he distinguishes the qualities of the various wines. His palate was as fine as could be, and he possessed the great qualification that he knew how to take each book on its own terms without expecting it to be some other book and was thus in a position to appreciate a great variety of kinds of writing. He was a man of strong social prejudices and peculiarly intransigent political views, but, so far as it is humanly possible, he kept them out of his literary criticism. The result is one of the most agreeable and most comprehensive commentaries on literature that have ever been written in English. Most scholars who have read as much as Saintsbury do not have Saintsbury's discriminating taste. Here is a critic who has covered the whole ground like any academic historian, yet whose account of it is not merely a chronology but a record of fastidious enjoyment. Since enjoyment is the only thing he is looking for, he does not need to know the causes of things, and the historial background of literature does not interest him very much.

There is, however, another tradition of criticism which dates from the beginning of the eighteenth century. In the year 1725, the Neapolitan philosopher Vico published *La Scienza Nuova*, a revolutionary work on the philosophy of history, in which he asserted for the first time that the social world was certainly the work of man, and attempted what is, so far as I know, the first social interpretation of a work of literature. This is what Vico says about Homer: "Homer composed the *Iliad* when Greece was young and consequently burning with sublime passions such as pride, anger and vengeance—passions which cannot allow dissimulation and which consort with generosity; so that she then admired Achilles, the hero of force. But, grown old, he composed the *Odyssey*, at a time when the passions of Greece

were already somewhat cooled by reflection, which is the mother of prudence—so that she now admired Ulysses, the hero of wisdom. Thus also, in Homer's youth, the Greek people liked cruelty, vituperation, savagery, fierceness, ferocity; whereas, when Homer was old, they were already enjoying the luxuries of Alcinoüs, the delights of Calypso, the pleasures of Circe, the songs of the sirens and the pastimes of the suitors, who went no further in aggression and combat than laying siege to the chaste Penelope—all of which practices would appear incompatible with the spirit of the earlier time. The divine Plato is so struck by this difficulty that, in order to solve it, he tells us that Homer had foreseen in inspired vision these dissolute, sickly and disgusting customs. But in this way he makes Homer out to have been but a foolish instructor for Greek civilization, since, however much he may condemn them, he is displaying for imitation these corrupt and decadent habits which were not to be adopted till long after the foundation of the nations of Greece, and accelerating the natural course which human events would take by spurring the Greeks on to corruption. Thus it is plain that the Homer of the *Iliad* must have preceded by many years the Homer who wrote the *Odyssey*; and it is plain that the former must belong to the northeastern part of Greece, since he celebrates the Trojan War, which took place in his part of the country, whereas the latter belongs to the southeastern part, since he celebrates Ulysses, who reigned there."

You see that Vico has here explained Homer in terms both of historical period and of geographical origin. The idea that human arts and institutions were to be studied and elucidated as the products of the geographical and climatic conditions in which the people who created them lived, and of the phase of their social development through which they were passing at the moment, made great progress during the eighteenth century. There are traces of it even in Dr. Johnson, that most orthodox and classical of critics—as, for example, when he accounts for certain characteristics of Shakespeare by the relative barbarity of the age in which he lived, pointing out, just as Vico had done, that "nations, like individuals, have their infancy." And by the eighties of the eighteenth century Herder, in his *Ideas on the Philosophy of History*, was writing of poetry that it was a kind of "Proteus among the people, which is always changing its form in response to the languages, manners, and habits, to the temperaments and climates, nay even to the accents of different nations." He said—what could still seem startling even so late as that—that "language was not a divine communication, but something men had produced themselves." In the lectures on the philosophy of history that Hegel delivered in Berlin in 1822–23, he discussed the national literatures as expressions of the societies which had produced them—societies which he conceived as great organisms continually transforming themselves under the influence of a succession of dominant ideas.

In the field of literary criticism, this historical point of view came to its first complete flower in the work of the French critic Taine, in the middle of the ninetenth century. The whole school of historian-critics to which Taine belonged—Michelet, Renan, Sainte-Beuve—had been occupied in interpreting books in terms of their historical origins. But Taine was the first of these to attempt to apply such principles systematically and on a large scale in a work devoted exclusively to literature. In the Introduction to his *History of English Literature*, published in 1863, he made his famous pronouncement that works of literature were to be understood as the upshot of three interfusing factors: *the moment, the race and the milieu*. Taine thought he was a scientist and a mechanist, who was examining works of literature from the same point of view as the chemist's in experimenting with chemical compounds. But the difference between the critic and the chemist is that the critic cannot first combine his elements and then watch to see what they will do: he can only examine phenomena which have already taken place. The

procedure that Taine actually follows is to pretend to set the stage for the experiment by describing the moment, the race and the milieu, and then to say: "Such a situation demands such and such a kind of writer." He now goes on to describe the kind of writer that the situation demands, and the reader finds himself at the end confronted with Shakespeare or Milton or Byron or whoever the great figure is—who turns out to prove the accuracy of Taine's prognosis by precisely living up to this description.

There was thus a certain element of imposture in Taine; but it was the rabbits he pulled out that saved him. If he had really been the mechanist that he thought he was, his work on literature would have had little value. The truth was that Taine loved literature for its own sake—he was at his best himself a brilliant artist—and he had very strong moral convictions which give his writing emotional power. His mind, to be sure, was an analytic one, and his analysis, though terribly oversimplified, does have an explanatory value. Yet his work was what we call creative. Whatever he may say about chemical experiments, it is evident when he writes of a great writer that the moment, the race and the milieu have combined, like the three sounds of the chord in Browning's poem about Abt Vogler, to produce not a fourth sound but a star.

To Taine's set of elements was added, dating from the middle of the century, a new element, the economic, which was introduced into the discussion of historical phenomena mainly by Marx and Engels. The non-Marxist critics themselves were at the time already taking into account the influence of the social classes. In his chapters on the Norman conquest of England, Taine shows that the difference between the literatures produced respectively by the Normans and by the Saxons was partly the difference between a ruling class, on the one hand, and a vanquished and repressed class, on the other. And Michelet, in his volume on the Regency, which was finished the

same year that the *History of English Literature* appeared, studies the *Manon Lescaut* of
the Abbé Prévost as a document representing
the point of view of the small gentry before the
French Revolution. But Marx and Engels derived the social classes from the way that people made or got their livings—from what they
called the *methods of production*; and they
tended to regard these economic processes as
fundamental to civilization.

The Dialectical Materialism of Marx and
Engels was not really so materialistic as it
sounds. There was in it a large element of the
Hegelian idealism that Marx and Engels
thought they had got rid of. At no time did
these two famous materialists take so mecha-
nistic a view of things as Taine began by professing; and their theory of the relation of
works of literature to what they called the *economic base* was a good deal less simple than
Taine's theory of the moment, the race and the
milieu. They thought that art, politics, religion,
philosophy and literature belonged to what
they called the *superstructure* of human activity; but they saw that the practitioners of
these various professions tended also to constitute social groups, and that they were always
pulling away from the kind of solidarity based
on economic classes in order to establish a professional solidarity of their own. Furthermore,
the activities of the superstructure could influence one another, and they could influence the
economic base. It may be said of Marx and
Engels in general that, contrary to the popular
impression, they were tentative, confused and
modest when it came down to philosophical
first principles, where a materialist like Taine
was cocksure. Marx once made an attempt to
explain why the poems of Homer were so good
when the society that produced them was from
his point of view—that is, from the point of
view of its industrial development—so primitive; and this gave him a good deal of trouble.
If we compare his discussion of this problem
with Vico's discussion of Homer, we see that
the explanation of literature in terms of a
philosophy of social history is becoming, instead of simpler and easier, more difficult and
more complex.

Marx and Engels were deeply imbued, moreover, with the German admiration for literature, which they had learned from the age of
Goethe. It would never have occurred to either
of them that *der Dichter* was not one of the
noblest and most beneficent of humankind.
When Engels writes about Goethe, he presents
him as a man equipped for "practical life,"
whose career was frustrated by the "misery" of
the historical situation in Germany in his time,
and reproaches him for allowing himself to
lapse into the "cautious, smug and narrow"
philistinism of the class from which he came;
but Engels regrets this, because it interfered
with the development of the "mocking, defiant, world-despising genius," "der geniale
Dichter," "der gewaltige Poet," of whom Engels would not even, he says, have asked that he
should have been a political liberal if Goethe
had not sacrificed to his bourgeois shrinkings
his truer esthetic sense. And the great critics
who were trained on Marx—Franz Mehring
and Bernard Shaw—had all this reverence for
the priesthood of literature. Shaw deplores the
absence of political philosophy and what he regards as the middle-class snobbery in Shakespeare; but he celebrates Shakespeare's poetry
and his dramatic imagination almost as en-
thusiastically as Swinburne does, describing
even those potboiling comedies, *Twelfth Night*
and *As You Like It*—the themes of which
seem to him most trashy—as "the Crown
Jewels of English dramatic poetry." Such a
critic may do more for a writer by showing him
as a real man dealing with a real world at a
definite moment of time than the impressionist
critic of Swinburne's type who flourished in the
same period of the late nineteenth century.
The purely impressionist critic approaches the
whole of literature as an exhibit of belletristic
jewels, and he can only write a rhapsodic catalogue. But when Shaw turned his spotlight on
Shakespeare as a figure in the Shavian drama
of history, he invested him with a new interest
as no other English critic had done.

* * *

The insistence that the man of letters should play a political role, the disparagement of works of art in comparison with political action, were thus originally no part of Marxism. They only became associated with it later. This happened by way of Russia, and it was due to special tendencies in that country that date from long before the Revolution or the promulgation of Marxism itself. In Russia there have been very good reasons why the political implications of literature should particularly occupy the critics. The art of Pushkin itself, with its marvelous power of implication, had certainly been partly created by the censorship of Nicholas I, and Pushkin set the tradition for most of the great Russian writers that followed him. Every play, every poem, every story, must be a parable of which the moral is *implied*. If it were stated, the censor would suppress the book as he tried to do with Pushkin's *Bronze Horseman*, where it was merely a question of the packed implications protruding a little too plainly. Right down through the writings of Chekhov and up almost to the Revolution, the imaginative literature of Russia presents the peculiar paradox of an art that is technically objective and yet charged with social messages. In Russia under the Tsar, it was inevitable that social criticism should lead to political conclusions, because the most urgent need from the point of view of any kind of improvement was to get rid of the tsarist regime. Even the neo-Christian moralist Tolstoy, who pretended to be non-political, was to exert a subversive influence, because his independent preaching was bound to embroil him with the Church, and the Church was an integral part of the tsardom. Tolstoy's pamphlet called *What Is Art?*, in which he throws overboard Shakespeare and a large part of modern literature, including his own novels, in the interest of his intransigent morality, is the example which is most familiar to us of the moralizing Russian criticism; but it was only the most sensational expression of a kind of approach which had been prevalent since Belinsky and Chernyshev-

sky in the early part of the century. The critics, who were usually journalists writing in exile or in a contraband press, were always tending to demand of the imaginative writers that they should dramatize bolder morals.

Even after the Revolution had destroyed the tsarist government, this state of things did not change. The old habits of censorship persisted in the new socialist society of the Soviets, which was necessarily made up of people who had been stamped by the die of the despotism. We meet here the peculiar phenomenon of a series of literary groups that attempt, one after the other, to obtain official recognition or to make themselves sufficiently powerful to establish themselves as arbiters of literature. Lenin and Trotsky and Lunacharsky had the sense to oppose these attempts: the comrade-dictators of Proletcult or Lef or Rapp would certainly have been just as bad as the Count Benckendorff who made Pushkin miserable, and when the Stalin bureaucracy, after the death of Gorky, got control of this department as of everything else, they instituted a system of repression that made Benckendorff and Nicholas I look like Lorenzo de' Medici. In the meantime, Trotsky, who was Commissar of War but himself a great political writer with an interest in belles-lettres, attempted, in 1924, apropos of one of these movements, to clarify the situation. He wrote a brilliant and valuable book called *Literature and Revolution*, in which he explained the aims of the government, analyzed the work of the Russian writers, and praised or rebuked the latter as they seemed to him in harmony or at odds with the former. Trotsky is intelligent, sympathetic; it is evident that he is really fond of literature and that he knows that a work of art does not fulfill its function in terms of the formulas of party propaganda. But Mayakovsky, the Soviet poet, whom Trotsky had praised with reservations, expressed himself in a famous joke when he was asked what he thought of Trotsky's book— a pun which implied that a Commissar turned critic was inevitably a Commissar still; and what a foreigner cannot accept in Trotsky is his

assumption that it is the duty of the government to take a hand in the direction of literature.

This point of view, indigenous to Russia, has
been imported to other countries through the
permeation of Communist influence. The
Communist press and its literary followers have
reflected the control of the Kremlin in all the
phases through which it has passed, down to
the wholesale imprisonment of Soviet writers
which has been taking place since 1935. But it
has never been a part of the American system
that our Republican or Democratic administration should lay down a political line for the
guidance of the national literature. A recent
gesture in this direction on the part of Archi-
bald MacLeish, who seems a little carried away
by his position as Librarian of Congress, was
anything but cordially received by serious
American writers. So long as the United States
remains happily a non-totalitarian country, we
can very well do without this aspect of the historical criticism of literature.

Another element of a different order has,
however, since Marx's time been added to the
historical study of the origins of works of literature. I mean the psychoanalysis of Freud.
This appears as an extension of something
which had already got well started before,
which had figured even in Johnson's *Lives of
the Poets*, and of which the great exponent had
been Sainte-Beuve: the interpretation of works
of literature in the light of the personalities
behind them. But the Freudians made this interpretation more exact and more systematic.
The great example of the psychoanalysis of an
artist is Freud's own essay on Leonardo da
Vinci; but this has little critical interest: it is
an attempt to construct a case history. One of
the best examples I know of the application of
Freudian analysis to literature is in Van Wyck
Brooks's book, *The Ordeal of Mark Twain*, in
which Mr. Brooks uses an incident of Mark
Twain's boyhood as a key to his whole career.
Mr. Brooks has since repudiated the method he
resorted to here, on the ground that no one but

an analyst can ever know enough about a writer
to make a valid psychoanalytic diagnosis. This
is true, and it is true of the method that it has
led to bad results where the critic has built a
Freudian mechanism out of very slender evidence, and then given us what is really merely a
romance exploiting the supposed working of
this mechanism, in place of an actual study
that sticks close to the facts and the documents
of the writer's life and work. But I believe that
Van Wyck Brooks really had hold of something important when he fixed upon that childhood incident of which Mark Twain gave so
vivid an account to his biographer—that scene
at the deathbed of his father when his mother
had made him promise that he would not
break her heart. If it was not one of those crucial happenings that are supposed to determine
the complexes of Freud, it has certainly a typical significance in relation to Mark Twain's
whole psychology. The stories that people tell
about their childhood are likely to be profoundly symbolic even when they have been
partly or wholly made up in the light of later
experience. And the attitudes, the compulsions,
the emotional "patterns" that recur in the work
of a writer are of great interest to the historical
critic.

These attitudes and patterns are embedded
in the community and the historical moment,
and they may indicate its ideals and its diseases
as the cell shows the condition of the tissue.
The recent scientific experimentation in the
combining of Freudian with Marxist method,
and of psychoanalysis with anthropology, has
had its parallel development in criticism. And
there is thus another element added to our
equipment for analyzing literary works, and the
problem grows still more complex.

The analyst, however, is of course not concerned with the comparative values of his patients any more than the surgeon is. He cannot
tell you why the neurotic Dostoevsky produces
work of immense value to his fellows while another man with the same neurotic pattern
would become a public menace. Freud himself
emphatically states in his study of Leonardo

that his method can make no attempt to account for Leonardo's genius. The problems of comparative artistic value still remain after we have given attention to the Freudian psychological factor just as they do after we have given attention to the Marxist economic factor and to the racial and geographical factors. No matter how thoroughly and searchingly we may have scrutinized works of literature from the historical and biographical points of view, we must be ready to attempt to estimate, in some such way as Saintsbury and Eliot do, the relative degrees of success attained by the products of the various periods and the various personalities. We must be able to tell good from bad, the first-rate from the second-rate. We shall not otherwise write literary criticism at all, but merely social or political history as reflected in literary texts, or psychological case histories from past eras, or, to take the historical point of view in its simplest and most academic form, merely chronologies of books that have been published.

And now how, in these matters of literary art, do we tell the good art from the bad? Norman Kemp Smith, the Kantian philosopher, whose courses I was fortunate enough to take at Princeton twenty-five years ago, used to tell us that this recognition was based primarily on an emotional reaction. For purposes of practical criticism this is a safe assumption on which to proceed. It is possible to discriminate in a variety of ways the elements that in any given department go to make a successful work of literature. Different schools have at different times demanded different things of literature: *unity, symmetry, universality, originality, vision, inspiration, strangeness, suggestiveness, improving morality, socialist realism,* etc. But you could have any set of these qualities that any school of writing has called for and still not have a good play, a good novel, a good poem, a good history. If you identify the essence of good literature with any one of these elements or with any combination of them, you simply shift the emotional reaction to the rec-

ognition of the element or elements. Or if you add to your other demands the demand that the writer must have *talent,* you simply shift this recognition to the talent. Once people find some grounds of agreement in the coincidence of their emotional reactions to books, they may be able to discuss these elements profitably; but if they do not have this basic agreement, the discussion will make no sense.

But how, you may ask, can we identify this élite who know what they are talking about? Well, it can only be said of them that they are self-appointed and self-perpetuating, and that they will compel you to accept their authority. Impostors may try to put themselves over, but these quacks will not last. The implied position of the people who know about literature (as is also the case in every other art) is simply that they know what they know, and that they are determined to impose their opinions by main force of eloquence or assertion on the people who do not know. This is not a question, of course, of professional workers in literature—such as editors, professors and critics, who very often have no real understanding of the products with which they deal—but of readers of all kinds in all walks of life. There are moments when a first-rate writer, unrecognized or out of fashion with the official chalkers-up for the market, may find his support in the demand for his work of an appreciative cultivated public.

But what is the cause of this emotional reaction which is the critic's divining rod? This question has long been a subject of study by the branch of philosophy called esthetics, and it has recently been made a subject of scientific experimentation. Both these lines of inquiry are likely to be prejudiced in the eyes of the literary critic by the fact that the inquiries are sometimes conducted by persons who are obviously deficient in literary feeling or taste. Yet one should not deny the possibility that something of value might result from the speculations and explorations of men of acute minds who take as their given data the esthetic emotions of other men.

Almost everybody interested in literature has

tried to explain to himself the nature of these emotions that register our approval of artistic works; and I of course have my own explanation.

In my view, all our intellectual activity, in whatever field it takes place, is an attempt to give a meaning to our experience—that is, to make life more practicable; for by understanding things we make it easier to survive and get around among them. The mathematician Euclid, working in a convention of abstractions, shows us relations between the distances of our unwieldy and cluttered-up environment upon which we are able to count. A drama of Sophocles also indicates relations between the various human impulses, which appear so confused and dangerous, and it brings out a certain justice of Fate—that is to say, of the way in which the interaction of these impulses is seen in the long run to work out—upon which we can also depend. The kinship, from this point of view, of the purposes of science and art appears very clearly in the case of the Greeks, because not only do both Euclid and Sophocles satisfy us by making patterns, but they make much the same kind of patterns. Euclid's *Elements* takes simple theorems and by a series of logical operations builds them up to a climax in the square on the hypotenuse. A typical drama of Sophocles develops in a similar way.

Some writers (as well as some scientists) have a different kind of explicit message beyond the reassurance implicit in the mere feat of understanding life or of molding the harmony of artistic form. Not content with such an achievement as that of Sophocles—who has one of his choruses tell us that it is better not to be born, but who, by representing life as noble and based on law, makes its tragedy easier to bear—such writers attempt, like Plato, to think out and recommend a procedure for turning it into something better. But other departments of literature—lyric poetry such as Sappho's, for example—have *less* philosophical content than Sophocles. A lyric gives us nothing but a pattern imposed on the expression of a feeling; but this pattern of metrical quantities

and of consonants and vowels that balance has the effect of reducing the feeling, however unruly or painful it may seem when we experience it in the course of our lives, to something orderly, symmetrical and pleasing; and it also relates this feeling to the more impressive scheme, works it into the larger texture, of the body of poetic art. The discord has been resolved, the anomaly subjected to discipline. And this control of his emotion by the poet has the effect at second-hand of making it easier for the reader to manage his own emotions. (Why certain sounds and rhythms gratify us more than others, and how they are connected with the themes and ideas that they are chosen as appropriate for conveying, are questions that may be passed on to the scientist.)

And this brings us back again to the historical point of view. The experience of mankind on the earth is always changing as man develops and has to deal with new combinations of elements; and the writer who is to be anything more than an echo of his predecessors must always find expression for something which has never yet been expressed, must master a new set of phenomena which has never yet been mastered. With each such victory of the human intellect, whether in history, in philosophy or in poetry, we experience a deep satisfaction: we have been cured of some ache of disorder, relieved of some oppressive burden of uncomprehended events.

This relief that brings the sense of power, and, with the sense of power, joy, is the positive emotion which tells us that we have encountered a first-rate piece of literature. But stay! you may at this point warn: are not people often solaced and exhilarated by literature of the trashiest kind? They are: crude and limited people do certainly feel some such emotion in connection with work that is limited and crude. The man who is more highly organized and has a wider intellectual range will feel it in connection with work that is finer and more complex. The difference between the emotion of the more highly organized man and the emotion of the less highly organized one is a matter of mere gradation. You sometimes discover books—the novels of John Steinbeck, for example—that seem to mark precisely the borderline between work that is definitely superior and work that is definitely bad. When I was speaking a little while back of the genuine connoisseurs who establish the standards of taste, I meant, of course, the people who can distinguish Grade A and who prefer it to the other grades.

Lionel Trilling

THE SENSE OF THE PAST (1942)

IN RECENT YEARS the study of literature in our universities has again and again been called into question, chiefly on the ground that what is being studied is not so much literature itself as the history of literature. John Jay Chapman was perhaps the first to state the case against the literary scholars when in 1927 he denounced the "archaeological, quasi-scientific, and documentary study of the fine arts" because, as he said, it endeavored "to express the fluid universe of many emotions in terms drawn from the study of the physical sciences." And since Chapman wrote, the issue in the universities has been clearly drawn in the form of an opposition of "criticism" to "scholarship." Criticism has been the aggressor, and its assault upon scholarship has been successful almost in proportion to the spiritedness with which it has been made; at the present time, although the archaeological and quasi-scientific and documentary study of literature is still the dominant one in our universities, it is clear to everyone that scholarship is on the defensive and is ready to share the rule with its antagonist.

This revision of the academic polity can be

regarded only with satisfaction. The world seems to become less and less responsive to literature; we can even observe that literature is becoming something like an object of suspicion, and it is possible to say of the historical study of literature that its very existence is an evidence of this mistrust. De Quincey's categories of *knowledge* and *power* are most pertinent here; the traditional scholarship, in so far as it takes literature to be chiefly an object of knowledge, denies or obscures that active power by which literature is truly defined. All sorts of studies are properly ancillary to the study of literature. For example, the study of the intellectual conditions in which a work of literature was made is not only legitimate but sometimes even necessary to our perception of its power. Yet when Professor Lovejoy in his influential book, *The Great Chain of Being*, tells us that for the study of the history of ideas a really dead writer is better than one whose works are still enjoyed, we naturally pull up short and wonder if we are not in danger of becoming like the Edinburgh body-snatchers who *saw to it* that there were enough cadavers for study in the medical school.

Criticism made its attack on the historians of literature in the name of literature as power. The attack was the fiercer because literary history had all too faithfully followed the lead of social and political history, which, having given up its traditional connection with literature, had allied itself with the physical sciences of the nineteenth century and had adopted the assumption of these sciences that the world was reflected with perfect literalness in the will-less mind of the observer. The new history had many successes and it taught literary study what it had itself learned, that in an age of science prestige is to be gained by approximating the methods of science. Of these methods the most notable and most adaptable was the investigation of genesis, of how the work of art came into being. I am not concerned to show that the study of genesis is harmful to the right experience of the work of art: I do not believe it is. Indeed, I am inclined to suppose that whenever the genetic method is attacked we ought to suspect that special interests are being defended. So far is it from being true that the genetic method is in itself inimical to the work of art, that the very opposite is so; a work of art, or any human thing, studied in its genesis can take on an added value. Still, the genetic method can easily be vulgarized, and when it is used in its vulgar form, it can indeed reduce the value of a thing; in much genetic study the implication is clear that to the scholar the work of art is nothing but its conditions.

One of the attractions of the genetic study of art is that it seems to offer a high degree of certainty. Aristotle tells us that every study has its own degree of certainty and that the well-trained man accepts that degree and does not look for a greater one. We may add that there are different kinds as well as different degrees of certainty, and we can say that the great mistake of the scientific-historical scholarship is that it looks for a degree and kind of certainty that literature does not need and cannot allow.

The error that is made by literary scholars when they seek for a certainty analogous with the certainty of science has been so often remarked that at this date little more need be said of it. Up to a point the scientific study of art is legitimate and fruitful; the great thing is that we should recognize the terminal point

and not try to push beyond it, that we should not expect that the scientific study of, say, literature will necessarily assure us of the experience of literature; and if we wish as teachers to help others to the experience of literature, we cannot do so by imparting the fruits of our scientific study. What the partisans of the so-called New Criticism revolted against was the scientific notion of the fact as transferred in a literal way to the study of literature. They wished to restore autonomy to the work of art, to see it as the agent of power rather than as the object of knowledge.

The faults of these critics we know. Perhaps their chief fault they share with the scientific-historical scholars themselves—they try too hard. No less than the scholars, the critics fall into an error that Chapman denounced, the great modern illusion "that anything whatever . . . can be discovered through hard intellectual work and concentration." We often feel of them that they make the elucidation of poetic ambiguity or irony a kind of intellectual calisthenic ritual. Still, we can forgive them their strenuousness, remembering that something has happened to our relation with language which seems to require that we make methodical and explicit what was once immediate and unformulated.

But there is another fault of the New Critics of which we must take notice. It is that in their reaction from the historical method they forget that the literary work is ineluctably a historical fact, and, what is more important, that its historicity is a fact in our aesthetic experience. Literature, we may say, must in some sense always be an historical study, for literature is an historical art. It is historical in three separate senses.

In the old days the poet was supposed to be himself an historian, a reliable chronicler of events. Thucydides said that he was likely to be an inaccurate historian, but Aristotle said that he was more accurate, because more general, than any mere annalist; and we, following Aristotle, suppose that a large part of literature is properly historical, the recording and interpreting of personal, national, and cosmological events.

Then literature is historical in the sense that it is necessarily aware of its own past. It is not always consciously aware of this past, but it is always practically aware of it. The work of any poet exists by reason of its connection with past work, both in continuation and in divergence, and what we call his originality is simply his special relation to tradition. The point has been fully developed by T. S. Eliot in his well-known essay "Tradition and the Individual Talent." And Mr. Eliot reminds us how each poet's relation to tradition changes tradition itself, so that the history of literature is never quiet for long and is never merely an additive kind of growth. Each new age makes the pattern over again, forgetting what was once dominant, finding new affinities; we read any work within a kaleidoscope of historical elements.

And in one more sense literature is historical, and it is with this sense that I am here chiefly concerned. In the existence of every work of literature of the past, its historicity, its *pastness*, is a factor of great importance. In certain cultures the pastness of a work of art gives it an extra-aesthetic authority which is incorporated into its aesthetic power. But even in our own culture with its ambivalent feeling about tradition, there inheres in a work of art of the past a certain quality, an element of its aesthetic existence, which we can identify as its pastness. Side by side with the formal elements of the work, and modifying these elements, there is the element of history, which, in any complete aesthetic analysis, must be taken into account.

The New Critics exercised their early characteristic method almost exclusively upon lyric poetry, a genre in which the historical element, although of course present, is less obtrusive than in the long poem, the novel, and the drama. But even in the lyric poem the factor of historicity is part of the aesthetic experience; it is not merely a negative condition of the other elements, such as prosody or diction, which, if they are old enough, are likely to be insufficiently understood—it is itself a positive

aesthetic factor with positive and pleasurable relations to the other aesthetic factors. It is a part of the *given* of the work, which we cannot help but respond to. The New Critics imply that this situation *should* not exist, but it cannot help existing, and we have to take it into account.

We are creatures of time, we are creatures of the historical sense, not only as men have always been but in a new way since the time of Walter Scott. Possibly this may be for the worse; we would perhaps be stronger if we believed that Now contained all things, and that we in our barbarian moment were all that had ever been. Without the sense of the past we might be more certain, less weighted down and apprehensive. We might also be less generous, and certainly we would be less aware. In any case, we have the sense of the past and must live with it, and by it.

And we must read our literature by it. Try as we will, we cannot be like Partridge at the play, wholly without the historical sense. The leap of the imagination which an audience makes when it responds to *Hamlet* is enormous, and it requires a comprehensive, although not necessarily a highly instructed, sense of the past. This sense does not, for most artistic purposes, need to be highly instructed; it can consist largely of the firm belief that there really is such a thing as the past.

In the New Critics' refusal to take critical account of the historicity of a work there is, one understands, the impulse to make the work of the past more immediate and more real, to deny that between Now and Then there is any essential difference, the spirit of man being one and continuous. But it is only if we are aware of the reality of the past as past that we can feel it as alive and present. If, for example, we try to make Shakespeare literally contemporaneous, we make him monstrous. He is contemporaneous only if we know how much a man of his own age he was; he is relevant to us only if we see his distance from us. Or to take a poet closer to us in actual time, Wordsworth's Immortality Ode is acceptable to us only when it is understood to have been written at a certain past moment; if it had appeared much later than it did, if it were offered to us now as a contemporary work, we would not admire it; and the same is true of *The Prelude*, which of all works of the Romantic Movement is closest to our present interest. In the pastness of these works lies the assurance of their validity and relevance.

The question is always arising: What is the real poem? Is it the poem we now perceive? Is it the poem the author consciously intended? Is it the poem the author intended and his first readers read? Well, it is all these things, depending on the state of our knowledge. But in addition the poem is the poem as it has existed in history, as it has lived its life from Then to Now, as it is a thing which submits itself to one kind of perception in one age and another kind of perception in another age, as it exerts in each age a different kind of power. This makes it a thing we can never wholly understand—other things too, of course, help to make it that—and the mystery, the unreachable part of the poem, is one of its aesthetic elements.

To suppose that we can think like men of another time is as much of an illusion as to suppose that we can think in a wholly different way. But it is the first illusion that is exemplified in the attitude of the anti-historical critics. In the admirable poetry textbook of Cleanth Brooks and Robert Penn Warren, the authors disclaim all historical intention. Their purpose being what it is, they are right to do so, but I wonder if they are right in never asking in their aesthetic analysis the question: What effect is created by our knowledge that the language of a particular poem is not such as would be uttered by a poet writing now? To read a poem of even a hundred years ago requires as much translation of its historical circumstance as of its metaphors. This the trained and gifted critic is likely to forget; his own historical sense is often so deeply ingrained that he is not wholly conscious of it, and sometimes, for reasons of his own, he prefers to keep it merely implicit. Yet whether or not it is made conscious and ex-

plicit, the historical sense is one of the aesthetic and critical faculties.

What more apposite reminder of this can we have than the early impulse of the New Critics themselves to discover all poetic virtue in the poetry of the seventeenth century, the impulse, only lately modified, to find the essence of poetic error in the poetry of Romanticism? Their having given rein to this impulse is certainly not illegitimate. They were doing what we all do, what we all must and even should do: they were involving their aesthetics with certain cultural preferences, they were implying choices in religion, metaphysics, politics, manners. And in so far as they were doing this by showing a preference for a particular period of the past, which they brought into comparison with the present, they were exercising their historical sense. We cannot question their preference itself; we can only question the mere implicitness of their historical sense, their attitude of making the historical sense irrelevant to their aesthetic.

But if the historical sense is always with us, it must, for just that reason, be refined and made more exact. We have, that is, to open our minds to the whole question of what we mean when we speak of causation in culture. Hume, who so shook our notions of causation in the physical sciences, raises some interesting questions of causation in culture. "There is no subject," he says, "in which we must proceed with more caution than in tracing the history of the arts and sciences; lest we assign causes which never existed and reduce what is merely contingent to stable and universal principles." The cultivators of the arts, he goes on to say, are always few in number and their minds are delicate and "easily perverted." "Chance, therefore, or secret and unknown causes must have great influence on the rise and progress of all refined arts." But there is one fact, he continues, which gives us the license to speculate—this is the fact that the choice spirits arise from and are related to the mass of the people of their time. "The question, therefore, is not altogether concerning the taste, genius, and spirit of a few, but concerning those of a whole people; and may, therefore, be accounted for, in some measure, by general causes and principles." This gives us our charter to engage in cultural history and cultural criticism, but we must see that it is a charter to deal with a mystery.

The refinement of our historical sense chiefly means that we keep it properly complicated. History, like science and art, involves abstraction: we abstract certain events from others and we make this particular abstraction with an end in view, we make it to serve some purpose of our will. Try as we may, we cannot, as we write history, escape our purposiveness. Nor, indeed, should we try to escape, for purpose and meaning are the same thing. But in pursuing our purpose, in making our abstractions, we must be aware of what we are doing; we ought to have it fully in mind that our abstraction is not perfectly equivalent to the infinite complication of events from which we have abstracted. I should like to suggest a few ways in which those of us who are literary scholars can give to our notion of history an appropriate complication.

It ought to be for us a real question whether, and in what way, human nature is always the same. I do not mean that we ought to settle this question before we get to work, but only that we insist to ourselves that the question is a real one. What we certainly know has changed is the *expression* of human nature, and we must keep before our minds the problem of the relation which expression bears to feeling. E. E. Stoll, the well-known Shakespearean critic, has settled the matter out of hand by announcing the essential difference between what he calls "convention" and what he calls "life," and he insists that the two may have no truck with each other, that we cannot say of Shakespeare that he is psychologically or philosophically acute because these are terms we use of "life," whereas Shakespeare was dealing only with "convention." This has the virtue of suggesting how important is the relation of "convention" to "life," but it misses the point that

"life" is always expressed through "convention" and in a sense always *is* "convention," and that convention has meaning only because of the intentions of life. Professor Stoll seems to go on the assumption that Shakespeare's audiences were conscious of convention; they were aware of it, but certainly not conscious of it; what they were conscious of was life, into which they made an instantaneous translation of all that took place on the stage. The problem of the interplay between the emotion and the convention which is available for it, and the reciprocal influence they exert on each other, is a very difficult one, and I scarcely even state its complexities, let alone pretend to solve them. But the problem with its difficulties should be admitted, and simplicity of solution should always be regarded as a sign of failure.

A very important step forward in the complication of our sense of the past was made when Whitehead and after him Lovejoy taught us to look not for the expressed but for the assumed ideas of an age, what Whitehead describes as the "assumptions which appear so obvious that people do not know that they are assuming them because no other way of putting things has ever occurred to them."

But a regression was made when Professor Lovejoy, in that influential book of his, assured us that "the ideas in serious reflective literature are, of course, in great part philosophical ideas in dilution." To go fully into the error of this common belief would need more time than we have now at our disposal. It is part of our suspiciousness of literature that we undertake thus to make it a dependent art. Certainly we must question the assumption which gives the priority in ideas to the philosopher and sees the movement of thought as always from the systematic thinker, who thinks up the ideas in, presumably, a cultural vacuum, to the poet who "uses" the ideas "in dilution." We must question this even if it means a reconstruction of what we mean by "ideas."

And this leads to another matter about which we may not be simple, the relation of the poet to his environment. The poet, it is true, is an effect of environment, but we must remember that he is no less a cause. He may be used as the barometer, but let us not forget that he is also part of the weather. We have been too easily satisfied by a merely elementary meaning of environment; we have been content with a simple quantitative implication of the word, taking a large and literally environing thing to be always the environment of a smaller thing. In a concert room the audience and its attitude are of course the environment of the performer, but also the performer and his music make the environment of the audience. In a family the parents are no doubt the chief factors in the environment of the child; but also the child is a factor in the environment of the parents and himself conditions the actions of his parents toward him.

Corollary to this question of environment is the question of influence, the influence which one writer is said to have had on another. In its historical meaning, from which we take our present use, *influence* was a word intended to express a mystery. It means a flowing-in, but not as a tributary river flows into the main stream at a certain observable point; historically the image is an astrological one and the meanings which the Oxford Dictionary gives all suggest "producing effects by *insensible* or *invisible* means"—"the infusion of any kind of divine, spiritual, moral, immaterial, or *secret* power or principle." Before the idea of influence we ought to be far more puzzled than we are; if we find it hard to be puzzled enough, we may contrive to induce the proper state of uncertainty by turning the word upon ourselves, asking, "What have been the influences that made me the person I am, and to whom would I entrust the task of truly discovering what they were?"

Yet another thing that we have not understood with sufficient complication is the nature of ideas in their relation to the conditions of their development and in relation to their transmission. Too often we conceive of an idea as being like the baton that is handed from runner to runner in a relay race. But an idea as a transmissible thing is rather like the sentence that in the parlor game is whispered about in a circle; the point of the game is the amusement that comes when the last version is compared with the original. As for the origin of ideas, we ought to remember that an idea is the formulation of a response to a situation; so, too, is the modification of an existing idea. Since the situations in which people or cultures find themselves are limited in number, and since the possible responses are also limited, ideas certainly do have a tendency to recur, and because people think habitually ideas also have a tendency to persist when the situation which called them forth is no longer present; so that ideas do have a certain limited autonomy, and sometimes the appearance of a complete autonomy. From this there has grown up the belief in the actual perfect autonomy of ideas. It is supposed that ideas think themselves, create themselves and their descendants, have a life independent of the thinker and the situation. And from this we are often led to conclude that ideas, systematic ideas, are directly responsible for events.

A similar feeling is prevalent among our intellectual classes in relation to words. Semantics is not now the lively concern that it was a few years ago, but the mythology of what we may call political semantics has become established in our intellectual life, the belief that we are betrayed by words, that words push us around against our will. "The tyranny of words" became a popular phrase and is still in use, and the semanticists offer us an easier world and freedom from war if only we assert our independence from words. But nearly a century ago Dickens said that he was tired of hearing about "the tyranny of words" (he used that phrase); he was, he said, less concerned with the way words abuse us than with the way we abuse words. It is not words that make our troubles, but our own wills. Words cannot control us unless we desire to be controlled by them. And the same is true of the control of systematic ideas. We have come to believe that some ideas can betray us, others save us. The educated classes are learning to blame ideas for our troubles, rather than blaming what is a very different thing—our own bad thinking. This is the great vice of academicism, that it is concerned with ideas rather than with thinking, and nowadays the errors of academicism do not stay in the academy; they make their way into the world, and what begins as a failure of perception among intellectual specialists finds its fulfillment in policy and action.

In time of war, when two different cultures, or two extreme modifications of the same culture, confront each other with force, this belief in the autonomy of ideas becomes especially strong and therefore especially clear. In any modern war there is likely to be involved a conflict of ideas which is in part factitious but which is largely genuine. But this conflict of ideas, genuine as it may be, suggests to both sides the necessity of believing in the fixed, immutable nature of the ideas to which each side owes allegiance. What gods were to the ancients at war, ideas are to us. Thus, in the last war, an eminent American professor of philosophy won wide praise for demonstrating that Nazism was to be understood as the inevitable outcome of the ideas of Schopenhauer and Nietzsche, while the virtues of American democracy were to be explained by tracing a direct line of descent from Plato and the Athenian polity. Or consider a few sentences from a biography of Byron, written when, not so long ago, the culture of Nazism was at its height. The author, a truly admirable English biographer, is making an estimate of the effect of the Romantic Movement upon our time. He concludes that the Romantic Movement failed. Well, we have all heard that before, and perhaps it is true, although I for one know less and less what it means. Indeed, I know less and less what is meant by the ascription of failure to any movement in literature. All movements fail, and perhaps the Romantic Movement failed more than most because it attempted more than most; possibly it attempted too much. To say that a literary movement failed

seems to suggest a peculiar view of both literature and history; it implies that literature ought to settle something for good and all, that life ought to be progressively completed. But according to our author, not only did the Romantic Movement fail—it left a terrible legacy:

Nationalism was essentially a Romantic movement, and from nationalism springs the half-baked racial theorist with his romantic belief in the superiority of "Aryan" blood and his romantic distrust of the use of reason. So far-reaching were the effects of the Romantic Revival that they still persist in shapes under which they are no longer recognized. . . . For Romantic literature appeals to that strain of anarchism which inhabits a dark corner of every human mind and is continually advancing the charms of extinction against the claims of life—the beauty of all that is fragmentary and youthful and half-formed as opposed to the compact achievement of adult genius.

It is of course easy enough to reduce the argument to absurdity—we have only to ask why Germany and not ourselves responded so fiercely to the romantic ideas which, if they be indeed the romantic ideas, were certainly available to everybody. The failure of logic is not however what concerns us, but rather what the logic is intended to serve: the belief that ideas generate events, that they have an autonomous existence, and that they can seize upon the minds of some men and control their actions independently of circumstance and will.

Needless to say, these violations of historical principle require a violation of historical fact. The Schopenhauer and the Nietzsche of the first explanation have no real reference to two nineteenth-century philosophers of the same names; the Plato is imaginary, the Athens out of a storybook, and no attempt is made to reconcile this fanciful Athens with the opinion of the real Athens held by the real Plato. As for the second explanation, how are we to connect anarchism, and hostility to the claims of life, and the fragmentary, and the immature, and the half-formed, with Kant, or Goethe, or

Wordsworth, or Beethoven, or Berlioz, or De-
lacroix? And how from these men, who *are*
Romanticism, dare we derive the iron rigidity
and the desperate centralization which the
New Order of the Nazis involved, or the systematic cruelty or the elaborate scientism with
which the racial doctrine was implicated?

The two books to which I refer are of course
in themselves harmless and I don't wish to put
upon them a weight which they should not
properly be made to bear. But they do suggest
something of the low estate into which history
has fallen among our educated classes, and
they are of a piece with the depreciation of
the claims of history which a good many literary people nowadays make, a depreciation
which has had the effect of leading young students of literature, particularly the more gifted
ones, to incline more and more to resist historical considerations, justifying themselves, as it
is natural they should, by pointing to the dullness and deadness and falsifications which have
resulted from the historical study of literature.
Our resistance to history is no doubt ultimately
to be accounted for by nothing less than the
whole nature of our life today. It was said by
Nietzsche—the real one, not the lay figure of
cultural propaganda—that the historical sense
was an actual faculty of the mind, "a sixth
sense," and that the credit for the recognition
of its status must go to the nineteenth century.
What was uniquely esteemed by the nineteenth century is not likely to stand in high favor with us: our coldness to historical thought
may in part be explained by our feeling that it
is precisely the past that caused all our troubles, the nineteenth century being the most
blameworthy of all the culpable centuries. Karl
Marx, for whom history was indeed a sixth
sense, expressed what has come to be the secret
hope of our time, that man's life in politics,
which is to say, man's life in history, shall come
to an end. History, as we now understand it,
envisions its own extinction—that is really
what we nowadays mean by "progress"—and
with all the passion of a desire kept secret even
from ourselves, we yearn to elect a way of life

which shall be satisfactory once and for all,
time without end, and we do not want to be
reminded by the past of the considerable possibility that our present is but perpetuating mistakes and failures and instituting new troubles.

And yet, when we come to think about it,
the chances are all in favor of our having to go
on making our choices and so of making our
mistakes. History, in its meaning of a continuum of events, is not really likely to come to an
end. There may therefore be some value in
bringing explicitly to mind what part in culture
is played by history in its other meaning of an
ordering and understanding of the continuum
of events. There is no one who is better able to
inform us on this point than Nietzsche. We
can perhaps listen to him with the more patience because he himself would have had considerable sympathy for our impatience with
history, for although he thought that the historical sense brought certain virtues, making
men "unpretentious, unselfish, modest, brave,
habituated to self-control and self-renuncia-
tion," he also thought that it prevented them
from having the ability to respond to the very
highest and noblest developments of culture,
making them suspicious of what is wholly completed and fully matured. This ambivalent
view of the historical sense gives him a certain
authority when he defines what the historical
sense is and does. It is, he said, "the capacity
for divining quickly the order of the rank of the
valuation according to which a people, a community, or an individual has lived." In the
case of a people or of a community, the valuations are those which are expressed not only by
the gross institutional facts of their life, what
Nietzsche called "the operating forces," but
also and more significantly by their morals and
manners, by their philosophy and art. And the
historical sense, he goes on to say, is "the 'divining instinct' for the relationships of these valuations, for the relation of the valuations to the
operating forces." The historical sense, that is,
is to be understood as the critical sense, as the
sense which life uses to test itself. And since
there never was a time when the instinct for

divining—and "quickly"!—the order of rank of cultural expressions was so much needed, our growing estrangement from history must be understood as the sign of our desperation.

Nietzsche's own capacity for quickly divining the order of rank of cultural things was, when he was at his best, more acute than that of any other man of his time or since. If we look for the explanation of his acuity, we find it in the fact that it never occurred to him to separate his historical sense from his sense of art. They were not two senses but one. And the merit of his definition of the historical sense, especially when it is taken in conjunction with the example of himself, is that it speaks to the historian and to the student of art as if they were one person. To that person Nietzsche's definition prescribes that culture be studied and judged as life's continuous evaluation of itself, the evaluation being understood as never finding full expression in the "operating forces" of a culture, but as never finding expression at all without reference to these gross, institutional facts.

FREUD AND LITERATURE (1947)

THE FREUDIAN psychology is the only systematic account of the human mind which, in point of subtlety and complexity, of interest and tragic power, deserves to stand beside the chaotic mass of psychological insights which literature has accumulated through the centuries. To pass from the reading of a great literary work to a treatise of academic psychology is to pass from one order of perception to another, but the human nature of the Freudian psychology is exactly the stuff upon which the poet has always exercised his art. It is therefore not surprising that the psychoanalytical theory has had a great effect upon literature. Yet the relationship is reciprocal, and the effect of Freud upon literature has been no greater than the effect of literature upon Freud. When, on the occasion of the celebration of his seventieth birthday, Freud was greeted as the "discoverer of the unconscious," he corrected the speaker and disclaimed the title. "The poets and philosophers before me discovered the unconscious," he said. "What I discovered was the scientific method by which the unconscious can be studied."

A lack of specific evidence prevents us from considering the particular literary "influences" upon the founder of psychoanalysis; and, besides, when we think of the men who so clearly anticipated many of Freud's own ideas—Schopenhauer and Nietzsche, for example—and then learn that he did not read their works until after he had formulated his own theories, we must see that particular influences cannot be in question here but that what we must deal with is nothing less than a whole *Zeitgeist*, a direction of thought. For psychoanalysis is one of the culminations of the Romanticist literature of the nineteenth century. If there is perhaps a contradiction in the idea of a science standing upon the shoulders of a literature which avows itself inimical to science in so many ways, the contradiction will be resolved if we remember that this literature, despite its avowals, was itself scientific in at least the sense of being passionately devoted to a research into the self.

In showing the connection between Freud and this Romanticist tradition, it is difficult to know where to begin, but there might be a certain aptness in starting even back of the tradition, as far back as 1762 with Diderot's *Rameau's Nephew*. At any rate, certain men at the heart of nineteenth-century thought were agreed in finding a peculiar importance in this brilliant little work: Goethe translated it, Marx admired it, Hegel—as Marx reminded Engels in the letter which announced that he was sending the book as a gift—praised and expounded it at length, Shaw was impressed by it, and Freud himself, as we know from a quotation in his *Introductory Lectures*, read it with the pleasure of agreement.

The dialogue takes place between Diderot himself and a nephew of the famous composer. The protagonist, the younger Rameau, is a despised, outcast, shameless fellow; Hegel calls him the "disintegrated consciousness" and credits him with great wit, for it is he who breaks down all the normal social values and makes new combinations with the pieces. As for Diderot, the deuteragonist, he is what Hegel calls the "honest consciousness," and Hegel considers him reasonable, decent, and dull. It is quite clear that the author does not despise his Rameau and does not mean us to. Rameau is lustful and greedy, arrogant yet self-abasing, perceptive yet "wrong," like a child. Still, Diderot seems actually to be giving the fellow a kind of superiority over himself, as though Rameau represents the elements which, dangerous but wholly necessary, lie beneath the reasonable decorum of social life. It would perhaps be pressing too far to find in Rameau Freud's id and in Diderot Freud's ego; yet the connection does suggest itself; and at least we have here the perception which is to be the common characteristic of both Freud and Romanticism, the perception of the hidden element of human nature and of the opposition between the hidden and the visible. We have too the bold perception of just what lies hidden: "If the little savage [i.e., the child] were left to himself, if he preserved all his foolishness and combined the violent passions of a man of thirty with the lack of reason of a child in the cradle, he'd wring his father's neck and go to bed with his mother."

From the self-exposure of Rameau to Rousseau's account of his own childhood is no great step; society might ignore or reject the idea of the "immorality" which lies concealed in the beginning of the career of the "good" man, just

as it might turn away from Blake struggling to expound a psychology which would include the forces beneath the propriety of social man in general, but the idea of the hidden thing went forward to become one of the dominant notions of the age. The hidden element takes many forms and it is not necessarily "dark" and "bad"; for Blake the "bad" was the good, while for Wordsworth and Burke what was hidden and unconscious was wisdom and power, which work in despite of the conscious intellect.

The mind has become far less simple; the devotion to the various forms of autobiography —itself an important fact in the tradition— provides abundant examples of the change that has taken place. Poets, making poetry by what seems to them almost a freshly discovered faculty, find that this new power may be conspired against by other agencies of the mind and even deprived of its freedom; the names of Wordsworth, Coleridge, and Arnold at once occur to us again, and Freud quotes Schiller on the danger to the poet that lies in the merely analytical reason. And it is not only the poets who are threatened; educated and sensitive people throughout Europe become aware of the depredations that reason might make upon the affective life, as in the classic instance of John Stuart Mill.

We must also take into account the preoccupation—it began in the eighteenth century, or even in the seventeenth—with children, women, peasants, and savages, whose mental life, it is felt, is less overlaid than that of the educated adult male by the proprieties of social habit. With this preoccupation goes a concern with education and personal development, so consonant with the historical and evolutionary bias of the time. And we must certainly note the revolution in morals which took place at the instance (we might almost say) of the *Bildungsroman*, for in the novels fathered by *Wilhelm Meister* we get the almost complete identification of author and hero and of the reader with both, and this identification almost inevitably suggests a leniency of moral judgment. The autobiographical novel has a further influence upon the moral sensibility by its exploitation of all the modulations of motive and by its hinting that we may not judge a man by any single moment in his life without taking into account the determining past and the expiating and fulfilling future.

It is difficult to know how to go on, for the further we look the more literary affinities to Freud we find, and even if we limit ourselves to bibliography we can at best be incomplete. Yet we must mention the sexual revolution that was being demanded—by Shelley, for example, by the Schlegel of *Lucinde*, by George Sand, and later and more critically by Ibsen; the belief in the sexual origin of art, baldly stated by Tieck, more subtly by Schopenhauer; the investigation of sexual maladjustment by Stendhal, whose observations on erotic feeling seem to us distinctly Freudian. Again and again we see the effective, utilitarian ego being relegated to an inferior position and a plea being made on behalf of the anarchic and self-indulgent id. We find the energetic exploitation of the idea of the mind as a divisible thing, one part of which can contemplate and mock the other. It is not a far remove from this to Dostoevski's brilliant instances of ambivalent feeling. Novalis brings in the preoccupation with the death wish, and this is linked on the one hand with sleep and on the other hand with the perception of the perverse, self-destroying impulses, which in turn leads us to that fascination by the horrible which we find in Shelley, Poe, and Baudelaire. And always there is the profound interest in the dream—"Our dreams," said Gerard de Nerval, "are a second life"—and in the nature of metaphor, which reaches its climax in Rimbaud and the later Symbolists, metaphor becoming less and less communicative as it approaches the relative autonomy of the dream life.

But perhaps we must stop to ask, since these are the components of the *Zeitgeist* from which Freud himself developed, whether it can be said that Freud did indeed produce a wide literary effect. What is it that Freud added that the tendency of literature itself would not have developed without him? If we were looking for a writer who showed the Freudian influence, Proust would perhaps come to mind as readily as anyone else; the very title of his novel, in French more than in English, suggests an enterprise of psychoanalysis and scarcely less so does his method—the investigation of sleep, of sexual deviation, of the way of association, the almost obsessive interest in metaphor; at these and at many other points the "influence" might be shown. Yet I believe it is true that Proust did not read Freud. Or again, exegesis of *The Waste Land* often reads remarkably like the psychoanalytic interpretation of a dream, yet we know that Eliot's methods were prepared for him not by Freud but by other poets.

Nevertheless, it is of course true that Freud's influence on literature has been very great. Much of it is so pervasive that its extent is scarcely to be determined; in one form or another, frequently in perversions or absurd simplifications, it has been infused into our life and become a component of our culture of which it is now hard to be specifically aware. In biography its first effect was sensational but not fortunate. The early Freudian biographers were for the most part Guildensterns who seemed to know the pipes but could not pluck out the heart of the mystery, and the same condemnation applies to the early Freudian critics. But in recent years, with the acclimatization of psychoanalysis and the increased sense of its refinements and complexity, criticism has derived from the Freudian system much that is of great value, most notably the license and the injunction to read the work of literature with a lively sense of its latent and ambiguous meanings, as if it were, as indeed it is, a being no less alive and contradictory than the man who created it. And this new response to the literary work has had a corrective effect upon our conception of literary biography. The literary critic or biographer who makes use of the Freudian theory is no less threatened by the dangers of theoretical systematization than he was in the early days, but he is likely to be more aware of these dangers; and I think it is true to say that now the

motive of his interpretation is not that of exposing the secret shame of the writer and limiting
the meaning of his work, but, on the contrary,
that of finding grounds for sympathy with the
writer and for increasing the possible significances of the work.

The names of the creative writers who have
been more or less Freudian in tone or assumption would of course be legion. Only a relatively
small number, however, have made serious use
of the Freudian ideas. Freud himself seems to
have thought this was as it should be: he is said
to have expected very little of the works that
were sent to him by writers with inscriptions
of gratitude for all they had learned from him.
The Surrealists have, with a certain inconsist-
ency, depended upon Freud for the "scientific"
sanction of their program. Kafka, with an apparent awareness of what he was doing, has explored the Freudian conceptions of guilt and
punishment, of the dream, and of the fear of
the father. Thomas Mann, whose tendency, as
he himself says, was always in the direction of
Freud's interests, has been most susceptible to
the Freudian anthropology, finding a special
charm in the theories of myths and magical
practices. James Joyce, with his interest in the
numerous states of receding consciousness, with
his use of words as things and of words which
point to more than one thing, with his pervading sense of the interrelation and interpenetration of all things, and, not least important, his
treatment of familial themes, has perhaps most
thoroughly and consciously exploited Freud's
ideas.

II

It will be clear enough how much of Freud's
thought has significant affinity with the anti-
rationalist element of the Romanticist tradition. But we must see with no less distinctness
how much of his system is militantly rationalistic. Thomas Mann is at fault when, in his first
essay on Freud, he makes it seem that the
"Apollonian," the rationalistic, side of psychoanalysis is, while certainly important and wholly
admirable, somehow secondary and even acci-

dental. He gives us a Freud who is committed
to the "night side" of life. Not at all: the rationalistic element of Freud is foremost; before
everything else he is positivistic. If the interpreter of dreams came to medical science
through Goethe, as he tells us he did, he entered not by way of the *Walpurgisnacht* but by
the essay which played so important a part in
the lives of so many scientists of the nineteenth
century, the famous disquisition on Nature.

This correction is needed not only for accuracy but also for any understanding of Freud's
attitude to art. And for that understanding we
must see how intense is the passion with which
Freud believes that positivistic rationalism, in
its golden-age pre-Revolutionary purity, is the
very form and pattern of intellectual virtue.
The aim of psychoanalysis, he says, is the control of the night side of life. It is "to strengthen
the ego, to make it more independent of the
super-ego, to widen its field of vision, and so to
extend the organization of the id." "Where id
was,"—that is, where all the irrational, non-
logical, pleasure-seeking dark forces were—
"there shall ego be,"—that is, intelligence and
control. "It is," he concludes, with a reminiscence of Faust, "reclamation work, like the
draining of the Zuyder Zee." This passage is
quoted by Mann when, in taking up the subject of Freud a second time, he does indeed
speak of Freud's positivistic program; but even
here the bias induced by Mann's artistic interest in the "night side" prevents him from giving the other aspect of Freud its due emphasis.
Freud would never have accepted the role
which Mann seems to give him as the legiti-
mizer of the myth and the dark irrational ways
of the mind. If Freud discovered the darkness
for science he never endorsed it. On the contrary, his rationalism supports all the ideas of
the Enlightenment that deny validity to myth
or religion; he holds to a simple materialism, to
a simple determinism, to a rather limited sort
of epistemology. No great scientist of our day
has thundered so articulately and so fiercely
against all those who would sophisticate with
metaphysics the scientific principles that were

good enough for the nineteenth century. Conceptualism or pragmatism is anathema to him through the greater part of his intellectual career, and this, when we consider the nature of his own brilliant scientific methods, has surely an element of paradox in it.

From his rationalistic positivism comes much of Freud's strength and what weakness he has. The strength is the fine, clear tenacity of his positive aims, the goal of therapy, the desire to bring men a decent measure of earthly happiness. But upon the rationalism must also be placed the blame for the often naïve scientific principles which characterize his early thought —they are later much modified—and which consist largely of claiming for his theories a perfect correspondence with an external reality, a position which, for those who admire Freud and especially for those who take seriously his views on art, is troublesome in the extreme.

Now Freud has, I believe, much to tell us about art, but whatever is suggestive in him is not likely to be found in those of his works in which he deals expressly with art itself. Freud is not insensitive to art—on the contrary—nor does he ever intend to speak of it with contempt. Indeed, he speaks of it with a real tenderness and counts it one of the true charms of the good life. Of artists, especially of writers, he speaks with admiration and even a kind of awe, though perhaps what he most appreciates in literature are specific emotional insights and observations; as we have noted, he speaks of literary men, because they have understood the part played in life by the hidden motives, as the precursors and coadjutors of his own science.

And yet eventually Freud speaks of art with what we must indeed call contempt. Art, he tells us, is a "substitute gratification," and as such is "an illusion in contrast to reality." Unlike most illusions, however, art is "almost always harmless and beneficent" for the reason that "it does not seek to be anything but an illusion. Save in the case of a few people who are, one might say, obsessed by Art, it never dares make any attack on the realm of reality." One of its chief functions is to serve as a "nar-cotic." It shares the characteristics of the dream, whose element of distortion Freud calls a "sort of inner dishonesty." As for the artist, he is virtually in the same category with the neurotic. "By such separation of imagination and intellectual capacity," Freud says of the hero of a novel, "he is destined to be a poet or a neurotic, and he belongs to that race of beings whose realm is not of this world."

Now there is nothing in the logic of psychoanalytical thought which requires Freud to have these opinions. But there is a great deal in the practice of the psychoanalytical therapy which makes it understandable that Freud, unprotected by an adequate philosophy, should be tempted to take the line he does. The analytical therapy deals with illusion. The patient comes to the physician to be cured, let us say, of a fear of walking in the street. The fear is real enough, there is no illusion on that score, and it produces all the physical symptoms of a more rational fear, the sweating palms, pounding heart, and shortened breath. But the patient knows that there is no cause for the fear, or rather that there is, as he says, no "real cause": there are no machine guns, man traps, or tigers in the street. The physician knows, however, that there is indeed a "real" cause for the fear, though it has nothing at all to do with what is or is not in the street; the cause is within the patient, and the process of the therapy will be to discover, by gradual steps, what this real cause is and so free the patient from its effects.

Now the patient in coming to the physician, and the physician in accepting the patient, make a tacit compact about reality; for their purpose they agree to the limited reality by which we get our living, win our loves, catch our trains and our colds. The therapy will undertake to train the patient in proper ways of coping with this reality. The patient, of course, has been dealing with this reality all along, but in the wrong way. For Freud there are two ways of dealing with external reality. One is practical, effective, positive; this is the way of the conscious self, of the ego which must be made independent of the super-ego and extend its organization over the id, and it is the right way. The antithetical way may be called, for our purpose now, the "fictional" way. Instead of doing something about, or to, external reality, the individual who uses this way does something to, or about, his affective states. The most common and "normal" example of this is daydreaming, in which we give ourselves a certain pleasure by imagining our difficulties solved or our desires gratified. Then, too, as Freud discovered, sleeping dreams are, in much more complicated ways, and even though quite unpleasant, at the service of this same "fictional" activity. And in ways yet more complicated and yet more unpleasant, the actual neurosis from which our patient suffers deals with an external reality which the mind considers still more unpleasant than the painful neurosis itself.

For Freud as psychoanalytic practitioner there are, we may say, the polar extremes of reality and illusion. Reality is an honorific word, and it means what is *there*; illusion is a pejorative word, and it means a response to what is *not there*. The didactic nature of a course of psychoanalysis no doubt requires a certain firm crudeness in making the distinction; it is after all aimed not at theoretical refinement but at practical effectiveness. The polar extremes are practical reality and neurotic illusion, the latter judged by the former. This, no doubt, is as it should be; the patient is not being trained in metaphysics and epistemology.

This practical assumption is not Freud's only view of the mind in its relation to reality. Indeed what may be called the essentially Freudian view assumes that the mind, for good as well as bad, helps create its reality by selection and evaluation. In this view, reality is malleable and subject to creation; it is not static but is rather a series of situations which are dealt with in their own terms. But beside this conception of the mind stands the conception which arises from Freud's therapeutic-practical assumptions; in this view, the mind deals with a reality which is quite fixed and static, a reality that is wholly

"given" and not (to use a phrase of Dewey's) "taken." In his epistemological utterances, Freud insists on this second view, although it is not easy to see why he should do so. For the reality to which he wishes to reconcile the neurotic patient is, after all, a "taken" and not a "given" reality. It is the reality of social life and of value, conceived and maintained by the human mind and will. Love, morality, honor, esteem—these are the components of a created reality. If we are to call art an illusion then we must call most of the activities and satisfactions of the ego illusions; Freud, of course, has no desire to call them that.

What, then, is the difference between, on the one hand, the dream and the neurosis, and, on the other hand, art? That they have certain common elements is of course clear; that unconscious processes are at work in both would be denied by no poet or critic; they share too, though in different degrees, the element of fantasy. But there is a vital difference between them which Charles Lamb saw so clearly in his defense of the sanity of true genius: "The . . . poet dreams being awake. He is not possessed by his subject but he has dominion over it."

That is the whole difference: the poet is in command of his fantasy, while it is exactly the mark of the neurotic that he is possessed by his fantasy. And there is a further difference which Lamb states; speaking of the poet's relation to reality (he calls it Nature), he says, "He is beautifully loyal to that sovereign directness, even when he appears most to betray her"; the illusions of art are made to serve the purpose of a closer and truer relation with reality. Jacques Barzun, in an acute and sympathetic discussion of Freud, puts the matter well: "A good analogy between art and *dreaming* has led him to a false one between art and *sleeping*. But the difference between a work of art and a dream is precisely this, that the work of art *leads us back to the outer reality by taking account of it*." Freud's assumption of the almost exclusively hedonistic nature and purpose of art bar him from the perception of this.

Of the distinction that must be made between the artist and the neurotic Freud is of course aware; he tells us that the artist is not like the neurotic in that he knows how to find a way back from the world of imagination and "once more get a firm foothold in reality." This however seems to mean no more than that reality is to be dealt with when the artist suspends the practice of his art; and at least once when Freud speaks of art dealing with reality he actually means the rewards that a successful artist can win. He does not deny to art its function and its usefulness; it has a therapeutic effect in releasing mental tension; it serves the cultural purpose of acting as a "substitute gratification" to reconcile men to the sacrifices they have made for culture's sake; it promotes the social sharing of highly valued emotional experiences; and it recalls men to their cultural ideals. This is not everything that some of us would find that art does, yet even this is a good deal for a "narcotic" to do.

III

I started by saying that Freud's ideas could tell us something about art, but so far I have done little more than try to show that Freud's very conception of art is inadequate. Perhaps, then, the suggestiveness lies in the application of the analytic method to specific works of art or to the artist himself? I do not think so, and it is only fair to say that Freud himself was aware both of the limits and the limitations of psychoanalysis in art, even though he does not always in practice submit to the former or admit the latter.

Freud has, for example, no desire to encroach upon the artist's autonomy; he does not wish us to read his monograph on Leonardo and then say to the "Madonna of the Rocks" that it is a fine example of homosexual, autoerotic painting. If he asserts that in investigation the "psychiatrist cannot yield to the author," he immediately insists that the "author cannot yield to the psychiatrist," and he warns the latter not to "coarsen everything" by using for all human manifestations the "substantially useless and awkward terms" of clinical procedure. He ad-

mits, even while asserting that the sense of beauty probably derives from sexual feeling, that psychoanalysis "has less to say about beauty than about most other things." He confesses to a theoretical indifference to the form of art and restricts himself to its content. Tone, feeling, style, and the modification that part makes upon part he does not consider. "The layman," he says, "may expect perhaps too much from analysis . . . for it must be admitted that it throws no light upon the two problems which probably interest him the most. It can do nothing toward elucidating the nature of the artistic gift, nor can it explain the means by which the artist works—artistic technique."

What, then, does Freud believe that the analytical method can do? Two things: explain the "inner meanings" of the work of art and explain the temperament of the artist as man.

A famous example of the method is the attempt to solve the "problem" of *Hamlet* as suggested by Freud and as carried out by Dr. Ernest Jones, his early and distinguished follower. Dr. Jones's monograph is a work of painstaking scholarship and of really masterly ingenuity. The research undertakes not only the clearing up of the mystery of Hamlet's character, but also the discovery of "the clue to much of the deeper workings of Shakespeare's mind." Part of the mystery in question is of course why Hamlet, after he had so definitely resolved to do so, did not avenge upon his hated uncle his father's death. But there is another mystery to the play—what Freud calls "the mystery of its effect," its magical appeal that draws so much interest toward it. Recalling the many failures to solve the riddle of the play's charm, he wonders if we are to be driven to the conclusion "that its magical appeal rests solely upon the impressive thoughts in it and the splendor of its language." Freud believes that we can find a source of power beyond this.

We remember that Freud has told us that the meaning of a dream is its intention, and we may assume that the meaning of a drama is its intention, too. The Jones research undertakes to discover what it was that Shakespeare intended to say about Hamlet. It finds that the intention was wrapped by the author in a dreamlike obscurity because it touched so deeply both his personal life and the moral life of the world; what Shakespeare intended to say is that Hamlet cannot act because he is incapacitated by the guilt he feels at his unconscious attachment to his mother. There is, I think, nothing to be quarreled with in the statement that there is an Oedipus situation in *Hamlet*; and if psychoanalysis has indeed added a new point of interest to the play, that is to its credit.[1] And, just so, there is no reason to quarrel with Freud's conclusion when he undertakes to give us the meaning of *King Lear* by a tortuous tracing of the mythological implications of the theme of the three caskets, of the relation of the caskets to the Norns, the Fates, and the Graces, of the connection of these triadic females with Lear's daughters, of the transmogrification of the death goddess into the love goddess and the identification of Cordelia with both, all to the conclusion that the meaning of *King Lear* is to be found in the tragic refusal of an old man to "renounce love, choose death, and make friends with the necessity of dying." There is something both beautiful and suggestive in this, but it is not *the* meaning of *King Lear* any more than the Oedipus motive is *the* meaning of *Hamlet*.

It is not here a question of the validity of the evidence, though that is of course important. We must rather object to the conclusions of Freud and Dr. Jones on the ground that their proponents do not have an adequate conception of what an artistic meaning is. There is no single meaning to any work of art; this is true

[1] However, A. C. Bradley, in his discussion of Hamlet (*Shakespearean Tragedy*), states clearly the intense sexual disgust which Hamlet feels and which, for Bradley, helps account for his uncertain purpose; and Bradley was anticipated in this view by Löning. It is well known, and Dover Wilson has lately emphasized the point, that to an Elizabethan audience Hamlet's mother was not merely tasteless, as to a modern audience she seems, in hurrying to marry Claudius, but actually adulterous in marrying him at all because he was, as her brother-in-law, within the forbidden degrees.

not merely because it is better that it should be true, that is, because it makes art a richer thing, but because historical and personal experience show it to be true. Changes in historical context and in personal mood change the meaning of a work and indicate to us that artistic understanding is not a question of fact but of value. Even if the author's intention were, as it cannot be, precisely determinable, the meaning of a work cannot lie in the author's intention alone. It must also lie in its effect. We can say of a volcanic eruption on an inhabited island that it "means terrible suffering," but if the island is uninhabited or easily evacuated it means something else. In short, the audience partly determines the meaning of the work. But although Freud sees something of this when he says that in addition to the author's intention we must take into account the mystery of *Hamlet*'s effect, he nevertheless goes on to speak as if, historically, *Hamlet*'s effect had been single and brought about solely by the "magical" power of the Oedipus motive to which, unconsciously, we so violently respond. Yet there was, we know, a period when *Hamlet* was relatively in eclipse, and it has always been scandalously true of the French, a people not without filial feeling, that they have been somewhat indifferent to the "magical appeal" of *Hamlet*.

I do not think that anything I have said about the inadequacies of the Freudian method of interpretation limits the number of ways we can deal with a work of art. Bacon remarked that experiment may twist nature on the rack to wring out its secrets, and criticism may use any instruments upon a work of art to find its meanings. The elements of art are not limited to the world of art. They reach into life, and whatever extraneous knowledge of them we gain—for example, by research into the historical context of the work—may quicken our feelings for the work itself and even enter legitimately into those feelings. Then, too, anything we may learn about the artist himself may be enriching and legitimate. But one research into the mind of the artist is simply not practicable, however legitimate it may theoretically be. That is, the investigation of his unconscious intention as it exists apart from the work itself. Criticism understands that the artist's statement of his conscious intention, though it is sometimes useful, cannot finally determine meaning. How much less can we know from his unconscious intention considered as something apart from the whole work? Surely very little that can be called conclusive or scientific. For, as Freud himself points out, we are not in a position to question the artist; we must apply the technique of dream analysis to his symbols, but, as Freud says with some heat, those people do not understand his theory who think that a dream may be interpreted without the dreamer's free association with the multitudinous details of his dream.

We have so far ignored the aspect of the method which finds the solution to the "mystery" of such a play as *Hamlet* in the temperament of Shakespeare himself and then illuminates the mystery of Shakespeare's temperament by means of the solved mystery of the play. Here it will be amusing to remember that by 1935 Freud had become converted to the theory that it was not Shakespeare of Stratford but the Earl of Oxford who wrote the plays, thus invalidating the important bit of evidence that Shakespeare's father died shortly before the composition of *Hamlet*. This is destructive enough to Dr. Jones's argument, but the evidence from which Dr. Jones draws conclusions about literature fails on grounds more relevant to literature itself. For when Dr. Jones, by means of his analysis of *Hamlet*, takes us into "the deeper workings of Shakespeare's mind," he does so with a perfect confidence that he knows what *Hamlet* is and what its relation to Shakespeare is. It is, he tells us, Shakespeare's "chief masterpiece," so far superior to all his other works that it may be placed on "an entirely separate level." And then, having established his ground on an entirely subjective literary judgment, Dr. Jones goes on to tell us that *Hamlet* "probably expresses the core of Shakespeare's philosophy and outlook as no

other work of his does." That is, all the contradictory or complicating or modifying testimony of the other plays is dismissed on the basis of Dr. Jones's acceptance of the peculiar position which, he believes, *Hamlet* occupies in the Shakespeare canon. And it is upon this quite inadmissible judgment that Dr. Jones bases his argument: "It may be expected *therefore* that anything which will give us the key to the inner meaning of the play will *necessarily* give us the clue to much of the deeper workings of Shakespeare's mind." (The italics are mine.)

I should be sorry if it appeared that I am trying to say that psychoanalysis can have nothing to do with literature. I am sure that the opposite is so. For example, the whole notion of rich ambiguity in literature, of the interplay between the apparent meaning and the latent—not "hidden"—meaning, has been reinforced by the Freudian concepts, perhaps even received its first impetus from them. Of late years, the more perceptive psychoanalysts have surrendered the early pretensions of their teachers to deal "scientifically" with literature. That is all to the good, and when a study as modest and precise as Dr. Franz Alexander's essay on *Henry IV* comes along, an essay which pretends not to "solve" but only to illuminate the subject, we have something worth having. Dr. Alexander undertakes nothing more than to say that in the development of Prince Hal we see the classic struggle of the ego to come to normal adjustment, beginning with the rebellion against the father, going on to the conquest of the super-ego (Hotspur, with his rigid notions of honor and glory), then to the conquests of the *id* (Falstaff, with his anarchic self-indulgence), then to the identification with the father (the crown scene) and the assumption of mature responsibility. An analysis of this sort is not momentous and not exclusive of other meanings; perhaps it does no more than point up and formulate what we all have already seen. It has the tact to *accept* the play and does not, like Dr. Jones's study of *Hamlet*, search for a "hidden motive" and a "deeper working," which implies that there is a reality to which the play stands in the relation that a dream stands to the wish that generates it and from which it is separable; it is this reality, this "deeper working," which, according to Dr. Jones, produced the play. But *Hamlet* is not merely the product of Shakespeare's thought, it is the very instrument of his thought, and if meaning is intention, Shakespeare did not intend the Oedipus motive or anything less than *Hamlet*; if meaning is effect then it is *Hamlet* which affects us, not the Oedipus motive. *Coriolanus* also deals, and very terribly, with the Oedipus motive, but the effect of the one drama is very different from the effect of the other.

IV

If, then, we can accept neither Freud's conception of the place of art in life nor his application of the analytical method, what is it that he contributes to our understanding of art or to its practice? In my opinion, what he contributes outweighs his errors; it is of the greatest importance, and it lies in no specific statement that he makes about art but is, rather, implicit in his whole conception of the mind.

For, of all mental systems, the Freudian psychology is the one which makes poetry indigenous to the very constitution of the mind. Indeed, the mind, as Freud sees it, is in the greater part of its tendency exactly a poetry-making organ. This puts the case too strongly, no doubt, for it seems to make the working of the unconscious mind equivalent to poetry itself, forgetting that between the unconscious mind and the finished poem there supervene the social intention and the formal control of the conscious mind. Yet the statement has at least the virtue of counterbalancing the belief, so commonly expressed or implied, that the very opposite is true, and that poetry is a kind of beneficent aberration of the mind's right course.

Freud has not merely naturalized poetry; he has discovered its status as a pioneer settler, and he sees it as a method of thought. Often enough he tries to show how, as a method of thought, it is unreliable and ineffective for conquering reality; yet he himself is forced to use it in the very shaping of his own science, as when he speaks of the topography of the mind and tells us with a kind of defiant apology that the metaphors of space relationship which he is using are really most inexact since the mind is not a thing of space at all, but that there is no other way of conceiving the difficult idea except by metaphorical, imagistic language of the early stages of culture; it was left to Freud to discover how, in a scientific age, we still feel and think in figurative formations, and to create, what psychoanalysis is, a science of tropes, of metaphor and its variants, synecdoche and metonomy.

Freud showed, too, how the mind, in one of its parts, could work without logic, yet not without that directing purpose, that control of intent from which, perhaps it might be said, logic springs. For the unconscious mind works without the syntactical conjunctions which are logic's essence. It recognizes no *because*, no *therefore*, no *but*; such ideas as similarity, agreement, and community are expressed in dreams imagistically by compressing the elements into a unity. The unconscious mind in its struggle with the conscious always turns from the general to the concrete and finds the tangible trifle more congenial than the large abstraction. Freud discovered in the very organization of the mind those mechanisms by which art makes its effects, such devices as the condensations of meanings and the displacement of accent.

All this is perhaps obvious enough and, though I should like to develop it in proportion both to its importance and to the space I have given to disagreement with Freud, I will not press it further. For there are two other elements in Freud's thought which, in conclusion, I should like to introduce as a great weight in their bearing on art.

Of these, one is a specific idea which, in the middle of his career (1920), Freud put forward in his essay *Beyond the Pleasure Principle*. The essay itself is a speculative attempt to solve a perplexing problem in clinical analysis, but its relevance to literature is inescapable, as Freud sees well enough, even though his perception of its critical importance is not sufficiently strong to make him revise his earlier views of the nature and function of art. The idea is one which stands besides Aristotle's notion of the catharsis, in part to supplement, in part to modify it.

Freud has come upon certain facts which are not to be reconciled with his earlier theory of the dream. According to this theory, all dreams, even the unpleasant ones, could be understood upon analysis to have the intention of fulfilling the dreamer's wishes. They are in the service of what Freud calls the pleasure principle, which is opposed to the reality principle. It is, of course, this explanation of the dream which had so largely conditioned Freud's theory of art. But now there is thrust upon him the necessity for reconsidering the theory of the dream, for it was found that in cases of war neurosis—what we once called shellshock—the patient, with the utmost anguish, recurred in his dreams to the very situation, distressing as it was, which had precipitated his neurosis. It seemed impossible to interpret these dreams by any assumption of a hedonistic intent. Nor did there seem to be the usual amount of distortion in them: the patient recurred to the terrible initiatory situation with great literalness. And the same pattern of psychic behavior could be observed in the play of children; there were some games which, far from fulfilling wishes, seemed to concentrate upon the representation of those aspects of the child's life which were most unpleasant and threatening to his happiness.

To explain such mental activities Freud evolved a theory for which he at first refused to claim much but to which, with the years, he attached an increasing importance. He first makes the assumption that there is indeed in the psychic life a repetition-compulsion which goes beyond the pleasure principle. Such a compulsion cannot be meaningless, it must have an intent. And that intent, Freud comes to believe, is exactly and literally the develop-

ing of fear. "These dreams," he says, "are attempts at restoring control of the stimuli by developing apprehension, the pretermission of which caused the traumatic neurosis." The dream, that is, is the effort to reconstruct the bad situation in order that the failure to meet it may be recouped; in these dreams there is no obscured intent to evade but only an attempt to meet the situation, to make a new effort of control. And in the play of children it seems to be that "the child repeats even the unpleasant experiences because through his own activity he gains a far more thorough mastery of the strong impression than was possible by mere passive experience."

Freud, at this point, can scarcely help being put in mind of tragic drama; nevertheless, he does not wish to believe that this effort to come to mental grips with a situation is involved in the attraction of tragedy. He is, we might say, under the influence of the Aristotelian tragic theory which emphasizes a qualified hedonism through suffering. But the pleasure involved in tragedy is perhaps an ambiguous one; and sometimes we must feel that the famous sense of cathartic resolution is perhaps the result of glossing over terror with beautiful language rather than an evacuation of it. And sometimes the terror even bursts through the language to stand stark and isolated from the play, as does Oedipus's sightless and bleeding face. At any rate, the Aristotelian theory does not deny another function for tragedy (and for comedy, too) which is suggested by Freud's theory of the traumatic neurosis—what might be called the mithridatic function, by which tragedy is used as the homeopathic administration of pain to inure ourselves to the greater pain which life will force upon us. There is in the cathartic theory of tragedy, as it is usually understood, a conception of tragedy's function which is too negative and which inadequately suggests the sense of active mastery which tragedy can give.

In the same essay in which he sets forth the conception of the mind embracing its own pain for some vital purpose, Freud also expresses a provisional assent to the idea (earlier stated, as he reminds us, by Schopenhauer) that there is perhaps a human drive which makes of death the final and desired goal. The death instinct is a conception that is rejected by many of even the most thoroughgoing Freudian theorists (as, in his last book, Freud mildly noted); the late Otto Fenichel in his authoritative work on the neurosis argues cogently against it. Yet even if we reject the theory as not fitting the facts in any operatively useful way, we still cannot miss its grandeur, its ultimate tragic courage in acquiescence to fate. The idea of the reality principle and the idea of the death instinct form the crown of Freud's broader speculation on the life of man. Their quality of grim poetry is characteristic of Freud's system and the ideas it generates for him.

And as much as anything else that Freud gives to literature, this quality of his thought is important. Although the artist is never finally determined in his work by the intellectual systems about him, he cannot avoid their influence; and it can be said of various competing systems that some hold more promise for the artist than others. When, for example, we think of the simple humanitarian optimism which, for two decades, has been so pervasive, we must see that not only has it been politically and philosophically inadequate, but also that it implies, by the smallness of its view of the varieties of human possibility, a kind of check on the creative faculties. In Freud's view of life no such limitation is implied. To be sure, certain elements of his system seem hostile to the usual notions of man's dignity. Like every great critic of human nature—and Freud is that—he finds in human pride the ultimate cause of human wretchedness, and he takes pleasure in knowing that his ideas stand with those of Copernicus and Darwin in making pride more difficult to maintain. Yet the Freudian man is, I venture to think, a creature of far more dignity and far more interest than the man which any other modern system has been able to conceive. Despite popular belief to the contrary, man, as Freud conceives him, is not to be understood by any simple formula (such as sex) but is rather an inextricable tangle of culture and biology. And not being simple, he is not simply good; he has, as Freud says somewhere, a kind of hell within him from which rise everlastingly the impulses which threaten his civilization. He has the faculty of imagining for himself more in the way of pleasure and satisfaction than he can possibly achieve. Everything that he gains he pays for in more than equal coin; compromise and the compounding with defeat constitute his best way of getting through the world. His best qualities are the result of a struggle whose outcome is tragic. Yet he is a creature of love; it is Freud's sharpest criticism of the Adlerian psychology that to aggression it gives everything and to love nothing at all.

One is always aware in reading Freud how little cynicism there is in his thought. His desire for man is only that he should be human, and to this end his science is devoted. No view of life to which the artist responds can insure the quality of his work, but the poetic qualities of Freud's own principles, which are so clearly in the line of the classic tragic realism, suggest that this is a view which does not narrow and simplify the human world for the artist but on the contrary opens and complicates it.

THE MORALITY OF CRITICISM

F. R. Leavis

From *Revaluation: Tradition and Development in English Poetry*. Reprinted by permission of the author and of Chatto and Windus, Ltd.

SHELLEY (1935)

IF SHELLEY HAD not received some distinguished attention in recent years (and he has been differed over by the most eminent critics) there might, perhaps, have seemed little point in attempting a restatement of the essential critical observations—the essential observations, that is, in the reading and appreciation of Shelley's poetry. For they would seem to be obvious enough. Yet it is only one incitement out of many when a critic of peculiar authority, contemplating the common change from being "intoxicated by Shelley's poetry at the age of fifteen" to finding it now "almost unreadable," invokes for explanation the nature of Shelley's "ideas" and, in reference to them, that much-canvassed question of the day, "the question of belief or disbelief":

It is not so much that thirty years ago I was able to read Shelley under an illusion which experience has dissipated, as that because the question of belief or disbelief did not arise I was in a much better position to enjoy the poetry. I can only regret that Shelley did not live to put his poetic gifts, which were certainly of the first order, at the service of more tenable beliefs—which need not have been, for my purposes, beliefs more acceptable to me.

This is, of course, a personal statement; but perhaps if one insists on the more obvious terms of literary criticism—more strictly critical terms—in which such a change might be explained, and suggests that the terms actually used might be found unfortunate in their effect, the impertinence will not be unpardonable. It does, in short, seem worth endeavouring to make finally plain that, when one dissents from persons who, sympathizing with Shelley's revolutionary doctrines and with his idealistic ardours and fervours—with his "beliefs," exalt him as a poet, it is strictly the "poetry" one is criticizing. There would also appear to be some reason for insisting that in finding Shelley almost unreadable one need not be committing

oneself to a fashionably limited taste—an inability to appreciate unfashionable kinds of excellence or to understand a use of words that is
unlike Hopkins's or Donne's.

It will be well to start, in fact, by examining
the working of Shelley's poetry—his characteristic modes of expression—as exemplified in
one of his best poems.

Thou on whose stream, mid the steep sky's com-
    motion,
Loose clouds like earth's decaying leaves are shed,
Shook from the tangled boughs of Heaven and
    Ocean,

Angels of rain and lightning: there are spread
On the blue surface of thine aëry surge,
Like the bright hair uplifted from the head

Of some fierce Maenad, even from the dim verge
Of the horizon to the zenith's height,
The locks of the approaching storm.

The sweeping movement of the verse, with the
accompanying plangency, is so potent that, as
many can testify, it is possible to have been for
years familiar with the Ode—to know it by
heart—without asking the obvious questions.
In what respects are the "loose clouds" like
"decaying leaves"? The correspondence is certainly not in shape, colour or way of moving. It
is only the vague general sense of windy tumult
that associates the clouds and the leaves; and,
accordingly, the appropriateness of the metaphor "stream" in the first line is not that it
suggests a surface on which, like leaves, the
clouds might be "shed," but that it contributes
to the general "streaming" effect in which the
inappropriateness of "shed" passes unnoticed.
What again, are those "tangled boughs of
Heaven and Ocean"? They stand for nothing
that Shelley could have pointed to in the scene
before him; the "boughs," it is plain, have
grown out of the "leaves" in the previous line,
and we are not to ask what the tree is. Nor are
we to scrutinize closely the "stream" metaphor
as developed: that "blue surface" must be the
concave of the sky, an oddly smooth surface for
a "surge"—if we consider a moment. But in

this poetic surge, while we let ourselves be
swept along, there is no considering, the image
doesn't challenge any inconvenient degree of
realization, and the oddness is lost. Then again,
in what ways does the approach of a storm
("loose clouds like earth's decaying leaves,"
"like ghosts from an enchanter fleeing") suggest streaming hair? The appropriateness of the
Maenad, clearly, lies in the pervasive suggestion of frenzied onset, and we are not to ask
whether her bright hair is to be seen as streaming out in front of her (as, there is no need to
assure ourselves, it might be doing if she were
running before a still swifter gale: in the kind
of reading that got so far as proposing to itself
this particular reassurance no general satisfaction could be exacted from Shelley's imagery).

Here, clearly, in these peculiarities of imagery and sense, peculiarities analysable locally
in the mode of expression, we have the manifestation of essential characteristics—the Shelleyan characteristics as envisaged by the criticism that works on a philosophical plane and
makes judgments of a moral order. In the
growth of those "tangled boughs" out of the
leaves, exemplifying as it does a general tendency of the images to forget the status of the
metaphor or simile that introduced them and
to assume an autonomy and a right to propa-
gate, so that we lose in confused generations
and perspectives the perception or thought that
was the ostensible *raison d'être* of imagery, we
have a recognized essential trait of Shelley's:
his weak grasp upon the actual. This weakness,
of course, commonly has more or less creditable accounts given of it—idealism, Platonism
and so on; and even as unsentimental a judge
as Mr. Santayana correlates Shelley's inability
to learn from experience with his having been
born a "nature preformed," a "spokesman of
the *a priori*," "a dogmatic, inspired, perfect and
incorrigible creature."[1] It seems to me that
Mr. Santayana's essay, admirable as it is, rates
the poetry too high. But for the moment it will
be enough to recall limitations that are hardly

---

[1] See the essay on Shelley in *Winds of Doctrine*.

disputed: Shelley was not gifted for drama or narrative. Having said this, I realize that I had forgotten the conventional standing of *The Cenci*; but controversy may be postponed: it is at any rate universally agreed that (to shift tactfully to positive terms) Shelley's genius was "essentially lyrical."

This predicate would, in common use, imply a special emotional intensity—a vague gloss, but it is difficult to go further without slipping into terms that are immediately privative and limiting. Thus there is certainly a sense in which Shelley's poetry is peculiarly emotional, and when we try to define this sense we find ourselves invoking an absence of something. The point may be best made, perhaps, by recalling the observation noted above, that one may have been long familiar with the *Ode to the West Wind* without ever having asked the obvious questions; questions that propose themselves at the first critical inspection. This poetry induces—depends for its success on inducing—a kind of attention that doesn't bring the critical intelligence into play: the imagery feels right, the associations work appropriately, if (as it takes conscious resistance not to do) one accepts the immediate feeling and doesn't slow down to think.

Shelley himself can hardly have asked the questions. Not that he didn't expend a great deal of critical labour upon his verse. "He composed rapidly and attained to perfection by intensive correction. He would sometimes write down a phrase with alterations and rejections time after time until it came within a measure of satisfying him. Words are frequently substituted for others and lines interpolated." The *Ode to the West Wind* itself, as is shown in the repository[2] of fragments the preface to which supplies these observations, profited by the process described, which must be allowed to have been in some sense critical. But the critical part of Shelley's creative labour was a matter of getting the verse to feel right, and

feeling, for Shelley as a poet, had—as the insistent concern for "rightness," the typical final product being what it is, serves to emphasize—little to do with thinking (though Shelley was in some ways a very intelligent man).

We have here, if not sufficient justification for the predicate "essentially lyrical," certainly a large part of the reason for Shelley's being found essentially poetical by the succeeding age. He counted, in fact, for a great deal in what came to be the prevailing idea of "the poetical"—the idea that had its latest notable statement in Professor Housman's address, *The Name and Nature of Poetry*. The Romantic conceptions of genius and inspiration[3] developed (the French Revolution and its ideological background must, of course, be taken into account) in reaction against the Augustan insistence on the social and the rational. When Wordsworth says that "all good poetry is the spontaneous overflow of powerful feelings" he is of his period, though the intended force of this dictum, the force it has in its context and in relation to Wordsworth's own practice, is very different from that given it when Shelley assents, or when it is assimilated to Byron's "poetry is the lava of the imagination, whose eruption prevents an earthquake."[4] But Byron was for the young Tennyson (and the Ruskin parents)[5] the poet, and Shelley (Browning's "Sun-treader") was the idol of the undergraduate Tennyson and his fellow Apostles, and, since the poetry of "the age of Wordsworth" became canonical, the assent given to Wordsworth's dictum has commonly been Shelleyan.

---

[2] *Verse and Prose from the Manuscripts of Percy Bysshe Shelley.* Edited by Sir John C. E. Shelley-Rolls, Bart., and Roger Ingpen.

[3] See *Four Words* (now reprinted in *Words and Idioms*), by Logan Pearsall Smith.

[4] *Letters and Journals*, ed. R. E. Prothero, vol. iii, p. 405 (1900). (I am indebted for this quotation to Mr. F. W. Bateson's *English Poetry and the English Language*.)

[5] "His ideal of my future,—now entirely formed in conviction of my genius,—was that I should enter at college into the best society, take all the best prizes every year, and a double first to finish with; marry Lady Clara Vere de Vere; write poetry as good as Byron's, only pious; preach sermons as good as Bossuet's, only Protestant; be made, at forty, Bishop of Winchester, and at fifty, Primate of England." *Praeterita*, vol. i, p. 340 (1886).

The force of Shelley's insistence on spontaneity is simple and unequivocal. It will be enough to recall a representative passage or two from the *Defence of Poetry*:

for the mind in creation is as a fading coal, which some invisible influence, like an inconstant wind, awakes to transitory brightness; this power arises from within, like the colour of a flower which fades and changes as it is developed, and the conscious portions of our nature are unprophetic either of its approach or its departure.

"Inspiration" is not something to be tested, clarified, defined and developed in composition,

but when composition begins, inspiration is already on the decline, and the most glorious poetry that has ever been communicated to the world is probably a feeble shadow of the original conceptions of the poet. . . . The toil and delay recommended by critics can be justly interpreted to mean no more than a careful observation of the inspired moments, and an artificial connexion of the spaces between their suggestions, by the intertexture of conventional expressions; a necessity only imposed by the limitedness of the poetical faculty itself. . . .

The "poetical faculty," we are left no room for doubting, can, of its very nature, have nothing to do with any discipline, and can be associated with conscious effort only mechanically and externally, and when Shelley says that Poetry

is not subject to the control of the active powers of the mind, and that its birth and recurrence have no necessary connexion with consciousness or will

he is not saying merely that the "active powers of the mind" are insufficient in themselves for creation—that poetry cannot be written merely by taking thought. The effect of Shelley's eloquence is to hand poetry over to a sensibility that has no more dealings with intelligence than it can help; to a "poetic faculty" that, for its duly responsive vibrating (though the poet must reverently make his pen as sensitive an instrument as possible to "observe"—in the scientific sense—the vibrations), demands that

active intelligence shall be, as it were, switched off.

Shelley, of course, had ideas and ideals; he wrote philosophical essays, and it need not be irrelevant to refer, in discussing his poetry, to Plato, Godwin and other thinkers. But there is nothing grasped in the poetry—no object offered for contemplation, no realized presence to persuade or move us by what it is. A. C. Bradley, remarking that "Shelley's ideals of good, whether as a character or as a mode of life, resting as they do on abstraction from the mass of real existence, tend to lack body and individuality," adds: "But we must remember that Shelley's strength and weakness are closely allied, and it may be that the very abstractness of his ideal was a condition of that quivering intensity of aspiration towards it in which his poetry is unequalled." [6] That is the best that can be respectably said. Actually, that "quivering intensity," offered in itself apart from any substance, offered instead of any object, is what, though it may make Shelley intoxicating at fifteen makes him almost unreadable, except in very small quantities of his best, to the mature. Even when he is in his own way unmistakably a distinguished poet, as in *Prometheus Unbound*, it is impossible to go on reading him at any length with pleasure; the elusive imagery, the high-pitched emotions, the tone and movement, the ardours, ecstasies and despairs, are too much the same all through. The effect is of vanity and emptiness (Arnold was right) as well as monotony.

The force of the judgment that feeling in Shelley's poetry is divorced from thought needs examining further. Any suspicion that Donne is the implied criterion will, perhaps, be finally averted if for the illuminating contrast we go to Wordsworth. Wordsworth is another "Romantic" poet; he too is undramatic; and he too invites the criticism (Arnold, his devoted admirer, made it) that he lacks variety. "Thought" will hardly be found an assertive presence in his best poetry; in so far as the term

---

[6] *Oxford Lectures on Poetry*, p. 167.

suggests an overtly active energy it is decidedly inappropriate. "Emotion," his own word, is the word most readers would insist on, though they would probably judge Wordsworth's emotion to be less lyrical than Shelley's. The essential difference, however—and it is a very important one—seems, for present purposes, more relevantly stated in the terms I used in discussing Wordsworth's "recollection in tranquillity." The process covered by this phrase was one of emotional discipline, critical exploration of experience, pondered valuation and maturing reflection. As a result of it an organization is engaged in Wordsworth's poetry, and the activity and standards of critical intelligence are implicit.

An associated difference was noted in the sureness with which Wordsworth grasps the world of common perception. The illustration suggested was *The Simplon Pass* in comparison with Shelley's *Mont Blanc*. The element of Wordsworth in *Mont Blanc* (it is perceptible in these opening lines) serves only to enhance the contrast:

The everlasting universe of things
Flows through the mind, and rolls its rapid
waves,
Now dark—now glittering—now reflecting
gloom—
Now lending splendour, where from secret
springs
The source of human thought its tribute brings
Of waters—with a sound but half its own,
Such as a feeble brook will oft assume
In the wild woods, among the mountains lone,
Where waterfalls around it leap for ever,
Where woods and winds contend, and a vast
river
Over its rocks ceaselessly bursts and raves.

The metaphorical and the actual, the real and the imagined, the inner and the outer, could hardly be more unsortably and indistinguishably confused. The setting, of course, provides special excuse for bewildered confusion; but Shelley takes eager advantage of the excuse and the confusion is characteristic—what might be found unusual in *Mont Blanc* is a certain compelling vividness. In any case, Wordsworth himself is explicitly offering a sense of sublime bewilderment, similarly inspired:

Black drizzling crags that spake by the wayside
As if a voice were in them, the sick sight
And giddy prospect of the raving stream,
The unfettered clouds and region of the heavens,
Tumult and peace, the darkness and the light—
Were all like workings of one mind, the features
Of the same face . . .

He is, of course, recollecting in tranquillity; but the collectedness of those twenty lines (as against Shelley's one hundred and forty) does not belong merely to the record; it was present (or at least the movement towards it was) in the experience, as those images, "one mind," "the same face"—epitomizing, as they do, the contrast with Shelley's ecstatic dissipation—may fairly be taken to testify.

This comparison does not aim immediately at a judgment of relative value. *Mont Blanc* is very interesting as well as idiosyncratic, and is not obviously the product of the less rare gift. There are, nevertheless, critical judgments to be made—judgments concerning the emotional quality of Wordsworth's poetry and of Shelley's: something more than mere description of idiosyncrasy is in view. What should have come out in the comparison that started as a note on Wordsworth's grasp of the outer world is the unobtrusiveness with which that "outer" turns into "inner": the antithesis, clearly, is not altogether, for present purposes, a simple one to apply. What is characteristic of Wordsworth is to grasp surely (which, in the nature of the case, must be delicately and subtly) what he offers, whether this appears as belonging to the outer world—the world as perceived, or to inner experience. He seems always to be presenting an object (wherever this may belong) and the emotion seems to derive from what is presented. The point is very obviously and impressively exemplified in *A slumber did my spirit seal*, which shows Wordsworth at his supreme height. Here (compare it with the *Ode to the West Wind*, where we have Shelley's genius at its best; or, if something more obviously comparable is required, with Tennyson's *Break, break, break*) there is no emotional comment—nothing "emotional" in phrasing, movement or tone; the facts seem to be presented barely, and the emotional force to be generated by them in the reader's mind when he has taken them in—generated by the two juxtaposed stanzas, in the contrast between the situations or states they represent.

Shelley, at his best and worst, offers the emotion in itself, unattached, in the void. "In itself" "for itself"—it is an easy shift to the pejorative implications of "for its own sake"; just as, for a poet with the habit of sensibility and expression described, it was an easy shift to deserving them. For Shelley is obnoxious to the pejorative implications of "habit": being inspired was, for him, too apt to mean surrendering to a kind of hypnotic rote of favourite images, associations and words. "Inspiration," there not being an organization for it to engage (as in Wordsworth, whose sameness is of a different order from Shelley's, there was), had only poetical habits to fall back on. We have them in their most innocent aspect in those favourite words: *radiant, aërial, odorous, daedal, faint, sweet, bright, wingèd, -inwoven*, and the rest of the fondled vocabulary that any reader of Shelley could go on enumerating. They manifest themselves as decidedly deplorable in *The Cloud* and *To a Skylark*, which illustrate the dangers of fostering the kind of inspiration that works only when critical intelligence is switched off. These poems may be not unfairly described as the products of switching poetry on.[7] There has been in recent years some controversy about particular points in *To a Skylark*, and there are a score or more points inviting adverse criticism. But this need hardly be offered; it is, or should be, so plain that the poem is a mere tumbled out spate

("spontaneous overflow") of poeticalities, the place of each one of which Shelley could have filled with another without the least difficulty and without making any essential difference. They are held together by the pervasive "lyrical emotion," and that this should be capable of holding them together is comment enough on the nature of its strength.

Cheaper surrenders to inspiration may easily be found in the collected Shelley; there are, for instance, gross indulgences in the basest Regency album taste.[8] But criticism of Shelley has something more important to deal with than mere bad poetry; or, rather, there are badnesses inviting the criticism that involves moral judgments. It must have already appeared (it has virtually been said) that surrendering to inspiration cannot, for a poet of Shelley's emotional habits, have been very distinguishable from surrendering to temptation. The point comes out in an element of the favoured vocabulary not exemplified above: *charnel, corpse, phantom, liberticide, aghast, ghastly* and so on. The wrong approach to emotion, the approach from the wrong side or end (so to speak), is apparent here; Shelley would clearly have done well not to have indulged these habits and these likings: the viciousness and corruption are immediately recognizable. But viciousness and corruption do not less attend upon likings for tender ("I love Love"),[9] sympathetic, exalted and ecstatic emotions, and may be especially expected to do so in a mind as little able to hold an object in front of it as Shelley's was.

The transition from the lighter concerns of literary criticism to the diagnosis of radical disabilities and perversions, such as call for moral comment, may be conveniently illustrated from a favourite anthology-piece, *When the lamp is shattered*:

> When the lamp is shattered
> The light in the dust lies dead—

---

[7]   Poesy's unfailing river
       Which through Albion winds forever
       Lashing with melodious wave
       Many a sacred Poet's grave . . .
       —*Lines Written Among the Euganean Hills*

[8] See, for instance, the poem beginning, "That time is dead for ever, child."

[9] See the last stanza of "Rarely, rarely comest thou."

When the cloud is scattered
The rainbow's glory is shed.
When the lute is broken,
Sweet tones are remembered not;
When the lips have spoken,
Loved accents are soon forgot.

As music and splendour
Survive not the lamp and the lute,
The heart's echoes render
No song when the spirit is mute:—
No song but sad dirges,
Like the wind through a ruined cell;
Or the mournful surges
That ring the dead seaman's knell.

When hearts have once mingled
Love first leaves the well-built nest;
The weak one is singled
To endure what it once possessed.
O Love! who bewailest
The frailty of all things here,
Why choose you the frailest
For your cradle, your home, and your bier?

Its passions will rock thee
As the storms rock the ravens on high;
Bright reason will mock thee,
Like the sun from a wintry sky.
From thy nest every rafter
Will rot, and thine eagle home
Leave thee naked to laughter,
When leaves fall and cold winds come.

The first two stanzas call for no very close attention—to say so, indeed, is to make the main criticism, seeing that they offer a show of insistent argument. However, reading with an unsolicited closeness, one may stop at the second line and ask whether the effect got with "lies dead" is legitimate. Certainly, the emotional purpose of the poem is served, but the emotional purpose that went on being served in that way would be suspect. Leaving the question in suspense, perhaps, one passes to "shed"; "shed" as tears, petals and coats are shed, or as light is shed? The latter would be a rather more respectable use of the word in connexion with a rainbow's glory, but the context indicates the former. Only in the vaguest

and slackest state of mind—of imagination and thought—could one so describe the fading of a rainbow; but for the right reader "shed" sounds right, the alliteration with "shattered" combining with the verse-movement to produce a kind of inevitability. And, of course, suggesting tears and the last rose of summer, it suits with the general emotional effect. The nature of this is by now so unmistakable that the complete nullity of the clinching "so," when it arrives—of the two lines that justify the ten preparatory lines of analogy—seems hardly worth stopping to note:

The heart's echoes render
No song when the spirit is mute.

Nor is it surprising that there should turn out to be a song after all, and a pretty powerful one—for those who like that sort of thing; the "sad dirges," the "ruined cell," the "mournful surges" and the "dead seaman's knell" being immediately recognizable as currency values. Those who take pleasure in recognizing and accepting them are not at the same time exacting about sense.

The critical interest up to this point has been to see Shelley, himself (when inspired) so unexacting about sense, giving himself so completely to sentimental banalities. With the next stanza it is much the same, though the emotional *clichés* take on a grosser unction and the required abeyance of thought (and imagination) becomes more remarkable. In what form are we to imagine Love leaving the well-built nest? For readers who get so far as asking, there can be no acceptable answer. It would be unpoetically literal to suggest that, since the weak one is singled, the truant must be the mate, and, besides, it would raise unnecessary difficulties. Perhaps the mate, the strong one, is what the weak one, deserted by Love, whose alliance made possession once possible, now has to endure? But the suggestion is frivolous; the sense is plain enough—enough, that is, for those who respond to the sentiment. Sufficient recognition of the sense depends neither on thinking, nor on realization of the metaphors, but on response to the sentimental common-places: it is only when intelligence and imagination insist on intruding that difficulties arise. So plain is this that there would be no point in contemplating the metaphorical complexity that would develop if we could take the tropes seriously and tried to realize Love making of the weak one, whom it (if we evade the problem of sex) leaves behind in the well-built nest, a cradle, a home and a bier.

The last stanza brings a notable change; it alone in the poem has any distinction, and its personal quality, characteristically Shelleyan, stands out against the sentimental conventionality of the rest. The result is to compel a more radical judgment on the poem than has yet been made. In "Its passions will rock thee" the "passions" must be those of Love, so that it can no longer be Love that is being apostrophized. Who, then, is "thee"? The "frailest"—the "weak one"—it would appear. But any notion one may have had that the "weak one," as the conventional sentiments imply, is the woman must be abandoned: the "eagle home," to which the "well-built nest" so incongruously turns, is the Poet's. The familiar timbre, the desolate intensity (note particularly the use of "bright" in "bright reason"), puts it beyond doubt that Shelley is, characteristically, addressing himself—the "pardlike Spirit beautiful and swift," the "Love in desolation masked," the "Power girt round with weakness."

Characteristically: that is, Shelley's characteristic pathos is self-regarding, directed upon an idealized self in the way suggested by the tags just quoted.[10] This is patently so in some of his best poetry; for instance, in the *Ode to the West Wind*. Even there, perhaps, one may find something too like an element of luxury in the poignancy (at any rate, one's limiting criticism of the Ode would move towards such a judgment); and that in general there must be dangers and weakness attending upon such a habit will hardly be denied. The poem just examined shows how gross may be, in Shelley, the corruptions that are incident. He can make self-pity a luxury at such a level that the conventional pathos of album poeticizing, not excluding the banalities about (it is plainly so in the third stanza) the sad lot of woman, can come in to gratify the appetite.

The abeyance of thought exhibited by the first three stanzas now takes on a more sinister aspect. The switching-off of intelligence that is necessary if the sentiments of the third stanza are to be accepted has now to be invoked in explanation of a graver matter—Shelley's ability to accept the grosser, the truly corrupt, gratifications that have just been indicated. The antipathy of his sensibility to any play of the critical mind, the uncongeniality of intelligence to inspiration, these clearly go in Shelley, not merely with a capacity for momentary self-deceptions and insincerities, but with a radical lack of self-knowledge. He could say of Wordsworth, implying the opposite of himself, that

> he never could
> Fancy another situation
> From which to dart his contemplation
> Than that wherein he stood.

But, for all his altruistic fervours and his fancied capacity for projecting his sympathies, Shelley is habitually—it is no new observation—his own hero: Alastor, Laon, The Sensitive Plant

> (It loves, even like Love, its deep heart is full,
> It desires what it has not, the Beautiful)

and Prometheus. It is characteristic that he should say to the West Wind

> A heavy weight of hours has chained and bowed
> One too like thee: tameless, and swift, and proud,

and conclude:

> Be thou, Spirit fierce,
> My spirit! Be thou me, impetuous one!

---

[10] Cf. Senseless is the breast, and cold,
Which relenting love would fold;
Bloodless are the veins and chill
Which the pulse of pain did fill;
Every little living nerve
That from bitter words did swerve
Round the tortured lips and brow,
Are like sapless leaflets now,
Frozen upon December's brow.
—*Lines Written Among the Euganean Hills*

About the love of such a nature there is likely at the best to be a certain innocent selfishness. And it is with fervour that Shelley says, as he is always saying implicitly, "I love Love." Mr. Santayana acutely observes: "In him, as in many people, too intense a need of loving excludes the capacity for intelligent sympathy." Perhaps love generally has less in it of intelligent sympathy than the lover supposes, and is less determined by the object of love; but Shelley, we have seen, was, while on the one hand conscious of ardent altruism, on the other peculiarly weak in his hold on objects—peculiarly unable to realize them as existing in their own natures and their own right. His need of loving (in a sense that was not, perhaps, in the full focus of Mr. Santayana's intention) comes out in the erotic element that, as already remarked in these pages, the texture of the poetry pervasively exhibits. There is hardly any need to illustrate here the tender, caressing, voluptuous effects and suggestions of the favourite vocabulary and imagery. The consequences of the need, or "love," of loving, combined, as it was, with a notable lack of self-knowledge and a capacity for ecstatic idealizing, are classically extant in *Epipsychidion*.

The love of loathing is, naturally, less conscious than the love of Love. It may fairly be said to involve a love of Hate, if not of hating: justification enough for putting it this way is provided by *The Cenci*, which exhibits a perverse luxury of insistence, not merely upon horror, but upon malignity. This work, of course, is commonly held to require noting as, in the general account of Shelley, a remarkable exception: his genius may be essentially lyrical, but he can, transcending limitations, write great drama. This estimate of *The Cenci* is certainly a remarkable instance of *vis inertiae*—of the power of conventional valuation to perpetuate itself, once established. For it takes no great discernment to see that *The Cenci* is very bad and that its badness is characteristic. Shelley, as usual, is the hero—here the heroine; his relation to Beatrice is of the same order as his relation to Alastor and Prometheus, and the

usual vices should not be found more acceptable because of the show of drama.

Nor is this show the less significantly bad because Shelley doesn't know where it comes from—how he is contriving it. He says in his *Preface* that an idea suggested by Calderon is "the only plagiarism which I have intentionally committed in the whole piece." Actually, not only is the "whole piece" Shakespearian in inspiration (how peculiarly dubious an affair inspiration was apt to be for Shelley we have seen), it is full of particular echoes of Shakespeare—echoes protracted, confused and woolly; plagiarisms, that is, of the worst kind. This Shakespearianizing, general and particular is—and not the less so for its unconsciousness —quite damning. It means that Shelley's drama and tragedy do not grow out of any realized theme; there is nothing grasped at the core of the piece. Instead there is Beatrice-Shelley, in whose martyrdom the Count acts Jove— with more than Jovian gusto:

> I do not feel as if I were a man,
> But like a fiend appointed to chastise
> The offences of some unremembered world.
> My blood is running up and down my veins;
> A fearful pleasure makes it prick and tingle:
> I feel a giddy sickness of strange awe;
> My heart is beating with an expectation
> Of horrid joy.

The pathos is of corresponding corruptness. The habits that enable Shelley to be unconscious about this kind of indulgence enable him at the same time to turn it into tragic drama by virtue of an unconscious effort to be Shakespeare.

There are, of course, touches of Webster: Beatrice in the trial scene is commonly recognized to have borrowed an effect or two from the White Devil. But the Shakespearian promptings are everywhere, in some places almost ludicrously assorted, obvious and thick. For instance, Act III, Sc. ii starts (stage direction: "Thunder and the sound of a storm") by being at line two obviously Lear. At line eight Othello comes in and carries on for ten lines;

and he reasserts himself at line fifty. At line fifty-five Hamlet speaks. At line seventy-eight we get an effect from *Macbeth*, to be followed by many more in the next act, during which, after much borrowed suspense, the Count's murder is consummated.

The quality of the dramatic poetry and the relation between Shelley and Shakespeare must, for reasons of space, be represented—the example is a fair one—by a single brief passage (Act V, Sc. iv, l. 48):

O

My God! Can it be possible I have
To die so suddenly? So young to go
Under the obscure, cold, rotting wormy ground!
To be nailed down into a narrow place;
To see no more sweet sunshine; hear no more
Blithe voice of living thing; muse not again
Upon familiar thoughts, sad, yet thus lost—
How fearful! to be nothing! Or to be . . .
What? Oh, where am I? Let me go not mad!
Sweet Heaven, forgive weak thoughts! If there
    should be
No God, no Heaven, no Earth in the void world;
The wide, gray, lampless, deep, unpeopled
    world!

This patently recalls Claudio's speech in *Measure for Measure* (Act III, Sc. i):

Ay, but to die, and go we know not where;
To lie in cold obstruction and to rot;
This sensible warm motion to become
A kneaded clod; and the delighted spirit
To bathe in fiery floods, or to reside
In thrilling region of thick-ribbed ice;
To be imprisoned in the viewless winds,
And blown with restless violence round about
The pendent world; or to be worse than worst
Of those that lawless and incertain thoughts
Imagine howling:—'tis too horrible!
The weariest and most loathed worldly life
That age, ache, penury, and imprisonment
Can lay on nature is a paradise
To what we fear of death.

The juxtaposition is enough to expose the vague, generalizing externality of Shelley's rendering. Claudio's words spring from a vividly realized particular situation; from the imagined experience of a given mind in a given critical

moment that is felt from the inside—that is lived—with sharp concrete particularity. Claudio's "Ay, but to die . . ." is not insistently and voluminously emotional like Beatrice's ("wildly")

O

My God! Can it be possible . . .

but it is incomparably more intense. That "cold obstruction" is not abstract; it gives rather the essence of the situation in which Claudio shrinkingly imagines himself—the sense of the warm body (given by "cold") struggling ("obstruction" takes an appropriate effort to pronounce) in vain with the suffocating earth. Sentience, warmth and motion, the essentials of being alive as epitomized in the next line, recoil from death, realized brutally in the concrete (the "clod" is a vehement protest, as "clay," which "kneaded" nevertheless brings appropriately in, would not have been). Sentience, in the "delighted spirit," plunges, not into the delightful coolness suggested by "bathe," but into the dreadful opposite, and warmth and motion shudder away from the icy prison ("reside" is analogous in working to "bathe"). The shudder is there in "thrilling," which also—such alliteration as that of "thrilling region" and "thick-ribbed" is not accidental in a Shakespearian passage of this quality— gives the sharp reverberating report of the ice as, in the intense cold, it is forced up into ridges or ribs (at which, owing to the cracks, the thickness of the ice can be seen).

But there is no need to go on. The point has been sufficiently enforced that, though this vivid concreteness of realization lodged the passage in Shelley's mind, to become at the due moment "inspiration," the passage inspired is nothing but wordy emotional generality. It does not grasp and present anything, but merely makes large gestures towards the kind of effect deemed appropriate. We are told emphatically what the emotion is that we are to feel; emphasis and insistence serving instead of realization and advertising its default. The intrusion of the tag from Lear brings out the

vague generality of that unconscious set at being Shakespeare which Shelley took for dramatic inspiration.

Inspection of *The Cenci*, then, confirms all
the worst in the account of Shelley. Further
confirmation would not need much seeking;
but, returning to the fact of his genius, it is
pleasanter, and more profitable, to recall what
may be said by way of explaining how he
should have been capable of the worst. His upbringing was against him. As Mr. Santayana
says: "Shelley seems hardly to have been
brought up; he grew up in the nursery among
his young sisters, at school among the rude
boys, without any affectionate guidance, without imbibing any religious or social tradition."
Driven in on himself, he nourished the inner
life of adolescence on the trashy fantasies and
cheap excitements of the Terror school. The
phase of serious tradition in which, in incipient
maturity, he began to practise poetry was, in a
subtler way, as unfavourable: Shelley needed
no encouragement to cultivate spontaneity of
emotion and poetical abeyance of thought.
Then the state of the world at the time must,
in its effect on a spirit of Shelley's sensitive humanity and idealizing bent, be allowed to account for a great deal—as the sonnet, *England
in 1819*, so curiously intimates:

An old, mad, blind, despised, and dying king,—
Princes, the dregs of their dull race, who flow
Through public scorn,—mud from a muddy
    spring,—
Rulers who neither see, nor feel, nor know,
But leech-like to their fainting country cling,
Till they drop, blind in blood, without a blow,—
A people starved and stabbed in the untilled
    field,—
An army, which liberticide and prey
Makes as a two-edged sword to all who wield,—
Golden and sanguine laws which tempt and slay;
Religion Christless, Godless—a book sealed;
A Senate,—Time's worst statute unrepealed,—
Are graves, from which a glorious Phantom may
Burst, to illumine our tempestuous day.

The contrast between the unusual strength
(for Shelley) of the main body of the sonnet

and the pathetic weakness of the final couplet
is eloquent. Contemplation of the actual world
being unendurable, Shelley devotes himself to
the glorious Phantom that may (an oddly ironical stress results from the rime position) work
a sudden miraculous change but is in any case
as vague as Demogorgon and as unrelated to
actuality—to which Shelley's Evil is correspondingly unrelated.

The strength of the sonnet, though unusual
in kind for Shelley, is not of remarkably distinguished quality in itself; the kindred strength
of *The Mask of Anarchy* is. Of this poem Professor Elton says: [11] "There is a likeness in it
to Blake's [gift] which has often been noticed;
the same kind of anvil-stroke, and the same
use of an awkward simplicity for the purposes
of epigram." The likeness to Blake is certainly
there—much more of a likeness than would
have seemed possible from the characteristic
work. It lies, not in any assumed broadsheet
naïveté or crudity such as the account cited
might perhaps suggest, but in a rare emotional integrity and force, deriving from a
clear, disinterested and mature vision.

> When one fled past, a maniac maid,
> And her name was Hope, she said:
> But she looked more like Despair,
> And she cried out in the air:
>
> 'My father Time is weak and gray
> With waiting for a better day;
> See how idiot-like he stands,
> Fumbling with his palsied hands!
>
> He has had child after child,
> And the dust of death is piled
> Over every one but me—
> Misery, oh, Misery!'
>
> Then she lay down in the street,
> Right before the horses' feet,
> Expecting, with a patient eye,
> Murder, Fraud, and Anarchy.

These stanzas do not represent all the virtue
of the poem, but they show its unusual purity
and strength. In spite of "Murder, Fraud, and

[11] *Survey of English Literature, 1780–1830*, Vol.
II, p. 202.

Anarchy," there is nothing of the usual Shelleyan emotionalism—no suspicion of indulgence, insistence, corrupt will or improper approach. The emotion seems to inhere in the vision communicated, the situation grasped: Shelley sees what is in front of him too clearly, and with too pure a piety and indignation, to have any regard for his emotions as such; the emotional value of what is presented asserts itself, or rather, does not need asserting. Had he used and developed his genius in the spirit of *The Mask of Anarchy* he would have been a much greater, and a much more readable, poet.

But *The Mask of Anarchy* is little more than a marginal throw-off, and gets perhaps too much stress in even so brief a distinguishing mention as this. The poetry in which Shelley's genius manifests itself characteristically, and for which he has his place in the English tradition, is much more closely related to his weaknesses. It would be perverse to end without recognizing that he achieved memorable things in modes of experience that were peculiarly congenial to the European mind in that phase of its history and are of permanent interest. The sensibility expressed in the *Ode to the West Wind* is much more disablingly limited than current valuation allows, but the consummate expression is rightly treasured. The Shelleyan confusion appears, perhaps, at its most poignant in *The Triumph of Life*, the late unfinished poem. This poem has been paralleled with the revised *Hyperion*, and it is certainly related by more than the *terza rima* to Dante. There is in it a profounder note of disenchantment than before, a new kind of desolation, and, in its questioning, a new and profoundly serious concern for reality:

. . . their might
Could not repress the mystery within,
And for the morn of truth they feigned, deep
  night

Caught them ere evening . . .

For in the battle Life and they did wage,
She remained conqueror . . .

"Whence camest thou? and whither goest thou?
How did thy course begin?" I said, "and why?

Mine eyes are sick of this perpetual flow
Of people, and my heart sick of one sad
  thought—
Speak!"

       as one between desire and shame
Suspended, I said—If, as it doth seem,
Thou comest from the realm without a name

Into this valley of perpetual dream,
Show whence I came and where I am, and
  why—
Pass not away upon the passing stream.

But in spite of the earnest struggle to grasp something real, the sincere revulsion from personal dreams and fantasies, the poem itself is a drifting phantasmagoria—bewildering and bewildered. Vision opens into vision, dream unfolds within dream, and the visionary perspectives, like those of the imagery in the passage of *Mont Blanc*, shift elusively and are lost; and the failure to place the various phases or levels of visionary drift with reference to any grasped reality is the more significant because of the palpable effort. Nevertheless, *The Triumph of Life* is among the few things one can still read and go back to in Shelley when he has become, generally, "almost unreadable."

Shelley's part in the later notion of "the poetical" has been sufficiently indicated. His handling of the medium assimilates him readily, as an influence, to the Spenserian-Miltonic line running through *Hyperion* to Tennyson. Milton is patently present in *Alastor*, the earliest truly Shelleyan poem; and *Adonais*—

Afar the melancholy thunder moaned,
Pale Ocean in unquiet slumber lay

—relates him as obviously to *Hyperion* as to *Lycidas*. Indeed, to compare the verse of *Hyperion*, where the Miltonic Grand Style is transmuted by the Spenserianizing Keats, with that of *Adonais* is to bring out the essential relation between the organ resonances of *Para-*

dise Lost and the pastoral melodizing [12] of *Ly-cidas*. Mellifluous mourning in *Adonais* is a more fervent luxury than in *Lycidas*, and more declamatory ("Life like a dome of many-coloured glass"—the famous imagery is hap-

[12] O Golden tongued Romance, with serene lute!
  Fair plumed Syren, Queen of far-away!
  Leave melodizing on this wintry day,
  Shut up thine olden pages, and be mute:
    —Keats' *Sonnet: On Sitting Down to Read*
    King Lear *Once Again*

pily conscious of being impressive, but the impressiveness is for the spell-bound, for those sharing the simple happiness of intoxication); and it is, in the voluptuous self-absorption with which the medium enjoys itself, rather nearer to Tennyson.

But, as was virtually said in the discussion of imagery from the *Ode to the West Wind*, the Victorian poet with whom Shelley has some peculiar affinities is Swinburne.

THE IRONY OF SWIFT (1934)

SWIFT is a great English writer. For opening with this truism I have a reason: I wish to discuss Swift's writings—to examine what they are; and they are (as the extant commentary bears witness) of such a kind that it is peculiarly difficult to discuss them without shifting the focus of discussion to the kind of man that Swift was. What is most interesting in them does not so clearly belong to the realm of things made and detached that literary criticism, which has certainly not the less its duties towards Swift, can easily avoid turning—unawares, and that is, degenerating—into something else. In the attempt to say what makes these writings so remarkable, reference to the man who wrote is indeed necessary; but there are distinctions. For instance, one may (it appears), having offered to discuss the nature and import of Swift's satire, find oneself countering imputations of misanthropy with the argument that Swift earned the love of Pope, Arbuthnot, Gay, several other men and two women: this should not be found necessary by the literary critic. But the irrelevancies of Thackeray and of his castigator, the late Charles Whibley—irrelevancies not merely from the point of view of literary criticism—are too gross to need placarding; more insidious

deviations are possible.

The reason for the opening truism is also the reason for the choice of title. To direct the attention upon Swift's irony gives, I think, the best chance of dealing adequately, without deviation or confusion, with what is essential in his work. But it involves also (to anticipate an objection) a slight to the classical status of *Gulliver's Travels*, a book which, though it may represent Swift's most impressive achievement in the way of complete creation—the thing achieved and detached—does not give the best opportunities for examining his irony. And *Gulliver's Travels*, one readily agrees, hasn't its classical status for nothing. But neither is it for nothing that, suitably abbreviated, it has become a classic for children. What for the adult reader constitutes its peculiar force—what puts it in so different a class from *Robinson Crusoe*—resides for the most part in the fourth book (to a less extent in the third). The adult may re-read the first two parts, as he may *Robinson Crusoe*, with great interest, but his interest, apart from being more critically conscious, will not be of a different order from the child's. He will, of course, be aware of an ingenuity of political satire in *Lilliput*, but the political satire is, unless for historians, not very much alive today. And even the more general satire characteristic of the second book will not strike him as very subtle. His main satisfaction, a great deal enhanced, no doubt, by the ironic seasoning, will be that which Swift, the student of the *Mariner's Magazine* and of travellers' relations, aimed to supply in the bare precision and the matter-of-fact realness of his narrative.

But what in Swift is most important, the disturbing characteristic of his genius, is a peculiar emotional intensity; that which, in *Gulliver*, confronts us in the Struldbrugs and the Yahoos. It is what we find ourselves contemplating when elsewhere we examine his irony. To lay the stress upon an emotional intensity should be matter of commonplace: actually, in routine usage, the accepted word for Swift is "intellectual." We are told, for instance, that his is pre-eminently "intellectual satire" (though we are not told what satire is). For this formula the best reason some commentators can allege is the elaboration of analogies—their "exact and elaborate propriety" [1]—in *Gulliver*. But a muddled perception can hardly be expected to give a clear account of itself; the stress on Swift's "intellect" (Mr Herbert Read alludes to his "mighty intelligence") [2] registers, it would appear, a confused sense, not only of the mental exercise involved in his irony, but of the habitually critical attitude he maintains toward the world, and of the negative emotions he specializes in.

From "critical" to "negative" in this last sentence is, it will be observed, a shift of stress. There are writings of Swift where "critical" is the more obvious word (and where "intellectual" may seem correspondingly apt)—notably, the pamphlets or pamphleteering essays in which the irony is instrumental, directed and limited to a given end. The *Argument Against Abolishing Christianity* and the *Modest Proposal*, for instance, are discussible in the terms in which satire is commonly discussed: as the criticism of vice, folly, or other aberration, by some kind of reference to positive standards. But even here, even in the *Argument*, where Swift's ironic intensity undeniably directs itself

to the defence of something that he is intensely concerned to defend, the effect is essentially negative. The positive itself appears only negatively—a kind of skeletal presence, rigid enough, but without life or body; a necessary pre-condition, as it were, of directed negation. The intensity is purely destructive.

The point may be enforced by the obvious contrast with Gibbon—except that between Swift's irony and Gibbon's the contrast is so complete that any one point is difficult to isolate. Gibbon's irony, in the fifteenth chapter, may be aimed against, instead of for, Christianity, but contrasted with Swift's it is an assertion of faith. The decorously insistent pattern of Gibbonian prose insinuates a solidarity with the reader (the implied solidarity in Swift is itself ironical—a means to betrayal), establishes an understanding and habituates to certain assumptions. The reader, it is implied, is an eighteenth-century gentleman ("rational," "candid," "polite," "elegant," "humane"); eighteen hundred years ago he would have been a pagan gentleman, living by these same standards (those of absolute civilization); by these standards (present everywhere in the stylized prose and adroitly emphasized at key points in such phrases as "the polite Augustus," "the elegant mythology of the Greeks") the Jews and early Christians are seen to have been ignorant fanatics, uncouth and probably dirty. Gibbon as a historian of Christianity had, we know, limitations; but the positive standards by reference to which his irony works represent something impressively realized in eighteenth-century civilization; impressively "there" too in the grandiose, assured and ordered elegance of his history. (When, on the other hand, Lytton Strachey, with a Gibbonian period or phrase or word, a "remarkable," "oddly," or "curious," assures us that he feels an amused superiority to these Victorian puppets, he succeeds only in conveying his personal conviction that he feels amused and superior.)

Gibbon's irony, then, habituates and reassures, ministering to a kind of judicial certitude

---

[1] Churton Collins.
[2] *English Prose Style.*

or complacency. Swift's is essentially a matter of surprise and negation; its function is to defeat habit, to intimidate and to demoralize. What he assumes in the *Argument* is not so much a common acceptance of Christianity as that the reader will be ashamed to have to recognize how fundamentally unchristian his actual assumptions, motives, and attitudes are. And in general the implication is that it would shame people if they were made to recognize themselves unequivocally. If one had to justify this irony according to the conventional notion of satire, then its satiric efficacy would be to make comfortable non-recognition, the unconsciousness of habit, impossible.

A method of surprise does not admit of description in an easy formula. Surprise is a perpetually varied accompaniment of the grave, dispassionate, matter-of-fact tone in which Swift delivers his intensities. The dissociation of emotional intensity from its usual accompaniments inhibits the automatic defence-reaction:

He is a Presbyterian in politics, and an atheist in religion; but he chooses at present to whore with a Papist.

What bailiff would venture to arrest Mr Steele, now he has the honour to be your representative? and what bailiff ever scrupled it before?

Or inhibits, let us say, the normal response; since "defence" suggests that it is the "victim" whose surprise we should be contemplating, whereas it is our own, whether Swift's butt is Wharton or the atheist or mankind in general. "But satire, being levelled at all, is never resented for an offence by any, since every individual makes bold to understand it of others, and very wisely removes his particular part of the burden upon the shoulders of the World, which are broad enough and able to bear it." [3] There is, of course, no contradiction here; a complete statement would be complex. But, actually, the discussion of satire in terms of

[3] *A Tale of a Tub*: the Preface.

offence and castigation, victim and castigator, is unprofitable, though the idea of these has to be taken into account. What we are concerned with (the reminder is especially opportune) is an arrangement of words on the page and their effects—the emotions, attitudes and ideas that they organize.

Our reaction, as Swift says, is not that of the butt or victim; nevertheless, it necessarily entails some measure of sympathetic self-projection. We more often, probably, feel the effect of the words as an intensity in the castigator than as an effect upon a victim: the dissociation of animus from the usual signs defines for our contemplation a peculiarly intense contempt or disgust. When, as sometimes we have to do, we talk in terms of effect on the victim, then "surprise" becomes an obviously apt word; he is to be betrayed, again and again, into an incipient acquiescence:

Sixthly. This would be a great Inducement to Marriage, which all wise Nations have either encouraged by Rewards, or enforced by Laws and Penalties. It would increase the Care and Tenderness of Mothers towards their Children, when they were sure of a Settlement for Life, to the poor Babes, provided in some Sort by the Publick, to their annual Profit instead of Expence; we should soon see an honest Emulation among the married Women, *which of them could bring the fattest Child to the Market*. Men would become as *fond* of their Wives, during the Time of their Pregnancy, as they are now of their *Mares* in Foal, their *Cows* in Calf, or *Sows* when they are ready to farrow, nor offer to beat or kick them (as is too *frequent* a Practice) for fear of a Miscarriage.

The implication is: "This, as you so obligingly demonstrate, is the only kind of argument that appeals to you; here are your actual faith and morals. How, on consideration, do you like the smell of them?"

But when in reading the *Modest Proposal* we are most engaged, it is an effect directly upon ourselves that we are most disturbingly aware of. The dispassionate, matter-of-fact tone induces a feeling and a motion of assent, while the burden, at the same time, compels the feelings appropriate to rejection, and in the contrast—the tension—a remarkably disturbing energy is generated. A sense of an extraordinary energy is the general effect of Swift's irony. The intensive means just indicated are reinforced extensively in the continuous and unpredictable movement of the attack, which turns this way and that, comes now from one quarter and now from another, inexhaustibly surprising—making again an odd contrast with the sustained and level gravity of the tone. If Swift does for a moment appear to settle down to a formula it is only in order to betray; to induce a trust in the solid ground before opening the pitfall.

"His *Tale of a Tub* has little resemblance to his other pieces. It exhibits a vehemence and rapidity of mind, a copiousness of images, a vivacity of diction, such as he afterwards never possessed, or never exerted. It is of a mode so distinct and peculiar, that it must be considered by itself; what is true of that, is not true of anything else he has written." What Johnson is really testifying to here is the degree in which the *Tale of a Tub* is characteristic and presents the qualities of Swift's genius in concentrated form. "That he has in his works no metaphors, as has been said, is not true," says Johnson a sentence or two later, "but his few metaphors seem to be received rather by necessity than choice." This last judgment may at any rate serve to enforce Johnson's earlier observation that in the *Tale of a Tub* Swift's powers function with unusual freedom. For the "copiousness of images" that Johnson constates is, as the phrase indicates, not a matter of choice but of essential genius. And, as a matter of fact, in this "copiousness of images" the characteristics that we noted in discussing Swift's pamphleteering irony have their supreme expression.

It is as if the gift applied in *Gulliver* to a very limiting task—directed and confined by a scheme uniting a certain consistency in analogical elaboration with verisimilitude—were here enjoying free play. For the bent expressing

itself in this "copiousness" is clearly fundamental. It shows itself in the spontaneous metaphorical energy of Swift's prose—in the image, action or blow that, leaping out of the prosaic manner, continually surprises and disconcerts the reader: "such a man, truly wise, creams off Nature, leaving the sour and the dregs for philosophy and reason to lap up." It appears with as convincing a spontaneity in the sardonic vivacity of comic vision that characterizes the narrative, the presentment of action and actor. If, then, the continual elaborate play of analogy is a matter of cultivated habit, it is a matter also of cultivated natural bent, a congenial development. It is a development that would seem to bear a relation to the Metaphysical fashion in verse (Swift was born in 1667). The spirit of it is that of a fierce and insolent game, but a game to which Swift devotes himself with a creative intensity.

And whereas the mind of man, when he gives the spur and bridle to his thoughts, does never stop, but naturally sallies out into both extremes of high and low, of good and evil, his first flight of fancy commonly transports him to ideas of what is most perfect, finished, and exalted, till, having soared out of his own reach and sight, not well perceiving how near the frontiers of height and depth border upon each other, with the same course and wing he falls down plump into the lowest bottom of things, like one who travels the east into the west, or like a straight line drawn by its own length into a circle. Whether a tincture of malice in our natures makes us fond of furnishing every bright idea with its reverse, or whether reason, reflecting upon the sum of things, can, like the sun, serve only to enlighten one half of the globe, leaving the other half by necessity under shade and darkness, or whether fancy, flying up to the imagination of what is highest and best, becomes over-short, and spent, and weary, and suddenly falls, like a dead bird of paradise, to the ground. . . .

One may (without difficulty) resist the temptation to make the point by saying that this is poetry; one is still tempted to say that the use to which so exuberant an energy is put is a poet's. "Exuberant" seems, no doubt, a paradoxical word to apply to an energy used as Swift uses his; but the case is essentially one for paradoxical descriptions.

In his use of negative materials—negative emotions and attitudes—there is something that it is difficult not to call creative, though the aim always is destructive. Not all the materials, of course, are negative; the "bird of paradise" in the passage above is alive as well as dead. Effects of this kind, often much more intense, are characteristic of the *Tale of a Tub*, where surprise and contrast operate in modes that there is some point in calling poetic. "The most heterogeneous ideas are yoked by violence together"—and in the juxtaposition intensity is generated.

"Paracelsus brought a squadron of stink-pot-flingers from the snowy mountains of Rhaetia" —this (which comes actually from the *Battle of the Books*) does not represent what I have in mind; it is at once too simple and too little charged with animus. Swift's intensities are intensities of rejection and negation; his poetic juxtapositions are, characteristically, destructive in intention, and when they most seem creative of energy are most successful in spoiling, reducing, and destroying. Sustained "copiousness," continually varying, and concentrating surprise in sudden local foci, cannot be represented in short extracts; it must suffice here to say that this kind of thing may be found at a glance on almost any page:

Meantime it is my earnest request that so useful an undertaking may be entered upon (if their Majesties please) with all convenient speed, because I have a strong inclination before I leave the world to taste a blessing which we mysterious writers can seldom reach till we have got into our graves, whether it is that fame, being a fruit grafted on the body, can hardly grow and much less ripen till the stock is in the earth, or whether she be a bird of prey, and is lured among the rest to pursue after the scent of a carcass, or whether she conceives her trumpet sounds best and farthest when she stands on a tomb, by the advantage of a rising ground and the echo of a hollow vault.

It is, of course, possible to adduce Swift's authority for finding that his negations carry with them a complementary positive—an implicit assertion. But (*pace* Charles Whibley) the only thing in the nature of a positive that most readers will find convincingly present is self-assertion—*superbia*. Swift's way of demonstrating his superiority is to destroy, but he takes a positive delight in his power. And that the reader's sense of the negativeness of the *Tale of a Tub* is really qualified comes out when we refer to the Yahoos and the Struldbrugs for a test. The ironic detachment is of such a kind as to reassure us that this savage exhibition is mainly a game, played because it is the insolent pleasure of the author: "demonstration of superiority" is as good a formula as any for its prevailing spirit. Nevertheless, about a superiority that asserts itself in this way there is something disturbingly odd, and again and again in the *Tale of a Tub* we come on intensities that shift the stress decisively and remind us how different from Voltaire Swift is, even in his most complacent detachment.

I propose to examine in illustration a passage from the *Digression Concerning the Original, the Use, and Improvement of Madness in a Commonwealth* (i.e. Section IX). It will have, in the nature of the case, to be a long one, but since it exemplifies at the same time all Swift's essential characteristics, its length will perhaps be tolerated. I shall break up the passage for convenience of comment, but, except for the omission of nine or ten lines in the second instalment, quotation will be continuous:

For the brain in its natural position and state of serenity disposeth its owner to pass his life in the common forms, without any thought of subduing multitudes to his own power, his reasons, or his visions, and the more he shapes his understanding by the pattern of human learning, the less he is inclined to form parties after his particular notions, because that instructs him in his private infirmities, as well as in the stubborn ignorance of the people. But when a man's fancy gets astride on his reason, when imagination is at cuffs with the senses, and common understanding as well as common sense is kicked out of doors, the first proselyte he makes is himself; and when that is once compassed, the difficulty is not so great in bringing over others, a strong delusion always operating from without as vigorously as from within. For cant and vision are to the ear and the eye the same that tickling is to the touch. Those entertainments and pleasures we most value in life are such as dupe and play the wag with the senses. For if we take an examination of what is generally understood by happiness, as it has respect either to the understanding or to the senses, we shall find all its properties and adjuncts will herd under this short definition, that it is a perpetual possession of being well deceived.

Swift's ant-like energy—the business-like air, obsessed intentness and unpredictable movement—have already had an effect. We are not, at the end of this instalment, as sure that we know just what his irony is doing as we were at the opening. Satiric criticism of sectarian "enthusiasm" by reference to the "common forms"—the Augustan standards—is something that, in Swift, we can take as very seriously meant. But in the incessant patter of the argument we have (helped by such things as, at the end, the suggestion of animus in that oddly concrete "herd") a sense that direction and tone are changing. Nevertheless, the change of tone for which the next passage is most remarkable comes as a disconcerting surprise:

And first, with relation to the mind or understanding, it is manifest what mighty advantages fiction has over truth, and the reason is just at our elbow; because imagination can build nobler scenes and produce more wonderful revolutions than fortune or Nature will be at the expense to furnish. . . . Again, if we take this definition of happiness and examine it with reference to the senses, it will be acknowledged wonderfully adapt. How sad and insipid do all objects accost us that are not conveyed in the vehicle of delusion! How shrunk is everything as it appears in the glass of Nature, so that if it were not for the assistance of artificial mediums, false lights, refracted angles, varnish, and tinsel, there would be a mighty level in the felicity and enjoyments of mortal men. If this were seriously considered by the world, as I have a certain reason to sus-

pect it hardly will, men would no longer reckon among their high points of wisdom the art of exposing weak sides and publishing infirmities— an employment, in my opinion, neither better nor worse than that of unmasking, which, I think, has never been allowed fair usage, either in the world or the playhouse.

The suggestion of changing direction does not, in the first part of this passage, bring with it anything unsettling: from ridicule of "enthusiasm" to ridicule of human capacity for self-deception is an easy transition. The reader, as a matter of fact, begins to settle down to the habit, the steady drift of this irony, and is completely unprepared for the sudden change of tone and reversal of attitude in the two sentences beginning "How sad and insipid do all objects," etc. Exactly what the change means or is, it is difficult to be certain (and that is of the essence of the effect). But the tone has certainly a personal intensity and the ironic detachment seems suddenly to disappear. It is as if one found Swift in the place—at the point of view—where one expected to find his butt. But the ambiguously mocking sentence with which the paragraph ends reinforces the uncertainty.

The next paragraph keeps the reader for some time in uneasy doubt. The irony has clearly shifted its plane, but in which direction is the attack going to develop? Which, to be safe, must one dissociate oneself from, "credulity" or "curiosity"?

In the proportion that credulity is a more peaceful possession of the mind than curiosity, so far preferable is that wisdom which converses about the surface to that pretended philosophy which enters into the depths of things and then comes gravely back with informations and discoveries, that in the inside they are good for nothing. The two senses to which all objects first address themselves are the sight and the touch; these never examine further than the colour, the shape, the size, and whatever other qualities dwell or are drawn by art upon the outward of bodies; and then comes reason officiously, with tools for cutting, and opening, and mangling, and piercing, offering to demonstrate that they are not of the same consistence quite through. Now I take all this to be the last degree of perverting Nature, one of whose eternal laws is to put her best furniture forward. And therefore, in order to save the charges of all such expensive anatomy for the time to come, I do here think fit to inform the reader that in such conclusions as these reason is certainly in the right; and that in most corporeal beings which have fallen under my cognisance the outside hath been infinitely preferable to the in, whereof I have been further convinced from some late experiments. Last week I saw a woman flayed, and you will hardly believe how much it altered her person for the worse.

The peculiar intensity of that last sentence is, in its own way, so decisive that it has for the reader the effect of resolving uncertainty in general. The disturbing force of the sentence is a notable instance of a kind already touched on: repulsion is intensified by the momentary co-presence, induced by the tone, of incipient and incompatible feelings (or motions) of acceptance. And that Swift feels the strongest animus against "curiosity" is now beyond all doubt. The natural corollary would seem to be that "credulity," standing ironically for the "common forms"—the sane, socially sustained, common-sense illusions—is the positive that the reader must associate himself with and rest on for safety. The next half-page steadily and (to all appearances) unequivocally confirms this assumption:

Yesterday I ordered the carcass of a beau to be stripped in my presence, when we were all amazed to find so many unsuspected faults under one suit of clothes. Then I laid open his brain, his heart, and his spleen, but I plainly perceived at every operation that the farther we proceeded, we found the defects increase upon us in number and bulk; from all of which I justly formed this conclusion to myself, that whatever philosopher or projector can find out an art to sodder and patch up the flaws and imperfections of Nature, will deserve much better of mankind and teach us a much more useful science than that, so much in present esteem, of widening and exposing them (like him who held anatomy to be the ultimate end of physic). And he whose

fortunes and dispositions have placed him in a convenient station to enjoy the fruits of this noble art, he that can with Epicurus content his ideas with the films and images that fly off upon his senses from the superficies of things, such a man, truly wise, creams off Nature, leaving the sour and the dregs for philosophy and reason to lap up.

Assumption has become habit, and has been so nourished that few readers note anything equivocal to trouble them in that last sentence: the concrete force of "creams off," "sour," "dregs" and "lap up" seems unmistakably to identify Swift with an intense animus against "philosophy and reason" (understood implicitly to stand for "curiosity" the anatomist). The reader's place, of course, is with Swift.

The trap is sprung in the last sentence of the paragraph:

This is the sublime and refined point of felicity called the possession of being well-deceived, the serene peaceful state of being a fool among knaves.

What is left? The next paragraph begins significantly: "But to return to madness." This irony may be critical, but "critical" turns out, in no very long run, to be indistinguishable from "negative." The positives disappear. Even when, as in the Houyhnhnms, they seem to be more substantially present, they disappear under our "curiosity." The Houyhnhnms, of course, stand for Reason, Truth and Nature, the Augustan positives, and it was in deadly earnest that Swift appealed to these; but how little at best they were anything solidly realized, comparison with Pope brings out. Swift did his best for the Houyhnhnms, and they may have all the reason, but the Yahoos have all the life. Gulliver's master "thought Nature and reason were sufficient guides for a reasonable animal," but nature and reason as Gulliver exhibits them are curiously negative, and the reasonable animals appear to have nothing in them to guide. "They have no fondness for their colts or foals, but the care they take in educating them proceeds entirely from the dictates of reason." This freedom from irrational feelings and impulses simplifies other matters too: "their language doth not abound in variety of words, because their wants and passions are fewer than among us." And so conversation, in this model society, is simplified: "nothing passed but what was useful, expressed in the fewest and most significant words . . ." "Courtship, love, presents, jointures, settlements, have no place in their thoughts, or terms whereby to express them in their language. The young couple meet and are joined, merely because it is the determination of their parents and friends: it is what they see done every day, and they look upon it as one of the necessary actions of a reasonable being." The injunction of "temperance, industry, exercise, and cleanliness . . . the lessons enjoined to the young ones of both sexes," seems unnecessary; except possibly for exercise, the usefulness of which would not, perhaps, be immediately apparent to the reasonable young.

The clean skin of the Houyhnhnms, in short, is stretched over a void; instincts, emotions and life, which complicate the problem of cleanliness and decency, are left for the Yahoos with the dirt and the indecorum. Reason, Truth and Nature serve instead; the Houyhnhnms (who scorn metaphysics) find them adequate. Swift too scorned metaphysics, and never found anything better to contend for than a skin, a surface, an outward show. An outward show is, explicitly, all he contends for in the quite unironical *Project for the Advancement of Religion,* and the difference between the reality of religion and the show is, for the author of the *Tale of a Tub,* hardly substantial. Of Jack we are told, "nor could all the world persuade him, as the common phrase is, to eat his victuals like a Christian." It is characteristic of Swift that he should put in these terms, showing a complete incapacity even to guess what religious feeling might be, a genuine conviction that Jack should be made to kneel when receiving the Sacrament.

Of the intensity of this conviction there can be no doubt. The Church of England was the established "common form," and, moreover, was Swift's church: his insane egotism reinforced the savagery with which he fought to maintain this cover over the void, this decent surface. But what the savagery of the passage from the *Digression* shows mainly is Swift's sense of insecurity and of the undisguisable flimsiness of any surface that offered.

The case, of course, is more complex. In the passage examined the "surface" becomes, at the most savage moment, a human skin. Swift's negative horror, at its most disturbing, becomes one with his disgust-obsession: he cannot bear to be reminded that under the skin there is blood, mess and entrails; and the skin itself, as we know from *Gulliver,* must not be seen from too close. Hypertrophy of the sense of uncleanness, of the instinct of repulsion, is not uncommon; nor is its association with what accompanies it in Swift. What is uncommon is Swift's genius and the paradoxical vitality with which this self-defeat of life—life turned against itself—is manifested. In the *Tale of a Tub* the defeat is also a triumph; the genius delights in its mastery, in its power to destroy, and negation is felt as self-assertion. It is only when time has confirmed Swift in disappointment and brought him to more intimate contemplation of physical decay that we get the Yahoos and the Struldbrugs.

Here, well on this side of pathology, literary criticism stops. To attempt encroachments would be absurd, and, even if one were qualified, unprofitable. No doubt psychopathology and medicine have an interesting commentary to offer, but their help is not necessary. Swift's genius belongs to literature, and its appreciation to literary criticism.

We have, then, in his writings probably the most remarkable expression of negative feelings and attitudes that literature can offer—the spectacle of creative powers (the paradoxical description seems right) exhibited consistently in negation and rejection. His verse demands an essay to itself, but fits in readily with what has been said. "In poetry," he reports of the Houyhnhnms, "they must be allowed to excel all other mortals; wherein the justness of their similes and the minuteness as well as exactness of their descriptions are, indeed, inimitable. Their verses abound very much in both of these . . ." The actuality of presentment for which Swift is notable, in prose as well as verse, seems always to owe its convincing "justness" to, at his least actively malicious, a coldly intense scrutiny, a potentially hostile attention. "To his domesticks," says Johnson, "he was naturally rough; and a man of rigorous temper, with that vigilance of minute attention which his works discover, must have been a master that few could bear." *Instructions to Servants* and the *Polite Conversation* enforce obviously the critical bearing and felicity of Johnson's remark.

A great writer—yes; that account still imposes itself as fitting, though his greatness is no matter of moral grandeur or human centrality; our sense of it is merely a sense of great force. And this force, as we feel it, is conditioned by frustration and constriction; the channels of life have been blocked and perverted. That we should be so often invited to regard him as a moralist and an idealist would seem to be mainly a witness to the power of vanity, and the part that vanity can play in literary appreciation: *saeva indignatio* is an indulgence that solicits us all, and the use of literature by readers and critics for the projection of nobly suffering selves is familiar. No doubt, too, it is pleasant to believe that unusual capacity for egotistic animus means unusual distinction of intellect; but, as we have seen, there is no reason to lay stress on intellect in Swift. His work does indeed exhibit an extraordinary play of mind; but it is not great intellectual force that is exhibited in his indifference to the problems raised—in, for instance, the *Voyage to the Houyhnhnms*—by his use of the concept, or the word "Nature." It is not merely that he had an Augustan contempt for metaphysics; he shared the shallowest complacencies of Augustan common sense: his irony might destroy these, but there is no conscious criticism.

He was, in various ways, curiously unaware —the reverse of clairvoyant. He is distinguished by the intensity of his feelings, not by insight into them, and he certainly does not impress us as a mind in possession of its experience.

We shall not find Swift remarkable for intelligence if we think of Blake.

Yvor Winters

THE MORALITY OF POETRY (1937)

BEFORE ATTEMPTING TO ELUCIDATE or to criticize a poetry so difficult and evasive as that of the best moderns, it would appear wise to summarize as clearly as possible those qualities for which one looks in a poem. We may say that a poem in the first place should offer us new

From *In Defense of Reason*, Swallow Press, Chicago (Copyright 1947).

perceptions, not only of the exterior universe, but of human experience as well; it should add, in other words, to what we have already seen. This is the elementary function for the reader. The corresponding function for the poet is a sharpening and training of his sensibilities; the very exigencies of the medium as he employs it in the act of perception should force him to the discovery of values which he never would have found without the convening of all the conditions of that particular act, conditions one or more of which will be the necessity of solving some particular difficulty such as the location of a rhyme or the perfection of a cadence without disturbance to the remainder of the poem. The poet who suffers from such difficulties instead of profiting by them is only in a rather rough sense a poet at all.

If, however, the difficulties of versification are a stimulant merely to the *poet*, the reader may argue that he finds them a hindrance to himself and that he prefers some writer of prose who appears to offer him as much with less trouble to all concerned. The answer to such a reader is that the appearance of equal richness in the writer of prose is necessarily deceptive.

For language is a kind of abstraction, even at its most concrete; such a word as "cat," for instance, is generic and not particular. Such a word becomes particular only in so far as it gets into some kind of experiential complex, which qualifies it and limits it, which gives it, in short, a local habitation as well as a name. Such a complex is the poetic line or other unit, which, in turn, should be a functioning part of the larger complex, or poem. This is, I imagine, what Mallarmé should have had in mind when he demanded that the poetic line be a new word, not found in any dictionary, and partaking of the nature of incantation (that is, having the power to materialize, or perhaps it would be more accurate to say, *being*, a new experience.)

The poem, to be perfect, should likewise be a new word in the same sense, a word of which the line, as we have defined it, is merely a syllable. Such a word is, of course, composed of much more than the sum of its words (as one normally uses the term) and its syntax. It is composed of an almost fluid complex, if the adjective and the noun are not too nearly contradictory, of relationships between words (in the normal sense of the term), a relationship involving rational content, cadences,

rhymes, juxtapositions, literary and other connotations, inversions, and so on, almost indefinitely. These relationships, it should be obvious, extend the poet's vocabulary incalculably. They partake of the fluidity and unpredictability of experience and so provide a means of treating experience with precision and freedom. If the poet does not wish, as, actually, he seldom does, to reproduce a given experience with approximate exactitude, he can employ the experience as a basis for a new experience that will be just as real, in the sense of being particular, and perhaps more valuable.

Now verse is more valuable than prose in this process for the simple reasons that its rhythms are faster and more highly organized than are those of prose, and so lend themselves to a greater complexity and compression of relationship, and that the intensity of this convention renders possible a greater intensity of other desirable conventions, such as poetic language and devices of rhetoric. The writer of prose must substitute bulk for this kind of intensity; he must define his experience ordinarily by giving all of its past history, the narrative logic leading up to it, whereas the experiential relations given in a good lyric poem, though particular in themselves, are applicable without alteration to a good many past histories. In this sense, the lyric is general as well as particular; in fact, this quality of transferable or generalized experience might be regarded as the defining quality of lyrical poetry.

What I have just said should make plain the difficulty of comprehending a poem exactly and fully; its total intention may be very different from its paraphrasable, or purely logical content. If one take, for example, Mr. Allen Tate's sonnet, *The Subway*, and translate it into good scholarly prose, using nothing but the rational content of the poem as a reference, one will find the author saying that as a result of his ideas and of his metropolitan environment, he is going mad. Now as a matter of fact, the poem says nothing of the sort:

Dark accurate plunger down the successive knell
Of arch on arch, where ogives burst a red
Reverberance of hail upon the dead
Thunder, like an exploding crucible!
Harshly articulate, musical steel shell
Of angry worship, hurled religiously
Upon your business of humility
Into the iron forestries of hell!

Till broken in the shift of quieter
Dense altitudes tangential of your steel,
I am become geometries—and glut
Expansions like a blind astronomer
Dazed, while the worldless heavens bulge and reel
In the cold revery of an idiot.

The sonnet indicates that the author has faced and defined the possibility of the madness that I have mentioned (a possibility from the consideration of which others as well as himself may have found it impossible to escape) and has arrived at a moral attitude toward it, an attitude which is at once defined and communicated by the poem. This attitude is defined only by the entire poem, not by the logical content alone; it is a matter not only of logical content, but of feeling as well. The feeling is particular and unparaphrasable, but one may indicate the nature of it briefly by saying that it is a feeling of dignity and of self-control in the face of a situation of major difficulty, a difficulty which the poet fully apprehends. This feeling is inseparable from what we call poetic form, or unity, for the creation of a form is nothing more nor less than the act of evaluating and shaping (that is, controlling) a given experience. It should be obvious that any attempt to reduce the rational content of such a poem would tend to confuse or even to eliminate the feeling: the poem consists in the relationship between the two.

To reënforce my point, I shall take the liberty of quoting another poem, this one by Mr. Howard Baker, in which something comparable occurs. The title is *Pont Neuf:*

Henry the Fourth rides in bronze,
His shoulders curved and pensive, thrust
Enormously into electric
Blazonments of a Christmas trust.

Children pass him aghast and pleased,
Reflective of the flickerings
Of jerky bears and clowns. Alone,
Astute to all the bickerings

Of age and death rides Henry the Grand.
A lean tug shudders in the Seine;
And Notre Dame is black, a relic
Of the blood of other men.

Peace to the other men! And peace
To the mind that has no century,
And sees the savage pull the statue down,
And down the bear and clown.

The spiritual control in a poem, then, is simply a manifestation of the spiritual control within the poet, and, as I have already indicated, it may have been an important means by which the poet arrived at a realization of spiritual control. This conception must not be confused with the conception of the poem as a safety valve, by which feeling is diverted from action, by which the writer escapes from an attitude by pouring it into his work and leaving it behind him. The conception which I am trying to define is a conception of poetry as a technique of contemplation, of comprehension, a technique which does not eliminate the need of philosophy or of religion, but which, rather, completes and enriches them.

One feels, whether rightly or wrongly, a correlation between the control evinced within a poem and the control within the poet behind it. The laxity of the one ordinarily appears to involve laxity in the other. The rather limp versification of Mr. Eliot and of Mr. MacLeish is inseparable from the spiritual limpness that one feels behind the poems, as the fragmentary, ejaculatory, and over-excited quality of a great many of the poems of Hart Crane is inseparable from the intellectual confusion upon which these particular poems seem to rest (for examples, *The Dance, Cape Hatteras,* and *Atlantis*). Crane possessed great energy, but his faculties functioned clearly only within a limited range of experience (*Repose of Rivers, Voyages II, Faustus and Helen II*). Outside of that range he was either numb (*My Grandmother's Loveletters* and *Harbor Dawn*) or unsure of himself and hence uncertain in his detail (as in *The River*, a very powerful poem in spite of its poor construction and its quantities of bad writing) or both (see *Indiana*, probably one of the worst poems in modern literature). Many of the poems of Mr. Eliot and of Mr. MacLeish could be reduced by paraphrase to about the same thing as my paraphrase of Mr. Tate's sonnet; the difference between them and Mr. Tate in this connection is that, as the form of nearly all of their poems is much looser to start with, the process of paraphrasing would constitute a much slighter act of betrayal. And we must not forget that this quality, form, is not something outside the poet, something "aesthetic," and superimposed upon his moral content; it is essentially a part, in fact it may be the decisive part, of the moral content, even though the poet may be arriving at the final perfection of the condition he is communicating while he communicates it and in a large measure as a result of the act and technique of communication. For the communication is first of all with himself: it is, as I have said, the last refinement of contemplation.

I should pause here to remark that many writers have sought to seize the fluidity of experience by breaking down the limits of form, but that in so doing, they defeat their own ends. For, as I have shown, writing, as it approaches the looseness of prose and departs from the strictness of verse, tends to lose the capacity for fluid or highly complex relationships between words; language, in short, reapproaches its original stiffness and generality; and one is forced to recognize the truth of what appears a paradox, that the greatest fluidity of statement is possible where the greatest clarity of form prevails. It is hard to see how the existence of such a work as Mr. Joyce's latest creation [1] can be anything but precarious, in spite of its multitudes of inci-

[1] Entitled at this writing (1935) *Work in Progress.* (Ultimately published as *Finnegans Wake.*)

dental felicities; for it departs from the primary condition of prose—coherent and cumulative logic or narrative—without, since it is, finally, prose, achieving the formal precision of verse. These remarks should not be construed, however, as an argument against free verse, though, with proper qualification, they could be brought to bear in such an argument. The free verse that is really verse—the best, that is, of W. C. Williams, H. D., Miss Moore, Wallace Stevens, and Ezra Pound—is, in its peculiar fashion, the antithesis of free, and the evaluation of this verse is a difficult problem in itself.

Thus we see that the poet, in striving toward an ideal of poetic form at which he has arrived through the study of other poets, is actually striving to perfect a moral attitude toward that range of experience of which he is aware. Such moral attitudes are contagious from poet to poet, and, within the life of a single poet, from poem to poem. The presence of Hardy and Arnold, let us say, in so far as their successful works offer us models and their failures warnings or unfulfilled suggestions, should make it easier to write good poetry; they should not only aid us, by providing standards of sound feeling, to test the soundness of our own poems, but, since their range of experience is very wide, they should aid us, as we are able to enter and share their experience, to grow into regions that we had not previously mastered or perhaps even discovered. The discipline of imitation is thus valuable if it leads to understanding and assimilation. Too often a minor poet or other reader will recognize in such a master the validity of only that part of the master's experience which corresponds to his own limited range, and will rule out the poetry to which he is consequently numb as sentimental or otherwise imperfect. Inflexibility of critical opinion in such matters is not particularly conducive to growth.

Random experiment may have a related value: one may hit on a form (perhaps the rough idea or draft of a form) which induces some new state or states of mind. I regard as fallacious the notion that form is determined by a precedent attitude or a precedent subject matter, at least invariably: the form (that is, the general idea of a certain type of form) *may* precede, and the attitude, in any case, is never definite till the form is achieved.[2] It does not follow that any attitude resulting from random experiment is intrinsically desirable; undesirable attitudes, like desirable, are contagious and may spread widely; it is here that criticism becomes necessary. A failure, however, to achieve something valuable may offer a valuable suggestion to someone else. The poet who has succeeded once or twice in mastering difficult and central emotions and in recording his mastery for future reference should find it easier to succeed again.

I am not endeavoring in the two foregoing paragraphs to establish poetry as a substitute for philosophy or for religion. Religion is highly desirable if it is really available to the individual; the study of philosophy is always available and is of incalculable value as a preliminary and as a check to activities as a poet and as a critic (that is, as an intelligent reader). I am, then, merely attempting to define a few of the things which poetry does.

It would perhaps be wise to add another caution: I suffer from no illusion that any man who can write a good poem has a naturally sweet moral temper or that the man who has written three good poems is a candidate for canonization. Literary history is packed with sickening biographies. But it is worth noting that the poetry of such a man, say, as Rochester (who in this is typical of his age) displays a mastery of an extremely narrow range of experience, and that his moral brutality falls almost wholly in those regions (nearly every region save that of worldly manners, if we except some few poems, notably *Upon Noth-*

[2] As a single example, consider the manner in which the Petrarchan experimenters in England, most of them feeble poets and the best of them given to empty and inflated reasoning, worked out the technique of reasoning elaborately in graceful lyrical verse and bequeathed that technique to the 17th century: the form preceded the matter.

ing, Absent from Thee, and, possibly, *A Song of a Young Lady to Her Ancient Lover,* in which last there is a curious blending of the erotic with deep moral feeling) with which his poetry fails to deal or with which it deals badly.

This statement requires elucidation. Rochester frequently writes of his debauchery, and sometimes writes well of it, but in the best poems on the subject, in such poems as *The Maim'd Debauchee* and *Upon Drinking in a Bowl,* he writes, as do his contemporaries in the comedy, as a witty and satirical gentleman: the wit inspired by the material is mastered, and other aspects of the material are ignored. In the worst poems on more or less similar material (for examples, the numerous lampoons upon Charles II and upon Nell Gwyn) we have a grossness of feeling comparable to that of his worst actions. All of this, however, detracts not in the least from the quality of Rochester's best poetry, which is remarkably fine; Rochester seldom extends the standards which he recognizes into fields to which they are inapplicable, and hence he is seldom guilty of false evaluation. In reading him, one is aware that he is a sound and beautiful poet, and that there are greater poets. That is all of which one has a right to be aware.

If a poem, in so far as it is good, represents the comprehension on a moral plane of a given experience, it is only fair to add that some experiences offer very slight difficulties and some very great, and that the poem will be the most valuable, which, granted it achieves formal perfection, represents the most difficult victory. In the great tragic poets, such as Racine or Shakespeare, one feels that a victory has been won over life itself, so much is implicated in the subject matter; that feeling is the source of their power over us, whereas a slighter poet will absorb very little of our experience and leave the rest untouched.

This requisite seems to be ignored in a large measure by a good many contemporary poets of more or less mystical tendencies, who avoid the difficult task of mastering the more complex forms of experience by setting up a theoretic escape from them and by then accepting that escape with a good deal of lyrical enthusiasm. Such an escape is offered us, I fear, by Hart Crane, in one of the most extraordinary sections of his volume, *The Bridge*, in the poem called *The Dance*, and such escapes are often employed by Mr. Yeats. In the religious poets of the past, one encounters this vice very seldom; the older religions are fully aware that the heart, to borrow the terms of a poem by Janet Lewis, is untranslatable, whatever may be true of the soul, and that one can escape from the claims of the world only by understanding those claims and by thus accustoming oneself to the thought of eventually putting them by. This necessity is explicitly the subject of one of Sidney's greatest sonnets, *Leave me, O Love, which reachest but to dust*, and of the greatest poem by George Herbert, *Church Monuments*; one can find it elsewhere. The attitude is humane, and does not belittle nor evade the magnitude of the task; it is essentially a tragic attitude.

For this reason, the religious fervor of Gerard Hopkins, of John Donne, or of George Herbert should weaken but little the force of most of their poems for the non-believer, just as the deterministic doctrines, whatever their nature and extent, to be found in Hardy, should not weaken for us those poems which do not deal too pugnaciously with the doctrines, and for the same reason. Though a belief in any form of determinism should, if the belief is pushed to its logical ends, eliminate the belief in, and consequently the functioning of, whatever it is that we call the will, yet there is no trace of any kind of disintegration in Hardy's poetic style, in his sense of form, which we have seen to be, so far as writing is concerned, identical with the will or the ability to control and shape one's experience. The tragic necessity of putting by the claims of the world without the abandonment of self-control, without loss of the ability to go on living, for the present, intelligently and well, is just as definitely the subject of Hardy's poetry as of Her-

bert's. We have in both poets a common moral territory which is far greater than are the theological regions which they do not share; for, on the one hand, the fundamental concepts of morality are common to intelligent men regardless of theological orientation, except in so far as morality may be simply denied or ignored, and, on the other hand, the Absolute is in its nature inscrutable and offers little material for speculation, except in so far as it is a stimulus to moral speculation. It would be difficult, I think, to find a devotional poem of which most of the implications were not moral and universal. So with Hardy: his determinism was mythic and animistic and tended to dramatize the human struggle, whereas a genuinely rational and coherent determinism would have eliminated the human struggle. He was thrown back upon traditional literary and folk wisdom in working out moral situations, and for these situations his mythology provided a new setting, sometimes magnificent, sometimes melodramatic, but, thanks to its rational incompleteness, not really destructive of a working morality. Like many another man who has been unable to think clearly, he was saved by the inability to think coherently: had he been coherent, he would probably have been about as interesting as Godwin; as it is, his professed beliefs and his working beliefs have only a little in common, and the former damage his work only in a fragmentary way, as when satires of circumstance are dragged into a novel or isolated in a poem to prove a point (and they can prove nothing, of course) and usually to the detriment of coherent feeling and understanding.

Crane's attitude, on the other hand, often suggests a kind of theoretic rejection of all human endeavor in favor of some vaguely apprehended but ecstatically asserted existence of a superior sort. As the exact nature of the superior experience is uncertain, it forms a rather uncertain and infertile source of material for exact poetry; one can write poetry about it only by utilizing in some way more or less metaphorical the realm of experience from which one is trying to escape; but as one *is* endeavoring to escape from this realm, not to master it and understand it, one's feelings about it are certain to be confused, and one's imagery drawn from it is bound to be largely formulary and devoid of meaning. That is, in so far as one endeavors to deal with the Absolute, not as a means of ordering one's moral perception but as the subject itself of perception, one will tend to say nothing, despite the multiplication of words. In *The Dance* there seems to be an effort to apply to each of two mutually exclusive fields the terms of the other. This is a vice of which Rochester was not guilty.

Crane's best work, such as *Repose of Rivers* and *Voyages II*, is not confused, but one feels that the experience is curiously limited and uncomplicated: it is between the author, isolated from most human complications, and Eternity. Crane becomes in such poems a universal symbol of the human mind in a particular situation, a fact which is the source of his power, but of the human mind in very nearly the simplest form of that situation, a fact which is the source of his limitation.

Objective proof of this assertion cannot be found in the poems, any more than proof of the opposite quality can be found in Hardy; it is in each poet a matter of feeling invading the poetry mainly by way of the non-paraphrasable content: one feels the fragility of Crane's finest work, just as one feels the richness of Hardy's. Hardy is able to utilize, for example, great ranges of literary, historical, and other connotations in words and cadences; one feels behind each word the history of the word and the generations of men who embodied that history; Hardy gets somehow at the wealth of the race. It should be observed again how the moral discipline is involved in the literary discipline, how it becomes, at times, almost a matter of living philology. From the greater part of this wealth Crane appears to be isolated and content to remain isolated. His isolation, like Hardy's immersion, was in part social and unavoidable, but a clearer mind and a more fixed

intention might have overcome much of the handicap.

I should like to forestall one possible objection to the theory of poetry which I am trying to elucidate. Poetry, as a moral discipline, should not be regarded as one more means of escape. That is, moral responsibility should not be transferred from action to paper in the face of a particular situation. Poetry, if pursued either by the poet or by the reader, in the manner which I have suggested, should offer a means of enriching one's awareness of human experience and of so rendering greater the possibility of intelligence in the course of future action; and it should offer likewise a means of inducing certain more or less constant habits of feeling, which should render greater the possibility of one's acting, in a future situation, in accordance with the findings of one's improved intelligence. It should, in other words, increase the intelligence and strengthen the moral temper; these effects should naturally be carried over into action, if, through constant discipline, they are made permanent acquisitions. If the poetic discipline is to have steadiness and direction, it requires an antecedent discipline of ethical thinking and of at least some ethical feeling, which may be in whole or in part the gift of religion or of a social tradition, or which may be largely the result of individual acquisition by way of study. The poetic discipline includes the antecedent discipline and more: it is the richest and most perfect technique of contemplation.

This view of poetry in its general outline is not original, but is a restatement of ideas that have been current in English criticism since the time of Sidney, that have appeared again in most of the famous apologists for poetry since Sidney, especially in Arnold and in Newman. In summarizing these ideas, I have merely endeavored to illuminate a few of the more obscure relationships and to dispose of them in such a way as to prepare the reader for various analyses of poetic method which I intend, in other essays, to undertake. Poetic morality and poetic feeling are inseparable; feeling and technique, or structure, are inseparable. Technique has laws which govern poetic (and perhaps more general) morality more widely than is commonly recognized. It is my intention to examine them.

PRELIMINARY PROBLEMS (1943)

FIRST PROBLEM

Is it possible to say that Poem A (one of Donne's *Holy Sonnets,* or one of the poems of Jonson or of Shakespeare) is better than Poem B (Collins' *Ode to Evening*) or vice versa?

If not, is it possible to say that either of these is better than Poem C (*The Cremation of Sam Magee,* or something comparable)?

If the answer is no in both cases, then any poem is as good as any other. If this is true, then all poetry is worthless; but this obviously is not true, for it is contrary to all our experience.

If the answer is yes in both cases, then there follows the question of whether the answer implies merely that one poem is better than another for the speaker, or whether it means that one poem is intrinsically better than another. If the former, then we are impressionists, which is to say relativists; and are either mystics of the type of Emerson, or hedonists of the type of Stevens and Ransom. If the latter, then we assume that constant principles govern the poetic experience, and that the poem (as likewise the judge) must be judged in relationship to those principles. It is important, therefore, to discover the consequences of assuming each of these positions.

If our answer to the first question is no and to the second yes, then we are asserting that we can distinguish between those poems which are of the canon and those which are not, but that within the canon all judgment is impossible. This view, if adopted, will require serious elucidation, for on the face of it, it appears in-

explicable. On the other hand, one cannot deny that within the canon judgment will become more difficult, for the nearer two poems may be to the highest degrees of excellence, the harder it will be to choose between them. Two poems, in fact, might be so excellent that there would be small profit in endeavoring to say that one was better, but one could arrive at this conclusion only after a careful examination of both.

SECOND PROBLEM

If we accept the view that one poem can be regarded as better than another, the question then arises whether this judgment is a matter of inexplicable intuition, or whether it is a question of intuition that can be explained, and consequently guided and improved by rational elucidation.

If we accept the view that the judgment in question is inexplicable, then we are again forced to confess ourselves impressionists and relativists, unless we can show that the intuitions of all men agree at all times, or that intuitions of one man are invariably right and those of all others wrong whenever they differ. We obviously can demonstrate neither of these propositions.

If we start, then, with the proposition that one poem may be intrinsically superior to another, we are forced to account for differences of opinion regarding it. If two critics differ, it is possible that one is right and the other wrong, more likely that both are partly right and partly wrong, but in different respects: neither the native gifts nor the education of any man have ever been wholly adequate to many of the critical problems he will encounter, and no two men are ever the same in these respects or in any others. On the other hand, although the critic should display reasonable humility and caution, it is only fair to add that few men possess either the talent or the education to justify their being taken very seriously, even of those who are nominally professional students of these matters.

But if it is possible by rational elucidation to give a more or less clear account of what one finds in a poem and why one approves or disapproves, then communication between two critics, though no doubt imperfect, becomes possible, and it becomes possible that they may in some measure correct each other's errors and so come more near to a true judgment of the poem.

THIRD PROBLEM

If rational communication about poetry is to take place, it is necessary first to determine what we mean by a poem.

A poem is first of all a statement in words.

But it differs from all such statements of a purely philosophical or theoretical nature, in that it has by intention a controlled content of feeling. In this respect, it does not differ from many works written in prose, however.

A poem differs from a work written in prose by virtue of its being composed in verse. The rhythm of verse permits the expression of more powerful feeling than is possible in prose when such feeling is needed, and it permits at all times the expression of finer shades of feeling.

A poem, then, is a statement in words in which special pains are taken with the expression of feeling. This description is merely intended to distinguish the poem from other kinds of writing; it is not offered as a complete description.

FOURTH PROBLEM

What, however, are words?

They are audible sounds, or their visual symbols, invented by man to communicate his thoughts and feelings. Each word has a conceptual content, however slight; each word, exclusive, perhaps, of the particles, communicates

vague associations of feeling.

The word *fire* communicates a concept; it also connotes very vaguely certain feelings, depending on the context in which we happen to place it—depending, for example, on whether we happen to think of a fire on a hearth, in a furnace, or in a forest. These feelings may be rendered more and more precise as we render the context more and more precise; as we come more and more near to completing and perfecting our poem.

FIFTH PROBLEM

But if the poem, as compared to prose, pays especial attention to feeling, are we to assume that the rational content of the poem is unimportant to its success?

The rational content cannot be eliminated from words; consequently the rational content cannot be eliminated from poetry. It is there. If it is unsatisfactory in itself, a part of the poem is unsatisfactory; the poem is thus damaged beyond argument. If we deny this, we must surely explain ourselves very fully.

If we admit this, we are faced with another problem: is it conceivable that rational content and feeling-content may both be perfect, and yet that they may be unrelated to each other, or imperfectly related? To me this is inconceivable, because the emotional content of words is generated by our experience with the conceptual content, so that a relationship is necessary.

This fact of the necessity of such relationship may fairly return us for a moment to the original question: whether imperfection of rational content damages the entire poem. If there is a necessary relationship between concept and feeling, and concept is unsatisfactory, then feeling must be damaged by way of the relationship.

SIXTH PROBLEM

If there is a relationship between concept and feeling, what is the nature of that relationship?

To answer this, let us return to the basic unit, the word. The concept represented by the word, motivates the feeling which the word communicates. It is the concept of fire which generates the feelings communicated by the word, though the sound of the word may modify these feelings very subtly, as may other accidental qualities, especially if the word be used skillfully in a given context. The accidental qualities of a word, however, such as its literary history, for example, can only modify, cannot essentially change, for these will be governed ultimately by the concept; that is, *fire* will seldom be used to signify *plum-blossom,* and so will have few opportunities to gather connotations from the concept, *plum-blossom.* The relationship, in the poem, between rational statement and feeling, is thus seen to be that of motive to emotion.

SEVENTH PROBLEM

But has not this reasoning brought us back to the proposition that all poems are equally good? For if each word motivates its own feeling, because of its intrinsic nature, will not any rational statement, since it is composed of words, motivate the feeling exactly proper to it?

This is not true, for a good many reasons, of which I shall enumerate only a few of the more obvious. In making a rational statement, in purely theoretical prose, we find that our statement may be loose or exact, depending upon the relationships of the words to each other. The precision of a word depends to some extent upon its surroundings. This is true likewise with respect to the connotations of words. Two words, each of which has several usably close rational synonyms, may reinforce and clarify each other with respect to their connotations or they may not do so.

Let me illustrate with a simple example from Browning's *Serenade at the Villa:*

So wore night; the East was gray,
    White the broad-faced hemlock flowers.

The lines are marred by a crowding of long syllables and difficult consonants, but they have great beauty in spite of the fault. What I wish to point out, for the sake of my argument, is the relationship between the words *wore* and

gray. The verb *wore* means literally that the night passed, but it carries with it connotations of exhaustion and attrition which belong to the condition of the protagonist; and grayness is a color which we associate with such a condition. If we change the phrase to read: "Thus night passed," we shall have the same rational meaning, and a meter quite as respectable, but no trace of the power of the line: the connotation of *wore* will be lost, and the connotation of *gray* will remain merely in a state of ineffective potentiality. The protagonist in seeing his feeling mirrored in the landscape is not guilty of motivating his feeling falsely, for we know his general motive from the poem as a whole; he is expressing a portion of the feeling motivated by the total situation through a more or less common psychological phenomenon. If the poem were such, however, that we did not know why the night *wore* instead of *passed,* we should have just cause for complaint; in fact, most of the strength of the word would probably be lost. The second line contains other fine effects, immediately with reference to the first line, ultimately with reference to the theme; I leave the reader to analyze them for himself, but he will scarcely succeed without the whole poem before him.

Concepts, as represented by particular words, are affected by connotations due to various and curious accidents. A word may gather connotations from its use in folk-poetry, in formal poetry, in vulgar speech, or in technical prose: a single concept might easily be represented by four words with these distinct histories; and any one of the words might prove to be proper in a given poetic context. Words gain connotation from etymological accidents. Something of this may be seen in the English word *outrage,* in which is commonly felt, in all likelihood, something associated with *rage,* although there is no rage whatever in the original word. Similarly the word *urchin,* in modern English, seldom connotes anything related to hedgehogs, or the familiars of the witches, by whose intervention the word arrived at its modern meaning and feeling. Yet the connotation proper to any stage in the history of such a word might be resuscitated, or a blend of connotations effected, by skillful use. Further, the connotation of a word may be modified very strongly by its function in the metrical structure, a matter which I shall discuss at length in connection with the theories of Ransom.

This is enough to show that exact motivation of feeling by concept is not inherent in any rational statement. Any rational statement will govern the general possibilities of feeling derivable from it, but the task of the poet is to adjust feeling to motive precisely. He has to select words containing not only the right relationships within themselves, but the right relationships to each other. The task is very difficult; and this is no doubt the reason why the great poetry of a great poet is likely to be very small in bulk.

EIGHTH PROBLEM

Is it not possible, however, to escape from this relationship of motive to emotion by confining ourselves very largely to those words which denote emotion: love, envy, anger, and the like?

This is not possible, for these words, like others, represent concepts. If we should confine ourselves strictly to such a vocabulary, we should merely write didactic poetry: poetry about love in general, or about anger in general. The emotion communicated would result from our apprehension of the ideas in question. Such poetry is perfectly legitimate, but it is only one kind of poetry, and it is scarcely the kind which the Romantic theorist is endeavoring to define.

Such poetry has frequently been rendered particular by the use of allegory. The playful allegorizing of minor amoristic themes which one encounters in the Renaissance and which is possibly descended from certain neo-Platonic elements in medieval poetry may serve as illustration. Let us consider these and the subsequent lines by Thomas Lodge:

Love in my bosom like a bee
    Doth suck his sweet;
Now with his wings he plays with me,
    Now with his feet.

Love itself is a very general idea and might include many kinds of experience; the idea is limited by this allegory to the sentimental and sensual, but we still have an idea, the subdivision of the original idea, and the feeling must be appropriate to the concept. The concept is rendered concrete by the image of Cupid, whose actions, in turn, are rendered visible by comparison to the bee: it is these actions which make the poem a kind of anticipatory meditation on more or less sensual love, a meditation which by its mere tone of expression keeps the subject in its proper place as a very minor one. Sometimes the emphasis is on the mere description of the bee, sometimes on the description of Cupid, sometimes on the lover's feeling; but the feeling motivated in any passage is governed by this emphasis. The elements, once they are united in the poem, are never really separated, of course. In so far as the poet departs from his substantial theme in the direction of mere bees and flowers, he will achieve what Ransom calls irrelevance; but if there is much of this the poem will be weakened. Whether he so departs or not, the relation of motive to emotion must remain the same, within each passage. I have discussed this problem in my essay on Ransom.

A common romantic practice is to use words denoting emotions, but to use them loosely and violently, as if the very carelessness expressed emotion. Another is to make a general statement, but seem to refer it to a particular occasion, which, however, is never indicated: the poet thus seems to avoid the didactic, yet he is not forced to understand the particular motive. Both these faults may be seen in these lines from Shelley:

Out of the day and night
A joy has taken flight;
    Fresh spring, and summer, and winter hoar,
Move my faint heart with grief, but with delight
    No more—oh, never more.

The poet's intention is so vague, however, that he achieves nothing but stereotypes of a very crude kind.

The Romantics often tried other devices. For example, it would be possible to write a poem on fear in general, but to avoid in some measure the effect of the purely didactic by illustrating the emotion along the way with various experiences which might motivate fear. There is a danger here, though it is merely a danger, that the general idea may not dominate the poem, and that the poem may thus fall apart into a group of poems on particular experiences. There is the alternative danger, that the particular quality of the experiences may be so subordinated to the illustrative function of the experiences, that within each illustration there is merely a stereotyped and not a real relationship of motive to feeling: this occurs in Collins' *Ode to Fear*, though a few lines in the Epode come surprisingly to life. But the methods which I have just described really offer no semblance of an escape from the theory of motivation which I am defending.

Another Romantic device, if it is conscious enough to be called a device, is to offer instead of a defensible motive a false one, usually culled from landscape. This kind of writing represents a tacit admission of the principle of motivation which I am defending, but a bad application of the principle. It results in the kind of writing which I have called pseudo-reference in my volume, *Primitivism and Decadence*. One cannot believe, for example, that Wordsworth's passions were charmed away by a look at the daffodils, or that Shelley's were aroused by the sight of the leaves blown about in the autumn wind. A motive is offered, and the poet wants us to accept it, but we recognize it as inadequate. In such a poem there may be fragments of good description, which motivate a feeling more or less purely appropriate to the objects described, and these fragments may sustain our liking for the poem: this happens in Collins' *Ode to Evening*; but one will find also an account of some kind of emotion essentially irrelevant to the objects described, along with the attempt, more or less explicit, to deduce the emotion from the object.

There remains the method of the Post-Romantics, whether French Symbolists or American Experimentalists: the method of trying to extinguish the rational content of language while retaining the content of association. This method I have discussed in *Primitivism and Decadence*, and I shall discuss it again in this book.

NINTH PROBLEM

The relationship in the poem of rational meaning to feeling we have seen to be that of motive to emotion; and we have seen that this must be a satisfactory relationship. How do we determine whether such a relationship is satisfactory? We determine it by an act of moral judgment. The question then arises whether moral judgments can be made, whether the concept of morality is or is not an illusion.

If morality can be considered real, if a theory of morality can be said to derive from reality, it is because it guides us toward the greatest happiness which the accidents of life permit: that is, toward the fullest realization of our nature, in the Aristotelian or Thomistic sense. But is there such a thing, abstractly considered, as full realization of our nature?

To avoid discussion of too great length, let us consider the opposite question: is there such a thing as obviously unfulfilled human nature? Obviously there is. We need only turn to the feeble-minded, who cannot think and so cannot perceive or feel with any clarity; or to the insane, who sometimes perceive and feel with great intensity, but whose feelings and perceptions are so improperly motivated that they are classed as illusions. At slightly higher levels, the criminal, the dissolute, the unscrupulously selfish, and various types of neurotics are likely to arouse but little disagreement as examples.

Now if we are able to recognize the fact of insanity—if in fact we are forced to recognize it—that is, the fact of the obvious maladjustment of feeling to motive, we are forced to admit the possibility of more accurate adjustment, and, by necessary sequence, of absolutely accurate adjustment, even though we admit the likelihood that most people will attain to a final adjustment but very seldom indeed. We can guide ourselves toward such an adjustment in life, as in art, by means of theory and the critical examination of special instances; but the final act of judgment is in both life and art a unique act—it is a relationship between two elements, the rational understanding and the feeling, of which only one is classificatory and of which the other has infinite possibilities of variation.

TENTH PROBLEM

If the final act of adjustment is a unique act of judgment, can we say that it is more or less right, provided it is demonstrably within the general limits prescribed by the theory of morality which has led to it? The answer to this question is implicit in what has preceded; in fact the answer resembles exactly that reached at the end of the first problem examined. We can say that it is more or less nearly right. If extreme deviation from right judgment is obvious, then there is such a thing as right judgment. The mere fact that life may be conducted in a fairly satisfactory manner, by means of inaccurate judgment within certain limits, and that few people ever bother to refine their judgment beyond the stage which enables them to remain largely within those limits, does not mean that accurate judgment has no reality. Implicit in all that has preceded is the concept that in any moral situation, there is a right judgment as an ultimate possibility; that the human judge, or actor, will approximate it more or less nearly; that the closeness of his approximation will depend upon the accuracy of his rational understanding and of his intuition, and upon the accuracy of their interaction upon each other.

ELEVENTH PROBLEM

Nothing has thus far been said about human action, yet morality is supposed to guide human action. And if art is moral, there should be a relationship between art and human action.

The moral judgment, whether good, bad, or indifferent, is commonly the prelude and instigation to action. Hastily or carefully, intelligently or otherwise, one arrives at some kind of general idea of a situation calling for action, and one's idea motivates one's feeling: the act results. The part played by will, or the lack of it, between judgment and act, the possibility that action may be frustrated by some constitutional or habitual weakness or tendency, such as cowardice or a tendency to anger, in a person of a fine speculative or poetic judgment, are subjects for a treatise on ethics or psychology; a treatise on poetry stops with the consideration of the speculative judgment, which reaches its best form and expression in poetry. In the situations of daily life, one does not, as a rule, write a poem before acting: one makes a more rapid and simple judgment. But if the poem does not individually lead to a particular act, it does not prevent action. It gives us a better way of judging representative acts than we should otherwise have. It is thus a civilizing influence: it trains our power of judgment, and should, I imagine, affect the quality of daily judgments and actions.

TWELFTH PROBLEM

What, then, is the nature of the critical process?

It will consist (1) of the statement of such historical or biographical knowledge as may be necessary in order to understand the mind and method of the writer; (2) of such analysis of his literary theories as we may need to understand and evaluate what he is doing; (3) of a rational critique of the paraphrasable content (roughly, the motive) of the poem; (4) of a rational critique of the feeling motivated—that is, of the details of style, as seen in language and technique; and (5) of the final act of judgment, a unique act, the general nature of which can be indicated, but which cannot be communicated precisely, since it consists in receiving from the poet his own final and unique judgment of his matter and in judging that judgment. It should be noted that the purpose of the first four processes is to limit as narrowly as possible the region in which the final unique act is to occur.

In the actual writing of criticism, a given task may not require all of these processes, or may not require that all be given equal emphasis; or it may be that in connection with a certain writer, whether because of the nature of the writer or because of the way in which other critics have treated him previously, one or two of these processes must be given so much emphasis that others must be neglected for lack of space. These are practical matters to be settled as the occasions arise.

THE ANALYSIS
OF FORM

Kenneth Burke

THE POETIC PROCESS (1931)

IF WE WISH to indicate a gradual rise to a crisis, and speak of this as a climax, or a crescendo, we are talking in intellectualistic terms of a mechanism which can often be highly emotive. There is in reality no such general thing as a crescendo. What does exist is a multiplicity of individual art-works each of which may be arranged as a whole, or in some parts, in a manner which we distinguish as climactic. And there is also in the human brain the potentiality for reacting favorably to such a climactic arrangement. Over and over again in the history of art, different material has been arranged to embody the principle of the crescendo; and this must be so because we "think" in a crescendo, because it parallels certain psychic and physical processes which are at the roots of our experience. The accelerated motion of a falling body, the cycle of a storm, the procedure of the sexual act, the ripening of crops—growth here is not merely a linear progression, but a frui-

From *Counter-Statement* by Kenneth Burke. Reprinted by permission of Hermes Publications, Los Altos, California.

tion. Indeed, natural processes are, inevitably, "formally" correct, and by merely recording the symptoms of some physical development we can obtain an artistic development. Thomas Mann's work has many such natural forms converted into art forms, as, in *Death in Venice*, his charting of a sunrise and of the progressive stages in a cholera epidemic. And surely, we may say without much fear of startling anyone, that the work of art utilizes climactic arrangement because the human brain has a pronounced potentiality for being arrested, or entertained, by such an arrangement.

But the concept "crescendo" does not have the emotive value of a crescendo. To arouse the human potentiality for being moved by the crescendo, I must produce some particular experience embodying a crescendo, a story, say, about A and B, where A becomes more and more involved in difficulties with B and finally shoots him. Here I have replaced the concept by a work of art illustrating it, and now for the first time I have an opportunity of making the crescendo play upon the human emotions.

In this way the work of art is seen to involve a principle of individuation. A shoots B in a crescendo, X weathers a flood and rescues Y in a crescendo—the artist may particularize, or individuate, the crescendo in any of the myriad aspects possible to human experience, localizing or channelizing it according to the chance details of his own life and vision. And similarly, throughout the permutations of history, art has always appealed, by the changing individuations of changing subject matter, to certain potentialities of appreciation which would seem to be inherent in the very germ plasm of man, and which, since they are constant, we might call innate forms of the mind. These forms are the "potentiality for being interested by certain processes or arrangements," or the "feeling for such arrangements of subject matter as produce crescendo, contrast, comparison, balance, repetition, disclosure, reversal, contraction, expansion, magnification, series, and so on." Such "forms of the mind" might be listed at greater length. But I shall stop at the ones given, as I believe they illustrate to the extent of being a definition of my meaning. At bottom these "forms" may be looked upon as minor divisions of the two major "forms," unity and diversity. In any case, both unity and diversity will be found intermingling in any example of such forms. Contrast, for instance, is the use of elements which conflict in themselves but are both allied to a broader unity (as laughter on one page, tears on the next, but each involving an incident which furthers the growth of the plot). But the emotions cannot enjoy these forms, or laws (naturally, since they are merely the *conditions of emotional response*) except in their concreteness, in their quasivitiating material incorporation, in their specification or individuation.

This statement can be made clearer by comparing and contrasting it with the doctrines of Plato. Plato taught that the world of our senses is the manifestation of divine law through material. Thus, he supposed certain archetypes, or pure ideas, existing in heaven, while the objects of sensuous experience were good, true, and beautiful in proportion as they exemplified the pure form or idea behind them. Physical, or sensuous beauty, is valuable in so far as it gives us glimpses of the divine beauty, the original form, of which it is an imperfect replica.

Scholastic philosophy concerned itself principally with the problems raised by this teaching. The divine forms were called universals, and the concept of a principle of individuation was employed to describe the conditions under which we could experience these divine forms. "*Universale intelligitur, singulare sentitur,*" their position was finally stated: "We think in terms of universals, but we feel particulars." Or, to illustrate, "We may make an intellectual concept of goodness, but we can experience only some particular good thing."

Thus, the Platonic teaching was gradually reversed, and finally became branded as representative of a typically erroneous attitude. To say that an object is good in that it reflects the divine idea, or archetype, of goodness is, according to the nominalists, the mistake of hypostatization, of mistaking a linguistic convenience for a metaphysical reality. What really happens, they say, is that we find certain objects appealing in one way or another (tasty, beneficial, mild, obedient) and in the economy of speech use the word "good" for all these aspects of appeal. And since another economy of speech is the conversion of adjectives into nouns, we next turn "good" into "goodness" and suppose that there is some actual thing, sitting somewhere, which corresponds to this word. This is to misunderstand the nature of language, they assert: and this misunderstanding results from the naive supposition that, since each object has a word to designate it, so each word designates an object. Thus, they see no need for going from the particular to the universal; and they might, rather, define goodness as a complex of conditions in the human mind, body, and environment which makes some objects, through a variety of ways, more appealing than others.

So eager were the nominalists to disavow Plato in detail, that they failed to discover the justice of his doctrines in essence. For we need but take his universals out of heaven and situate them in the human mind (a process begun by Kant), making them not metaphysical, but psychological. Instead of divine forms, we now have "conditions of appeal." There need not be a "divine contrast" in heaven for me to appreciate a contrast; but there *must be* in my mind the sense of contrast. The researches of anthropologists indicate that man has "progressed" in cultural cycles which repeat themselves in essence (in form) despite the limitless variety of specific details to embody such essences, or forms. Speech, material traits (for instance, tools), art, mythology, religion, social systems, property, government, and war—these are the nine "potentials" which man continually re-individuates into specific cultural channels, and which anthropologists call the "universal pattern." And when we speak of psychological universals, we mean simply that just as there is inborn in the germ plasm of a dog the potentiality of barking, so there is inborn in the germ plasm of man the potentiality of speech, art, mythology, and so on. And while these potentialities are continually changing their external aspects, their "individuations," they do not change in essence. Given the potentiality for speech, the child of any culture will speak the language which it hears. There is no mental equipment for speaking Chinese which is different from the mental equipment for speaking English. But the potentiality externalizes itself in accordance with the traditions into which the individual happens to be born. And by education we do not mean the "awaking" of a moral, or religious, or social, or artistic sense, but the leading of such potentialities into one specific channel. We cannot teach the moral sense any more than we can teach abstract thought to a dog. But we can individuate the moral sense by directing it into a specific code or tradition. The socialists today imply this fact when they object to the standard *bourgeois* education, meaning that it channelizes the potentialities of the child into a code which protects the *bourgeois* interests,

whereas they would have these same potentialities differently individuated to favor the proletarian revolution.

This, I hope, should be sufficient to indicate that there is no hypostatization in speaking of innate forms of the mind, and mentioning "laws" which the work of art makes accessible to our emotions by individuation. And for our purposes we might translate the formula *"universale intelligitur, singulare sentitur"* into some such expansion as this: "We can discuss the basic forms of the human mind under such concepts as crescendo, contrast, comparison, and so on. But to experience them emotionally, we must have them singularized into an example, an example which will be chosen by the artist from among his emotional and environmental experiences."

Whereupon, returning to the Poetic Process, let us suppose that while a person is sleeping some disorder of the digestion takes place, and he is physically depressed. Such depression in the sleeper immediately calls forth a corresponding psychic depression, while this psychic depression in turn translates itself into the invention of details which will more or less adequately symbolize this depression. If the sleeper has had some set of experiences strongly marked by the feeling of depression, his mind may summon details from this experience to symbolize his depression. If he fears financial ruin, his depression may very reasonably seize upon the cluster of facts associated with this fear in which to individuate itself. On the other hand, if there is no strong set of associations in his mind clustered about the mood of depression, he may invent details which, on waking, seem inadequate to the mood. This fact accounts for the incommunicable wonder of a dream, as when at times we look back on the dream and are mystified at the seemingly unwarranted emotional responses which the details "aroused" in us. Trying to convey to others the emotional overtones of this dream, we laboriously recite the details, and are compelled at every turn to put in such confessions of defeat as "There was something strange about the room," or "For some reason or other I was afraid of this boat, although there doesn't seem to be any good reason now." But the details were not the cause of the emotion; the emotion, rather, dictated the selection of the details. Especially when the emotion was one of marvel or mystery, the invented details seem inadequate—the dream becoming, from the standpoint of communication, a flat failure, since the emotion failed to individuate itself into adequate symbols. And the sleeper himself, approaching his dream from the side of consciousness after the mood is gone, feels how inadequate are the details for conveying the emotion that caused them, and is aware that even for him the wonder of the dream exists only in so far as he still remembers the quality pervading it. Similarly, a dreamer may awaken himself with his own hilarious laughter, and be forthwith humbled as he recalls the witty saying of his dream. For the delight in the witty saying came first (was causally prior) and the witty saying itself was merely the externalization, or individuation, of this delight. Of a similar nature are the reminiscences of old men, who recite the facts of their childhood, not to force upon us the trivialities and minutiae of these experiences, but in the forlorn hope of conveying to us the "overtones" of their childhood, overtones which, unfortunately, are beyond reach of the details which they see in such an incommunicable light, looking back as they do upon a past which is at once themselves and another.

The analogy between these instances and the procedure of the poet is apparent. In this way the poet's moods dictate the selection of details and thus individuate themselves into one specific work of art.

However, it may have been noticed that in discussing the crescendo and the dream I have been dealing with two different aspects of the art process. When art externalizes the human sense of crescendo by inventing one specific crescendo, this is much different from the dream externalizing depression by inventing a combination of details associated with depression. If

the artist were to externalize his mood of horror by imagining the facts of a murder, he would still have to externalize his sense of crescendo by the arrangement of these facts. In the former case he is individuating an "emotional form," in the latter a "technical form." And if the emotion makes for the consistency of his details, by determining their selection, technique makes for the vigor, or saliency, or power of the art-work by determining its arrangement.[1]

We now have the poet with his moods to be individuated into subject matter, and his feeling for technical forms to be individuated by the arrangement of this subject matter. And as our poet is about to express himself, we must now examine the nature of self-expression.

First, we must recognize the element of self-expression which is in all activity. In both metaphysics and the sphere of human passions, the attraction of two objects has been called

---

[1] This saliency is, of course, best maintained by the shifting of technical forms. Any device for winning the attention, if too often repeated, soon becomes wearisome. Chesterton's constant conversion of his thoughts into paradox, for instance, finally inoculates us against the effect intended. Yet any one thought, given this form, is highly salient. The exploitation of a few technical forms produces *mannerism*, while the use of many produces *style*. A page of Shakespeare can be divided endlessly into technical devices (no doubt, for the most part, spontaneously generated): shifting rhythms within the blank verse, coincidences and contrasts of vowel quantity, metaphors, epigrams, miniature plot processes where in a few lines some subject rises, blossoms, and drops—while above the whole is the march and curve of the central plot itself. Yet even Shakespeare tends to bludgeon us at times with the too frequent use of metaphor, until what was an allurement threatens to become an obstacle. We might say that the hypertrophy of metaphor is Shakespeare at his worst, and fills in those lapses of inspiration when he is keeping things going as best as he can until the next flare-up. And thus, as with the music of Bach, if he at times attains the farthest reaches of luminosity and intensity, he never falls beneath the ingenious. . . . A writer like Proust, any single page of whom is astounding, becomes wearisome after extended reading. Proust's technical forms, one might say, are limited to the exploitation of parenthesis within parenthesis, a process which is carried down from whole chapters, through parts of chapters, into the paragraph, and thence into the halting of the single sentence.

will, love, gravitation. Does water express itself when it seeks its level? Does the formation of a snow crystal satisfy some spiritual hunger awakened by the encroachment of chill upon dormant clouds? Forgoing these remoter implications, avoiding what need not here be solved, we may be content with recognizing the element of self-expression in all human activities. There is the expression of racial properties, types of self-expression common to all mankind, as the development from puberty to adolescence, the defense of oneself when in danger, the seeking of relaxation after labor. And there is the self-expression of personal characteristics: the development from puberty to adolescence manifesting itself in heightened religiosity, cruelty, sentimentality, or cynicism; the defense of oneself being procured by weapons, speech, law, or business; the relaxation after labor being sought in books rather than alcohol, alcohol rather than books, woman rather than either—or perhaps by a long walk in the country. One man attains self-expression by becoming a sailor, another by becoming a poet.

Self-expression today is too often confused with pure utterance, the spontaneous cry of distress, the almost reflex vociferation of triumph, the clucking of the pheasant as he is startled into flight. Yet such utterance is obviously but one small aspect of self-expression. And, if it is a form of self-expression to utter our emotions, it is just as truly a form of self-expression to provoke emotion in others, if we happen to prefer such a practice, even though the emotions aimed at were not the predominant emotions of our own lives. The maniac attains self-expression when he tells us that he is Napoleon; but Napoleon attained self-expression by commanding an army. And, transferring the analogy, the self-expression of the artist, *qua* artist, is not distinguished by the uttering of emotion, but by the evocation of emotion. If, as humans, we cry out that we are Napoleon, as artists we seek to command an army.

Mark Twain, before setting pen to paper, again and again transformed the bitterness that he *wanted* to utter into the humor that he *could* evoke. This would indicate that his desire to evoke was a powerful one; and an event which is taken by Mr. Van Wyck Brooks as an evidence of frustration can just as easily be looked upon as the struggle between two kinds of self-expression. We might say that Mark Twain, as artist, placed so much greater emphasis upon evocation than utterance that he would even change the burden of his message, evoking what he best could, rather than utter more and evoke less. Certain channels of expression will block others. To become an athlete, for instance, I must curb my appetite for food and drink; or I may glut and carouse, and regret to the end of my days the flabbiness of my muscles. Perhaps those critics, then, who would see us emancipated, who would show us a possible world of expression without frustration, mean simply that we are now free to go and storm a kingdom, to go and become Napoleons? In this they provide us with a philosophy of action rather than a method, and in the last analysis I fear that their theories are the self-expression of utterance, not a rigid system for compelling conviction, but a kind of standard for those of their own mind to rally about.

Thus, we will suppose that the artist, whom we have left for some time at the agonizing point of expressing himself, discovers himself not only with a message, but also with a desire to produce effects upon his audience. He will, if fortunate, attempt to evoke the feelings with which he himself is big; or else these feelings will undergo transformations (as in the case of Twain) before reaching their fruition in the art-work. Indeed, it is inevitable that all initial feelings undergo some transformation when being converted into the mechanism of art, and Mark Twain differs from less unhappy artists not in kind, but in degree. Art is a translation, and every translation is a compromise (although, be it noted, a compromise which may have new virtues of its own, virtues not part of the original). The mechanism invented to reproduce the original mood of the artist in turn develops independent requirements. A certain theme of itself calls up a counter-theme; a certain significant moment must be prepared for. The artist will add some new detail of execution because other details of his mechanism have created the need for it; hence while the originating emotion is still in ferment, the artist is concerned with impersonal mechanical processes.

This leads to another set of considerations: *the artist's means are always tending to become ends in themselves.* The artist begins with his emotion, he translates this emotion into a mechanism for arousing emotion in others, and thus his interest in his own emotion transcends into his interest in the treatment. If we called beauty the artist's means of evoking emotion, we could say that the relationship between beauty and art is like that between logic and philosophy. For if logic is the implement of philosophy, it is just as truly the end of philosophy. The philosopher, as far as possible, erects his convictions into a logically progressive and well-ordered system of thought, because he would rather have such a system than one less well-ordered. So true is this, that at certain stages in the world's history when the content of philosophy has been thin, philosophers were even more meticulous than usual in their devotion to logical pastimes and their manipulation of logical processes. Which is to say that the philosopher does not merely use logic to convince others; he uses logic because he loves logic, so that logic is to him as much an end as a means. Others will aim at conviction by oratory, because they prefer rhetoric as a channel of expression. While in the Inquisition conviction was aimed at through the channel of physical torture, and presumably because the Inquisitors categorically enjoyed torture.[2] This

consideration shows the poet as tending towards two extremes, or unilaterals: the extreme of utterance, which makes for the ideal of spontaneity and "pure" emotion, and leads to barbarism in art; and the extreme of pure beauty, or means conceived exclusively as end, which leads to virtuosity, or decoration. And, in that fluctuating region between pure emotion and pure decoration, humanity and craftsmanship, utterance and performance, lies the field of art, the evocation of emotion by mechanism, a norm which, like all norms, is a conflict become fusion.

The poet steps forth, and his first step is the translation of his original mood into a symbol. So quickly has the mood become something else, no longer occupying the whole of the artist's attention, but serving rather as a mere indicator of direction, a principle of ferment. We may imagine the poet to suffer under a feeling of inferiority, to suffer sullenly and mutely until, being an artist, he spontaneously generates a symbol to externalize this suffering. He will write, say, of the King and the Peasant. This means simply that he has attained articulacy by linking his emotion to a technical form, and it is precisely this junction of emotion and technical form which we designate as the "germ of a plot," or "an idea for a poem." For such themes are merely the conversion of one's mood into a relationship, and the consistent observance of a relationship is the conscious or unconscious observance of a technical form. To illustrate:

In "The King and the Peasant" the technical form is one of contrast: the Humble and the Exalted. We might be shown the King and the Peasant, each in his sphere, each as a human being; but the "big scene" comes when the King is convoyed through the streets, and the Peasant bows speechless to the passing of the royal cortège. The Peasant, that is, despite all the intensity and subtlety of his personal experiences, becomes at this moment Peasant in the abstract—and the vestiture of sheer kingliness moves by . . . This basic relationship may be carried by variation into a new episode.

---

[2] Such a position, it has been contended, does not explain Demosthenes employing eloquence in his defense. We answer that it explains Demosthenes at a much earlier period when, with pebbles in his mouth, he struggled to perfect that medium which was subsequently to make his defense necessary. The medium which got him into trouble, he had to call upon to get him out of trouble.

The poet may arrange some incidents, the outcome of which is that the King and the Peasant find themselves in a common calamity, fleeing from some vast impersonal danger, a plague or an earthquake, which, like lightning, strikes regardless of prestige. Here King and Peasant are leveled as in death: both are Humble before the Exalted of unseen forces . . . The basic relationship may now be inverted. The King and the Peasant, say, are beset by brigands. There is a test of personal ingenuity or courage, it is the Peasant who saves the day, and lo! the Peasant is proved to be a true King and the King a Peasant.[3]

Our suppositional poet is now producing furiously, which prompts us to realize that his discovery of the symbol is no guaranty of good writing. If we may believe Jules Gaultier, Flaubert possessed genius in that he so ardently desired to be a genius; and we might say that this ratio was re-individuated into the symbol of Madame Bovary, a person trying to live beyond her station. This symbol in turn had to be carried down into a myriad details. But the symbol itself made for neither good writing nor bad. George Sand's symbols, which seemed equally adequate to encompass certain emotional and ideological complexities of her day, did not produce writing of such beauty. While as for Byron, we approach him less through the beauty of his workmanship than through our interest in, sympathy with, or aversion to, Byronism—Byronism being the quality behind such symbols as Manfred, Cain, and Childe Harold: the "man against the sky."

This brings up the matter of relationship between the symbol and the beautiful.

[3] This is, of course, an overly simplified example of technical form as a generative principle, yet one can cite the identical procedure in a noble poem, *Lycidas.* After repeating for so long in varying details the idea that Lycidas is dead while others are left behind to mourn him ("But, oh! the heavy change, now thou art gone . . .") Milton suddenly reverses the ratio:

"Weep no more, woeful shepherds, weep no more,
  For Lycidas, your sorrow, is not dead."

Lycidas lives on in Heaven. Which is to say, it is Lycidas, and not his mourners, who is truly alive!

This symbol, I should say, attracts us by its power of formula, exactly as a theory of history or science. If we are enmeshed in some nodus of events and the nodus of emotions surrounding those events, and someone meets us with a diagnosis (simplification) of our partially conscious, partially unconscious situation, we are charmed by the sudden illumination which this formula throws upon our own lives. Mute Byrons (potential Byrons) were waiting in more or less avowed discomfiture for the formulation of Byronism, and when it came they were enchanted. Again and again through Byron's pages they came upon the minutiae of their Byronism (the ramifications of the symbol) and continued enchanted. And thus, the symbol being so effective, they called the work of Byron beautiful. By which they meant that it was successful in winning their emotions.

But suppose that I am not Byronic, or rather that the Byronic element in me is subordinated to other much stronger leanings. In proportion as this is so, I shall approach Byron, not through his Byronism, but through his workmanship (not by the ramifications of the symbol, but by the manner in which these ramifications are presented). Byronism will not lead me to accept the workmanship; I may be led, rather, by the workmanship to accept Byronism. Calling only those parts of Byron beautiful which lead me to accept Byronism, I shall find less of such beauty than will all readers who are potential Byrons. Here technical elements mark the angle of my approach, and it will be the technical, rather than the symbolic, elements of the poet's mechanism that I shall find effective in evoking my emotions, and thus it will be in these that I shall find beauty. For beauty is the term we apply to the poet's success in evoking our emotions.

Falstaff may, I think, be cited as an almost perfect symbol from the standpoint of approach through workmanship, for nearly all readers are led to Falstaff solely through the brilliancy of his presentation. The prince's first speech, immediately before Falstaff himself has entered, strikes a theme and a pace which startles us into attention. Thereafter, again and again the enormous obligations which the poet has set himself are met with, until the character of this boisterous "bedpresser" becomes for us one of the keenest experiences in all literature. If one needs in himself the itch of Byronism to meet Byron halfway, for the enjoyment of Falstaff he needs purely the sense of literary values.

Given the hour, Flaubert must share the honors with George Sand. But when the emphasis of society has changed, new symbols are demanded to formulate new complexities, and the symbols of the past become less appealing of themselves. At such a time Flaubert, through his greater reliance upon style, becomes more "beautiful" than Sand. Although I say this realizing that historical judgments are not settled once and for all, and some future turn of events may result in Sand's symbols again being very close to our immediate concerns, while Flaubert might by the same accident become remote: and at such a time Flaubert's reputation would suffer. In the case of his more romantic works, this has already happened. In these works we feel the failures of workmanship, especially his neglect of an organic advancement or progression, a neglect which permits only our eye to move on from page to page while our emotions remain static, the lack of inner co-ordination making it impossible for us to accumulate momentum in a kind of work which strongly demands such momentum, such "anticipation and remembering." This becomes for us an insurmountable obstacle, since the symbols have ceased to be the "scandals" they were for his contemporaries, so that we demand technique where they inclined more to content themselves with "message." And thus only too often we find the *Temptations of Saint Anthony* not beautiful, but decorative, less an experience than a performance.

Yet we must not consider the symbol, in opposition to style, as outside of technical form. The technical appeal of the symbol lies in the fact that it is a principle of logical guidance, and makes for the repetition of itself in chang-

ing details which preserve as a constant the original ratio. A study of evolution, for instance, may be said to repeat again and again, under new aspects, the original proposition of evolution. And in the same way the symbol of art demands a continual restatement of itself in all the ramifications possible to the artist's imagination.[4]

In closing: We have the original emotion, which is channelized into a symbol. This symbol becomes a generative force, a relationship to be repeated in varying details, and thus makes for one aspect of technical form. From a few speeches of Falstaff, for instance, we advance unconsciously to a synthesis of Falstaff; and thereafter, each time he appears on the stage, we know what to expect of him in essence, or quality, and we enjoy the poet's translation of this essence, or quality, into particulars, or quantity. The originating emotion makes for *emotional* consistency within the

[4] It is usually in works of fantasy that this repetition of the symbol under varying aspects can be followed most easily. In *Gulliver's Travels*, for instance, the ratio of discrepancy between Gulliver and his environment is repeated again and again in new subject matter. The ratio of the *Odyssey* is ramified in a manner which is equally obvious, being, we might say, the discovery of the propositions which were, for Homer, inherent in the idea of "man in the wide, wide world." In its purity, this repetition of the symbol's ratio usually makes for episodic plot, since precisely this repetition is the *primum mobile* of the story. Baudelaire's sonnet, *La Géante*, is a perfect instance of the episodic in miniature. Thus, in the more exuberant days, when nature created monsters, the poet would have liked to live with a giantess, like a cat with a queen; he would have peered into the fogs of her eyes; he would have crawled over the slope of her enormous knees; and when, tired, she stretched out across the countryside, he would have "slept nonchalantly beneath the shadows of her breasts, like a peaceful hamlet at the foot of a mountain.". . . This same deduction is, of course, at the bottom of every successful art-work, although where accumulation is more in evidence than linear progression (incidents of plot being "brought to a head") these simple ratios are more deeply embedded, and thus less obvious. In his monologues, his conversations with the ghost, with Polonius, with Ophelia, with his mother—in each of these instances Hamlet repeats, under a new aspect, the same "generative ratio," that symbol and enigma which is Hamlet. "A certain kind of person" is a static symbol; a murder is a dynamic one; but beneath the dynamic we will find the static.

parts; the symbol demands a *logical* consistency within this emotional consistency. In a horror story about a murder, for instance, the emotion of horror will suggest details associated with horror, but the specific symbol of murder will limit the details of horror to those adapted to murder.[5]

The symbol faces two ways, for in addition to the technical form just mentioned (an "artistic" value) it also applies to life, serving here as a formula for our experiences, charming us by finding some more or less simple principle underlying our emotional complexities. For the symbol here affects us like a work of science, like the magic formula of the savage, like the medicine for an ill. But the symbol is also like a "message," in that once we know it we feel no call to return to it, except in our memories, unless some new element of appeal is to be found there. If we read again and again some textbook on evolution, and enjoy quoting

[5] Some modern writers have attempted, without great success, to eliminate the symbol, and thus to summon the *emotional* cluster without the further limitation of a *logical* unit. This is also true of modern music. Compare, for instance, the constant circulation about a theme in classical music with the modern disregard of this "arbitrary" unity. As story today gravitates towards lyric, so sonata gravitates towards suite.

aloud pages of it, this is because, beyond the message, there is style. For in addition to the symbol, and the ramifications of the symbol, poetry also involves the *method of presenting* these ramifications. We have already shown how a person who does not avidly need the symbol can be led to it through the excellence of its presentation. And we should further realize that the person who does avidly need the symbol loses this need the more thoroughly the symbol is put before him. I may be startled at finding myself Faust or Hamlet, and even be profoundly influenced by this formulation, since something has been told me that I did not know before. But I cannot repeat this new and sudden "illumination." Just as every religious experience becomes ritualized (artistic values taking the place of revelation), so when I return to the symbol, no matter how all-sufficient it was at the first, the test of repetition brings up a new factor, which is style.

"What we find words for," says Nietzsche, "is that for which we no longer have use in our own hearts. There is always a kind of contempt in the act of speaking." Contempt, indeed, so far as the original emotion was concerned, but not contempt for the act of speaking.

R. P. Blackmur

THE ENABLING ACT OF CRITICISM (1940)

THERE IS a kind of resolute candor necessary to a full approach to literature which is impossible to any particular approach. The best that the individual can do positively is to insist that his particular work aims in the general direction of

From *American Issues, II: The Literary Record*, ed. Willard Thorp, Merle Curti, and Carlos Baker, J. B. Lippincott Co. Reprinted by permission of the Estate of R. P. Blackmur.

that candor, and the least that he can do negatively is not only to admit but to insist that other particular approaches also aim in that direction. Failure to make either insistence leads to irrelevance and arrogance of judgment, and if persisted in at the level of practice—whether in book-reviewing or in major criticism—tends to complete the separation of the literary critic from his proper subject-matter. Instead of practicing literary criticism he will find himself practicing self-expression or casual philosophy, practices which will be deceptive in the degree that they were not candidly undertaken. Thus when the critic takes Criticism itself as his subject—when he faces his own practice, when he confronts other critics with their own practice —he must concern himself sooner or later with the relative stage of candor or deception which that practice discloses. And the sooner he does this the better, because for the life of me I cannot see how the critic judging of Criticism can do much more. Further, if he takes his job seriously, I cannot see how he can content himself with attempting less. Surely it is a tenable view that criticism must in the end come back to the task of saying what its objects are in terms of themselves; as surely, then, it is of first importance to distinguish in the work of a critic what is criticism from what is something else.

To put the matter quite practically, on the level where we actually use criticism, which is to say in our efforts towards a better understanding of literature, let us set up a series of questions designed to show the distinctions we want. We have a critic before us. What, when he is all done, does he tell us about the works he says he is examining? Is what he tells us everywhere subordinated to what we may call the interests of the works themselves: precisely, what it is within the work that interests us or defeats its own interest? Or, on the contrary, is what he tells us subordinated to some interest, no doubt worthy in itself, independent of the work in hand? If so, which interest predominates? And, if the extra-literary interest does predominate, can it yet be said that it nevertheless enlightens the literary interest, by situating it, say, among all the interests that go to make up a culture? This last, if we rephrase it, makes up the crucial question; for does it not ask, really, whether we can accept or reject a literary work by the application of literary standards alone? That is, to make one more rephrasing, do we in fact ever understand literature only by literary means?

If we can answer these questions as it were backwards, it is possible that we may come out somewhere near right in the end. At least we should have a beginning not merely provisional or wayward but with an end already and firmly in view: namely, a focus for literary experience, and a vantage for looking. We can think of the whole backward process as the enabling act of criticism.

Well, then it is plain that we never do in fact understand literature solely by literary means any more than we understand water solely by drinking it, solely by chemical analysis, solely by looking at it, or solely by damming it up. It is the unified mind and sensibility that is engaged in the act of understanding; the act is imaginative; and to try to compartmentalize the act so as to emphasize one faculty over another is to invalidate the imagination and abort the act. Looked at in this way, the question of the final understanding of literature becomes either an artificial or an irrelevant question. If we do not use the whole mind we shall understand nothing; if we do use it, we do so as it were inarticulately, as the product of our whole culture: that is, we take it for granted.

But what is taken for granted must be attended just the same, like breathing; and in this case especially; for the unified, imaginative character of the understanding was not brought up here for nothing but indifferent acceptance. It was brought up in order to emphasize the fact that at the other end of the rod from criticism—in the act of the composition of literature itself—the process is the same. Serious writing is done under the full tolerable weight of mind and sensibility. Imagination is in that sense absolute. All that can be made to bear, bears. That is why the critic must bring his full tolerable imagination to bear before judgment is possible.

In the word tolerable we introduce a consideration which brings us to the next question in our backwards moving series; the question whether, really, we can accept or reject a literary work by the application of literary standards alone. Here the answer is double; partly yes and partly no, only good sense—the taste of practice—determining which. T. S. Eliot's remark is initially in order, that while we can only tell that a work is literature by literary standards, we cannot tell whether it is great literature except by other than literary standards. A first qualifying reflection is that there is not very much great literature; and a second is that, even when a critic is concerned with great literature, most of the problems he handles will not directly affect his estimate of its greatness. Greatness is come up to, felt, discovered; not handled. A critic who tried to handle merely the greatness of Shakespeare or Dante would see it disappear before his eyes. And a critic who attempted to establish the greatness of Joyce or Eliot or Yeats would be largely wasting his time; for greatness is established by custom, by time, by the apprehension in the minds of many men of inexhaustibility, and even so greatness is transitory and variable. Milton is not so great to-day as a century ago. Dante is greater. And I use the copulative deliberately, for greatness is an act of estimation not an assertion of fact, and hence may be expected to vary, but not, once estimated, ever to disappear irrecoverably. It would be intolerable as well as impossible for us today to look at Milton either with our own full mind and sensibility or with those of his own generation, or with those of the eighteenth century. We use of our own what will bear, of the others only what will elucidate—and then only putatively. On the other hand—and this is the aspect of critical activity to which we shall return—it would be intolerable if we did not bring the full force of our literary standards to bear in order to determine what of Milton is literature and what is not. Equally, the other way round, we should bring as much as possible of Milton's literary achievement to bear on the products of our own time; and the extent to which this can be done will constitute a literary judgment on both Milton and our own time. Those other, extra-literary standards, the standards of the convictions of our whole culture, will thus tend to disappear or be transformed into the literary standards.

A very different thing happens—at this time; though it may not be at another—in the example of Dante, whose greatness has grown so in our estimation that the force of his work seems almost a quality of the air that poets must breathe to invigorate their own verse. Dante, said Yeats, was the chief imagination of Christendom; and I think it may be hazarded that his greatness lies in the fact that he showed the highest and fullest unity the Christian order ever reached actually at work in light and air and earth. As Eliot says, the Divine Comedy is a vast ordering of actual human feelings and emotions; which are our own feelings and emotions, and as we apprehend them expose us, as little in our own poetry is able to do, to the conviction of our own fate. This is to say, perhaps, that no matter how much of our extra-literary standards we bring to bear on Dante, it is not enough; it is rather that Dante's standards enlighten ours; so that, as far as actually accepting or rejecting Dante goes, we have only our literary standards to resort to. (I suggest that it is not our Christianity that brings us to Dante, but our desperate lack of it.) If this statement of present affairs is provisionally correct it constitutes a profound judgment of defect in our culture, established, in the fact, by literary means alone. Thus, in effect, we witness literary standards operating the Christian order as a "mere" principle of composition. This is not offered with approval or disapproval, but hazarded as a possible mode of approaching the problem of judging literature: namely, by the transformation of literary standards to the level of general conviction. It should be added that there does not seem to be any other poet—certainly not Shakespeare, who dramatized inertia rather than order—where such a possibility shows itself. Dante is alone in achievement.

You would not think so from a quick rereading of the principal literary critics since the middle of the nineteenth century—since, that is, the specific decay of the Christian order began to be felt as a shifting towards disorder, towards dismay, towards corruption, in the general order of culture. In Taine and Saint Beuve; in Arnold and Pater; in Babbitt and More; in the psychologists, the aestheticians, and the Marxists; in the critics associated with the *Action Française,* and in the secular neo-Thomists as well; indeed almost everywhere that men have taken literature seriously, you will find the tendency prevalent, at varying intensities, to estimate the value of writers in the degree that their *literary* standards did or did not operate in the place of other standards. Writers have been generally judged, along the lines of the critic's particular interest, as to whether or not they were able to effect deliberately such a transformation of standards as we have just been suggesting that Dante effected as it were inadvertently. There is not a writer of the last century of any stature who has not been condemned, or at least run down, for his failure in this direction by one or more of these our most eminent and best trained critics.

Now it may be that these critics are right in their preoccupation. It may be that the vast task of ordering human feelings and emotions has been imposed upon the arts and especially upon literature by the present lack of any authority otherwise derived. It may be that we are committed—I will not say condemned—to a wholly secular culture. Faced with the immediate alternatives in the wave, as Mrs. Lindbergh calls it, of fascist and soviet culture, we may even hope for a secular culture. But if assent is given to that idea, it does not follow that the literary critic in emphasizing the Dantesque aspect of literature can escape his obligation to explore and to master the primary aspect of literature: that aspect in which it represents the experience of the actual which is beneath and beyond merely moral experience, and which alone grounds or situates moral experience. Eliot's remark holds true that as morals are only a primary consideration for the saint, so they are only a secondary consideration for the artist.

This brings us up sharp on our next question, as to whether the extra-literary interest, if it predominates in the critic's mind, enlightens the literary interest. With regard to the general mass of critics to whom we referred above, the answer is plainly negative, and may be drawn from two approximate facts about their work. They seem, in the mass, seldom to have enjoyed literature, and they seem as individuals, and especially when concerned with the literature of their own times, to have been concerned with what a given work did not do to the virtual exclusion of what it did do. In short, and this is what makes one most suspicious of their candor, they not only made their criticism autonomous, which is a sin of pride, but they also made criticism appear to do the work of literature, which is the sin of putting God in second place. They defiled their literary knowledge to the point where it hardly seems recogniseable as knowledge of literature at all; with the curious but natural result that their morals or politics or sociology or theology seemed second-rate, vitiated by isolation from the actual world which lay before them in the literature which was their declared subject-matter. That the literature has survived in spite of its criticism and continues to arouse the same sort of attention suggests that it was not that the intent of the critics was mistaken but that their method was inefficient and their attention inadequate.

It is not the business of this paper to decide to what uses literature may be put, and it is not the predilection of this writer to see literature made into a kind of Pandora's box of panaceas, or even into the source of a merely moral order; but if there is a demand for that sort of thing, and there is, then it had better be done along lines that admit the possibility of success at the beginning. Those lines exist, are available, and may be taught; they are indicated in the frame of questions around which these paragraphs have been laid down. Assuming that literature, being imaginative, is understood if at all by the whole imagination before it is understood or used in any other way, acknowledging that many interests not literary but moral, political, spiritual, are nevertheless imaginatively present in literature, and even insisting that it is in the light of those interests that literature shows its stature (thereby adding to our own) and must be judged, it remains necessary to approach those other interests through the interests of the works themselves: through what is told, shown, expressed. It is there, in the interest of the actual, shaped and composed by what Santayana calls the enormous burden of perception—all that the intellect ignores or merely schematises —it is there, straight in front of you, in the words and the motions of the words, that the artist has focussed, or failed to focus, those interests you want. It could not be otherwise.

If you think otherwise, there is a primary defect in your contact with literature such as you would not permit yourself, say, in your contact with philosophy where it is a commonplace that the words are important and often difficult: where a universe is heaped in a phrase. If you think it is so but easy, you are rash and inexperienced. In the very degree that the work of literature does focus the interests you want it will be difficult—indeed an inexhaustible labor —to grasp the text. And until you have grasped the text you cannot paraphrase it; and to paraphrase in intellectual terms an imaginative experience is I suppose a generalized description of what you mean to do. But if you can grasp the text the rest will either come naturally,

though arduously, or will seem irrelevant or superfluous. You will have either the labor of articulating your judgment of interest, or you will see that, so far as literature is concerned, it does not count.

The real difficulty lies further back, and is double in character. It consists, first, in being willing to concentrate your maximum attention upon the work which the words and the motions of the words—and by motions I mean all the technical devices of literature—perform upon each other. Secondly, it consists in submitting, at least provisionally, to whatever authority your attention brings to light in the words. In doing this you will be following in pretty close parallel the procedure which the writer followed. Whether your submission is permanent or must be withdrawn will be determined by the judgment of all the standards and all the interests you can bring to bear. These will differ with the work in hand. But the act of submission must be made before you can tell; it is an act of imagination, not of will; and it is the enabling act of criticism. If it does not provide you with another Dante, it will at least provide you with an interest in literature; and without that you would not know a Dante if he appeared.

THE CHAIN OF OUR OWN NEEDLES:
CRITICISM AND OUR CULTURE (1961)

It HOPEFULLY seems to me that an intimate commentary on the following passages from Montaigne, all but the last from his essay on Cato the Younger, would provide every approach and much of the substance we need in thinking about what criticism must be up to in our own culture, both its problems and its chances.

I am singular in my desire that we should all be judged apart from others, and that I may not

From *The Critical Matrix*, ed. Paul R. Sullivan, Georgetown University Press. Reprinted by permission of the Estate of R. P. Blackmur.

be expected to conform to the general pattern.

Give me the most excellent and blameless action, and I will straightway provide it with fifty vicious intentions, all having a semblance of likelihood. God knows, if one tried to multiply them, how many interpretations may be placed on our real intentions [our secret will]! In all their calumnies their ingenuity is not so much malicious as clumsy and ignorant.

It is matter for astonishment that we have many more poets than critics and interpreters of poetry. It is easier to write than to recognize it. At a certain low stage it may be judged by precepts and by art. But the good, the supreme, the divine, is above rules and reason. Whoever is able to discern the beauty of it with firm and steady sight sees it no more than he sees the splendour of a lightning flash. It does not beguile our judgment, it transports and overwhelms it. The frenzy that spurs him who is able to penetrate into it also strikes a third person on hearing him discuss and recite it; as a magnet not only attracts a needle, but refuses into it the power of attracting others. This is more clearly seen in the theatre, where the sacred inspiration of the Muses, having first stirred the poet to anger, grief, hatred; and transported them at their will outside of himself, through the poet again strikes the actor, and through the actor consecutively a whole people. It is the chain of our needles hanging one from the other.

From my earliest childhood poetry has had this power to transpierce and transport me. But this very lively feeling that is natural to me has been differently affected by differing styles, not so much higher and lower (for they were ever the highest of each kind), as differing in colour: first, a sprightly and witty fluency; afterwards, a pointed and exalted subtlety; lastly, a mature and constant power.

One thinks at once how Montaigne has swept away all the old nonsense about styles which did so much to cut an author's force and to impair the pleasures of reading. Every great style has been mixed. Every purity is a simple well-compounded. But intimate commentaries belong to the reader, and I will say here only that none of the passages quoted formed part of the original essay; Montaigne added them late in life—his own commentary on his first thoughts. What I now add is not commentary on Montaigne, but I should like it to be read in the presence of his remarks, for that is how I now put them down.

The great risk of criticism is that it may operate when literature has been forgotten, and seem an independent mode of the mind; and this is especially so in a culture where will and choice give way to wilfulness and chance irritation. Every skill breeds its own passion, and what lasts after the skill is gone—as jealousy lasts after love—may be all the more passion-

ately obsessive the more the point is gone. This may be why we distrust criticism and deny it all serious application to the experience of reading. We do not think jealousy valid—though we know it may be fatal.

Yet we must have criticism (even if it is *only* appreciation) or we might not know otherwise that we had a literature. It may be that providence could have given us some other means than criticism for getting hold of literature and keeping it alive and renewing it: some means free of fashion and carping and infatuation, above all some means free of error and partiality. Providence has not done so. We could be reasonably sure, if we could somehow survive so long, of seeing our own errors in the light of the errors of kingdom come. In the meantime, we can trace the recurrence of what looks like error and what acts like truth along some of the regular paths of literary history.

We accept criticism because we have it, and we will accept the risk of criticism (that it may supplant or ignore the literature it was supposed to criticize) because we think we can minimize that risk by constant resort to the trick of keeping literature in sight, among the right and wrong in whose endless jar justice resides. Let us keep in mind, say, *Antony and Cleopatra, Lycidas,* and *The Dead:* a play, a special kind of lyric, and a long story or nouvelle. The play and the poem have a long history of controversy, and the story would have it if it were older and if it were not overshadowed by its author's other works. There is hardly a rule of the older schools of criticism, and hardly a prejudice of any of the more recent schools, which each of these works might not be held to have broken. On the other hand, there is hardly an insight of these same schools which these works do not exemplify. I do not say rules are errors and insights truths; only that it seems likely that when rules are made to act like insights error results—and it may be that when insights are made the chief *source* of rules we sometimes catch sight of truth. We seldom remember our insights when we do not have rules.

What I am getting at is this. If we can really apply the lessons of literary history to the works in front of us, then I think we shall see that it is the permanent inescapable business of criticism to explain and to justify—or to condemn—the total irresponsibility of the work of art. This is not my phrase but Thomas Mann's, towards the end of *Dr. Faustus*; and of course what he had in mind was not at all what you might think. He had not at all in mind the irresponsibility of children or young animals; nor irresponsibility in any form of life. Art is not life, but an abstraction of its nakedness; art is a response to life, but not necessary to any one form or institution of that life, and with more or less in the way between the response and the life. The purer the response, and the more complete the response, the more totally irresponsible it is to any of the means whereby we control life or keep it going. There is a mystery here—because art is also the most *prescriptive* of all our activities at the formal level: we can learn ahead of time how it will be done, but we can only learn afterwards what has been done. It is this aspect and this mystery of literature and art that many have condemned—from Plato to Tolstoi; it is also what some have been troubled by—from Johnson to Paul Elmer More; and it is what others have justified and explained—from Aristotle to Eliot. It is this, too, I believe, that makes the most useful criticism in our time in the job of relating literature to society and to ourselves. It makes a bridge between those who read and what is written.

But we have a history to think of in which certain types of criticism have been persistent or at least recurrent, and none of them have been very satisfactory for very long at a time. Why, then, should there be a criticism at all? If art and society were either wholly settled in their relations, or were perfect in themselves—that is, if we ever wholly understood each other the first time—then there would be no need for criticism. Then art and society would be very different from anything we know. One of the great and steady subjects of literature is our

failure to understand ourselves; another is a new, or an old recurring shift, in our unsettled states; and a third is our aspiration towards one or another impossible form of perfection. Art and especially the art of literature may be described as the effort to put into concert some of our conflicts about these relations. It expresses our experience of these conflicts. The art is imperfect in itself; and the audience has an imperfect—or at least a debatable—relation to the imperfect art; and the art and its audience change their attitudes towards each other—and change themselves too—at different rates. The moments of being in step are accidental and transitory and incalculable.

Men have wanted to clear up this incongruity for at least 2500 years—for themselves as individuals, as élites, and as whole societies. There has seldom been a living literature for long at a time without its criticism, though there have sometimes been criticisms which sought for literatures to come, or contorted the literature at hand from the past. Different types of relation between literature and its audience produced different types, and sets of types, of criticism to clarify the relation or to bridge the gap. Sometimes a single type had to carry the burden once carried by several types; sometimes a number of types have cut each other's throats, and very nearly that of literature. An example of the single type is the almost exclusive dominance of Rhetoric from Quintilian roughly to Dante; some of that time Rhetoric did a pretty full job extraordinarily well. A set of types committing suicide and nearly murder, might be found in American genteel criticism of the late 19th and early 20th centuries, which either ignored or attacked living literature as in Melville, the early Eliot, the middle Yeats. And so on.

For convenience, I think we can separate out the persistent types of criticism into three kinds: those which have to do with us and literature; those which have to do with literature in relation to itself; and those which have to do with the relation between literature and us or society. Presumably there ought to be a fourth kind which would triangulate the relations between the first three. When that happens we get great criticism, but we can hardly call it a type.

The first kind—those types which relate us to literature—roughly halves itself into a concern for genesis and a concern for history. What they have in common is interest in what is variously called Inspiration, Authority, and the Nature of Authorship. They make some answer to the questions: Who wrote it? Where did he get it? The notions that collect around these questions give some sense of the types, and the deepest and perhaps the oldest notion is that of Wooing the Muse—as in our own day Robert Graves has written a book about The White Goddess, the Muse who gives and destroys, which attracts the backward demons in us. A milder form, found in Plato, Shakespeare, Milton, and Henry James, is the notion of the presiding guardian or Genius; as we would say (or some of us) a dominant neurosis or obsession with one's role. Then we have the ancient notion of the frenzied poet, the madman, the drunk—for which the 19th century invented the "pure" poet, and the 20th century invented expressionism, and both found solace in the idea of the artist as hero. Or again there is the notion, no doubt older than history, that poetry is direct intuition—where Freud would give us the relation between the preconscious and the conscious, Jung that between the collective unconscious and the conscious, and Croce would give us poetry as the theoretic form of feelings. All of these notions involve some idea of possession, of a seeking or wooing of possession, or a cult or cultivation of possession. There is a relatively early rational form of these notions in Dante's invocation of the Muse for aid in his Comedy, which is always worth quoting again:

> O Muse, o alto ingegno, or m'aiutate!
> O mente, che scrivesti ciò ch'io vidi,
> Qui si parrà la tua nobilitate.
> —*Inferno* II

This is a rational notion of Memory that may be acquired, wooed, invoked, revealed, but above all acquired, and this, with a little jump,

brings us to our own general attitude in literary criticism. We have turned the wooing of the muses into the study of genetics. We have turned the notion of memory—the current of tradition—into the study of history.

This explains (for the old addictions are still at work, as our poets and our scientists show)— this explains our wide practice of genetic and historical criticism. We try to find in the poet's own life and in the conditions of his own time what previous ages tried to find outside the poet and outside the time. We justify the poet's strength by the trouble in his soul or with his family, and we explain his weaknesses as the result of his environment—usually by his isolation from or in that environment—as Dante said he was a Florentine by birth but not by character. That is, we deal with poetry by finding correspondences for it in the life of the poet and the life of his time, and we judge him by his relative success in expressing both. This is how we get at (or make up for) a doctrine of inspiration, the source of authority, and the nature of authorship. We like to find the genesis of the poem and the biography of the man who wrote it, which allows a high degree of relativism and makes difficult the ascertainment of judgment in the appreciation of a particular work.

The other or historical half of this first kind of criticism is composed of a larger and more varied set of types. Since we are a race that has come to live much in time—and with 2500 years of literature simultaneously on our hands —it is not surprising that we should have invented historical criticism even if we did not thereby take care of inspiration. Historical criticism takes care of two problems which are always of pressing importance as soon as recognized. It shows us what the poet did not have to put into his work—explicitly, in detail, so that another generation can recognize it—because it was taken for granted in the state of culture, the climate of ideas, the temperature of the soul, or the topical interests, under the influence of which he wrote. Secondly, historical criticism shows us what the poet got into his work by conventions, assumptions, symbols, uses of language, of which we have lost the native skill. It is these two ideas of historical criticism which have developed the whole race of literary scholars, all of whom in their specific tasks provide types of criticism under our general head. We have a scholarship in interpretation, in the establishment of texts, in history for itself (as a corrective), and in genesis both biographical and environmental and that having to do with the technical situation. Historical criticism is our way of dealing with those aspects of the radical imperfection of the poetry of the past. So also, historical criticism—if we take it as our cultivated and acknowledged memory—our way of wooing the muse as readers—should suggest how to deal with the radical imperfection of the poetry of the present—of all poetry: to let it sink in, to bring to it all we can: to ask Who wrote it, Where did he get it?

Perhaps the sum of what is meant by historical criticism and scholarship is this: it gives a body of conscious knowledge to occupy our minds while we acquire—or re-acquire—the deep unconscious skills of combination and selection of perception of which literature is made. No skill is *known* in the arts until it has run down into the fingertips of second nature. Meanwhile we have to busy ourselves at the portals, as if we were inside.

What we have been talking about is a general rehearsal of facts about the body of literature taken as granted—all having to do with our relation to literature from the outside. The direction of thought is *from* us *to* literature—with a mass of theory or attitude about the source of literature, of inspiration, authority, and authorship, attracting us, so to speak, from the other side. But none of these types of criticism inquire whether a work in question is or is not literature at all, which belongs to our second batch of types, those which have to do with literature in relation to itself. Here we want to deal with facts concerned with the medium and the form of literature. We get into questions of standards of taste, of interest, and skill. Above all we get into the question of genuineness, which depends on the answer to the other questions and something more. We

ask here, How did he write? and What, as a thing written, did he write?

It must be emphasized—always—that unlike the questions of history and genesis—we are concerned with matters largely prescribed though gradually changing; with matters that must be learned and may be modified. The medium of literature is language; most of it, with respect to its immediately preceding state, is unchanged: yet that little change is what keeps it alive. The form of literature is the corpus of technical matters as they get into language; technique may change more sharply than language in a given time, but changes within a narrower compass on the whole. The technique of Chaucer is nearer that of Hardy than the language; so with Virgil and Dante, Shakespeare and O'Neill. We deal then with prescriptive studies when we deal with the inner relations of literature.

As we had genesis and history as names for our first batch, we have even more venerable names for our second. Rhetoric deals with matters of the medium of language; Poetics deals with matters of the form of literature, though of course these cannot be segregated in practice, only in theory and analysis. But rhetoric comes first, as it is anterior to and larger than the poetic use of it.

In Rhetoric we have these types of criticism or what sometimes is criticism: We have grammar or the means of the declaration of the subject; syntax or the ordnance of relations; figures and tropes or the means of expansion; semantics, or the recovery of the seed, and history brought to bear; meaning or the creation and discovery of specific experience; communication versus expression, or the characteristic problem of discrimination; the purification of the language of the tribe, or the *merely* primary obligation; the reality in language, or the inexhaustible reservoir of what we did not know that we knew; and the logos, or the word within a word unable to utter a word: the mystery in the medium. In short we are dealing with the control of the medium: the endless thing which requires true and everlasting cooperation.

In Poetics we have these types of criticism

under the following words and phrases: We have genre, which asks what kind is this? with what is it cognate? with what incongruous? We have comparative criticism, which asks How does this illustrate what? We have technical analysis, which handles the questions of such things as rhyme, rhythm, metre; plot, surprise, recognition, discovery, etc.; point of view, mode, etc. We have non-technical analysis, which deals with the questions of habit and possibility and scope with iconography, symbolism, story, character, and psychology. We have also the confusion of genres, or ambiguity of intent, and confusion of technical forms, or ambiguity of execution. And we have, if we like (for we do not need it till we come to philosophy) a theory of the imagination. In short, we are dealing with execution in the medium: the specific thing, done alone, and for once, but an example, perhaps seen with others, or against others, whether good or bad. Here we are enormously aware of standards, of prescriptions, of their arbitrariness and of their necessity: of the interminable training and practice that goes with them. And we come blank on the need for gift, for genuineness, if anything is to be done with them. We are back wooing the Muses; with the greater sense of incentive and the more haunted.

We also come upon the institutions of literature—which is how we come on our third batch of criticism: those which have to do with the relation between literature and us or society; between literature and the powers that be; between literature and the censor; between literature and the individual who is faced with—and is not merely escaping—society.

Here the question is neither one of the history of what has happened nor prescription of what ought to be done. It is the question of determining between prescription for, and assent to, what has been done, what has come out of the affair between men and the muses. And this is locked up with a kind of lock-jaw locking in the question of value. We ask of what use is it? What will it do? It is because these questions cannot be avoided, because

other people ill-equipped will rush in to ask them, that some at least among the body of critics must train themselves to ask these questions and force themselves to answer them. It is no defense that in a really decent society they would not come up, for the conventions and institutions of a decent society would be constantly refreshed with reality, and such a society we have never had.

These last types of criticism divide, like the other batches, roughly in halves: into those which are pragmatic in relation to existing society and those which have to do with the principle of any possible society, though the two halves may become confused and shift their roles, depending on the kind of gap there is to be bridged between the audience and the society. My orders, then, are provisional, schemes for discussion.

Of the pragmatic types, where we have to do with unabashed direct use, there is first literature as news. Here is the book-review and the topical interest. Then there is literature as the carrier of ideas, which is literature taken as propaganda high or low or indifferent. Near that, but older, is literature as active psychology (as Ortega says of the novel that it may provide us with new psychologies) where we deal with knowledge of character and "practical" human relations. Beyond this is social or political literature where we see how the general causes of society are enacted, frustrated, or recruited. Then there is literature taken as the exhibition of epistemology, as a contribution to the general means of access to experience. Last in this group there is the type of criticism which we may call creative where one writer reacts in his own work to the work of his ancestors and his peers. These are the neutral uses of literature, the supplemental uses which few believe wholly legitimate but everybody uses and argues.

In parallel to these there are the uses by principle, having to do with ultimate or aspiring use. There is the defensive use, the assertion of the voice of passion, the voice of the poet, of the inspiration of the muse. This has its correlative in moral criticism, or the relation of literature to conduct. Aesthetic criticism comes next, which deals with the problem of created perception, of perception at a remove. Then there is philosophic criticism which assesses what happens to our systems of ideas when these are incorporated in experience. In the same way religious criticism examines what happens to vision and mystery and piety when these are found in experience. Lastly there is judicial criticism, the establishment of identity in truth, purpose, or inspiration. These are the "committed" uses of literature which are believed deeply but are in our society difficult to prove.

To learn to do sums about criticism is hard. None of the digits or numbers used seem to belong to the same kind—as analysis, comparison, elucidation, and judgment. These are all moneys, or all forms of criticism, and even with the best standard of conversion you can add them up only with a sense of loss and wild injustice with regard to their particular values. What is analysis if taken as judgment? It is the insistence on rhyme or alliteration. What is comparison taken as judgment? It is the insistence on the unities, on heroes in high places, or on purity of genre. What is elucidation taken as judgment? It defeats every judgment which is not genetic and puts a greater premium on sincerity than on truth. And so on. Let us try one more from the other end. What happens to judgment if it is taken as analysis? Morals (usually in the guise of charged immorality) get forced into art instead of being found there. Whoever heard of a judicial critic given to moral analysis as a preliminary obligation who could judge favorably the characteristic literature of his own time? Not Plato, not Irving Babbitt. What is wanted is tact: the delicate submission of the arrogance of thought to the movements of life.

Various combinations and permutations, with their subtypes and small heresies, could be continued to some unknown position of "n"; and the more we put down the more surely we would approach the conviction that criticism, so soon as it touches theory, is a mass of contradictory, incongruous, and untenable positions. Yet literature has got along no matter what the theory of criticism. Art has a vitality and a momentum, a kind of habit of survival, like society itself; though according to every law and every rational expectation both ought to have perished long since. Art and life are rebelliously themselves. What is much more surprising is that the works of intellect including criticism, though mortal in the given instance, also have a way of surviving in the *next* instance; and they do so by reminding us that the job is always to do over again. We can always see that the criticism of the past, though useless and wrong-headed to us, was for itself right and just; it is rightness and justness gone by that give us incentive for our own renewals. What we need is always the same: some sort of intellectual account of the transactions between us and the arts.

If art does not in itself substitute for or serve or transform or transcend all the matters that daily and greatly concern us, yet it does something to the felt experience of them. It discovers or creates and then gives conventional and memorable form to the felt experience of them. Sometimes the form leads to the feeling, sometimes the feeling leads to the form. Most likely the motion is double and the relation mutual. In any case, the process is dubious, confused, problematic, equivocal, and radically imperfect with regard both to the feeling and the form, the experience and the intent, so far as they reach the arbitrary conventional medium of the art. That is where criticism comes in: to get into those feelings in art, to get the art back to life, and to determine the uses to be made of the art as understood in both ways; and all along to fill in the gaps where that is possible and to make jumps where it is not. It is a fact, whether of poverty or of riches, that the great activity of criticism will be on past art in terms of the present world, and on present art in terms of past art, which are not at all the same thing. The future drags us along.

This is our chain of needles.

R. S. Crane

TOWARD A MORE ADEQUATE CRITICISM
OF POETIC STRUCTURE (1953)

WE CAN JUDGE of the adequacy of any procedure in practical criticism only by considering the concepts and the methods of reasoning which it presupposes and asking ourselves what important aspects, if any, of the objects we are examining they force us to leave out of account. And when this test is applied not merely to the two contemporary schools of criticism discussed in the last lecture but to the long tradition of critical language from which they have emerged, it becomes apparent, I think, that there are nowhere present in this tradition any means for dealing precisely and particularly with what I shall call the forming principle or immediate shaping cause of structure in individual poems.

The principle I speak of is one that operates in much the same way in all the arts; and there is nothing mysterious about it—nothing which any one who has ever written anything, however unpoetic, cannot verify for himself by reflecting a little upon his own experience. The process of literary composition has often been rather crudely divided, especially by authors of textbooks on English writing, into two stages: a stage of preparatory reading, thinking, planning, incubation, and a stage of putting the materials thus assembled into words; and what

Professor Crane's notes have been omitted from this printing of the essay, since many of them refer to other chapters in *The Languages of Criticism and the Structure of Poetry.*

Reprinted from *The Languages of Criticism and the Structure of Poetry* by R. S. Crane by permission of University of Toronto Press. Copyright, Canada, 1953 by University of Toronto Press.

happens in the second stage has usually been represented as a direct transference to paper of the ideas or imaginations which the writer has come into possession of in the first stage—as a simple matter, that is, of giving to an acquired content an appropriate verbal form. I have myself taught this easy doctrine to students; but never, I believe, since I began to meditate on the disturbing fact that all too frequently, when I have attempted to write an essay after a long and interested concentration on the subject, and the noting of many exciting ideas and patterns of key terms, and the construction of what looked like a perfect outline, I have found myself unable to compose the first sentence, or even to know what it ought to be about, or, having forced myself to go on, to bring the thing to a satisfying conclusion, whereas, on other occasions, with no more complete preparation, no greater desire to write, and no better state of nerves, I have discovered, to my delight, that nearly everything fell speedily into place, the right words came (or at any rate words which I couldn't change later on), and the sentences and paragraphs followed one another with scarcely a hitch and in an order that still seemed to me the inevitable one when I came to reread the essay in cold blood.

I have had so many more experiences of the first sort than of the second that I have tried to isolate the reason for the difference. And the best way I can explain it is to say that what I failed to attain in the former cases and did attain somehow, at one moment or another of the total process, in the latter was a kind of intuitive glimpse of a possible subsuming form for the materials, or at least those I attached most importance to, which I had assembled in my mind and notes—a form sufficiently coherent and intelligible, as a form in my mind, so that I could know at once what I must or could do, and what I need not or ought not to do, in what order and with what emphasis in the various parts, in developing my arguments and putting them into words. I have never been able to write anything which seemed to me, in retrospect, to possess any quality of organic wholeness, however uninteresting or thin, except in response to such a synthesizing idea. It is more than a general intention, more than a "theme," and more than an outline in the usual sense of that word; it is, as I have said, a shaping or directing cause, involving at the same time, and in some sort of correlation, the particular conceptual form my subject is to take in my essay, the particular mode of argument or of rhetoric I am to use in discussing it, and the particular end my discussion is to serve: I must know, in some fashion, at least these three things before I can proceed with any ease or success. As a conception my idea may be tight or loose, complex or simple; I call it a shaping cause for the very good reason that, once such a principle has come to me for a particular essay, it generates consequences and problems in the detailed working out of my subject which I cannot well escape so long as I remain committed to writing the essay as I see it ought to be written. It exerts, that is, a kind of impersonal and objective power, which is at once compulsive and suggestive, over everything I attempt to do, until in the end I come out with a composition which, if my execution has been adequate, is quite distinct, as an ordered whole, from anything I myself completely intended or foresaw when I began to write, so that afterwards I sometimes wonder, even when I applaud, how I could ever have come to say what I have said.

I do not believe that this experience of mine is unique among writers of prose, and I have been told by friends who are novelists, playwrights, or lyric poets that something like this is a true description of what happens also to them whenever they are successfully creative. The point indeed has often been hinted at by artists in the too infrequent moments when they talk in practical terms, undistorted by *a priori* critical doctrines, about their own or others' work. Most of the published criticism of T. S. Eliot has been more concerned with the qualities of poets than with the construction of poems; but what I have been saying about the all-importance and compulsive power of formal causes in writing is at least adumbrated in his famous "Impersonal theory of poetry" and more than adumbrated in his remark, in an early essay, that "No artist produces great art by a deliberate attempt to express his personality. He expresses his personality indirectly through concentrating upon a task which is a task in the same sense as the making of an efficient engine or the turning of a jug or a table-leg." There is interesting testimony to the same effect, too, in some observations by Mr. Joyce Cary on the writing of novels. "Every professional artist," he says, "has met the questioner who asks of some detail: 'Why did you do it so clumsily like that, when you could have done it so neatly like this?' And smiles, as on a poor dreamer without logic or understanding, when he gets the answer: 'It might have been better your way, but I couldn't do it because it wouldn't have belonged.'" This is well understood, he adds, by critics like Horace and Boileau, who, being also artists, had "learned in practice that there are rules of construction, mysterious relations in technique, which exist apparently in the nature of the art itself"—or, as I should say, in the nature of the particular work of art in hand—"and which oblige the artist to respect them," though these are by no means the same as the abstract notions of literary kinds which most critics insist upon when they discuss, for instance, the novel.

Here then—in the artist's intuition of a form capable of directing whatever he does with his materials in a particular work—is an essential cause of poetic structure, the most decisive, indeed, of all the causes of structure in poetry because it controls in an immediate way the act of construction itself. Without it, no poetic whole; with it, a poetic whole of a certain kind and emotional quality, which will be excellent in proportion to the intrinsic possibilities of the form the poet has conceived and to his success in doing with his materials in his medium all that it requires or permits him to do if its full possibilities, as a form of a certain kind, are to be realized.

If form, however, in this constructive sense of the word, is thus an indispensable first principle for writers, it would seem that it might also be taken, with fruitful results, as a first principle in the practical criticism of their works. I do not find, unfortunately, although I have looked widely in the applied criticism of the past and present, that this has ever been knowingly and systematically done by any of the critics, in the tradition I have been speaking of in the last two lectures, who have thought the problem of structure in poetry to be an important concern. And there are at least two major reasons why this has been the case.

In the first place, as should be clear from my example, the shaping cause of any given literary work—the principle which determines for its writer the necessities and opportunities he must consider in composing it—is something over and above and, as a principle, causally distinct from any of the potentialities he or anyone else can attribute in advance to either the materials he has assembled in his mind or the technical devices at his disposal. He can know what he can do, in fact, only after he has done it; and the doing is an act of synthesis which, if it is successful, inevitably imposes a new character on the materials and devices out of which it is effected. If we are to talk, therefore, about formal principles in poetry and be able to trace their consequences in the structures of particular poems, we must have terms in our criticism for more than the materials of subject-matter and language which poets use and the technical procedures possible in their art. Yet it is almost wholly on the basis of assumptions limited to these non-formal aspects of poetry that the

critics in the tradition we have been discussing have undertaken to deal with problems of structure in poems. Some of them, as a consequence, have confined their attention entirely or mainly to questions of technique in the sense either of devices of prosody or diction (the rest of poetry being thought of as a matter of inspiration, invention, or subject-matter) or of representational devices in the drama and the novel (the problem of what is represented or why being thought of either as the business of particular writers or as not amenable to art): a good example of both the virtues and limitations of this latter approach is Percy Lubbock's *The Craft of Fiction,* in which the problem of structure or "form" in the novel is reduced to the problem of the different possible ways— some of them assumed to be intrinsically better than others—in which stories may be shaped in the telling.

For the many other critics in the modern tradition whose preoccupations have been not so much technical as aesthetic, the approach to poetic structure has been by way of a dialectic in which, as we have seen, the "inseparable properties" of poetic thought and poetic expression have been derived by negative and positive analogies from the known or assumed characteristics of other modes of discourse, with the result that these critics have been able to distinguish only such attributes of form in poetry as can be discovered by asking how the elements of any discourse can be or have been related to one another in a composition. They have given us in this way many approximations to poetic form, which fail nevertheless, since they necessarily consist merely in possible or observed configurations of the poetic matter, to constitute in any complete sense shaping principles of structure. Some of the approximations have been very general indeed; as when structure, or the best structure, in poetry is identified with abstract relations of symmetry or balance (or their artful avoidance), of repetition with variation, or of oppositions reconciled, and the structural analysis of particular poems is directed to the subsumption of their details of content and diction under one or another of these schemes; or as when some figure of speech, such as metaphor, synecdoche, or irony, is fixed upon as the basic model of poetic structure and the analysis of poems determined accordingly. The approximations, however, can easily be more specific than these. A good many poetic patterns, thus, have been derived by deduction from the known possibilities of grammatical or rhetorical arrangement in discourse of whatever kind; such is Mr. Yvor Winters' resolution of possible modes of organization in poetry into seven major types: the method of repetition, the logical method, the narrative method, pseudo-reference, qualitative progression, alternation of method, and double mood; the significant thing about these and other similar classifications is their equal applicability to writings which the critics who make them would undoubtedly hold to be non-poetic. And other relatively particularized formulae have been arrived at by finding correspondences between the arrangement of parts in poems and the arrangement of parts in paintings or musical compositions; by analogizing poetic organization to the simpler and more evident structures of rituals or myths; and very often, especially among the historical critics, by imputing to poems, as structural principles, whatever conventions of design can be attributed to the earlier works which served their writers as models. Whether general or particular, however, what these expedients give us are merely signs or manifestations or qualities of order in poems rather than the causes from which, in individual poems, the order springs; they call attention to "patterns" in poems of often great intrinsic interest, but they provide no means, since none are available in the critical language these critics are using, for helping us to understand why the "patterns" are there or what their precise function is. For this we require something more than any method can supply that is content to infer conceptions of form solely from the characteristics and possibilities of poetic materials.

In the second place, as my initial example

also perhaps suggests, the question of shaping principles in poetry is a question not of deductive theory but of empirical fact; the problem, in any given poem, is what actually was, for its poet, the primary intuition of form which enabled him to synthesize his materials into an ordered whole. Until we have some idea of that we cannot proceed to inquire into its consequences in the poet's invention and rendering of details; and this means that the first principle of our analysis must be an induction of which the only warrant is the evidence of the poem itself. We may be assisted in making this by our knowledge of other poems, and we need general concepts, moreover, to guide us, since it is only through concepts that we are ever able to understand particular things. But what we are looking for is, first of all, a fact— possibly a fact of a kind that has no complete parallel in the earlier or later history of poetry, inasmuch as it is the mark of good poets that they try to avoid repeating too often the inventions of others. It is fatal therefore to think that we can know the shaping principle of any poem in advance or, what amounts to the same thing in practice, that we can get at it in terms of any predetermined conception or model of what structure in poetry or in this or that special branch of poetry in general either is or ought to be. Yet this is exactly what most of the critics who have concerned themselves with questions of structure in practical criticism have attempted to do. They have come to poems equipped, so to speak, with paradigms of poetry, or of epic, tragedy, lyric, and so on, and hence with more or less definite specifications concerning the nature of the structural patterns they ought to look for; and they have as a consequence been unable to see any structural principles in poems except those already contained in their preferred definitions and models.

Let me give one more example of this paradigm method in operation; I take it from a recent essay on *Othello* by Professor Robert Heilman. Now the question of the structure of *Othello* could surely be approached inductively through a comparison of the material data of action, character, and motive supplied to Shakespeare by Cinthio's *novella* with what happened to these in the completed play. We could then ask what particular shaping principle, among principles possible in serious dramas, we must suppose to have governed Shakespeare's construction of the tragedy if we are to account with a maximum completeness and economy both for the new uses to which he put his borrowed materials and for the differences between the succession of our expectations and desires when we read the *novella* and when we witness or read *Othello*. This is not, however, where Mr. Heilman starts. His problem is not to develop a hypothesis which will adequately explain the structural peculiarities of this play but to read the play in the light of a hypothesis (of the "abstract" sort) already formed in his mind and previously used as the basis of his interpretation of *King Lear*. *Othello* he knows is a "poetic drama" (since it is a dramatic representation in which the verse and diction are obviously important parts); it must therefore have the characteristic structure of "poetic drama," which is to say, according to Mr. Heilman, a structure composed of two elements—"drama" and "poetry"—which operate in "collusion," as two "languages" or "bearers of meaning," to the end of expressing symbolically a "total meaning" relative to a given subject or "theme." The argument of his essay is accordingly a simple application of this paradigm to the facts of the text which it enables him to select as significant data. "The most obvious approach to the structure of drama," he remarks in the beginning, "is to equate structure with plot and then to describe plot in terms of those familiar and yet somewhat elusive elements sometimes called rising action, climax, dénouement, etc." This would give us a number of observations, or guesses, about the stages of the action, the location of the climax, and so on, which might be true enough but which would yield at best, as he says, "only superficial information." Such information, we can agree, might well be superficial for any

critic; what makes it seem superficial to Mr. Heilman is of course the hypothesis he is engaged in applying. For if *Othello* is not merely a drama but a "poetic drama," then its structure must be "equated" with something else than plot—namely, the interaction of its "drama" and its "poetry." The subject of the dramatic action, he says, is primarily not jealousy (as many have supposed) but love; the advantage of this view is that it not only names the dominant theme but indicates "the forces which give the play a composition of a certain kind," inasmuch as the "central tension is between the love of Othello and the hate of Iago, the specific forms taken in this play"—and here we meet the familiar reduction terms—"by good and evil." This "dramatic structure," however, is constantly modified in the course of the play by the parallel and (in Mr. Heilman's sense) strictly "poetic" structure constituted, in the speeches, by the many patterns of imagery that turn on symbolic oppositions of black and white, darkness and light, hell and heaven, foul and fair, chaos and order. These, we are told, are not so many static antitheses merely, but form a kind of dialectical action, corresponding to and enriching the dramatic action, through the successive permutations and shifts which the basic pairs of terms, at least in Mr. Heilman's exposition, are made to undergo. Much of this is illuminating and provocative; one would not care to embark upon a discussion of the structure of *Othello* without first taking account of Mr. Heilman's observations. I do not think, however, that he comes very close to defining any principle of structure for *Othello* that could conceivably have guided Shakespeare in constructing the poetic whole which arouses in us such poignant tragic emotions. What he exhibits are rather some of the material antecedents of the tragic structure in the conceptions of love and jealousy which the writing of the play presupposed and some of the consequences of the structure in the imagery and thought by which it is made effective in the words; and his only warrant for "equating" the combination of these aspects with the structure of the play is his prior assumption, which controls his examination of the text, that the structure of *Othello* must be of this sort.

These, then, are the main reasons why the dominant languages of modern criticism, for all the many insights into poetry which those who use them have attained, are inadequate means for dealing with the causes and aspects of structure in particular poems that have their bases in the productive acts of poets. We need for this purpose, if the question happens to interest or seem important to us, a language in which we can envisage our questions as questions of fact rather than of relations of ideas (such as "drama" and "poetry" or "poetry" and "prose"); in which we can talk about the internal necessities and possibilities in poems and the problems these posed for their poets rather than merely about the necessities and problems defined for us by our special choice of dialectical premises; in which we can develop terms for distinguishing the formal causes of poems from their material constituents and technical mechanisms; and in which, finally, we can achieve a precision of differentiation in speaking of the structures of different poems which is not glaringly incommensurate with the formal inventiveness of poets. The only near approach to such a critical language, however, is that made long ago by Aristotle; it would be foolish not to avail ourselves of his contribution, in its methodological aspects, so far as possible; and we have therefore to consider to what extent we can still profit, in practical criticism, by attempting to adapt to our current needs the principles and analytical devices which he was the first and almost the last to use.

II

It is not a question of regarding the *Poetics*, in Mr. Blackmur's phrase, as a "sacred book" and certainly not of looking upon ourselves, in any exclusive sense, as forming an "Aristotelian" or "Neo-Aristotelian" school. It would be a desirable thing, indeed, if we could do away with "schools" in criticism as they have been done away with in most of the disciplines in which learning as distinguished from doctrine has been advanced. But our loyalty at any rate should be to problems rather than to ancient masters; and if it happens that we have problems for which Aristotle can give us the means, or some of the means, of solution, we should be prepared to benefit from his initiative in precisely the same way as many of our contemporaries have benefited from the more recent initiatives of Coleridge, Richards, Frazer, and Freud without necessarily becoming disciples of any of these men. And it is not difficult to see what there is in Aristotle, or what we can develop out of him, that is immediately pertinent to the problem of poetic structure in the particular form in which I have defined it at the beginning of this lecture.

I should put first in the list the conception of poetic works as "concrete wholes." Now anything is a concrete whole, as I have said before, the unity of which can be adequately stated only by saying that it "is such and such a form embodied in this or that matter, or such and such a matter with this or that form; so that its shape and structure must be included in our description" as well as that out of which it is constituted or made. And of the two natures which must join in any such whole, or in our account of it, "the formal nature is of greater importance than the material nature" inasmuch as the "form" of any individual object, such as a man or a couch, is the principle or cause "by reason of which the matter is some definite thing." In spite of the now somewhat unfamiliar language in which the conception is stated in Aristotle, the underlying insight is one that we can easily translate into the terms of common experience. I take, for instance, a piece of modelling clay. There are many things which I cannot do with it—of which, as Aristotle would say, it cannot be the matter; but on the other hand the potentialities it does hold out, within these limits, are indefinite in number: I can make of it, if I wish, a geographical globe, with all its continents indicated, or the model of a house, or the bust of a sinister-looking man, and so on through a vast range of similar possibilities that is bounded only by my invention and skill. In any of these realizations the thing I make remains a thing of clay, having all the permanent characteristics of such a thing; but it remains this only in a partial sense; in itself, as a particular object to which we may respond practically or aesthetically, it is at the same time something else—a globe, a house, a sinister-looking man; and any description we may give of it, though it must obviously specify its clayness—that is, its material nature—would be of no use to anybody unless it also specified the definite kind of thing into which the clay has been shaped— that is, its formal nature. And the latter is clearly more important than the former since it is what accounts, in any particular case, for the clay being handled thus and not otherwise and for our response being of such and such a quality rather than any other.

It is not difficult to see how the conception fits the work of the poet or of any other writer. Here is a speech in a famous novel:

"Ah, my poor dear child, the truth is, that in London it is always a sickly season. Nobody is healthy in London—nobody can be. It is a dreadful thing to have you forced to live there; so far off! and the air so bad!"

Taken in isolation, this may be described simply as an expression of regret that the person addressed has to live in London, based on the commonplace thought that the air of London, as compared with the air of the country, is far from healthy. The speech, we may say, is made out of this matter; but it is a matter, obviously, that permits of a variety of particular uses: it might be a speech in an idyll, or in a satire, or in a moral epistle in the manner of Cowper; and in each case its formal nature and hence our response would be different. It is actually, of course, a speech by Mr. Woodhouse in *Emma*; and when it is so read, in its position in the dialogue of Chapter 12 and in the light of what we have already seen of Emma's father,

it assumes the nature of a characteristic comic act, wherein the most important thing is not the commonplace thought itself, but the excessive and inappropriate emotion, at the prospect of Isabella's coming departure for home, which this is made to express, and which is the formal principle shaping the matter of the speech into a definite, though not self-contained, artistic unit capable of directing our thoughts in a particular way.

Or here again is a whole poem, the material nature of which is comprised of the following sequence of happenings:

A young Italian duke, influenced by his idle companions, dismisses the wise counsellor his father had recommended to him, refuses the advice of his fiancée, and devotes himself to a life of private pleasure and neglect of public duty. A Turkish corsair takes advantage of this situation to storm the Duke's castle and to reduce him and all his court to slavery; and the Duke falls into despair when he learns that his fiancée is destined for the conqueror's harem. She, however, deceives the corsair into giving her a delay of three days and a chance to speak to her lover. She uses this time to rouse the Duke to repentance for his past errors and to work out with him a plan whereby he and his father's counsellor will attempt a rescue before the three days are up. The plan succeeds; the Duke and his friends overcome the corsair's troops and make him prisoner. The Duke's false companions then demand that the Turk be executed; but the Duke, grateful for the lesson his captivity has taught him, responds by banishing them and allowing the corsair to depart unharmed; whereupon he marries his fiancée and resolves to rule more wisely in the future.

As an action this is clearly not without some form, being a coherent and complete chain of possible events, to which we are likely to respond by taking sides with the Duke and the girl against their captors. I am sure, however, that anyone who reads *The Duke of Benevento* for the first time after hearing my summary will think that I have given a very indefinite account of what happens in Sir John Henry Moore's poem and hence misled him completely as to the poem's distinctive nature and effect. He will probably be prepared to read a vaguely tragicomic romance or drama of a kind common enough in the 1770's; what he will actually find is a short piece of 204 lines beginning as follows:

I hate the prologue to a story
Worse than the tuning of a fiddle,
   Squeaking and dinning;
Hang order and connection,
I love to dash into the middle;
   Exclusive of the fame and glory,
There is a comfort on reflection
   To think you've done with the beginning.

And so at supper one fine night,
   Hearing a cry of Alla, Alla,
The Prince was damnably confounded,
   And in a fright,
But more so when he saw himself surrounded
By fifty Turks; and at their head the fierce
   Abdalla,

And then he look'd a little grave
To find himself become a slave, . . .

And so on consistently to the end, in a rapidly narrated episode of which the formal nature is the kind of anti-romantic comedy clearly foreshadowed in these lines—a form that is only potentially in the story of the poem (since this could yield several other forms) and is created out of it, partly indeed by Moore's pre-Byronic language and manner of narration, but also, as a reading of the whole poem will show, by the notably unheroic qualities of character and thought which he gives to his hero and heroine, with the result that we are unable to take their predicament any more tragically than they themselves do.

It can be seen from these illustrations how different is such a conception of the internal relations of form and matter in a "concrete whole" from the later and much commoner analytic in which form or art is set over against content or subject-matter in one or another of the many ways we have already illustrated. A poem, on the view of its structure suggested by

Aristotle, is not a composite of *res* and *verba* but a certain matter formed in a certain way or a certain form imposed upon or wrought out of a certain matter. The two are inseparable aspects of the same individual thing, though they are clearly distinct analytically as principles or causes, and though, of the two, the formal nature is necessarily the more important as long as our concern is with the poem as a concrete object. On the one hand, we do not cease to talk about the matter of a poem when we examine its formal structure, and, on the other hand, there is a sense in which nothing in a completed poem, or any distinguishable part thereof, is matter or content merely, in relation to which something else is form. In a well-made poem, everything is formed, and hence rendered poetic (whatever it may have been in itself), by virtue simply of being made to do something definite in the poem or to produce a definitely definable effect, however local, which the same materials of language, thought, character-traits, or actions would be incapable of in abstraction from the poem, or the context in the poem, in which they appear. We are not speaking poetically but only materially of anything in a poem, therefore, when we abstract it from its function or effect in the poem; we speak poetically, or formally, only when we add to a description of the thing in terms of its constituent elements (for example, the content of a metaphor or the events of a plot) an indication of the definite quality it possesses or of that in the poem for the sake of which it is there. In an absolute sense, then, nothing in a successful poem is non-formal or non-poetic; but it is also true that structure of any kind necessarily implies a subordination of some parts to others; and in this relative sense we may intelligibly say of one formed element of a poem that it is material to something else in the same poem, the existence and specific effectiveness of which it makes possible. We may thus speak of the words of a poem as the material basis of the thought they express, although the words also have form as being ordered in sentences and rhythms; and similarly we may speak of thought as the matter of character, of character and thought in words as the matter of action or emotion, and so on up to but not including the over-all form which synthesizes all these subordinate elements, formally effective in themselves, into a continuous poetic whole. Or we can reverse the order of consideration, and ask what matter of action, character, and thought a poem requires if its plot or lyric structure is to be formally of a certain kind, or what kind of character a speech ought to suggest if it is to serve adequately its function in a scene, or what selection and arrangement of words will render best or most economically a given state of mind.

Here then is an intelligible, universally applicable, and analytically powerful conception of the basic structural relations in poems which we can take over from Aristotle without committing ourselves to the total philosophy in which it was evolved. We can also take over, in the second place, the method of investigation and reasoning which he found appropriate to structures of this kind. The conception and the method, indeed, can hardly be divorced. For if we are to consider poetic works, in practical criticism, from the point of view of their concrete wholeness, then our central problem is to make their elements and subordinate structures causally intelligible in the light of their respective organizing forms. This can be done, however, only by means of general concepts embodying answers to two major questions relative to such kinds of poetry as we may be interested in: first, what different forms can go with what different matters, and, second, what parts, and what constructions of each of them, are necessary to the achievement of any given form. But these, it is obvious, are questions of fact, the answers to which can never be given by any "abstract" method but must depend upon inquiries of an *a posteriori* type which move inductively (in Aristotle's sense of induction) from particulars to the universals they embody and from ends or forms thus defined, by hypothetical necessity to the essential conditions of their realization in poetic matter. The method, of course, is not Aristotelian in any unique sense, but no one has shown as fully as he did how it may be applied to poetics or how completely it depends, in this application, upon an adequate knowledge of literary history.

The method is factual, but it is not indifferent to values; and the third thing we can learn from Aristotle is a manner of considering questions of better and worse in poetry which is likewise appropriate to the conception of poems as concrete wholes organized by formal principles. As things made by and for men, poems, as I have said before, can have a great variety of uses and be judged not improperly in terms of many different criteria, moral, political, intellectual, grammatical, rhetorical, historical. To judge them as poems, however, is to judge them in their distinctive aspect as wholes of certain kinds, in the light of the assumption that the poet's end—the end which makes him a poet—is simply the perfecting of the poem as a beautiful or intrinsically excellent thing. I do not mean by this that poems are ever perfected in an absolute sense. We need not quarrel with R. G. Collingwood when he remarks, in his *Autobiography*, that as a boy living in a household of artists he "learned to think of a picture not as a finished product exposed for the admiration of virtuosi, but as the visible record, lying about the house, of an attempt to solve a definite problem in painting, so far as the attempt has gone." "I learned," he adds, "what some critics and aestheticians never know to the end of their lives, that no 'work of art' is ever finished, so that in that sense of the phrase there is no such thing as a 'work of art' at all. Work ceases upon the picture or manuscript, not because it is finished, but because sending-in day is at hand, or because the printer is clamorous for copy, or because 'I am sick of working at this thing' or 'I can't see what more I can do to it.'" This is sound sense, which critics and aestheticians ought to learn if they do not know it; but it is clearly not incompatible with the assumption that what a poet seeks to do, as a poet, is to make as good a work poetically speaking as he can; and this goodness, we can surely agree with Aristotle, must always consist in a mean between doing too much and not doing enough in his invention and handling of all its parts. The criterion, again, is not an absolute one; the mean in art, as in morals, is a relative mean, which has to be determined in adjustment to the particular necessities and possibilities of the form the artist is trying to achieve. And just as the poet can know these only by trial and error plus reflection upon the general conditions of his art and on what other poets have been able to do, so the critic can know them, and the ends to which they are relative, only by similar *ex post facto* means. He must therefore leave to other critics with less strictly "poetic" preoccupations the task of formulating criteria for poetry on the basis of general "abstract" principles; his business is to take the point of view of the poet and his problems and to judge what he has done, as sympathetically as possible, in terms of what must and what might be done *given* the distinctive form, new or old, which the poet is trying to work out of his materials. And here, once more, the procedure of Aristotle can be of use.

We can still profit, moreover, not merely from these general features of his approach—all of them relevant also to other than critical problems—but likewise from many of the more particular applications of his method in the *Poetics*, including, first of all, the fundamental distinction, on which the whole treatise is based, between poetry which is "imitation" and poetry which is not. The former, for Aristotle, is poetry in the most distinctive sense, since its principles are not the principles of any other art; but to insist on this is not to question the possibility of discussing as "poetry" other kinds of works of which the materials and devices, though not the forms, are those of poems in the stricter meaning of the word; the difference is not one of relative dignity or value but purely of constructive principle, and hence of the kinds of hypotheses and terms that are required, respectively, for the analysis and judgment of works belonging to each. The distinction, as Aristotle understood it, has played no

important part in the subsequent history of criticism. A class of "didactic" poems has, it is true, been more or less constantly recognized, but the differentiation between these and other poems has most often been made in terms of purpose, content, and technique rather than of matter and form, a "didactic" poem being distinguished sometimes as one in which the end of instruction is more prominent than that of delight, sometimes as one that uses or springs from or appeals to the reason rather than the imagination, sometimes as one that relies mainly on precepts instead of fictions and images or that uses direct rather than indirect means of expression. This breakdown of the original distinction was natural enough in the periods of criticism in which the ends of poetry were defined broadly as instruction and pleasure, and it is still natural in a period, such as our own, when the great preoccupation is with "meaning" and with poetry as a special kind of language for expressing special modes of signification. In both periods, although some classes of poems have been set apart as "didactic" in a peculiar and frequently pejorative sense, all poetry, or all poetry except that which can be described as "entertainment" merely, has tended to assume an essentially didactic character and function. The prevalence nowadays of "thematic analysis" as a method of discussion applicable to all poetic works that can be taken seriously at all is a clear sign of this, as is also the currency of "archetypal" analogies. The result, however, has been to banish from criticism, or to confuse beyond clear recognition, a distinction which has as much validity now as when it was first made and which has not been supplanted by any of the later distinctions, since these all rest on quite different bases of principle. The distinction is simply between works, on the one hand, in which the formal nature is constituted of some particular human activity or state of feeling qualified morally and emotionally in a certain way, the beautiful rendering of this in words being the sufficient end of the poet's effort, and works, on the other hand (like the *Divine Comedy, Ab-*

salom and Achitophel, Don Juan, 1984, etc.),
in which the material nature is "poetic" in the
sense that it is made up of parts similar to those
of imitative poems and the formal nature is
constituted by some particular thesis, intellectual or practical, relative to some general
human interest, the artful elaboration and en-
forcement of this by whatever means are available and appropriate being the sufficient end of
the poet's effort. Great and serious works can
be and have been written on either of these
basic principles of construction, but the principles themselves, it must be evident, are
sharply distinct, and the difference is bound to
be reflected, in innumerable subtle as well as
obvious ways, in everything that poets have to
do or can do in the two major kinds. To continue to neglect the distinction, therefore, is
merely to deprive ourselves unnecessarily of an
analytical device—however hard to apply in
particular cases—which can only serve, when
intelligently used, to introduce greater exactness into our critical descriptions and greater
fairness into our critical judgments.

Of the many other distinctions and concepts
in the *Poetics* which are still valid and useful
—at least for the kind of discussion of poetic
structure we now have in mind—nearly all are
limited, in their strict applicability, to imitative
works. For any inquiry into such forms we cannot neglect, to begin with, the all-important
distinctions of object, means, manner, and *dynamis* upon which the definition of tragedy in
Chapter 6 is based. They are, as I have tried to
show in the second lecture, the essential and
basic determinants of the structure of any species of imitative works when these are viewed
as concrete wholes, for we can conceive adequately of such a whole only when we consider
as precisely as possible what kind of human experience is being imitated, by the use of what
possibilities of the poetic medium, through
what mode of representation, and for the sake
of evoking and resolving what particular sequence of expectations and emotions relative
to the successive parts of the imitated object.
It is always some definite combination of these

four things that defines, for the imitative
writer, the necessities and possibilities of any
work he may have in hand; for what he must
and can do at any point will differ widely according as he is imitating a character, a state of
passion, or an action, and if an action (with
character, thought, and passion inevitably involved), whether one of which the central figures are men and women morally better than
we are, or like ourselves, or in some sense worse;
and according as he is doing this in verse of a
certain kind or in prose or in some joining of
the two; and according as he is doing it in a
narrative or a dramatic or a mixed manner; and
according, finally, as he is shaping his incidents
and characters and their thoughts and feelings,
his language, and his technique of representation (whatever it may be) so as to give us, let
us say, the peculiar kind of comic pleasure we
get from *Tom Jones* or that we get from *The
Alchemist* or, to add still another possible
nuance of comic effect, from *Volpone*. These,
then, are indispensable distinctions for the
critic who wishes to grasp the principles of construction and the consequences thereof in any
imitative work; and he will be sacrificing some
of the precision of analysis possible to him if he
fails to take them all into consideration as independent variables—if he talks, for instance,
about the plot of a novel or the pattern of images in a lyric poem without specifying the
emotional "working or power" which is its controlling form, or if, in dealing with any kind of
imitative work, he neglects to distinguish
clearly between the "things" being imitated,
upon which the *dynamis* primarily depends,
and the expedients of representational manner
by which the writer has sought to clarify or
maximize their peculiar effect.

There remains, lastly, the detailed analytic
of imitative forms which is represented in the
Poetics by the chapters on tragedy and epic. I
need not repeat what I have said in the second
lecture about Aristotle's distinctive conceptions
—which have largely vanished from later criticism—of plot, character, thought, and diction
—or about the relationships of causal subordi-

nation in which these "parts" are made to stand to one another in the tragic and epic structures, so that the last three (together with music and spectacle in tragedy), while being capable of form themselves, have the status of necessary material conditions of the plot, which, in the most specific sense of the synthesis of things done and said in a work as determined to a certain "working or power," is the principal part or controlling form of the whole. I have said why this analysis seems to me sound, given the assumptions on which it is based and its limited applicability to works of which the subjects are actions of the more or less extended sort Aristotle here had in mind. We can therefore still use it, and the many constituent definitions and distinctions it involves, in the criticism of the larger poetic forms; and we can profit particularly, I think, from the discussion of tragic plot-form in Chapter 13, not only because it gives us a clue to the structure of many later "tragic" works (this plot-form is clearly the formula, for example, of *Othello*, though not quite of *Macbeth*, and certainly not of *Richard III*) but also, and chiefly, because it suggests the four general questions we have to ask ourselves about any work having a plot as its principle of construction if we are to see clearly what problems its writer faced in composing it: as to precisely what the change is, from what it starts and to what it moves; in what kind of man it takes place; by reason of what causes in the man's thoughts and actions or outside him; and with what succession of emotional effects in the representation.

III

We should be merely "Aristotelians," however, rather than independent scholars were we to remain content with what we can thus extract from Aristotle for present-day critical use; and we should be able to deal only crudely and inadequately with a great many of the most interesting structural problems raised by modern works. We need therefore to push the Aristotelian type of theoretical analysis far beyond the point where Aristotle himself left off, and this in several different directions.

There are, to begin with, the many non-imitative species of poetry or imaginative literature with which the *Poetics* does not deal at all. A large number of these have been roughly distinguished in the nomenclature and theories of subsequent criticism under such heads as: philosophical poems, moral essays, epigrams, treatises in verse, occasional poems; Horatian satires, Juvenalian satires, Varronian or Menippean satires; allegories, apologues, fables, parables, exempla, thesis or propaganda dramas and novels. But though a vast deal of critical and historical discussion has been devoted to these forms, we have as yet only fragments and beginnings of a usable inductive analytic of their structural principles as distinguished from their material conventions.

Again, there are all the shorter imitative forms, most of them later in origin or artistic development than Aristotle, which we commonly group together as lyric poems; much of the best criticism of these has been concerned either with their techniques and fixed conventional patterns or with a dialectical search for the qualities of subject-matter and expression which are thought to differentiate lyric poetry, as a homogeneous type, from other poetic kinds. What we need to have, therefore, is a comprehensive study, free from "abstract" assumptions, of the existing species of such poems in terms both of the different "proper pleasures" achievable in them and of the widely variant material structures in which the pleasures may inhere. Lyrics, it is plain, do not have plots, but any successful lyric obviously has something analogous to a plot in the sense of a specific form which synthesizes into a definite emotional whole what is said or done in the poem and conditions the necessities and probabilities which the poet must embody somehow in his lines; and the nature of this formal principle—whether it is, for example, a man in an evolving state of passion interpreted for him by his thought (as in the "Ode to a Nightingale") or a man adjusting himself voluntarily to an emotionally significant discovery about his life (as in the "Ode on Intimations of Immortality")—has to be grasped with some precision if we are to be able to speak appropriately and adequately about the poem's construction in all its parts and the degree of its artistic success. And here too most of the necessary analytical work still remains to be done.

We are much better off, thanks to Aristotle, with respect to the full-length imitative forms of narrative and drama; but even in this field of theory there are many important outstanding questions. Except for one suggestive paragraph in Chapter 5 on the general nature of the ridiculous, the *Poetics* as we have it is silent on comedy; and although there is much to be learned from the innumerable later discussions, especially since the eighteenth century, the insights these make available still have to be translated out of the rhetorical and psychological languages in which they are, for the most part, embodied into the more consistently "poetic" language we are committed to using. That there are a good many distinguishable comic plot-forms, both in drama and in narrative, must be evident to every one; but as to what they are, and what different artistic necessities and possibilities each of them involves, we have as yet, I think, only rather vague general notions; and the problem has not been greatly advanced by the traditional classifications into comedy of intrigue, comedy of manners, comedy of character, and so on. The same thing is true of the many intermediate forms between comedy in the stricter sense and tragedy proper: of tragicomedy, for example, or the "serious" and "tender" comedy which emerged in the eighteenth century, or the kind of domestic novel which Jane Austen wrote in *Pride and Prejudice, Mansfield Park*, and *Persuasion*, or the adventure romance in its earlier as well as its contemporary forms, or even the detective novel, much as has been written about the "poetics" of that. Nor is tragedy itself in much better case. What the *Poetics* gives us is an analytic of only one among the many plot-forms which the critical opinion as

well as the common sense of later times has thought proper to call "tragic"; and it is one of the unfortunate results of the respect which Aristotle has always commanded that critics have tended to blur the distinctive principles of construction and effect, or to impair the artistic integrity, of these "non-Aristotelian" tragic forms in their eagerness to bring them in some fashion under his definition. We need therefore a fresh attempt at analysis, by the same method but in more appropriate terms, for such plot-forms, among others, as are represented severally by *Richard III* and *The Duchess of Malfi*, by *The Orphan*, by *The Brothers Karamazov*, and by *A Passage to India*.

It is not merely of the forms of drama and narrative, however, that we require a better theory but also of many of their characteristic structural devices. We still tend to think of plot in its material aspects in the limited terms in which it is treated in the *Poetics* on the basis of the somewhat elementary practice of the Greeks, with the result that when we have to deal with works that combine in various ways two or many lines of action or concern themselves primarily not with external actions but with changes in thought and feeling or with the slow development or degeneration of moral character or with the fortunes of groups rather than of individuals, we often fall into the confusion which has led many modern critics to reject the concept of plot altogether. This is clearly no solution, but the remedy can be only a more comprehensive and discriminating induction of possible dramatic and narrative structures than Aristotle was able to provide. And there is also the complex question of how plots of whatever kind, or their equivalents in other forms, have to be or can be represented in the words—the question, in short, of imitative manner in a sense that goes beyond, while still depending upon, Aristotle's distinction of the three manners in his third chapter. Of all the topics I have mentioned, this is perhaps the one on which the largest body of precise and useful observation has been accumulated, by all those critics from the Renaissance to our day who have devoted themselves to the "tech-niques" first of the drama and epic and then of the novel, short-story, and lyric. Even here, however, much remains to be done; and one of the chief requisites, I think, is a clearer posing of the whole problem in such a way as to cor-relate the many devices of manner which these critics have discriminated, as well as others that have escaped them, with the distinguish-able functions which manner has to serve with respect to form. I have touched upon some of these functions in the second lecture, and I will add only the suggestion that there are likely to be, in all richly developed imitative works, incidents, characters, speeches, and images which are not parts of the plot-form but must be viewed by the critic as elements of "thought" in a sense akin to but distinct from that intended by Aristotle in Chapters 6 and 19. We may treat as "thought" of this kind anything permitting of inference in a poetic work, over and above the direct working of the imitated object, that functions as a device, vis-à-vis the audience, for disclosing or hinting at relevant traits of character or situation, awaken-ing or directing expectations, conditioning states of mind, emphasizing essential issues, suggesting in what light something is to be viewed, or, more broadly still, setting the action or some part of it in a larger context of ideas or analogies so that it may come to seem, in its universal implications for human beings, not simply the particular and untypical action it might otherwise be taken to be. Every novelist or dramatist—or lyric poet, for that matter—who reflects on his own work will understand what this means; but the conception has still to become widely recognized among critics, or it surely would have been applied long since to such things as the apparently superfluous epi-sodes and characters and the recurrent general words and patterns of images in Shakespeare—the dialectic of "Nature" in *King Lear*, for in-stance—concerning which most recent writers have thought it necessary to offer much more profound explanations.

It would be well, finally, if we could carry our method of inductive and causal analysis into some of the larger questions of theory—com-mon to both imitative and non-imitative poetry —to which these writers and other contem-porary critics have given special prominence: we could profit greatly, for example, from a re-examination, in our distinctive language, of poetic images, of the elements and functions of diction in poetry, of the various modes and uses of symbols, and of the structural charac-teristics of myths.

We need not wait, however, for the comple-tion of these possible studies before beginning to use such theory of poetic forms as we now possess in the service of practical criticism. There is after all a close mutual interdepend-ence, in the method we are considering, be-tween theoretical analysis and the investiga-tion of particular works; and as our attempts at application become more numerous and more varied in their objects, so will our grasp of the necessary general distinctions and principles tend to improve.

IV

In these attempts, as should be clear from what I have said, we shall be making a pretty complete break with the tradition of practical criticism discussed in the last two lectures—a tradition in which it has always been neces-sary, before individual works of poetic art can be analysed or judged, to conceive of poetry as a homogeneous whole and to define its nature in some kind of dialectical relation to other modes of discourse and thought. We shall not need, for our purposes, to commit ourselves to any of the numerous and apparently inconsist-ent theories of poetry, tragedy, lyric, or the like, based on such a presupposition, which this tra-dition has developed. We shall not need to worry, as so many contemporaries have done, about how poetry differs from science or prose, or about what its mission is in the modern world. We shall not need to decide in advance of our studies of poems whether poetry in general is best defined as a kind of language or a kind of subject-matter; whether its end is pleasure or some species of knowledge or practical good; whether its proper domain includes all the kinds of imaginative writing or only · some of these; whether it is most closely akin to rhetoric and dialectic or to ritual, myth, or dream; or whether it is or is not a separable element in prose fiction and drama. Nor shall we need to assume that all good poems have "themes" or that poetic expression is always indirect, metaphorical, and symbolic. Not merely would such speculative commitments be useless to us, given our empirical starting-point, but they would be fatal, in proportion as we allowed our analyses to be directed by them, to our very effort, since they would inevitably blind us to all those aspects of our problem which our particular doctrine of poetry failed to take into account.

I do not mean that we shall not have to make some assumptions of our own, but only that these need not and ought not to be particularized assumptions about the intrinsic nature and necessary structure of our objects considered as a unitary class of things. We shall have to assume that any poetic work, like any other production of human art, has, or rather is, a definite structure of some kind which is determined immediately by its writer's intuition of a form to be achieved in its materials by the right use of his medium, and, furthermore, that we can arrive at some understanding of what this form actually is and use our understanding as a principle in the analysis and criticism of the work. We shall have to come to some agreement, moreover, as to what we will mean by "poetic works"; but here again the fewer specifications we impose on ourselves in advance the better. It will be sufficient for all our purposes if we begin, simply, by taking as "poems" or "works of literary art" all those kinds of productions which have been commonly called such at different times, but without any supposition that, because these have the same name, they are all "poems" or "works of literary art" in the same fundamental structural sense—that the art necessary to write *The Divine Comedy* or *The Faerie Queene* is the

same art, when viewed in terms of its peculiar principles of form, as the art which enabled Shakespeare to write *King Lear* and *Othello*. And for such productions we shall need to assume, in addition, only one common characteristic: that they are all works which, in one degree or another, justify critical consideration primarily for their own sake, as artistic structures, rather than merely for the sake of the knowledge or wisdom they express or the practical utility we may derive from them, though either or both of these other values may be importantly involved in any particular case.

The problem of structure, for any individual work of this kind, is the problem—to give it its most general statement—of how the material nature of the work is related to its formal nature, when we understand by form that principle, or complex of principles, which gives to the subject-matter the power it has to affect our opinions and emotions in a certain definite way such as would not have been possible had the synthesizing principle been of a different kind. The question, as I have said, is primarily one of fact and cause; and it is answered, for a given work, when we have made as intelligible as we can the fashion in which its material elements of whatever kind—words, images, symbols, thoughts, character-traits, incidents, devices of representation—are made to function in relation to a formal whole which we can warrantably assert was the actual final cause of its composition. By "actual final cause" I mean simply a cause without the assumption of which, as somehow effective in the writing, the observable characteristics of the parts, their presence in the poem, their arrangement and proportioning, and their interconnections cannot be adequately understood. In discovering what this shaping principle is in any work we must make use of such evidence as there may be concerning the history of its conception and writing, including any statements the writer may have made about his intentions. Our task, however, is not to explain the writer's activity but the result thereof; our problem is not psychological but artistic; and hence the causes that centrally concern us are the internal causes of which the only sufficient evidence is the work itself as a completed product. What we want to know is not the actual process but the actual rationale of the poem's construction in terms of the poetic problems the writer faced and the reasons which determined his solutions. And in looking for these we shall assume that if the poem holds together as an intelligibly effective whole, in which a certain form is realized in a certain matter which never before had this form, the result can be understood fully only by supposing that such and such problems were involved and were solved by the writer in accordance with reasons which, in part at least, we can state; and this clearly does not commit us to holding that the problems and reasons we uncover in our analysis, as necessarily implied by the completed poem, must have presented themselves to the writer explicitly as such in a continuous movement of self-conscious deliberation; it will be sufficient if we can show that the poem could hardly have been written as it is or have the effect it does on our minds had the writer not done, somehow or at some time, what these particular problems and reasons dictate.

We can never, of course, know such things directly, but only by inference from the consequences of the conceived form, whether of the whole or of any of its parts, in the details of the completed work; and there can be no such inference except by way of hypotheses which both imply and are implied by the observable traits of the work. There are, however, hypotheses and hypotheses, and the character of those we shall have to make is determined by the nature of our problem. We propose to consider poems as unique existent things the structural principles of which are to be discovered, rather than as embodiments of general truths about the structure of poetry already adequately known. Hence our procedure must be the reverse of that procedure by way of preferred paradigms or models of structure which we have seen to be so characteristic of contemporary practical criticism. Our task is not to show the reflection in poems of complex or "ironical" attitudes, interactions of prose and poetry or of logical structure and irrelevant texture, patterns of ritual drama, or basic mythical themes, on the assumption that if the poem is a good poem it will inevitably have whichever of these or other similarly derived general structures we happen to be interested in finding examples of; it is rather the task of making formal sense out of any poetic work before us on the assumption that it may in fact be a work for whose peculiar principles of structure there are nowhere any usable parallels either in literary theory or in our experience of other works. The hypotheses we have to make, therefore, will not be of the fixed and accredited kind which scientists employ only when their problem is not to find out something still unknown but to "demonstrate" a classic experiment to beginners, but rather of the tentative kind—to be modified or rejected altogether at the dictation of the facts—which are the proper means to any serious inductive inquiry. They will be particular working hypotheses for the investigation of the structures of individual poems, not general hypotheses about such things as poetry or "poetic drama" in which the specific nature of the individual structures to be examined is already assumed.

We must also distinguish between critical hypotheses in the strict sense and interpretative hypotheses concerning the details of literary works in their material aspects. It is not one of our presuppositions that "form" in poetry is "meaning"; we should hold, rather, that meaning is something involved in poems as a necessary, but not sufficient, condition of the existence in them of poetic form, and hence that the recovery of meaning is an essential prerequisite to the discovery of form though not in itself such a discovery. Before we can understand a poem as an artistic structure we must understand it as a grammatical structure made up of successive words, sentences, paragraphs, and speeches which give us both meanings in the ordinary sense of that term and signs from which we may infer what the speakers, whether characters or narrators, are like and what they are thinking, feeling, or doing. The great temptation for critics who are not trained and practising scholars is to take this understanding for granted or to think that it may easily be obtained at second hand by consulting the works of scholars. This is an illusion, just as it is an illusion in scholars to suppose that they can see, without training in criticism, all the problems which their distinctive methods are fitted to solve. The ideal would be that all critics should be scholars and all scholars critics; but, although there ought to be the closest correlation of the two functions in practice, they are nevertheless distinct in nature and in the kinds of hypotheses to which they lead. The hypotheses of interpretation are concerned with the meanings and implications in texts that result from their writers' expressive intentions in setting down particular words and constructions and arranging these in particular sequences. Such meanings and implications, indeed, are forms, of which words and sentences are the matter; but they are forms of a kind that can appear in any sort of discourse, however unpoetic. They are to be interpreted by resolving the forms into the elements which poems share with the common speech or writing and the common thought and experience of the times when they were written; and this requires the use of techniques and principles quite different from any that poetic theory can afford: the techniques and principles of historical grammar of the analysis and history of ideas, of the history of literary conventions, manners, and so on, and the still more general techniques and principles, seldom methodized, by which we construe characters and actions in everyday life.

The hypotheses of criticism, on the contrary, are concerned with the shaping principles, peculiar to the poetic arts, which account in any work for the power of its grammatical materials, in the particular ordering given to these, to move our opinions and feelings in such-and-such a way. They will be of two sorts according as the questions to which they are answers re-late to the principles by which poetic works have been constructed as wholes of certain definite kinds or to the reasons which connect a particular part of a given work, directly or indirectly, with such a principle by way of the poetic problems it set for the writer at this point. And there can be no good practical criticism in this mode in which both sorts are not present; for although the primary business of the critic is with the particulars of any work he studies down to its minuter details of diction and rhythm, he can never exhibit the artistic problems involved in these or find other than extra-poetic reasons for their solutions without the guidance of an explicit definition of the formal whole which they have made possible.

A single work will suffice to illustrate both kinds of critical hypotheses as well as the relation between them, and I will begin by considering what idea of the governing form of *Macbeth* appears to accord best with the facts of that play and the sequence of emotions it arouses in us. I need not say again why it seems to me futile to look for an adequate structural formula for *Macbeth* in any of the more "imaginative" directions commonly taken by recent criticism; I shall assume, therefore, without argument, that we have to do, not with a lyric "statement of evil" or an allegory of the workings of sin in the soul and the state or a metaphysical myth of destruction followed by recreation or a morality play with individualized characters rather than types, but simply with an imitative tragic drama based on historical materials. To call it an imitative tragic drama, however, does not carry us very far; it merely limits roughly the range of possible forms we have to consider. Among these are the contrasting plot-forms embodied respectively in *Othello* and in *Richard III*: the first a tragic plot-form in the classic sense of Aristotle's analysis in *Poetics* 13; the second a plot-form which Aristotle rejected as non-tragic but which appealed strongly to tragic poets in the Renaissance—a form of serious action designed to arouse moral indignation for the deliberately unjust and seemingly prospering acts of the protagonist and moral satisfaction at his subsequent ruin. The plot-form of *Macbeth* clearly involves elements which assimilate it now to the one and now to the other of both these kinds. The action of the play is twofold, and one of its aspects is the punitive action of Malcolm, Macduff, and their friends which in the end brings about the protagonist's downfall and death. The characters here are all good men, whom Macbeth has unforgivably wronged, and their cause is the unqualifiedly just cause of freeing Scotland from a bloody tyrant and restoring the rightful line of kings. All this is made clear in the representation not only directly through the speeches and acts of the avengers but indirectly by those wonderfully vivid devices of imagery and general thought in which modern critics have found the central value and meaning of the play as a whole; and our responses, when this part of the action is before us, are such as are clearly dictated by the immediate events and the poetic commentary: we desire, that is, the complete success of the counter-action and this as speedily as possible before Macbeth can commit further horrors. We desire this, however—and that is what at once takes the plot-form out of the merely retributive class—not only for the sake of humanity and Scotland but also for the sake of Macbeth himself. For what most sharply distinguishes our view of Macbeth from that of his victims and enemies is that, whereas they see him from the outside only, we see him also, throughout the other action of the play—the major action—from the inside, as he sees himself; and what we see thus is a moral spectacle the emotional quality of which, for the impartial observer, is not too far removed from the tragic *dynamis* specified in the *Poetics*. This is not to say that the main action of *Macbeth* is not significantly different, in several respects, from the kind of tragic action which Aristotle envisages. The change is not merely from good to bad fortune, but from a good state of character to a state in which the hero is almost, but not quite, transformed into a monster; and the tragic act which initi-

ates the change, and still more the subsequent unjust acts which this entails, are acts done—unlike Othello's killing of Desdemona—in full knowledge of their moral character. We cannot, therefore, state the form of this action in strictly Aristotelian terms, but the form is none the less one that involves, like tragedy in Aristotle's sense, the arousal and catharsis of painful emotions for, and not merely with respect to, the protagonist—emotions for which the terms pity and fear are not entirely inapplicable.

Any adequate hypothesis about the structure of *Macbeth*, then, would have to take both of these sets of facts into account. For both of the views we are given of the hero are true: he is in fact, in terms of the nature and objective consequences of his deeds, what Macduff and Malcolm say he is throughout Acts IV and V, but he is also—and the form of the play is really the interaction of the two views in our opinions and emotions—what we ourselves see him to be as we witness the workings of his mind before the murder of Duncan, then after the murder, and finally when, at the end, all his illusions and hopes gone, he faces Macduff. He is one who commits monstrous deeds without becoming wholly a monster, since his knowledge of the right principle is never altogether obscured, though it is almost so in Act IV. We can understand such a person and hence feel fear and pity of a kind for him because he is only doing upon a grander scale and with deeper guilt and more terrifying consequences for himself and others what we can, without too much difficulty, imagine ourselves doing, however less extremely, in circumstances generally similar. For the essential story of *Macbeth* is that of a man, not naturally depraved, who has fallen under the compulsive power of an imagined better state for himself which he can attain only by acting contrary to his normal habits and feelings; who attains this state and then finds that he must continue to act thus, and even worse, in order to hold on to what he has got; who persists and becomes progressively hardened morally in the process;

and who then, ultimately, when the once alluring good is about to be taken away from
him, faces the loss in terms of what is left of
his original character. It is something like this
moral universal that underlies, I think, and
gives emotional form to the main action of
Macbeth. It is a form that turns upon the difference between what a seemingly advan-
tageous crime appears to be in advance to a
basically good but incontinent man and what
its moral consequences for such a man inevitably are; and the catharsis is effected not merely
by the man's deserved overthrow but by his
own inner suffering and by his discovery, before it is too late, of what he had not known
before he began to act. If we are normal human beings we must abhor his crimes; yet we
cannot completely abhor but must rather pity
the man himself, and even when he seems
most the monster (as Macbeth does in Act IV)
we must still wish for such an outcome as will
be best, under the circumstances, not merely
for Scotland but for him.

But if this, or something close to it, is indeed
the complex emotional structure intended in
Macbeth, then we have a basis for defining with
some precision the various problems of incident, character, thought, imagery, diction,
and representation which confronted Shakespeare in writing the play, and hence a starting-
point for discussing, in detail, the rationale of
its parts. Consider—to take only one instance
—the final scene. In the light of the obvious
consequences of the form I have attributed to
the play as a whole, it is not difficult to state
what the main problems at this point are. If
the catharsis of the tragedy is to be complete,
we must be made to feel both that Macbeth
is being killed in a just cause and that his state
of mind and the circumstances of his death are
such as befit a man who, for all his crimes, has
not altogether lost our pity and goodwill. We
are of course prepared for this double response
by all that has gone before, and, most immediately, in the earlier scenes of Act V, by the fresh
glimpses we are given of the motivation of the
avengers and by Macbeth's soliloquies. But it

will clearly be better if the dual effect can be
sustained until the very end; and this requires,
on the one hand, that we should be vividly reminded once more of Macbeth's crimes and
the justified hatred they have caused and of the
prospect of a new and better time which his
death holds out for Scotland, and, on the other
hand, that we should be allowed to take satisfaction, at last, in the manner in which Macbeth himself behaves. The artistic triumph of
the scene lies in the completeness with which
both problems are solved: the first in the words
and actions of Macduff, the speeches about
young Siward, and Malcolm's closing address;
the second by a variety of devices, both of invention and of representation, the appropriateness of which to the needed effect can be seen if
we ask what we would not want Macbeth to do
at this moment. We want him to be killed, as I
have said, for his sake no less than that of Scotland; but we would not want him either to
seek out Macduff or to flee the encounter when
it comes or to "play the Roman fool"; we would
not want him to show no recognition of the
wrongs he has done Macduff or, when his last
trust in the witches has gone, to continue to
show fear or to yield or to fight with savage
animosity; and he is made to do none of these
things, but rather the contraries of all of them,
so that he acts in the end as the Macbeth whose
praises we have heard in the second scene of
the play. And I would suggest that the cathartic
effect of these words and acts is reinforced indirectly, in the representation, by the analogy
we can hardly help drawing between his conduct now and the earlier conduct of young
Siward, for of Macbeth too it can be said that
"he parted well and paid his score"; the implication of this analogy is surely one of the functions, though not the only one, which the lines
about Siward are intended to serve.

Such are the kinds of hypotheses we shall
need to make if we are to have critical knowledge of the shaping principles of poetic works
or of the artistic reasons governing the character and interrelation of their parts. They are
working suppositions which, as I have said,

both imply and are implied by the particulars of the works for which they are constructed; and they can never be made well by any critic who is not naturally sensitive to such particulars and in the habit of observing them closely. These, however, though indispensable, are not sufficient conditions. It never happens in any inquiry into matters of fact that the particulars we observe determine their own meaning automatically; the concrete or the individual is never intelligible except through the general and the abstract; and if we are to allow the facts to speak for themselves, we must in some fashion supply them with a language in which to talk. Hypotheses, in short, are not made out of nothing, but presuppose on the part of the inquirer who forms them a systematic body of concepts relative to the subject-matter with which he is dealing. The critic who proposes to explore hypothetically the structures of individual poems is in the same predicament; he must bring to his task, inescapably, general ideas about poetic structure, or he can never construct a workable hypothesis about the structure of any poem.

Hence the crucial importance for the practical critic of poetic forms, in the sense we are now giving to this term, of the kind of analytic of poetry which was outlined earlier in this lecture. From the point of view of the criticism of individual poems, the concepts and distinctions involved in that analytic differ from those which most contemporary critics have been content to use: they supply, not a unified set of terms for constituting structural patterns in poems (like Mr. Heilman's formula for "poetic drama" or the theories that make all good poetry a species of "ironical" or "paradoxical" structure), but a great variety of terms designating distinct and alternative principles, devices, and functions in poetry from which the critic need select only such combinations as appear to be relevant to the poems he is examining. What he thus acquires are not hypotheses ready formed but elements out of which he may form such hypotheses as the facts of his poems seem to warrant—in short, knowledge of structural possibilities only, resting on inductive inquiry into the principles poets have actually used in building poems and hence expanding with the development and progressive differentiation of poetry itself, so that he brings to the discussion of individual poems merely conceptual materials for framing pertinent questions about them without any predetermination of the substance of his answers, much as a physician uses the alternatives given him by medical theory in diagnosing symptoms in one of his patients. In the other mode of criticism the relation of theory to a particular poem is the relation of a previously selected idea or pattern of structure to its embodiment or reflection in a given work; here the relation is one of many known possibilities of structural patterning in poetry to the actualization in the poem examined of some one or more of these.

A critic using the first type of theory might argue somewhat as follows, for example, about the structure of Gray's *Elegy*. We must assume, he might say, the language of poetry being what it is, that the principle of structure in any good poem is a principle of balancing and harmonizing discrepant connotations, attitudes, and meanings; we must look therefore for a structure of this kind in Gray's poem or be content to relegate it to an inferior class of poetry; and our quest, indeed, is not in vain, for when we examine the text in the light of our general hypothesis of "ironical" structure, we quickly find that all the details of the *Elegy* can be subsumed under the theme of a continuous contrast of two modes of burial—in the church itself and in the churchyard—in which, as in all good poetry, opposing meanings are finally resolved. A critic, however, whose theory was of the second type, would proceed in an altogether different way. He would have no favourite hypothesis of structure as such, but would know merely that among short poems which, like the *Elegy*, evoke in us serious emotions, the shaping principle may be of several essentially distinct types, each of them generating distinct artistic problems for the poet; and he would use this knowledge as a basis for asking himself some such questions as these: Is what happens in the *Elegy* best explained by supposing, as the other critic has clearly done, that the poem is intended to be read as an emotionalized argument in verse (whether about modes of burial or something else), the personal qualities of the speaker and the setting of his meditation being simply devices for enforcing the unifying dialectic? Or is the poem better read—better, that is, with respect to the actual shaping principle of its construction—as an imitative lyric? And if it is this latter kind of structure, is the form one in which the speaker is conceived as being merely moved in a certain way by his situation (as in Gray's "Ode on a Distant Prospect of Eton College"), or as acting in a certain manner in relation to it (as in Marvell's "To His Coy Mistress"), or as deliberating morally in a certain state of mind on what is for him a serious issue in life? Weighing these possibilities (which give us perhaps the major forms which short serious imitative poems can have), our second critic would probably conclude that it is the last possibility which best explains both the constructed matter and the arrangement of the *Elegy* and the peculiar quality of the emotions which Gray's words and rhythms arouse in us. He might then describe the *Elegy* as an imitative lyric of moral choice rather than of action or of mood, representing a situation in which a virtuous, sensitive, and ambitious young man of undistinguished birth confronts the possibility of his death while still to "Fortune and to Fame unknown," and eventually, after much disturbance of mind (hinted at in the Swain's description of him), reconciles himself to his probable fate by reflecting that none of the rewards of successful ambition can "sooth the dull cold ear of Death," which comes as inevitably to the great as to the obscure; that a life passed "far from the madding crowd's ignoble strife," though circumscribing the exercise of virtue and talent, may yet be a means of preserving innocence; and that he can at any rate look forward to—what all men desire as a minimum—living on in the memory of at least one friend, while his merits and frailties

alike repose "in trembling hope" on the bosom of his Father and his God. Something like this, I think (pedantic as any brief statement of it must sound), is the answer our second critic would give; but the point is that in arriving at it he would be using his theory of possible principles of structure in short poems simply to furnish him with the distinctions he needs if he is not to substitute a structure of his own for the structure Gray achieved.

The more extensive and discriminating such general knowledge, therefore, the better the critic's hypotheses are likely to be. But it is also the nature of this kind of theoretical knowledge to be always inadequate, though in varying degrees, to the particulars we use it to illuminate. We can never know in advance all the possibilities, and we can never, consequently, form a hypothesis about a work of any artistic complexity or even about many simpler works without making a shorter or longer inductive leap from the words and sentences before us to the peculiar combination of universals which defines their poetic form. And that is why, in this mode of criticism, we can make no separation except analytically between theory and application, the latter being possible only if the former already exists at least up to a certain point and the former being constantly refined and enlarged as we proceed with the latter.

Application, however, is our main problem here, and its success depends upon the extent to which the universal terms of our hypotheses and the perceived and felt particulars of the texts for which they are constructed can be made to fit together. The general conditions are two: first, our ability to keep our explanatory formulae fluid and to submit them to constant revisions in principle or in detail before we transform them into conclusions; and, second, our willingness to use systematically what has been called "the method of multiple working hypotheses." We have to remember, that is, that the value of a hypothesis is always relative, not merely to the facts it is intended to explain, but to all the other variant hypotheses which the same facts might suggest if only we gave them a chance; that the best hypothesis is simply the best among several possible hypotheses, relevant to the same work or problem, with which we have actually compared it; and that unless we make such comparisons a regular part of our procedure, we always court the danger of missing either slightly or altogether what our author was really attempting to do.

There are also, in addition to these very general rules, several more particular criteria. Our aim is an explanation and judgment of poetic works in terms of their structural causes; hence, in the first place, the necessity of so framing our hypotheses that they are not descriptive formulae merely but clearly imply practical artistic consequences, in what the writers must or cannot or might well do in the act of writing, for the details of the works they are being used to explain; that is the character, for example, of Aristotle's definition of tragic plot-form in *Poetics* 13, and I have tried to impart a similar character to the statements above about *Macbeth*. The ideal is to have a central principle of explanation that will enable us to see precisely the functional relations between all the particular problems a writer has attempted to solve and the form of his work as a whole, even though we may have to conclude, in some cases, that the relation is a very tenuous one. In the second place, our aim is an explanation and judgment in terms adapted as closely as possible to the peculiar structure and power of the work before us; hence the necessity of trying to go beyond formulae that imply the work as a whole or any of its parts only generically; as when, for instance, we neglect to distinguish between the different material structures possible in lyrics and treat a particular lyric without regard to such distinctions, or as when we discuss a work like Jane Austen's *Emma* merely as a comedy, failing to see how little this can tell us about its distinctive comic construction. In the third place, we aspire to completeness of explanation; and this means that in framing a hypothesis about any work we must consider everything in the text as significant evidence that involves in

any way a free choice on the writer's part between possible alternative things to be done with his materials or ways of doing them at any point. The hypothesis must therefore be complex rather than simple; it must recognize that the same parts may have different functions, including that of mere adornment; and, above all, it cannot be arrived at by giving a privileged position, on *a priori* grounds, to a particular variety of signs of artistic intention, in a complex work, to the exclusion of other and often conflicting signs of the same thing. This last is conspicuously the error of those interpreters of *Macbeth* who have inferred the central form of that play chiefly from the thought and imagery that serve to emphasize the "unnatural" character of the hero's crimes and the inevitability of a just retribution, without attempting to correlate with this the many signs, both in the construction of the plot and in its extraordinarily artful representation, of the distinctive moral quality of Macbeth's actions when these are seen from the inside. There will always be incompleteness in any hypothesis, moreover, or in any criticism that follows its use, that leaves out of account, as one of the crucial facts, the peculiar sequence of emotions we feel when we read the work unbiased by critical doctrine; for, as we have seen, the most important thing about any poetic production is the characteristic power it has to affect us in this definite way rather than that. Completeness, however, is impossible without coherence; hence our hypotheses, in the fourth place, must aim at a maximum of internal unity, on the assumption that, although many works are episodic and although many predominantly imitative works, for example, also have didactic or topical parts, this can best be seen if we begin by presuming that literary artists usually aim at creating wholes.

The only proof there can be of a hypothesis about any particular thing lies in its power of completeness and coherence of explanation within the limits of the data it makes significant —and this always relatively to the other hypotheses pertinent to the same data with which it has been compared. We must be guided, however, in choosing among alternative hypotheses, by a further criterion—the classic criterion of economy: that that hypothesis is the best, other things being equal, which requires the fewest supplementary hypotheses to make it work or which entails the least amount of explaining away; it is no recommendation, thus, for Mr. Knights's interpretation of *Macbeth* that he has to say of the emotion aroused in most readers as well as in Bradley by Macbeth's soliloquies in Act V, that this is mere "conventional 'sympathy for the hero,' " which ought not to be allowed to distort that dialectical system of values in the play that is for him "the pattern of the whole." And we must be careful, further, not to construe our "data" in too narrow a sense and so be satisfied with hypotheses that clearly conflict with facts external to the works we are considering but relevant nevertheless to their interpretation; I mean not only such particular evidences as we can often find of writers' intentions—for example, Coleridge's statements about the kind of poem he designed *The Rime of the Ancient Mariner* to be—but also such general probabilities with respect to the works of a given period or genre or with respect to poetic works of any kind or age as are supplied by either our historical knowledge or our common sense. It is not likely, for instance, that a Shakespearean tragedy intended for the popular stage should really have a kind of basic structure which practising playwrights of any time would find it difficult or impossible to make effective for their audiences. Nor is it ever a sensible thing in a critic to cultivate indifference to common opinion about the works he is discussing. The opinion may be wrong or, as often happens, it may need to be corrected and refined; but in such conflicts—at least when they involve the larger aspects and effects of works—the burden of proof is on him. For the secrets of art are not, like the secrets of nature, things lying deeply hid, inaccessible to the perception and understanding of all who have not mastered the special techniques their discovery requires. The critic does, indeed, need special techniques, but for the sake of building upon common sense apprehensions of his objects,

not of supplanting these; and few things have done greater harm to the practice and repute of literary criticism in recent times than the assumption that its discoveries, like those of the physical sciences, must gain in importance and plausibility as they become more and more paradoxical in the ancient sense of that word: as if—to adapt a sharp saying of Professor Frank Knight about social studies—now that everybody is agreed that natural phenomena are not like works of art, the business of criticism must be to show that works of art are like natural phenomena.

It remains, finally, to consider the bearing of all this on judgments of poetic value. And the first thing to observe is that, if our hypothesis concerning the shaping principle of any work is adequate, it will give us a basis for saying with some precision (as my example of Act V of *Macbeth* will perhaps suggest) what are the necessities which such a form imposes on any artist whose aim is its successful realization in his materials. Some of them will be necessities common to all self-contained poetic works of no matter what kind, such as the necessity, if the parts are to cohere, of devices for effecting continuity from beginning through middle to end; others will be more and more specific necessities determined by the nature of the form we assume to have been intended, such as the necessity, if a comic effect like that of *Tom Jones* is to be obtained, of keeping the ridiculous mistakes of the hero from obscuring the sympathetic traits that make us wish him ultimate good fortune. These will all be consequences inferable from our basic definition of the form, and our primary task will be to trace them, in detail, throughout the particulars of the work at all its levels from plot or lyric situation down to the imagery and words. A kind of judgment of value will thus emerge in the very process of our analysis: if the writer has indeed done, somehow, all the essential things he would need to do on the assumption that he is actually writing the kind of work we have defined, then to that extent the work is good, or at least not artistically bad; and we should have to use very little rhetoric in addition to make this clear. But this is only half of the problem, for it is true of most mediocre writers that they usually do, in some fashion, a great part or all of the things their particular forms require, but do little more besides. The crucial question, therefore, concerns not so much the necessities of the assumed form as its possibilities. What is it that the writer might have done, over and above the minimum requirements of his task, which he has not done, or what is it that we have not expected him to do which he has yet triumphantly accomplished? These are the things our analyses ought peculiarly to attend to if they are to be adequate to their objects.

The possible in this sense, as distinguished from the necessary, is that which tends to perfect—to warrant praise of a positive rather than a merely negative kind. We can know it in two ways: by having our minds stored with memories of what both the most and the least perfect of artists have done when confronted with similar problems of invention, representation, and writing; and by considering theoretically the conditions under which any particular effect aimed at in a given work might be better or worse achieved—by asking, for instance, what would in general make a predicament like that of Tom Jones on the discovery of his first affair with Molly seem most completely comic, and then discussing the episode, as it is actually developed by Fielding, in these terms. Both methods are comparative, but the comparisons, if they are not to result in unfair impositions on the writer whose work we are considering, must take account of the fact that the desirable or admirable in literature is never something absolute but is always relative, in any given part of a work, to the requirements of the over-all form and to the function of the part as only one part along with many others: forgetting this, we should make the mistake of Mr. Joyce Cary's critic and demand neatness where clumsiness is what "belongs," vividness and particularity where faintness and generality are needed, doing more than is done when this would be doing too much.

The judgments of value we should thus be trying to make would for this reason always be judgments in kind, grounded on a prior definition of the writer's problems as problems peculiar, at least in their concrete determination, to the formal nature of the work he is writing. They would also be judgments in terms of intentions—what is it that the writer aimed to do here and how well has he succeeded in doing it?—but the intentions we should take as principles would not be those, except accidentally, which the writer had stated explicitly before or after writing or those which can be defined for the writer by saying that he must have intended to write this work because this is what he has written. The common objections to criticism based on "intention" in either of these senses are unanswerable. They do not hold, however, when we identify intention with the hypothesized form of a poetic work and then consider how fully what we know of the necessities and possibilities of this form are achieved in the work, on the assumption that, if the work shows any serious concern with art at all, the writer must have wished or been willing to be judged in this way. There is nothing unfair to the writer in such an approach, inasmuch as we are not engaged in a judicial process of bringing his work under a previously formulated general theory of literary value but in a free inquiry whose aim is simply the discovery of those values in his work—among them, we always hope, unprecedented values—which he has been able to put there. They will always be values incident to the relation between the form of the work and its matter at all of its structural levels; and it will be appropriate to interpret what we find in terms of a distinction between three classes of works considered from this point of view: works that are well conceived as wholes but contain few parts the formal excellence of which remains in our memory or invites us to another reading; works that are rich in local virtues but have only a loose or tenuous over-all form; and works that satisfy Coleridge's criterion for a poem, that it aims at "the production of as much immediate pleasure in parts, as is compatible with the largest sum of pleasure in the whole." These last are the few relatively perfect productions in the various literary kinds, and as between the other two we shall naturally prefer the second to the first.

V

All methods, in any field of study, have their characteristic corruptions when they fall into the hands of incompetent practitioners. The corruption of the historical critic is thus typically some kind of antiquarian irrelevance, as when texts are annotated more learnedly than they need to be or with only a loose pertinence to the problems and difficulties they present. The corruption of the literary critic in the modes of criticism we are chiefly familiar with at the present time is most commonly perhaps a cult of the paradoxical, along with which go, often enough, an addiction to irresponsible analogizing, a preference for metaphorical over literal statement, and a tendency to substitute rhetoric for inquiry as a guiding aim. The critic whose portrait I am drawing in this lecture is less likely, I think, to give way to any of these perversions than to certain others which, though different in kind, are no less to be deplored. In his concern with form, he can all too easily become merely formalistic, attending less to what gives life to poems than to the mechanism of their structural parts; in his concern with poetic wholes, he can be tempted to forget that the wholes have no existence apart from the words through which they are made actual; in his concern with development of theory, he can readily persuade himself that the enunciation of theory, however well established, is more important than the solution of the concrete problems to which it is relevant and so fall into a methodological pedantry as bad as the factual pedantry of the antiquarians.

I do not think, however, that these are inevitable faults, given a certain flexibility of mind, a sensitivity to literary particulars, an ability to resist the spirit of routine and self-satisfaction, and an understanding of the right relation between methods and problems. And when they are not allowed to distort the results, I should contend that the approach I have been describing is capable of giving us more nearly

adequate insights into the structural principles and characteristics of poetic works than any of the other modes of critical language with which we have compared it. We may say of these other methods, in terms borrowed from our own, that what they have chiefly concentrated on, in their analyses of structure, has been the matter of poetic works and its generic figurations and techniques rather than their forms. These are essential aspects of the problem, but they are aspects with which we too can deal. We can consider how any element in a poem "works with the other elements to create the effect intended by the poet"; we can discuss the "meaning" of poems in the sense of the thought that is presupposed by or expressed through any of their characteristic devices of statement and representation; we can treat of images and patterns of images and of the subtleties of poetic diction and rhythm; we can find a place for what is sound in the distinction between "structure" and "texture"; and we can make use of all that the "archetypal" critics can tell us about the cultural and psychological universals which poems imply. We can do all these things; but we can also do more, and as a consequence be able to do these things with greater precision and intelligibility.

For we possess what these other methods have conspicuously lacked: a means of isolating and defining those principles of structure in individual poems which distinguish them from other poems or kinds of poems and determine thus in highly specific ways what their distinctive elements are and the artistic reasons that justify the particular configurations we observe them to have. In contrast with our constructive and differentiating procedure, the procedures of these other critical schools have been, in varying degrees, generalizing and reductive. There is reduction, and hence a loss of causal particularity, whenever the only terms critics use in talking about literary structures are terms applicable primarily to the writer as distinct in some way from his product (as in F. R. Leavis' discussions of novels as direct reflections of the "complexity" of the novelists' "interests") or whenever the only source of terms is the psychology of readers (as in Miss Bodkin's definition of the "archetypal pattern" of rebirth evoked for her by *The Ancient Mariner*): what can be discovered in such cases is merely a kind of structure that many poems can have, or even other species of writing. There is reduction similarly in any method that draws its only structural formulae from such things as the common figures of poetical or rhetorical language (as in Cleanth Brooks and the Shakespearean critics who speak of plays as "metaphors"), or the non-poetic forms of myth and ritual, or the supposed patterns of psychic activity. And there is still reduction, though of a less extreme variety, in the critics who equate poetic structure, in all except the most general sense of "aesthetic pattern," exclusively with the conventions of verbal form or thematic arrangement which poets derive from earlier poetic tradition; in the critics, again, who look for fixed and unitary definitions of the poetic genres and discuss individual tragedies, comedies, epics, novels, and lyrics as more or less typical or perfect examples of these various quasi-Platonic forms; in the critics who identify the principles of structure in poems with the "themes" which are either their germinal ideas or moral bases or their underlying schemes of probability; and in the many critics, lastly, who fix their attention on some part of the total structure—on one phase of the action or on the framework of its representation, on a principal character, a "key" passage of thought, a conspicuous train of imagery—and proceed to derive from this their formula for the whole.

What these critics all leave out is thus the very principle we have taken as our starting-point: the shaping principle of form and emotional "power" without which no poem could come into existence as a beautiful and effective whole of a determinate kind. We can therefore talk with a fullness and precision of distinction impossible to them about the particular and widely variant relations which exist in different poems between their formal and their material natures. We are not limited to any one conception of poetic unity or to any one set of concepts for defining structure. We are not forced to speak of the working together of the parts of a poem merely in terms of simple contrarieties of theme or tone or in vocabulary of which the most exact words are expressions like "goes with," is "associated with," or is "related to" or "carries out," "reflects," "repeats," "qualifies," "balances," "contrasts with," "contradicts," and so on. We are not compelled, in order to show our recognition that the best poetry is not indifferent to thought or "meaning," to interpret all poetic masterpieces in which ideas are contained or evoked as if they were compositions of the same order as *The Divine Comedy*, or, at any rate, in some sense or in some degree, metaphorical or symbolic expressions, or, at the very least, "studies" of something or other. We shall be aware that there are indeed many poetic works to which such descriptions can be applied, but we shall go on the assumption—which all experience and literary history surely warrants—that ideas can function in poems in radically different ways: sometimes as sources of inspiration, sometimes as formal and shaping ends, sometimes as means for constituting the characters, purposes, or states of mind of the *dramatis personae*, sometimes as choric devices for enhancing or universalizing the actions; and the distinctions of our theoretic analysis, and notably our distinction between imitative and non-imitative forms, will enable us to discriminate these various uses when we come upon them and to judge of the significance of the thought in any poem or passage according as one or another of them is its primary cause. And finally, in dealing with the problems of imagery that have been so prominent during the past generation, especially in the criticism of Shakespeare, we are not restricted to either a merely material classification and psychological interpretation of images (as in Miss Spurgeon and her followers) or to a merely generalized and indefinite discussion of their functions in drama (as in some of the more recent Shakespeareans): with our basic distinction of object, manner, and means and our more specific devices for relating the parts of individual works to their controlling forms, we should be able, at the very least, to introduce greater particularity and artistic intelligibility into the subject than are apparent in most of the current discussions.

I look upon this approach, therefore, as one likely to repay a more concentrated effort of research and application than it has received in modern times. It is not a method that lends itself too easily, perhaps, to the immediate purposes of reviewers and professional critics of current productions, but it is not without its utility even here: there must be many readers of such criticism who would be grateful for more precise indications than they usually get of what are the formal as well as the material and technical novelties to be found in the latest serious novels, plays, and volumes of verse, and above all of the kinds of "peculiar pleasures" they are fitted to give us and why. The method is undoubtedly better suited, however, to the more ample and considered criticism of the literature of the past or of contemporary literature when this is made an object of elaborated study; and there is excellent reason to think that the writing of literary history in particular might be radically transformed, and to great advantage, through the inclusion of what I have called the immediate artistic causes of literary productions along with the relatively more external and remote causes to which historians of literature have mainly confined themselves.

And there is another realm in which these principles might be expected to yield peculiar benefits—that of literary education. They can give us, for one thing, the basis of a teachable discipline of reading and appreciation which would be exempt, on the one hand, from mere impressionism and the evocation of irresponsible opinion and, on the other hand, from the imposition on students of ready-made literary doctrines or canons of taste. Its essence would be simply the communication to students of a comprehensive scheme of questions to be asked about all the different kinds of literary works they might be studying and of criteria for discussing the appropriateness and adequacy of

the answers in the light of the particulars of texts and of the students' responses as human beings to what is going on in them. The development of such a discipline, centred, as it would be, in the statement and free comparison of hypotheses, would help to bring into literary studies something they have commonly lacked—a subject-matter, namely, in the sense not merely of facts but of compendent general concepts for their interpretation; concepts, moreover, that can be translated into habits of observation and reflection such as will tend to make the student independent of his teacher: a potential scholar in criticism rather than a disciple or member of a school, and a scholar who would do credit to his training precisely in proportion as he was able to correct and develop further the things he had been taught. I think that this could be done by a kind of practical and inductive teaching which would keep the student's mind centred on the concrete aspects of works and his feelings about them rather than on theoretical matters as such and which would, at the same time, build up in him an increasingly clear understanding of what it means to give a reasoned and warranted answer to a critical question and also, to an extent greater than has been common in the teaching of criticism, of how essential it is, if the answer is to be valid, that it accord with whatever truths the student has learned in the linguistic and historical parts of his education. For it is hard to see how the training I am suggesting could be carried on successfully without bringing criticism and these other disciplines into closer mutual relations than have existed between them for a long time.

We might expect, moreover, that such training would encourage a kind of appreciation of literary masterpieces that has been largely neglected in the critical tradition upon which our teaching has hitherto, in the main, been founded. The strength of that tradition has been its sensitiveness to the qualities and values which literary works share with one another or with other modes of expression—to these rather than to the differentiated characteristics of works which are what they are by virtue primarily of their writers' individual acts of poetic making. And it is not at all to minimize the importance of analogies and common principles in criticism to suggest that any literary culture is incomplete that does not lead also to a discriminating understanding, such as the training I propose is suited to give, of the peculiar principles of construction that contribute to make poetry the complex and richly diversified experience we all feel it to be. We may say indeed that what chiefly distinguishes the genius of literary study, as of the humanities in general, from the genius of science is that it naturally aspires to this kind of completion, not being permanently satisfied with reductions of the individual and the specific to the common, and perpetually feeling the need for distinctions and methods that will help us to do justice to the inventiveness of man and the uniqueness of his works.

And along with this would go a third benefit, in the capacity of our principles to maintain the integrity of literary appreciation without cutting it off formalistically from the life which literary works represent or attempt to guide. It is difficult to keep this balance in any of the critical languages in which the basic distinction for the analysis and judgment of works is some variant of the ancient dichotomy of *verba* and *res*; for if we distinguish thus between art and what art expresses, between poetic language and poetic thought, structure and idea, technique and meaning, symbol and concept, "presentment" and the moral "interests" of writers, we inevitably tend to regard one or the other of these two aspects as primary in importance. Our teaching of literature, consequently, in so far as it is "literary," appears far removed from common experience and human emotion, and in so far as it throws the emphasis on content, on questions of knowledge and behaviour, runs the risk of becoming merely an amateur branch of ethics, psychology, sociology, anthropology, or the history of ideas.

These disadvantages very largely disappear, I think, when we bring to the discussion of poetic works our radically different distinction of matter and form. For form as we conceive it is simply that which gives definite shape, emotional power, and beauty to the materials of man's experience out of which the writer has composed his work. Hence it cannot be separated as mere "form" from the matter in which it exists, nor can we talk about it adequately (as I have tried to illustrate in my discussions of *Macbeth* and of Gray's *Elegy*) without talking at the same time about the human qualities of the actions, persons, feelings, and thoughts the work brings before us and the very human, but no less poetic, responses these evoke in our minds. There can thus be no good "literary" criticism, in this language, that does not presuppose a constant making of moral and psychological discriminations and a constant concern with nuances of thought, as well as with subtleties of language and technique; what keeps it "literary" or "poetic" and prevents it from degenerating into either "studies in character" or excursions into philosophy and social history is the direction imposed on all our questions about the "content" of works by our hypotheses concerning their shaping principles of form. We can agree, therefore, with the critics who hold that we ought to deal with poetry as poetry and not another thing, and we can agree no less with those who insist that one of the main tasks of criticism is to show the "relevance" of poems to "life"; only these, for us, are not two tasks but one. And I would state a further point in the same connection, the bearing of which will be easily evident to those who have grown impatient with the current tendency to reduce all questions of morals and politics to questions of ideologies and beliefs. The counterpart of this "rationalism" in literary studies is the assumption that "relevance to life" in poetry is a matter primarily of "themes" and "imaginative visions," so that no imaginative work can be taken seriously from which we cannot extract a "total meaning" over and above the human particulars it exhibits, which we then set forth as what the work is intending to say. From this narrowing of the scope of literary values to such values as only earnest modern intellectuals can think of greater importance than the spectacle of individual men doing and suffering, we have, fortunately, an effective way of escape in our distinction between imitative and didactic forms. We can accord a proper appreciation, in their own terms, to works of which the formal principles are clearly ideas. But we are free to discuss the others, including notably the tragedies of Shakespeare, in a way that fully respects their seriousness, and the implication of universals in the working out of their plots, without being committed to the dehumanizing supposition that the moral habits and dispositions of individual persons and the qualities and circumstances of their actions are things less valuable for us, as men and citizens, to contemplate in literature than the pale abstractions by which they have been overlaid in the prevailing modes of interpretation. And so we might contribute not only to a more discriminating understanding of what literature as literature can do but to a kind of training in concrete moral and social perception, unbiased by doctrine, such as all who live in a free society would be the better for having.

VI

When all this is said, however, it is still true that what I have been talking about in this lecture is only one out of many possible legitimate approaches to the question of poetic structure, not to speak of the innumerable other questions with which critics can profitably concern themselves. I should not want to leave the impression, therefore, that I think it the only mode of criticism seriously worth cultivation at the present time by either teachers of literature or critics, but simply that its development, along with the others, might have many fruitful consequences for our teaching and criticism generally. What distinguishes it from the other modes is its preoccupation with the immediate constructive problems of writers in the making of individual works and with the artistic reasoning necessarily involved in their successful solution; and its great claim to consideration is that it can deal with these matters more precisely and adequately, and with a more complete

reliance on the canons of inductive inquiry, unhampered by doctrinal preconceptions, than any of the other existing critical languages. It can give us, consequently, a body of primary literary facts about literary works, in their aspect as concrete wholes, in the light of which we can judge the relevance and validity—or see the precise bearing—of such observations and statements of value as result from the application to the same works of other critical principles and procedures: if the structural principles of *Macbeth* or of Gray's *Elegy* are actually what we have taken them to be, then whatever else may be truly said about these same works, in answer to other questions or in the context of other ways of reasoning about them, must obviously be capable of being brought into harmony with this prior factual knowledge of the distinctive how and why of their construction. Here is something, therefore, which critics who prefer a more generalizing or a more speculative approach to literary works can hardly neglect if they wish to be responsible students of literature rather than merely rhetoricians bent on exploiting favourite theses at any cost. For though it is true enough, for example, that what writers do is conditioned by their personal lives and complexes, their social circumstances, and their literary traditions, there is always a risk that exclusive explanations of literary peculiarities in terms of such remoter causes will collapse and seem absurd as soon as we consider, for any work to which they have been applied, what are the immediate artistic exigencies which its writer faced because of his choice of form or manner in this particular work. These exigencies can never be safely disregarded so long as the genetic relation between art and its sources and materials in life remains the very indirect relation we know it is; and it is perhaps not the least of the utilities to be found in the criticism of forms that its cultivation, in a context of the many other kinds of critical inquiry, would help to keep critics of all schools constantly reminded of their existence and importance.

But the other kinds ought to be there. Of the truth about literature, no critical language can ever have a monopoly or even a distant approach to one; and there are obviously many things which the language I have been speaking of cannot do. It is a method not at all suited, as is criticism in the grand line of Longinus, Coleridge, and Matthew Arnold, to the definition and appreciation of those general qualities of writing—mirroring the souls of writers—for the sake of which most of us read or at any rate return to what we have read. It is a method that necessarily abstracts from history and hence requires to be supplemented by other very different procedures if we are to replace the works we study in the circumstances and temper of their times and see them as expressions and forces as well as objects of art. It is a method, above all, that completely fails, because of its essentially differentiating character, to give us insights into the larger moral and political values of literature or into any of the other organic relations with human nature and human experience in which literature is involved. And yet who will say that these are not as compelling considerations for criticism as anything comprised in the problem of poetic structure as we have been discussing it in these lectures? The moral is surely that we ought to have at our command, collectively at least, as many different critical methods as there are distinguishable major aspects in the construction, appreciation, and use of literary works. The multiplicity of critical languages is therefore something not to be deplored but rather rejoiced in, as making possible a fuller exploration of our subject in its total extent than we could otherwise attain; and for my part I have as fond a regard for Longinus and for the masters of historical criticism as I have for Aristotle, and as strong a conviction of their continuing utility. Nor will there ever cease to be employment for criticism of the less rigorous or more imaginative types—in directing attention to aspects of poems which only a new model or analogy can bring into view, in formulating and promoting new ideals of poetic excellence or new poetic styles, in suggesting to poets unrealized possibilities in subject-matter and language, in relating poetry, for readers, to large non-poetic human contexts of emotion and meaning, in keeping the life of poetry and of taste from declining into orthodoxy and routine.

The best hope for criticism in the future, indeed, lies in the perpetuation of this multiplicity; nothing could be more damaging than the practical success of any effort to define authoritatively the frontiers and problems of our subject or to assign to each of its variant languages a determinate place in a single hierarchy of critical modes. Better far than that the chaos of schools and splinter parties we have with us now! But there need be no such choice; for the great obstacle to advance in criticism is not the existence of independent groups of critics each pursuing separate interests, but the spirit of exclusive dogmatism which keeps them from learning what they might from one another; and for that the only effective remedy, I think, is to take to heart the two lessons which the persistence throughout history of many distinct critical languages ought to teach us. The first is the lesson of self-knowledge: we can attempt to become more clearly aware than we have usually been of just what it is that we ourselves are doing—and why—when we make critical statements of any kind, and at the same time try to extend that clarity, in as intellectually sympathetic a way as possible, to the statements of other critics, and especially to those that appear to be most inconsistent with our own. And it will be all the easier to attain this self-understanding, with its natural discouragements to doctrinal prejudice, if we also learn the second lesson, and come habitually to think of the various critical languages of the past and present, including our own, no longer as rival attempts to foreclose the "real" or "only profitable" truth about poetry, so that we have to choose among them as we choose among religious dogmas or political causes, but simply as tools of our trade—as so many distinct conceptual and logical means, each with its peculiar capacities and limitations, for solving truly the many distinct kinds of problems which poetry, in its magnificent variety of aspects, presents to our view.

PART III

Continental Criticism

INTRODUCTION

T HE GULF that separates the continent of Europe from England
and the English-speaking peoples has always been deep. It extends
beyond differences of language and customs to different habits of mind.
To the British and the Americans, Europeans have often seemed over-
refined or exhausted; to Europeans, the British and Americans have
often seemed innocent or provincial. In moving from English literary
criticism to the continent, we enter a world with its own peculiar traditions and its own internal logic. Criticism takes on a different cast there
—more self-conscious, fiercer, more subtle. Yet modern continental
criticism cannot be ignored; precisely because its suppositions do not
resemble ours, we can go there for new kinds of language, new modes of
seeing.

Turning from English literary criticism to European, we are likely to
be struck first by its fascination with theory. The leading English and
American philosophers have not, with a few exceptions, excelled as men
of letters; but the leading European philosophers of modern times
constitute an honor roll of criticism: Nietzsche, Bergson, Croce, Gilson,
Heidegger, Sartre, Camus. English literary critics have often prided
themselves on their common sense; but European literary critics often
seem to write in a private or acroamatic language. As a result, continental criticism tends to move away from poems to poetics, from works
of art to the philosophy of art. It risks specialization and rarefaction
for the sake of achieving a higher perspective. And at their best, continental critics can attain a level of sophistication and insight that

makes the practical concerns of much English literary criticism seem small.

Moreover, they can also command a much wider culture. One virtue of continental criticism is its readiness to draw upon other intellectual disciplines outside literature. We have already noted its close ties with philosophy—vitalism, phenomenology, metaphysics, existentialism—and we must equally note the influence of the political theory of Marx, the psychology of Jung and Freud, the anthropology of Lévi-Strauss. European literary criticism has rarely, like American criticism after Eliot and Pound, insisted on the autonomy or "objectivity" of literature. Rather it has sought to relate poetry to other human concerns, and to construct a literary theory that is coordinated with all the major movements of intellectual history.

Just because of this fullness of reference, however, modern continental criticism is not easy to present in excerpts. An understanding of Heidegger's criticism, for instance, depends upon some knowledge of the development of European philosophy, his own idiosyncratic terminology, the difficult poetry (especially Hölderlin's) that he considers, and (many would argue) the counter-arguments of such critics as Emil Staiger. We have not attempted so hopeless a task. Instead we have tried to select criticism that, while thoroughly European in spirit, has influenced English and American critics, is intelligible in itself, and offers methods of approach that can be put to use.

To begin with, continental critics have been far more active than the English in searching for a general system of aesthetics. Benedetto Croce spent his life pursuing, in philosophical and historical studies, the essence of art, and Croce's theory remains the starting place for contemporary aestheticians. Fundamentally, it is a theory based on expression, or more precisely on "intuition-expression," the fusion of the artist's feeling with its outward symbol or manifestation. The form of each work of art, according to Croce, combines an intuition (feeling, idea, statement) with an image (symbol, picture, word) in indivisible unity. From this insight (which Croce thought revolutionary) spring many critical assumptions, such as the identity of form and content, which have become familiar to modern readers. Even critics who have not read Croce may well derive some of their basic principles from his analysis.

Certainly every modern reader, willingly or not, has been influenced by Freud. Literature helped contemporary psychology to many of its formulations—as Oedipus fathered the Oedipus Complex—and psychology has returned the favor by offering literature a new kind of criticism. In spite of Freud's suspicion of creative fantasies, he profoundly admired such prophetic Freudians as Shakespeare, and many of his finest essays verge on literary criticism. From the interpretation of dreams one takes only a short step to the interpretation of poems. If such an approach seems too concerned with pathology, it has been helpful nevertheless (as Lionel Trilling argues in an essay reprinted above) in deepening the resources of poets and critics for dealing with the human dimension of art. Moreover, the complementary psychology of Carl Jung, which views artistic creation not as pathology but as the satisfaction of a spiritual need, has also profoundly affected modern criticism. Jung's description of images and archetypes which flow from a "collective unconscious" has stimulated a whole school of criticism devoted to myths; Northrop Frye, though he does not accept Jung's explanation of myths, has profited from a similar mode of analysis. The search for a literary criticism based on modern psychology continues to occupy many of the best young critics in Europe and America.

Far fewer English-speaking critics have embraced, as yet, another mode of continental criticism: structuralism. Associated originally with the vogue of Lévi-Strauss's ideas in France, structuralism has gradually won more and more European converts—indeed, as I. A. Richards' essay on Jakobson (reprinted above) indicates, it can even excite critics who have spent a life working in other modes. What structuralism offers above all is a methodology. Like Richards and Frye, though often more dogmatically, it envisions a future science of criticism, in which the critic will be able to analyze works of literature into their basic structures. Although such structural models cannot be identical with literary works, any more than the physical world is identical with the principles defined by the physicist, they can furnish categories for every literary possibility. Eventually, according to some structuralists, the field of literature may be formulated into an abstract system sufficiently exact to be analyzed on a computer. Thus Lévi-Strauss and Jakobson, in their famous analysis of Baudelaire's "Les Chats" (*L'Homme*, 1962), point toward a complete survey of the poem: its grammatical, phonetic, rhythmic, textual, and semantic features. From many such surveys, a general theory of poetry might begin to emerge, and the critical method itself become refined. Obviously such a theory remains in the future. The essays by Barthes and Todorov in this section are both introductory, suggesting that the conclusions made possible by structural analysis must be as yet provisional. Yet the methods of structuralism have already begun to be applied to a broad spectrum of literary works; and in coming years we can expect it to establish a firmer and firmer ground in theory.

The work of Walter Benjamin belongs to an older kind of continental criticism, a kind without a name (though we might call it phenomenological). Immensely cultured, artistic, multilingual, a collector of books and ideas, he represents the traditions of Europe at their most sensitive and intellectual. Even as a Marxist he is more a connoisseur than a convert. Indeed, the criticism he writes seems more *experienced* than anything in English, more seasoned by time. In one essay, Benjamin speaks of the critic as an alchemist, who refines the work of art into pure truth. We reprint "The Storyteller" not as an example of a school but as the product of such alchemy.

Finally, continental criticism differs from that of England and America because it follows its own traditions and debates. We have chosen to present one such debate: the long argument about the novels of Gustave Flaubert. Flaubert seems singularly well suited to be a touchstone of critical opinions. Himself a supremely deliberate artist, he helped to define the modern theory of the novel, and later theories have often used him as a point of departure. Thus Henry James, who promoted serious criticism of fiction in English, referred to Flaubert as "*the* novelist, intent and typical," "the novelist's novelist." European critics have similarly thought of *Madame Bovary* as *the* novel; to summarize their opinions of Flaubert is to summarize the most searching continental discussion of the art of fiction.

That discussion has been rich and diverse. Flaubert's own comments on his work (some of them quoted below by Walter Pater) stress its artistic detachment, the purity and objectivity of good style. But many later critics have chosen to emphasize different aspects of his novels. Erich Auerbach studies him against the background of Western art as a whole, in its efforts to develop accurate representations of reality. Georges Poulet uses forms and patterns in *Madame Bovary* to locate Flaubert's consciousness at a particular point in time and space. Georg Lukács, subtly combining Marxist and linguistic analysis, stresses the way that the artist has been conditioned by the dialectic of history. Jean-Paul Sartre analyzes the novel existentially as a project through which the author defines himself. Each of these critics brings to his analysis not only a knowledge of what Flaubert has meant to European theories of the novel, but his own individual philosophy of art. One by one, they see fiction as a means of making new demands and setting new standards for the quality of life. Together, they represent the variety and the depth of modern continental criticism.

A Note on Sources

Benedetto Croce (1866–1952), a dominant force in Italian philosophy and literary criticism for more than half a century, is widely regarded as the founder of modern aesthetics. His first major work, *Estetica* (1902), was especially influential in the translation by Douglas Ainslie, *Aesthetic* (1909). Other important statements on this subject include *The Breviary of Aesthetic* (written in 1912) and the *Encyclopaedia Britannica* article reprinted below. The variety of Croce's interests in philosophy, politics, criticism, and history is excellently represented by *Philosophy, Poetry, History,* tr. Cecil Sprigge (1966).

Sigmund Freud (1856–1939), Austrian psychoanalyst and "Copernicus of the mind," took many excursions into literary criticism; his brilliant essay on *King Lear*, "The Theme of the Three Caskets" (1913), is one of several *On Creativity and the Unconscious*, ed. B. Nelson (1958). Among Freud's books, *The Interpretation of Dreams* (1900) has influenced interpretations of literature, and *Jokes and Their Relation to the Unconscious* (1905) has influenced views of comedy.

Carl Gustav Jung (1875–1961), Swiss psychiatrist, broke with Freud to found a psychological school based on archetypes which emanate from a collective unconscious. His writings, emphasizing the persistence of myths in human life, have greatly affected literary criticism; see especially *The Spirit in Man, Art, and Literature,* tr. R. F. C. Hull (1966), part of a series of Jung's works being published by the Bollingen Foundation.

Roland Barthes (1915–   ) is one of the leading contemporary French critics. *Writing Degree Zero* (1953; tr. 1967), the work which established his reputation, has been succeeded by a series of books on literature, semiology, and structural analysis, among them *On Racine,* tr. Richard Howard (1964).

Tzvetan Todorov (1939–   ), a young Bulgarian literary critic who lives in Paris, has recently published several books in French on the theory and practice of structuralism, including *Littérature et signification* (1967) and *Introduction à la littérature fantastique* (1970).

Walter Benjamin (1892–1940), who died a refugee and a suicide, has become recognized in the last fifteen years as perhaps the greatest literary critic of modern Germany. Several essays from *Schriften,* ed. T. W. Adorno (1955), have been published in English as *Illuminations,* tr. Harry Zohn, with a long introduction by Hannah Arendt (1968).

Gustave Flaubert (1821–1880), the great French novelist, is best known for *Madame Bovary* (1857), *Salammbô* (1862), *L'Éducation sentimentale* (1869), and *La tentation de Saint Antoine* (1874). His correspondence—some excerpts from which are translated below by Walter Pater (1839–1894), the leading English critic of his time—is filled with penetrating literary criticism; a useful collection is available in *Selected Letters,* tr. Francis Steegmuller (1953).

Erich Auerbach (1892–1957), German scholar and critic, wrote *Mimesis: The Representation of Reality in Western Literature* while in exile in Turkey during World War II; the book was published in German in 1946, in English, tr. W. R. Trask, in 1953. Other works in English include *Scenes from the Drama of European Literature* (1959) and *Introduction to Romance Languages and Literature* (1961).

Georges Poulet (1902–   ), Belgian literary critic now resident in Switzerland, has taught at many universities in Europe and America. His books in English, translated by Elliott Coleman, are *Studies in Human Time* (1956), *The Interior Distance* (1959), and *Metamorphoses of the Circle* (1967).

Georg Lukács (1885–1971), a Hungarian who usually writes in German, is universally regarded as the greatest Marxist literary critic. His early theoretical writings, especially *History and Class Consciousness* (1923; tr. 1971), define a philosophy of social action. Literary essays are collected in *Writer and Critic* (tr. 1970), *The Historical Novel* (1937; tr. 1962), and *Studies in European Realism* (written in the late 1930's; tr. 1964).

Jean-Paul Sartre (1905–   ), the great French novelist, philosopher, and playwright, has written a series of books that mingle literary criticism with biography, existential philosophy, and Marxist dialectic. Of the many volumes of *Situations,* an essay from *Situations II* translated by Bernard Frechtman, *What Is Literature?* (1949), has been most influential. Other notable essays are *Baudelaire* (1947; tr. 1949) and *Saint Genet, Actor and Martyr* (1952; tr. 1963). *Search for a Method* (tr. 1963) introduces Sartre's long *Critique de la Raison dialectique* and prepares for a full-length study of Flaubert.

AESTHETICS AND LITERATURE

Benedetto Croce

AESTHETICS (1928)

IF WE EXAMINE a poem in order to determine what it is that makes us feel it to be a poem, we at once find two constant and necessary elements: a complex of *images,* and a *feeling* that animates them. Let us, for instance, recall a passage learnt at school: Virgil's lines (*Aeneid,* iii, 294, *sqq.*), in which Aeneas describes how on hearing that in the country to whose shores he had come the Trojan Helenus was reigning, with Andromache, now his wife, he was overcome with amazement and a great desire to see this surviving son of Priam and to hear of his strange adventures. Andromache, whom he meets outside the walls of the city, by the waters of a river renamed Simois, celebrating funeral rites before a cenotaph of green turf and two altars to Hector and Astyanax; her astonishment on seeing him, her hesitation, the halting words in which she questions him, uncertain whether he is a man or a ghost; Aeneas's no less agitated replies and interrogations, and the pain and confusion with which

From *Encyclopaedia Britannica,* 14th edition (1929).

she recalls the past—how she lived through scenes of blood and shame, how she was assigned by lot as slave and concubine to Pyrrhus, abandoned by him and united to Helenus, another of his slaves, how Pyrrhus fell by the hand of Orestes and Helenus became a free man and a king; the entry of Aeneas and his men into the city, and their reception by the son of Priam in this little Troy, this mimic Pergamon with its new Xanthus, and its Scaean Gate whose threshold Aeneas greets with a kiss —all these details, and others here omitted, are images of persons, things, attitudes, gestures, sayings, joy and sorrow; mere images, not history or historical criticism, for which they are neither given nor taken. But through them all there runs a feeling, a feeling which is our own no less than the poet's, a human feeling of bitter memories, of shuddering horror, of melancholy, of home-sickness, of tenderness, of a kind of childish *pietas* that could prompt this vain revival of things perished, these playthings fashioned by a religious devotion, the *parva Troia,* the *Pergama simulata magnis,* the *arentem Xanthi cognomine rivum*: something inexpressible in logical terms, which only poetry can express in full. Moreover, these two elements may appear as two in a first abstract analysis, but they cannot be regarded as two distinct threads, however intertwined; for, in effect, the feeling is altogether converted into images, into this complex of images, and is thus a feeling that is contemplated and therefore resolved and transcended. Hence poetry must be called neither feeling, nor image, nor yet the sum of the two, but "contemplation of feeling" or "lyrical intuition" or (which is the same thing) "pure intuition"—pure, that is, of all historical and critical reference to the reality or unreality of the images of which it is woven, and apprehending the pure throb of life in its ideality. Doubtless, other things may be found in poetry besides these two elements or moments and the synthesis of the two; but these other things are either present as extraneous elements in a compound (reflections, exhortations, polemics, allegories, etc.), or else they are just these image-feelings themselves taken in abstraction from their context as so much material, restored to the condition in which it was before the act of poetic creation. In the former case, they are non-poetic elements merely interpolated into or attached to the poem; in the latter, they are divested of poetry, rendered unpoetical by a reader either unpoetical or not at the moment poetical, who has dispelled the poetry, either because he cannot live in its ideal realm, or for the legitimate ends of historical enquiry or other practical purposes which involve the degradation—or rather, the conversion—of the poem into a document or an instrument.

ARTISTIC QUALITIES

What has been said of "poetry" applies to all the other "arts" commonly enumerated; painting, sculpture, architecture, music. Whenever the artistic quality of any product of the mind is discussed, the dilemma must be faced, that either it is a lyrical intuition, or it is something else, something just as respectable, but not art. If painting (as some theorists have maintained) were the imitation or reproduction of a given object, it would be, not art, but something mechanical and practical; if the task of the painter (as other theorists have held) were to combine lines and lights and colours with ingenious novelty of invention and effect, he would be, not an artist, but an inventor; if music consisted in similar combinations of notes, the paradox of Leibniz and Father Kircher would come true, and a man could write music without being a musician; or alternatively we should have to fear (as Proudhon did for poetry and John Stuart Mill for music) that the possible combinations of words or notes would one day be exhausted, and poetry or music would disappear. As in poetry, so in these other arts, it is notorious that foreign elements sometimes intrude themselves; foreign either *a parte objecti* or *a parte subjecti,* foreign either in fact or from the point of view of an inartistic spectator or listener. Thus the critics of these arts advise the artist to exclude, or at least not to rely upon what they call the "literary" elements in painting, sculpture and music, just as the critic of poetry advises the writer to look for "poetry" and not be led astray by mere literature. The reader who understands poetry goes straight to this poetic heart and feels its beat upon his own; where this beat is silent, he denies that poetry is present, whatever and however many other things may take its place, united in the work, and however valuable they may be for skill and wisdom, nobility of intellect, quickness of wit and pleasantness of effect. The reader who does not understand poetry loses his way in pursuit of these other things. He is wrong not because he admires them, but because he thinks he is admiring poetry.

OTHER FORMS OF ACTIVITY AS DISTINCT FROM ART

By defining art as lyrical or pure intuition we have implicitly distinguished it from all other forms of mental production. If such distinctions are made explicit, we obtain the following negations:

1. *Art is not philosophy*, because philosophy is the logical thinking of the universal categories of being, and art is the unreflective intuition of being. Hence, while philosophy transcends the image and uses it for its own purposes, art lives in it as in a kingdom. It is said that art cannot behave in an irrational manner and cannot ignore logic; and certainly it is neither irrational nor illogical; but its own rationality, its own logic, is a quite different thing from the dialectical logic of the concept, and it was in order to indicate this peculiar and unique character that the name "logic of sense" or "aesthetic" was invented. The not uncommon assertion that art has a logical character, involves either an equivocation between conceptual logic and aesthetic logic, or a symbolic expression of the latter in terms of the former.

2. *Art is not history*, because history implies the critical distinction between reality and unreality; the reality of the passing moment and the reality of a fancied world: the reality of fact and the reality of desire. For art, these distinctions are as yet unmade; it lives, as we have said, upon pure images. The historical existence of Helenus, Andromache and Aeneas makes no difference to the poetical quality of Virgil's poem. Here, too, an objection has been raised: namely that art is not wholly indifferent to historical criteria, because it obeys the laws of "verisimilitude"; but, here again, "verisimilitude" is only a rather clumsy metaphor for the mutual coherence of images, which without this internal coherence would fail to produce their effect as images, like Horace's *delphinus in silvis* and *aper in fluctibus*.

3. *Art is not natural science*, because natural science is historical fact classified and so made abstract; nor is it *mathematical science*, because mathematics performs operations with abstractions and does not contemplate. The analogy sometimes drawn between mathematical and poetical creation is based on merely external and generic resemblances; and the alleged necessity of a mathematical or geometrical basis for the arts is only another metaphor, a symbolic expression of the constructive, cohesive and unifying force of the poetic mind building itself a body of images.

4. *Art is not the play of fancy*, because the play of fancy passes from image to image, in search of variety, rest or diversion, seeking to amuse itself with the likenesses of things that give pleasure or have an emotional and pathetic interest; whereas in art the fancy is so dominated by the single problem of converting chaotic feeling into clear intuition, that we recognize the propriety of ceasing to call it fancy and calling it imagination, poetic imagination or creative imagination. Fancy as such is as far removed from poetry as are the works of Mrs. Radcliffe or Dumas *père*.

5. *Art is not feeling in its immediacy*. Andromache, on seeing Aeneas, becomes *amens, diriguit visu in medio, labitur, longo vix tempore fatur*, and when she speaks *longos ciebat incassum fletus*; but the poet does not lose his wits or grow stiff as he gazes; he does not totter or weep or cry; he expresses himself in harmonious verses, having made these various perturbations the object of which he sings. Feelings in their immediacy are "expressed" for if they were not, if they were not also sensible and bodily facts ("psycho-physical phenomena," as the positivists used to call them) they would not be concrete things, and so they would be nothing at all. Andromache expressed herself in the way described above. But "expression" in this sense, even when accompanied by consciousness, is a mere metaphor from "mental" or "aesthetic expression" which alone really expresses, that is, gives to feeling a theoretical form and converts it into words, song and outward shape. This distinction between contemplated feeling, or poetry, and feeling enacted or endured, is the source of the power, ascribed to art, of "liberating us from the passions" and "calming" us (the power of *catharsis*), and of the consequent condemnation, from an aesthetic point of view, of works of art, or parts of them, in which immediate feeling has a place or finds a vent.

Hence, too, arises another characteristic of poetic expression—really synonymous with the last—namely its "infinity" as opposed to the "finitude" of immediate feeling or passion; or, as it is also called, the "universal" or "cosmic" character of poetry. Feeling, not crushed but contemplated by the work of poetry, is seen to diffuse itself in widening circles over all the realm of the soul, which is the realm of the universe, echoing and re-echoing endlessly; joy and sorrow, pleasure and pain, energy and lassitude, earnestness and frivolity, and so forth, are linked to each other and lead to each other through infinite shades and gradations; so that the feeling, while preserving its individual physiognomy and its original dominating motive, is not exhausted by or restricted to this original character. A comic image, if it is poetically comic, carries with it something that is not comic, as in the case of Don Quixote or Falstaff; and the image of something terrible is never, in poetry, without an atoning element of loftiness, goodness and love.

6. *Art is not instruction or oratory:* it is not circumscribed and limited by service to any practical purpose whatever, whether this be the inculcation of a particular philosophical, historical or scientific truth, or the advocacy of a particular way of feeling and the action corresponding to it. Oratory at once robs expression of its "infinity" and independence, and, by making it the means to an end, dissolves it in this end. Hence arises what Schiller called the "non-determining" character of art, as opposed to the "determining" character of oratory; and hence the justifiable suspicion of "political poetry"—political poetry being, proverbially, bad poetry.

7. As art is not to be confused with the form of practical action most akin to it, namely instruction and oratory, so *a fortiori*, it must not be confused with other forms directed to the production of certain effects, whether these consist in pleasure, enjoyment and utility, or in goodness and righteousness. We must exclude from art not only meretricious works, but also those inspired by a desire for goodness, as

equally, though differently, inartistic and repugnant to lovers of poetry. Flaubert's remark that indecent books lacked *vérité*, is parallel to Voltaire's gibe that certain "poésies sacrées" were really "sacrées, car personne n'y touche."

ART IN ITS RELATIONS

The "negations" here made explicit are obviously, from another point of view, "relations"; for the various distinct forms of mental activity cannot be conceived as separate each from the rest and acting in self-supporting isolation. This is not the place to set forth a complete system of the forms or categories of the mind in their order and their dialectic; confining ourselves to art, we must be content to say that the category of art, like every other category, mutually presupposes and is presupposed by all the rest: it is conditioned by them all and conditions them all. How could the aesthetic synthesis, which is poetry, arise, were it not preceded by a state of mental commotion? *Si vis me flere, dolendum est,* and so forth. And what is this state of mind which we have called feeling, but the whole mind, with its past thoughts, volitions and actions, now thinking and desiring and suffering and rejoicing, travailing within itself? Poetry is like a ray of sunlight shining upon this darkness, lending it its own light and making visible the hidden forms of things. Hence it cannot be produced by an empty and dull mind; hence those artists who embrace the creed of pure art or art for art's sake, and close their hearts to the troubles of life and the cares of thought, are found to be wholly unproductive, or at most rise to the imitation of others or to an impressionism devoid of concentration. Hence the basis of all poetry is human personality, and, since human personality finds its completion in morality, the basis of all poetry is the moral consciousness. Of course this does not mean that the artist must be a profound thinker or an acute critic; or that he must be a pattern of virtue or a hero; but he must have a share in the world of thought and action which will enable him, either in his own person or by sympathy with others, to live the whole drama of human life. He may sin, lose the purity of his heart, and expose himself, as a practical agent, to blame; but he must have a keen sense of purity and impurity, righteousness and sin, good and evil. He may not be endowed with great practical courage; he may even betray signs of timidity and cowardice; but he must feel the dignity of courage. Many artistic inspirations are due, not to what the artist, as a man, is in practice, but to what he is not, and feels that he ought to be, admiring and enjoying the qualities he lacks when he sees them in others. Many, perhaps the finest, pages of heroic and warlike poetry are by men who never had the nerve or the skill to handle a weapon. On the other hand, we are not maintaining that the possession of a moral personality is enough to make a poet or an artist. To be a *vir bonus* does not make a man even an orator, unless he is also *dicendi peritus*. The *sine qua non* of poetry is poetry, that form of theoretical synthesis which we have defined above; the spark of poetical genius without which all the rest is mere fuel, not burning because no fire is at hand to light it. But the figure of the pure poet, the pure artist, the votary of pure Beauty, aloof from contact with humanity, is no real figure but a caricature.

That poetry not only presupposes the other forms of human mental activity but is presupposed by them, is proved by the fact that without the poetic imagination which gives contemplative form to the workings of feeling, intuitive expression to obscure impressions, and thus becomes representations and words, whether spoken or sung or painted or otherwise uttered, logical thought could not arise. Logical thought is not language, but it never exists without language, and it uses the language which poetry has created; by means of concepts, it discerns and dominates the representations of poetry, and it could not dominate them unless they, its future subjects, had first an existence of their own. Further, without the discerning and criticizing activity of thought, action would be impossible; and if action, then

good action, the moral consciousness, duty. Every man, however much he may seem to be all logical thinker, critic, scientist, or all absorbed in practical interests or devoted to duty, cherishes at the bottom of his heart his own private store of imagination and poetry; even Faust's pedantic *famulus*, Wagner, confessed that he often had his "grillenhafte Stunden." Had this element been altogether denied him, he would not have been a man, and therefore not even a thinking or acting being. This extreme case is an absurdity; but in proportion as this private store is scanty, we find a certain superficiality and aridity in thought, and a certain coldness in action.

THE SCIENCE OF ART, OR AESTHETICS, AND ITS PHILOSOPHICAL CHARACTER

The concept of art expounded above is in a sense the ordinary concept, which appears with greater or less clarity in all statements about art, and is constantly appealed to, explicitly or implicitly, as the fixed point round which all discussions on the subject gravitate: and this, not only nowadays, but at all times, as could be shown by the collection and interpretation of things said by writers, poets, artists, laymen and even the common people. But it is desirable to dispel the illusion that this concept exists as an innate idea, and to replace this by the truth, that it operates as an *a priori* concept. Now an *a priori* concept does not exist by itself, but only in the individual products which it generates. Just as the *a priori* reality called Art, Poetry or Beauty does not exist in a transcendent region where it can be perceived and admired in itself, but only in the innumerable works of poetry, of art and of beauty which it has formed and continues to form, so the logical *a priori* concept of art exists nowhere but in the particular judgments which it has formed and continues to form, the refutations which it has effected and continues to effect, the demonstrations it makes, the theories it constructs, the problems and groups of problems, which it solves and has solved. The definitions and distinctions and negations and relations expounded above have each its own history, and have been progressively worked out in the course of centuries, and in them we now possess the fruits of this complex and unremitting toil. Aesthetic, or the science of art, has not therefore the task (attributed to it by certain scholastic conceptions) of defining art once for all and deducing from this conception its various doctrines, so as to cover the whole field of aesthetic science; it is only the perpetual systematization, always renewed and always growing, of the problems arising from time to time out of reflection upon art, and is identical with the solutions of the difficulties and the criticisms of the errors which act as stimulus and material to the unceasing progress of thought. This being so, no exposition of aesthetic (especially a summary exposition such as can alone be given here) can claim to deal exhaustively with the innumerable problems which have arisen and may arise in the course of the history of aesthetics; it can only mention and discuss the chief, and among these, by preference, those which still make themselves felt and resist solution in ordinary educated thought; adding an implied "et cetera," so that the reader may pursue the subject according to the criteria set before him, either by going again over old discussions, or by entering into those of to-day, which change and multiply and assume new shapes almost daily. Another warning must not be omitted: namely that aesthetics, though a special philosophical science, having as its principle a special and distinct category of the mind, can never, just because it is philosophical, be detached from the main body of philosophy; for its problems are concerned with the relations between art and the other mental forms, and therefore imply both difference and identity. Aesthetics is really the whole of philosophy, but with special emphasis on that side of it which concerns art. Many have demanded or imagined or desired a self-contained aesthetics, devoid of any general philosophical implications, and consistent with more than one, or with any, philosophy; but the project is impossible of execution because self-contradictory. Even those who promise to expound a naturalistic, inductive, physical, physiological or psychological aesthetics—in a word, a non-philosophical aesthetics—when they pass from promise to performance surreptitiously introduce a general positivistic, naturalistic or even materialistic philosophy. And anyone who thinks that the philosophical ideas of positivism, naturalism and materialism are false and out of date, will find it an easy matter to refute the aesthetic or pseudo-aesthetic doctrines which mutually support them and are supported by them, and will not regard their problems as problems still awaiting solution or worthy of discussion —or, at least, protracted discussion. For instance, the downfall of psychological associationism (or the substitution of mechanism for *a priori* synthesis) implies the downfall not only of logical associationism but of aesthetics also, with its association of "content" and "form," or of two "representations," which (unlike Campanella's *tactus intrinsecus*, effected *cum magna suavitate*) was a *contactus extrinsecus* whose terms were no sooner united than they *discedebant*. The collapse of biological and evolutionary explanations of logical and ethical values implies the same collapse in the case of aesthetic value. The proved inability of empirical methods to yield knowledge of reality, which in fact they can only classify and reduce to types, involves the impossibility of an aesthetics arrived at by collecting aesthetic facts in classes and discovering their laws by induction.

INTUITION AND EXPRESSION

One of the first problems to arise, when the work of art is defined as "lyrical image," concerns the relation of "intuition" to "expression" and the manner of the transition from the one to the other. At bottom this is the same problem which arises in other parts of philosophy: the problem of inner and outer, of mind and matter, of soul and body, and, in ethics, of intention and will, will and action, and so forth. Thus stated, the problem is insoluble;

for once we have divided the inner from the outer, body from mind, will from action, or intuition from expression, there is no way of passing from one to the other or of reuniting them, unless we appeal for their reunion to a third term, variously represented as God or the Unknowable. Dualism leads necessarily either to transcendence or to agnosticism. But when a problem is found to be insoluble in the terms in which it is stated the only course open is to criticize these terms themselves, to inquire how they have been arrived at, and whether their genesis was logically sound. In this case, such inquiry leads to the conclusion that the terms depend not upon a philosophical principle, but upon an empirical and naturalistic classification, which has created two groups of facts called internal and external respectively (as if internal facts were not also external, and as if an external fact could exist without also being internal), or souls and bodies, or images and expressions; and everyone knows that it is hopeless to try to find a dialectical unity between terms that have been distinguished not philosophically or formally but only empirically and materially. The soul is only a soul in so far as it is a body; the will is only a will in so far as it moves arms and legs, or is action; intuition is only intuition in so far as it is, in that very act, expression. An image that does not express, that is not speech, song, drawing, painting, sculpture or architecture—speech at least murmured to oneself, song at least echoing within one's own breast, line and colour seen in imagination and colouring with its own tint the whole soul and organism—is an image that does not exist. We may assert its existence, but we cannot support our assertion; for the only thing we could adduce in support of it would be the fact that the image was embodied or expressed. This profound philosophical doctrine, the *identity of intuition and expression* is, moreover, a principle of ordinary common sense, which laughs at people who claim to have thoughts they cannot express or to have imagined a great picture which they cannot paint. *Rem tene, verba sequentur;* if there are

no *verba,* there is no *res.* This identity, which applies to every sphere of the mind, has in the sphere of art a clearness and self-evidence lacking, perhaps, elsewhere. In the creation of a work of poetry, we are present, as it were, at the mystery of the creation of the world; hence the value of the contribution made by aesthetics to philosophy as a whole, or the conception of the One that is All. Aesthetics, by denying in the life of art an abstract spiritualism and the resulting dualism, prepares the way and leads the mind towards idealism or absolute spiritualism.

EXPRESSION AND COMMUNICATION

Objections to the identity of intuition and expression generally arise from psychological illusions which lead us to believe that we possess at any moment a profusion of concrete and lively images, when in fact we only possess signs and names for them; or else from faulty analysis of cases like that of the artist who is believed to express mere fragments of a world of images that exists in his mind in its entirety, whereas he really has in his mind only these fragments, together with—not the supposed complete world, but at most an aspiration or obscure working towards it, towards a greater and richer image which may take shape or may not. But these objections also arise from a confusion between *expression* and *communication,* the latter being really distinct from the image and its expression. Communication is the fixation of the intuition-expression upon an object metaphorically called material or physical; in reality, even here we are concerned not with material or physical things but with a mental process. The proof that the so-called physical object is unreal, and its resolution into terms of mind, is primarily of interest for our general philosophical conceptions, and only indirectly for the elucidation of aesthetic questions; hence for brevity's sake we may let the metaphor or symbol stand and speak of matter or nature. It is clear that the poem is complete as soon as the poet has expressed it in words which he repeats to himself. When he comes to repeat them aloud, for others to hear, or looks for someone to learn them by heart and repeat them to others as in a *schola cantorum*, or sets them down in writing or in printing, he has entered upon a new stage, not aesthetic but practical, whose social and cultural importance need not, of course, be insisted upon. So with the painter; he paints on his panel or canvas, but he could not paint unless at every stage in his work, from the original blur or sketch to the finishing touches, the intuited image, the line and colour painted in his imagination, preceded the brush-stroke. Indeed, when the brush-stroke outruns the image, it is cancelled and replaced by the artist's correction of his own work. The exact line that divides expression from communication is difficult to draw in the concrete case, for in the concrete case the two processes generally alternate rapidly and appear to mingle, but it is clear in idea, and it must be firmly grasped. Through overlooking it, or blurring it through insufficient attention, arise the confusions between *art* and *technique*. Technique is not an intrinsic element of art but has to do precisely with the concept of communication. In general it is a cognition or complex of cognitions disposed and directed to the furtherance of practical action; and, in the case of art, of the practical action which makes objects and instruments for the recording and communicating of works of art; *e.g.*, cognitions concerning the preparation of panels, canvases or walls to be painted, pigments, varnishes, ways of obtaining good pronunciation and declamation and so forth. Technical treatises are not aesthetic treatises, nor yet parts or chapters of them. Provided, that is, that the ideas are rigorously conceived and the words used accurately in relation to them it would not be worth while to pick a quarrel over the use of the word "technique" as a synonym for the artistic work itself, regarded as "inner technique" or the formation of intuition-expressions. The confusion between art and technique is especially beloved by impotent artists, who hope to obtain from practical things and practical

devices and inventions the help which their strength does not enable them to give themselves.

ARTISTIC OBJECTS: THE THEORY OF THE SPECIAL ARTS, AND THE BEAUTY OF NATURE

The work of communicating and conserving artistic images, with the help of technique, produces the material objects metaphorically called "*artistic objects*" or "*works of art*": pictures, sculptures and buildings, and, in a more complicated manner, literary and musical writings, and, in our own times, gramophones and records which make it possible to reproduce voices and sounds. But neither these voices and sounds nor the symbols of writing, sculpture and architecture, are works of art; works of art exist only in the minds that create or re-create them. To remove the appearance of paradox from the truth that beautiful objects, beautiful things, do not exist, it may be opportune to recall the analogous case of economic science, which knows perfectly well that in the sphere of economics there are no naturally or physically *useful* things, but only demand and labour, from which physical things acquire, metaphorically, this epithet. A student of economics who wished to deduce the economic value of things from their physical qualities would be perpetrating a gross *ignoratio elenchi*.

Yet this same *ignoratio elenchi* has been, and still is, committed in aesthetic, by the theory of special *arts*, and the limits or peculiar aesthetic character of each. The divisions between the arts are merely technical or physical, according as the artistic objects consist of physical sounds, notes, coloured objects, carved or modelled objects, or constructed objects having no apparent correspondence with natural bodies (poetry, music, painting, sculpture, architecture, etc.). To ask what is the artistic character of each of these arts, what it can and cannot do, what kinds of images can be expressed in sounds, what in notes, what in colours, what in lines, and so forth, is like asking in economics what things are entitled by their physical qualities to have a value and what are not, and what relative values they are entitled to have; whereas it is clear that physical qualities do not enter into the question, and anything may be desired or demanded or valued more than another, or more than anything else at all, according to circumstances and needs. Even Lessing found himself slipping down the slope leading to this truth, and was forced to such strange conclusions as that actions belonged to poetry and bodies to sculpture; even Richard Wagner attempted to find a place in the list for a comprehensive art, namely Opera, including in itself by a process of aggregation the powers of all the arts. A reader with any artistic sense finds in a single solitary line from a poet at once musical and picturesque qualities, sculpturesque strength and architectural structure; and the same with a picture, which is never a mere thing of the eyes but an affair of the whole soul, and exists in the soul not only as colour but as sound and speech. But when we try to grasp these musical or picturesque or other qualities, they elude us and turn into each other, and melt into a unity, however we may be accustomed to distinguish them by different names; a practical proof that art is one and cannot be divided into arts. One, and infinitely varied; not according to the technical conceptions of the several arts, but according to the infinite variety of artistic personalities and their states of mind.

With this relation (and confusion) between artistic creations and instruments of communication or *objets d'art* must be connected the problem of *natural beauty*. We shall not discuss the question, raised by certain aestheticians, whether there are in nature other poets, other artistic beings, beside man; a question which ought to be answered in the affirmative not only out of respect for the song-birds, but, still more, out of respect for the idealistic conception of the world as life and spirituality throughout; even if (as the fairy-tale goes) we have lost the magic herb which when we put it in our mouth, gives us the power of understanding the language of animals and plants. The phrase *natural beauty* properly refers to persons, things, and places whose effect is comparable to that of poetry, painting, sculpture and the other arts. There is no difficulty in allowing the existence of such "natural *objets d'art*," for the process of poetic communication may take place by means of objects naturally given as well as by means of objects artificially produced. The lover's imagination creates a woman beautiful to him, and personifies her in Laura; the pilgrim's imagination creates the charming or sublime landscape, and embodies it in the scene of a lake or a mountain; and these creations of theirs are sometimes shared by more or less wide social circles, thus becoming the "professional beauties" admired by everyone and the famous "views" before which all experience a more or less sincere rapture. No doubt, these creations are mortal; ridicule sometimes kills them, satiety may bring neglect, fashion may replace them by others; and—unlike works of art—they do not admit of authentic interpretation. The bay of Naples, seen from the height of one of the most beautiful Neapolitan villas, was after some time described by the Russian lady who owned the villa as *une cuvette bleue*, whose blue encircled by green so wearied her that she sold the villa. But even the *cuvette bleue* was a legitimate poetical creation.

LITERARY KINDS AND AESTHETIC CATEGORIES

Effects at once greater and more detrimental upon the criticism and historical study of art and literature have been produced by a theory of similar but slightly different origin, the theory of *literary and artistic kinds*. This, like the foregoing, is based on a classification in itself justifiable and useful. The foregoing is based on a technical or physical classification of artistic objects; this is based on a classification according to the feelings which form their content or motive, into *tragic, comic, lyrical, heroic, erotic, idyllic, romantic* and so on, with divisions and subdivisions. It is useful in practice to distribute an artist's works, for purposes of publication, into these classes, putting lyrics in one volume, dramas in another, poems in a third and romances in a fourth; and it is convenient, in fact, indispensable, to refer to works and groups of works by these names in speaking and writing of them. But here again we must deny and pronounce illegitimate the transition from these classificatory concepts to the poetic laws of composition and aesthetic criteria of judgment, as when people try to decide that a tragedy must have a subject of a certain kind, characters of a certain kind, a plot of a certain kind and a certain length; and, when confronted by a work, instead of looking for and appraising its own poetry, ask whether it is a tragedy or a poem, and whether it obeys the "laws" of one or other "kind." The literary criticism of the 19th century owed its great progress largely to its abandonment of the criteria of kinds, in which the criticism of the Renaissance and the French classicists had always been entangled, as may be seen from the discussions arising out of the poems of Dante, Ariosto and Tasso, Guarini's *Pastor fido*, Corneille's *Cid*, and Lope de Vega's *comedias*. Artists have profited by this liberation less than critics; for anyone with artistic genius bursts the fetters of such servitude, or even makes them the instruments of his power; and the artist with little or no genius turns his very freedom into a new slavery.

It has been thought that the divisions of kinds could be saved by giving them a philosophical significance; or at any rate one such division, that of lyric, epic and dramatic, regarded as the three moments of a process of objectification passing from the lyric, the outpouring of the ego, to the epic, in which the ego detaches its feeling from itself by narrating it, and thence to the drama, in which it allows this feeling to create of itself its own mouthpieces, the *dramatis personae*. But the lyric is not a pouring-forth; it is not a cry or a lament; it is an objectification in which the ego sees itself on the stage, narrates itself, and dramatizes itself; and this lyrical spirit forms the poetry both of epic and of drama, which are therefore distinguished from the lyric only by external signs. A work which is altogether poetry, like *Macbeth* or *Antony and Cleopatra*, is substantially a lyric in which the various tones and successive verses are represented by characters and scenes.

In the old aesthetics, and even to-day in those which perpetuate the type, an important place is given to the so-called categories of beauty: the *sublime*, the *tragic*, the *comic*, the *graceful*, the *humorous* and so forth, which German philosophers not only claimed to treat as philosophical concepts, whereas they are really mere psychological and empirical concepts, but developed by means of that dialectic which belongs only to pure or speculative concepts, philosophical categories. Thus they arranged them in an imaginary progress culminating now in the Beautiful, now in the Tragic, now in the Humorous. Taking these concepts at their face value, we may observe their substantial correspondence with the concepts of the literary and artistic kinds; and this is the source from which, as excerpts from manuals of literature, they have found their way into philosophy. As psychological and empirical concepts, they do not belong to aesthetics; and as a whole, in their common quality, they refer merely to the world of feelings, empirically grouped and classified, which forms the permanent matter of artistic intuition.

RHETORIC, GRAMMAR AND PHILOSOPHY OF LANGUAGE

Every error has in it an element of truth, and arises from an arbitrary combination of things which in themselves are legitimate. This principle may be confirmed by an examination of other erroneous doctrines which have been prominent in the past and are still to a less degree prominent to-day. It is perfectly legitimate, in teaching people to write, to make use of distinctions like that between simple style, ornate style and metaphorical style and its forms, and to point out that here the pupil ought to express himself literally and there metaphorically, or that here the metaphor used is incoherent or drawn out to excessive length, and that here the figure of "preterition," there "hypotyposis" or "irony," would have been suitable. But when people lose sight of the merely practical and didactic origin of these distinctions and construct a philosophical theory of form as divisible into simple form and ornate form, logical form and affective form, and so forth, they are introducing elements of rhetoric into aesthetics and vitiating the true concept of expression. For expression is never logical, but always affective, that is, lyrical and imaginative; and hence it is never metaphorical but always "proper"; it is never simple in the sense of lacking elaboration, or ornate in the sense of being loaded with extraneous elements; it is always adorned with itself, *simplex munditiis*. Even logical thought or science, so far as it is expressed, becomes feeling and imagination, which is why a philosophical or historical or scientific book can be not only true but beautiful and must always be judged not only logically but also aesthetically. Thus we sometimes say that a book is a failure as theory, or criticism, or historical truth, but a success as a work of art, in view of the feeling animating it and expressed in it. As for the element of truth which is obscurely at work in this distinction between logical form and metaphorical form, dialectic and rhetoric, we may detect in it the need of a science of aesthetics side by side with that of logic; but it was a mistake to try to distinguish the two sciences within the sphere of expression which belongs to one of them alone.

Another element in education, namely the teaching of languages, has no less legitimately, ever since ancient times, classified expressions into periods, propositions and words, and words into various species, and each species according to the variations and combinations of roots and suffixes, syllables and letters; and hence have arisen alphabets, grammars and vocabularies, just as in another way for poetry has arisen a science of prosody, and for music and the figurative and architectural arts there have arisen musical and pictorial grammars and so forth. But here, too, the ancients did not succeed in avoiding an illegitimate transition *ab intellectu ad rem*, from abstractions to reality, from the empirical to the philosophical, such as we have already observed elsewhere; and this involved thinking of speech as an ag-gregation of words, and words as aggregations of syllables or of roots and suffixes; whereas the *prius* is speech itself, a continuum, resembling an organism, and words and syllables and roots are a *posterius*, an anatomical preparation, the product of the abstracting intellect, not the original or real fact. If grammar, like rhetoric in the case above considered, is transplanted into aesthetic, the result is a distinction between expression and the means of expression, which is a mere reduplication; for the means of expression are just expression itself, broken into pieces by grammarians. This error, combined with the error of distinguishing between simple and ornate form, has prevented people from seeing that the philosophy of language is not a philosophical grammar, but is wholly devoid of grammatical elements. It does not raise grammatical classifications to a philosophical level; it ignores them, and, when they get in its way, destroys them. The philosophy of language, in a word, is identical with the philosophy of poetry and art, the science of intuition-expression, aesthetics; which embraces language in its whole extension, passing beyond the limits of phonetic and syllabic language, and in its unimpaired reality as living and completely significant expression.

CLASSICAL AND ROMANTIC

The problems reviewed above belong to the past—a past extending through centuries—rather than to the present; of their misstated questions and misconceived solutions there now remain mere relics and superstitions which affect academic treatises more than they do the consciousness and culture of ordinary people. But it is necessary to watch carefully for new shoots from the old stock, which still appear from time to time, in order to cut them down. Such is, in our own time, the theory of styles applied to the history of art (Wölfflin and others) and extended to the history of poetry (Strick and others), a new irruption of rhetorical abstractions into the judgment and history of works of art. But the chief problem of our time, to be overcome by aesthetics, is connected with the crisis in art and in judgments upon art produced by the romantic period. Not that this crisis was not foreshadowed by precedents and parallels in earlier history, like Alexandrian art and that of the late Roman period, and in modern times the Baroque art and poetry which followed upon that of the Renaissance. The crisis of the romantic period, together with sources and characteristics peculiar to itself, had a magnitude all its own. It asserted an antithesis between *naive* and *sentimental* poetry, *classical* and *romantic* art, and thus denied the unity of art and asserted a duality of two fundamentally different arts, of which it took the side of the second, as that appropriate to the modern age, by upholding the primary importance in art of feeling, passion and fancy. In part this was a justifiable reaction against the rationalistic literature of classicism in the French manner, now satirical, now frivolous, weak in feeling and imagination and deficient in a deep poetic sense; but in part, *romanticism* was a rebellion not against *classicism* but against the classical as such: against the idea of the serenity and infinity of the artistic image, against catharsis and in favour of a turbid emotionalism that could not and would not undergo purification. This was very well understood by Goethe, the poet both of passion and of serenity, and therefore, because he was a poet, a classical poet; who opposed romantic poetry as "hospital poetry." Later, it was thought that the disease had run its course and that romanticism was a thing of the past; but though some of its contents and some of its forms were dead, its soul was not: its soul consisting in this tendency on the part of art towards an immediate expression of passions and impressions. Hence it changed its name but went on living and working. It called itself "realism," "verism," "symbolism," "artistic style," "impressionism," "sensualism," "imagism," "decadentism," and nowadays, in its extreme forms, "expressionism" and "futurism." The very conception of art is attacked by these doctrines, which tend to replace it by the conception of one or other kind of non-art; and the statement that they are fighting against art is confirmed by the hatred of the extremists of

this movement for museums and libraries and all the art of the past—that is, for the idea of art which on the whole corresponds with art as it has been historically realized. The connection of this movement, in its latest modern form, with industrialism and the psychology produced and fostered by industrialism is obvious. What art is contrasted with is practical life as lived to-day; and art, for this movement, is not the expression of life and hence the transcending of life in the contemplation of the infinite and universal, but the cries and gesticulations and broken colours of life itself. The real poets and artists, on the other hand, rare at any time, naturally continue, nowadays as always, to work according to the old and only idea of what art is, expressing their feelings in harmonious forms; and the real connoisseurs (rarer, these also, than people think) continue to judge their work according to this same idea. In spite of this, the tendency to destroy the idea of art is a characteristic of our age; and this tendency is based on the *proton pseudos* which confuses mental or aesthetic expression with natural or practical expression—the expression which passes confusedly from sensation to sensation and is a mere effect of sensation, with the expression which art elaborates, as it builds, draws, colours or models, and which is its beautiful creation. The problem for aesthetics to-day is the reassertion and defence of the classical as against romanticism: the synthetic, formal theoretical element which is the *proprium* of art, as against the affective element which it is the business of art to resolve into itself, but which to-day has turned against it and threatens to displace it. Against the inexhaustible fertility of creative mind, the gates of hell shall not prevail; but the hostility which endeavours to make them prevail is disturbing, even if only in an incidental manner, the artistic taste, the artistic life and consequently the intellectual and moral life of to-day.

THE CRITICISM AND HISTORY OF ART AND LITERATURE

Another group of questions raised in works on aesthetics, though not unsuitable to such works, properly belongs to logic and the theory of historical thought. These concern the aesthetic judgment and the history of poetry and the arts. By showing that the aesthetic activity (or art) is one of the forms of mind, a value, a category, or whatever we choose to call it, and not (as philosophers of various schools have thought) an empirical concept referable to certain orders of utilitarian or mixed facts, by establishing the *autonomy of aesthetic value,* aesthetics has also shown that it is the predicate of a special judgment, the *aesthetic judgment,* and the subject-matter of history, of a special history, the history of poetry and the arts, *artistic and literary history*.

The questions that have been raised concerning the aesthetic judgment and artistic and literary history are making allowance for the peculiar character of art, identical with the methodological questions that arise in every field of historical study. It has been asked whether the aesthetic judgment is *absolute* or *relative*; but every historical judgment (and the aesthetic judgment affirming the reality and quality of aesthetic facts is an historical judgment) is always both absolute and relative at once: absolute, in so far as the category involved in the construction possesses universal truth; relative, in so far as the object constructed by that category is historically conditioned: hence in the historical judgment the category is individualized and the individual becomes absolute. Those who in the past have denied the absoluteness of the aesthetic judgment (sensationalistic, hedonistic or utilitarian aestheticians) denied in effect the quality, reality and autonomy of art. It has been asked whether a knowledge of the history of the time —the whole history of the time in question—is necessary for the aesthetic judgment of the art of that time; it certainly is, because, as we know, poetic creation presupposes all the rest of the mind which it is converting into lyrical imagery, and the one aesthetic creation presupposes all the other creations (passions, feelings, customs, etc.) of the given historical moment. Hence may be seen the error both of those who advocate a merely historical judg-

ment upon art (historical critics) and of those who advocate a merely aesthetic (aesthetic critics). The former would find in art all the rest of history (social conditions, biography of the artist, etc.), but would omit that part which is proper to art; the latter would judge the work of art in abstraction from history, depriving it of its real meaning and giving it an imaginary meaning or testing it by arbitrary standards. Lastly, there has appeared a kind of scepticism or pessimism as to the possibility of understanding the art of the past; a scepticism or pessimism which in that case ought to extend to every part of history (history of thought, politics, religion and morality), and refutes itself by a *reductio ad absurdum*, since what we call contemporary art and history really belong to the past as much as those of more distant ages, and must, like them, be re-created in the present, in the mind that feels them and the intellect that understands them. There are artistic works and periods that remain to us unintelligible; but this only means that we are not now in a position to enter again into their life and to understand them, and the same is true of the ideas and customs and actions of many peoples and ages. Humanity, like the individual, remembers some things and forgets many others; but it may yet, in the course of its mental development, reach a point where its memory of them revives.

A final question concerns the form proper to artistic and literary history, which, in the form that arose in the romantic period, and still prevails to-day, expounds the history of works of art as a function of the concepts and social needs of its various periods, regarding them as aesthetic expressions of these things and connecting them closely with civil history. This tends to obscure and almost to render invisible the peculiar character of the individual work of art, the character which makes it impossible to confuse one work of art with any other, and results in treating them as documents of social life. In practice no doubt this method is tempered by what may be called the "individualizing" method, which emphasizes the individual character of the works; but the mixture has the defects of all eclecticism. To escape this, there is nothing to do but consistently to develop individualizing history, and to treat works of art not in relation to social history but as each a world in itself, into which from time to time the whole of history is concentrated, transfigured and imaginatively transcended in the individuality of the poetic work, which is a creation, not a reflection, a monument, not a document. Dante is not simply a document of the middle ages, nor Shakespeare of the English Renaissance; as such, they have many equals or superiors among bad poets and non-poets. It has been objected that this method imposed on artistic and literary history the form of a series of disconnected essays or monographs; but, obviously, the connection is provided by human history as a whole, of which the personalities of poets constitute a part, and a somewhat conspicuous part (Shakespearian poetry is an event no less important than the Reformation or the French Revolution), and, precisely because they are a part of it, they ought not to be submerged and lost in it, that is, in its other parts, but ought to retain their proper proportions and their original character.

HISTORY OF AESTHETICS

From the character of aesthetics as a philosophical science (*see* above) it follows that its history cannot be separated from that of philosophy at large, from which aesthetics receives light and guidance, and gives back light and guidance in its turn. The so-called subjectivist tendency which modern philosophy acquired with Descartes, for instance, by promoting enquiry into the creative power of the mind, indirectly promoted enquiry into the aesthetic power; and conversely, as an example of the influence of aesthetic on the rest of philosophy, it is enough to recall the effect which the mature consciousness of creative imagination and poetic logic had in liberating philosophical logic from the traditional intellectualism and formalism, and raising it to the level of speculative or dialectical logic in the philosophies

of Schelling and Hegel. But if the history of aesthetics must be seen as a part of the entire history of philosophy, it must on the other hand be enlarged beyond its boundaries as ordinarily defined, which would restrict it almost entirely to the series of works by so-called professional philosophers and of the academic treatises known as "systems of philosophy." Genuine and original philosophical thought is often to be found, alive and energetic in books not written by professional philosophers and not outwardly systematic; ethical thought, in works of asceticism and religion; political, in the works of historians; aesthetic, in those of art-critics, and so forth. Further, it must be remembered that, strictly speaking, the subject-matter of the history of aesthetics is not the problem, the single problem, of the definition of art, a problem exhausted when that definition has been or shall have been attained; but the innumerable problems which are perpetually springing up in connection with art, in which this one problem, the problem of defining art, acquires particularity and concreteness, and in which alone it truly exists. Subject to these warnings, which must be carefully borne in mind, a general sketch of the history of aesthetics may be given, to provide a preliminary orientation, without running the risk of being understood in an unduly rigid and simplificatory manner.

A sketch of this kind must accept, not merely as convenient for purposes of exposition but as historically true, the common statement that aesthetics is a modern science. Graeco-Roman antiquity did not speculate about art, or speculated very little; its chief concern was to create a method of artistic instruction, not a "philosophy" but an "empirical science" of art. Such are the ancient treatises on "grammar," "rhetoric," "institutions of oratory," "architecture," "music," "painting" and "sculpture"; the basis of all later methods of instruction, even those of to-day, in which the old principles are restated and interpreted *cum grano salis*, but not abandoned, because in practice they are indispensable. The philosophy of art did not find favourable or stimulating conditions in ancient philosophy, which was primarily "physics" and "metaphysics," and only secondarily and intermittently "psychology" or more precisely "philosophy of mind." To the philosophical problems of aesthetics it only referred in passing, either negatively, in Plato's denial of the value of poetry, or positively, in Aristotle's defence, which attempted to secure for poetry a realm of its own between that of history and that of philosophy, or again in the speculations of Plotinus, who for the first time united the previously disconnected concepts of "art" and "the beautiful." Other important thoughts of the ancients were that to poetry belonged "tales" (*mythoi*) and not "arguments" (*logoi*), and that "semantic" (rhetorical or poetical) propositions were to be distinguished from "apophantic" (logical). Lately an almost wholly unexpected strain of ancient aesthetic thought has come to light, in the Epicurean doctrines expounded by Philodemus, in which imagination is conceived in what seems almost a romantic way. But these observations remained, for the time being, practically sterile; and the ancients' firm and sure judgment in artistic matters was never raised to the level and consistency of a theory, owing to an obstacle of a general nature—the objectivistic or naturalistic character of ancient philosophy, whose removal was only commenced, or demanded, by Christianity when it brought the problems of the soul into the focus of thought.

But even Christian philosophy, partly through its predominating transcendence, mysticism and asceticism, partly through the scholastic form which it borrowed from ancient philosophy and with which it remained content, while it raised the problems of morality in an acute form, and handled them with delicacy, did not penetrate deeply into the mental region of imagination and taste, just as it avoided the region which corresponds to it in the sphere of practice, the region of passions, interests, utility, politics and economics. Just as politics and economics were conceived moralistically, so art was subordinated to moral and re-ligious allegory; and the germs of aesthetics scattered through the ancient writers were forgotten or only superficially remembered. The philosophy of the Renaissance, with its return to naturalism, revived, interpreted and adapted the ancient poetics and rhetorics and treatises on the arts; but though it laboured long at "verisimilitude" and "truth," "imitation" and "the idea," "beauty" and the mystical theory of beauty and love, "catharsis" or the purgation of passion, and the problems of the literary kinds, traditional and modern, it never reached a new and fruitful principle. No thinker arose capable of doing for the Renaissance treatises on poetry and art what Machiavelli did for political science, asserting with emphasis, not merely by the way and as an admission, its original and autonomous character.

Much more important in this respect, though its importance was long overlooked by historians, was the thought of the later Renaissance, known in Italy as the *seicento*, Baroque, or the literary and artistic decadence. This was the time at which the distinction was first insisted upon between the "intellect" and a faculty called *ingegno, ingenium,* "wit" or "genius," as especially inventive of art; and, corresponding to this, a faculty of judgment, which was not ratiocination or logical judgment, because it judged "without discourse" or "without concepts," and came to be called "taste." These terms were reinforced by another, which appeared to denote something not determinable in logical concepts and in some way mysterious: "*nescio quid*" or "*je ne sais quoi*"; an expression particularly frequent in Italy (*non so che*), and imitated in other countries. At the same time were sung the praises of the enchantress "imagination," of the "sensible" or "sensuous" element in poetic imagery, and of the miracles of "colour," in painting, as opposed to "drawing" which seemed not altogether free from an element of cold logic. These new intellectual tendencies were somewhat turbid, but at times were purified and raised to the level of reasoned theory, *e.g.,* Zuccolo (1623), who criticized "metric art" and replaced its criteria by the "judgment of sense," which to him meant not the eye or the ear but a higher power united to the senses; Mascardi (1636), who rejected the objective and rhetorical distinction between the styles, and reduced style to the particular individual manner arising out of the particular "wit" of each writer, thus asserting the existence of as many styles as there are writers; Pallavicino (1644), who criticized "verisimilitude" and assigned to poetry as its proper domain that of "first apprehensions" or imaginations, "neither true nor false"; and Tesauro (1654), who tried to work out a logic of rhetoric as opposed to the logic of dialectic, and extended the rhetorical forms beyond merely verbal form, to pictorial and plastic form.

Cartesianism, to which we have already referred, though, in the hands of Descartes and his successors, hostile to poetry and imagination, from another point of view, as stimulating enquiry into the subject or the mind, helped these scattered efforts (as we have said) to consolidate themselves into a system and to search for a principle to which the arts could be reduced; and here too the Italians, welcoming Descartes' method but not his rigid intellectualism or his contempt for poetry, art and imagination, wrote the first treatises on poetry in which the concept of imagination played a central or leading part (Calopreso 1691, Gravina 1692 and 1708, Muratori 1704 and others). These had considerable influence on Bodmer and the Swiss school, and, through them, on the new German criticism and aesthetics and that of Europe at large; so that a recent writer (Robertson) could speak of "the Italian origin of romantic aesthetics."

These minor theorists led to the work of G. B. Vico, who in his *Scienza nuova* (1725–1730) propounded a "poetic logic" which he distinguished from "intellectual logic"; regarded poetry as a mode of consciousness or theoretic form preceding the philosophical or reasoning form, and asserted as its sole principle the imagination, which is strong in proportion as it is free from ratiocination, its

enemy and destroyer; praised as father and prince of all true poets the barbaric Homer, and with him, though impaired by theological and scholastic culture, the half-barbaric Dante; and attempted, though without success, to discern English tragedy and Shakespeare, who, though undiscovered by Vico, would, had he known him, certainly have been his third barbaric and supreme poet. But in aesthetics as elsewhere, Vico in his lifetime founded no school, because he was before his time, and also because his philosophical thought was concealed beneath a kind of historical symbolism. "Poetic logic" only began to make progress when it reappeared in a far less profound shape, but in a more favourable environment, in the works of Baumgarten, who systematized an aesthetics of a somewhat hybrid Leibnitzian origin, and gave it various names, including *ars analogi rationis, scientia cognitionis sensitivae, gnoseologia inferior*, and the name it has retained, *aesthetica* (*Meditationes*, 1735; *Aesthetica*, 1750–58).

The school of Baumgarten, or (more correctly) of Leibnitz, which both did and did not distinguish imaginative from logical form (for it regarded it as *cognitio confusa* and none the less ascribed to it a *perfectio* of its own), and the current of English aesthetics (Shaftesbury, Hutcheson, Hume, Home, Gerard, Burke, Alison, etc.), together with the essays on beauty and art which abounded at this time, and the theoretical and historical works of Lessing and Winckelmann, contributed to provide the stimulus, partly positive and partly negative, to the formation of the other masterpiece of 18th century aesthetics, the *Critique of Judgment* (1790) by Immanuel Kant, in which the author (after doubting it in the first *Critique*) discovered that beauty and art afford subject-matter for a special philosophical science—in other words, discovered the autonomy of the aesthetic activity. As against the utilitarians he showed that the beautiful pleases "without interest" (*i.e.*, utilitarian interest); against the intellectualists, that it pleases "without concepts"; and further, against both, that it has "the form of purposiveness" without "representation of a purpose": and, against the hedonists, that it is "the object of a universal pleasure." In substance, Kant never went further than this negative and generic assertion of the beautiful, just as, in the *Critique of Practical Reason*, once he had vindicated the moral law, he did not go beyond the generic form of duty. But the principles he had laid down were laid down once for all. After the *Critique of Judgment*, a return to hedonistic and utilitarian explanations of art and beauty could (and did) take place only through ignorance of Kant's demonstrations. Even the return to Leibnitz and Baumgarten's theory of art as confused or fanciful thinking would have been impossible, had Kant been able to link up his own theory of the beautiful, as pleasing apart from concepts, and as purposiveness without representation of purpose, with Vico's imperfect and inconsistent but powerful theory of the logic of imagination, which was to some extent represented in Germany at this time by Hamann and Herder. But Kant himself prepared the way for the reassertion of the "confused concept" when he ascribed to genius the virtue of combining intellect and fancy, and distinguished art from "pure beauty" by defining it as "adherent beauty."

This return to the tradition of Baumgarten is apparent in post-Kantian philosophy when it regards poetry and art as a form of the knowledge of the Absolute or the Idea, whether equal to philosophy, inferior and preparatory to it, or superior to it as in Schelling's philosophy (1800) where it becomes the organ of the Absolute. In the richest and most striking work of this school, the *Lectures on Aesthetic* of Hegel (1765–1831), art, with religion and philosophy, is placed in the "sphere of absolute mind," where the mind is set free from empirical knowledge and practical action, and enjoys the beatific thought of God or the Idea. It remains doubtful whether the first moment in this triad is art or religion; different expositions of his doctrine by Hegel himself differ in this respect; but it is clear that both, art and religion alike, are at once transcended and included in the final synthesis which is philosophy. This means that art, like religion, is substantially an inferior or imperfect philosophy, a philosophy expressed in imagery, a contradiction between a content and a form inadequate to it which only philosophy can resolve. Hegel, who tended to identify the system of philosophy, the dialectic of concepts, with actual history, expressed this by his famous paradox of the death of art in the modern world, as incapable of subserving the highest interests of the age.

This conception of art as philosophy, or intuitive philosophy, or a symbol of philosophy, or the like, reappears throughout the idealistic aesthetics of the first half of the 19th century, with rare exceptions, e.g., Schleiermacher's *Lectures on Aesthetic* (1825, 1832–33) which we possess in a very incomplete form. In spite of the high merit of these works, and the enthusiasm for poetry and art which they express, the reaction against this type of aesthetics was, at bottom, a reaction against the artificial character of the principle on which they were based. This reaction took place in the second half of the century, simultaneously with the general reaction against the idealistic philosophy of the great post-Kantian systems. This antiphilosophical movement certainly had its significance as a symptom of discontent and of a desire to find new paths; but it did not produce an aesthetics correcting the errors of its predecessors and carrying the problem a stage further. In part, it was a breach in the continuity of thought; in part, a hopeless attempt to solve the problems of aesthetics, which are philosophical problems, by the methods of empirical science (e.g., Fechner); in part, a revival of hedonistic and utilitarian aesthetic by a utilitarianism resting on association of ideas, evolution and a biological theory of heredity (e.g., Spencer). Nothing of real value was added by the *epigoni* of idealism (Vischer, Schasler, Carriere, Lotze, etc.), or the followers of the other early 19th century philosophical movements, e.g., the so-called formalistic aesthetics (Zimmermann) derived from Herbart, or the eclectics and psychologists, who, like all the rest, laboured at two abstractions, "content" and "form" ("aesthetics of content" and "aesthetics of form"), and sometimes tried to fasten the two together, failing to see that by so doing they were only uniting two fictions into a third. The best thoughts on art in this period are to be found not in the professional philosophers or aestheticians but in the critics of poetry and art, *e.g.*, De Sanctis in Italy, Baudelaire and Flaubert in France, Pater in England, Hanslick and Fiedler in Germany, Julius Lange in Holland, etc. These writers alone make amends for the aesthetic trivialities of the positivistic philosophers and the empty artificiality of the so-called idealists.

The general revival of speculative thought led to greater successes in aesthetics in the first decades of the 20th century. Especially noteworthy is the union which is taking place between aesthetics and the philosophy of language, facilitated by the difficulties under which linguistics, conceived as the naturalistic and positivistic science of the phonetic laws of language and similar abstractions, is labouring. But the most recent aesthetic productions, because they are recent and still in process of development, cannot as yet be historically placed and judged.

POETRY, THE WORK OF TRUTH: LITERATURE, THE WORK OF CIVILIZATION (1948)

You MIGHT SUPPOSE that the argument of this lecture, the relation between poetry and literature, is destined for those of you who are pursuing the vocation of literary and artistic history and criticism, and that it is of small interest to students of political and moral history. I will not pause to remind you of the grand principle that all truths coexist in a relation of mutual demonstration, support, clarification, or to recall the advice of Plato to his faithful but unpolished disciple Xenocrates to "sacrifice to the Graces," which in our case might mean to cultivate poetry and literature as necessities for the historian worthy of that name. I will only say now that you will receive in this lecture some new information on a concept which is bound to interest you historians: the concept of civilization.

In the distant age of Greek antiquity poetry

From *Philosophy, Poetry, History* by Benedetto Croce, translated by Cecil Sprigge, published by Oxford University Press. Originally a lecture to the Naples School of Historical Studies.

and literature were already being studied theoretically, giving rise to two separate branches of learning, exemplified in Aristotle's *Poetics* and *Rhetoric*, of which the former is partly and the latter wholly preserved for us. Treatises on Rhetoric had the nature of textbooks for lawyers and for public men in general. You may be interested to know why in Italian we can write not only Retorica but also, in defiance of etymology, Rettorica. The reason is that in the eleventh and twelfth centuries this branch of learning was considered necessary for the "rectors" or magistrates entrusted with the *rettoria*, rectorship or governorship of lands, as I myself learned some time ago from an appendix to a book by the French scholar Pézard on Brunetto Latini's role in the Inferno of Dante. I read it in manuscript and as far as I know it has not yet been published, so that this curious piece of information may constitute an indiscretion, for which the author will surely pardon me.

The *Poetics* and the *Rhetoric* were linked by the fact that the latter part of this second branch of learning, concerned with the Art of Speech (περὶ τῆς λέξεως), began in later times to be detached and to form, nearer to our own age, a separate body which came to be regarded as a sequel and conclusion of the *Poetics*, this last being concerned with the literary genres or kinds, while the Art of Speech was supposed to lay down the rules of fair speech just as grammar gave those of correct speech. Thus all the concepts of Rhetoric came to flow into the Poetic: the distinctions between *content* and *form*, between the *nude* and the *ornate* style, between *proper* and *metaphorical* discourse, and further the various modes of metaphors and figures, and the general law governing the use of all those distinctions, which was the concept of the πρέπον or suitable.

When I set to work to elaborate afresh the doctrine of Aesthetics, among other ingredients which I rejected, such as the "literary genres," the theory of the "modifications of the beautiful," and that of the "divisions of the arts," I expelled, from the field of poetry and the arts, "Rhetoric," and did so with particular ruthlessness, because I thought I discerned in every one of its lineaments a disregard of and an offence against the true nature of poetry.

Take for instance the distinction and separation of content from form. Wherever, I asked, is there in poetry a content distinct from the poetical form? No doubt there is a pre-existing *matter* for poetry, namely men's feelings. But this matter receives poetic form, and he who would pronounce upon the character of poetry has no other course open to him than to read or repeat the poem without losing a syllable, a comma, an accent, because all these and other elements are conjoined in determining its character. For instructional purposes we may stress this or that particular, but neither jointly nor severally can these ever avail to make us know the poem and trace its true and individual physiognomy. For this nothing else will serve except direct vision or intuition. Content and form are in poetry fused indistinguishably as in a single act. Were it otherwise, poetry

would be not truth but the allegorical disguise of truth, that is, not poetry. The word of poetry is not a garment donned by poetry, it is poetry's own self. I mean here the spiritual word, not that abstract physical sound which aroused the strange and perhaps jocular admiration of Gautier for "Minos et Pasiphaë," and gave rise to the unhappy charlatanries of Mallarmé and other decadents. Again, what is "adorned" or "naked" expression? How, if an expression is expressive, can it be naked, and how, on the other hand, can it be adorned, if this means laden with something over and above and extraneous to the expression? How can "proper" words be distinguished from those which are "metaphorical" or imaginous? Poetic expression is always both proper and imaginous, the image being the work of the creative fancy. What is this πρέπον, this "aptness" or "suitability" to which is committed the value of the expressive form, the standard of judgement, whereas the sole value and standard of poetry is beauty? Now beauty is a mental brightness, while suitability is a practical matter, as in the question whether a shoe fits or whether certain behaviour is helpful in producing a desired effect. In fact, whoever wishes to deny poetry has but to recite, giving them out for attributes of poetry, all the qualities of rhetorical and literary expression. This will be the death of poetry. If, on the contrary, one wishes to give a true account of poetry, it suffices to attribute to it the very opposite of such qualities.

After I had thus reclaimed poetry from the attachments of rhetoric or literature, rescuing and safeguarding what was dear to me, I gave little further heed to "literature," which was then for me a secondary interest. This is the usual way with philosophical enquiries. They proceed from pause to pause, and the next pause is interrupted, the task resumed, only when a new problem arises in us to excite our intellect. Such a new problem means a new torment, but also a new pleasure, a "sweet love" as Saint Thomas says in the poem when announcing to Dante the next point of doctrine which he is going to unravel:

. . . Quando l'una paglia è trita,
quando la sua semenza è già riposta
a batter l'altra dolce amor m'invita.[1]

In truth, I had rolled back the invasions and usurpations of the rhetorical or literary theory of expression in the field of the theory of poetry, little recking if I had at the same time rolled back literature and even a theory which, however false in relation to poetry, might well not be false in another sphere. But the rejection of literature itself required a denial of positivity, of value, an affirmation of an intrinsic negativity in literature, the treatment of the concept of literature as the concept of an error. It is true that in my youth the word "literature" was often used in a pejorative sense (compare: "Et tout le reste est littérature"). But this did not and could not mean anything else than that poetry is not literature but is music ("De la musique avant toute chose"), that is, pure art. There was talk also of "bad literature" and this implied that there was also a literature which is good. For that matter everyone of us does his best to turn out works consisting of the most adequate literature that his skill, his deliberate studies, his constant efforts, his repeated corrections of first drafts, enable him to provide. Nobody, in fact, likes being called unlettered, barbaric, awkward, tasteless. The respectability and the claims of literature are thus beyond all question. Rhetoric too had got itself a bad name, specially from the Romantics, who for that matter endowed the world with a Rhetoric of their own, less careful and less useful than that of Quintilian, to mention for example one who might with advantage still be read and studied in our schools. Alessandro Manzoni, the classical, the Virgilian Manzoni, made fun of the rhetoric of his "Seventeenth-Century Anonymous Author" and of his strings of conceits and metaphors, yet he too acknowledged that a touch of rhetoric, "discreet, subtle, tasteful," is indispensable.

Our present question is rather different and

may for convenience be divided into the three queries: 1. what need is met by literature; 2. how does literature originate; 3. what form of the spirit is it which fashions it? I have discussed this subject in a book designed as an introduction to the study of literature and poetry (*La Poesia*), and I return to it now, not only for the sake of expounding it to you, but also in order to add to the argument of the book some thoughts which had not then occurred to me. Like all those who feel a responsibility for the work they perform, I am accustomed to turn back to what I have already written and published, to dip into my own books to see whether I discover errors or deficiencies and whether there are suggestions which could be further developed. With some surprise I have sometimes found myself accused in consequence of that scrupulous re-examination and correction of my works, of contradicting myself and failing in coherence. Does coherence, then, consist in standing still, or does it not consist in advancing by movement towards an ever richer coherency? A proverb of Naples has it that man is not born a master of his trade, he does not start with the knowledge which has to be acquired in the course of life. I would add that man does not even die a perfectly accomplished master. Let me recall how long ago a Neapolitan surgeon whom I knew as a fellow member of the Senate suddenly felt himself mortally stricken while performing an operation: his dying gesture was to pass the lancet to his assistant saying "Now you carry on."

Well then, as to the first query I will say that the human soul being poetical, musical, or however we express this responsiveness to the power of harmony and beauty, feels the need to extend the domain of beauty as widely as possible, and to expel or to modify whatever by its presence detracts from or disturbs and offends beauty. This is not always actually possible. Suffering, when not extreme, may find an appropriate utterance, but great suffering is either silent or finds an outlet in rough language and gestures. In the heat of the battle the leader, as Parini puts it, "shouts insup-

---

[1]   . . . Since one sheaf is threshed,
its grain already stored,
sweet love invites me to beat out the other.
—*Paradiso*, XIII, 34–36

portably for ears refined." Only in the pages of the historians of antiquity, who delighted in such ornaments, does he deliver a well-phrased harangue. He who is in the grip of violent feelings would be ashamed, even were he able, to work up a beautiful expression which would tame what is to him the sacred rage of his passion. One pressing eagerly to attain his end will not pause to discover a wealth of words in which to clothe his demand and his ideal. Even the thinker, when an idea dawns in his mind, must often resign himself to renouncing the search for a fine and adequate expression, in favour of some sign, mark, line, scratch, or even conventional word with which to fix it in his mind so that in due season it may flash forth again when he is at ease and in a suitable frame of mind. In these cases we yield to obstacles just as we yield to an illness, not as welcoming and cultivating it, but with sighs and groans, vowing to get rid of it all as soon as possible, so as to be able to array one's feelings and volitions and thoughts in the light which poetry has kindled in one's soul—an immortal light! That light which has arrayed or will array them, softens them, eliminates all that is barbarous, renders them urbane or, as the Greeks said, citizenly (ἀστεῖοι). Literature, which performs this office, civilizing those expressions which are immediate or natural, is in itself a large part of what we call "Civilization."

We pass on to the second query. What has hitherto been said cannot be doubted: the existence of our faculties of letters itself attests it. But the manner in which Literature accomplishes this office is not so clear, and as far as I know the theorists keep silent about it, and perhaps few have ever considered this with attention or sought to formulate it. The civilizing effect we are speaking of is evidently not procured by the intervention or requested mediation of the spirit or genius of poetry. This cannot strictly speaking be bent or turned to any use, being, like the love of Carmen, *un oiseau sauvage que l'on ne peut apprivoiser.* When it intervenes, it does so by its own impulse, drawing and resolving into itself every affection, every volition, every thought. We

needs must, then, ascribe to the practical activity of the spirit the adoption—for the use of that which in itself is unpoetic—of poetic or aesthetic form, abstracted from poetry. Is that possible? And, to start with, is there any other example outside the aesthetic field of a similar or analogous operation, by which we may explain and justify such a transference of formal or more accurately speaking formalistic character?

There is such an example, and I marvel that it has not been thought of before. In the field of logic there exists besides the deep and substantial logic whereby the universal is conceived in the individual, a logic which we might call superficial, a purely syllogistic and formalistic logic which may clothe with itself affirmations that are untrue, indeed not only tolerates but sometimes requires that this should happen, for the sake of an abbreviation of argument and an easier arrival, by the critical method, at an establishment or re-establishment of the truth; or at the very least, as happens in practical affairs, secures a pseudological, lawyerish agreement bringing to a temporary or final end a dispute which was dragging on harmfully—a better occasion will arise some day for a proper solution. Such is that *logica utens* which European civilization owes mainly to the Aristotelian *Organon* and to the great use and enrichment of this by the mediaeval scholastics. It is no doubt an ill, maybe even a great ill calling for correction, when a truth has been left unspoken or an error has been spoken. But worse still is it when an error is presented in confused, disordered, incorrect, and perpetually contradictory shape, wrapped up at every point in the language of the passions, so that the critic or corrector loses heart, unable to cope with the constancy and violence of such ignorance, and turns his back without having overcome it, leaving it to its own fate. By comparison it is better that the error should remain provisionally in command of the argument, if only it be consecutively set forth, set forth, in fact, with such stringency that this very stringency will at a given moment halt and arrest and execute it at the conclusion of that well-spun argument which will have rendered the original fallacy transparent, bringing it to a confession of its fault. The education in "formal" reasoning which during two thousand years Europe received first from the Greek sophists and philosophers and later from the Catholic universities of the Middle Ages, and finally from the secular schools and universities, has not always been appraised at its full value, whether because advantages which have become common property are always undervalued, or because minds which were turned to that other speculative, dialectical, profound logic, turned away from the periodical distractions and unfair competition of the formalistic logic. However, where the want of the formal discipline was obvious and harmful, this did not pass unnoticed. I remember the Russian Chadaiev, in 1828, noted this as a deficiency in the Russian people, remarking sadly, "Le syllogisme de l'Occident nous est inconnu."

Now this function of formalistic logic which arrays the truth and renders it more easily communicable, but similarly arrays error, rendering it more limpid and therefore easier to see through—so that both truth and error are left intact beneath the veil of logical method whose benefits are conferred impartially, maintaining the argument at a rational level and excluding recourse to the stirring of feelings or other irrelevancies—this or the same sort of function is performed analogously by that aesthetic formalism which treats matters of judgement and philosophy, of history, of science, and matters too of exhortation, menace, flattery, love, pain—in a word the whole range of the intrinsically non-poetic—as though they were poetic, attending to harmony of diction, rhythm, melody, coherence, and proportion of images, in a word to all those details and all those minutiae which are needful in good prose, that is good literature. Should it happen that suddenly an inspiration of true poetry should spring out of this, the heart will rejoice, but will at the same time withdraw and ward it off like a temptation or defer it: this not being a permitted occasion for poetry. The man of literature or prose has no wish to compose poetry, feeling indeed that the mere touch of this adversary would undo the web that he has skilfully woven. Yet he wants to adopt for his own use the "idea" of poetry, or as one might say the "Aestheticity" without the "poeticity," its depthless surface, its form which, in being severed from the content, is severed from itself, is no more itself but an external vesture, utilizable as such, a coat of all those colours and shades which may from time to time be suited to the spirit of the man of literature, of prose, according as his mood is austere, calm, solemn, conversational, or gay. Sometimes it happens that he despises or thinks he despises literature, proclaiming that he means to write just those words which come to his lips, the words of common and popular speech. Do not believe him. Not that he is a liar, but he certainly deceives himself. Just on such an occasion he is likely to be more of a man of letters than ever. Good literature will have become a second nature to him, so that the more subtle and shy and aristocratic his art, the more he will seem to himself to be borne on the current of the natural and popular. At other times he may show disdain and haughtiness towards poetry as being by comparison with literature a frivolity. Had I time, I might quote examples of this attitude. It has been remarked that the Greeks and Romans strictly practised the separation of the writers of poetry from the writers of prose. We have no knowledge of prose works of Sophocles or Euripides, of Virgil or Lucretius or Propertius, while the verses composed by the supreme man of prose and literature, Cicero, became proverbial as ridiculous attempts, *ridenda poëmata*. The modern poets have been more versatile composing, as they still do, worthy and important prose works. I merely remark on this fact in passing, and do not draw any consequences from it, though it may be worth someone else's attention. Instead I will observe that in the sphere of the pictorial and plastic arts, and of music and architecture, as well as in that of the "spoken word" or articulated utterance, there are to be found "literary" works. Connoisseurs and critics recognize these at once, but are wrong in despising them, for they have their own value and serve their purpose excellently.

I come to the third query. Whose handiwork is this prose or literature? We must of course discard the suggestion that it is the joint work of the poet and the non-poet when they *coniurent amice*. Such an agreement is not strictly speaking possible, and, were it, the products of the collaboration would be feeble in the extreme, the result of a series of transactions and mis-tones. But neither may we attribute it to the poet alone, for we have already delineated his impatient and tempestuous, domineering and disdainful treatment of any content which resists and holds its own ground. And here the content, whether of philosophic and historic thought, of scientific construction, of deliberate effort to induce in others a state of mind propitious to some action, or of utterance for the relief of one's own mental turmoil, has to be fully respected in all its weightiness and precision. Indeed if the satisfaction of the aesthetic urge is accomplished in a measure exceeding what is felt to be the complement and perfection of the thought or the excitement of the feelings which is at stake, then the content resists assimilation to an aesthetic form which flies asunder like an ill-fitting garment. Indeed a true fit can be accomplished only by dint of a long training in that, as it were, diplomatic capacity to accord two wills in such manner that neither abases itself but each finds in the other some interest common to both, the energy of natural expression sacrificing as much of itself as does not help on the purpose in hand, and acquiring a brightness of beauty which shines not for its own sake but for the help which it can render. Such "practical tact" plays in literature the same sort of role as the "aesthetic taste" plays in poetical composition. Its part is not that of the creative genius operating with *quodam sensu sine ratione et arte*, but is an operation with a calculating and selective adroitness, as in the handling of a technical instrument. The author of this handiwork is, then, the practical mind, which works identically in every practical business save for the variations called for in the different tasks

presented to it: in our case, then, not the practical spirit of the engineer building a machine, the chemist compounding a drug, the soldier planning a bombardment or an air-raid, but that of the man who would present in fine array, and at the same time in the fullness of their being, the results of his efforts as a philosopher, historian, scientist, orator, politician, or maybe simply his agitations, his affections, his feelings.

So now the present lecturer, that old foe of Rhetoric, which he once abhorred for having penetrated or having been introduced into the sacred precincts of poetry, takes up such an attitude as one of the poets of the Italian Risorgimento advised his countrymen to take up towards the Germans: once they had been driven back across the Alps they should be treated again as brothers. Having expelled Rhetoric from those precincts, I feel it my duty and pleasure to make peace and to suggest to my former foe lines of defence which were not previously available. I will observe that Rhetoric unwittingly tended to provide a theory, not of poetry, but of literature, offering or furnishing to this end the concepts proper to Rhetoric, first and foremost the fundamental practical concept of the $\pi\rho\acute{\epsilon}\pi o\nu$, the suitable or appropriate. Not without reason Rhetoric then went on to distinguish in literature form and content, the raiment and the body which it clothed, calling the former the ornament. And I will not now be too strait-laced or severe about that description of a "proper" or "naked" expression contrasted with the ornate or metaphorical expression, but will understand it as meaning the natural, savage, or barbarian expression which not having undergone an aesthetic elaboration and clarification remains in its previous condition as non-aesthetic fact.

Before closing this lecture, let me dwell again for a moment on the concept of civilization as the process of redemption of humanity from barbarism, a process in which the formation and progress of literary expression is, as we have said, an important factor. Truth to tell, the radiation of poetic or aesthetic virtue works not only at one point but throughout the body of civilization. From it come all those customs and relations in human societies which we call gentle and gallant, and thus (to take perhaps the most striking and imaginatively convincing example), those ceremonial features of capital executions, in ancient if not in modern times, according to which the executor of high purposes (for by such a title was his function ennobled), before seizing upon the condemned, went down on his knees to him to ask pardon since what he was about to do was done not in hatred but in obedience to the guardians of the law. In one of my essays I have attributed to Aesthetics (considered by professorial philosophers to be a specialized science of secondary importance, not to be taken too seriously) an outstanding importance for all the other branches of philosophy, for their problems have analogues and correspondences with those of aesthetics the solution of which can help on the solution of their own. To this I must now add an affirmation of the importance of poetry and art, not in their theory but in their concreteness, for the social, political, and moral institutions of men. I should be sorry if this efficacy which I attribute to the philosophy of art, in the field of theory, and to art itself in the field of practice, were regarded as a paradox in which I indulge merely because I have myself delighted in those studies. Let me say then that this idea, far from being paradoxical, lives already in the ancient conception of the poet as the teacher of peoples whom he drew forward out of a condition of barbarism and set to build their city to the tune of his lyre.

Speaking of this powerful efficacy of poetry in the origination of literature and of civilized behaviour, I may here appropriately comment upon an important observation of Goethe. I have mentioned it on another occasion, but it still remains little known and unutilized even in France, where it should have roused much attention seeing that it refers directly to a particular aspect of the French spirit. As far as I know the only critic to mention it was Sainte-Beuve in his *Tableau de la poésie française au*

XVI siècle, though he read it and took his version from a French translation fantastic rather than incomprehensible, the work of two ignoramuses—hence the passage is in France as good as unknown. It is a note to a German edition of Diderot's *Neveu de Rameau* entitled *Geschmack* (taste). Goethe points out that in France, especially since Louis XIV, "the various kinds of poetry were treated as if they were various grades of society, each one having its own code of manners," much as there are different conventions according as one is in exclusively male or in mixed or in highly distinguished company. Now the *convenances* which prevail in such a well-ordered society were transferred to tragedy, comedy, odes, and other literary types, and according to a supposed code of manners certain images and words were admitted or excluded in each class. Hence *goût* in French came to have an altogether different and almost opposite significance to that of *Geschmack* in German, which meant poetic taste. Now such an application of the rules of good society to poetry was doubtless still more absurd and harmful than those mistaken but practically inoffensive distinctions prescribed by Rhetoric. For they were the torment of the great poets and the comfort of the minor and feeble. But it was the fact that both sets of rules, those of literature and those of good behaviour in society, came from the same source, that is from the aesthetic formalistic adornment both of immediate, natural expression, and of social relations, which facilitated such an application in France of drawing-room conventions to poetry. This remark of Goethe on French *goût* I have chosen for the conclusion of my talk today in the course of which I have been obliged to insist upon a number of difficult because highly unaccustomed distinctions, knowing well that I could not and cannot implant my solutions in your minds unless for your part, by dint of meditating these problems and theories, you discover them for yourselves, or for that matter discover better ones to pass beyond them and take their place.

PSYCHOLOGY AND LITERATURE

Sigmund Freud

[CREATIVE WRITERS AND DAY-DREAMING] (1908)

WE LAYMEN have always been intensely curious to know—like the Cardinal who put a similar question to Ariosto [1]—from what sources that strange being, the creative writer, draws his material, and how he manages to make such an impression on us with it and to arouse in us emotions of which, perhaps, we had not even thought ourselves capable. Our interest is only heightened the more by the fact that, if we ask him, the writer himself gives us no explanation, or none that is satisfactory; and it is not at all weakened by our knowledge that not even the clearest insight into the determinants of his choice of material and into the nature of the art of creating imaginative form will ever help to make creative writers of *us*.

If we could at least discover in ourselves or in people like ourselves an activity which was in some way akin to creative writing! An ex-

amination of it would then give us a hope of obtaining the beginnings of an explanation of the creative work of writers. And, indeed, there is some prospect of this being possible. After all, creative writers themselves like to lessen the distance between their kind and the common run of humanity; they so often assure us that every man is a poet at heart and that the last poet will not perish till the last man does.

Should we not look for the first traces of imaginative activity as early as in childhood? The child's best-loved and most intense occupation is with his play or games. Might we not say that every child at play behaves like a creative writer, in that he creates a world of his own, or, rather, rearranges the things of his world in a new way which pleases him? It would be wrong to think he does not take that world seriously; on the contrary, he takes his play very seriously and he expends large amounts of emotion on it. The opposite of play is not what is serious but what is real. In spite of all the emotion with which he cathects his world of play, the child distinguishes it quite

Chapter IX, "The Relation of the Poet to Day-Dreaming," of Volume IV of *The Collected Papers of Sigmund Freud*, edited by Ernest Jones, M.D., Basic Books, Inc., Publishers, New York, 1959.

[1] "Where did you find so many stories, Lodovico?"

well from reality; and he likes to link his imagined objects and situations to the tangible and visible things of the real world. This linking is all that differentiates the child's "play" from "phantasying."

The creative writer does the same as the child at play. He creates a world of phantasy which he takes very seriously—that is, which he invests with large amounts of emotion—while separating it sharply from reality. Language has preserved this relationship between children's play and poetic creation. It gives [in German] the name of "*Spiel*" ["play"] to those forms of imaginative writing which require to be linked to tangible objects and which are capable of representation. It speaks of a "*Lustspiel*" or "*Trauerspiel*" ["comedy" or "tragedy": literally, "pleasure play" or "mourning play"] and describes those who carry out the representation as *Schauspieler* ["players": literally "show-players"]. The unreality of the writer's imaginative world, however, has very important consequences for the technique of his art; for many things which, if they were real, could give no enjoyment, can do so in the play of phantasy, and many excitements which, in themselves, are actually distressing, can become a source of pleasure for the hearers and spectators at the performance of a writer's work.

There is another consideration for the sake of which we will dwell a moment longer on this contrast between reality and play. When the child has grown up and has ceased to play, and after he has been labouring for decades to envisage the realities of life with proper seriousness, he may one day find himself in a mental situation which once more undoes the contrast between play and reality. As an adult he can look back on the intense seriousness with which he once carried on his games in childhood; and, by equating his ostensibly serious occupations of to-day with his childhood games, he can throw off the too heavy burden imposed on him by life and win the high yield of pleasure afforded by *humour*.

As people grow up, then, they cease to play, and they seem to give up the yield of pleasure which they gained from playing. But whoever understands the human mind knows that hardly anything is harder for a man than to give up a pleasure which he has once experienced. Actually, we can never give anything up; we only exchange one thing for another. What appears to be a renunciation is really the formation of a substitute or surrogate. In the same way, the growing child, when he stops playing, gives up nothing but the link with real objects; instead of *playing*, he now *phantasies*. He builds castles in the air and creates what are called *day-dreams*. I believe that most people construct phantasies at times in their lives. This is a fact which has long been overlooked and whose importance has therefore not been sufficiently appreciated.

People's phantasies are less easy to observe than the play of children. The child, it is true, plays by himself or forms a closed psychical system with other children for the purposes of a game; but even though he may not play his game in front of the grown-ups, he does not, on the other hand, conceal it from them. The adult, on the contrary, is ashamed of his phantasies and hides them from other people. He cherishes his phantasies as his most intimate possessions, and as a rule he would rather confess his misdeeds than tell anyone his phantasies. It may come about that for that reason he believes he is the only person who invents such phantasies and has no idea that creations of this kind are widespread among other people. This difference in the behaviour of a person who plays and a person who phantasies is accounted for by the motives of these two activities, which are nevertheless adjuncts to each other.

A child's play is determined by wishes: in point of fact by a single wish—one that helps in his upbringing—the wish to be big and grown up. He is always playing at being "grown up," and in his games he imitates what he knows about the lives of his elders. He has no reason to conceal this wish. With the adult, the case is different. On the one hand, he knows that he is expected not to go on playing or phantasying any longer, but to act in the real world; on the other hand, some of the wishes which give rise to his phantasies are of a kind which it is essential to conceal. Thus he is ashamed of his phantasies as being childish and as being unpermissible.

But, you will ask, if people make such a mystery of their phantasying, how is it that we know such a lot about it? Well, there is a class of human beings upon whom, not a god, indeed, but a stern goddess—Necessity—has allotted the task of telling what they suffer and what things give them happiness.[2] These are the victims of nervous illness, who are obliged to tell their phantasies, among other things, to the doctor by whom they expect to be cured by mental treatment. This is our best source of knowledge, and we have since found good reason to suppose that our patients tell us nothing that we might not also hear from healthy people.

Let us now make ourselves acquainted with a few of the characteristics of phantasying. We may lay it down that a happy person never phantasies, only an unsatisfied one. The motive forces of phantasies are unsatisfied wishes, and every single phantasy is the fulfilment of a wish, a correction of unsatisfying reality. These motivating wishes vary according to the sex, character and circumstances of the person who is having the phantasy; but they fall naturally into two main groups. They are either ambitious wishes, which serve to elevate the subject's personality; or they are erotic ones. In young women the erotic wishes predominate almost exclusively, for their ambition is as a rule absorbed by erotic trends. In young men egoistic and ambitious wishes come to the fore clearly enough alongside of erotic ones. But we will not lay stress on the opposition between the two trends; we would rather emphasize the

fact that they are often united. Just as, in many altar-pieces, the portrait of the donor is to be seen in a corner of the picture, so, in the majority of ambitious phantasies, we can discover in some corner or other the lady for whom the creator of the phantasy performs all his heroic deeds and at whose feet all his triumphs are laid. Here, as you see, there are strong enough motives for concealment; the well-brought-up young woman is only allowed a minimum of erotic desire, and the young man has to learn to suppress the excess of self-regard which he brings with him from the spoilt days of his childhood, so that he may find his place in a society which is full of other individuals making equally strong demands.

We must not suppose that the products of this imaginative activity—the various phantasies, castles in the air and day-dreams—are stereotyped or unalterable. On the contrary, they fit themselves in to the subject's shifting impressions of life, change with every change in his situation, and receive from every fresh active impression what might be called a "date-mark." The relation of a phantasy to time is in general very important. We may say that it hovers, as it were, between three times—the three moments of time which our ideation involves. Mental work is linked to some current impression, some provoking occasion in the present which has been able to arouse one of the subject's major wishes. From there it harks back to a memory of an earlier experience (usually an infantile one) in which this wish was fulfilled; and it now creates a situation relating to the future which represents a fulfilment of the wish. What it thus creates is a day-dream or phantasy, which carries about it traces of its origin from the occasion which provoked it and from the memory. Thus past, present and future are strung together, as it were, on the thread of the wish that runs through them.

A very ordinary example may serve to make what I have said clear. Let us take the case of a poor orphan boy to whom you have given the address of some employer where he may per-

[2] [This is an allusion to some well-known lines spoken by the poet-hero in the final scene of Goethe's *Torquato Tasso:*
   Und wenn der Mensch in seiner Qual verstummt,
      Gab mir ein Gott, zu sagen, wie ich leide.
"And when mankind is dumb in its torment, a god granted me to tell how I suffer."]

haps find a job. On his way there he may indulge in a day-dream appropriate to the situation from which it arises. The content of his
phantasy will perhaps be something like this.
He is given a job, finds favour with his new
employer, makes himself indispensable in the
business, is taken into his employer's family,
marries the charming young daughter of the
house, and then himself becomes a director of
the business, first as his employer's partner and
then as his successor. In this phantasy, the
dreamer has regained what he possessed in his
happy childhood—the protecting house, the
loving parents and the first objects of his affectionate feelings. You will see from this example
the way in which the wish makes use of an
occasion in the present to construct, on the
pattern of the past, a picture of the future.

There is a great deal more that could be said
about phantasies; but I will only allude as
briefly as possible to certain points. If phantasies become over-luxuriant and over-powerful,
the conditions are laid for an onset of neurosis
or psychosis. Phantasies, moreover, are the
immediate mental precursors of the distressing
symptoms complained of by our patients. Here
a broad by-path branches off into pathology.

I cannot pass over the relation of phantasies
to dreams. Our dreams at night are nothing
else than phantasies like these, as we can demonstrate from the interpretation of dreams.[3]
Language, in its unrivalled wisdom, long ago
decided the question of the essential nature of
dreams by giving the name of "day-dreams" to
the airy creations of phantasy. If the meaning
of our dreams usually remains obscure to us in
spite of this pointer, it is because of the circumstance that at night there also arise in us
wishes of which we are ashamed; these we must
conceal from ourselves, and they have consequently been repressed, pushed into the unconscious. Repressed wishes of this sort and
their derivatives are only allowed to come to
expression in a very distorted form. When
scientific work had succeeded in elucidating
this factor of *dream-distortion*, it was no longer

difficult to recognize that night-dreams are
wish-fulfilments in just the same way as day-
dreams—the phantasies which we all know so
well.

So much for phantasies. And now for the
creative writer. May we really attempt to compare the imaginative writer with the "dreamer
in broad daylight," and his creations with day-
dreams? Here we must begin by making an
initial distinction. We must separate writers
who, like the ancient authors of epics and
tragedies, take over their material ready-made,
from writers who seem to originate their own
material. We will keep to the latter kind, and,
for the purposes of our comparison, we will
choose not the writers most highly esteemed by
the critics, but the less pretentious authors of
novels, romances and short stories, who nevertheless have the widest and most eager circle of
readers of both sexes. One feature above all
cannot fail to strike us about the creations of
these story-writers: each of them has a hero
who is the centre of interest, for whom the
writer tries to win our sympathy by every possible means and whom he seems to place under
the protection of a special Providence. If, at
the end of one chapter of my story, I leave the
hero unconscious and bleeding from severe
wounds, I am sure to find him at the beginning
of the next being carefully nursed and on the
way to recovery; and if the first volume closes
with the ship he is in going down in a storm at
sea, I am certain, at the opening of the second
volume, to read of his miraculous rescue—a
rescue without which the story could not proceed. The feeling of security with which I follow the hero through his perilous adventures is
the same as the feeling with which a hero in
real life throws himself into the water to save a
drowning man or exposes himself to the enemy's fire in order to storm a battery. It is the
true heroic feeling, which one of our best writers has expressed in an inimitable phrase:
"Nothing can happen to *me!*"[4] It seems to me,

[3] Cf. Freud, *The Interpretation of Dreams.*

[4] ["Es kann dir nix g'schehen!" This phrase from
Anzengruber, the Viennese dramatist, was a favourite
one of Freud's.]

however, that through this revealing characteristic of invulnerability we can immediately recognize His Majesty the Ego, the hero alike of every day-dream and of every story.

Other typical features of these egocentric stories point to the same kinship. The fact that all the women in the novel invariably fall in love with the hero can hardly be looked on as a portrayal of reality, but it is easily understood as a necessary constituent of a day-dream. The same is true of the fact that the other characters in the story are sharply divided into good and bad, in defiance of the variety of human characters that are to be observed in real life. The "good" ones are the helpers, while the "bad" ones are the enemies and rivals, of the ego which has become the hero of the story.

We are perfectly aware that very many imaginative writings are far removed from the model of the naïve day-dream; and yet I cannot suppress the suspicion that even the most extreme deviations from that model could be linked with it through an uninterrupted series of transitional cases. It has struck me that in many of what are known as "psychological" novels only one person—once again the hero—is described from within. The author sits inside his mind, as it were, and looks at the other characters from outside. The psychological novel in general no doubt owes its special nature to the inclination of the modern writer to split up his ego, by self-observation, into many part-egos, and, in consequence, to personify the conflicting currents of his own mental life in several heroes. Certain novels, which might be described as "eccentric," seem to stand in quite special contrast to the type of the day-dream. In these, the person who is introduced as the hero plays only a very small active part; he sees the actions and sufferings of other people pass before him like a spectator. Many of Zola's later works belong to this category. But I must point out that the psychological analysis of individuals who are not creative writers, and who diverge in some respects from the so-called norm, has shown us analogous variations of the day-dream, in which the ego contents itself with the role of spectator.

If our comparison of the imaginative writer with the day-dreamer, and of poetical creation with the day-dream, is to be of any value, it must, above all, show itself in some way or other fruitful. Let us, for instance, try to apply to these authors' works the thesis we laid down earlier concerning the relation between phantasy and the three periods of time and the wish which runs through them; and, with its help, let us try to study the connections that exist between the life of the writer and his works. No one has known, as a rule, what expectations to frame in approaching this problem; and often the connection has been thought of in much too simple terms. In the light of the insight we have gained from phantasies, we ought to expect the following state of affairs. A strong experience in the present awakens in the creative writer a memory of an earlier experience (usually belonging to his childhood) from which there now proceeds a wish which finds its fulfilment in the creative work. The work itself exhibits elements of the recent provoking occasion as well as of the old memory.

Do not be alarmed at the complexity of this formula. I suspect that in fact it will prove to be too exiguous a pattern. Nevertheless, it may contain a first approach to the true state of affairs; and, from some experiments I have made, I am inclined to think that this way of looking at creative writings may turn out not unfruitful. You will not forget that the stress it lays on childhood memories in the writer's life—a stress which may perhaps seem puzzling—is ultimately derived from the assumption that a piece of creative writing, like a day-dream, is a continuation of, and a substitute for, what was once the play of childhood.

We must not neglect, however, to go back to the kind of imaginative works which we have to recognize, not as original creations, but as the re-fashioning of ready-made and familiar material. Even here, the writer keeps a certain amount of independence, which can express itself in the choice of material and in changes in it which are often quite extensive. In so far as the material is already at hand, however, it is derived from the popular treasure-house of myths, legends and fairy tales. The study of constructions of folk-psychology such as these is far from being complete, but it is extremely probable that myths, for instance, are distorted vestiges of the wishful phantasies of whole nations, the *secular dreams* of youthful humanity.

You will say that, although I have put the creative writer first in the title of my paper, I have told you far less about him than about phantasies. I am aware of that, and I must try to excuse it by pointing to the present state of our knowledge. All I have been able to do is to throw out some encouragements and suggestions which, starting from the study of phantasies, lead on to the problem of the writer's choice of his literary material. As for the other problem—by what means the creative writer achieves the emotional effects in us that are aroused by his creations—we have as yet not touched on it at all. But I should like at least to point out to you the path that leads from our discussion of phantasies to the problems of poetical effects.

You will remember how I have said that the day-dreamer carefully conceals his phantasies from other people because he feels he has reasons for being ashamed of them. I should now add that even if he were to communicate them to us he could give us no pleasure by his disclosures. Such phantasies, when we learn them, repel us or at least leave us cold. But when a creative writer presents his plays to us or tells us what we are inclined to take to be his personal day-dreams, we experience a great pleasure, and one which probably arises from the confluence of many sources. How the writer accomplishes this is his innermost secret; the essential *ars poetica* lies in the technique of overcoming the feeling of repulsion in us which is undoubtedly connected with the barriers that rise between each single ego and the others. We can guess two of the methods used by this technique. The writer softens the character of his egoistic day-dreams by altering and disguising it, and he bribes us by the purely formal— that is, aesthetic—yield of pleasure which he offers us in the presentation of his phantasies. We give the name of an *incentive bonus*, or a *fore-pleasure*, to a yield of pleasure such as this, which is offered to us so as to make possible the release of still greater pleasure arising from deeper psychical sources. In my opinion, all the aesthetic pleasure which a creative writer affords us has the character of a fore-pleasure of this kind, and our actual enjoyment of an imaginative work proceeds from a liberation of tensions in our minds. It may even be that not a little of this effect is due to the writer's enabling us thenceforward to enjoy our own day-dreams without self-reproach or shame. This brings us to the threshold of new, interesting and complicated enquiries; but also, at least for the moment, to the end of our discussion.

Carl Jung

PSYCHOLOGY AND LITERATURE (1929)

It is obvious enough that psychology, being the study of psychic processes, can be brought to bear upon the study of literature, for the human psyche is the womb of all the sciences and arts. We may expect psychological research, on the one hand, to explain the formation of a work of art, and on the other to reveal the factors that make a person artistically creative. The psychologist is thus faced with two separate and distinct tasks, and must approach them in radically different ways.

In the case of the work of art we have to deal with a product of complicated psychic activities —but a product that is apparently intentional and consciously shaped. In the case of the artist we must deal with the psychic apparatus itself. In the first instance we must attempt the psychological analysis of a definitely circumscribed and concrete artistic achievement, while in the second we must analyse the living and creative human being as a unique personality. Although these two undertakings are closely related and even interdependent, neither of them can yield the explanations that are sought by the other. It is of course possible to draw inferences about the artist from the work of art, and *vice versa*, but these inferences are never conclusive. At best they are probable surmises or lucky guesses. A knowledge of Goethe's particular relation to his mother throws some light upon Faust's exclamation: "The mothers—mothers —how very strange it sounds!" But it does not enable us to see how the attachment to his mother could produce the Faust drama itself,

From *Modern Man in Search of a Soul* by Carl G. Jung. Reprinted by permission of Harcourt Brace Jovanovich, Inc.

however unmistakably we sense in the man Goethe a deep connection between the two. Nor are we more successful in reasoning in the reverse direction. There is nothing in *The Ring of the Nibelungs* that would enable us to recognize or definitely infer the fact that Wagner occasionally liked to wear womanish clothes, though hidden connections exist between the heroic masculine world of the Nibelungs and a certain pathological effeminacy in the man Wagner.

The present state of development of psychology does not allow us to establish those rigorous causal connections which we expect of a science. It is only in the realm of the psycho-physiological instincts and reflexes that we can confidently operate with the idea of causality. From the point where psychic life begins—that is, at a level of greater complexity—the psychologist must content himself with more or less widely ranging descriptions of happenings and with the vivid portrayal of the warp and weft of the mind in all its amazing intricacy. In doing this, he must refrain from designating any one psychic process, taken by itself, as "necessary." Were this not the state of affairs, and could the psychologist be relied upon to uncover the causal connections within a work of art and in the process of artistic creation, he would leave the study of art no ground to stand on and would reduce it to a special branch of his own science. The psychologist, to be sure, may never abandon his claim to investigate and establish causal relations in complicated psychic events. To do so would be to deny psychology the right to exist. Yet he can never make good this claim in the fullest sense, because the creative aspect of life which finds its clearest expression in art baffles all attempts at rational formulation. Any reaction to stimulus may be causally explained; but the creative act, which is the absolute antithesis of mere reaction, will for ever elude the human understanding. It can only be described in its manifestations; it can be obscurely sensed, but never wholly grasped. Psychology and the study of art will always have to turn to one another for help, and the one will not invalidate the other. It is an important principle of psychology that psychic events are derivable. It is a principle in the study of art that a psychic product is something in and for itself whether the work of art or the artist himself is in question. Both principles are valid in spite of their relativity.

THE WORK OF ART

There is a fundamental difference of approach between the psychologist's examination of a literary work, and that of the literary critic. What is of decisive importance and value for the latter may be quite irrelevant for the former. Literary products of highly dubious merit are often of the greatest interest to the psychologist. For instance, the so-called "psychological novel" is by no means as rewarding for the psychologist as the literary-minded suppose. Considered as a whole, such a novel explains itself. It has done its own work of psychological interpretation, and the psychologist can at most criticize or enlarge upon this. The important question as to how a particular author came to write a particular novel is of course left unanswered, but I wish to reserve this general problem for the second part of my essay.

The novels which are most fruitful for the psychologist are those in which the author has not already given a psychological interpretation of his characters, and which therefore leave room for analysis and explanation, or even invite it by their mode of presentation. Good examples of this kind of writing are the novels of Benoît, and English fiction in the manner of Rider Haggard, including the vein exploited by Conan Doyle which yields that most cherished article of mass-production, the detective story. Melville's *Moby Dick*, which I consider the greatest American novel, also comes within this class of writings. An exciting narrative that is apparently quite devoid of psychological exposition is just what interests the psychologist most of all. Such a tale is built upon a groundwork of implicit psychological assumptions, and, in the measure that the author is unconscious of them, they reveal themselves, pure and unalloyed, to the critical discernment. In the psychological novel, on the other hand, the author himself attempts to reshape his material so as to raise it from the level of crude contingency to that of psychological exposition and illumination—a procedure which all too often clouds the psychological significance of the work or hides it from view. It is precisely to novels of this sort that the layman goes for "psychology"; while it is novels of the other kind that challenge the psychologist, for he alone can give them deeper meaning.

I have been speaking in terms of the novel, but I am dealing with a psychological fact which is not restricted to this particular form of literary art. We meet with it in the works of the poets as well, and are confronted with it when we compare the first and second parts of the Faust drama. The love-tragedy of Gretchen explains itself; there is nothing that the psychologist can add to it that the poet has not already said in better words. The second part, on the other hand, calls for explanation. The prodigious richness of the imaginative material has so overtaxed the poet's formative powers that nothing is self-explanatory and every verse adds to the reader's need of an interpretation. The two parts of *Faust* illustrate by way of extremes this psychological distinction between works of literature.

In order to emphasize the distinction, I will call the one mode of artistic creation *psychological*, and the other *visionary*. The psychological mode deals with materials drawn from the realm of human consciousness—for instance, with the lessons of life, with emotional shocks, the experience of passion and the crises of human destiny in general—all of which go to make up the conscious life of man, and his feeling life in particular. This material is psychically assimilated by the poet, raised from the commonplace to the level of poetic experience, and given an expression which forces the reader to greater clarity and depth of human insight by bringing fully into his consciousness what he ordinarily evades and overlooks or senses only with a feeling of dull discomfort. The poet's work is an interpretation and illumination of the contents of consciousness, of the ineluctable experiences of human life with its eternally recurrent sorrow and joy. He leaves nothing over for the psychologist, unless, indeed, we expect the latter to expound the reasons for which Faust falls in love with Gretchen, or which drive Gretchen to murder her child! Such themes go to make up the lot of humankind; they repeat themselves millions of times and are responsible for the monotony of the police-court and of the penal code. No obscurity whatever surrounds them, for they fully explain themselves.

Countless literary works belong to this class: the many novels dealing with love, the environment, the family, crime and society, as well as didactic poetry, the larger number of lyrics, and the drama, both tragic and comic. Whatever its particular form may be, the psychological work of art always takes its materials from the vast realm of conscious human experience—from the vivid foreground of life, we might say. I have called this mode of artistic creation psychological because in its activity it nowhere transcends the bounds of psychological intelligibility. Everything that it embraces—the experience as well as its artistic expression—belongs to the realm of the understandable. Even the basic experiences themselves, though non-rational, have nothing strange about them; on the contrary, they are that which has been known from the beginning of time—passion and its fated outcome, man's subjection to the turns of destiny, eternal nature with its beauty and its horror.

The profound difference between the first and second parts of *Faust* marks the difference between the psychological and the visionary modes of artistic creation. The latter reverses all the conditions of the former. The experience that furnishes the material for artistic expression is no longer familiar. It is a strange something that derives its existence from the hinterland of man's mind—that suggests the abyss of time separating us from pre-human ages, or evokes a super-human world of contrasting light and darkness. It is a primordial experience which surpasses man's understanding, and to which he is therefore in danger of succumbing. The value and the force of the experience are given by its enormity. It arises from timeless depths; it is foreign and cold, many-sided, demonic and grotesque. A grimly ridiculous sample of the eternal chaos—a *crimen laesae majestatis humanae,* to use Nietzsche's words—it bursts asunder our human standards of value and of aesthetic form. The disturbing vision of monstrous and meaningless happenings that in every way exceed the grasp of human feeling and comprehension makes quite other demands upon the powers of the artist than do the experiences of the foreground of life. These never rend the curtain that veils the cosmos; they never transcend the bounds of the humanly possible, and for this reason are readily shaped to the demands of art, no matter how great a shock to the individual they may be. But the primordial experiences rend from top to bottom the curtain upon which is painted the picture of an ordered world, and allow a glimpse into the unfathomed abyss of what has not yet become. Is it a vision of other worlds, or of the obscuration of the spirit, or of the beginning of things before the age of man, or of the unborn generations of the future? We cannot say that it is any or none of these.

> Shaping—re-shaping—
> The eternal spirit's eternal pastime.[1]

[1] *Gestaltung, Umgestaltung,*
Des ew'gen Sinnes ew'ge Unterhaltung.
　　　　　　　　　　　　—Goethe

We find such vision in *The Shepherd of Hermas*, in Dante, in the second part of *Faust*, in Nietzsche's Dionysian exuberance, in Wagner's *Nibelungenring*, in Spitteler's *Olympischer Frühling*, in the poetry of William Blake, in the *Ipnerotomachia* of the monk Francesco Colonna, and in Jacob Boehme's philosophic and poetic stammerings. In a more restricted and specific way, the primordial experience furnishes material for Rider Haggard in the fiction-cycle that turns upon *She*, and it does the same for Benoît, chiefly in *L'Atlantide*, for Kubin in *Die Andere Seite*, for Meyrink in *Das Grüne Gesicht*—a book whose importance we should not undervalue—for Goetz in *Das Reich ohne Raum*, and for Barlach in *Der Tote Tag*. This list might be greatly extended.

In dealing with the psychological mode of artistic creation, we never need ask ourselves what the material consists of or what it means. But this question forces itself upon us as soon as we come to the visionary mode of creation. We are astonished, taken aback, confused, put on our guard or even disgusted—and we demand commentaries and explanations. We are reminded in nothing of everyday, human life, but rather of dreams, night-time fears and the dark recesses of the mind that we sometimes sense with misgiving. The reading public for the most part repudiates this kind of writing—unless, indeed, it is coarsely sensational—and even the literary critic feels embarrassed by it. It is true that Dante and Wagner have smoothed the approach to it. The visionary experience is cloaked, in Dante's case, by the introduction of historical facts, and, in that of Wagner, by mythological events—so that history and mythology are sometimes taken to be the materials with which these poets worked. But with neither of them does the moving force and the deeper significance lie there. For both it is contained in the visionary experience. Rider Haggard, pardonably enough, is generally held to be a mere inventor of fiction. Yet even with him the story is primarily a means of giving expression to significant material. However much the tale may seem to overgrow the content, the latter outweighs the former in importance.

The obscurity as to the sources of the material in visionary creation is very strange, and the exact opposite of what we find in the psychological mode of creation. We are even led to suspect that this obscurity is not unintentional. We are naturally inclined to suppose—and Freudian psychology encourages us to do so—that some highly personal experience underlies this grotesque darkness. We hope thus to explain these strange glimpses of chaos and to understand why it sometimes seems as though the poet had intentionally concealed his basic experience from us. It is only a step from this way of looking at the matter to the statement that we are here dealing with a pathological and neurotic art—a step which is justified in so far as the material of the visionary creator shows certain traits that we find in the fantasies of the insane. The converse also is true; we often discover in the mental output of psychotic persons a wealth of meaning that we should expect rather from the works of a genius. The psychologist who follows Freud will of course be inclined to take the writings in question as a problem in pathology. On the assumption that an intimate, personal experience underlies what I call the "primordial vision"—an experience, that is to say, which cannot be accepted by the conscious outlook—he will try to account for the curious images of the vision by calling them cover-figures and by supposing that they represent an attempted concealment of the basic experience. This, according to his view, might be an experience in love which is morally or aesthetically incompatible with the personality as a whole or at least with certain fictions of the conscious mind. In order that the poet, through his ego, might repress this experience and make it unrecognizable (unconscious), the whole arsenal of a pathological fantasy was brought into action. Moreover, this attempt to replace reality by fiction, being unsatisfactory, must be repeated in a long series of creative embodiments. This would explain the proliferation of imaginative forms, all monstrous, demonic, grotesque and perverse. On the one hand they are substitutes for the unacceptable experience, and on the other they help to conceal it.

Although a discussion of the poet's personality and psychic disposition belongs strictly to the second part of my essay, I cannot avoid taking up in the present connection this Freudian view of the visionary work of art. For one thing, it has aroused considerable attention. And then it is the only well-known attempt that has been made to give a "scientific" explanation of the sources of the visionary material or to formulate a theory of the psychic processes that underlie this curious mode of artistic creation. I assume that my own view of the question is not well known or generally understood. With this preliminary remark, I will now try to present it briefly.

If we insist on deriving the vision from a personal experience, we must treat the former as something secondary—as a mere substitute for reality. The result is that we strip the vision of its primordial quality and take it as nothing but a symptom. The pregnant chaos then shrinks to the proportions of a psychic disturbance. With this account of the matter we feel reassured and turn again to our picture of a well-ordered cosmos. Since we are practical and reasonable, we do not expect the cosmos to be perfect; we accept these unavoidable imperfections which we call abnormalities and diseases, and we take it for granted that human nature is not exempt from them. The frightening revelation of abysses that defy the human understanding is dismissed as illusion, and the poet is regarded as a victim and perpetrator of deception. Even to the poet, his primordial experience was "human—all too human," to such a degree that he could not face its meaning but had to conceal it from himself.

We shall do well, I think, to make fully explicit all the implications of that way of accounting for artistic creation which consists in reducing it to personal factors. We should see clearly where it leads. The truth is that it takes us away from the psychological study of the work of art, and confronts us with the psychic disposition of the poet himself. That the latter presents an important problem is not to be denied, but the work of art is something in its own right, and may not be conjured away. The question of the significance to the poet of his own creative work—of his regarding it as a trifle, as a screen, as a source of suffering or as an achievement—does not concern us at the moment, our task being to interpret the work of art psychologically. For this undertaking it is essential that we give serious consideration to the basic experience that underlies it—namely, to the vision. We must take it at least as seriously as we do the experiences that underlie the psychological mode of artistic creation, and no one doubts that they are both real and serious. It looks, indeed, as if the visionary experience were something quite apart from the ordinary lot of man, and for this reason we have difficulty in believing that it is real. It has about it an unfortunate suggestion of obscure metaphysics and of occultism, so that we feel called upon to intervene in the name of a well-intentioned reasonableness. Our conclusion is that it would be better not to take such things too seriously, lest the world revert again to a benighted superstition. We may, of course, have a predilection for the occult; but ordinarily we dismiss the visionary experience as the outcome of a rich fantasy or of a poetic mood—that is to say, as a kind of poetic license psychologically understood. Certain of the poets encourage this interpretation in order to put a wholesome distance between themselves and their work. Spitteler, for example, stoutly maintained that it was one and the same whether the poet sang of an Olympian Spring or to the theme: "May is here!" The truth is that poets are human beings, and that what a poet has to say about his work is often far from being the most illuminating word on the subject. What is required of us, then, is nothing less than to defend the importance of the visionary experience against the poet himself.

It cannot be denied that we catch the reverberations of an initial love-experience in *The Shepherd of Hermas*, in the *Divine Comedy* and in the *Faust* drama—an experience which is completed and fulfilled by the vision. There is no ground for the assumption that the second part of *Faust* repudiates or conceals the normal, human experience of the first part, nor are we justified in supposing that Goethe was normal at the time when he wrote *Part I*, but in a neurotic state of mind when he composed *Part II*. *Hermas*, Dante and Goethe can be taken as three steps in a sequence covering nearly two thousand years of human development, and in each of them we find the personal love-episode not only connected with the weightier visionary experience, but frankly subordinated to it. On the strength of this evidence which is furnished by the work of art itself and which throws out of court the question of the poet's particular psychic disposition, we must admit that the vision represents a deeper and more impressive experience than human passion. In works of art of this nature —and we must never confuse them with the artist as a person—we cannot doubt that the vision is a genuine, primordial experience, regardless of what reason-mongers may say. The vision is not something derived or secondary, and it is not a symptom of something else. It is true symbolic expression—that is, the expression of something existent in its own right, but imperfectly known. The love-episode is a real experience really suffered, and the same statement applies to the vision. We need not try to determine whether the content of the vision is of a physical, psychic or metaphysical nature. In itself it has psychic reality, and this is no less real than physical reality. Human passion falls within the sphere of conscious experience, while the subject of the vision lies beyond it. Through our feelings we experience the known, but our intuitions point to things that are unknown and hidden—that by their very nature are secret. If ever they become conscious, they are intentionally kept back and concealed, for which reasons they have been regarded from earliest times as mysterious, uncanny and deceptive. They are hidden from the scrutiny of man, and he also hides himself from them out

of *deisidaemonia*. He protects himself with the shield of science and the armour of reason. His enlightenment is born of fear; in the day-time he believes in an ordered cosmos, and he tries to maintain this faith against the fear of chaos that besets him by night. What if there were some living force whose sphere of action lies beyond our world of every day? Are there human needs that are dangerous and unavoidable? Is there something more purposeful than electrons? Do we delude ourselves in thinking that we possess and command our own souls? And is that which science calls the "psyche" not merely a question-mark arbitrarily confined within the skull, but rather a door that opens upon the human world from a world beyond, now and again allowing strange and unseizable potencies to act upon man and to remove him, as if upon the wings of the night, from the level of common humanity to that of a more than personal vocation? When we consider the visionary mode of artistic creation, it even seems as if the love-episode had served as a mere release—as if the personal experience were nothing but the prelude to the all-important "divine comedy."

It is not alone the creator of this kind of art who is in touch with the night-side of life, but the seers, prophets, leaders and enlighteners also. However dark this nocturnal world may be, it is not wholly unfamiliar. Man has known of it from time immemorial—here, there, and everywhere; for primitive man today it is an unquestionable part of his picture of the cosmos. It is only we who have repudiated it because of our fear of superstition and metaphysics, and because we strive to construct a conscious world that is safe and manageable in that natural law holds in it the place of statute law in a commonwealth. Yet, even in our midst, the poet now and then catches sight of the figures that people the night-world—the spirits, demons and gods. He knows that a purposiveness out-reaching human ends is the life-giving secret for man; he has a presentiment of incomprehensible happenings in the pleroma. In short, he sees something of that psychic world that strikes terror into the savage and the barbarian.

From the very first beginnings of human society onward man's efforts to give his vague intimations a binding form have left their traces. Even in the Rhodesian cliff-drawings of the Old Stone Age there appears, side by side with the most amazingly life-like representations of animals, an abstract pattern—a double cross contained in a circle. This design has turned up in every cultural region, more or less, and we find it today not only in Christian churches, but in Tibetan monasteries as well. It is the so-called sun-wheel, and as it dates from a time when no one had thought of wheels as a mechanical device, it cannot have had its source in any experience of the external world. It is rather a symbol that stands for a psychic happening; it covers an experience of the inner world, and is no doubt as lifelike a representation as the famous rhinoceros with the tick-birds on its back. There has never been a primitive culture that did not possess a system of secret teaching, and in many cultures this system is highly developed. The men's councils and the totem-clans preserve this teaching about hidden things that lie apart from man's daytime existence—things which, from primeval times, have always constituted his most vital experiences. Knowledge about them is handed on to younger men in the rites of initiation. The mysteries of the Graeco-Roman world performed the same office, and the rich mythology of antiquity is a relic of such experiences in the earliest stages of human development.

It is therefore to be expected of the poet that he will resort to mythology in order to give his experience its most fitting expression. It would be a serious mistake to suppose that he works with materials received at second-hand. The primordial experience is the source of his creativeness; it cannot be fathomed, and therefore requires mythological imagery to give it form. In itself it offers no words or images, for it is a vision seen "as in a glass, darkly." It is merely a deep presentiment that strives to find expression. It is like a whirlwind that seizes everything within reach and, by carrying it aloft, assumes a visible shape. Since the particular expression can never exhaust the possibilities of the vision, but falls far short of it in richness of content, the poet must have at his disposal a huge store of materials if he is to communicate even a few of his intimations. What is more, he must resort to an imagery that is difficult to handle and full of contradictions in order to express the weird paradoxicality of his vision. Dante's presentiments are clothed in images that run the gamut of Heaven and Hell; Goethe must bring in the Blocksberg and the infernal regions of Greek antiquity; Wagner needs the whole body of Nordic myth; Nietzsche returns to the hieratic style and recreates the legendary seer of prehistoric times; Blake invents for himself indescribable figures, and Spitteler borrows old names for new creatures of the imagination. And no intermediate step is missing in the whole range from the ineffably sublime to the perversely grotesque.

Psychology can do nothing towards the elucidation of this colourful imagery except bring together materials for comparison and offer a terminology for its discussion. According to this terminology, that which appears in the vision is the collective unconscious. We mean by collective unconscious, a certain psychic disposition shaped by the forces of heredity; from it consciousness has developed. In the physical structure of the body we find traces of earlier stages of evolution, and we may expect the human psyche also to conform in its make-up to the law of phylogeny. It is a fact that in eclipses of consciousness—in dreams, narcotic states and cases of insanity—there come to the surface psychic products or contents that show all the traits of primitive levels of psychic development. The images themselves are sometimes of such a primitive character that we might suppose them derived from ancient, esoteric teaching. Mythological themes clothed in modern dress also frequently appear. What is of particular importance for the study of literature in these manifestations of the collective unconscious is that they are compensatory to the conscious attitude. This is to say that they can bring a one-sided, abnormal, or dangerous state of consciousness into equilibrium in an apparently purposive way. In dreams we can see this process very clearly in its positive aspect. In cases of insanity the compensatory process is often perfectly obvious, but takes a negative form. There are persons, for instance, who have anxiously shut themselves off from all the world only to discover one day that their most intimate secrets are known and talked about by everyone.[2]

If we consider Goethe's *Faust*, and leave aside the possibility that it is compensatory to his own conscious attitude, the question that we must answer is this: In what relation does it stand to the conscious outlook of his time? Great poetry draws its strength from the life of mankind, and we completely miss its meaning if we try to derive it from personal factors. Whenever the collective unconscious becomes a living experience and is brought to bear upon the conscious outlook of an age, this event is a creative act which is of importance to everyone living in that age. A work of art is produced that contains what may truthfully be called a message to generations of men. So *Faust* touches something in the soul of every German. So also Dante's fame is immortal, while *The Shepherd of Hermas* just failed of inclusion in the New Testament canon. Every period has its bias, its particular prejudice and its psychic ailment. An epoch is like an individual; it has its own limitations of conscious outlook, and therefore requires a compensatory adjustment. This is effected by the collective unconscious in that a poet, a seer or a leader allows himself to be guided by the unexpressed desire of his times and shows the way, by word or deed, to the attainment of that which everyone blindly craves and expects—whether this attainment results in good or evil, the healing of an epoch or its destruction.

[2] See my article: "Mind and the Earth," in *Contributions to Analytical Psychology*. Harcourt, Brace, New York, 1928.

It is always dangerous to speak of one's own times, because what is at stake in the present is too vast for comprehension. A few hints must therefore suffice. Francesco Colonna's book is cast in the form of a dream, and is the apotheosis of natural love taken as a human relation; without countenancing a wild indulgence of the senses, he leaves completely aside the Christian sacrament of marriage. The book was written in 1453. Rider Haggard, whose life coincides with the flowering-time of the Victorian era, takes up this subject and deals with it in his own way; he does not cast it in the form of a dream, but allows us to feel the tension of moral conflict. Goethe weaves the theme of Gretchen-Helen-Mater-Gloriosa like a red thread into the colourful tapestry of Faust. Nietzsche proclaims the death of God, and Spitteler transforms the waxing and waning of the gods into a myth of the seasons. Whatever his importance, each of these poets speaks with the voice of thousands and ten thousands, foretelling changes in the conscious outlook of his time.

THE POET

Creativeness, like the freedom of the will, contains a secret. The psychologist can describe both these manifestations as processes, but he can find no solution of the philosophical problems they offer. Creative man is a riddle that we may try to answer in various ways, but always in vain, a truth that has not prevented modern psychology from turning now and again to the question of the artist and his art. Freud thought that he had found a key in his procedure of deriving the work of art from the personal experiences of the artist.[3] It is true that certain possibilities lay in this direction, for it was conceivable that a work of art, no less than a neurosis, might be traced back to those knots in psychic life that we call the complexes. It was Freud's great discovery that neuroses have a causal origin in the psychic realm—that they take their rise from emotional

[3] See Freud's essay on Jensen's *Gradiva* and on Leonardo da Vinci.

states and from real or imagined childhood experiences. Certain of his followers, like Rank and Stekel, have taken up related lines of enquiry and have achieved important results. It is undeniable that the poet's psychic disposition permeates his work root and branch. Nor is there anything new in the statement that personal factors largely influence the poet's choice and use of his materials. Credit, however, must certainly be given to the Freudian school for showing how far-reaching this influence is and in what curious ways it comes to expression.

Freud takes the neurosis as a substitute for a direct means of gratification. He therefore regards it as something inappropriate—a mistake, a dodge, an excuse, a voluntary blindness. To him it is essentially a shortcoming that should never have been. Since a neurosis, to all appearances, is nothing but a disturbance that is all the more irritating because it is without sense or meaning, few people will venture to say a good word for it. And a work of art is brought into questionable proximity with the neurosis when it is taken as something which can be analysed in terms of the poet's repressions. In a sense it finds itself in good company, for religion and philosophy are regarded in the same light by Freudian psychology. No objection can be raised if it is admitted that this approach amounts to nothing more than the elucidation of those personal determinants without which a work of art is unthinkable. But should the claim be made that such an analysis accounts for the work of art itself, then a categorical denial is called for. The personal idiosyncrasies that creep into a work of art are not essential; in fact, the more we have to cope with these peculiarities, the less is it a question of art. What is essential in a work of art is that it should rise far above the realm of personal life and speak from the spirit and heart of the poet as man to the spirit and heart of mankind. The personal aspect is a limitation—and even a sin—in the realm of art. When a form of "art" is primarily personal it deserves to be treated as if it were a neurosis. There may be some validity in the idea held by the Freudian school that

artists without exception are narcissistic—by which is meant that they are undeveloped persons with infantile and auto-erotic traits. The statement is only valid, however, for the artist as a person, and has nothing to do with the man as an artist. In his capacity of artist he is neither auto-erotic, nor hetero-erotic, nor erotic in any sense. He is objective and impersonal—even inhuman—for as an artist he is his work, and not a human being.

Every creative person is a duality or a synthesis of contradictory aptitudes. On the one side he is a human being with a personal life, while on the other side he is an impersonal, creative process. Since as a human being he may be sound or morbid, we must look at his psychic make-up to find the determinants of his personality. But we can only understand him in his capacity of artist by looking at his creative achievement. We should make a sad mistake if we tried to explain the mode of life of an English gentleman, a Prussian officer, or a cardinal in terms of personal factors. The gentleman, the officer and the cleric function as such in an impersonal rôle, and their psychic make-up is qualified by a peculiar objectivity. We must grant that the artist does not function in an official capacity—the very opposite is nearer the truth. He nevertheless resembles the types I have named in one respect, for the specifically artistic disposition involves an overweight of collective psychic life as against the personal. Art is a kind of innate drive that seizes a human being and makes him its instrument. The artist is not a person endowed with free will who seeks his own ends, but one who allows art to realize its purposes through him. As a human being he may have moods and a will and personal aims, but as an artist he is "man" in a higher sense—he is "collective man"—one who carries and shapes the unconscious, psychic life of mankind. To perform this difficult office it is sometimes necessary for him to sacrifice happiness and everything that makes life worth living for the ordinary human being.

All this being so, it is not strange that the artist is an especially interesting case for the psychologist who uses an analytical method. The artist's life cannot be otherwise than full of conflicts, for two forces are at war within him—on the one hand the common human longing for happiness, satisfaction and security in life, and on the other a ruthless passion for creation which may go so far as to override every personal desire. The lives of artists are as a rule so highly unsatisfactory—not to say tragic—because of their inferiority on the human and personal side, and not because of a sinister dispensation. There are hardly any exceptions to the rule that a person must pay dearly for the divine gift of the creative fire. It is as though each of us were endowed at birth with a certain capital of energy. The strongest force in our make-up will seize and all but monopolize this energy, leaving so little over that nothing of value can come of it. In this way the creative force can drain the human impulses to such a degree that the personal ego must develop all sorts of bad qualities—ruthlessness, selfishness and vanity (so-called "auto-erotism")—and even every kind of vice, in order to maintain the spark of life and to keep itself from being wholly bereft. The auto-erotism of artists resembles that of illegitimate or neglected children who from their tenderest years must protect themselves from the destructive influence of people who have no love to give them—who develop bad qualities for that very purpose and later maintain an invincible egocentrism by remaining all their lives infantile and helpless or by actively offending against the moral code or the law. How can we doubt that it is his art that explains the artist, and not the insufficiencies and conflicts of his personal life? These are nothing but the regrettable results of the fact that he is an artist—that is to say, a man who from his very birth has been called to a greater task than the ordinary mortal. A special ability means a heavy expenditure of energy in a particular direction, with a consequent drain from some other side of life.

It makes no difference whether the poet knows that his work is begotten, grows and matures with him, or whether he supposes that by taking thought he produces it out of the void. His opinion of the matter does not change the fact that his own work outgrows him as a child its mother. The creative process has feminine quality, and the creative work arises from unconscious depths—we might say, from the realm of the mothers. Whenever the creative force predominates, human life is ruled and moulded by the unconscious as against the active will, and the conscious ego is swept along on a subterranean current, being nothing more than a helpless observer of events. The work in process becomes the poet's fate and determines his psychic development. It is not Goethe who creates *Faust*, but *Faust* which creates Goethe. And what is *Faust* but a symbol? By this I do not mean an allegory that points to something all too familiar, but an expression that stands for something not clearly known and yet profoundly alive. Here it is something that lives in the soul of every German, and that Goethe has helped to bring to birth. Could we conceive of anyone but a German writing *Faust* or *Also sprach Zarathustra*? Both play upon something that reverberates in the German soul—a "primordial image," as Jacob Burckhardt once called it—the figure of a physician or teacher of mankind. The archetypal image of the wise man, the saviour or redeemer, lies buried and dormant in man's unconscious since the dawn of culture; it is awakened whenever the times are out of joint and a human society is committed to a serious error. When people go astray they feel the need of a guide or teacher or even of the physician. These primordial images are numerous, but do not appear in the dreams of individuals or in works of art until they are called into being by the waywardness of the general outlook. When conscious life is characterized by one-sidedness and by a false attitude, then they are activated—one might say, "instinctively"—and come to light in the dreams of individuals and the visions of artists and seers, thus restoring the psychic equilibrium of the epoch.

In this way the work of the poet comes to meet the spiritual need of the society in which he lives, and for this reason his work means more to him than his personal fate, whether he is aware of this or not. Being essentially the instrument for his work, he is subordinate to it, and we have no reason for expecting him to interpret it for us. He has done the best that in him lies in giving it form, and he must leave the interpretation to others and to the future. A great work of art is like a dream; for all its apparent obviousness it does not explain itself and is never unequivocal. A dream never says: "You ought," or: "This is the truth." It presents an image in much the same way as nature allows a plant to grow, and we must draw our own conclusions. If a person has a nightmare, it means either that he is too much given to fear, or else that he is too exempt from it; and if he dreams of the old wise man it may mean that he is too pedagogical, as also that he stands in need of a teacher. In a subtle way both meanings come to the same thing, as we perceive when we are able to let the work of art act upon us as it acted upon the artist. To grasp its meaning, we must allow it to shape us as it once shaped him. Then we understand the nature of his experience. We see that he has drawn upon the healing and redeeming forces of the collective psyche that underlies consciousness with its isolation and its painful errors; that he has penetrated to that matrix of life in which all men are embedded, which imparts a common rhythm to all human existence, and allows the individual to communicate his feeling and his striving to mankind as a whole.

The secret of artistic creation and of the effectiveness of art is to be found in a return to the state of *participation mystique*—to that level of experience at which it is man who lives, and not the individual, and at which the weal or woe of the single human being does not count, but only human existence. This is why every great work of art is objective and impersonal, but none the less profoundly moves us each and all. And this is also why the personal life of the poet cannot be held essential to his art—but at most a help or a hindrance to his creative task. He may go the way of a Philistine, a good citizen, a neurotic, a fool or a criminal. His personal career may be inevitable and interesting, but it does not explain the poet.

STRUCTURALISM

Roland Barthes

CRITICISM AS LANGUAGE (1963)

It is always possible to promulgate certain major critical principles in the light of contemporary ideology, especially in France, where theoretical formulations carry great weight, no doubt because they give the practising critic the assurance that he is, at one and the same time, taking part in a fight, making history and exemplifying a philosophical system. We can say that, during the last fifteen years, French criticism has developed, with various degrees of success, with four great "philosophies." There is, first of all, Existentialism, or what is generally so called, although the appropriateness of the term is debatable; it has produced Sartre's critical works, his studies of Baudelaire and Flaubert, his shorter articles on Proust, Mauriac, Giraudoux and Ponge, and above all his outstanding book on Genet. Next Marxism; it is well known by now (the matter was thrashed out long ago) that orthodox Marxism has proved critically sterile through offering a

Reproduced from *The Times Literary Supplement*, Sept. 27, 1963, by permission.

purely mechanical explanation of works of literature and providing slogans rather than criteria of value. It follows that the most fruitful criticism has to be looked for, as it were, on the frontiers of Marxism, not at its recognized centre. The work of Lucien Goldmann on Racine, Pascal, the "New Novel," the avantgarde theatre and Malraux owes a large and explicit debt to Lukács, and it would be difficult to imagine a more flexible and ingenious form of criticism based on political and social history. Then there is psychoanalysis; at the moment, the best representative of Freudian psychoanalytical criticism is Charles Mauron, who has written on Racine and Mallarmé. But here again, "marginal" activities have proved more fruitful. Gaston Bachelard, starting from an analysis of substances rather than of works and tracing the dynamic distortions of imagery in a great many poets, founded a whole critical school which is, indeed, so prolific that present-day French criticism in its most flourishing aspect can be said to be Bachelardian in inspiration (G. Poulet, J. Starobinski, J.-P. Richard).

Lastly, there is structuralism (which, if reduced to extremely simple, perhaps excessively simple, terms, might be called formalism); the movement has been important, one might almost say fashionable, in France since Claude Lévi-Strauss brought it into the social sciences and philosophical reflection. So far, it has produced very few critical works, but such works are in preparation and they will no doubt show the influence of the linguistic model worked out by de Saussure and elaborated by Roman Jakobson (who, in his earlier years, belonged to a literary critical movement, the Russian formalist school). It would seem possible, for instance, to develop a variety of literary criticism on the basis of the two rhetorical categories established by Jakobson, metaphor and metonymy.

As can be seen, this French criticism is both "national" (it owes little or nothing to Anglo-American, Spitzerian or Crocian criticism) and up-to-date or—if the expression seems preferable—"unfaithful to the past" (since it belongs entirely to an aspect of contemporary ideology, it can hardly consider itself as being indebted to any critical tradition, whether founded by Sainte-Beuve, Taine or Lanson). However, the last-named type of criticism raises a particular problem in this connexion. Lanson was the prototype of the French teacher of literature and, during the last fifty years, his work, method and mentality, as transmitted by innumerable disciples, have continued to govern academic criticism. Since the principles, or at least the declared principles, of this kind of criticism are accuracy and objectivity in the establishment of facts, it might be thought that there would be no incompatibility between Lansonianism and the various forms of ideological criticism, which are all interpretative. But although most present-day French critics (I am thinking of those who deal with structure, not those concerned with current reviewing) are themselves teachers, there is a certain amount of tension between interpretative and positivistic (academic) criticism. The reason is that Lansonianism is itself an ideology; it is

not simply content to demand the application of the objective rules of all scientific research, it also implies certain general convictions about man, history, literature and the relationship between the author and his work. For instance, Lansonian psychology is quite out of date, since it consists fundamentally of a kind of analogical determinism, according to which the details of a given work must resemble the details of the author's life, the characters the innermost being of the author, and so on. This makes it a very peculiar ideology because, since it was invented, psychology has, among other things, imagined the opposite relationship of negation between the work and the author. Of course, it is inevitable that an ideology should be based on philosophical postulates; the argument against Lansonianism is not that it has assumptions, but that instead of admitting them, it drapes them in a moral cloak of rigorous and objective investigation; it is as if ideology were being smuggled surreptitiously into the scientific approach.

Since these different ideological principles can coexist *simultaneously* (and for my part, I can, in a certain sense, accept both *simultaneously*), we have to conclude that the ideological choice is not the essence of criticism nor "truth" its ultimate test. Criticism is something other than making correct statements in the light of "true" principles. It follows that the major sin in criticism is not to have an ideology but to keep quiet about it. There is a name for this kind of guilty silence; it is self-deception or bad faith. How can anyone believe that a given work is an *object* independent of the psyche and personal history of the critic studying it, with regards to which he enjoys a sort of extraterritorial status? It would be a very remarkable thing if the profound relationship that most critics postulate between the author they are dealing with and his works were nonexistent in the case of their own works and their own situation in time. It is inconceivable that the creative laws governing the writer should not also be valid for the critic. All criticism must include (although it may do so in the most indirect and discreet way) an implicit comment on itself; all criticism is criticism both of the work under consideration and of the critic; to quote Claudel's pun, it is knowledge (connaissance) of the other and co-birth (co-naissance) of oneself to the world. Or, to express the same thing in still another way, criticism is not in any sense a table of results or a body of judgments; it is essentially an activity, that is to say a series of intellectual acts inextricably involved with the historical and subjective (the two terms are synonymous) existence of the person who carries them out and has to assume responsibility for them. It is pointless to ask whether or not an activity is "true"; the imperatives governing it are quite different.

Whatever the complexities of literary theory, a novelist or a poet is supposed to speak about objects and phenomena which, whether imaginary or not, are external and anterior to language. The world exists and the writer uses language; such is the definition of literature. The object of criticism is very different; it deals not with "the world," but with the linguistic formulations made by others; it is a comment on a comment, a secondary language or *meta* language (as the logicians would say), applied to a primary language (or language-as-object). It follows that critical activity must take two kinds of relationships into account: the relationship between the critical language and the language of the author under consideration and the relationship between the latter (language-as-object) and the world. Criticism is defined by the interaction of these two languages and so bears a close resemblance to another intellectual activity, logic, which is also entirely founded on the distinction between language-as-object and meta-language.

Consequently, if criticism is only a meta-language, its task is not to discover forms of "truth" but forms of "validity." In itself, a language cannot be true or false; it is either valid or non-valid. It is valid when it consists of a coherent system of signs. The rules governing the language of literature are not con-

cerned with the correspondence between that language and reality (whatever the claims made by schools of realism), but only with its being in line with the system of signs that the author has decided on (of course, in this connexion great stress must be laid on the term *system*). It is not the business of criticism to decide whether Proust told "the truth"—whether, for instance, Baron de Charlus was really Montesquiou or Françoise, Céleste or even, more generally, whether the society Proust describes is an adequate representation of the historical conditions in which the aristocracy was finally eliminated at the end of the nineteenth century—its function is purely to evolve its own language and to make it as coherent and logical, that is as systematic, as possible, so that it can render an account of, or better still "integrate" (in the mathematical sense) the greatest possible quantity of Proust's language just as a logical equation tests the validity of a piece of reasoning, without taking sides about the "truth" of the arguments used. We might say that the task of criticism (and this is the only guarantee of its universality) is purely formal; it does not consist in "discovering" in the work or the author under consideration something "hidden" or "profound" or "secret" which has so far escaped notice (through what miracle? Are we more perceptive than our predecessors?) but only in *fitting together*—as a skilled cabinet maker, by a process of "intelligent" fumbling, interlocks two parts of a complicated piece of furniture—the language of the day (Existentialism, Marxism or psychoanalysis) and the language of the author, that is, the formal system of logical rules that he evolved in the conditions of his time. The "proof" of a given form of criticism is not "alethiological" in nature (i.e., is not concerned with the truth), since critical writing, like logical writing, can never be other than tautology; in the last resort, it consists in the delayed statement (but the delay, through being fully accepted, is itself significant) that "Racine is Racine," "Proust is Proust." If there is such a thing as a critical proof, it lies not in the ability to *discover* the work under consideration but, on the contrary, to *cover* it as completely as possible with one's own language.

In this respect too, then, criticism is an essentially formal activity, not in the aesthetic, but in the logical sense of the term. It might be said that the only means by which criticism can avoid the self-deception or bad faith referred to earlier is to set itself the moral aim not to deciphering the meaning of the work under consideration, but of reconstituting the rules and compulsions which governed the elaboration of that sense; provided always it is also agreed that a work of literature is a very special semantic system, the aim of which is to put "meaning" into the world, but not "a meaning." A work of literature, at least of the kind that is normally considered by the critics (and this itself may be a possible definition of "good" literature) is neither ever quite meaningless (mysterious or "inspired") nor ever quite clear; it is, so to speak, *suspended* meaning; it offers itself to the reader as a declared system of significance, but as a signified object it eludes his grasp. This kind of *dis-appointment* or *deception* (de-capio: un-take) inherent in the meaning explains how it is that a work of literature has such power to ask questions of the world (by undermining the definite meanings that seem to be the apanage of beliefs, ideologies and commonsense) without, however, supplying any answers (no great work is "dogmatic"): it also explains how a work can go on being reinterpreted indefinitely, since there is no reason why critics should ever stop discussing Racine or Shakespeare (except through an act of abandonment which would itself be a kind of language). Literature, since it con-

sists at one and the same time of the insistent offering of a meaning and the persistent elusiveness of that meaning, is definitely no more than a language, that is, a system of signs; its being lies not in the message but in the system. This being so, the critic is not called upon to reconstitute the message of the work, but only its system, just as the business of the linguist is not to decipher the meaning of a sentence but to determine the formal structure which permits the transmission of its meaning.

It is precisely through the admission, on the part of criticism, that it is only a language (or, more accurately, a meta-language) that it can, paradoxically yet genuinely, be objective and subjective, historical and existential, totalitarian and liberal. The language that a critic chooses to speak is not a gift from heaven; it is one of the range of languages offered by his situation in time and, objectively, it is the latest stage of a certain historical development of knowledge, ideas and intellectual passions; it is a *necessity*. On the other hand, each critic chooses this necessary language, in accordance with a certain existential pattern, as the *means of exercising* an intellectual function which is his, and his alone, putting into the operation his "deepest self," that is, his preferences, pleasures, resistances and obsessions. In this way the critical work contains within itself a dialogue between two historical situations and two subjectivities, those of the author and those of the critic. But this dialogue shows a complete egotistical bias towards the present; criticism is neither a "tribute" to the truth of the past nor to the truth of "the other"; it is the ordering of that which is intelligible in our own time.

Tzvetan Todorov

STRUCTURAL ANALYSIS OF NARRATIVE (1969)

THE THEME I propose to deal with is so vast that the few pages which follow will inevitably take the form of a résumé. My title, moreover, contains the word "structural," a word more misleading than enlightening today. To avoid misunderstandings as much as possible, I shall proceed in the following fashion. First, I shall give an abstract description of what I conceive to be the structural approach to literature. This approach will then be illustrated by a concrete problem, that of narrative, and more specifically, that of plot. The examples will all be taken from the *Decameron* of Boccaccio. Finally, I shall attempt to make several general conclusions about the nature of narrative and the principles of its analysis.

First of all, one can contrast two possible attitudes toward literature: a theoretical attitude and a descriptive attitude. The nature of structural analysis will be essentially theoretical and non-descriptive; in other words, the aim of such a study will never be the description of a concrete work. The work will be considered as the manifestation of an abstract structure, merely one of its possible realizations; an understanding of that structure will be the real goal of structural analysis. Thus, the term "structure" has, in this case, a logical rather than spatial significance.

Another opposition will enable us to focus more sharply on the critical position which concerns us. If we contrast the internal approach to a literary work with the external

From *Novel: A Forum on Fiction*, Fall 1969. Reprinted by permission of the editor.

one, structural analysis would represent an internal approach. This opposition is well known to literary critics, and Wellek and Warren have used it as the basis for their *Theory of Literature*. It is necessary, however, to recall it here, because, in labeling all structural analysis "theoretical," I clearly come close to what is generally termed an "external" approach (in imprecise usage, "theoretical" and "external," on the one hand, and "descriptive" and "internal," on the other, are synonyms). For example, when Marxists or psychoanalysts deal with a work of literature, they are not interested in a knowledge of the work itself, but in the understanding of an abstract structure, social or psychic, which manifests itself through that work. This attitude is therefore both theoretical and external. On the other hand, a New Critic (imaginary) whose approach is obviously internal, will have no goal other than an understanding of the work itself; the result of his efforts will be a paraphrase of the work, which is supposed to reveal the meaning better than the work itself.

Structural analysis differs from both of these attitudes. Here we can be satisfied neither by a pure description of the work nor by its interpretation in terms that are psychological or sociological or, indeed, philosophical. In other words, structural analysis coincides (in its basic tenets) with theory, with poetics of literature. Its object is the literary discourse rather than works of literature, literature that is virtual rather than real. Such analysis seeks no longer to articulate a paraphrase, a rational résumé of the concrete work, but to propose a theory of the structure and operation of the literary discourse, to present a spectrum of literary possibilities, in such a manner that the existing works of literature appear as particular instances that have been realized.

It must immediately be added that, in practice, structural analysis will also refer to real works: the best stepping-stone toward theory is that of precise, empirical knowledge. But such analysis will discover in each work what it has in common with others (study of genres, of periods, for example), or even with all other works (theory of literature); it would be unable to state the individual specificity of each work. In practice, it is always a question of going continually back and forth, from abstract literary properties to individual works and vice versa. Poetics and description are in fact two complementary activities.

On the other hand, to affirm the internal nature of this approach does not mean a denial of the relation between literature and other homogeneous series, such as philosophy or social life. It is rather a question of establishing a hierarchy: literature must be understood in its specificity, as literature, before we seek to determine its relation with anything else.

It is easily seen that such a conception of literary analysis owes much to the modern notion of science. It can be said that structural analysis of literature is a kind of propaedeutic for a future science of literature. This term "science," used with regard to literature, usually raises a multitude of protests. It will therefore perhaps be fitting to try to answer some of those protests right now.

Let us first of all reread that page from Henry James's famous essay on "The Art of Fiction," which already contains several criticisms: "Nothing, for instance, is more possible than that he [the novelist] be of a turn of mind for which this odd, literal opposition of description and dialogue, incident and description, has little meaning and light. People often talk of these things as if they had a kind of internecine distinctness, instead of melting into each other

at every breath, and being intimately associated parts of one general effort of expression. I cannot imagine composition existing in a series of blocks, nor conceive, in any novel worth discussing at all, of a passage of description that is not in its intention narrative, a passage of dialogue that is not in its intention descriptive, a touch of truth of any sort that does not partake of the nature of incident, or an incident that derives its interest from any other source than the general and only source of the success of a work of art—that of being illustrative. A novel is a living thing, all one and continuous, like any other organism, and in proportion as it lives will it be found, I think, that in each of the parts there is something of each of the other parts. The critic who over the close texture of a finished work shall pretend to trace a geography of items will mark some frontiers as artificial, I fear, as any that have been known to history."

In this excerpt, the critic who uses such terms as "description," "narration," "dialogue," is accused by Henry James of committing two sins. First, there will never be found, in a real text, a pure dialogue, a pure description, and so on. Secondly, the very use of these terms is unnecessary, even harmful, since the novel is "a living thing, all one and continuous."

The first objection loses all its weight as soon as we put ourselves in the perspective of structural analysis; although it does aim at an understanding of concepts like "description" or "action," there is no need to find them in a pure state. It seems rather natural that abstract concepts cannot be analyzed directly, at the level of empirical reality. In physics, for example, we speak of a property such as temperature although we are unable to isolate it by itself and are forced to observe it in bodies possessing many other qualities also, like resistance and volume. Temperature is a theoretical concept, and it does not need to exist in a pure state; such is also true for description.

The second objection is still more curious. Let us consider the already dubious comparison between a work and a living thing. We all know that any part of our body will contain blood, nerves, muscles—all at the same time; we nonetheless do not require the biologist to abandon these misleading abstractions, designated by the words: blood, nerves, muscles. The fact that we find them together does not prevent us from distinguishing them. If the first argument of James had a positive aspect (it indicated that our objective should be composed of abstract categories and not concrete works), the second represents an absolute refusal to recognize the existence of abstract categories, of whatever is not visible.

There is another very popular argument against the introduction of scientific principles in literary analysis. We are told in this instance that science must be objective, whereas the interpretation of literature is always subjective. In my opinion this crude opposition is untenable. The critic's work can have varying degrees of subjectivity; everything depends on the perspective he has chosen. This degree will be much lower if he tries to ascertain the properties of the work rather than seeking its significance for a given period or milieu. The degree of subjectivity will vary, moreover, when he is examining different strata of the same work. There will be very few discussions concerning the metrical or phonic scheme of a poem; slightly more concerning the nature of its images; still more with regard to the more complex semantic patterns.

On the other hand there is no social science (or science whatsoever) which is totally free of subjectivity. The very choice of one group of theoretical concepts instead of another presupposes a subjective decision; but if we do not make this choice, we achieve nothing at all. The economist, the anthropologist, and the linguist must be subjective also; the only difference is that they are aware of it and they try to limit this subjectivity, to make allowance for it within the theory. One can hardly attempt to repudiate the subjectivity of the social sciences at a time when even the natural sciences are affected by it.

It is now time to stop these theoretical spec-

ulations and to give an example of the structural approach to literature. This example will serve as illustration rather than proof: the theories which I have just exposed will not be necessarily contested if there are some imperfections in the concrete analysis based on them.

The abstract literary concept I would like to discuss is that of plot. Of course, that does not mean that literature, for me, is reduced to plot alone. I do think, however, that plot is a notion that critics undervalue and, hence, often disregard. The ordinary reader, however, reads a book above all as the narration of a plot; but this naive reader is uninterested in theoretical problems. My aim is to suggest a certain number of useful categories for examining and describing plots. These categories can thus implement the meager vocabulary at our command with regard to the analysis of narrative; it consists of such terms as action, character, recognition.

The literary examples that I shall use are taken from the *Decameron* of Boccaccio. I do not intend, however, to give an analysis of the *Decameron*: these stories will be used only to display an abstract literary structure, that is, plot. I shall begin by stating the plots of several of the tales.

A monk introduces a young girl into his cell and makes love to her. The abbot detects this misbehavior and plans to punish him severely. But the monk learns of the abbot's discovery and lays a trap for him by leaving his cell. The abbot goes in and succumbs to the charms of the girl, while the monk tries his turn at watching. At the end when the abbot intends to punish him, the monk points out that he has just committed the same sin. Result: the monk is not punished (I,4).

Isabetta, a young nun, is with her lover in her cell. Upon discovering this, the other nuns become jealous and go to wake up the abbess and have Isabetta punished. But the abbess was in bed with an abbot; because she has to come out quickly, she puts the under-shorts of the abbot on her head instead of her coif.

Isabetta is led into the church; as the abbess begins to lecture her, Isabetta notices the garment on her head. She brings this evidence to everyone's attention and thus escapes punishment (IX,2).

Peronnella receives her lover while her husband, a poor mason, is absent. But one day he comes home early. Peronnella hides the lover in a cask; when the husband comes in, she tells him that somebody wanted to buy the cask and that this somebody is now in the process of examining it. The husband believes her and is delighted with the sale. The lover pays and leaves with the cask (.VII,2).

A married woman meets her lover every night in the family's country house, where she is usually alone. But one night the husband returns from town; the lover has not come yet; he arrives a little later and knocks at the door. The wife asserts that this is a ghost who comes to annoy her every night and must be exorcised. The husband pronounces the formula which the wife has improvised; the lover figures out the situation and leaves, pleased with the ingenuity of his mistress (VII,1).

It is easy to recognize that these four plots (and there are many others like them in the *Decameron*) have something in common. In order to express that, I shall use a schematic formulation which retains only the common elements of these plots. The sign → will indicate a relation of entailment between two actions.

X violates a law → Y must punish X → X tries to avoid being punished →

$$\rightarrow \begin{cases} \text{Y violates a law} \\ \\ \text{Y believes that X is not violating the law} \end{cases} \rightarrow \text{Y does not punish X}$$

This schematic representation requires several explanations.

1. We first notice that the minimal schema of the plot can be shown naturally by a clause. Between the categories of language and those of narrative there is a profound analogy which must be explored.

2. Analysis of this narrative clause leads us to discover the existence of two entities which correspond to the "parts of speech." a) The agents, designated here by X and Y, correspond to proper nouns. They serve as subject or object of the clause; moreover, they permit identification of their reference without its being described. b) The predicate, which is always a verb here: violate, punish, avoid. The verbs have a semantic characteristic in common: they denote an action which modifies the preceding situation. c) An analysis of other stories would have shown us a third part of narrative speech, which corresponds to quality and does not alter the situation in which it appears: the adjective. Thus in I,8: at the beginning of the action Ermino is stingy, whereas Guillaume is generous. Guillaume finds a way to ridicule Ermino's stinginess, and since then Ermino is "the most generous and pleasant of gentlemen." The qualities of the two characters are examples of adjectives.

3. Actions (violate, punish) can have a positive or a negative form; thus, we shall also need the category of status, negation being one possible status.

4. The category of modality is also relevant here. When we say "X must punish Y," we denote thereby an action which has not yet taken place (in the imaginary universe of the story) but which is nonetheless present in a virtual state. André Jolles suggested that entire genres could be characterized by their mood; legends would be the genre of the imperative, to the extent that they offer us an example to follow; the fairy tale is, as is often said, the genre of the optative, of the fulfilled wish.

5. When we write "Y believes that X is not violating the law," we have an example of a verb ("believe") which differs from the others. It is not a question of a different action here but of a different perception of the same action. We could therefore speak of a kind of "point of view" which refers not only to the relation between reader and narrator, but also to the characters.

6. There are also relations between the clauses; in our example this is always a causal

relation; but a more extensive study would distinguish at least between entailment and presupposition (for example, the relation introducing modal punishment). Analysis of other stories shows that there are also purely temporal relations (succession) and purely spatial ones (parallelism).

7. An organized succession of clauses forms a new syntagmatic pattern, sequence. Sequence is perceived by the reader as a finished story; it is the minimal narrative in a completed form. This impression of completion is caused by a modified repetition of the initial clause; the first and the last clause will be identical but they will either have a different mood or status, for instance, or they will be seen from different points of view. In our example it is punishment which is repeated: first changed in modality, then denied. In a sequence of temporal relations, repetition can be total.

8. We might also ask: is there a way back? How does one get from the abstract, schematic representation to the individual tale? Here, there are three answers:

a) The same kind of organization can be studied at a more concrete level: each clause of our sequence could be rewritten as an entire sequence itself. We would not thereby change the nature of the analysis, but rather the level of generality.

b) It is also possible to study the concrete actions that incorporate our abstract pattern. For instance, we may point out the different laws that become violated in the stories of the *Decameron* or the different punishments that are meted out. That would be a thematic study.

c) Finally, we can examine the verbal medium which composes our abstract patterns. The same action can be expressed by means of dialogue or description, figurative or literal discourse; moreover, each action can be seen from a different point of view. Here we are dealing with a rhetorical study.

These three directions correspond to the three major categories of narrative analysis: study of narrative syntax, study of theme, study of rhetoric.

At this point we may ask: what is the purpose of all this? Has this analysis taught us anything about the stories in question? But that would be a bad question. Our goal is not a knowledge of the *Decameron* (although such analysis will also serve that purpose), but rather an understanding of literature or, in this specific instance, of plot. The categories of plot mentioned here will permit a more extensive and precise description of other plots. The object of our study must be narrative mood, or point of view, or sequence, and not this or that story in and for itself.

From such categories we can move forward and inquire about the possibility of a typology of plots. For the moment it is difficult to offer a valid hypothesis; therefore I must be content to summarize the results of my research on the *Decameron*.

The minimal complete plot can be seen as the shift from one equilibrium to another. This term "equilibrium," which I am borrowing from genetic psychology, means the existence of a stable but not static relation between the members of a society; it is a social law, a rule of the game, a particular system of exchange. The two moments of equilibrium, similar and different, are separated by a period of imbalance, which is composed of a process of degeneration and a process of improvement.

All of the stories of the *Decameron* can be entered into this very broad schema. From that point, however, we can make a distinction between two kinds of stories. The first can be labeled "avoided punishment"; the four stories I mentioned at the beginning are examples of it. Here we follow a complete cycle: we begin with a state of equilibrium which is broken by a violation of the law. Punishment would have restored the initial balance; the fact that punishment is avoided establishes a new equilibrium.

The other type of story is illustrated by the tale about Ermino (I,8), which we may label "conversion." This story begins in the middle of a complete cycle, with a state of imbalance created by a flaw in one of the characters. The story is basically the description of an improvement process—until the flaw is no longer there.

The categories which help us to describe these types tell us much about the universe of a book. With Boccaccio, the two equilibriums symbolize (for the most part) culture and nature, the social and the individual; the story usually consists in illustrating the superiority of the second term over the first.

We could also seek even greater generalizations. It is possible to contrast a specific plot typology with a game typology and to see them as two variants of a common structure. So little has been done in this direction that we do not even know what kinds of questions to ask.[1]

I would like to return now to the beginning argument and to look at the initial question again: what is the object of structural analysis of literature (or, if you wish, of poetics)? At first glance, it is literature or, as Jakobson would have said, literariness. But let us look more closely. In our discussion of literary phenomena, we have had to introduce a certain number of notions and to create an image of literature;

this image constitutes the constant preoccupation of all research on poetics. "Science is concerned not with things but with the system of signs it can substitute for things," wrote Ortega y Gasset. The virtualities which make up the object of poetics (as of all other sciences), these abstract qualities of literature exist only in the discourse of poetics itself. From this perspective, literature becomes only a mediator, a language, which poetics uses for dealing with itself.

We must not, however, conclude that literature is secondary for poetics or that it is not, in a certain sense, the object of poetics. Science is characterized precisely by this ambiguity concerning its object, an ambiguity that need not be resolved, but rather used as the basis for analysis. Poetics, like literature, consists of an uninterrupted movement back and forth between the two poles: the first is auto-reference, preoccupation with itself; the second is what we usually call its object.

There is a practical conclusion to be drawn from these speculations. In poetics as elsewhere, discussions of methodology are not a minor area of the larger field, a kind of accidental by-product: they are rather its very center, its principal goal. As Freud said, "The important thing in a scientific work is not the nature of the facts with which it is concerned, but the rigor, the exactness of the method which is prior to the establishment of these facts, and the research of a synthesis as large as possible."

---

[1] A few bibliographical suggestions: I deal more at length with the same problems in the chapter "Poétique" of the collective work *Qu'est-ce que le structuralisme?* (Paris, Editions du Seuil, 1968); and in my book *Grammaire du Décaméron*, published by Mouton, The Hague. Several studies using a similar perspective have been published in the periodical *Communications* (Paris, Editions du Seuil), Nos. 4, 8, 11 (articles of Barthes, Bremond, Genette, *etc.*).

CRITICISM OF FICTION

Walter Benjamin

THE STORYTELLER: REFLECTIONS ON THE WORKS OF NIKOLAI LESKOV (1936)

FAMILIAR though his name may be to us, the storyteller in his living immediacy is by no means a present force. He has already become something remote from us and something that is getting even more distant. To present someone like Leskov as a storyteller does not mean bringing him closer to us but, rather, increasing our distance from him. Viewed from a certain distance, the great, simple outlines which define the storyteller stand out in him, or rather, they become visible in him, just as in a rock a human head or an animal's body may appear to an observer at the proper distance and angle of vision. This distance and this angle of vision are prescribed for us by an experience which we may have almost every day. It teaches us that the art of storytelling is coming to an end. Less and less frequently do we encounter people with the ability to tell a tale properly. More and more often there is

embarrassment all around when the wish to hear a story is expressed. It is as if something that seemed inalienable to us, the securest among our possessions, were taken from us: the ability to exchange experiences.

One reason for this phenomenon is obvious: experience has fallen in value. And it looks as if it is continuing to fall into bottomlessness. Every glance at a newspaper demonstrates that it has reached a new low, that our picture, not only of the external world but of the moral world as well, overnight has undergone changes which were never thought possible. With the [First] World War a process began to become apparent which has not halted since then. Was it not noticeable at the end of the war that men returned from the battlefield grown silent —not richer, but poorer in communicable experience? What ten years later was poured out in the flood of war books was anything but experience that goes from mouth to mouth. And there was nothing remarkable about that. For never has experience been contradicted more thoroughly than strategic experience by tactical warfare, economic experience by inflation, bodily experience by mechanical warfare, moral experience by those in power. A generation that had gone to school on a horse-drawn streetcar now stood under the open sky in a countryside in which nothing remained unchanged but the clouds, and beneath these clouds, in a field of force of destructive torrents and explosions, was the tiny, fragile human body.

II

Experience which is passed on from mouth to mouth is the source from which all storytellers have drawn. And among those who have written down the tales, it is the great ones whose written version differs least from the speech of the many nameless storytellers. Incidentally, among the last named there are two groups which, to be sure, overlap in many ways. And the figure of the storyteller gets its full corporeality only for the one who can picture them both. "When someone goes on a trip, he has something to tell about," goes the German saying, and people imagine the storyteller as someone who has come from afar. But they enjoy no less listening to the man who has stayed at home, making an honest living, and who knows the local tales and traditions. If one wants to picture these two groups through their archaic representatives, one is embodied in the resident tiller of the soil, and the other in the trading seaman. Indeed, each sphere of life has, as it were, produced its own tribe of storytellers. Each of these tribes preserves some of its characteristics centuries later. Thus, among nineteenth-century German storytellers, writers like Hebel and Gotthelf stem from the first tribe, writers like Sealsfield and Gerstäcker from the second. With these tribes, however, as stated above, it is only a matter of basic types. The actual extension of the realm of storytelling in its full historical breadth is inconceivable without the most intimate interpenetration of these two archaic types. Such an interpenetration was achieved particularly by the Middle Ages in their trade structure.

The resident master craftsman and the traveling journeymen worked together in the same rooms; and every master had been a traveling journeyman before he settled down in his home town or somewhere else. If peasants and seamen were past masters of storytelling, the artisan class was its university. In it was combined the lore of faraway places, such as a much-traveled man brings home, with the lore of the past, as it best reveals itself to natives of a place.

III

Leskov was at home in distant places as well as distant times. He was a member of the Greek Orthodox Church, a man with genuine religious interests. But he was a no less sincere opponent of ecclesiastic bureaucracy. Since he was not able to get along any better with secular officialdom, the official positions he held were not of long duration. Of all his posts, the one he held for a long time as Russian representative of a big English firm was presumably the most useful one for his writing. For this firm he traveled through Russia, and these trips advanced his worldly wisdom as much as they did his knowledge of conditions in Russia. In this way he had an opportunity of becoming acquainted with the organization of the sects in the country. This left its mark on his works of fiction. In the Russian legends Leskov saw allies in his fight against Orthodox bureaucracy. There are a number of his legendary tales whose focus is a righteous man, seldom an ascetic, usually a simple, active man who becomes a saint apparently in the most natural way in the world. Mystical exaltation is not Leskov's forte. Even though he occasionally liked to indulge in the miraculous, even in piousness he prefers to stick with a sturdy nature. He sees the prototype in the man who finds his way about the world without getting too deeply involved with it.

He displayed a corresponding attitude in worldly matters. It is in keeping with this that he began to write late, at the age of twenty-nine. That was after his commercial travels.

His first printed work was entitled "Why Are Books Expensive in Kiev?" A number of other writings about the working class, alcoholism, police doctors, and unemployed salesmen are precursors of his works of fiction.

IV

An orientation toward practical interests is characteristic of many born storytellers. More pronouncedly than in Leskov this trait can be recognized, for example, in Gotthelf, who gave his peasants agricultural advice; it is found in Nodier, who concerned himself with the perils of gas light; and Hebel, who slipped bits of scientific instruction for his readers into his *Schatzkästlein*, is in this line as well. All this points to the nature of every real story. It contains, openly or covertly, something useful. The usefulness may, in one case, consist in a moral; in another, in some practical advice; in a third, in a proverb or maxim. In every case the storyteller is a man who has counsel for his readers. But if today "having counsel" is beginning to have an old-fashioned ring, this is because the communicability of experience is decreasing. In consequence we have no counsel either for ourselves or for others. After all, counsel is less an answer to a question than a proposal concerning the continuation of a story which is just unfolding. To seek this counsel one would first have to be able to tell the story. (Quite apart from the fact that a man is receptive to counsel only to the extent that he allows his situation to speak.) Counsel woven into the fabric of real life is wisdom. The art of storytelling is reaching its end because the epic side of truth, wisdom, is dying out. This, however, is a process that has been going on for a long time. And nothing would be more fatuous than to want to see in it merely a "symptom of decay," let alone a "modern" symptom. It is, rather, only a concomitant symptom of the secular productive forces of history, a concomitant that has quite gradually removed narrative from the realm of living speech and at the same time is making it possible to see a new beauty in what is vanishing.

V

The earliest symptom of a process whose end is the decline of storytelling is the rise of the novel at the beginning of modern times. What distinguishes the novel from the story (and from the epic in the narrower sense) is its essential dependence on the book. The dissemination of the novel became possible only with the invention of printing. What can be handed on orally, the wealth of the epic, is of a different kind from what constitutes the stock in trade of the novel. What differentiates the novel from all other forms of prose literature—the fairy tale, the legend, even the novella—is that it neither comes from oral tradition nor goes into it. This distinguishes it from storytelling in particular. The storyteller takes what he tells from experience—his own or that reported by others. And he in turn makes it the experience of those who are listening to his tale. The novelist has isolated himself. The birthplace of the novel is the solitary individual, who is no longer able to express himself by giving examples of his most important concerns, is himself uncounseled, and cannot counsel others. To write a novel means to carry the incommensurable to extremes in the representation of human life. In the midst of life's fullness, and through the representation of this fullness, the novel gives evidence of the profound perplexity of the living. Even the first great book of the genre, *Don Quixote*, teaches how the spiritual greatness, the boldness, the helpfulness of one of the noblest of men, Don Quixote, are completely devoid of counsel and do not contain the slightest scintilla of wisdom. If now and then, in the course of the centuries, efforts have been made—most effectively, perhaps, in *Wilhelm Meisters Wanderjahre*—to implant instruction in the novel, these attempts have always amounted to a modification of the novel form. The *Bildungsroman*, on the other hand, does not deviate in any way from the basic structure of the novel. By integrating the social process with the development of a person, it bestows the most frangible justification on the order determining it. The legitimacy it provides stands in direct opposition to reality. Particularly in the *Bildungsroman*, it is this inadequacy that is actualized.

VI

One must imagine the transformation of epic forms occurring in rhythms comparable to those of the change that has come over the earth's surface in the course of thousands of centuries. Hardly any other forms of human communication have taken shape more slowly, been lost more slowly. It took the novel, whose beginnings go back to antiquity, hundreds of years before it encountered in the evolving middle class those elements which were favorable to its flowering. With the appearance of these elements, storytelling began quite slowly to recede into the archaic; in many ways, it is true, it took hold of the new material, but it was not really determined by it. On the other hand, we recognize that with the full control of the middle class, which has the press as one of its most important instruments in fully developed capitalism, there emerges a form of communication which, no matter how far back its origin may lie, never before influenced the epic form in a decisive way. But now it does exert such an influence. And it turns out that it confronts storytelling as no less of a stranger than did the novel, but in a more menacing way, and that it also brings about a crisis in the novel. This new form of communication is information.

Villemessant, the founder of *Le Figaro*, characterized the nature of information in a famous formulation. "To my readers," he used to say, "an attic fire in the Latin Quarter is more important than a revolution in Madrid." This makes strikingly clear that it is no longer intelligence coming from afar, but the information which supplies a handle for what is nearest that gets the readiest hearing. The intelligence that came from afar—whether the spatial kind from foreign countries or the temporal kind of tradition—possessed an authority which gave

it validity, even when it was not subject to verification. Information, however, lays claim to prompt verifiability. The prime requirement is that it appear "understandable in itself." Often it is no more exact than the intelligence of earlier centuries was. But while the latter was inclined to borrow from the miraculous, it is indispensable for information to sound plausible. Because of this it proves incompatible with the spirit of storytelling. If the art of storytelling has become rare, the dissemination of information has had a decisive share in this state of affairs.

Every morning brings us the news of the globe, and yet we are poor in noteworthy stories. This is because no event any longer comes to us without already being shot through with explanation. In other words, by now almost nothing that happens benefits storytelling; almost everything benefits information. Actually, it is half the art of storytelling to keep a story free from explanation as one reproduces it. Leskov is a master at this (compare pieces like "The Deception" and "The White Eagle"). The most extraordinary things, marvelous things, are related with the greatest accuracy, but the psychological connection of the events is not forced on the reader. It is left up to him to interpret things the way he understands them, and thus the narrative achieves an amplitude that information lacks.

VII

Leskov was grounded in the classics. The first storyteller of the Greeks was Herodotus. In the fourteenth chapter of the third book of his *Histories* there is a story from which much can be learned. It deals with Psammenitus.

When the Egyptian king Psammenitus had been beaten and captured by the Persian king Cambyses, Cambyses was bent on humbling his prisoner. He gave orders to place Psammenitus on the road along which the Persian triumphal procession was to pass. And he further arranged that the prisoner should see his daughter pass by as a maid going to the well with her pitcher. While all the Egyptians were lamenting and bewailing this spectacle, Psammenitus stood alone, mute and motionless, his eyes fixed on the ground; and when presently he saw his son, who was being taken along in the procession to be executed, he likewise remained unmoved. But when afterwards he recognized one of his servants, an old, impoverished man, in the ranks of the prisoners, he beat his fists against his head and gave all the signs of deepest mourning.

From this story it may be seen what the nature of true storytelling is. The value of information does not survive the moment in which it was new. It lives only at that moment; it has to surrender to it completely and explain itself to it without losing any time. A story is different. It does not expend itself. It preserves and concentrates its strength and is capable of releasing it even after a long time. Thus Montaigne referred to this Egyptian king and asked himself why he mourned only when he caught sight of his servant. Montaigne answers: "Since he was already over-full of grief, it took only the smallest increase for it to burst through its dams." Thus Montaigne. But one could also say: The king is not moved by the fate of those of royal blood, for it is his own fate. Or: We are moved by much on the stage that does not move us in real life; to the king, this servant is only an actor. Or: Great grief is pent up and breaks forth only with relaxation. Seeing this servant was the relaxation. Herodotus offers no explanations. His report is the driest. That is why this story from ancient Egypt is still capable after thousands of years of arousing astonishment and thoughtfulness. It resembles the seeds of grain which have lain for centuries in the chambers of the pyramids shut up air-tight and have retained their germinative power to this day.

VIII

There is nothing that commends a story to memory more effectively than that chaste compactness which precludes psychological analysis. And the more natural the process by which the storyteller forgoes psychological shading,

the greater becomes the story's claim to a place in the memory of the listener, the more completely is it integrated into his own experience, the greater will be his inclination to repeat it to someone else someday, sooner or later. This process of assimilation, which takes place in depth, requires a state of relaxation which is becoming rarer and rarer. If sleep is the apogee of physical relaxation, boredom is the apogee of mental relaxation. Boredom is the dream bird that hatches the egg of experience. A rustling in the leaves drives him away. His nesting places—the activities that are intimately associated with boredom—are already extinct in the cities and are declining in the country as well. With this the gift for listening is lost and the community of listeners disappears. For storytelling is always the art of repeating stories, and this art is lost when the stories are no longer retained. It is lost because there is no more weaving and spinning to go on while they are being listened to. The more self-forgetful the listener is, the more deeply is what he listens to impressed upon his memory. When the rhythm of work has seized him, he listens to the tales in such a way that the gift of retelling them comes to him all by itself. This, then, is the nature of the web in which the gift of storytelling is cradled. This is how today it is becoming unraveled at all its ends after being woven thousands of years ago in the ambience of the oldest forms of craftsmanship.

IX

The storytelling that thrives for a long time in the milieu of work—the rural, the maritime, and the urban—is itself an artisan form of communication, as it were. It does not aim to convey the pure essence of the thing, like information or a report. It sinks the thing into the life of the storyteller, in order to bring it out of him again. Thus traces of the storyteller cling to the story the way the handprints of the potter cling to the clay vessel. Storytellers tend to begin their story with a presentation of the circumstances in which they themselves have learned what is to follow, unless they simply pass it off as their own experience. Leskov begins his "Deception" with the description of a train trip on which he supposedly heard from a fellow passenger the events which he then goes on to relate; or he thinks of Dostoevsky's funeral, where he sets his acquaintance with the heroine of his story "A Propos of the Kreutzer Sonata"; or he evokes a gathering of a reading circle in which we are told the events that he reproduces for us in his "Interesting Men." Thus his tracks are frequently evident in his narratives, if not as those of the one who experienced it, then as those of the one who reports it.

This craftsmanship, storytelling, was actually regarded as a craft by Leskov himself. "Writing," he says in one of his letters, "is to me no liberal art, but a craft." It cannot come as a surprise that he felt bonds with craftsmanship, but faced industrial technology as a stranger. Tolstoy, who must have understood this, occasionally touches this nerve of Leskov's storytelling talent when he calls him the first man "who pointed out the inadequacy of economic progress. . . . It is strange that Dostoevsky is so widely read. . . . But I simply cannot comprehend why Leskov is not read. He is a truthful writer." In his artful and high-spirited story "The Steel Flea," which is midway between legend and farce, Leskov glorifies native craftsmanship through the silversmiths of Tula. Their masterpiece, the steel flea, is seen by Peter the Great and convinces him that the Russians need not be ashamed before the English.

The intellectual picture of the atmosphere of craftsmanship from which the storyteller comes has perhaps never been sketched in such a significant way as by Paul Valéry. "He speaks of the perfect things in nature, flawless pearls, full-bodied, matured wines, truly developed creatures, and calls them 'the precious product of a long chain of causes similar to one another.'" The accumulation of such causes has its temporal limit only at perfection. "This patient process of Nature," Valéry continues, "was once imitated by men. Miniatures, ivory carvings, elaborated to the point of greatest perfection, stones that are perfect in polish and engraving, lacquer work or paintings in which a series of thin, transparent layers are placed one on top of the other—all these products of sustained, sacrificing effort are vanishing, and the time is past in which time did not matter. Modern man no longer works at what cannot be abbreviated."

In point of fact, he has succeeded in abbreviating even storytelling. We have witnessed the evolution of the "short story," which has removed itself from oral tradition and no longer permits that slow piling one on top of the other of thin, transparent layers which constitutes the most appropriate picture of the way in which the perfect narrative is revealed through the layers of a variety of retellings.

x

Valéry concludes his observations with this sentence: "It is almost as if the decline of the idea of eternity coincided with the increasing aversion to sustained effort." The idea of eternity has ever had its strongest source in death. If this idea declines, so we reason, the face of death must have changed. It turns out that this change is identical with the one that has diminished the communicability of experience to the same extent as the art of storytelling has declined.

It has been observable for a number of centuries how in the general consciousness the thought of death has declined in omnipresence and vividness. In its last stages this process is accelerated. And in the course of the nineteenth century bourgeois society has, by means of hygienic and social, private and public institutions, realized a secondary effect which may have been its subconscious main purpose: to make it possible for people to avoid the sight of the dying. Dying was once a public process in the life of the individual and a most exemplary one; think of the medieval pictures in which the deathbed has turned into a throne toward which the people press through the wide-open doors of the death house. In the course of modern times dying has been pushed further and further out of the perceptual world of the living. There used to be no house, hardly a room, in which someone had not once died. (The Middle Ages also felt spatially what makes that inscription on a sun dial of Ibiza, *Ultima multis* [the last day for many], significant as the temper of the times.) Today people live in rooms that have never been touched by death, dry dwellers of eternity, and when their end approaches they are stowed away in sanatoria or hospitals by their heirs. It is, however, characteristic that not only a man's knowledge or wisdom, but above all his real life—and this is the stuff that stories are made of—first assumes transmissible form at the moment of his death. Just as a sequence of images is set in motion inside a man as his life comes to an end—unfolding the views of himself under which he has encountered himself without being aware of it—suddenly in his expressions and looks the unforgettable emerges and imparts to everything that concerned him that authority which even the poorest wretch in dying possesses for the living around him. This authority is at the very source of the story.

XI

Death is the sanction of everything that the storyteller can tell. He has borrowed his authority from death. In other words, it is natural history to which his stories refer back. This is expressed in exemplary form in one of the most beautiful stories we have by the incomparable Johann Peter Hebel. It is found in the *Schatzkästlein des rheinischen Hausfreundes*, is entitled "Unexpected Reunion," and begins with the betrothal of a young lad who works in the mines of Falun. On the eve of his wedding he dies a miner's death at the bottom of his tunnel. His bride keeps faith with him after his death, and she lives long enough to become a wizened old woman; one day a body is brought up from the abandoned tunnel which, saturated with iron vitriol, has escaped decay, and she recognizes her betrothed. After this reunion she too is called away by death. When Hebel,

in the course of this story, was confronted with the necessity of making this long period of years graphic, he did so in the following sentences: "In the meantime the city of Lisbon was destroyed by an earthquake, and the Seven Years' War came and went, and Emperor Francis I died, and the Jesuit Order was abolished, and Poland was partitioned, and Empress Maria Theresa died, and Struensee was executed. America became independent, and the united French and Spanish forces were unable to capture Gibraltar. The Turks locked up General Stein in the Veteraner Cave in Hungary, and Emperor Joseph died also. King Gustavus of Sweden conquered Russian Finland, and the French Revolution and the long war began, and Emperor Leopold II went to his grave too. Napoleon captured Prussia, and the English bombarded Copenhagen, and the peasants sowed and harvested. The millers ground, the smiths hammered, and the miners dug for veins of ore in their underground workshops. But when in 1809 the miners at Falun . . ."

Never has a storyteller embedded his report deeper in natural history than Hebel manages to do in this chronology. Read it carefully. Death appears in it with the same regularity as the Reaper does in the processions that pass around the cathedral clock at noon.

XII

Any examination of a given epic form is concerned with the relationship of this form to historiography. In fact, one may go even further and raise the question whether historiography does not constitute the common ground of all forms of the epic. Then written history would be in the same relationship to the epic forms as white light is to the colors of the spectrum. However this may be, among all forms of the epic there is not one whose incidence in the pure, colorless light of written history is more certain than the chronicle. And in the broad spectrum of the chronicle the ways in which a story can be told are graduated like shadings of one and the same color. The chronicler is the historyteller. If we think back to the passage from Hebel, which has the tone of a chronicle throughout, it will take no effort to gauge the difference between the writer of history, the historian, and the teller of it, the chronicler. The historian is bound to explain in one way or another the happenings with which he deals; under no circumstances can he content himself with displaying them as models of the course of the world. But this is precisely what the chronicler does, especially in his classical representatives, the chroniclers of the Middle Ages, the precursors of the historians of today. By basing their historical tales on a divine plan of salvation—an inscrutable one—they have from the very start lifted the burden of demonstrable explanation from their own shoulders. Its place is taken by interpretation, which is not concerned with an accurate concatenation of definite events, but with the way these are embedded in the great inscrutable course of the world.

Whether this course is eschatologically determined or is a natural one makes no difference. In the storyteller the chronicler is preserved in changed form, secularized, as it were. Leskov is among those whose work displays this with particular clarity. Both the chronicler with his eschatological orientation and the storyteller with his profane outlook are so represented in his works that in a number of his stories it can hardly be decided whether the web in which they appear is the golden fabric of a religious view of the course of things, or the multicolored fabric of a worldly view.

Consider the story "The Alexandrite," which transports the reader into "that old time when the stones in the womb of the earth and the planets at celestial heights were still concerned with the fate of men, and not today when both in the heavens and beneath the earth everything has grown indifferent to the fates of the sons of men and no voice speaks to them from anywhere, let alone does their bidding. None of the undiscovered planets play any part in horoscopes any more, and there are a lot of

new stones, all measured and weighed and examined for their specific weight and their density, but they no longer proclaim anything to us, nor do they bring us any benefit. Their time for speaking with men is past."

As is evident, it is hardly possible unambiguously to characterize the course of the world that is illustrated in this story of Leskov's. Is it determined eschatologically or naturalistically? The only certain thing is that in its very nature it is by definition outside all real historical categories. Leskov tells us that the epoch in which man could believe himself to be in harmony with nature has expired. Schiller called this epoch in the history of the world the period of naïve poetry. The storyteller keeps faith with it, and his eyes do not stray from that dial in front of which there moves the procession of creatures of which, depending on circumstances, Death is either the leader or the last wretched straggler.

XIII

It has seldom been realized that the listener's naïve relationship to the storyteller is controlled by his interest in retaining what he is told. The cardinal point for the unaffected listener is to assure himself of the possibility of reproducing the story. Memory is the epic faculty *par excellence*. Only by virtue of a comprehensive memory can epic writing absorb the course of events on the one hand and, with the passing of these, make its peace with the power of death on the other. It is not surprising that to a simple man of the people, such as Leskov once invented, the Czar, the head of the sphere in which his stories take place, has the most encyclopedic memory at his command. "Our Emperor," he says, "and his entire family have indeed a most astonishing memory."

Mnemosyne, the rememberer, was the Muse of the epic art among the Greeks. This name takes the observer back to a parting of the ways in world history. For if the record kept by memory—historiography—constitutes the creative matrix of the various epic forms (as great prose is the creative matrix of the various metrical forms), its oldest form, the epic, by virtue of being a kind of common denominator includes the story and the novel. When in the course of centuries the novel began to emerge from the womb of the epic, it turned out that in the novel the element of the epic mind that is derived from the Muse—that is, memory—manifests itself in a form quite different from the way it manifests itself in the story.

Memory creates the chain of tradition which passes a happening on from generation to generation. It is the Muse-derived element of the epic art in a broader sense and encompasses its varieties. In the first place among these is the one practiced by the storyteller. It starts the web which all stories together form in the end. One ties on to the next, as the great storytellers, particularly the Oriental ones, have always readily shown. In each of them there is a Scheherazade who thinks of a fresh story whenever her tale comes to a stop. This is epic remembrance and the Muse-inspired element of the narrative. But this should be set against another principle, also a Muse-derived element in a narrower sense, which as an element of the novel in its earliest form—that is, in the epic—lies concealed, still undifferentiated from the similarly derived element of the story. It can, at any rate, occasionally be divined in the epics, particularly at moments of solemnity in the Homeric epics, as in the invocations to the Muse at their beginning. What announces itself in these passages is the perpetuating remembrance of the novelist as contrasted with the short-lived reminiscences of the storyteller. The first is dedicated to *one* hero, *one* odyssey, *one* battle; the second, to *many* diffuse occurrences. It is, in other words, *remembrance* which, as the Muse-derived element of the novel, is added to reminiscence, the corresponding element of the story, the unity of their origin in memory having disappeared with the decline of the epic.

XIV

"No one," Pascal once said, "dies so poor that he does not leave something behind."

Surely it is the same with memories too—although these do not always find an heir. The novelist takes charge of this bequest, and seldom without profound melancholy. For what Arnold Bennett says about a dead woman in one of his novels—that she had had almost nothing in the way of real life—is usually true of the sum total of the estate which the novelist administers. Regarding this aspect of the matter we owe the most important elucidation to Georg Lukács, who sees in the novel "the form of transcendental homelessness." According to Lukács, the novel is at the same time the only art form which includes time among its constitutive principles.

"Time," he says in his *Theory of the Novel*, "can become constitutive only when connection with the transcendental home has been lost. Only in the novel are meaning and life, and thus the essential and the temporal, separated; one can almost say that the whole inner action of a novel is nothing else but a struggle against the power of time. . . . And from this . . . arise the genuinely epic experiences of time: hope and memory. . . . Only in the novel . . . does there occur a creative memory which transfixes the object and transforms it. . . . The duality of inwardness and outside world can here be overcome for the subject 'only' when he sees the . . . unity of his entire life . . . out of the past life-stream which is compressed in memory. . . . The insight which grasps this unity . . . becomes the divinatory-intuitive grasping of the unattained and therefore inexpressible meaning of life."

The "meaning of life" is really the center about which the novel moves. But the quest for it is no more than the initial expression of perplexity with which its reader sees himself living this written life. Here "meaning of life"—there "moral of the story": with these slogans novel and story confront each other, and from them the totally different historical co-ordinates of these art forms may be discerned. If *Don Quixote* is the earliest perfect specimen of the novel, its latest exemplar is perhaps the *Éducation sentimentale*.

In the final words of the last-named novel, the meaning which the bourgeois age found in its behavior at the beginning of its decline has settled like sediment in the cup of life. Frédéric and Deslauriers, the boyhood friends, think back to their youthful friendship. This little incident then occurred: one day they showed up in the bordello of their home town, stealthily and timidly, doing nothing but presenting the *patronne* with a bouquet of flowers which they had picked in their own gardens. "This story was still discussed three years later. And now they told it to each other in detail, each supplementing the recollection of the other. 'That may have been,' said Frédéric when they had finished, 'the finest thing in our lives.' 'Yes, you may be right,' said Deslauriers, 'that was perhaps the finest thing in our lives.' "

With such an insight the novel reaches an end which is more proper to it, in a stricter sense, than to any story. Actually there is no story for which the question as to how it continued would not be legitimate. The novelist, on the other hand, cannot hope to take the smallest step beyond that limit at which he invites the reader to a divinatory realization of the meaning of life by writing "Finis."

XV

A man listening to a story is in the company of the storyteller; even a man reading one shares this companionship. The reader of a novel, however, is isolated, more so than any other reader. (For even the reader of a poem is ready to utter the words, for the benefit of the listener.) In this solitude of his, the reader of a novel seizes upon his material more jealously than anyone else. He is ready to make it completely his own, to devour it, as it were. Indeed, he destroys, he swallows up the material as the fire devours logs in the fireplace. The suspense which permeates the novel is very much like the draft which stimulates the flame in the fireplace and enlivens its play.

It is a dry material on which the burning interest of the reader feeds. "A man who dies at the age of thirty-five," said Moritz Heimann once, "is at every point of his life a man who dies at the age of thirty-five." Nothing is more dubious than this sentence—but for the sole reason that the tense is wrong. A man—so says the truth that was meant here—who died at thirty-five will appear to *remembrance* at every point in his life as a man who dies at the age of thirty-five. In other words, the statement that makes no sense for real life becomes indisputable for remembered life. The nature of the character in a novel cannot be presented any better than is done in this statement, which says that the "meaning" of his life is revealed only in his death. But the reader of a novel actually does look for human beings from whom he derives the "meaning of life." Therefore he must, no matter what, know in advance that he will share their experience of death: if need be their figurative death—the end of the novel—but preferably their actual one. How do the characters make him understand that death is already waiting for them—a very definite death and at a very definite place? That is the question which feeds the reader's consuming interest in the events of the novel.

The novel is significant, therefore, not because it presents someone else's fate to us, perhaps didactically, but because this stranger's fate by virtue of the flame which consumes it yields us the warmth which we never draw from our own fate. What draws the reader to the novel is the hope of warming his shivering life with a death he reads about.

XVI

"Leskov," writes Gorky, "is the writer most deeply rooted in the people and is completely untouched by any foreign influences." A great storyteller will always be rooted in the people, primarily in a milieu of craftsmen. But just as this includes the rural, the maritime, and the urban elements in the many stages of their economic and technical development, there are many gradations in the concepts in which their store of experience comes down to us. (To say nothing of the by no means insignificant share which traders had in the art of storytelling;

their task was less to increase its didactic content than to refine the tricks with which the attention of the listener was captured. They have left deep traces in the narrative cycle of *The Arabian Nights*.) In short, despite the primary role which storytelling plays in the household of humanity, the concepts through which the yield of the stories may be garnered are manifold. What may most readily be put in religious terms in Leskov seems almost automatically to fall into place in the pedagogical perspectives of the Enlightenment in Hebel, appears as hermetic tradition in Poe, finds a last refuge in Kipling in the life of British seamen and colonial soldiers. All great storytellers have in common the freedom with which they move up and down the rungs of their experience as on a ladder. A ladder extending downward to the interior of the earth and disappearing into the clouds is the image for a collective experience to which even the deepest shock of every individual experience, death, constitutes no impediment or barrier.

"And they lived happily ever after," says the fairy tale. The fairy tale, which to this day is the first tutor of children because it was once the first tutor of mankind, secretly lives on in the story. The first true storyteller is, and will continue to be, the teller of fairy tales. Whenever good counsel was at a premium, the fairy tale had it, and where the need was greatest, its aid was nearest. This need was the need created by the myth. The fairy tale tells us of the earliest arrangements that mankind made to shake off the nightmare which the myth had placed upon its chest. In the figure of the fool it shows us how mankind "acts dumb" toward the myth; in the figure of the youngest brother it shows us how one's chances increase as the mythical primitive times are left behind; in the figure of the man who sets out to learn what fear is it shows us that the things we are afraid of can be seen through; in the figure of the wiseacre it shows us that the questions posed by the myth are simple-minded, like the riddle of the Sphinx; in the shape of the animals which come to the aid of the child in the fairy tale it shows

that nature not only is subservient to the myth, but much prefers to be aligned with man. The wisest thing—so the fairy tale taught mankind in olden times, and teaches children to this day —is to meet the forces of the mythical world with cunning and with high spirits. (This is how the fairy tale polarizes *Mut*, courage, dividing it dialectically into *Untermut*, that is, cunning, and *Übermut*, high spirits.) The liberating magic which the fairy tale has at its disposal does not bring nature into play in a mythical way, but points to its complicity with liberated man. A mature man feels this complicity only occasionally, that is, when he is happy; but the child first meets it in fairy tales, and it makes him happy.

XVII

Few storytellers have displayed so profound a kinship with the spirit of the fairy tale as did Leskov. This involves tendencies that were promoted by the dogmas of the Greek Orthodox Church. As is well known, Origen's speculation about *apokatastasis*—the entry of all souls into Paradise—which was rejected by the Roman Church plays a significant part in these dogmas. Leskov was very much influenced by Origen and planned to translate his work *On First Principles*. In keeping with Russian folk belief he interpreted the Resurrection less as a transfiguration than as a disenchantment, in a sense akin to the fairy tale. Such an interpretation of Origen is at the bottom of "The Enchanted Pilgrim." In this, as in many other tales by Leskov, a hybrid between fairy tale and legend is involved, not unlike that hybrid which Ernst Bloch mentions in a connection in which he utilizes our distinction between myth and fairy tale in his fashion.

"A hybrid between fairy tale and legend," he says, "contains figuratively mythical elements, mythical elements whose effect is certainly captivating and static, and yet not outside man. In the legend there are Taoist figures, especially very old ones, which are 'mythical' in this sense. For instance, the couple Philemon and Baucis: magically escaped though in natural repose.

And surely there is a similar relationship between fairy tale and legend in the Taoist climate of Gotthelf, which, to be sure, is on a much lower level. At certain points it divorces the legend from the locality of the spell, rescues the flame of life, the specifically human flame of life, calmly burning, within as without."

"Magically escaped" are the beings that lead the procession of Leskov's creations: the righteous ones. Pavlin, Figura, the toupee artiste, the bear keeper, the helpful sentry—all of them embodiments of wisdom, kindness, comfort the world, crowd about the storyteller. They are unmistakably suffused with the *imago* of his mother.

This is how Leskov describes her: "She was so thoroughly good that she was not capable of harming any man, nor even an animal. She ate neither meat nor fish, because she had such pity for living creatures. Sometimes my father used to reproach her with this. But she answered: 'I have raised the little animals myself, they are like my children to me. I can't eat my own children, can I?' She would not eat meat at a neighbor's house either. 'I have seen them alive,' she would say; 'they are my acquaintances. I can't eat my acquaintances, can I?' "

The righteous man is the advocate for created things and at the same time he is their highest embodiment. In Leskov he has a maternal touch which is occasionally intensified into the mythical (and thus, to be sure, endangers the purity of the fairy tale). Typical of this is the protagonist of his story "Kotin the Provider and Platonida." This figure, a peasant named Pisonski, is a hermaphrodite. For twelve years his mother raised him as a girl. His male and female organs mature simultaneously, and his bisexuality "becomes the symbol of God incarnate."

In Leskov's view, the pinnacle of creation has been attained with this, and at the same time he presumably sees it as a bridge established between this world and the other. For these earthily powerful, maternal male figures which again and again claim Leskov's skill as a storyteller have been removed from obedience to the sex-

ual drive in the bloom of their strength. They do not, however, really embody an ascetic ideal; rather, the continence of these righteous men has so little privative character that it becomes the elemental counterpoise to uncontrolled lust which the storyteller has personified in *Lady Macbeth of Mzensk*. If the range between a Pavlin and this merchant's wife covers the breadth of the world of created beings, in the hierarchy of his characters Leskov has no less plumbed its depth.

XVIII

The hierarchy of the world of created things, which has its apex in the righteous man, reaches down into the abyss of the inanimate by many gradations. In this connection one particular has to be noted. This whole created world speaks not so much with the human voice as with what could be called "the voice of Nature" in the title of one of Leskov's most significant stories.

This story deals with the petty official Philip Philipovich who leaves no stone unturned to get the chance to have as his house guest a field marshal passing through his little town. He manages to do so. The guest, who is at first surprised at the clerk's urgent invitation, gradually comes to believe that he recognizes in him someone he must have met previously. But who is he? He cannot remember. The strange thing is that the host, for his part, is not willing to reveal his identity. Instead, he puts off the high personage from day to day, saying that the "voice of Nature" will not fail to speak distinctly to him one day. This goes on until finally the guest, shortly before continuing on his journey, must grant the host's public request to let the "voice of Nature" resound. Thereupon the host's wife withdraws. She "returned with a big, brightly polished, copper hunting horn which she gave to her husband. He took the horn, put it to his lips, and was at the same instant as though transformed. Hardly had he inflated his cheeks and produced a tone as powerful as the rolling of thunder when the field marshal cried: 'Stop, I've got it now, brother.

This makes me recognize you at once! You are the bugler from the regiment of jaegers, and because you were so honest I sent you to keep an eye on a crooked supplies supervisor.' 'That's it, Your Excellency,' answered the host. 'I didn't want to remind you of this myself, but wanted to let the voice of Nature speak.' "

The way the profundity of this story is hidden beneath its silliness conveys an idea of Leskov's magnificent humor. This humor is confirmed in the same story in an even more cryptic way. We have heard that because of his honesty the official was assigned to watch a crooked supplies supervisor. This is what we are told at the end, in the recognition scene. At the very beginning of the story, however, we learn the following about the host: "All the inhabitants of the town were acquainted with the man, and they knew that he did not hold a high office, for he was neither a state official nor a military man, but a little supervisor at the tiny supply depot, where together with the rats he chewed on the stale rusks and boot soles, and in the course of time had chewed himself together a nice little frame house." It is evident that this story reflects the traditional sympathy which storytellers have for rascals and crooks. All the literature of farce bears witness to it. Nor is it denied on the heights of art; of all Hebel's characters, the Brassenheim Miller, Tinder Frieder, and Red Dieter have been his most faithful companions. And yet for Hebel, too, the righteous man has the main role in the *theatrum mundi*. But because no one is actually up to this role, it keeps changing hands. Now it is the tramp, now the haggling Jewish peddler, now the man of limited intelligence who steps in to play this part. In every single case it is a guest performance, a moral improvisation. Hebel is a casuist. He will not for anything take a stand with any principle, but he does not reject it either, for any principle can at some time become the instrument of the righteous man. Compare this with Leskov's attitude. "I realize," he writes in his story "A Propos of the Kreutzer Sonata," "that my thinking is based much more on a practical view of life than on abstract philosophy or lofty morality; but I am nevertheless used to thinking the way I do." To be sure, the moral catastrophes that appear in Leskov's world are to the moral incidents in Hebel's world as the great, silent flowing of the Volga is to the babbling, rushing little millstream. Among Leskov's historical tales there are several in which passions are at work as destructively as the wrath of Achilles or the hatred of Hagen. It is astonishing how fearfully the world can darken for this author and with what majesty evil can raise its scepter. Leskov has evidently known moods—and this is probably one of the few characteristics he shares with Dostoevsky—in which he was close to antinomian ethics. The elemental natures in his *Tales from Olden Times* go to the limit in their ruthless passion. But it is precisely the mystics who have been inclined to see this limit as the point at which utter depravity turns into saintliness.

XIX

The lower Leskov descends on the scale of created things the more obviously does his way of viewing things approach the mystical. Actually, as will be shown, there is much evidence that in this, too, a characteristic is revealed which is inherent in the nature of the storyteller. To be sure, only a few have ventured into the depths of inanimate nature, and in modern narrative literature there is not much in which the voice of the anonymous storyteller, who was prior to all literature, resounds so clearly as it does in Leskov's story "The Alexandrite." It deals with a semi-precious stone, the chrysoberyl. The mineral is the lowest stratum of created things. For the storyteller, however, it is directly joined to the highest. To him it is granted to see in this chrysoberyl a natural prophecy of petrified, lifeless nature concerning the historical world in which he himself lives. This world is the world of Alexander II. The storyteller—or rather, the man to whom he attributes his own knowledge—is a gem engraver named Wenzel who has achieved the greatest conceivable skill in his art. One can juxtapose him with the silversmiths of Tula and say that—in the spirit of Leskov—the perfect artisan has access to the innermost chamber of the realm of created things. He is an incarnation of the devout. We are told of this gem cutter: "He suddenly squeezed my hand on which was the ring with the alexandrite, which is known to sparkle red in artificial light, and cried: 'Look, here it is, the prophetic Russian stone! O crafty Siberian. It was always green as hope and only toward evening was it suffused with blood. It was that way from the beginning of the world, but it concealed itself for a long time, lay hidden in the earth, and permitted itself to be found only on the day when Czar Alexander was declared of age, when a great sorcerer had come to Siberia to find the stone, a magician. . . .' 'What nonsense are you talking,' I interrupted him; 'this stone wasn't found by a magician at all, it was a scholar named Nordenskjöld!' 'A magician! I tell you, a magician!' screamed Wenzel in a loud voice. 'Just look; what a stone! A green morning is in it and a bloody evening . . . This is fate, the fate of noble Czar Alexander!' With these words old Wenzel turned to the wall, propped his head on his elbows, and . . . began to sob."

One can hardly come any closer to the meaning of this significant story than by some words which Paul Valéry wrote in a very remote context. "Artistic observation," he says in reflections on a woman artist whose work consisted in the silk embroidery of figures, "can attain an almost mystical depth. The objects on which it falls lose their names. Light and shade form very particular systems, present very individual questions which depend upon no knowledge and are derived from no practice, but get their existence and value exclusively from a certain accord of the soul, the eye, and the hand of someone who was born to perceive them and evoke them in his own inner self."

With these words, soul, eye, and hand are brought into connection. Interacting with one another, they determine a practice. We are no longer familiar with this practice. The role of the hand in production has become more modest, and the place it filled in storytelling lies waste. (After all, storytelling, in its sensory aspect, is by no means a job for the voice alone. Rather, in genuine storytelling the hand plays a part which supports what is expressed in a hundred ways with its gestures trained by work.) That old co-ordination of the soul, the eye, and the hand which emerges in Valéry's words is that of the artisan which we encounter wherever the art of storytelling is at home. In fact, one can go on and ask oneself whether the relationship of the storyteller to his material, human life, is not in itself a craftsman's relationship, whether it is not his very task to fashion the raw material of experience, his own and that of others, in a solid, useful, and unique way. It is a kind of procedure which may perhaps most adequately be exemplified by the proverb if one thinks of it as an ideogram of a story. A proverb, one might say, is a ruin which stands on the site of an old story and in which a moral twines about a happening like ivy around a wall.

Seen in this way, the storyteller joins the ranks of the teachers and sages. He has counsel —not for a few situations, as the proverb does, but for many, like the sage. For it is granted to him to reach back to a whole lifetime (a life, incidentally, that comprises not only his own experience but no little of the experience of others; what the storyteller knows from hearsay is added to his own). His gift is the ability to relate his life; his distinction, to be able to tell his entire life. The storyteller: he is the man who could let the wick of his life be consumed completely by the gentle flame of his story. This is the basis of the incomparable aura about the storyteller, in Leskov as in Hauff, in Poe as in Stevenson. The storyteller is the figure in which the righteous man encounters himself.

Perspectives on Flaubert

Walter Pater

[FLAUBERT ON ART] (1889)

IN CONTRAST with the majority of writers, apt to make a false pretence of facility, it is of his labour that Flaubert boasts. That was because, after all, labour did but set free the innate lights of a true diamond; it realized, was a ministry to, the great imaginative gift of which he was irresistibly conscious. It was worth his while!

As for me, the more I feel the difficulties of good writing, the more my boldness grows. It is this preserves me from the pedantry into which I should otherwise fall. I have plans for books, the composition of which would occupy the rest of my life: and if there happen to me, sometimes, cruel moments, which well-nigh make me weep with anger (so great do I feel my weakness to be), there are others also when I can scarce contain myself for joy: something from the depths within me, for which voluptuous is no word,

overflows for me in sudden leaps. I feel transported, almost inebriate, with my own thoughts, as if there came to me, at some window within, a puff of warm perfumes. I shall never go very far, and know how much I lack; but the task I undertake will surely be executed by another. I shall have put on the true road some one better endowed, better born, for the purpose, than myself. The determination to give to prose the rhythm of verse, leaving it still veritable prose; to write the story of common life as history or the epic gets written (that is to say, without detriment to the natural truth of the subject), is perhaps impossible. I ask myself the question sometimes. Yet it is perhaps a considerable, an original thing, to have tried. I shall have had my permanent value for my obstinacy. And who knows? One day I may find a good *motif*, an air entirely within the compass of my voice: and at any rate I shall have passed my life not ignobly, often with delight. Yet still it is saddening to think how many great men arrive easily at the desired effect, by means beyond the limits of conscious art. What could be worse built than many things

From "Correspondance de Gustave Flaubert," *Athenaeum*, 3 August 1889. Review and translations by Walter Pater.

in Rabelais, Cervantes, Molière, Hugo? But, then, what sudden thrusts of power! What power in a single word!

Impersonality in art, the literary ideal of Gustave Flaubert, is perhaps no more possible than realism. The artist *will* be felt; his subjectivity must and will colour the incidents, as his very bodily eye *selects* the aspects of things. By force of an immense and continuous effort, however, the whole scope of which these letters enable us to measure, Flaubert did keep *Madame Bovary* at a great distance from himself; the author might be thought to have been completely hidden out of sight in his work. Yet even here he transpires, clearly enough, from time to time; and the morbid sense of life, everywhere impressed in the very atmosphere of that sombre history, came certainly of the writer himself. The cruelty of the ways of things—that is a conviction of which the development is partly traceable in these letters.

Provided the brain remains! That is the chief thing. But how nothingness invades us! We are scarcely born ere decay begins for us, in such a way that the whole of life is but one long combat with it, more and more triumphant, on its part, to the consummation, namely, death; and then the reign of decay is exclusive. There have been at most two or three years in which I was really entire—from seventeen to nineteen. I was splendid just then, though I scarce like to say so now; enough to attract the eyes of a whole assembly of spectators, as happened to me at Rouen, on the first presentation of *Ruy Blas*. Ever since then I have deteriorated at a furious pace. There are mornings when I feel afraid to look at myself, so worn and used-up am I grown.

Madame Bovary, of course, was a tribute to science; and Flaubert had no dread, great hopes rather, of the service of science in imaginative literature, though the combat between scientific truth—mental physiology and the like—and that perfectly finished academic style he preferred, might prove a hard one. We might be all of us, since Sophocles—well, "tattooed savages!" but still, there was "something else in art besides rectitude of line and the well-polished surface." The difficulty lay in the limitations of language, which it would be the literary artist's true contention to enlarge. "We have too many things, too few words. 'Tis from that comes the torture of the fine literary conscience." But it was one's duty, none the less, to accept all, "imprint all, and, above all, fix one's *point d'appui* in the present." Literature, he held, would take more and more the modes of action which now seem to belong exclusively to science. It would be, above all, *exposante*—by way of exposition; by which, he was careful to point out, he by no means intended *didactic*. One must make pictures, by way of showing nature as she really is; only, the pictures must be complete ones. We must paint both sides, the upper and under. Style—what it might be, if writers faithfully cherished it—that was the subject of his perpetual consideration. Here is a sketch of the prose style of the future:—

Style, as I conceive it, style as it will be realized some day—in ten years, or ten generations! It would be rhythmical as verse itself, precise as the language of science; and with undulations—a swelling of the violin! plumage of fire! A style which would enter into the idea like the point of a lancet; when thought would travel over the smooth surfaces like a canoe with fair winds behind it. Prose is but of yesterday, it must be confessed. Verse is *par excellence* the form of the ancient literatures. All possible prosodic combinations have been already made; those of prose are still to make.

The effort, certainly, cost him much; how much we may partly see in these letters, the more as *Madame Bovary*, on which he was then mainly at work, made a large demand also on his impersonality:—

The cause of my going so slowly is just this, that nothing in that book [*Madame Bovary*] is drawn from myself. Never has my own personality been so useless to me. It may be, perhaps, that hereafter I shall do stronger things. I hope so, but I can hardly imagine I shall do anything more skilful. Here everything is of the head. If it has been false in aim, I shall always feel that it has been a good mental exercise. But after all, what is the non-natural to others is the natural to me—the extraordinary, the fantastic, the wild chase, mythologic, or metaphysic. *Saint Antoine* did not require of me one quarter of the tension of mind *Madame Bovary* has caused me. *Saint Antoine* was a discharge: I had nothing but pleasure in writing it; and the eighteen months devoted to the composition of its five hundred pages were the most thoroughly voluptuous of my life, hitherto. Judge, then, of my condition in writing *Madame Bovary*. I must needs put myself every minute into a skin not mine, and antipathetic to me. For six months now I have been making love Platonically; and at the present moment my exaltation of mind is that of a good Catholic: I am longing to go to confession.

A constant reader of Montaigne, Flaubert pushed to the utmost the habit of doubt, as

leading to artistic detachment from all practical ends:—

Posterity will not be slow in cruel desertion of those who have determined to be useful, and have sung "for a cause." It cares very little for Chateaubriand, and his resuscitation of mediaeval religion; for Béranger, with his libertine philosophy; will soon care little for Lamartine and his religious humanitarianism. Truth is never in the present; and if one attaches oneself to the present, there comes an end of one. At the present moment, I believe that even a thinker (and the artist, surely, is three times a thinker) should have no convictions.

Flaubert himself, whatever we may think of that, had certainly attained a remarkable degree of detachment from the ordinary interests of mankind.

Erich Auerbach

SERIOUS IMITATION OF EVERYDAY LIFE (1937)

Mais c'était surtout aux heures des repas qu'elle n'en pouvait plus, dans cette petite salle au rez-de-chaussée, avec le poêle qui fumait, la porte qui criait, les murs qui suintaient, les pavés humides; toute l'amertume de l'existence lui semblait servie sur son assiette, et, à la fumée du bouilli, il montait du fond de son âme comme d'autres bouffées d'affadissement. Charles était long à manger; elle grignotait quelques noisettes, ou bien, appuyée du coude, s'amusait, avec la pointe de son couteau, de faire des raies sur la toile cirée.

(But it was above all at mealtimes that she

could bear it no longer, in that little room on the ground floor, with the smoking stove, the creaking door, the oozing walls, the damp floor-tiles; all the bitterness of life seemed to be served to her on her plate, and, with the steam from the boiled beef, there rose from the depths of her soul other exhalations as it were of disgust. Charles was a slow eater; she would nibble a few hazel-nuts, or else, leaning on her elbow, would amuse herself making marks on the oilcloth with the point of her table-knife.) [1]

The paragraph forms the climax of a presentation whose subject is Emma Bovary's dissatisfaction with her life in Tostes. She has long hoped for a sudden event which would give a new turn to it—to her life without elegance,

From Erich Auerbach, *Mimesis: The Representation of Reality in Western Literature*, translated by Willard R. Trask (copyright 1953 by Princeton University Press); pp. 482–491. Reprinted by permission of Princeton University Press.

[1] *Madame Bovary*, Part 1, chapter 9.

adventure, and love, in the depths of the provinces, besides a mediocre and boring husband; she has even made preparations for such an event, has lavished care on herself and her house, as if to earn that turn of fate, to be worthy of it; when it does not come, she is seized with unrest and despair. All this Flaubert describes in several pictures which portray Emma's world as it now appears to her; its cheerlessness, unvaryingness, grayness, staleness, airlessness, and inescapability now first become clearly apparent to her when she has no more hope of fleeing from it. Our paragraph is the climax of the portrayal of her despair. After it we are told how she lets everything in the house go, neglects herself, and begins to fall ill, so that her husband decides to leave Tostes, thinking that the climate does not agree with her.

The paragraph itself presents a picture—man and wife together at mealtime. But the picture is not presented in and for itself; it is subordinated to the dominant subject, Emma's despair. Hence it is not put before the reader directly: here the two sit at table—there the reader stands watching them. Instead, the reader first sees Emma, who has been much in evidence in the preceding pages, and he sees the picture first through her; directly, he sees only Emma's inner state; he sees what goes on at the meal indirectly, from within her state, in the light of her perception. The first words of the paragraph, *Mais c'était surtout aux heures des repas qu'elle n'en pouvait plus* . . . state the theme, and all that follows is but a development of it. Not only are the phrases dependent upon *dans* and *avec*, which define the physical scene, a commentary on *elle n'en pouvait plus* in their piling up of the individual elements of discomfort, but the following clause too, which tells of the distaste aroused in her by the food, accords with the principal purpose both in sense and rhythm. When we read further, *Charles était long à manger*, this, though grammatically a new sentence and rhythmically a new movement, is still only a resumption, a variation, of the principal theme; not until we

come to the contrast between his leisurely eating and her disgust and to the nervous gestures of her despair, which are described immediately afterward, does the sentence acquire its true significance. The husband, unconcernedly eating, becomes ludicrous and almost ghastly; when Emma looks at him and sees him sitting there eating, he becomes the actual cause of the *elle n'en pouvait plus*; because everything else that arouses her desperation—the gloomy room, the commonplace food, the lack of a tablecloth, the hopelessness of it all—appears to her, and through her to the reader also, as something that is connected with him, that emanates from him, and that would be entirely different if he were different from what he is.

The situation, then, is not presented simply as a picture, but we are first given Emma and then the situation through her. It is not, however, a matter—as it is in many first-person novels and other later works of a similar type—of a simple representation of the content of Emma's consciousness, of *what* she feels *as* she feels it. Though the light which illuminates the picture proceeds from her, she is yet herself part of the picture, she is situated within it. In this she recalls the speaker in the scene from Petronius discussed in our second chapter; but the means Flaubert employs are different. Here it is not Emma who speaks, but the writer. *Le poêle qui fumait, la porte qui criait, les murs qui suintaient, les pavés humides*—all this, of course, Emma sees and feels, but she would not be able to sum it all up in this way. *Toute l'amertume de l'existence lui semblait servie sur son assiette*—she doubtless has such a feeling; but if she wanted to express it, it would not come out like that; she has neither the intelligence nor the cold candor of self-accounting necessary for such a formulation. To be sure, there is nothing of Flaubert's life in these words, but only Emma's; Flaubert does nothing but bestow the power of mature expression upon the material which she affords, in its complete subjectivity. If Emma could do this herself, she would no longer be what she is, she would have outgrown herself and thereby saved herself. So she does not simply see, but is herself seen as one seeing, and is thus judged, simply through a plain description of her subjective life, out of her own feelings. Reading in a later passage (part 2, chapter 12): *jamais Charles ne lui paraissait aussi désagréable, avoir les doigts aussi carrés, l'esprit aussi lourd, les façons si communes . . .* , the reader perhaps thinks for a moment that this strange series is an emotional piling up of the causes that time and again bring Emma's aversion to her husband to the boiling point, and that she herself is, as it were, inwardly speaking these words; that this, then, is an example of *erlebte Rede.* But this would be a mistake. We have here, to be sure, a number of paradigmatic causes of Emma's aversion, but they are put together deliberately by the writer, not emotionally by Emma. For Emma feels much more, and much more confusedly; she sees other things than these—in his body, his manners, his dress; memories mix in, meanwhile she perhaps hears him speak, perhaps feels his hand, his breath, sees him walk about, good-hearted, limited, unappetizing, and unaware; she has countless confused impressions. The only thing that is clearly defined is the result of all this, her aversion to him, which she must hide. Flaubert transfers the clearness to the impressions; he selects three, apparently quite at random, but which are paradigmatically taken from Bovary's physique, his mentality, and his behavior; and he arranges them as if they were three shocks which Emma felt one after the other. This is not at all a naturalistic representation of consciousness. Natural shocks occur quite differently. The ordering hand of the writer is present here, deliberately summing up the confusion of the psychological situation in the direction toward which it tends of itself—the direction of "aversion to Charles Bovary." This ordering of the psychological situation does not, to be sure, derive its standards from without, but from the material of the situation itself. It is the type of ordering which must be employed if the situation itself is to be translated into language without admixture.

In a comparison of this type of presentation with those of Stendhal and Balzac, it is to be observed by way of introduction that here too the two distinguishing characteristics of modern realism are to be found; here too real everyday occurrences in a low social stratum, the provincial petty bourgeoisie, are taken very seriously (we shall discuss the particular character of this seriousness later); here too everyday occurrences are accurately and profoundly set in a definite period of contemporary history (the period of the bourgeois monarchy)—less obviously than in Stendhal or Balzac, but unmistakably. In these two basic characteristics the three writers are at one, in contradistinction to all earlier realism; but Flaubert's attitude toward his subject is entirely different. In Stendhal and Balzac we frequently and indeed almost constantly hear what the writer thinks of his characters and events; sometimes Balzac accompanies his narrative with a running commentary—emotional or ironic or ethical or historical or economic. We also very frequently hear what the characters themselves think and feel, and often in such a manner that, in the passage concerned, the writer identifies himself with the character. Both these things are almost wholly absent from Flaubert's work. His opinion of his characters and events remains unspoken; and when the characters express themselves it is never in such a manner that the writer identifies himself with their opinion, or seeks to make the reader identify himself with it. We hear the writer speak; but he expresses no opinion and makes no comment. His role is limited to selecting the events and translating them into language; and this is done in the conviction that every event, if one is able to express it purely and completely, interprets itself and the persons involved in it far better and more completely than any opinion or judgment appended to it could do. Upon this conviction—that is, upon a profound faith in the truth of language responsibly, candidly, and carefully employed—Flaubert's artistic practice rests.

This is a very old, classic French tradition. There is already something of it in Boileau's line concerning the power of the rightly used word (on Malherbe: *D'un mot mis en sa place enseigna le pouvoir*); there are similar statements in La Bruyère. Vauvenargues said: *Il n'y aurait point d'erreurs qui ne périssent d'elles-mêmes, exprimées clairement.* Flaubert's faith in language goes further than Vauvenargues's: he believes that the truth of the phenomenal world is also revealed in linguistic expression. Flaubert is a man who works extremely consciously and possesses a critical comprehension of art to a degree uncommon even in France; hence there occur in his letters, particularly of the years 1852–1854, during which he was writing *Madame Bovary* (*Troisième Série* in the *Nouvelle édition augmentée* of the *Correspondance*, 1927), many highly informative statements on the subject of his aim in art. They lead to a theory—mystical in the last analysis, but in practice, like all true mysticism, based upon reason, experience, and discipline—of a self-forgetful absorption in the subjects of reality which transforms them (*par une chimie merveilleuse*) and permits them to develop to mature expression. In this fashion subjects completely fill the writer; he forgets himself, his heart no longer serves him save to feel the hearts of others, and when, by fanatical patience, this condition is achieved, the perfect expression, which at once entirely comprehends the momentary subject and impartially judges it, comes of itself; subjects are seen as God sees them, in their true essence. With all this there goes a view of the mixture of styles which proceeds from the same mystical-realistic insight: there are no high and low subjects; the universe is a work of art produced without any taking of sides, the realistic artist must imitate the procedures of Creation, and every subject in its essence contains, before God's eyes, both the serious and the comic, both dignity and vulgarity; if it is rightly and surely reproduced, the level of style which is proper to it will be rightly and surely found; there is no need either for a general theory of levels, in which subjects are arranged according to their dignity, or for any analysis by the writer commenting upon the subject, after its presentation, with a view to better comprehension and more accurate classification; all this must result from the presentation of the subject itself.

It is illuminating to note the contrast between such a view and the grandiloquent and ostentatious parading of the writer's own feelings, and of the standards derived from them, of the type inaugurated by Rousseau and continued after him; a comparative interpretation of Flaubert's *Notre coeur ne doit être bon qu'à sentir celui des autres*, and Rousseau's statement at the beginning of the Confessions, *Je sens mon coeur, et je connais les hommes*, could effectually represent the change in attitude which had taken place. But it also becomes clear from Flaubert's letters how laboriously and with what tensity of application he had attained to his convictions. Great subjects, and the free, irresponsible rule of the creative imagination, still have a great attraction for him; from this point of view he sees Shakespeare, Cervantes, and even Hugo wholly through the eyes of a romanticist, and he sometimes curses his own narrow petty-bourgeois subject which constrains him to tiresome stylistic meticulousness (*dire à la fois simplement et proprement des choses vulgaires*); this sometimes goes so far that he says things which contradict his basic views: *... et ce qu'il y a de désolant, c'est de penser que, même réussi dans la perfection, cela* [*Madame Bovary*] *ne peut être que passable et ne sera jamais beau, à cause du fond même.* Withal, like so many important nineteenth-century artists, he hates his period; he sees its problems and the coming crises with great clarity; he sees the inner anarchy, the *manque de base théologique*, the beginning menace of the mob, the lazy eclectic Historism, the domination of phrases, but he sees no solution and no issue; his fanatical mysticism of art is almost like a substitute religion, to which he clings convulsively, and his candor very often becomes sullen, petty, choleric, and neurotic. But this sometimes perturbs his impartiality and that love of his subjects which is comparable to the Creator's love. The paragraph which we have analyzed, however, is untouched by such deficiencies and weaknesses in his nature; it permits us to observe the working of his artistic purpose in its purity.

The scene shows man and wife at table, the most everyday situation imaginable. Before Flaubert, it would have been conceivable as literature only as part of a comic tale, an idyl, or a satire. Here it is a picture of discomfort, and not a momentary and passing one, but a chronic discomfort, which completely rules an entire life, Emma Bovary's. To be sure, various things come later, among them love episodes; but no one could see the scene at table as part of the exposition for a love episode, just as no one would call *Madame Bovary* a love story in general. The novel is the representation of an entire human existence which has no issue; and our passage is a part of it, which, however, contains the whole. Nothing particular happens in the scene, nothing particular has happened just before it. It is a random moment from the regularly recurring hours at which the husband and wife eat together. They are not quarreling, there is no sort of tangible conflict. Emma is in complete despair, but her despair is not occasioned by any definite catastrophe; there is nothing purely concrete which she has lost or for which she has wished. Certainly she has many wishes, but they are entirely vague— elegance, love, a varied life; there must always have been such unconcrete despair, but no one ever thought of taking it seriously in literary works before; such formless tragedy, if it may be called tragedy, which is set in motion by the general situation itself, was first made conceivable as literature by romanticism; probably Flaubert was the first to have represented it in people of slight intellectual culture and fairly low social station; certainly he is the first who directly captures the chronic character of this psychological situation. Nothing happens, but that nothing has become a heavy, oppressive, threatening something. How he accomplishes this we have already seen; he organizes into compact and unequivocal discourse the confused impressions of discomfort which arise in Emma at sight of the room, the meal, her hus-

band. Elsewhere too he seldom narrates events which carry the action quickly forward; in a series of pure pictures—pictures transforming the nothingness of listless and uniform days into an oppressive condition of repugnance, boredom, false hopes, paralyzing disappointments, and piteous fears—a gray and random human destiny moves toward its end.

The interpretation of the situation is contained in its description. The two are sitting at table together; the husband divines nothing of his wife's inner state; they have so little communion that things never even come to a quarrel, an argument, an open conflict. Each of them is so immersed in his own world—she in despair and vague wish-dreams, he in his stupid philistine self-complacency—that they are both entirely alone; they have nothing in common, and yet they have nothing of their own, for the sake of which it would be worthwhile to be lonely. For, privately, each of them has a silly, false world, which cannot be reconciled with the reality of his situation, and so they both miss the possibilities life offers them. What is true of these two, applies to almost all the other characters in the novel; each of the many mediocre people who act in it has his own world of mediocre and silly stupidity, a world of illusions, habits, instincts, and slogans; each is alone, none can understand another, or help another to insight; there is no common world of men, because it could only come into existence if many should find their way to their own proper reality, the reality which is given to the individual—which then would be also the true common reality. Though men come together for business and pleasure, their coming together has no note of united activity; it becomes one-sided, ridiculous, painful, and it is charged with misunderstanding, vanity, futility, falsehood, and stupid hatred. But what the world would really be, the world of the "intelligent," Flaubert never tells us; in his book the world consists of pure stupidity, which completely misses true reality, so that the latter should properly not be discoverable in it at all; yet it is there; it is in the writer's language, which unmasks the stupidity by pure statement; language, then, has criteria for stupidity and thus also has a part in that reality of the "intelligent" which otherwise never appears in the book.

Emma Bovary, too, the principal personage of the novel, is completely submerged in that false reality, in *la bêtise humaine*, as is the "hero" of Flaubert's other realistic novel, Frédéric Moreau in the *Éducation sentimentale*. How does Flaubert's manner of representing such personages fit into the traditional categories "tragic" and "comic"? Certainly Emma's existence is apprehended to its depths, certainly the earlier intermediate categories, such as the "sentimental" or the "satiric" or the "didactic," are inapplicable, and very often the reader is moved by her fate in a way that appears very like tragic pity. But a real tragic heroine she is not. The way in which language here lays bare the silliness, immaturity, and disorder of her life, the very wretchedness of that life, in which she remains immersed (*toute l'amertume de l'existence lui semblait servie sur son assiette*), excludes the idea of true tragedy, and the author and the reader can never feel as one with her as must be the case with the tragic hero; she is always being tried, judged, and, together with the entire world in which she is caught, condemned. But neither is she comic; surely not; for that, she is understood far too deeply from within her fateful entanglement—though Flaubert never practices any "psychological understanding" but simply lets the state of the facts speak for itself. He has found an attitude toward the reality of contemporary life which is entirely different from earlier attitudes and stylistic levels, including—and especially—Balzac's and Stendhal's. It could be called, quite simply, "objective seriousness." This sounds strange as a designation of the style of a literary work. Objective seriousness, which seeks to penetrate to the depths of the passions and entanglements of a human life, but without itself becoming moved, or at least without betraying that it is moved—this is an attitude which one expects from a priest, a teacher, or a psychologist rather than from an artist. But priest, teacher, and psychologist wish to accomplish something direct and practical—which is far from Flaubert's mind. He wishes, by his attitude—*pas de cris, pas de convulsion, rien que la fixité d'un regard pensif*—to force language to render the truth concerning the subjects of his observation: "style itself and in its own right being an absolute manner of viewing things" (*Corr.* 2, 346). Yet this leads in the end to a didactic purpose: criticism of the contemporary world; and we must not hesitate to say so, much as Flaubert may insist that he is an artist and nothing but an artist. The more one studies Flaubert, the clearer it becomes how much insight into the problematic nature and the hollowness of nineteenth-century bourgeois culture is contained in his realistic works; and many important passages from his letters confirm this. The demonification of everyday social intercourse which is to be found in Balzac is certainly entirely lacking in Flaubert; life no longer surges and foams, it flows viscously and sluggishly. The essence of the happenings of ordinary contemporary life seemed to Flaubert to consist not in tempestuous actions and passions, not in demonic men and forces, but in the prolonged chronic state whose surface movement is mere empty bustle, while underneath it there is another movement, almost imperceptible but universal and unceasing, so that the political, economic, and social subsoil appears comparatively stable and at the same time intolerably charged with tension. Events seem to him hardly to change; but in the concretion of duration, which Flaubert is able to suggest both in the individual occurrence (as in our example) and in his total picture of the times, there appears something like a concealed threat: the period is charged with its stupid issuelessness as with an explosive.

Through his level of style, a systematic and objective seriousness, from which things themselves speak and, according to their value, classify themselves before the reader as tragic or comic, or in most cases quite unobtrusively as both, Flaubert overcame the romantic vehemence and uncertainty in the treatment of contemporary subjects; there is clearly something of the earlier positivism in his idea of art, although he sometimes speaks very derogatorily of Comte. On the basis of this objectivity, further developments became possible . . . However, few of his successors conceived the task of representing contemporary reality with the same clarity and responsibility as he; though among them there were certainly freer, more spontaneous, and more richly endowed minds than his.

The serious treatment of everyday reality, the rise of more extensive and socially inferior human groups to the position of subject matter for problematic-existential representation, on the one hand; on the other, the embedding of random persons and events in the general course of contemporary history, the fluid historical background—these, we believe, are the foundations of modern realism. . . .

Georges Poulet

THE CIRCLE AND THE CENTER:
REALITY AND MADAME BOVARY (1955)

In his book *Mimesis*, for almost a decade the standard study of the concept of reality in Western literature and recently translated into English for the first time, Professor Erich Auerbach quotes the following passage from *Madame Bovary*:

But it was above all at mealtimes that she could bear it no longer, in that little room on the ground floor, with the smoking stove, the creaking door, the oozing walls, the damp floor-tiles; all the bitterness of life seemed to be served to her on her plate, and, with the steam from the boiled beef, there rose from the depths of her soul other exhalations as it were of disgust. Charles was a slow eater; she would nibble a few hazel-nuts, or else, leaning on her elbow, would amuse herself making marks on the oilcloth with the point of her table-knife.

This passage, Auerbach declares, forms the climax of a presentation whose subject is

From *Metamorphoses of the Circle* by Georges Poulet. Reprinted by permission of Georges Poulet and The Johns Hopkins Press.

Emma Bovary's dissatisfaction with her life at Tostes. In several cumulative pictures Flaubert describes the cheerlessness, drabness, unvaryingness, narrowness of Emma's world. This paragraph is therefore the climax of the portrayal of her despair. In itself it presents a picture: man and wife together at mealtime. But the picture is not represented in and for itself; it is subordinated to the dominant subject, Emma's despair. We are first given Emma, and then the situation through her. It is not, however, Mr. Auerbach continues, a matter of a simple representation of the content of Emma's consciousness, of what she feels, as she feels it. Though the light which illuminates the picture proceeds from her, she is yet herself part of the picture, she is situated within it.

It may be useful to reflect upon these enlightening, yet not completely satisfying remarks. No doubt, Flaubert's method consists in presenting, as an object for our contemplation, a subjective being which, in its stead, has for its own object of contemplation the surrounding reality of things. Emma, as Mr. Auerbach points out, "does not simply see, but is herself seen as one seeing." If Flaubert had simply decided to paint her from the outside, she would be merely an object among objects. With the room, the stove, the walls, the plate and the husband, she would be part and parcel of the plurality of things. If, on the other hand, Flaubert had wanted to make of her somebody like Bloom in *Ulysses*, or Clarissa Dalloway in *Mrs. Dalloway*, i.e., a purely subjective being, then there would have been no husband, plate, walls, stove or room. Nothing would have been left, except the sensations and emotions caused in Emma by these objects; and there would have been no Emma, or at least in us no consciousness of her as a person standing against a background of things, since she would have been reduced to the status of a stream of thoughts and feelings. In both cases something essential in Flaubert's novel would have been lost, in one case the objective world, in the other the subjective mind, and in both, the extremely delicate relationship between objective and subjective, which is the very substance of the novel. It is this constant relation which not only links together the dual aspects of the novel, but which also keeps each of these two realities from fragmenting itself into a sheer multiplicity, here of thoughts and emotions, there of objects. There is in *Madame Bovary* an inner coherence, and this coherence is due to the fact that things, simultaneous or successive, are constantly fused together in the unity of a single perceptive mind, and that conversely this mind is kept from disappearing in the flux of its own consciousness by the objectivity of a world with which it is in constant touch. This essential interrelation is excellently commented upon by Mr. Auerbach in his examination of the paragraph of Madame Bovary quoted above. But it seems to me that there is still something to be done. For in this paragraph there is not only a theoretical representation of reality; there is also a concrete medium through which this representation has been achieved. It is the business of the critic to examine, within the text, by

what action Flaubert accomplished his purpose, i.e., to show vividly the interrelation of a consciousness and its environment.

Let us therefore go back to the text. First we read: *Mais c'était surtout aux heures des repas. . . .* What is given to us at first, is time. This time is not a continuity. It is a moment which repeats itself again and again, but which is also, when it happens, the present moment of Emma's life; the moment, above all moments, when actually she cannot bear her existence any more. Thus what we have at first, is something purely and intensely subjective, an awareness of time, an awareness of despair. But as soon as this awareness is revealed, it is immediately located within a place, *la petite salle*, and surrounded with a long enumeration of details, all objective in themselves, but all endowed with affective powers: a stove that smokes, a door that creaks, walls oozing, floor-tiles which are damp. To these details there must be added all the other particulars, which the author does not mention in this paragraph, but which were described at great length in the preceding pages, and which are present in the memory of the reader, as they are indeed in the memory of Emma herself. Thus what is given here is greatly swollen by what was given before. Details have an enormous cumulative power. This is the power of number, or, to use an Aristotelian distinction, this is a numbering and not a numbered number. The multiplicity—in itself meaningless—of all these details, takes force and meaning from the fact that they all affect in the same way the same person. Therefore, from their outside location around Emma, they combine their force and their weight, in order to come down and bring pressure upon her. To express this coming down and in, of the outside reality, crowding on consciousness, Flaubert writes this sentence: "All the bitterness of life seemed to be served to her on her plate, and, with the steam from the boiled beef, there rose from the depths of her soul other exhalations as it were of disgust."

Let us consider successively the two balanced

parts of this sentence. The first one is straight and to the point. One can feel in the directness with which it rushes toward its goal, the very motion by which the influx of despair, emanating from the surrounding objects, passes through a sort of tangible space, in order to reach the subject. To give this effect, Flaubert has purposely inverted the objective and the subjective. Instead of a room, a stove, a door, a tiled floor, there is now a "bitterness of life." The multiple objects have been transformed into their subjective equivalents; just as, conversely, the soul of Emma, which is the goal of the combined offensive carried out by things, has been symbolically represented by the narrow objective circumference of her plate. Thus a deliberate confusion has been created between the subjective and the objective; as if, by penetrating into Emma's soul, the images of things had lost their objectivity and been transformed into feelings, or as if Emma, by becoming affected by material things, had become also somehow material.

But there are still more discoveries to be made in this wonderful sentence. Its beauty consists in rendering exactly by the physical motion of the words, the psychic motion of the meaning. First the general expression, all the bitterness of life, substitutes to the manifold of things a subjective totality encompassing the whole of existence. Then, through the rapid flow of the following words, "seemed to be served to her on her plate," this peripheral reality shrinks down from all sides to lodge itself within the narrowest place, the plate of Emma. So the psychic motion, which in itself is invisible, has become a local and therefore a perceptible motion, through the figure of a space crossed over by the bitterness of existence finding its final home in the object on which is concentrated the attention of Emma. We are witnessing here an extraordinary narrowing of space, a rush of all causal forces, gathering from the depth of the past and from the three dimensions of external space, to converge on a central point, Emma's consciousness. But as soon as Flaubert has created this

motion from the periphery to the center, he gives us a reverse motion from the center toward the periphery: "and, with the steam from the boiled beef, there rose from the depths of her soul other exhalations as it were of disgust." After the contraction the dilation. We do not doubt but that these exhalations go upward and outward, to join the outer regions wherefrom the condensed bitterness of existence came downward into Emma's plate. Thus, crossed over in both directions, the Flaubertian *milieu* appears as a vast surrounding space which spreads from Emma to an indeterminate circumference, and from the circumference to the consciousness of Emma.

This circular character of Flaubert's representation of reality is not a mere metaphor; or, if it is one, it is not one invented for the sake of the argument. On the contrary this metaphor occurs so often, and, when it occurs, fits so well and plays such an important part in the context, that we must consider it as the essential image by which Flaubert expresses the interrelation of objective world and subjective being. My purpose is to examine the different aspects and meanings presented by this metaphor in the work of Flaubert.

Let us take another passage from *Madame Bovary*. It can be found in a first draft of the novel, published in 1936 by Mlle. Leleu. The moment of Emma's life here described belongs to a period slightly antecedent to the passage examined previously. Here she is shown during a walk she takes with her dog, a little Italian greyhound, in the country near Tostes:

She began by *looking round her mechanically* to see if nothing had changed, since last she had been there. She found the same wall flowers on the stones, on the slabs of the wall the same patches of dried up lichen, the same pebbles in the beds of nettles, and the three windows, always closed, which were rotting away. . . . Her thoughts, aimless at first, were wandering at random, like the handsome greyhound who, unleashed, was *running round and round in the field*, chasing a rat in a furrow, or bringing himself to a stop in order to nibble the poppies. . . . But when she had thus let her eyes roam over the horizon, whereas her *diffused* attention had barely skimmed a thousand ideas following each other, then, *as two concentric circles at once contracting their circumferences,* her thoughts retired within herself, her wavering glances became transfixed, and sitting on the ground under the beeches, prodding the grass with the ivory tip of her sunshade, she was always coming back to this question: Why, oh dear, why did I marry?

Here, beyond question, the metaphor of the circle cannot be overlooked. It plays a conspicuous part. At first everything tends to become peripheral. Emma's thoughts wander at random, her eyes roam over the horizon, her attention is spread on a thousand ideas. The things that she perceives, the thoughts that she thinks, gets farther and farther in the distance, and finally they distribute themselves in such a way that they form two concentric circles whose central point is Emma's consciousness. To give the right emphasis to this general impression of circularity, Flaubert has taken care to prefigure it by another circle, the one physically described by the dog running round and round in the field. But this is not all. Let us read again the beginning of the long sentence which constitutes the second half of the paragraph: "But when she had thus let her eyes roam over the horizon, whereas her diffused attention had barely skimmed a thousand ideas following each other. . . ." No doubt, these long undulating clauses, progressively opening, are shaped in this particular form, so as to give a physical impression of the corresponding widening of Emma's thoughts and feelings. But if we read the second part of the sentence, we detect a striking difference of rhythm. The clauses are shorter, straighter and faster; her thoughts retired within herself, her wavering glances became transfixed . . . she was always coming back to this question. Here, manifestly, diffusion has been replaced by contraction. The circles are shrinking, the thoughts from all sides are coming back, the words are running, as if impatient to reach their goal and to come to a full

stop. This final fixation of all motions is represented in two, or even in three distinct ways. Just as the dog, who was running round in the field, comes to a full stop in order to nibble the poppies, so Emma's mind, which was wandering far away in circles among her memories and dreams, comes back to an idea on which it concentrates. And, in a way, this idea is different from all preceding ones, since it is not diffuse, remote and infinitely varied, but precise, intimate and absolutely unique. It is not circumferential, it is central. However this one central thought is closely connected with the previous multiplicity. It is out of this multiplicity that it was issued. It was this very multiplicity which, by fusion, contraction and inward motion, produced finally the central thought, as the result and summing up. Thus the center contains the circumference. And this center is represented once more, symbolically, by a single dimensionless object, which has replaced in the picture the whole landscape: the pointed tip of a sunshade, digging the ground. The circular horizon has shrunk to a mere point.

This infinite contraction of the mental and external spaces is in no way mysterious, either in itself or in its occurrence. It is the most natural motion of the human mind. We know that it is because the diffused attention of Emma, wandering aimlessly, has touched many ideas, that these ideas have awakened, echoed in her mind, evoked the picture of her whole existence, and given expression finally to the question which was at the core of her consciousness. Nothing was more genuine than this moving inward from the circumference to the center. And, on the other hand, nothing was less instantaneous. From extreme eccentricity to extreme concentricity, it is step by step, by a slow and repeated process, that the thought goes back to the self. From the circumference to the center of the psychic circle, we see a gradual progress, we feel the time, we measure the distance.

We have seen space gradually contracting. Let us now see space completely contracted, space which cannot expand. All his life, Flaubert was intensely conscious of the narrowness of existence. Already in one of his earlier books, *Smarh*, he had spoken of "his sickly thought, *running in an iron circle*." In *November* we find the following sentence: "Returning ceaselessly to my starting-point, I was *going round and round in an impassable circle*." In August 1847, he wrote to Louise Colet: "I am attached to a patch of land, to a *circumscribed point* in the world, and the more I feel myself attached to it, the more I turn again and again furiously toward the sun and sky." Nor was this feeling in Flaubert confined to his youth. On April 6, 1858, in his full maturity, he wrote to Mlle. Leroyer de Chantepie:

For the fourth time I am going to find myself again in Marseilles, and, this time, I shall be alone, absolutely alone. *The circle has shrunk.* The reflections I was making in 1849 when about to embark for Egypt, I am going to make again in a few days, when tramping the same streets. Thus our life *goes round continually* in the same train of miseries, like a squirrel in a cage, and each new step makes us gasp.

Similarly all the works of Flaubert's old age have for their main theme circumscribed existence. For instance, *A Simple Heart*, the story of Félicité, the maid-servant, from which I quote this passage:

The small circle of her ideas shrank even more, and the chiming of bells, the bellowing of cattle did not exist any more. All living things now were moving as silently as ghosts. Only one sound still reached her ears: the voice of her parrot.

This parrot, first as a pet, then as a stuffed bird, becomes gradually the central object in the old maid's circle of existence. At the end there is no more circle. There is only the stuffed bird, which is the unique point on which the old maid's look is fixed at the moment of her death. Another story from that period is the legend of St. Julian the Hospitaller. Julian is a great hunter, pursuing his quarry in many countries, until, in a culminat-

ing scene, the animals at bay turn upon him, *"making around him a narrow circle."* The same feeling of suffocation can be found in *Salammbô*, where a whole army is shut in, to perish by starvation, in a narrow mountain-pass. And the same picture of narrow activity, running blindly around in a small circle, is to be found in *Bouvard and Pécuchet*. Everywhere in the work of Flaubert there is the obsession of narrow, endless circularity. But nowhere does it appear more strikingly than in the story of Emma Bovary. Emma is essentially a person who feels herself enclosed and stifled within the bounds of the place where she lives and of the moment in which she thinks. Her whole existence at Tostes or at Yonville seems to her a shutting up within walls, a groping around inside narrow limits; limits so narrow that sometimes they seem to join each other, to condense into a point, the point of time and space where she is constrained to live. She is here, here only, in the dimensionless *here*; she is forbidden forever to escape outside, into the infinite *elsewhere*. Nevertheless this *elsewhere* exists, it exists everywhere else, it is spreading on every side, and it is toward that *elsewhere* that her longing irradiates incessantly. The extraordinary constriction of Emma's existence, reduced to a mere punctum, is described by Flaubert in this passage, taken from the first version of *Madame Bovary*:

Then the train of the same days started again. They were going to follow each other in the same manner, in Indian file, always similar, innumerable, bringing nothing. And they were before her, hundreds and thousands of them, enough for ten or twenty years! It will never finish, it will last until her death. The other lives, constricted, flat, cramped as they were, had at least some chance of an adventure, of a broadening *of their limits*. Sometimes there dropped an accident which shook their surface. An unexpected happening could *create peripeties ad infinitum*. . . . But, for her, nothing would happen.

First of all, the beauty of this passage is due to the intense feeling of duration which impregnates it: Then the train of the same days started again. Duration appears here as a mere prolongation of the past into the present. But it appears also as a prolongation of the present into the future: They were going to follow each other in the same manner, in Indian file. The three dimensions of time, past, present and future, identify themselves with one another, in such a way, that they become a uniform and continuous texture. As far as the eye can reach, duration extends, forward, backward, always the same, forming a homogeneous bulk of temporal matter. But by a process which, in his famous sonnet *The Swan*, Mallarmé will repeat, this vast extent of duration, spread uniformly on all sides, is also experienced by Emma as the narrowest possible span of time. The very uniformity of all past, present and future moments of existence, transforms and contracts all of them into a single moment; and this moment, incessantly rediscovered along the retrospective and prospective expanse of time, is never discovered but as the same narrow span infinitely repeated. So time is just an endless void of duration, in the middle of which life appears constricted, identical to itself, bringing nothing. However, this life is compared by Emma to others. These other lives, "constricted, flat, cramped as they were, had at least some chance of an adventure, of a broadening of their limits." Adventure considered as a widening of existence, is described by a symbol well-known since the Stoics: "Sometimes there dropped an accident which shook their surface. An unexpected happening could create peripeties ad infinitum." No doubt the image suggested here is the one of a stone dropped in a pool. From the point where it strikes the surface, concentric waves go out in all directions. The circles widen, multiply, get farther from the center. So an adventure, an accident, something unprovoked, uncalled for, may fall suddenly into the pool of life, burst into its stillness, produce circles of events going outward. The accident in itself is nothing; just a piece of gravel thrown in the water. But the small whirlpool it creates

breaks the limits of the still narrow circle of existence, to replace them by an infinite circumference.[1] The most insignificant event may be the starting point of an immense future.

Everything, therefore, depends on these occurrences. But, thinks Emma, they only happen to other people, they will never happen to me. Now, in spite of Emma's forebodings, it is precisely Flaubert's purpose to make things happen to her. Not many happenings, just three or four. Emma's life is a pool in which, occasionally, stones are thrown. Or, more exactly, it is a series of pools, each one a little bigger than the preceding one, first the father's farm, then Tostes, then Yonville, finally Yonville plus Rouen. In the stillness of each of these pools, at a particular time, a stone is thrown. This throwing of the stone is invariably the appearance of a new lover. From the moment he comes out, there start waves of emotion, which for a time broaden Emma's life; up to the moment when, the lover having gone, the emotion being spent, Emma is brought back by a retrogressive process to her starting point.

Let us examine this starting point in the first and most fugitive of Emma's love affairs.

Invited with her husband to a ball in an aristocratic country house, *le château de la Vaubyessard*, Emma has been deeply moved by this incidental excursion in a *milieu* so different from hers. She has danced in the arms of a Parisian Viscount, whose elegance has made on her a profound expression: "All things turning around them, the lamps, the furniture, the wainscoting, the floor like a disc on a pivot." Let us keep in mind these physical gyrations in which we must see a prefiguration of the mental gyrations which, later on, will proceed in Emma's mind. The day after, Emma leaves the château and the Viscount, to come back to the narrow circle of her ordinary life. The only keepsake she has brought back from that memorable event is a cigar case which may, or may not, have belonged to

[1] See Marjorie Hope Nicolson, *The Breaking of the Circle*, Evanston, Ill., 1950.

the Viscount. Now this fortuitous dancing partner, whom Emma will not see any more, is a very small pebble in her life. Nevertheless we will see, starting from the point of its falling, waves and waves of dreams irradiating in Emma's imagination. To follow this phenomenon, we have not only the final version of the novel, but also some preliminary drafts, and even in the primitive scenario referring to Emma's life after her return, we find this sentence: "The Viscount is a center, he disappears, but the surroundings stay and widen." Another version, more elaborated, gives the explanation of this cryptic statement. First we are informed that sometimes Emma looks at the cigar case, which makes her dream of the Viscount. She wants to imagine his life in Paris, and she reads books about life in the capital. These books are mostly novels. Then comes the important passage:

The memory of the Viscount was always passing, like a ghost, into what she was reading. She found his picture on every page. Examining the imaginary personages, she was always making parallels and comparisons with him. Thus he was enhanced by their poetry and he reflected his reality upon their fiction. Then *the circle of which he was the center, where all rays converged, gradually widened round him,* and, spreading equally in this expanse, the Viscount's personality became more and more diluted, like a drop of red wine that one lets fall in a glass of water.

The image of the drop of wine corresponds closely to the one of the pebble. In both instances a fallen object, by dilation or dilution, becomes the center and generating point of a circular motion. In the final version the image changes once again, but still represents the figure of a circle:

The memory of the Viscount always returned as she read. Between him and the imaginary personages she made comparisons. But the circle of which he *was the center gradually widened round him,* and the *halo* that he bore, drawing away from his head, broadened out beyond, lighting up other dreams.

Here, instead of the pebble, or the drop of wine, we have the halo. The circle, narrow at first, becomes progressively so wide that it loses touch with the center, and, identifying itself with other dreams, irradiates confusedly in the distance toward a sort of peripheral happiness:

At the far end of life's vista, high above, she thus saw happiness lying in a marvellous abode.

Here again we have a fundamental process of the Flaubertian mind, just the opposite of the one which makes the mind contract within narrow limits. It is the process of expansion, which generates innumerable reveries, leading from a central thought to a profusion of eddying images. As often as not, the starting point is a recollection. For instance, in a letter from Flaubert to Louise Colet, dated August 22, 1853, from Trouville, we find the following passage:

All the memories of my youth are crying out under my feet, like shells on the beach. Each wave that I see breaking on the seashore awakens in me distant *resounding echoes.*

As in Proust, we can often find in Flaubert a whole world of reminiscences, "sortant d'une tasse de thé." But in Flaubert, contrarily to Proust, this springing forth of the past is never directed toward the recapture of any distinct reality. It is a spreading outward, a processus of indetermination. Thus, at the tinkling of a bell, stirring memories of Emma's youth, "Gentle vibrations made her thoughts quiver and *go widening in the infinite vagueness of retrospections.*" The distinctness of each recollection is thus progressively replaced by their multiplicity, their vibratility, and, finally, by the vastness of the place they have indistinctly filled up by their resonances. In *Smarh,* as in the three *Temptations,* we experience at a cosmic scale this feeling of expansion:

How vast is creation! I see the planets rising and the stars running, carried away with their lights. *The dome of the sky is widening as I go upward with it,* the worlds are rolling around me. So I am *the center* of this moving creation.

And in the 1849 version of the *Temptation:*

The Devil:—Diffuse, expand, spread out.

Anthony:—I see the *circles widening*, I hear the rumbling sound of the spheres.

Or:

Thy joy will grow unceasingly, according to the increases of thy love, like the vibrations of seraphic harps, which, widening from sphere to sphere, unfold in the Infinite the praise of God.

Thus, independently of any religious or philosophical belief, by the essential trend of his imagination, Flaubert's soul, like the soul of St. Anthony, tends to become "diffuse, universal, stretched out." In a letter written by Flaubert to Louise Colet on the 3rd of March, 1852, we read:

I have come across some old drawings that I colored when I was seven or eight years old, and that I have not seen since. There are rocks painted in blue and trees in green. Looking at them (at a wintering in an ice-field especially) I relived some of the terrors I experienced when I was a child. . . . My journeys, the recollections of my childhood, all these things reflect their colors on one another, they fall into line, dance in a prodigious blaze and *rise in a spiral.*

The theme of the spiral is frequent in Flaubert. It may have come from his friend Le Poittevin, whose novel, *Bélial,* is summed up in these words by Flaubert: "The general idea is the whirl, the *infinite spiral.*" Already in the youthful *Memoirs of a Madman* Flaubert writes these curious words: "Oh! the infinite! the infinite! immense gulf, *spiral* which rises from the abyss to the higher regions of the unknown, old idea within which *we go round, taken with giddiness.*" The first two *Temptations* are full of spirals. Thus the Ophits say, speaking of their snake-god: "His *spirals* are the *circles* of worlds spread out concentrically." And the Gnostics: "The mysterious Gnosis raises up endlessly its *spiral,* and, driven by us, thou shalt ascend ceaselessly toward the irradiating Syzygia, which will carry thee high above in the bosom of the perennial Bythos, in the immovable *circle* of the perfect Plerom." Moreover, we know that, on more than one occasion, Flaubert planned to write a novel precisely entitled *La Spirale,* which would have had for subject the transfiguration of reality through dream, and of which nothing remains except a few unprinted notes known through a German scholar, E. W. Fischer. Quoting from these notes the phrase "comme une spirale qui monte à l'infini," Mr. Fischer wonders about the meaning of the title: "Is it intended to mean that the thoughts of the hero are moving along circles which rise infinitely, fantastic circles around the reality, from which they fly, and to which, however, they are attached as to their starting-point?" It would be difficult to get closer to the spirit of the author. Very likely, through the symbol of an ever-rising spiral, Flaubert wanted once more to illustrate the circular widening of horizons, that we found already in *Madame Bovary.* If we want further proof, let us recall this other sentence from the *Correspondence:* "The heart in its affections, like mankind in its ideas, *spreads endlessly in widening circles.*" Elsewhere Flaubert writes: "All feeling is an extension." But in the whole of the *Correspondence* there is nothing nearer *Madame Bovary* than the following passage: "My existence, like a stagnant swamp, is so still that *the least event dropping in it, causes innumerable circles.* . . ."

Yet in spreading outward the mind runs risks of which Flaubert was well aware. The first one, that we have already seen, is the risk of losing touch with the center of one's thoughts, and therefore with all order and precision. In their famous discussion with Flaubert after the reading of the *Temptation,* Bouilhet and Du Camp were not entirely in the wrong when they told Flaubert: "You made an angle from which *diverging* figures spread out so far that one loses sight of them. . . . You proceed through expansion." Perhaps when using this particular metaphor, Bouilhet and Du Camp had in mind the words said, precisely in the *Temptation,* by the Heresies to Anthony: "We are the *diverging rays* which multiply the light, and all *converging* toward its base to increase its span." No doubt, in his desire of extending immensely the scope of his work, Flaubert, in the 1849 version, had developed divergency at the expense of convergency. But out of this multiplicity of directions and desegregation of all images in the void of space, a new danger appears, which is the danger of giddiness, madness, mental hemorrhage that nothing can stem. Flaubert writes: "I have often felt madness coming in for me. In my poor head there was a whirl of ideas and images, and it seemed to me that my consciousness, my very self, was sinking like a ship in the tempest." The ship sinks at the center of the whirl, while at the periphery there is a maddening circular motion. This is just such a psychic catastrophe as we witness in *Madame Bovary*, when Emma, rejected by Rodolphe, goes back through the fields. There is no center left in her, or, more exactly the mental center of her self is a bursting point, exploding and projecting itself in countless fragments in all directions:

She remained lost in stupor, and having no more consciousness of herself than through the beating of her arteries, that she seemed to hear bursting forth like a deafening music filling all the fields. The earth beneath her feet was more yielding than the sea, and the furrows seemed to be immense brown waves breaking into foam. Everything in her head, of memories, ideas, went off at once like a thousand fireworks . . .
Suddenly it seemed to her that fiery *spheres* were exploding in the air like detonating balls when they strike, and were whirling, whirling to melt at last upon the snow between the branches of the trees. In the midst of each of them appeared the face of Rodolphe. They multiplied and drew near her, penetrating her. Then all disappeared.

But at the opposite extreme of this ultimate state of mind, where there is no longer any circle, or center, or any existential coherence whatsoever, there are in *Madame Bovary* all the passages where the eccentric and concentric motions balance each other, and the circumference does not lose its relation to the center. In *Par les champs et par les grèves*, Flaubert writes: "A reverie can be great and give birth at least to fruitful melancholies, when, *starting from a fixed point and never losing touch with*

it, the imagination hovers within its luminous *circle*." This hovering of the dreams within a luminous circle, to the center of which they are closely related, is expressed in the first *Sentimental Education*, at the moment when the hero discovers that he is loved:

The universe appeared to him, through a luminous vista, full of glory and love, and his own life *surrounded by a halo*, like the face of a God; happiness spread over him; it was coming out of everything, it exuded even from the walls.

In a preceding passage, the halo, "drawing away from his head, broadened out beyond, lighting up other dreams." Here, instead of disappearing into the distance, the halo irradiated by love seems to reach a limit, from which its reflected light comes back toward the center of emanation. In our first example, we have seen all the surrounding bitterness of existence concentrate into Emma's plate. Here, through the same concentric approach, we see all the surrounding sweetness of the world reaching the soul.

The same process is repeated again and again in *Madame Bovary*. For instance, this description of the motion by which the image of Emma comes from the depths of the past into the center of Léon's consciousness:

It seemed to him that the face of this woman was *sending from far away on his present life a kind of reverberation*, like these setting suns, which, close to the ground, cast out as far as us their luminous undulations.

Or this admirable passage, which unfortunately Flaubert did not retain in the final version, where through the happiness of her present love, Emma not only unfolds herself to the external reality, but also experiences in the apex of actual love the fulfillment of past desires, kept at the periphery of her mind:

Besides, in loving him, not only did she fulfill her need of love, but she also satisfied all her old desires, which had been inhibited. . . . All the feelings of her soul *converged in this love, as the spokes of a wheel around the axle which supports them.*

Thus, what Flaubert intended to show in *Madame Bovary* is a life which at one moment contracts and at another unfolds; a life which sometimes is reduced to a moment without duration and a point without dimension; and which sometimes, from that moment and from that point, extends to a circular consciousness of all its duration, of all the depths of its dreams, of all the spatiality of its environment:

All these reminiscences were *widening her existence*. They seemed to form immensities of feelings, *to which she turned*.

The relation, here, is from a dimensionless present to the vastness of peripheral life. But it may also happen conversely that from the breadth of a present existence, now peripheral, all the activities of the soul converge on a single central object.

Thus in the *Correspondence*:

It is to you that my thought flows back, when I have been through the circles of my reveries; *I cast myself on this thought at full length*, like a weary traveller on the grass alongside the road.

But, above all, this admirable passage of the first *Madame Bovary*, where we find the same image:

She concentrated on this recollection; it became *the center* of her spleen; all her thoughts *converged upon it*. . . . The humblest details, the past, the future, memories of simple words, fancies, comparisons, disgusts, she piled everything into this recollection, *her soul stretched at full length toward this center of heat*.

All these texts prove clearly that what Flaubert conceived and succeeded in devising, is a new way of presenting the relations between the mind and all surrounding reality, a more convincing way than the one used by his predecessors. While eighteenth century novelists, and Stendhal himself, were satisfied to go with the hero along the narrow track of successive time, and while Balzac constructed most of his plots as a line of force projected very straight in time and space, Flaubert is the first who builds his novels around a series of centers encompassed by their environments.

For the first time in the history of the novel, human consciousness shows itself as it is, as a sort of core, around which sensations, thoughts and memories move in a perceptible space. Thus it becomes possible to discover and express the depth of the human mind; a depth which can be conceived as an expanse through which radiations diverge, or, conversely, as the convergence of all peripheral life upon the sentient being.

But there is yet a last form of circularity that must be examined. It is the *ordering* of all activities around an image which dwells permanently in the center of the soul. The whole novel becomes then the continuous reshaping of a reality in itself disordered, taking form, meaning and motion from the living center to which it is related. Such is, it seems to me, the true structure of the *Sentimental Education*. Critics often consider it as a formless novel, a novel which has precisely for its subject-matter the formlessness of existence. Charles Du Bos has written some beautiful pages on the "milieu intérieur" of this novel, in which, for him, "Nothing takes hold, everything is oozing, and it seems that we are inside the *flowing* motion of time." But in insisting on this flowing *away*, Du Bos failed to see that in the *Sentimental Education* there is also a constant flowing *in* and *around*. Here, clearly there is no progression of water going down stream. As Flaubert told himself of his novel, "There is no progression of effect." Thus it would be more exact to compare its motion to the one of a *circular* river. Again and again, in the works of Flaubert, the word *circulation* appears, weighted with meaning. For instance, in the *Temptation*:

The blood of man pulses in his heart and swells the veins of his feet. The breath of God *circulates* among the worlds and the contingencies of these worlds.

Dost thou see, like blood in an enormous body, the universal Haensoph *circulating* in the hidden veins of all the worlds?

Thus, in the *Sentimental Education*, Frédéric Moreau is constantly perceiving, around him, currents of life quickening the circumambient world:

> He stayed to contemplate the quadrille, blinking his eyes to see better, breathing the soft perfumes of women, which were *circulating* like a kiss endlessly diffused.
>
> The ceiling, rounded in the form of a cupola, gave to the boudoir the shape of a basket; and a scented draught was *circulating* under the fluttering of fans.
>
> When he came up again to his study, he looked at the armchair where she had been seated and at all the objects she had touched. Something of her was *circulating around*. The caress of her presence was still enduring.

But this incessant motion of peripheral life would have no meaning, and the novel no form, if at the center there were not a coordinating element. This element is the love of the hero. If Frédéric had not loved Madame Arnoux, the novel would have been formless and meaningless. But this is not the case. As Jean-Pierre Richard says in his study on *The Creation of Form in Flaubert*, in the *Sentimental Education*, "All objects are disposed around an oriented axle." Because, from the first page of the novel, Mme. Arnoux draws Frédéric's love, whatever amorphous elements

exist in Frédéric's life, begin to gravitate around her image, taking light from her:

> And as a traveller lost in the midst of a wood, whom all paths lead back to the same spot, continually, at the end of every idea, he was finding again the memory of Mme. Arnoux.
>
> All the streets were leading toward her house; all carriages were standing in the squares to bring him there more quickly; Paris was related to her person, and the great city, with its thousand voices, was murmuring like an immense orchestra, *around her*.

Thus the main purpose of Flaubert's novel is to create relation and order. This order is formal. From the center to the circumference, from the circumference to the center, there are constant relations. These are the relations set by the sentient subject between each moment of its consciousness and its total environment. Flaubert's novel belongs to a region explored, in a famous article, by Professor Leo Spitzer: the region of *milieu* and *ambiance*. Sensible and emotive elements form a tangible circle, at the core of which there is, to quote the most perfect expression of Flaubert, "A *luminous center, toward which the entirety of things converge*."

Georg Lukács

FROM
THE CRISIS OF BOURGEOIS REALISM (1937)

FLAUBERT'S *Salammbô* is the great representative work of [a] new phase of development in the historical novel. It combines all the high artistic qualities of Flaubert's style. Stylistically, it is the paradigm of Flaubert's artistic aims;

From *The Historical Novel* by Georg Lukács. Reprinted by permission of The Merlin Press Ltd., London.

which is why it shows so much more clearly than the writings of the mediocre and untalented writers of this period the unresolved contradictions, the irremovable inner "problematic" of the new historical novel.

Flaubert formulated his aims programmatically. He says that he wished to apply the procedure and method of the modern novel to antiquity. And this programme was fully acknowledged by the important representatives of the new trend of naturalism. Zola's criticism of *Salammbô* is essentially a realization of this statement by Flaubert. Zola, admittedly, finds fault with a number of details, but accepts that Flaubert has applied the methods of the new realism correctly to historical material.

Outwardly *Salammbô* has not had the outstanding success of *Madame Bovary*. Nevertheless its echo has been quite strong. The leading French critic of the period, Sainte-Beuve, devoted a whole series of articles to it. Flaubert himself considered this critique so important that in a letter to Sainte-Beuve, published later, he took up all his critic's points in detail. This controversy illuminates so sharply the new problems which had arisen in this new phase of the historical novel that we must deal at length with the main arguments of the polemic.

Sainte-Beuve's basic critical position is deprecatory, despite his respect for Flaubert's literary personality. What makes this depreciation so interesting for us is that the critic himself takes up a similar philosophical and literary position in many respects to the Flaubert he criticizes. The difference is that the older Sainte-Beuve is still somewhat bound to the traditions of the earlier period; he is more flexible and willing to compromise than Flaubert, particularly in artistic questions. Flaubert pursued his path to its logical conclusion with the radical disregard of a deeply convinced and important writer. Sainte-Beuve's criticism, therefore, of Flaubert's creative method is certainly not that of the Scott-Balzac period, as we shall see. Indeed in this period Sainte-Beuve proposed and even realized artistic views which in many respects approached those of Flaubert and sharply contrasted with those of Balzac.

Flaubert keenly felt this affinity between his own basic position and that of his critic. Thus, in his letter to Sainte-Beuve, the author of *Port-Royal*, he presents his critic with the following *argumentum ad hominem*: "One last question, master, an improper question: why do you find Schahabarim almost comic and your good fel-

lows of Port Royal so serious? For me M. Singlin is funereal beside my elephants . . . And it is precisely because [the characters of Port Royal] are very distant from me that I admire your talent in trying to make them intelligible to me. For I believe and wish to live in Port Royal even less than I do in Carthage. Port Royal, too, was exclusive, unnatural, forced, all of a piece and yet true. Why do you not want two truths to exist, two contrary excesses, two different monstrosities?"

It is interesting to compare Flaubert's praise for Sainte-Beuve here with Balzac's entirely negative judgment on *Port-Royal*. Balzac and Flaubert are fairly close to one another in their judgment of the world which Sainte-Beuve, as an historian with artistic pretensions, presents. Both see the fragmented, eccentric, bagatelle nature of Sainte-Beuve's picture of history. But while Balzac passionately rejects such a conception of history, Flaubert regards it with an interested and sceptical curiosity. And there is no question here of simple politeness on the part of Flaubert towards the famous critic. His discussion in his correspondence of the Goncourts' historical pictures of the eighteenth century, for example, clearly proves the sincerity of these remarks, for there these Sainte-Beuve tendencies are pushed to the extreme. What comes out in all these cases is the new feeling of the leading ideologists towards history.

Of course, Flaubert's position in this process is not an average one. His literary greatness is expressed in the fact that the general tendency of the time appears in his work with an honest, passionate consistency. While in most other writers of the time, a negative attitude towards the contemporary prose of bourgeois life was simply a matter of aesthetic amusement or, frequently, of reactionary feeling, in Flaubert it is an intense disgust, a vehement hatred.

This disgust and hatred are behind Flaubert's interest in history: "I am weary of ugly things and sordid surroundings. Bovary has disgusted me with bourgeois morals for some time to come. I am going to live, for several years perhaps, inside a subject of splendour, far from the modern world of which I am heartily sick." And in another letter, also written while he was at work on *Salammbô:* "When one reads *Salammbô,* one will not, I hope, think of the Author. Few will guess how sad one had to be in order to resuscitate Carthage! There's a Thebaid to which disgust with modern life has driven me."

Thus Flaubert set himself a consistent programme: to reawaken a vanished world of no concern to us. It was precisely because of his deep hatred for modern society that he sought, passionately and paradoxically, a world which would in no way resemble it, which would have no connection with it, direct or indirect. Of course, this lack of connection—or rather the illusion of such—is at the same time the subjective factor which connects Flaubert's exotic historical subject matter with the everyday life of the present. For one must not forget that he tried to plan and execute his social novels, too, as a bystander, a non-participant. The letters he wrote while working on them testify to this again and again. And similarly one has to see that in both cases the programmatic non-partisanship, the famous "impassibilité" turns out to be an illusion: Flaubert reveals his attitude to both Emma Bovary and Salammbô through the atmosphere he creates. The only difference one can really discover in the treatment of the two themes is that the author is not in fact very emotionally involved with the masses of protectors and enemies of Carthage, while the everyday world of the contemporary novels kindles unceasing hatred and love in him. (It would be too superficial altogether to overlook this factor; it is enough to think of Dussarin in *L'Éducation sentimentale.*) This all explains why Flaubert could think it possible to use the same artistic means for both *Salammbô* and *Madame Bovary.* At the same time, however, it also explains the completely different artistic results: the artistic fruitfulness of genuine hatred and love, however hidden and suppressed in the one case, the transformation of disinterestedness into sterile exoticism in the other.

In the attempt to solve this task artistically the contradictions in Flaubert's position come out very plainly. Flaubert wishes to portray this world realistically, using the artistic means which he himself had discovered a few years earlier for *Madame Bovary* and there brought to perfection. But now it is not the grey everyday reality of French provincial life to which this realism of minutely observed and exactly described detail is to be applied; instead it is the alien and distant, incomprehensible but picturesque, decorative, grandiose, gorgeous, cruel and exotic world of Carthage which is to arise before us. This explains Flaubert's desperate struggle to evoke a graphic picture of old Carthage by means of exact study and exact production of archaeological detail.

Sainte-Beuve has a strong sense of the artistic discrepancy which results from this aim. He is always pointing out how the description of objects in Flaubert, the dead environment of men, overwhelms the portrayal of the men themselves: he criticizes the fact that, though all these details are correctly and brilliantly described in Flaubert, they do not add up to a whole, not even in relation to the dead objects. Flaubert describes doors, locks etc., all the components of a house, but the architect who builds the whole is nowhere to be seen. Sainte-Beuve sums up this criticism as follows: "the political side, the character of the persons, the genius of the people, the aspects whereby the particular history of this seafaring and, in its own way, civilizing people is of concern to history in general and of interest to the great current of civilization, are sacrificed here or subordinated to the exorbitant, descriptive side, to a dilettantism which, unable to apply itself to anything but rare ruins, is compelled to exaggerate them."

That these remarks hit a central defect in *Salammbô* is shown by Flaubert's despairing letters written while at work on the book. Thus he writes to a friend: "I am now full of doubts about the whole, about the general plan; I think there are too many soldiers. That is History, I know quite well. But if a novel is as tedious as a scientific potboiler, then Good Night, there's an end to Art . . . I am beginning the siege of Carthage now. I am lost among the machines of war, the balista and the scorpions, and I understand nothing of it, neither I nor anyone else."

But what can a world thus re-awakened mean to us? Granted that Flaubert successfully solved all the problems which he raised artistically—has a world so represented any real living significance for us? Flaubert's paradoxes with regard to subjects which do not concern us, and which are artistic because they do not concern us, are very characteristic of the author's moods, but they also have their objective aesthetic consequences which are already known to us. Sainte-Beuve denies that the world of *Salammbô* has this significance for us. He uses an interesting argument, which shows that something of the old tradition of the historical novel is still alive in him. He doubts whether one can treat antiquity artistically, whether it can be made the theme of a really living historical novel. "One can reconstruct antiquity, but one cannot bring it back to life." And he refers specifically to the living, continuous relation between Scott's themes and the present, to the many living links which make it possible for us to experience even the distant Middle Ages.

But his chief objection to the theme of *Salammbô* is not confined to this general doubt. Flaubert's subject, he says, occupies a special, remote, unrelated position even among the themes of antiquity. "What do I care about the duel between Tunis and Carthage? Speak to me of the duel between Carthage and Rome, that's a different matter! There I am attentive, there I am involved. In the bitter struggle between Rome and Carthage the whole of future civilization is at stake; our own depends on it . . .".

To this decisive objection Flaubert has no concrete answer. "Perhaps you are right in your considerations of the historical novel as applied to antiquity, and it is very possible that I have failed."

But he has nothing more concrete to say about this question and, while rejecting the artistic significance of archaeological authenticity, simply speaks of the immanent connections within the historical world he has so selected and portrayed. And he maintains that he is right or wrong according to whether he has been successful or not with regard to this immanent harmony.

Apart from which he defends his subject-matter and portrayal in a more lyrical and biographical vein. "I believe even," he says, "that I have been less hard on humanity in *Salammbô* than in *Madame Bovary*. The curiosity, the love which made me seek out vanished religions and peoples has something moral and sympathetic about it, so it seems to me."

The comparison between *Salammbô* and *Madame Bovary* does not derive from Flaubert himself; it occurs already in Sainte-Beuve's critique. Sainte-Beuve analyses the figure of *Salammbô*: "She talks to her nurse, confides to her her vague anxieties, her stifled sense of unease, her listlessness . . . She looks for, dreams of, calls to something unknown. It is the situation of more than one daughter of Eve, Carthaginian or otherwise; to some extent it is that of *Madame Bovary* at the beginning, when life has become too tedious for her and she goes off on her own to the beech-grove of Banneville . . . Well, poor Salammbô experiences in her own way the same feeling of vague yearning and oppressive desire. The author has only transposed, with great art, and *mythologised* this muffled lament of the heart and the senses." In another connection he compares Flaubert's general attitude to his historical characters with Chateaubriand's manner of portrayal. He says that Flaubert's Salammbô is less a sister of Hannibal than of Chateaubriand's Gallic maiden, Velléda.

The reproach of *modernization* is clearly contained in these comparisons, although Sainte-Beuve does not make an issue out of this question and often shows a great deal of tolerance towards modernization. Nor has

Flaubert's protest anything to do with the general methodological problem of modernization. This he takes to be self-evident. His disagreement is only with the concrete comparisons which Sainte-Beuve makes. "As for my heroine, I do not defend her. According to you she resembles . . . Velléda, Mme. Bovary. Not at all! Velléda is active, intelligent, European, Mme. Bovary is stirred by multiple passions; Salammbô, on the contrary, is rooted in a fixed idea. She is a maniac, a kind of Saint Theresa. What does it matter? I am not sure of her reality, for neither I, you, nor anyone, neither ancient nor modern can know the oriental woman, because it is impossible to associate with her."

Thus Flaubert is protesting only against the concrete form of modernization which Sainte-Beuve has attributed to the figure of Salammbô. The modernization itself he grants as self-evident; for it is really quite immaterial whether one attributes to Hannibal's sister the psychology of a French *petite bourgeoise* of the nineteenth century or of a Spanish nun of the seventeenth. To which must be added that Flaubert is, of course, also modernizing the psychology of Saint Theresa.

This is not a minor aspect of the work and influence of Flaubert. He chooses an historical subject whose inner social-historical nature is of no concern to him and to which he can only lend the appearance of reality in an external, decorative, picturesque manner by means of the conscientious application of archaeology. But at some point he is forced to establish a contact with both himself and the reader, and this he does by modernizing the psychology of his characters. The proud and bitter paradox which contends that the novel has nothing at all to do with the present, is simply a defensive paradox contending against the trivialities of his age. We see from Flaubert's explanations which we have already quoted that *Salammbô* was more than just an artistic experiment. It is for this reason that the modernization of the characters acquires central importance; it is the only source

of movement and life in this frozen, lunar landscape of archaeological precision.

Naturally it is a ghostly illusion of life. And an illusion which dissolves the hyper-objective reality of the objects. In describing the individual objects of an historical *milieu* Flaubert is much more exact and plastic than any other writer before him. But these objects have nothing to do with the inner life of the characters. When Scott describes a medieval town or the habitat of a Scottish clan, these material things are part and parcel of the lives and fortunes of people whose whole psychology belongs to the same level of historical development and is a product of the same social-historical ensemble as these material things. This is how the older epic writers produced their "totality of objects." In Flaubert there is no such connection between the outside world and the psychology of the principal characters. And the effect of this lack of connection is to degrade the archaeological exactness of the outer world: it becomes a world of historically exact *costumes and decorations*, no more than a pictorial frame within which a purely modern story is unfolded.

The actual influence of Salammbô is in fact also connected with this modernization. Artists have admired the accomplishment of Flaubert's descriptions. But the effect of Salammbô herself was to provide a heightened image, a decorative symbol, of the hysterical longings and torments of middle-class girls in large cities. History simply provided a decorative, monumental setting for this hysteria, which in the present spends itself in petty and ugly scenes, and which thus acquired a tragic aura quite out of keeping with its real character. The effect is powerful but it shows that Flaubert, because of his embitterment with the shallow prose of his time, had become objectively untruthful and distorted the real proportions of life. The artistic superiority of his bourgeois novels lies precisely in the fact that in them the proportions between emotion and event, between desire and its translation into deeds correspond to the real, social-historical character of emotion and desire. In *Salammbô* the emotions, in themselves quite unmonumental, are falsely and distortedly monumentalized and hence inwardly unequal to such artistic heightening. The way in which the figure of Salammbô was regarded as a symbol during the obvious decline of Royalism and the psychological reaction which set in against Zola's naturalism, is best shown by the analysis which Paul Bourget gives of her: "It is a constant law in his [Flaubert's] eyes that human effort must end abortively, first of all because external circumstances run counter to one's dreams, secondly because even favourable circumstances cannot prevent the soul from devouring itself in the gratification of its chimera. Our desire floats before us like the veil of Tanit, the embroidered *Zaïmph*, before Salammbô. While she cannot seize it, the girl languishes in despair. As soon as she touches it, she must die."

This modernizing determines the structure of the plot. Its basis is formed by two motifs which are only very externally connected: a "crown and state" conflict between Carthage and the rebellious mercenaries, and the love episode of Salammbô herself. Their involvement with one another is quite external and inevitably remains so. Salammbô is as much a stranger to the interests of her homeland, to the life-and-death struggle of her native city, as Madame Bovary is to the medical practice of her husband. But while in the bourgeois novel this indifference can be made the vehicle of a plot with Emma Bovary at the centre precisely because she is a stranger to provincial daily life, here instead we have a "crown and state" story, outwardly grandiose and requiring therefore extensive preparation, with which Salammbô's destiny has no organic connection. The links are all either pure accidents or external pretexts. But in the presentation of the story the external pretext must inevitably suppress and stifle the main theme. External occasions take up the major part of the novel; the main theme is reduced to a small episode.

This lack of relation between the human

tragedy, which is what kindles the reader's interest, and the political action clearly shows the change already undergone by historical feeling in this age. The political plot is not only lifeless because it is cluttered up with descriptions of inessential objects, but because it has no discernible connection with any concrete form of popular life that we may experience. The mercenaries in this novel are the same kind of wild, irrational, chaotic mass as the inhabitants of Carthage. True we are told in exhaustive detail how the quarrel arises, namely the fact that the mercenaries have not been paid, and by what circumstances this quarrel grows into a war; yet we have not the least idea of the real social-historical and human driving force which causes these clashes to take place in the way they do. These remain an irrational, historical fact despite Flaubert's detailed portrayal. And since the human motives do not spring organically out of a concrete social-historical basis, but are given to isolated figures in a modernized form, they only confuse the total picture still further, reduce still further the social reality of the entire story.

This comes out at its crudest in the love episode of Mâtho. Sainte-Beuve, in his analysis of this love-maddened mercenary, rightly recalls the so-called historical novels of the seventeenth century, in which Alexander the Great, Cyrus or Genserich appeared as love-stricken heroes. "But Mâtho in love, this African Goliath, who behaves so wildly and childishly in sight of Salammbô, seems just as false to me; he is as outside nature as he is outside history."

And Sainte-Beuve rightly remarks on the feature peculiar to Flaubert here, what is new in this distortion of history as compared with the seventeenth century: whereas the lovers of the old novels had been sweet and sentimental, Mâtho has a bestially savage character. In short, those brutal and animal features are emphasized and placed at the centre, which occur later in Zola as characteristics of the life of modern workers and peasants. Thus Flaubert's portrayal is "prophetic." Not, however, in the sense in which Balzac's works were prophetic, anticipating the actual, future development of social types, but merely in a literary-historical sense, anticipating the later distortion of modern life in the works of the Naturalists.

Flaubert's defence against this criticism of Sainte-Beuve is extremely interesting, illuminating yet another aspect of his method of approach to history. This is how he defends himself against the charge of modernization in the figure of Mâtho: "Mâtho *prowls like a madman* round Carthage. Madness is the right word. Wasn't love, as conceived by the ancients, a madness, a curse, an illness sent by the gods?"

This defence bases itself apparently on historical evidence. But only apparently; for Flaubert never examines the real nature of love within the social life of antiquity, the connection of its different psychological forms with other forms of ancient life. His starting point is an analysis of the isolated *idea* of love, as we find it in certain ancient tragedies. Flaubert is right when he says for instance that the love of Phaedra in Euripides' *Hippolytus* is presented as a sudden passion, innocently visited upon her by the Gods. But it is an entirely unhistorical modernization of ancient life to take merely the subjective side of such tragic conflicts and then to blow this up into a "psychological peculiarity" of the whole of antiquity. Obviously, in certain cases individual love and passion did irrupt "suddenly" into people's lives and cause great tragic collisions. It is also true that these collisions were far more unusual in ancient life than in the period of development from the Middle Ages until modern times, when similar problems occurred, though in a different form in keeping with the changed social circumstances. The special manifestation of passion in the portrayals of the ancients is connected in the closest possible way with the special forms of the break-up of gentile society in antiquity. But this is the final ideological result of a particular development. If this result is then torn out of its social-historical context, if its subjective-psychological

side is isolated from the causes which produce it, if therefore the artist's point of departure is not existence but an isolated idea, then whatever one's apparent historical evidence one's only approach to this idea is via modernization. Only in Flaubert's imagination does Mâtho embody ancient love. In reality, he is a prophetic model of the decadent drunkards and madmen of Zola.

This connection between approaching history from the standpoint of an idea and portraying it as a compound of outward exoticism and inner modernity is so important for the whole artistic development of the second half of the nineteenth century that we may be allowed to illustrate it by a further example. Richard Wagner, whose points of similarity with Flaubert Nietzsche disclosed with spiteful shrewdness, discovers the brother-and-sister love of Siegmund and Sieglinde in the Edda. This is an unusually interesting, exotic phenomenon, and is made "intelligible" by a lavish display of decorative pomp and modern psychology. Marx in few words revealed Wagner's falsification of the social-historical connections. Engels, in his *Origin of the Family*, quotes this letter of Marx: "Was it ever possible that brother embraced sister as a bride?" To these "lewd gods" of Wagner who, quite in the modern manner, spice their love intrigues with a little incest, Marx replied: "In primitive times the sister *was* the wife, and that was moral." Wagner's example shows even more clearly than Flaubert's, how, by starting from an isolated idea rather than from actual existence, one inevitably ends up by misrepresenting and distorting history. What remains are the outward, soulless facts of history (here love between brother and sister) which are injected with an entirely modern sensibility, and the old story, the old occurrence serves only to give picturesqueness to this modern sensibility, to add to it a decorative grandeur which, as we have seen, it does not deserve.

This question, has, however, still another side which is of exceptional importance for modern developments. As we have seen, the inner emptiness of social-historical events, left by the rift between the outward happenings and the modernized psychology of the characters, gives rise to the exotic historical *milieu*. The historical event, emptied in this subjectivist manner of its inner greatness has to acquire a pseudo-monumentality by other means. For it is precisely the longing to escape from the triviality of modern bourgeois life which produces these historical themes.

One of the most important means of producing this pseudo-monumentality is the emphasis on brutality. We have already seen how the most significant and influential critics of the period, Taine and Brandes, lament the absence of such brutality in Scott. Sainte-Beuve, belonging to an older generation, notes its presence and predominance in *Salammbô* with great unease: "he cultivates atrocity. The man is good, excellent, the book is cruel. He believes that it is a proof of strength to appear inhuman in his books."

For anyone who knows *Salammbô* it is hardly necessary to quote examples. I shall simply mention the great contrast during the siege of Carthage: while Carthage's supply of water is cut off and the whole city is dying of thirst, the most terrible hunger rages in the camp of the mercenaries. Flaubert takes delight in giving detailed and cruel pictures of the sufferings of the masses in and around Carthage. There is never any humanity in this suffering; it is simply horrible, senseless torment. No single member of the masses is individually characterized, the suffering yields no single conflict or action which might humanly interest or grip us.

Here we may see the sharp opposition between the old and the new representation of history. The writers of the classical period of the historical novel were only interested in the cruel and terrible happenings of previous history insofar as they were necessary expressions of definite forms of class struggle (e.g. the cruelty of the Chouans in Balzac) and also because they gave birth of a similar necessity to great human passions and conflicts etc. (the

heroism of the Republican officers during the Chouans' massacre of them in the same novel). The placing of the cruel processes of social development in a necessary and intelligible connection and the relationship between these and the human greatness of the combatants take from the events their cruelty and brutality. Which does not mean that the cruelty and brutality are in any way ironed out or mitigated —the reproach which Taine and Brandes levelled at Scott; they are simply given their rightful place inside the total context.

Flaubert begins a development where the inhumanity of subject-matter and presentation, where atrocity and brutality become ends in themselves. These features acquire their central position owing to the weak presentation of what is the chief issue—the social development of man; indeed for the same reason they assume even more importance than even this position warrants. Since real greatness is everywhere replaced by extensiveness—the decorative splendour of the contrasts replaces the social-human connections—inhumanity, cruelty, atrocity and brutality become substitutes for the lost greatness of real history. At the same time they spring from the morbid longing of modern man to escape from the suffocating narrowness of everyday life, a longing which he projects into this pseudo-monumentality. Disgust with small and petty office intrigues produces the ideal image of the mass poisoner, Cesare Borgia.

Flaubert felt deeply hurt by Sainte-Beuve's accusation. But his objections to the critic do not exceed a feeling of injury. And this is not accidental. For the extraordinarily sensitive and highly moral Flaubert has against his will become the initiator of the inhuman in modern literature. The development of capitalism not only levels and trivializes, it also brutalizes.

This brutalization of feeling manifests itself in literature to an ever increasing extent, most clearly of all in the description and portrayal of love, where the physical-sexual side gains growing ascendancy over the passion itself. Think how the greatest portrayers of love—Shakes-

peare, Goethe and Balzac—confined themselves to the merest intimations in their description of the physical act itself. The interest
shown by modern literature in this aspect of
love on the one hand derives from the increasing brutalization of the real emotions of love,
which occurs in life itself, and on the other has
the consequence that writers are forced to
search for more and more exquisite, abnormal,
perverse etc. themes in order to escape monotony.

Flaubert himself, in this respect, stands at
the beginning of this development. And it is
very characteristic both for him as well as for
the entire development of the historical novel
during the crisis of decline of bourgeois realism
that these tendencies are much more pronounced in his historical novels than in his
pictures of modern society. In both, hatred and
disgust for the pettiness, triviality and mean-
ness of modern bourgeois life are expressed with
equal force, yet very differently in keeping with
the difference of subject-matter. In his contemporary novels Flaubert concentrates his
ironic attack on the portrayal of everyday
bourgeois life and average bourgeois man. As
an outstanding realist artist he thus achieves an
infinitely nuanced picture of that dismal grey-
ness which is a real aspect of this everyday life.
Precisely his naturalist tendencies restrain
Flaubert from any eccentricity in his treatment
of the inhuman forms of capitalist life. But his
historical novel, as we have seen, he considered
a liberation from the fetters of this monotonous
flatness. All that his naturalist conscience had
forced him to renounce in his picture of contemporary reality found a place here. In terms
of form—the colourfulness, the decorative
monumentality of an exotic *milieu*; in terms
of content—eccentric passions in their fullest
extent and uniqueness. And it is here that we
clearly see the social, moral and ideological
limitations of this great and sincere artist: while
he sincerely hates the capitalist present, his
hatred has no roots in the great popular and
democratic traditions either of the past or
present and therefore has no future perspective.

His hatred does not historically transcend its
object. Thus if in the historical novels the
suppressed passions break open their fetters, it
is the eccentric-individualist side of capitalist
man which comes to the fore, that inhumanity
which everyday life hypocritically seeks to conceal and subdue. The later decadents already
portray this side of capitalist inhumanity with
boastful cynicism. In Flaubert it appears in the
Bengal illumination of a romantic-historical
monumentality. Thus the sides which Flaubert
here reveals of the new manner of portraying
life do not become widespread until later and
he himself was not yet aware of them as such
general tendencies.

But the contradiction between Flaubert's
ascetic disgust with modern life and these inhuman excesses of a riotous and demented
imagination does not alter the fact that he
appears here as one of the most important
precursors of dehumanization in modern literature. This inhumanity is not, of course, in
every instance a simple and straightforward
capitulation to the dehumanizing tendencies of
capitalism, which is the simple and most general case, in literature as in life. The important
personalities of this crisis of decline, Flaubert,
Baudelaire, Zola and even Nietzsche, suffer
from this development and savagely oppose it;
yet the manner of their opposition leads to an
intensification in literature of capitalist dehumanization in life.

This modernizing of feelings, ideas and
thoughts, combined with archaeological faith-
fulness towards things and customs of no concern to us, which can therefore only appear
exotic, is the sole basis on which the question
of *language* in the historical novel can be correctly and concretely raised theoretically. It is
customary to-day to treat linguistic problems
separately from general aesthetic questions,
questions of concrete genres etc. All that this
produces, however, are abstract "principles"
and (equally abstract) subjective judgments of
taste. Thus if we now proceed to the problems
of language in the work of the first important
writer to modernize and exoticize history then

we must view them as the final artistic consequence of those tendencies we have seen at work previously in the break-up of the classical historical novel as a whole.

It is obviously that linguistically the problem of "necessary anachronism" plays a decisive role. The sheer fact that all epic is an account of something *past* establishes a close linguistic relation to the present. For it is a present-day storyteller who speaks to present-day readers of Carthage or the Renaissance, of the English Middle Ages or Imperial Rome. It follows therefore that archaism must be ruled out of the general linguistic tone of the historical novel as a superfluous artificiality. The point is to bring a past period *near* to a present-day reader. And it is a universal law of great narrative art that this results from plastically presented events; that in order to understand the psychology of people in distant ages we must understand and feel ourselves close to their social and natural conditions of life, their customs etc.

It is certainly more difficult to do this with history than with the present. The epic task, however, is fundamentally the same. An important epic writer—say Gottfried Keller, Romain Rolland or Gorky—recounting his childhood, would never think of using baby language in order to convey his early attempts at orientation in life, his first childish gropings and babblings. Artistic truth consists in correctly rendering the feelings, ideas and thoughts of a child in a language in which all this can be readily understood by the adult reader. In principle there is no more reason why a medieval person should be better and more truthfully portrayed by the use of archaic language than a child by linguistic imitation of its first babblings. For this reason the linguistic means of the historical novel are *in principle* no different from those of the contemporary novel.

The Flaubertian attitude to history inevitably leads to a disintegration of epic language. This is true even for as great a stylist as Flaubert himself. Flaubert is too important an artist, and much too great an artist of the word

to wish to evoke historical authenticity by means of a consistent archaic tone. Lesser contemporaries, however, readily yield to this very tempting pseudo-historical language form. Thus, Meinhold in Germany cleverly imitated the old chronicles of the Thirty Years' War in his *Bernsteinhexe* (*The Amber Witch*) so that the reader should think he is reading not a narrative about the past, but the notes of a contemporary, a "genuine document."

It is, of course, natural for epic, particularly historical epic, to make the event narrated appear real and factual. But it is a naturalistic mistake to think that this authenticity can be brought about by imitating the old language. This is of as little help as external archaeological authenticity if the essential social-human relations are not brought close to the reader. And the achievement of the latter renders the naturalist authenticity superfluous in either case. Hebbel, who praised the *Bernsteinhexe* as a whole, with correct arguments, and attributed great artistic sensibility to its author in other respects, says of the so-called authenticity of language in the novel: "The real language of the hero has as much place in the novel and in literature in general as his real boot in a painting."

This authenticity is in any case pointless unless the characters belong to the same linguistic area, and this alone shows the naturalist character of any argument favouring the use of archaic language. Pushkin ridicules such theories of "probability" in poetry and asks ironically how, according to such a theory, is a Philoctetes in French drama supposed to rejoice at the sounds of his long missed native Greek. Hebbel, in his criticism of Meinhold from which we have just quoted, expressed a similar thought: "If Meinhold were right, then in novel and drama an old German would have to speak old German, a Greek Greek, a Roman Roman, and Troilus and Cressida, Julius Caesar and Coriolanus could not have been written, at least not by Shakespeare." Hebbel shows that the *Bernsteinhexe* exercises its artistic effect despite rather than because of its archaic language.

It is important to stress the naturalist character of this use of archaic language. For again it is not a problem peculiar to the historical novel (or drama), but merely a specific naturalist degeneration which replaces real characterization by picturesque bagatelles. If Gerhart Hauptmann in his play *Florian Geyer* was incapable of portraying the basic class antagonisms inside the camp of the rebellious peasants, if, therefore, Götz, Wendel, Hippler, Karlstatt, Bubenleben, Jacob Kohl etc. acquire no political and historical physiognomy, then how much use was the "authentic" language of the time? Goethe, on the other hand, is able without this "authenticity" of language to give a moving portrayal of the division among the knights in the destinies of Götz and Weislingen. Hauptmann is a particularly instructive example. He has an unusually sensitive ear for different idioms and dialects; he is nearly always successful when he can characterize in this way. But this very ability proves itself to be a secondary thing, for the liveliness of his characters varies enormously in spite of it, depending upon principles of portrayal far transcending the faithful linguistic reproduction of the intonation of a given person, time and place.

We have deliberately quoted dramatic examples here, because in drama, the form of "the present" (Gegenwärtigkeit—Goethe), there would appear to be a stronger compulsion to let a character speak his "real" (i.e. archaized) language than in epic, where a present-day storyteller speaks *about* figures of the past, and for whom he also provides the formal linguistic means of expression. We can see from this how especially absurd is the use of archaic language in the historical novel. It is of *past human beings* that the deeds, emotions, ideas and thoughts are communicated to us. The characters must be genuine both in content and form; but the language is necessarily not theirs, it is the narrator's own.

In drama it is different. However, the conclusion which naturalism draws from this difference is just as fallacious and possibly more dangerous. Quite apart from the absurd consequences which Pushkin and Hebbel pointed out, the fact that dramatic action, characters and dialogue have the form of the present means that they must be present for the spectator, *for us*. Thus the language of drama must be more immediately, more directly intelligible than that of narrative. The greater scope which is both possible and necessary for "necessary anachronism" in historical drama (which we have discussed at length in the previous section) also determines the language of drama.

But as with epic, the rejection of archaism does not mean modernization. The limits of "necessary anachronism" in drama are likewise set by the historical authenticity of the deeds, thoughts, emotions and ideas of men. Thus, while Shakespeare's Brutus or Caesar stay within this limit, Shaw's comedy *Caesar and Cleopatra* is, albeit brilliantly, modernized through and through.

In Flaubert this question is not nearly as acute as in the later naturalists. Yet Sainte-Beuve can already ridicule a whole series of "authentic" details—the use of dogs' milk and flies' feet as cosmetics and similar curiosities. But these are not accidental in Flaubert, nor simply an attempt to produce a striking effect; this would be quite foreign to so serious and sincere an artist of the word. They derive, in his case too, from naturalist principles. The principle of the photographic authenticity of description and dialogue etc. can lead to nothing else. The ever more furious ransacking of technical dictionaries which goes on in the contemporary novel in order on the one hand to reproduce each object with professional accuracy and on the other to render it in an appropriate specialist jargon must in the historical novel lead to archaeologism. In neither case does the writer wish his objects to be universally understood as the material basis, the material mediator of human actions. They appear before the reader, rather, on the one hand, strange and unfamiliar (the stranger, the more interesting) and on the other in the jargon of the initiated, which even the experts of neighbouring fields cannot be expected to understand.

In debates on the historical novel modernization of language often appears as an *antinomous opposite* of archaism. In fact they are *connected* tendencies, mutually conditioning and complementing one another. The need to modernize language likewise springs from an unhistorical or anti-historical conception of the feelings, ideas and thoughts of men. The livelier the concrete historical approach to the being and consciousness of a past epoch, as in the classical historical novel, the more natural it is to avoid the phraseology of an emotional and intellectual world which is foreign to the past period, which does not make the feelings, ideas and thoughts of *past human beings intelligible to us*, but attributes our feelings etc. to them.

While introjection is the psychological basis of naturalism, its social-historical basis is that of analogy. We have heard Flaubert's own words as to Salammbô and her modern models in his controversy with Sainte-Beuve. We see the same modernization all along the line. Sainte-Beuve, for example, complains of Flaubert's portrayal of the Council meeting in Carthage. Flaubert replies: "You ask me where

I got such an idea of the council of Carthage? But from all the analogous *milieux* of the time of the Revolution, from the convention to the American Parliament, where until recently they still exchanged blows with sticks and shot at one another with revolvers, which sticks and revolvers were carried (like daggers) in coat sleeves. And my Carthaginians have more propriety than the Americans, since there was no public present."

It is obvious that with such a conception of social basis and psychology the modernization of language is *unavoidable*. The conception itself is modernized by means of analogy; the Council of Carthage is an American parliament minus gallery, Salammbô a Saint Theresa under oriental conditions etc. It is only consistent that the feelings, ideas and thoughts which have been introjected into the characters should also receive a modernized language.

In *Salammbô* all the tendencies of decline in the historical novel appear in concentrated form: the decorative monumentalization, the devitalizing, dehumanizing and at the same time making private of history. History becomes a large, imposing scene for purely private, intimate and subjective happenings.

Jean-Paul Sartre

[TOWARD A STUDY OF FLAUBERT] (1961)

LET US SUPPOSE that I wish to make a study of Flaubert—who is presented in histories of literature as the father of realism. I learn that he said: "I myself am Madame Bovary." I discover that his more subtle contemporaries—in par-

From *Search for a Method*, by Jean-Paul Sartre, translated by Hazel Barnes. Copyright © 1963 by Alfred A. Knopf, Inc. Reprinted by permission of the publisher.

ticular Baudelaire, with his "feminine" temperament—had surmised this identification. I learn that the "father of realism" during his trip through the Orient dreamed of writing the story of a mystic virgin, living in the Netherlands, consumed by dreams, a woman who would have been the symbol of Flaubert's own cult of art. Finally, going back to his biography, I discover his dependence, his obedience, his "relative being," in short all the qualities which at that period were commonly called "feminine." At last I find out, a little late, that his physicians dubbed him a nervous old woman and that he felt vaguely flattered. Yet it is certain that he was *not to any degree at all* an invert.[1] Our problem then—without leaving the work itself; that is, the literary significations—is to ask ourselves why the author (that is, the pure synthetic activity which creates Madame Bovary) was able to metamorphose himself into a woman, what signification the metamorphosis possesses *in itself* (which presupposes a phenomenological study of Emma Bovary in the book), just what this woman is (of whom Baudelaire said that she possesses at once the folly and the will of a man), what the artistic transformation of male into female means in the nineteenth century (we must study the context of *Mlle de Maupin*, etc.), and finally, just who Gustave Flaubert *must have been* in order to have within the field of his possibles the possibility of portraying himself as a woman. The reply is independent of all biography, since this problem could be posed in Kantian terms: "Under what conditions is the feminization of experience possible?" In order to answer it, we must never forget that the author's style is directly bound up with a conception of the world; the sentence and paragraph structure, the use and position of the substantive, the verb, etc., the arrangement of the paragraphs, and the qualities of the narrative—to refer to only a few specific points —all express hidden presuppositions which can be determined *differentially* without as yet resorting to biography. Nevertheless, we shall never arrive at anything but *problems*. It is true that the statements of Flaubert's contemporaries will help us. Baudelaire asserted that the profound meaning of *The Temptation of St. Anthony*, a furiously "artistic" work which Bouilhet called "a diarrhea of pearls" and which in a completely confused fashion deals with the great metaphysical themes of the period (the destiny of man, life, death, God, religion, nothingness, etc.), is fundamentally identical with that of *Madame Bovary*, a work which is (on the surface) dry and objective. What kind of person, then, can Flaubert be, must he be, to express his own reality in the form of a frenzied idealism and of a realism more spiteful than detached? Who can he, must he, be in order to objectify himself in his work first as a mystic monk and then some years later as a resolute, "slightly masculine" woman?

At this point it is necessary to resort to biography—that is, to the facts *collected* by Flaubert's contemporaries and *verified* by historians. The work poses questions to the life. But we must understand in what sense; the work as the objectification of the person is, in fact, *more complete, more total* than the life. It has its roots in the life, to be sure; it illuminates the life, but it does not find its total explanation in the life alone. But it is too soon as yet for this total explanation to become apparent to us. The life is illuminated by the work as a reality whose total determination is found outside of it—both in the conditions which produce it and in the artistic creation which fulfills it and *completes it by expressing it*. Thus the work—when one has examined it —becomes a hypothesis and a research tool to clarify the biography. It questions and holds on to concrete episodes as replies to its questions.[2]

---

[1] His letters to Louise Colet show him to be narcissistic and onanist; but he boasts of amorous exploits, which must be true, since he is addressing the only person who can be both witness and judge of them.

[2] I do not recall that anyone has been surprised that the Norman giant projected himself in his work as a woman. But I do not recall either that anyone has studied Flaubert's femininity (his truculent, "loudmouthed" side has misled critics; but this is only a bit of camouflage, Flaubert has confirmed it a hundred times). Yet the order is discernible: the *logical scandal* is Madame Bovary, a masculine woman and feminized man, a lyric and realistic work. It is this scandal with its peculiar contradictions which must draw our attention to the life of Flaubert and to his lived femininity. We must detect it in his behavior—and first of all, in his sexual behavior. Now his letters to Louise Colet are sexual behavior; they are each one moments in the diplomacy of Flaubert with regard to this pertinacious poetess. We shall not find an embryonic *Mad-*

But these answers *are not complete.* They are insufficient and limited insofar as the objectification in art is irreducible to the objectification in everyday behavior. There is a hiatus between the work and the life. Nevertheless, the man, with his human relations thus clarified, appears to us in turn as a synthetic collection of questions. The work has revealed Flaubert's narcissism, his onanism, his idealism, his solitude, his dependence, his femininity, his passivity. But these qualities in turn are problems for us. They lead us to suspect at once both social structures (Flaubert is a property owner, he lives on unearned income, etc.) and a *unique* childhood drama. In short, these regressive questions provide us with the means to question his family group as a reality lived and denied by the child Flaubert. Our questions are based on two sorts of information: objective testimonies about the family (class characteristics, family type, individual aspect) and furiously subjective statements by Flaubert about his parents, his brother, his sister, etc. At this level we must be able constantly to refer back to the work and to know whether it contains a biographical truth such as the correspondence itself (falsified by its author) cannot contain. But we must know also that the work *never* reveals the secrets of the biography; the book can at most serve as a schema or conducting thread allowing us to discover the secrets in the life itself.

At this level, we study the early childhood as a way of living general conditions without clearly understanding or reflecting on them; consequently, we may find the meaning of the lived experience in the intellectual petite bourgeoisie, formed under the Empire, and in its way of living the evolution of French society. Here we pass over into the pure objective; that is, into the historical totalization. It is History itself which we must question—the halted advance of family capitalism, the return of the landed proprietors, the contradictions in the government, the misery of a still insufficiently developed Proletariat. But these interrogations are *constituting* in the sense in which the Kantian concepts are called "constitutive"; for they permit us to realize concrete syntheses there where we had as yet only abstract, general conditions. Beginning with an obscurely lived childhood, we can reconstruct the true character of petit bourgeois families. We compare Flaubert's with the family of Baudelaire (at a more "elevated" social level), with that of the Goncourt brothers (a petit bourgeois family which entered into the nobility about the end of the eighteenth century by the simple acquisition of "noble" property), with that of Louis Bouilhet, etc. In this connection we study the real relations between scientists and practitioners (the father Flaubert) and industrialists (the father of his friend, Le Poittevin). In this sense the study of the child Flaubert, as a universality lived in particularity, enriches the general study of the petite bourgeoisie in 1830. By means of the structures presiding over the particular family group, we enrich and make concrete the always too general characteristics of the class considered; in discontinuous "collectives," for example, we apprehend the complex relation between a petite bourgeoise of civil servants and intellectuals, on the one hand, and the "elite" of industrialists and landed proprietors on the other, or, again, the *roots* of this petite bourgeoisie, its peasant origin, etc., its relations with fallen aristocrats.[3] It is on this level that we are going to discover the major contradiction which the child, Gustave Flaubert, lived in his own way: the opposition between the bourgeois analytic mind and the synthetic myths of religion. Here again a systematic cross-reference is established between the particular anecdotes which clarify these vague contradictions (because the stories gather them together into a

---

ame Bovary in the correspondence, but we shall greatly clarify the correspondence by means of Madame Bovary (and, of course, by the other works).

[3] Flaubert's father, the son of a village veterinarian (a royalist), "distinguished" by the imperial administration, marries a girl whose family is connected with the nobility through marriage. He associates with rich industrialists; he buys land.

single exploding whole) and the general determination of living conditions which allows us to reconstruct *progressively* (because they have already been studied) the material existence of the groups considered.

The sum total of these procedures—regression and cross-reference—has revealed what I shall call the profundity of the lived. Recently an essayist, thinking to refute existentialism, wrote: "It is not man who is profound; it is the world." He was perfectly right, and we agree with him without reservation. Only we should add that the world is human, the profundity of man is the world; therefore profundity comes to the world through man. The exploration of this profundity is a descent from the absolute concrete (*Madame Bovary* in the hands of a reader contemporary with Flaubert—whether it be Baudelaire or the Empress or the Prosecuting Attorney) to its most abstract conditioning (material conditions, the conflict of productive forces and of the relations of production insofar as these conditions appear in their universality and are given as lived by all the members of an undefined group [4]—that is, practically, by *abstract* subjects). Across *Madame Bovary* we can and must catch sight of the movement of land-owners and capitalists, the evolution of the rising classes, the slow maturation of the Proletariat: everything is there. But the most concrete significations are radically irreducible to the most abstract significations. The "differential" at each signifying plane reflects the differential of the higher plane by impoverishing it and by contracting it; it clarifies the differential of the lower plane and serves as a rubric for the synthetic unification of our most abstract knowing. This *cross-reference* contributes to enrich the object with all the profundity of History; it determines, within the historical totalization, the still empty location for the object.

At this point in our research we have still not succeeded in revealing anything more than a hierarchy of heterogeneous significations: *Madame Bovary*, Flaubert's "femininity," his childhood in a hospital building, existing contradictions in the contemporary petite bourgeoisie, the evolution of the family, of property, etc.[5] Each signification clarifies the other, but their irreducibility creates a veritable discontinuity between them. Each serves as an encompassing framework for the preceding, but the included signification is richer than the including signification. In a word, we have only the outline for the dialectical movement, not the movement itself.

It is then and only then that we must employ the progressive method. The problem is to recover the totalizing movement of enrichment which engenders each moment in terms of the prior moment, the impulse which starts from lived obscurities in order to arrive at the final objectification—in short, the *project* by which Flaubert, in order to escape from the petite bourgeoisie, will launch himself across the various fields of possibles toward the alienated objectification of himself and will constitute himself inevitably and indissolubly as the author of *Madame Bovary* and as that petit bourgeois which he refused to be. This project has *a meaning*, it is not the simple negativity of flight; by it a man aims at the production of himself in the world as a certain objective totality. It is not the pure and simple abstract decision to write which makes up the peculiar quality of Flaubert, but the decision to write in a certain manner in order to manifest himself in the world in a particular way; in a word, it is the particular signification—within the framework of the contemporary ideology—which he gives to literature as the negation of

[4] In reality the petite bourgeoisie in 1830 is a numerically defined group (although there obviously exist unclassifiable intermediaries who unite it with the peasant, the bourgeois, the landowners). But *methodologically* this concrete universal will always remain indeterminate because the statistics are incomplete.

[5] Flaubert's wealth consisted exclusively of real estate: this hereditary landlord will be ruined by industry; at the end of his life he will sell his lands in order to save his son-in-law, who was involved in foreign trade and had connections with Scandinavian industry. Meanwhile we shall see him often complaining that his rental income is less than what the same investments would bring in if his father had put it into industry.

his original condition and as the objective solution to his contradictions. To rediscover the meaning of this "wrenching away from toward . . ." we shall be aided by our knowing all the signifying planes which he has traversed, which we have interpreted as his footprints, and which have brought him to the final objectification. We have the series: as we move back and forth between material and social conditioning and the work, the problem is to find the *tension* extending from objectivity to objectivity, to discover the law of expansion which surpasses one signification *by means of* the following one and which maintains the second in the first. In truth the problem is to invent a movement, to re-create it, but the hypothesis is immediately verifiable; the only valid one is that which will realize within a creative movement the transverse unity of *all* the heterogeneous structures.

Nevertheless, the project is in danger of being deviated, like Sade's project, by the collective instruments; thus the terminal objectification perhaps does not correspond exactly to the original choice. We must take up the regressive analysis again, making a still closer study of the instrumental field so as to determine the possible deviations; we must employ all that we have learned about the contemporary techniques of Knowledge as we look again at the unfolding life so as to examine the evolution of the choices and actions, their coherence or their apparent incoherence. *St. Anthony* expresses the whole Flaubert in his purity and in all the contradictions of his original project, but *St. Anthony* is a failure. Bouilhet and Maxime du Camp condemn it completely; they demand that it "tell a story." *There* is the deviation. Flaubert tells an anecdote, but he makes it support everything—the sky, hell, himself, St. Anthony, etc. The monstrous, splendid work which results from it, that in which he is objectified and alienated, is *Madame Bovary*. Thus the return to the biography shows us the hiatuses, the fissures, the accidents, at the same time that it confirms the hypothesis (the hypothesis of the original project) by revealing the direction and continu-

ity of the life. We shall define the method of the existentialist approach as a regressive-progressive and analytic-synthetic method. It is at the same time an enriching cross-reference between the object (which contains the whole period as hierarchized significations) and the period (which contains the object in its totalization). In fact, when the object is *rediscovered* in its profundity and in its particularity, then instead of remaining external to the totalization (as it was up until the time when the Marxists undertook to integrate it into history), it enters immediately into contradiction with it. In short, the simple inert juxtaposition of the epoch and the object gives way abruptly to a living conflict.

If one has lazily defined Flaubert as a realist and if one has decided that realism suited the public in the Second Empire (which will permit us to develop a brilliant, completely false theory about the evolution of realism between 1857 and 1957), one will never succeed in comprehending either that strange monster which is *Madame Bovary* or the author or the public. Once more one will be playing with shadows. But if one has taken the trouble, in a study which is going to be long and difficult, to demonstrate within this novel the objectification of the subjective and its alienation—in short, if one grasps it in the concrete sense which it still holds at the moment when it escapes from its author and *at the same time* from the outside as an object which is allowed to develop freely, then the book abruptly comes to oppose the objective reality which it will hold for public opinion, for the magistrates, for contemporary writers. This is the moment to return to the period and to ask ourselves, for example, this very simple question: There was at that time a realist school—Courbet in painting and Duranty in literature were its representatives. Duranty had frequently presented his credo and drafted his manifestos. Flaubert despised realism and said so over and over throughout his life; he loved only the absolute purity of art. Why did the public decide at the outset that Flaubert was the realist, and why did it love in him *that particu-*

lar realism; that is, that admirable faked confession, that disguised lyricism, that implicit metaphysic? Why did it so value as an admirable character portrayal of a woman (or as a pitiless description of woman) what was at bottom only a poor disguised man? Then we must ask ourselves *what kind of realism* this public demanded or, if you prefer, what kind of literature it demanded under that name and why. This last moment is of primary importance; it is quite simply the moment of alienation. Flaubert sees his work stolen away from him by the very success which the period bestows on it; he no longer recognizes his book, it is foreign to him. Suddenly he loses his own objective existence. But at the same time his work throws a new light upon the period; it enables us to pose a new question to History: Just what must that period have been in order that it should demand *this* book and mendaciously find there its own image. Here we are at the veritable moment of historical action or of what I shall willingly call the misunderstanding. But this is not the place to develop this new point. It is enough to say by way of conclusion that the man and his time will be integrated into the dialectical totalization when we have shown how History surpasses this contradiction.

PART IV

Poet-Critics

INTRODUCTION

N₀ ONE CARES, no one can care, so much about poetry as
poets do. Whether the poet thinks of himself as a prophet, a
craftsman, a lover, an entertainer, an oyster who secretes pearls, or the
creating conscience of his race, his immediate task is to serve his art. In
a world indifferent to poetry, he blows upon his spark to keep it from
going out. The first great work of English literary criticism is Sidney's
Apology, and ever since poets have led the way in defining and justifying
the work they do. Indeed, most of the great English and American critics
have also been important poets; and never has this relation been more
clear than in the twentieth century. Modern poetry and modern criticism are intimately bound together. This section will illustrate some of
the concern that modern poets have felt for their art, and some of their
conclusions about it.

A poet can be a critic in several ways. First of all, of course, he can
write critical essays on other poets, like William Carlos Williams' essay
(reprinted below) on Walt Whitman. The special quality of such criticism is likely to be its personal involvement, its attempt to find lessons
that can be used. When Williams (like D. H. Lawrence) praises Whitman's kind of poetry, he is also writing about his own. Perhaps no poet
can ever wholly avoid this sort of special critical pleading; and whatever
loss of objectivity it entails, it also promotes readings of a searching and
brilliant intensity.

A second kind of criticism, represented here in the selections from
Rainer Maria Rilke, Hart Crane, and Allen Tate, is the poet's analysis

of his own work. Modern critics have argued that such analysis possesses no final authority—"Critical inquiries are not settled by consulting the oracle" (W. K. Wimsatt, Jr., and Monroe Beardsley, "The Intentional Fallacy," *Sewanee Review*, 1946)—but its peculiar interest is self-evident: we learn not only about the poem but about the creative process. If poets cannot always tell us what a poem *is*, they can tell us a great deal about how it came to be. The quality of such introspection, caught in the image of Narcissus, informs much of the best modern poetry—for instance, the work of Paul Valéry and Wallace Stevens, whose poems turn upon a fine self-consciousness. And who is more likely than the poet to see into the depths of his poem?

A third kind of criticism written by poets is theoretical: an inquiry into the nature of poetry. The majority of the essays in the following section are of this kind, encompassing Housman's emphasis on the physical impact of poetry and Yeats's praise for its subtle spirituality, Thomas's love of mystery and Auden's systematic discriminations. The poet sights beyond his work to its larger meaning. For many artists, none more than the French, critical theory aims ultimately at a *poetics*, an idea of art that holds criticism and poetry as one. Thus the poems of Mallarmé, Valéry, Rilke, and Stevens often seem fragments of a greater whole, a single poem or poetic world that exists eternally in the imagination. The poetry and criticism of such authors are continuous, twin aspects of the same search for higher truth. For poets who do not share such a commitment to the ideal, theory can nevertheless help to stimulate creation. Indeed, according to Yeats, virtually all serious artists "have had some philosophy, some criticism of their art; and it has often been this philosophy, or this criticism, that has evoked their most startling inspiration."

Poets also write a fourth kind of criticism, more limited: the technical. The high ideal discussed by Mallarmé follows his practical experiments with certain rhythms, and Williams listens to Whitman to discover not only a vision of America but a new poetic line. Here the authority of great poets is hardly open to question; they prove their technical ability with every poem they write. As Ezra Pound says, "If you wanted to know something about an automobile, would you go to a man who had made one and driven it, or to a man who had merely heard about it?" From this point of view the ultimate critical act of modern times was Pound's own thorough revision of Eliot's *The Waste Land*. Unfortunately, technical criticism of poetry can scarcely be reproduced; a poet's best act of criticism is often the X with which he excises inferior writing. Indeed, a critic—Auden calls him the Censor—lives in every poet, keeping watch over his bad lines and self-deceptions. As our introduction to Pound has indicated, moreover, there is a sense in which most significant poetry can be considered an act of criticism. The translator, the imitator, even the innovator, criticize past achievements by adapting them to new creations. Yet such internal kinds of criticism, at once the poet's goad and his conscience, are too intimately tied to creation to be separated from the poet himself. If every poet is a critic, the great poet-critics remain those who have been able to give their critical intuitions an objective form in prose.

Nor have such poet-critics been rare in our century. No other section of this anthology offers such an embarrassment of riches. Perhaps an equally distinguished selection could have been made from names we have omitted: for instance, among the Americans, Robert Frost, Conrad Aiken, and Randall Jarrell; or among the British, Robert Graves and William Empson; or such French poet-critics as Guillaume Apollinaire, Paul Claudel, André Breton, and Yves Bonnefoy; from Spain, Miguel de Unamuno and Jorge Guillén; from Italy, Eugenio Montale; from Greece, George Seferis; from Russia, Osip Mandelstam; from Germany, Gottfried Benn; from Chile, Pablo Neruda; from Mexico, Octavio Paz. Our own selection tries to present a variety of approaches. We have given preference to criticism that only poets could have written: criticism that describes the author's own poetry or poetics, criticism that other poets have thought fruitful. Many of these essays lead back to the poet's work. We hope that the student will return to the poems of Rilke or Stevens with new ideas about them, and then return to the criticism with a better understanding of its genesis. Hopefully, too, this section may provoke some thought about the relations between poetry and discursive argument, and about the nature of the poetic enterprise itself.

A Note on Sources

Oscar Wilde (1854–1900), the author of *The Importance of Being Earnest* and *The Ballad of Reading Gaol,* published his novel *The Picture of Dorian Gray* in 1891, the same year as a book of literary criticism, *Intentions.* Its essays include "The Decay of Lying" and "The Critic as Artist." Richard Ellmann has edited his critical writings, *The Artist as Critic* (1969).

A. E. Housman (1859–1936), a distinguished English lyric poet and classical scholar, had a congenital aversion to literary criticism. His occasional essays are gathered in *Selected Prose* (1961).

W. B. Yeats (1865–1939), the great Irish poet, wrote literary criticism throughout his career, much of it collected in *Essays and Introductions* (1961). The student of Yeats's later phase will be especially interested in "A General Introduction for My Work" (1937) and *Letters on Poetry to Dorothy Wellesley* (1940).

Stéphane Mallarmé (1842–1898), French Symbolist poet, was influenced by Poe's essay "The Philosophy of Composition," and by Baudelaire, who had translated it. Much of Mallarmé's cryptic, poetic criticism has been translated by Bradford Cook, *Selected Prose Poems, Essays, & Letters* (1956).

Paul Valéry (1871–1945) was the most self-conscious of modern poets; he explored philosophical problems of aesthetics in relation to his own processes of composition. His analysis of his great poem "Le

Cimetière marin" is translated by Denise Folliot with other essays on *The Art of Poetry* (1958).

Rainer Maria Rilke (1875–1926), the Austrian lyric poet, translated and corresponded with Valéry. His most famous poems, the *Duino Elegies* and the *Sonnets to Orpheus,* were completed in an unparalleled burst of inspiration in February 1922. His theory of art is movingly expressed in *Letters to a Young Poet,* tr. M. D. Herter Norton (1954).

D. H. Lawrence (1885–1930), British novelist and poet, is best known as a critic for *Studies in Classic American Literature* (1923). Anthony Beal has edited his *Selected Literary Criticism* (1966).

Hart Crane (1899–1932), American poet, wrote little formal literary criticism. Brom Weber has included some literary essays with Crane's *Complete Poems* (1966).

John Crowe Ransom (1888–   ), the most prominent of that group of Southern poets called the "Fugitives," was a founder of *The Kenyon Review.* His influential books of literary essays include *God Without Thunder* (1930), *The World's Body* (1938), and *The New Criticism* (1941).

Allen Tate (1899–   ), an American poet whose early work was associated with Ransom's, has written an important novel about the Civil War, *The Fathers* (1938), as well as many volumes of poetry and criticism, the latter collected in *Essays of Four Decades* (1968).

Wallace Stevens (1879–1955) has come to be recognized as among the greatest American poets. In addition to his literary essays, collected in *The Necessary Angel* (1951) and *Opus Posthumous* (1957), his *Letters,* ed. Holly Stevens (1966), contain much practical criticism.

William Carlos Williams (1883–1963), author and physician, was with Whitman the most patriotic of major American poets. His attempt to write in a native poetic language and rhythm has profoundly influenced a generation of Americans. *Selected Essays* (1954) includes much of his prolific occasional criticism.

Dylan Thomas (1914–1953), Welsh lyric poet, left a few literary essays in *Quite Early One Morning* (1954). His *Letters to Vernon Watkins* (1957) and *Selected Letters,* ed. Constantine Fitzgibbon (1966), are rich in comments on poetry.

W. H. Auden (1907–   ), born in England, became an American citizen in 1946. In addition to many volumes of poems, he has published a study of the "iconography of the sea," *The Enchafèd Flood* (1950), and numerous essays on literature and the other arts, many of the best collected in *The Dyer's Hand* (1962).

Oscar Wilde

PREFACE TO
THE PICTURE OF DORIAN GRAY (1891)

THE ARTIST is the creator of beautiful things.

To reveal art and conceal the artist is art's aim. The critic is he who can translate into another manner or a new material his impression of beautiful things.

The highest, as the lowest, form of criticism is a mode of autobiography.

Those who find ugly meanings in beautiful things are corrupt without being charming. This is a fault.

Those who find beautiful meanings in beautiful things are the cultivated. For these there is hope.

They are the elect to whom beautiful things mean only Beauty.

There is no such thing as a moral or an immoral book. Books are well written, or badly written. That is all.

The nineteenth century dislike of Realism is the rage of Caliban seeing his own face in a glass.

The nineteenth century dislike of Romanticism is the rage of Caliban not seeing his own face in a glass.

The moral life of man forms part of the subject-matter of the artist, but the morality of art consists in the perfect use of an imperfect medium. No artist desires to prove anything. Even things that are true can be proved.

No artist has ethical sympathies. An ethical sympathy in an artist is an unpardonable mannerism of style.

No artist is ever morbid. The artist can express everything.

Thought and language are to the artist instruments of an art.

Vice and virtue are to the artist materials for an art.

From the point of view of form, the type of all the arts is the art of the musician. From the point of view of feeling, the actor's craft is the type.

All art is at once surface and symbol.

Those who go beneath the surface do so at their peril.

Those who read the symbol do so at their peril.

It is the spectator, and not life, that art really mirrors.

Diversity of opinion about a work of art shows that the work is new, complex, and vital.

When critics disagree the artist is in accord with himself.

We can forgive a man for making a useful thing as long as he does not admire it. The only excuse for making a useless thing is that one admires it intensely.

All art is quite useless.

A. E. Housman

FROM

THE NAME AND NATURE OF POETRY (1933)

IN THESE six simple words of Milton—

Nymphs and shepherds, dance no more—

what is it that can draw tears, as I know it can, to the eyes of more readers than one? What in the world is there to cry about? Why have the mere words the physical effect of pathos when the sense of the passage is blithe and gay? I can only say, because they are poetry, and find their way to something in man which is obscure and latent, something older than the present organisation of his nature, like the patches of fen which still linger here and there in the drained lands of Cambridgeshire.

Poetry indeed seems to me more physical than intellectual. A year or two ago, in common with others, I received from America a request that I would define poetry. I replied that I could no more define poetry than a terrier can define a rat, but that I thought we both recognised the object by the symptoms which it provokes in us. One of these symptoms was described in connexion with another object by Eliphaz the Temanite: "A spirit passed before my face: the hair of my flesh stood up." Experience has taught me, when I am shaving of a morning, to keep watch over my thoughts, because, if a line of poetry strays into my memory, my skin bristles so that the razor ceases to act. This particular symptom is accompanied by a shiver down the spine; there is another which consists in a constriction of the throat and a precipitation of water to the eyes; and there is a

From *Selected Prose*, edited by John Carter. Reprinted by permission of Cambridge University Press.

third which I can only describe by borrowing a phrase from one of Keats's last letters, where he says, speaking of Fanny Brawne, "everything that reminds me of her goes through me like a spear." The seat of this sensation is the pit of the stomach.

My opinions on poetry are necessarily tinged, perhaps I should say tainted, by the circumstance that I have come into contact with it on two sides. We were saying a while ago that poetry is a very wide term, and inconveniently comprehensive: so comprehensive is it that it embraces two books, fortunately not large ones, of my own. I know how this stuff came into existence; and though I have no right to assume that any other poetry came into existence in the same way, yet I find reason to believe that some poetry, and quite good poetry, did. Wordsworth for instance says that poetry is the spontaneous overflow of powerful feelings, and Burns has left us this confession, "I have two or three times in my life composed from the wish rather than the impulse, but I never succeeded to any purpose." In short I think that the production of poetry, in its first stage, is less an active than a passive and involuntary process; and if I were obliged, not to define poetry, but to name the class of things to which it belongs, I should call it a secretion; whether a natural secretion, like turpentine in the fir, or a morbid secretion, like the pearl in the oyster. I think that my own case, though I may not deal with the material so cleverly as the oyster does, is the latter; because I have seldom written poetry unless I was rather out of health, and the experience, though pleasurable, was generally agitating and exhausting. If only that you may know what to avoid, I will give some account of the process.

Having drunk a pint of beer at luncheon—beer is a sedative to the brain, and my afternoons are the least intellectual portion of my life—I would go out for a walk of two or three hours. As I went along, thinking of nothing in particular, only looking at things around me and following the progress of the seasons, there would flow into my mind, with sudden and unaccountable emotion, sometimes a line or two of verse, sometimes a whole stanza at once, accompanied, not preceded, by a vague notion of the poem which they were destined to form part of. Then there would usually be a lull of an hour or so, then perhaps the spring would bubble up again. I say bubble up, because, so far as I could make out, the source of the suggestions thus proffered to the brain was an abyss which I have already had occasion to mention, the pit of the stomach. When I got home I wrote them down, leaving gaps, and hoping that further inspiration might be forthcoming another day. Sometimes it was, if I took my walks in a receptive and expectant frame of mind; but sometimes the poem had to be taken in hand and completed by the brain, which was apt to be a matter of trouble and anxiety, involving trial and disappointment, and sometimes ending in failure. I happen to remember distinctly the genesis of the piece which stands last in my first volume. Two of the stanzas, I do not say which, came into my head, just as they are printed, while I was crossing the corner of Hampstead Heath between the Spaniard's Inn and the footpath to Temple Fortune. A third stanza came with a little coaxing after tea. One more was needed, but it did not come: I had to turn to and compose it myself, and that was a laborious business. I wrote it thirteen times, and it was more than a twelvemonth before I got it right.

W. B. Yeats

THE SYMBOLISM OF POETRY (1900)

SYMBOLISM, as seen in the writers of our day, would have no value if it were not seen also, under one "disguise or another, in every great imaginative writer," writes Mr. Arthur Symons in *The Symbolist Movement in Literature*, a subtle book which I cannot praise as I would, because it has been dedicated to me; and he goes on to show how many profound writers have in the last few years sought for a philosophy of poetry in the doctrine of symbolism, and how even in countries where it is almost scandalous to seek for any philosophy of poetry, new writers are following them in their search. We do not know what the writers of ancient times talked of among themselves, and one bull is all that remains of Shakespeare's talk, who was on the edge of modern times; and the journalist is convinced, it seems, that they talked of wine and women and politics, but never about their art, or never quite seriously about their art. He is certain that no one who had a philosophy of his art, or a theory of how he should write, has ever made a work of art, that people have no

Reprinted with permission of The Macmillan Company from *Essays and Introductions* by William Butler Yeats. © Mrs. W. B. Yeats, 1961.

imagination who do not write without fore-thought and afterthought as he writes his own articles. He says this with enthusiasm, because he has heard it at so many comfortable dinner-tables, where some one had mentioned through carelessness, or foolish zeal, a book whose diffi-culty had offended indolence, or a man who had not forgotten that beauty is an accusation. Those formulas and generalisations, in which a hidden sergeant has drilled the ideas of jour-nalists and through them the ideas of all but all the modern world, have created in their turn a forgetfulness like that of soldiers in battle, so that journalists and their readers have forgot-ten, among many like events, that Wagner spent seven years arranging and explaining his ideas before he began his most characteristic music; that opera, and with it modern music, arose from certain talks at the house of one Giovanni Bardi of Florence; and that the Pléiade laid the foundations of modern French literature with a pamphlet. Goethe has said, "a poet needs all philosophy, but he must keep it out of his work," though that is not always nec-essary; and almost certainly no great art, outside England, where journalists are more powerful and ideas less plentiful than elsewhere, has arisen without a great criticism, for its herald or its interpreter and protector, and it may be for this reason that great art, now that vulgarity has armed itself and multiplied itself, is perhaps dead in England.

All writers, all artists of any kind, in so far as they have had any philosophical or critical power, perhaps just in so far as they have been deliberate artists at all, have had some philoso-phy, some criticism of their art; and it has often been this philosophy, or this criticism, that has evoked their most startling inspiration, calling into outer life some portion of the divine life, or of the buried reality, which could alone extin-guish in the emotions what their philosophy or their criticism would extinguish in the intellect. They have sought for no new thing, it may be, but only to understand and to copy the pure in-spiration of early times, but because the divine life wars upon our outer life, and must needs

change its weapons and its movements as we change ours, inspiration has come to them in beautiful startling shapes. The scientific move-ment brought with it a literature which was al-ways tending to lose itself in externalities of all kinds, in opinion, in declamation, in pictur-esque writing, in word-painting, or in what Mr. Symons has called an attempt "to build in brick and mortar inside the covers of a book"; and now writers have begun to dwell upon the element of evocation, of suggestion, upon what we call the symbolism in great writers.

II

In "Symbolism in Painting," I tried to de-scribe the element of symbolism that is in pic-tures and sculpture, and described a little the symbolism in poetry, but did not describe at all the continuous indefinable symbolism which is the substance of all style.

There are no lines with more melancholy beauty than these by Burns:—

> The white moon is setting behind the white wave,[1]
> And Time is setting with me, O!

and these lines are perfectly symbolical. Take from them the whiteness of the moon and of the wave, whose relation to the setting of Time is too subtle for the intellect, and you take from them their beauty. But, when all are together, moon and wave and whiteness and setting Time and the last melancholy cry, they evoke an emotion which cannot be evoked by any other arrangement of colours and sounds and forms. We may call this metaphorical writing, but it is better to call it symbolical writing, be-cause metaphors are not profound enough to be moving, when they are not symbols, and when they are symbols they are the most perfect of all, because the most subtle, outside of pure sound, and through them one can best find out what symbols are. If one begins the reverie with any beautiful lines that one can remember, one

[1] [Burns actually wrote:—
"The wan moon is setting ayont the white wave."]

finds they are like those by Burns. Begin with this line by Blake:—

The gay fishes on the wave when the moon
   sucks up the dew;

or these lines by Nash:—

   Brightness falls from the air,
   Queens have died young and fair,
   Dust hath closed Helen's eye;

or these lines by Shakespeare:—

   Timon hath made his everlasting mansion
   Upon the beached verge of the salt flood;
   Who once a day with his embossed froth
   The turbulent surge shall cover;

or take some line that is quite simple, that gets its beauty from its place in a story, and see how it flickers with the light of the many symbols that have given the story its beauty, as a sword-blade may flicker with the light of burning towers.

All sounds, all colours, all forms, either because of their preordained energies or because of long association, evoke indefinable and yet precise emotions, or, as I prefer to think, call down among us certain disembodied powers, whose footsteps over our hearts we call emotions; and when sound, and colour, and form are in a musical relation, a beautiful relation to one another, they become, as it were, one sound, one colour, one form, and evoke an emotion that is made out of their distinct evocations and yet is one emotion. The same relation exists between all portions of every work of art, whether it be an epic or a song, and the more perfect it is, and the more various and numerous the elements that have flowed into its perfection, the more powerful will be the emotion, the power, the god it calls among us. Because an emotion does not exist, or does not become perceptible and active among us, till it has found its expression, in colour or in sound or in form, or in all of these, and because no two modulations or arrangements of these evoke the same emotion, poets and painters and musicians, and in a less degree because their effects are momentary, day and night and cloud and shadow, are continually making and unmaking mankind. It is indeed only those things which seem useless or very feeble that have any power, and all those things that seem useful or strong, armies, moving wheels, modes of architecture, modes of government, speculations of the reason, would have been a little different if some mind long ago had not given itself to some emotion, as a woman gives herself to her lover, and shaped sounds or colours or forms, or all of these, into a musical relation, that their emotion might live in other minds. A little lyric evokes an emotion, and this emotion gathers others about it and melts into their being in the making of some great epic; and at last, needing an always less delicate body, or symbol, as it grows more powerful, it flows out, with all it has gathered, among the blind instincts of daily life, where it moves a power within powers, as one sees ring within ring in the stem of an old tree. This is maybe what Arthur O'Shaughnessy meant when he made his poets say they had built Nineveh with their sighing; and I am certainly never sure, when I hear of some war, or of some religious excitement, or of some new manufacture, or of anything else that fills the ear of the world, that it has not all happened because of something that a boy piped in Thessaly. I remember once telling a seeress to ask one among the gods who, as she believed, were standing about her in their symbolic bodies, what would come of a charming but seeming trivial labour of a friend, and the form answering, "the devastation of peoples and the overwhelming of cities." I doubt indeed if the crude circumstance of the world, which seems to create all our emotions, does more than reflect, as in multiplying mirrors, the emotions that have come to solitary men in moments of poetical contemplation; or that love itself would be more than an animal hunger but for the poet and his shadow the priest, for unless we believe that outer things are the reality, we must believe that the gross is the shadow of the subtle, that things are wise before they become foolish, and secret before they cry out in the market-place. Solitary men in moments of contemplation receive, as I think, the creative impulse from the lowest of the Nine Hierarchies, and so make and unmake mankind, and even the world itself, for does not "the eye altering alter all"?

Our towns are copied fragments from our breast;
And all man's Babylons strive but to impart
The grandeurs of his Babylonian heart.

III

The purpose of rhythm, it has always seemed to me, is to prolong the moment of contemplation, the moment when we are both asleep and awake, which is the one moment of creation, by hushing us with an alluring monotony, while it holds us waking by variety, to keep us in that state of perhaps real trance, in which the mind liberated from the pressure of the will is unfolded in symbols. If certain sensitive persons listen persistently to the ticking of a watch, or gaze persistently on the monotonous flashing of a light, they fall into the hypnotic trance; and rhythm is but the ticking of a watch made softer, that one must needs listen, and various, that one may not be swept beyond memory or grow weary of listening; while the patterns of the artist are but the monotonous flash woven to take the eyes in a subtler enchantment. I have heard in meditation voices that were forgotten the moment they had spoken; and I have been swept, when in more profound meditation, beyond all memory but of those things that came from beyond the threshold of waking life. I was writing once at a very symbolical and abstract poem, when my pen fell on the ground; and as I stooped to pick it up, I remembered some fantastic adventure that yet did not seem fantastic, and then another like adventure, and when I asked myself when these things had happened, I found that I was remembering my dreams for many nights. I tried to remember what I had done the day before, and then what I had done that morning; but all my waking life had perished from me, and it was only after a struggle that I came to remember it again, and as I did so that more powerful and startling life perished in its turn. Had my pen not fallen on the ground and so made me turn from the images that I was weaving into verse, I would never have known that meditation had become trance, for I would have been like one who does not know that he is passing through a wood because his eyes are on the pathway. So I think that in the making and in the understanding of a work of art, and the more easily if it is full of patterns and symbols and music, we are lured to the threshold of sleep, and it may be far beyond it, without knowing that we have ever set our feet upon the steps of horn or of ivory.

IV

Besides emotional symbols, symbols that evoke emotions alone,—and in this sense all alluring or hateful things are symbols, although their relations with one another are too subtle to delight us fully, away from rhythm and pattern,—there are intellectual symbols, symbols that evoke ideas alone, or ideas mingled with emotions; and outside the very definite traditions of mysticism and the less definite criticism of certain modern poets, these alone are called symbols. Most things belong to one or another kind, according to the way we speak of them and the companions we give them, for symbols, associated with ideas that are more than fragments of the shadows thrown upon the intellect by the emotions they evoke, are the playthings of the allegorist or the pedant, and soon pass away. If I say "white" or "purple" in an ordinary line of poetry, they evoke emotions so exclusively that I cannot say why they move me; but if I bring them into the same sentence with such obvious intellectual symbols as a cross or a crown of thorns, I think of purity and sovereignty. Furthermore, innumerable meanings, which are held to "white" or to "purple" by bonds of subtle suggestion, and alike in the emotions and in the intellect, move visibly through my mind, and move invisibly beyond the threshold of sleep, casting lights and shadows of an indefinable wisdom on what had seemed before, it may be, but sterility and noisy violence. It is the intellect that decides where the reader shall ponder over the procession of the symbols, and if the symbols are merely emotional, he gazes from amid the accidents and destinies of the world; but if the symbols are intellectual too, he becomes himself a part of pure intellect, and he is himself mingled with the procession. If I watch a rushy pool in the moonlight, my emotion at its beauty is mixed with memories of the man that I have seen ploughing by its margin, or of the lovers I saw there a night ago; but if I look at the moon herself and remember any of her ancient names and meanings, I move among divine people, and things that have shaken off our mortality, the tower of ivory, the queen of waters, the shining stag among enchanted woods, the white hare sitting upon the hilltop, the fool of Faery with his shining cup full of dreams, and it may be "make a friend of one of these images of wonder," and "meet the Lord in the air." So, too, if one is moved by Shakespeare, who is content with emotional symbols that he may come the nearer to our sympathy, one is mixed with the whole spectacle of the world; while if one is moved by Dante, or by the myth of Demeter, one is mixed into the shadow of God or of a goddess. So, too, one is furthest from symbols when one is busy doing this or that, but the soul moves among symbols and unfolds in symbols when trance, or madness, or deep meditation has withdrawn it from every impulse but its own. "I then saw," wrote Gérard de Nerval of his madness, "vaguely drifting into form, plastic images of antiquity, which outlined themselves, became definite, and seemed to represent symbols of which I only seized the idea with difficulty." In an earlier time he would have been of that multitude whose souls austerity withdrew, even more perfectly than madness could withdraw his soul, from hope and memory, from desire and regret, that they might reveal those processions of symbols that men bow to before altars, and woo with incense and offerings. But being of our time, he has been like Maeterlinck, like Villiers de l'Isle-Adam in *Axël*, like all who are preoccupied with intellectual symbols in our time, a fore-shadower of the new sacred book, of which all the arts, as somebody has said, are beginning to dream. How can the arts overcome the slow dying of men's hearts that we call the progress of the world, and lay their hands upon men's heartstrings again, without becoming the garment of religion as in old times?

v

If people were to accept the theory that poetry moves us because of its symbolism, what change should one look for in the manner of our poetry? A return to the way of our fathers, a casting out of descriptions of nature for the sake of nature, of the moral law for the sake of the moral law, a casting out of all anecdotes and of that brooding over scientific opinion that so often extinguished the central flame in Tennyson, and of that vehemence that would make us do or not do certain things; or, in other words, we should come to understand that the beryl stone was enchanted by our fathers that it might unfold the pictures in its heart, and not to mirror our own excited faces, or the boughs waving outside the window. With this change of substance, this return to imagination, this understanding that the laws of art, which are the hidden laws of the world, can alone bind the imagination, would come a change of style, and we would cast out of serious poetry those energetic rhythms, as of a man running, which are the invention of the will with its eyes always on something to be done or undone; and we would seek out those wavering, meditative, organic rhythms, which are the embodiment of the imagination, that neither desires nor hates, because it has done with time, and only wishes to gaze upon some reality, some beauty; nor would it be any longer possible for anybody to deny the importance of form, in all its kinds, for although you can expound an opinion, or describe a thing, when your words are not quite well chosen, you cannot give a body to something that moves beyond the senses, unless your words are as subtle, as complex, as full of mysterious life, as the body of a flower or of a woman. The form of sincere poetry, unlike the form of the "popular poetry," may indeed be sometimes obscure, or ungrammatical as in some of the best of the *Songs of Innocence and Experience*, but it must have the perfections that escape analysis, the subtleties that have a new meaning every day, and it must have all this whether it be but a little song made out of a moment of dreamy indolence, or some great epic made out of the dreams of one poet and of a hundred generations whose hands were never weary of the sword.

Stéphane Mallarmé

FROM MUSIC AND LETTERS (1894)

LADIES AND GENTLEMEN:

I have been invited on your behalf to speak in some detail of our present literary situation. The time is especially appropriate.

For I bring news—the most amazing and unprecedented news.

We have been experimenting with verse.

Governments change; prosody remains ever intact; perhaps because during revolutions it goes unnoticed or because attack is not called for upon a dogma considered incapable of change.

There should be no delay in discussing this subject (think of the breathless guest, fresh from his travels, who has been witness to an extraordinary event; he will have no peace until he has poured forth his story). For verse is everything, from the moment we take pen in hand. As long as there is cadence, there will be style and versification. That is why the careful prose of discriminating writers—ornamental prose—can always be thought of as broken verse; it plays with its own tones and hidden rhymes, like a thyrsus of infinite complexity.

Such is the flowering of what we have come to call the *prose-poem*.

Meanwhile, the ancient and regular verse stands by with its very strict, numerical, and simple nature.

There can be no doubt that we have now reached the point of separation between the two.

At the beginning of this century, the keen and powerful poetic instinct of the Romantics combined these elements and created flowing alexandrines with regular pauses and run-on lines. Now, however, the combination is breaking up into two separate wholes. Our recent search has apparently been brought to a close by the fortunate discovery of *free verse*, which I like to call an individual modulation; for every soul is a knot of rhythm.

The inevitable result was disagreement. Naturally, certain of the pioneering spirits ventured far afield and thought they had done with what we must call "official" verse. They had not, however; for it will be used on special occasions; their attempt at divorce was overbold, but it was the only one and it will be tempered.

Those who looked askance at the whole affair probably think it was a waste of time.

On the contrary.

For authentic works of art were born, quite

Originally a lecture, delivered in French, at Oxford and Cambridge.

From *Selected Prose Poems, Essays & Letters*, translated by Bradford Cook. Reprinted by permission of The Johns Hopkins Press.

apart from the fight over form; and even if their value goes unrecognized, let us prize the special silence which will take their place and thus provide much-needed rest for the ancient instrument of our music. On special occasions verse will always thunder. Yet it should be exceptional, despite the fact that all measured writing, as we have just observed, *is* verse by definition. Similarly, Literature should continue to be the rarest of phenomena, despite our common desire to perpetuate it throughout the ages. French verse in particular is a delicate instrument and should be used sparingly. But now, after the recent interval of silence and hesitation, eternal verse may once again rise up with all its perfect tonalities and flow renewed —rise, accompanied by its newest elements, to the sublime.

Here, then, was a purifying storm; and it is entirely to the credit of the recent generation that, in the midst of all confusion, the act of writing was studied through to its very origin. The greatest progress was made in their answer to a question which I should ask quite simply in the following way: is there a reason for writing at all? It is not *description* which can unveil the efficacy and beauty of monuments, seas, or the human face in all their maturity and native state, but rather *evocation, allusion, suggestion.* These somewhat arbitrary terms reveal what may well be a very decisive tendency in modern literature, a tendency which limits literature and yet sets it free. For what is the magic charm of art, if not this: that, beyond the confines of a fistful of dust or of all other reality, beyond the book itself, beyond the very text, it delivers up that volatile scattering which we call the Spirit, Who cares for nothing save universal musicality.

So now you are up to date on the most recent poetic "fever," its sudden jumps and noble hesitations.

But we cannot let it go at that; for surely I have come here to speak to you of something far greater than the mere renewal of rites and rhymes—something which I scarcely grasp myself; indeed, we may finally *fail* to grasp it; but

let us hope at least to touch upon it. You bid me in your kindness to discuss my favorite theme; and fully realizing, as I do, your expectations, I am revisited by that vague desire of bygone days (which, in my solitude, I could never fulfill) to devote some special evening to an all-embracing discovery (from the heavens to the abyss) of that struggle with the Ideal which certain of my contemporaries are now waging—as others struggle with social problems, for example. And so, without further ado, let me ask a question which may seem startling to an audience long since devoted to literary elegance: does Literature exist? Exist in some form other than that convention of classical periods which was the art of etching and refining ideas in all fields? It is axiomatic that in order to perfect the building or the discovery, an architect, a jurist, or a doctor must finally raise them to the level of discourse. In short, everything which emanates from the human mind must be reintegrated. The subject is generally immaterial.

Very few people have faced up to this problem which looms large only late in life. I too have been tardy, and now I suddenly hesitate, when I should rather wish to speak with full confidence upon the subject. Perhaps this sort of inquiry has been complacently avoided because it was considered dangerous by gifted men who hastened to fulfill their promise— who feared its efficacy might be lost if they questioned it too deeply. All purposes endure: we force them into life through faith or facile self-persuasion; and so, for *us*, they do live. (Consider the shepherd, whose voice is echoed mockingly by neighboring rocks; yet, in his ear, never echoed so.) Be that as it may, I still find contentment and wisdom in shedding even a fading light on the basic reasons for this vocation.

So, now, to come back to that startling question I asked a few moments ago (when I boldly expressed my doubts about the legitimate function of literature—whereas I should perhaps have been content to wreathe its altar)—to come back to that sort of indefinable attack I made (bereft though I am of the power to make it), I would reply with conscious exaggeration (and now you are forewarned): *Yes,* Literature *does* exist and, I may add, exists alone and all-exclusively. Such, at least, is the best name we can give to the achievement I speak of.

At any moment in history, a man may appear who will be fully forgetful—and always remember that he will be *consciously* forgetful—of the intellectual impedimenta of his contemporaries. Using the most elemental and elementary of means, he will try to discover (for example) the symphonic equation of the seasons of the year, the habits of a sunbeam or a cloud. He will make one or two observations analogous to the undulant heat or other inclemencies of the changing climate, which are the multiple sources of our passions. But in order to do so, he must re-create verse, carefully eliminate its excess matter, and show perfect reverence for the twenty-four letters of the alphabet. These he shall transform, through the miracle of infinity, into some special language of his own. Then, with some gesture, some ray of light, he shall give meaning to their symmetry. And so, at last, he will achieve that transfiguration and reach that supernatural height which are Poetry. This truly polished initiate of paradise will then possess—beyond all other wealth—the means to happiness: a principle for knowledge. And he will have a native land. Through his initiative, or through their own virtual power, these divine characters will become a work of art.

They are our heritage from the ancient books of magic, from our age-old wealth of mind; they provide us with a method of notation which spontaneously becomes Literature. A method—no! They are our *principle!* The turn of some special phrase or the meshes of a couplet are patterned on our understanding of them, and thus insights and relationships are born in us.

Except for study-sheets, rubrics, parchment, and such, I consider reading to be a hopeless occupation. So it is that all attempts at the manufacture of happiness have failed for lack of proper means. I know of cases in which even

the most secret and careful of such means cannot, must not, satisfy us.

Something else! yes, it is as if the chance trembling of a page sought only hesitation and fluttered with impatience at the possibility of—something else. We know, of course, that we are subject to the absolute law which states that only what exists exists. Yet it would be obviously inconsistent to choose such an empty pretext as the basis for refusing all delusion, for we would then be refusing the very pleasure that we seek. The *beyond* is our means to that pleasure; I might almost say the "instrument" of our pleasure were it not repugnant to me to disassemble fiction in public (for it would be blasphemous to analyze the "mechanics" of literature and thus discover its chief cog—which is, in any case, nothingness). Yes, for me the miracle occurs when, in a dream of fiction, we seize the ideal which is absent here below, yet explosively present up above, and hurl it to some forbidden, thunderbolt height of heaven.

Why should we do this?

It is a game.

For just as we have the right to elicit emptiness from ourselves (hampered as we may be by reality too solidly, too preponderantly enthroned in us), so do we act that a sublime attraction may lovingly deliver us from that reality—and yet be filled with it and shed glittering lights upon it through empty space and in willful, solitary celebrations.

As for myself, I ask no less of literature. And now I am going to prove my point.

Nature exists; She will not be changed, although we may add cities, railroads, or other inventions to our material world.

Therefore, our eternal and only problem is to seize relationships and intervals, however few or multiple. Thus, faithful to some special vision deep within, we may extend or simplify the world at will.

To create is to conceive an object in its fleeting moment, in its absence.

To do this, we simply compare its facets and dwell lightly, negligently upon their multiplicity. We conjure up a scene of lovely, evanescent, intersecting forms. We recognize the entire and binding arabesque thus formed as it leaps dizzily in terror or plays disquieting chords; or, through a sudden digression (by no means disconcerting), we are warned of its likeness unto itself even as it hides. Then when the melodic line has given way to silence, we seem to hear such themes as are the very logic and substance of our soul. Yet whatever the agony may be in which the Monster writhes (as, through Her golden wounds, She pours the proof that She is always entire, always Herself), no vanquished throe may bend or cross the omnipresent Line which runs infinitely from point to point in Its creation of idea—creation perhaps unseen by man, mysterious, like some Harmony of perfect purity.

I am convinced that the constant grasp and realization of this ideal constitutes our obligation to Him Who once unleashed Infinity—Whose rhythm (as our fingers longingly seek it out among the keys of our verbal instrument) can be rendered by the fitting words of our daily tongue.

For in truth, what is Literature if not our mind's ambition (in the form of language) to define things; to prove to the satisfaction of our soul that a natural phenomenon corresponds to our imaginative understanding of it. And our hope, of course, is that we may ourselves be reflected in it.

I know that Music—at least in the usual sense of the word: that is, concert performances with strings, brass, wood winds, and occasionally libretti—has a similar though unexpressed ambition (She is never very confiding). And when, a moment ago, I was sketching those winding and mobile variations of the Idea which are the prerogative of the written word, some of you may have been reminded of certain orchestral phrasings in which we hear, first, a withdrawal to the shades, swirls and uneasy hesitation, and then suddenly the bursting, leaping, multiple ecstasy of Brilliance, like the approaching radiance of a sunrise. Yet this will all be useless until language, retempered and purified by the flight of song, has given it meaning.

So now we are reaching the end of our search.

There can be—or rather there *must* be—an exchange following this triumphant contribution of Music: the written word must rise and Music must receive it for a brief plaintive space, else the efficacies of life will be blind to their own brilliance, hidden, and without release. I am asking for a total restoration, in perfect and neutral silence, whereby the mind may seek its own native land again: let us have quakes and slippings, unlimited and unerring trajectories, rich revery in sudden flight, delightful unfulfillment, some special lunge or synthesis. But let there be no sonorous tumult which could be resorbed in dreams.

The greatest and most magical writers have always realized this ambition.

These, then, will be the precise and reciprocal elements of Mystery in our possession (we can forget the old distinction between Music and Literature—the one purposely separated from the other in preparation for their ultimate meeting): Music will release the powers lying within that abstract center of hearing, and even of vision, which is Comprehension; while Comprehension, in all its spaciousness, will lend equal power to the printed page.

I suggest, at my own esthetic risk, the following conclusion (and if I were fortunate enough to win your silent approval of it, I should feel fully honored this evening): namely, that Music and Literature constitute the moving facet —now looming toward obscurity, now glittering unconquerably—of that single, true phenomenon which I have called Idea.

The one bends toward the other, submerges, then returns to the surface with its treasure; another dive, another fluctuation, and the entire cycle is created to perfection. For humanity in general, this will be done theatrically: they will sit unconsciously and hear a performance of their own greatness. The individual, on the other hand, will be enlightened by the book, his teacher and constant companion. . . .

It will always be the pleasure and duty of the thoughtful critic to see through the ups and downs of a changing present and show the truly glorious artists in perspective. But in the meantime the disinterested poet, eschewing all virtuosity and bravado, must project his vision of the world and use the languages of the school, home, and market place which seem most fitting to that purpose. Then poetry will be lifted to some frightening, wavering, ecstatic pitch—like an orchestral wing spread wide in flight, but with its talons still rooted deep within your earth. Wherever you find it, you must deny the ineffable; for somehow it will speak.

Thus if the common man, neighbor to us all, has the gift of language on his lips and follows this very ordinary—or, rather, extraordinary!—method; and if an unheard echo joins his song, he will be able to communicate in the common vocabulary with all pomp and light. For it is fitting that to each of us Truth be revealed in Her native magnificence. And so, like a dutiful son or taxpayer, he willingly contributes what he owes to the common treasure of the fatherland.

Because (I must insist upon this last point— it all stems from that poetic Celebration we have been speaking about for the past hour; and, rather than divide it into the elements of Music and Literature, we can call it "Mystery" or perhaps "the evolutive context of the Idea" —I must insist) *because* . . .

Throughout the centuries, *our earthly society has been seriously handicapped* because we have failed to consider brute reality—city, government, laws—as a group of symbols. Or, to put it another way, we have turned them into cemeteries and thus destroyed the paradise they should be. We have made them a terrace, hardly higher than the earth. But, despite all appearances, it is not on earth, nor in tolls and elections, that we can find the lofty drama of the formalities which create a popular cult; for these are rather the representatives of the great Law as It is miraculously instituted with all transparent purity.

Whenever you are in danger of losing this perspective, you must destroy all material substructures. Or, better still, stream fairy lights along them all—and see! Your thoughts must ask an image of your earth.

If, in days to come, a new religion rises up in France, it will be the heavenly instinct within each one of us, expanded to the dimensions of infinite joy. A relatively harmless and elementary example of this can be found on the political level: voting (even for oneself) will not be satisfying until it becomes that expansive, trumpeting hymn of joy in which no name is chosen; nor can revolutions quite provide the broil and tempest in which we must stream and sink if we would rise and be reborn as heroes.

Paul Valéry

LITERATURE (1929)

A POEM MUST BE a holiday of Mind. It can be nothing else.

Holiday: it is a game, but solemn, ordered and significant; image of what one ordinarily is

not, partaking of a state where efforts are rhythms—are redeemed.

One celebrates something in accomplishing it, or representing it in its purest and fairest state.

Here we have the power of language and its inverse phenomenon, understanding, identity of the things it separates. One discards its poverty, its weaknesses, its everydayness. One organizes all the possibilities of language.

The holiday over, nothing must remain. Ashes, trampled garlands.

*

In the poet:
The ear speaks,
The mouth listens;
It is intelligence, vigilance, that gives birth to dream;
It is sleep that sees clearly;
It is the image and the phantom that look;
It is the lack and the blank that create.

*

Most people have such a vague idea about poetry that this vague feeling itself is their definition of poetry.

*

POETRY

It is the attempt to represent, or to restore, by means of articulated language those things, or that thing, which cries, tears, caresses, kisses, sighs, etc., try obscurely to express, and which objects seem to want to express in all that is lifelike in them or appears to have design.

In no other way can that thing be defined. It is of the nature of that energy which spends itself in responding to what is. . . .

*

Thought is hidden in verse like the nutritive virtue in fruit. A fruit is nourishment but it seems to be nothing but pure delight. One perceives only pleasure but one receives a substance. Enchantment veils this imperceptible nourishment it brings with it.

*

Poetry is only literature reduced to the essence of its active principle. It has been purged of idols of every sort and realistic illusions: of any possible ambiguity between the language of "truth" and the language of "creation," etc. . . .

And this half-creative, half-fictive role of language (itself of such a practical and veracious origin) is made perfectly evident by the fragility or arbitrary character of the subject.

*

The subject of a poem is as foreign to it and as important, as his name is to a man.

*

Some people, even poets and good poets, see in poetry an arbitrary luxury occupation, a special industry that can exist or not exist, flourish or perish—perfumers could very well be suppressed, liquor dealers, etc.

Others see in it a phenomenon whose nature and activity are altogether essential, profoundly related to the situation of the inner being in relation to knowledge, duration, hidden conflicts and endowments, memory, dream, etc.

*

While the interest in prose writings is, as it were, apart from the writings themselves and born of the consumption of the text, the interest in poems is an integral part of the poems and can never be separated from them.

*

Poetry is a survival.

Poetry, in a period of language simplification, of changing forms and insensibility in regard to them, of specialization—is a *thing preserved*. I mean that today verse would not be invented. Nor, indeed, rites of any kind.

*

The poet is also the one who looks for the comprehensible and conceivable system that would have a place in its expression for a beautiful accident of language: a certain word, a certain chord of words, a certain syntactic progression—a certain opening—that he has encountered, awakened, stumbled on by chance —thanks to his poet's nature.

*

Lyric poetry is the development of an exclamation.

*

Lyric poetry is the kind of poetry that thinks of the *voice in action*—the voice as direct issue of, or provoked by, things that one sees or that one feels as *present*.

*

It sometimes happens that the mind seeks poetry or the continuation of poetry in some source or hidden divinity.

But the ear demands a certain sound when

the mind demands a certain word whose sound does not conform to the ear's desire.

*

For a long, long time the *human voice* was the foundation and condition of *literature*. The presence of the voice explains the earliest literature from which classical literature derived its form and its admirable *temperament*. The whole human body present *beneath the voice*, as a support and necessary balance for the idea . . .

Then came the day when people knew how to read with their eyes, without spelling out the words, without hearing, and literature was thereby entirely altered. . . .

Evolution from the articulated to the glanced-at—from the flowing and progressive to the instantaneous—from that which is demanded by an audience to that which is demanded and snatched by a quick and avid eye running freely over the page.

*

CLASSICAL

To the ancients the celestial world seemed more orderly than it seems to us and, consequently, totally distinct from our terrestrial world; reciprocity between the two worlds did not occur to them.

The terrestrial world seemed very badly regulated.

Chance, liberty, caprice were the things that struck them (for chance is the liberty of things, the impression we have of the plurality and indifferent importance of solutions).

Their *Fatum* was something vague which undoubtedly won in the long run and as a whole (like the law of large numbers) but prayers, sacrifices, rites were feasible. Man still had some power over circumstances where his direct action is inapplicable.

And, therefore, to *set in order* seemed to him *divine*.

What differentiates Greek art and Oriental art is that the latter is concerned only with giving pleasure, Greek art with attaining *beauty*, that is, giving to things a form which will make

us think of universal order, divine wisdom, the domination of mind, things that do not exist in close, tangible, existing nature, all made up of *accidents*.

*

VARIATIONS ON THE CLASSICAL

A classical writer is a writer who dissimulates or reabsorbs associations of ideas.

*

CLASSICS

Thanks to the curious rules of French classical poetry the distance between the initial thought and the final expression is the greatest possible. This is important. A work is accomplished between the emotion received, or intention conceived, and the completion of the instrument which will restore it or an analogous *impression*. Everything is retraced, the thought is re-examined, etc.

Add to this the fact that the men who have raised poetry to its highest point were all translators. Skilled in transposing the ancients into our language.

Their poetry bears the mark of this practice. It is a translation, a *faithless beauty*—faithless to what is not in accord with the exigencies of a pure language.

*

Another and no more arbitrary definition of classical.

An art is classical if it is adapted not so much to individuals as to an organized society and one which is stable (as to customs).

Marriage in France was classical; and still is to some extent. It followed the same lines as stock comedy. There were stereotype roles. The drama began with an accidental and concerted meeting. "*Est-toi, chère Elise?*". . . The parents conversed with each other through the intermediary of their attorneys.

*

Under the heading of classical, people placidly and indiscriminately include writers who say very little in endless sentences; writers who have simply propounded old wives' verities;

others who show a crude vigor, or a defense counsel's verbosity, or an exquisite affected elegance; others who observe an obvious and very pronounced regularity, or the rules of the game.

*

Classical and cultivation—in the true sense of the word—trimming, grafting, selecting, pruning.

Thus Greek grafted on French, Tacitus on Jesuit, Euripides on Jansenist.

Abrupt returns of the fruit to the wild state.

*

Since the advent of romanticism *singularity* has been imitated instead of, as in the past, *mastery*.

The instinct of imitation has remained the same. But to it the modern adds a contradiction.

Mastery, as the word indicates, is to appear to have command over the technical resources of an art—instead of being visibly commanded by them.

The acquisition of mastery then presupposes the acquired habit of always thinking, or combining, with the technical means as *point of departure*, and of never thinking of a work except in terms of its *means*: of never beginning a work with a subject or an effect which has not

been imagined in relation to the technical means.

But it sometimes happens that mastery is taken off its guard and overcome by some innovator who by chance, or by gift, creates *new technical means* and seems at first to have given the world a new world. But it is never more than a question of technique.

*

The classical theatre deprived of description. But is it *natural* for a *character* to be always picturesquely expatiating?

A character should see only what is necessary and sufficient for him to see to further the action—and indeed that is all most men *see*. In that the classics are justified and confirmed by observation. The ordinary man is abstract, that is he is limited (in his own eyes and in those of his fellows) to his preoccupation of the moment. He sees only what is connected with it. . . .

Between classical and romantic the difference is very simple: it is the difference that separates the one who is ignorant of his technique and the one who has learned his.

A romantic who has learned his art becomes a classic. That is why romanticism ended in *Parnasse*.

Rainer Maria Rilke

[FROM A LETTER TO WITOLD VON HULEWICZ] (1925)

. . . And am *I* the one to give the Elegies their proper explanation? They reach out infinitely

Reprinted from *Letters of Rainer Maria Rilke, 1910–1926,* translated by Jane Bannard Greene and M. D. Herter Norton. By permission of W. W. Norton & Company, Inc. Copyright 1947, 1948 by W. W. Norton & Company, Inc.

Von Hulewicz was translating Rilke's great *Duino Elegies* into Polish.

beyond me. I regard them as a further elaboration of those essential premises that were already given in the *Book of Hours*, that in the two parts of the *New Poems* tentatively played with the image of the world and that then in the *Malte*, contracted in conflict, strike back into life and there almost lead to the proof that this life so suspended in the bottomless is impossible. In the *Elegies*, starting from the same postulates, life becomes possible again, indeed, it experiences here that ultimate *affirmation* to which young Malte, though on the difficult right path "des longues études," was as yet unable to conduct it. *Affirmation of life-AND-death appears as one in the "Elegies."* To grant one without the other is, so it is here learned and celebrated, a limitation which in the end shuts out all that is infinite. *Death is the side of life* averted from us, unshone upon by us: we must try to achieve the greatest consciousness of our existence which is at home in *both unbounded realms, inexhaustibly nourished from both . . .* The true figure of life extends through *both* spheres, the blood of the mightiest circulation flows through *both: there is neither a here nor a beyond, but the great unity* in which the beings that surpass us, the "angels," are at home. And now the place of the love problem, in this world extended by its greater half, in this world only now *whole*, only now *sound.* I am amazed that the *Sonnets to Orpheus*, which are at least as "*difficult*," filled with the same essence, are not more helpful to you in the understanding of the *Elegies*. These latter were begun in 1912 (at Duino), continued in Spain and Paris—fragmentarily—until 1914; the War interrupted this my greatest work altogether; when in 1922 I ventured to take them up again (here), the new elegies and their conclusion were preceded, in a few days, by the *Sonnets to Orpheus*, which imposed themselves tempestuously (and which had *not* been in my plan). They are, as could not have been otherwise, of the same "birth" as the *Elegies*, and their springing up, without my willing it, in connection with a girl who had died young, moves them even closer to the source of their origin: this connection being one more relation toward the center of *that* realm whose depth and influence we share, everywhere unboundaried, with the dead and those to come. We of the here and now are not for a moment hedged in the time-world, nor confined within it; we are incessantly flowing over and over to those who preceded us, to our

origins and to those who seemingly come after us. In that greatest "*open*" world all *are*, one cannot say "simultaneous," for the very falling away of time determines that they all *are*. Transiency everywhere plunges into a deep being. And so all the configurations of the here and now are to be used not in a time-bound way only, but, as far as we are able, to be placed in those superior significances in which we have a share. But *not in the Christian sense* (from which I am more and more passionately moving away), but, in a purely earthly, deeply earthly, blissfully earthly consciousness, we must introduce what is *here* seen and touched into the wider, into the widest orbit. Not into a beyond whose shadow darkens the earth, but into a whole, into *the whole*. Nature, the things of our intercourse and use, are provisional and perishable; but they are, as long as we are here, *our* property and our friendship, co-knowers of our distress and gladness, as they have already been the familiars of our forbears. So it is important not only not to run down and degrade all that is here, but just because of its provisionalness, which it shares with us, these phenomena and things should be understood and transformed by us in a most fervent sense. Transformed? Yes, for it is our task to imprint this provisional, perishable earth so deeply, so patiently and passionately in ourselves that its reality shall arise in us again "invisibly." *We are the bees of the invisible. Nous butinons éperdument le miel du visible, pour l'accumuler dans la grande ruche d'or de l'Invisible.* The *Elegies* show us at this work, at the work of these continual conversions of the beloved visible and tangible into the invisible vibrations and excitation of our own nature, which introduces new vibration-frequencies into the vibration-spheres of the universe. (Since different elements in the cosmos are only different vibration-exponents, we prepare for ourselves in this way not only intensities of a spiritual nature but also, who knows, new bodies, metals, nebulae and constellations.) And this activity is curiously supported and urged on by the ever more rapid fading away of so much of the visible that will no longer be replaced. Even for our grandparents a "house," a "well," a familiar tower, their very clothes, their coat: were infinitely more, infinitely more intimate; almost everything a vessel in which they found the human and added to the store of the human. Now, from America, empty indifferent things are pouring across, sham things, *dummy life* . . . A house, in the American sense, an American apple or a grapevine over there, has *nothing* in common with the house, the fruit, the grape into which went the hopes and reflections of our forefathers . . . Live things, things lived and conscient of us, are running out and can no longer be replaced. *We are perhaps the last still to have known such things.* On us rests the responsibility not alone of preserving *their* memory (that would be little and unreliable), but their human and laral value. ("Laral" in the sense of the household gods.) The earth has no way out other than to become invisible: *in* us who with a part of our natures partake of the invisible, have (at least) stock in it, and can increase our holdings in the invisible during our sojourn here,—*in* us alone can be consummated this intimate and lasting conversion of the visible into an invisible no longer dependent upon being visible and tangible, as our own destiny continually *grows at the same time* MORE PRESENT AND INVISIBLE in us. The elegies set up this norm of existence: they assure, they celebrate this consciousness. They cautiously fit it into its traditions, in that they claim for this supposition ancient traditions and rumors of traditions and even in the Egyptian cult of the dead evoke a foreknowledge of such relationships. (Although the "Land of Lamentation" through which the older "lamentation" leads the young dead is *not to be identified with* Egypt, but is only, in a sense, a mirroring of the Nile country in the desert clarity of the consciousness of the dead.) When one makes the mistake of holding up to the Elegies or Sonnets *Catholic* conceptions of death, of the beyond and of eternity, one is getting entirely away from their point of departure and preparing for oneself a more and more basic misunderstanding. The "angel" of the elegies has nothing to do with the angel of the Christian heaven (rather with the angel figures of Islam) . . . The angel of the *Elegies* is that creature in whom the transformation of the visible into the invisible, which we are accomplishing, appears already consummated. For the angel of the Elegies all past towers and palaces are existent, *because* long invisible, and the still standing towers and bridges of our existence *already* invisible, although (for us) still persisting physically. The angel of the Elegies is that being who vouches for the recognition in the invisible of a higher order of reality.—Hence "terrible" to us, because we, its lovers and transformers, do still cling to the visible.—All the worlds of the universe are plunging into the invisible as into their next deepest reality; *a few stars immediately intensify and pass away in the infinite consciousness of the angels—, others are dependent upon beings who slowly and laboriously transform them, in whose terrors and ecstasies they attain their next invisible realization. We are,* let it be emphasized once more, *in the sense of the Elegies, we are these transformers of the earth; our entire existence, the flights and plunges of our love, everything qualifies us for this task* (beside which there exists, essentially, no other). (The Sonnets show details from this activity which here appears placed under the name and protection of a dead girl whose incompletion and innocence holds open the gate of the grave so that, gone from us, she belongs to those powers that keep the one half of life fresh and open toward the other wound-open half.) Elegies and Sonnets support each other constantly—, and I see an infinite grace in the fact that, with the same breath, I was permitted to fill both these sails: the little rust-colored sail of the Sonnets and the Elegies' gigantic white canvas.

May you, dear friend, perceive here some advice and elucidation and, for the rest, help yourself along. For: I do not know whether I ever could say more . . .

D. H. Lawrence

INTRODUCTION TO NEW POEMS (1920)

IT SEEMS when we hear a skylark singing as if sound were running into the future, running so fast and utterly without consideration, straight on into futurity. And when we hear a nightingale, we hear the pause and the rich, piercing rhythm of recollection, the perfected past. The lark may sound sad, but with the lovely lapsing sadness that is almost a swoon of hope. The nightingale's triumph is a paean, but a death-paean.

So it is with poetry. Poetry is, as a rule, either the voice of the far future, exquisite and ethereal, or it is the voice of the past, rich, magnificent. When the Greeks heard the *Iliad* and the *Odyssey*, they heard their own past calling in their hearts, as men far inland sometimes hear the sea and fall weak with powerful, wonderful regret, nostalgia; or else their own future rippled its time-beats through their blood, as they followed the painful, glamorous progress of the Ithacan. This was Homer to the Greeks: their Past, splendid with battles won and death achieved, and their Future, the magic wandering of Ulysses through the unknown.

With us it is the same. Our birds sing on the horizons. They sing out of the blue, beyond us, or out of the quenched night. They sing at dawn and sunset. Only the poor, shrill, tame canaries whistle while we talk. The wild birds begin before we are awake, or as we drop into dimness, out of waking. Our poets sit by the gateways, some by the east, some by the

From *The Complete Poems of D. H. Lawrence,* Volume I, edited by Vivian de Sola Pinto and F. Warren Roberts. Reprinted by permission of The Viking Press, Inc.

west. As we arrive and as we go out our hearts surge with response. But whilst we are in the midst of life, we do not hear them.

The poetry of the beginning and the poetry of the end must have that exquisite finality, perfection which belongs to all that is far off. It is in the realm of all that is perfect. It is of the nature of all that is complete and consummate. This completeness, this consummateness, the finality and the perfection are conveyed in exquisite form: the perfect symmetry, the rhythm which returns upon itself like a dance where the hands link and loosen and link for the supreme moment of the end. Perfected bygone moments, perfected moments in the glimmering futurity, these are the treasured gem-like lyrics of Shelley and Keats.

But there is another kind of poetry: the poetry of that which is at hand: the immediate present. In the immediate present there is no perfection, no consummation, nothing finished. The strands are all flying, quivering, intermingling into the web, the waters are shaking the moon. There is no round, consummate moon on the face of running water, nor on the face of the unfinished tide. There are no gems of the living plasm. The living plasm vibrates unspeakably, it inhales the future, it exhales the past, it is the quick of both, and yet it is neither. There is no plasmic finality, nothing crystal, permanent. If we try to fix the living tissue, as the biologists fix it with formation, we have only a hardened bit of the past, the bygone life under our observation.

Life, the ever-present, knows no finality, no finished crystallisation. The perfect rose is only a running flame, emerging and flowing off, and never in any sense at rest, static, finished. Herein lies its transcendent loveliness. The whole tide of all life and all time suddenly heaves, and appears before us as an apparition, a revelation. We look at the very white quick of nascent creation. A water-lily heaves herself from the flood, looks around, gleams, and is gone. We have seen the incarnation, the quick of the ever-swirling flood. We have seen the invisible. We have seen, we have touched, we have partaken of the very substance of creative change, creative mutation. If you tell me about the lotus, tell me of nothing changeless or eternal. Tell me of the mystery of the inexhaustible, forever-unfolding creative spark. Tell me of the incarnate disclosure of the flux, mutation in blossom, laughter and decay perfectly open in their transit, nude in their movement before us.

Let me feel the mud and the heavens in my lotus. Let me feel the heavy, silting, sucking mud, the spinning of sky winds. Let me feel them both in purest contact, the nakedness of sucking weight, nakedly passing radiance. Give me nothing fixed, set, static. Don't give me the infinite or the eternal: nothing of infinity, nothing of eternity. Give me the still, white seething, the incandescence and the coldness of the incarnate moment: the moment, the quick of all change and haste and opposition: the moment, the immediate present, the Now. The immediate moment is not a drop of water running downstream. It is the source and issue, the bubbling up of the stream. Here, in this very instant moment, up bubbles the stream of time, out of the wells of futurity, flowing on to the oceans of the past. The source, the issue, the creative quick.

There is poetry of this immediate present, instant poetry, as well as poetry of the infinite past and the infinite future. The seething poetry of the incarnate. Now is supreme, beyond even the everlasting gems of the before and after. In its quivering momentaneity it surpasses the crystalline, pearl-hard jewels, the poems of the eternities. Do not ask for the qualities of the unfading timeless gems. Ask for the whiteness which is the seethe of mud, ask for that incipient putrescence which is the skies falling, ask for the never-pausing, never-ceasing life itself. There must be mutation, swifter than iridescence, haste, not rest, come-and-go, not fixity, inconclusiveness, immediacy, the quality of life itself, without denouement or close. There must be the rapid momentaneous association of things which meet and pass on the for ever incalculable journey of creation: everything left in its own rapid, fluid relationship with the rest of things.

This is the unrestful, ungraspable poetry of the sheer present, poetry whose very permanency lies in its wind-like transit. Whitman's is the best poetry of this kind. Without beginning and without end, without any base and pediment, it sweeps past for ever, like a wind that is for ever in passage, and unchainable. Whitman truly looked before and after. But he did not sigh for what is not. The clue to all his utterance lies in the sheer appreciation of the instant moment, life surging itself into utterance at its very well-head. Eternity is only an abstraction from the actual present. Infinity is only a great reservoir of recollection, or a reservoir of aspiration: man-made. The quivering nimble hour of the present, this is the quick of Time. This is the immanence. The quick of the universe is the *pulsating, carnal self*, mysterious and palpable. So it is always.

Because Whitman put this into his poetry, we fear him and respect him so profoundly. We should not fear him if he sang only of the "old unhappy far-off things," or of the "wings of the morning." It is because his heart beats with the urgent, insurgent Now, which is even upon us all, that we dread him. He is so near the quick.

From the foregoing it is obvious that the poetry of the instant present cannot have the same body or the same motion as the poetry of the before and after. It can never submit to the same conditions. It is never finished. There is no rhythm which returns upon itself, no serpent of eternity with its tail in its own mouth. There is no static perfection, none of that finality which we find so satisfying because we are so frightened.

Much has been written about free verse. But all that can be said, first and last, is that free verse is, or should be, direct utterance from the instant, whole man. It is the soul and the mind and body surging at once, nothing left out. They speak all together. There is some confusion, some discord. But the confusion and the discord only belong to the reality, as noise belongs to the plunge of water. It is no use inventing fancy laws for free verse, no use drawing a melodic line which all the feet must toe. Free verse toes no melodic line, no matter what drill-sergeant. Whitman pruned away his clichés—perhaps his clichés of rhythm as well as of phrase. And this is about all we can do, deliberately, with free verse. We can get rid of the stereotyped movements and the old hackneyed associations of sound or sense. We can break down those artificial conduits and canals through which we do so love to force our utterance. We can break the stiff neck of habit. We can be in ourselves spontaneous and flexible as flame, we can see that utterance rushes out without artificial form or artificial smoothness. But we cannot positively prescribe any motion, any rhythm. All the laws we invent or discover—it amounts to pretty much the same —will fail to apply to free verse. They will only apply to some form of restricted, limited unfree verse.

All we can say is that free verse does *not* have the same nature as restricted verse. It is not of the nature of reminiscence. It is not the past which we treasure in its perfection between our hands. Neither is it the crystal of the perfect future, into which we gaze. Its tide is neither the full, yearning flow of aspiration, nor the sweet, poignant ebb of remembrance and regret. The past and the future are the two great bournes of human emotion, the two great homes of the human days, the two eternities. They are both conclusive, final. Their beauty is the beauty of the goal, finished, perfected. Finished beauty and measured symmetry belong to the stable, unchanging eternities.

But in free verse we look for the insurgent naked throb of the instant moment. To break the lovely form of metrical verse, and to dish up the fragments as a new substance, called *vers libre*, this is what most of the free-versifiers accomplish. They do not know that free verse has its own *nature*, that it is neither star nor pearl, but instantaneous like plasm. It has no goal in either eternity. It has no finish. It has no satisfying stability, satisfying to those who like the immutable. None of this. It is the instant; the quick; the very jetting source of all will-be and has-been. The utterance is like a spasm, naked contact with all influences at once. It does not want to get anywhere. It just takes place.

For such utterance any externally applied law would be mere shackles and death. The law must come new each time from within. The bird is on the wing in the winds, flexible to every breath, a living spark in the storm, its very flickering depending upon its supreme mutability and power of change. Whence such a bird came: whither it goes: from what solid earth it rose up, and upon what solid earth it will close its wings and settle, this is not the question. This is a question of before and after. Now, *now*, the bird is on the wing in the winds.

Such is the rare new poetry. One realm we have never conquered: the pure present. One great mystery of time is *terra incognita* to us: the instant. The most superb mystery we have hardly recognised: the immediate, instant self. The quick of all time is the instant. The quick of all the universe, of all creation, is the incarnate, carnal self. Poetry gave us the clue: free verse: Whitman. Now we know.

The ideal—what is the ideal? A figment. An abstraction. A static abstraction, abstracted from life. It is a fragment of the before or the after. It is a crystallised aspiration, or a crystallised remembrance: crystallised, set, finished. It is a thing set apart, in the great storehouse of eternity, the storehouse of finished things.

We do not speak of things crystallised and set apart. We speak of the instant, the immediate self, the very plasm of the self. We speak also of free verse.

All this should have come as a preface to *Look! We Have Come Through!* But is it not better to publish a preface long after the book it belongs to has appeared? For then the reader will have had his fair chance with the book, alone.

Hart Crane

GENERAL AIMS AND THEORIES (1925)

WHEN I started writing Faustus & Helen it was my intention to embody in modern terms (words, symbols, metaphors) a contemporary approximation to an ancient human culture or mythology that seems to have been obscured rather than illumined with the frequency of poetic allusions made to it during the last century. The name of Helen, for instance, has become an all-too-easily employed crutch for evocation whenever a poet felt a stitch in his side. The real evocation of this (to me) very real and absolute conception of beauty seemed to consist in a reconstruction in these modern terms of the basic emotional attitude toward beauty that the Greeks had. And in so doing I found that I was really building a bridge between so-called classic experience and many divergent realities of our seething, confused cosmos of today, which has no formulated mythology yet for classic poetic reference or for religious exploitation.

So I found "Helen" sitting in a street car; the Dionysian revels of her court and her seduction were transferred to a Metropolitan roof garden with a jazz orchestra; and the *katharsis* of the fall of Troy I saw approximated in the recent World War. The importance of this scaffolding may easily be exaggerated, but it

Crane's commentary on his poem "For the Marriage of Faustus and Helen."
From *Hart Crane: The Life of an American Poet* by Philip Horton. Reprinted by permission of Philip Horton.

gave me a series of correspondences between two widely separated worlds on which to sound some major themes of human speculation—love, beauty, death, renascence. It was a kind of grafting process that I shall doubtless not be interested in repeating, but which is consistent with subsequent theories of mine on the relation of tradition to the contemporary creating imagination.

It is a terrific problem that faces the poet today—a world that is so in transition from a decayed culture toward a reorganization of human evaluations that there are few common terms, general denominators of speech that are solid enough or that ring with any vibration or spiritual conviction. The great mythologies of the past (including the Church) are deprived of enough façade to even launch good raillery against. Yet much of their traditions are operative still—in millions of chance combinations of related and unrelated detail, psychological reference, figures of speech, precepts, etc. These are all a part of our common experience and the terms, at least partially, of that very experience when it defines or extends itself.

The deliberate program, then, of a "break" with the past or tradition seems to me to be a sentimental fallacy. . . . The poet has a right to draw on whatever practical resources he finds in books or otherwise about him. He must tax his sensibility and his touchstone of experience for the proper selections of these themes and details, however,—and that is where he either stands, or falls into useless archeology.

I put no particular value on the simple objective of "modernity." The element of the temporal location of an artist's creation is of very secondary importance; it can be left to the impressionist or historian just as well. It seems to me that a poet will accidentally define his time well enough simply by reacting honestly and to the full extent of his sensibilities to the states of passion, experience and rumination that fate forces on him, first hand. He must, of course, have a sufficiently universal basis of experience to make his imagination selective and valuable. His picture of the "period," then, will simply be a by-product of his curiosity and the relation of his experience to a postulated "eternity."

I am concerned with the future of America, but not because I think that America has any so-called par value as a state or as a group of people. . . . It is only because I feel persuaded that here are destined to be discovered certain as yet undefined spiritual quantities, perhaps a new hierarchy of faith not to be developed so completely elsewhere. And in this process I like to feel myself as a potential factor; certainly I must speak in its terms and what discoveries I may make are situated in its experience.

But to fool one's self that definitions are being reached by merely referring frequently to skyscrapers, radio antennae, steam whistles, or other surface phenomena of our time is merely to paint a photograph. I think that what is interesting and significant will emerge only under the conditions of our submission to, and examination and assimilation of the organic effects on us of these and other fundamental factors of our experience. It can certainly not be an organic expression otherwise. And the expression of such values may often be as well accomplished with the vocabulary and blank verse of the Elizabethans as with the calligraphic tricks and slang used so brilliantly at times by an impressionist like Cummings.

It may not be possible to say that there is, strictly speaking, any "absolute" experience. But it seems evident that certain aesthetic experience (and this may for a time engross the total faculties of the spectator) can be called absolute, inasmuch as it approximates a formally convincing statement of a conception or apprehension of life that gains our unquestioning assent, and under the conditions of which our imagination is unable to suggest a further detail consistent with the design of the aesthetic whole.

I have been called an "absolutist" in poetry, and if I am to welcome such a label it should be under the terms of the above definition. It is really only a *modus operandi*, however, and as such has been used organically before by at least a dozen poets such as Donne, Blake, Baudelaire, Rimbaud, etc. I may succeed in defining it better by contrasting it with the impressionistic method. The impressionist is interesting as far as he goes—but his goal has been reached when he has succeeded in projecting certain selected factual details into his reader's consciousness. He is really not interested in the *causes* (metaphysical) of his materials, their emotional derivations or their utmost spiritual consequences. A kind of retinal registration is enough, along with a certain psychological stimulation. And this is also true of your realist (of the Zola type), and to a certain extent of the classicist, like Horace, Ovid, Pope, etc.

Blake meant these differences when he wrote:

> We are led to believe in a lie
> When we see *with* not *through* the eye.

The impressionist creates only with the eye and for the readiest surface of the consciousness, at least relatively so. If the effect has been harmonious or even stimulating, he can stop there, relinquishing entirely to his audience the problematic synthesis of the details into terms of their own personal consciousness.

It is my hope to go *through* the combined materials of the poem, using our "real" world somewhat as a spring-board and to give the poem *as a whole* an orbit or predetermined direction of its own. I would like to establish it as free from my own personality as from any chance evaluation on the reader's part. (This is, of course, an impossibility, but it is a characteristic worth mentioning.) Such a poem is at least a stab at a truth, and to such an extent may be differentiated from other kinds of poetry and called "absolute." Its evocation will not be toward decoration or amusement, but rather toward a state of consciousness, an "innocence" (Blake) or absolute beauty. In this condition there may be discoverable under new forms certain spiritual illuminations, shining with a morality essentialized from experience directly, and not from previous precepts or preconceptions. It is as though a poem gave the reader as he left it a single, new *word*, never before spoken and impossible to actually enunciate, but self-evident as an active principle in the reader's consciousness henceforward.

As to technical considerations: the motivation of the poem must be derived from the implicit emotional dynamics of the materials used, and the terms of expression employed are often selected less for their logical (literal) significance than for their associational meanings. Via this and their metaphorical inter-relationships, the entire construction of the poem is raised on the organic principle of a "logic of metaphor," which antedates our so-called pure logic, and which is the genetic basis of all speech, hence consciousness and thought-extension.

These dynamics often result, I'm told, in certain initial difficulties in understanding my poems. But on the other hand I find them at times the only means possible for expressing certain concepts in any forceful or direct way whatever. To cite two examples:—when, in Voyages (II), I speak of "adagios of islands," the reference is to the motion of a boat through islands clustered thickly, the rhythm of the motion, etc. And it seems a much more direct and creative statement than any more logical employment of words such as "coasting slowly through the islands," besides ushering in a whole world of music. Similarly in Faustus and Helen (III) the speed and tense altitude of an aeroplane are much better suggested by the idea of "nimble blue plateaus"—*implying* the aeroplane and its speed against a contrast of stationary elevated earth. Although the statement is pseudo in relation to formal logic—it *is* completely logical in relation to the truth of the imagination, and there is expressed a concept of speed and space that could not be handled so well in other terms.

In manipulating the more imponderable phenomena of psychic motives, pure emotional crystallizations, etc. I have had to rely even more on these dynamics of inferential mention, and I am doubtless still very unconscious of having committed myself to what seems nothing but obscurities to some minds. A poem like Possessions really cannot be technically explained. It must rely (even to a large extent with myself) on its organic impact on the imagination to successfully imply its meaning. This seems to me to present an exceptionally difficult problem, however, considering the real clarity and consistent logic of many of the other poems.

I know that I run the risk of much criticism by defending such theories as I have, but as it is part of a poet's business to risk not only criticism—but folly—in the conquest of consciousness I can only say that I attach no intrinsic value to what means I use beyond their practical service in giving form to the living stuff of the imagination.

New conditions of life germinate new forms of spiritual articulation. And while I feel that my work includes a more consistent extension of traditional literary elements than many contemporary poets are capable of appraising, I realize that I am utilizing the gifts of the past as instruments principally; and that the voice of the present, if it is to be known, must be caught at the risk of speaking in idioms and circumlocutions sometimes shocking to the scholar and historians of logic. Language has built towers and bridges, but itself is inevitably as fluid as always.

John Crowe Ransom

PREFACE TO *THE WORLD'S BODY* (1938)

To ADVERTISE scrupulously the nature of my book, I must say that these are not altogether papers in criticism; many of them will have to come under some other heading. For the author their relation to criticism, and their value, has been this: they are preparations for criticism, for the understanding and definition of the poetic effects. They are about poetic theory itself. That is one of the most fascinating fields of speculation; I suppose it can be one of the idlest.

It is my impression that the serious critic should serve a sort of apprenticeship with his general principles. But the studies can scarcely afford to be pursued in any way except in the constant company of the actual poems. About ten years ago, when I did not know this, I wrote out and sent to a publisher a general aesthetic of poetry, a kind of Prolegomena to Any Future Poetic, thinking that the public needed one, as perhaps it does. The intelligent publisher declined my project politely and returned my manuscript, which the other day I had the pleasure of consigning to the flames.

But for the animating idea which informed my little effort of that time I have no repentance. I was concerned with urging that it is not a pre-scientific poetry but a post-scientific one to which we must now give our consent. I suppose I was rationalizing my own history, for I came late into an interest in poetry, after I had been stuffed with the law if not the letter of our modern sciences, and quickly I had the

difficulty of finding a poetry which would not deny what we in our strange generation actually are: men who have aged in these pure intellectual disciplines, and cannot play innocent without feeling very foolish. The expense of poetry is greater than we will pay if it is something to engage in without our faculties. I could not discover that this mortification was required.

Among these papers the general ones offer various versions of what approaches, I hope, to a fairly single and coherent poetic doctrine. And I will supplement them here with still another version, a last one as I now believe, shorter and more dogmatic, for the benefit of some unusually close and generous reader who is disposed to make the most of my essays, and by way of a preface.

The kind of poetry which interests us is not the act of a child, or of that eternal youth which is in some women, but the act of an adult mind; and I will add, the act of a fallen mind, since ours too are fallen. It has been forgotten by most of the formal aestheticians that poetry is an event in time. Under the present circumstances it is an inevitable and perhaps spectacular event, which interrupts the history of men officially committed under civilization to their effective actions and abstract studies. It is revulsive, or revolutionary, by intention.

But I would like to suggest a distinction. First we should see what poetry properly is not, though it is what poetry has often been declared to be. There is a kind of poetry which proceeds out of failure. To its author the natural world has dispensed too liberally of its blows, privations, humiliations, and silences in answer to his prayers for sympathy. He therefore invents a private world where such injustice cannot be, and enjoys it as men enjoy their dream. The impulse is known very well, and has had many celebrations, as this one:

Ah, Love, could thou and I with Fate conspire
To grasp this sorry scheme of things entire,
Would we not shatter it to bits, and then
Remould it nearer to the heart's desire?

The poetry I am disparaging is a heart's-desire poetry. If another identification is needed, it is the poetry written by romantics, in a common sense of that term. It denies the real world by idealizing it: the act of a sick mind. A modern psychologist puts a blunt finger in a rather nasty manner upon this sort of behavior. It indicates in the subject a poor adaptation to reality; a sub-normal equipment in animal courage; flight and escapism; furtive libido. It is only reasonable if such acts, even if they are performed in the name of poetry, should be treated under the pathological categories. But it is unfortunate that some theorists, who would not know better because of their comparative unacquaintance with poetry, have concluded that it is all of this order.

There is a tragedy of success which is more teasing, and not much less bleak, than the tragedy of failure. See CXXIX among Shakespeare's sonnets, and Ecclesiastes, *passim*. For even though we have our heart's desire, as happens frequently enough, it tastes like ashes; there is little to it. The presumption is that we desired it too exclusively, and that the maximum efficiency with which we toiled for it was too much efficiency. In the labor we sacrificed nearly everything, and naturally the reward is as tenuous as the labor. Where is the body and solid substance of the world? It seems to have retired into the fulness of memory, but out of this we construct the fulness of poetry, which is counterpart to the world's fulness.

The true poetry has no great interest in improving or idealizing the world, which does well enough. It only wants to realize the world, to see it better. Poetry is the kind of knowledge by which we must know what we have arranged that we shall not know otherwise. We have elected to know the world through our science, and we know a great deal, but science is only the cognitive department of our animal life, and by it we know the world only as a scheme of abstract conveniences. What we cannot know constitutionally as scientists is the world which is made of whole and indefeasible objects, and this is the world which poetry recovers for us. Men become poets, or at least they read poets, in order to atone for having been hard practical men and hard theoretical scientists.

For such moderns as we are the poetry must be modern. It is not as in a state of innocence, to receive the fragrance of the roses on the world's first morning, that our moderns the scarred veterans may enact their poetry, but in the violence of return and regeneration. They re-enter the world, but it is the world which they have marked with their raids, and there is no other world they can enter. It is by its thickness, stubbornness, and power that it must impress them. First must come respect, and then, if then, love.

It is a paradox that poetry has to be a technical act, of extreme difficulty, when it wants only to know the untechnical homely fulness of the world. The race in its unconscious strategy pushes its sciences always harder, and they grow more and more exclusive as they prosper. But at the same time it devises the arts, and even sets them up in a sort of honor as an equal and opposite activity, and keeps them always changing their forms in order to have their full effect. They are probably the best devices there could be for the purpose, and the way they work is the proper object of critical studies.

Allen Tate

NARCISSUS AS NARCISSUS (1938)

ON THIS FIRST OCCASION, which will probably be the last, of my writing about my own verse, I could plead in excuse the example of Edgar Allan Poe, who wrote about himself in an essay called "The Philosophy of Composition." But in our age the appeal to authority is weak, and I am of my age. What I happen to know about the poem that I shall discuss is limited. I remember merely my intention in writing it; I do not know whether the poem is good; and I do not know its obscure origins.

How does one happen to write a poem: where does it come from? That is the question asked by the psychologists or the geneticists of poetry. Of late I have not read any of the genetic theories very attentively: years ago I read one by Mr. Conrad Aiken; another, I think, by Mr. Robert Graves; but I have forgotten them. I am not ridiculing verbal mechanisms, dreams, or repressions as origins of poetry; all three of them and more besides may have a great deal to do with it. Other psychological theories say a good deal about compensation. A poem is an indirect effort of a shaky man to justify himself to happier men, or to present a superior account of his relation to a world that allows him but little certainty, and would allow equally little to the happier men if they did not wear blinders—according to the poet. For example, a poet might be a man who could not get enough self-justifica-

tion out of being an automobile salesman (whose certainty is a fixed quota of cars every month) to rest comfortably upon it. So the poet, who wants to be something that he cannot be, and is a failure in plain life, makes up fictitious versions of his predicament that are interesting even to other persons because nobody is a perfect automobile salesman. Everybody, alas, suffers a little . . . I constantly read this kind of criticism of my own verse. According to its doctors, my one intransigent desire is to have been a Confederate general, and because I could not or would not become anything else, I set up for poet and began to invent fictions about the personal ambitions that my society has no use for.

Although a theory may not be "true," it may make certain insights available for a while; and I have deemed it proper to notice theories of the genetic variety because a poet talking about himself is often expected, as the best authority, to explain the origins of his poems. But persons interested in origins are seldom quick to use them. Poets, in their way, are practical men; they are interested in results. What is the poem, after it is written? That is the question. Not where it came from, or why. The Why and Where can never get beyond the guessing stage because, in the language of those who think it can, poetry cannot be brought to "laboratory conditions." The only real evidence that any critic may bring before his gaze is the finished poem. For some reason most critics have a hard time fixing their minds directly under their noses, and before

Tate's commentary on his poem "Ode to the Confederate Dead."

From *Essays of Four Decades* by Allen Tate, Swallow Press, Chicago (1969).

they see the object that is there they use a telescope upon the horizon to see where it came from. They are wood-cutters who do their job by finding out where the ore came from in the iron of the steel of the blade of the ax that Jack built. I do not say that this procedure is without its own contributory insights; but the insights are merely contributory and should not replace the poem, which is the object upon which they must be focused. A poem may be an instance of morality, of social conditions, of psychological history; it may instance all its qualities, but never one of them alone, nor any two or three; never less than all.

Genetic theories, I gather, have been cherished academically with detachment. Among "critics" they have been useless and not quite disinterested: I have myself found them applicable to the work of poets whom I do not like. That is the easiest way.

I say all this because it seems to me that my verse or anybody else's is merely a way of knowing something: if the poem is a real creation, it is a kind of knowledge that we did not possess before. It is not knowledge "about" something else; the poem is the fullness of that knowledge. We know the particular poem, not what it says that we can restate. In a manner of speaking, the poem is its own knower, neither poet nor reader knowing anything that the poem says apart from the words of the poem. I have expressed this view elsewhere in other terms, and it has been accused of aestheticism or art for art's sake. But let the reader recall the historic position of Catholicism: *nulla salus extra ecclesiam*. That must be religion*ism*. There is probably nothing wrong with art for art's sake if we take the phrase seriously, and not take it to mean the kind of poetry written in England forty years ago. Religion always ought to transcend any of its particular uses; and likewise the true art for art's sake view can be held only by persons who are always looking for things that they can respect apart from use (though they may be useful), like poems, fly rods, and formal gardens. . . . These are negative postulates, and I am going to illustrate

them with some commentary on a poem called "Ode to the Confederate Dead."

II

That poem is "about" solipsism, a philosophical doctrine which says that we create the world in the act of perceiving it; or about Narcissism, or any other *ism* that denotes the failure of the human personality to function objectively in nature and society. Society (and "nature" as modern society constructs it) appears to offer limited fields for the exercise of the whole man, who wastes his energy piecemeal over separate functions that ought to come under a unity of being. (Until the last generation, only certain women were whores, having been set aside as special instances of sex amid a social scheme that held the general belief that sex must be part of a whole; now the general belief is that sex must be special.) Without unity we get the remarkable self-consciousness of our age. Everybody is talking about this evil, and a great many persons know what ought to be done to correct it. As a citizen I have my own prescription, but as a poet I am concerned with the experience of "solipsism." And an experience *of* it is not quite the same thing as a philosophical statement *about* it.

I should have trouble connecting solipsism and the Confederate dead in a rational argument; I should make a fool of myself in the discussion, because I know no more of the Confederate dead or of solipsism than hundreds of other people. (Possibly less: the dead Confederates may be presumed to have a certain privacy; and as for solipsism, I blush in the presence of philosophers, who know all about Bishop Berkeley; I use the term here in its strict etymology.) And if I call this interest in one's ego Narcissism, I make myself a logical ignoramus, and I take liberties with mythology. I use Narcissism to mean only preoccupation with self; it may be either love or hate. But a good psychiatrist knows that it means self-love only, and otherwise he can talk about it more coherently, knows more about it than I shall ever hope or desire to know. He would look at me professionally if I uttered the remark that the modern squirrel cage of our sensibility, the extreme introspection of our time, has anything whatever to do with the Confederate dead.

But when the doctor looks at literature it is a question whether he sees it: the sea boils and pigs have wings because in poetry all things are possible—if you are man enough. They are possible because in poetry the disparate elements are not combined in logic, which can join things only under certain categories and under the law of contradiction; they are combined in poetry rather as experience, and experience has decided to ignore logic, except perhaps as another field of experience. Experience means conflict, our natures being what they are, and conflict means drama. Dramatic experience is not logical; it may be subdued to the kind of coherence that we indicate when we speak, in criticism, of form. Indeed, as experience, this conflict is always a logical contradiction, or philosophically an antinomy. Serious poetry deals with the fundamental conflicts that cannot be logically resolved: we can state the conflicts rationally, but reason does not relieve us of them. Their only final coherence is the formal re-creation of art, which "freezes" the experience as permanently as a logical formula, but without, like the formula, leaving all but the logic out.

Narcissism and the Confederate dead cannot be connected logically, or even historically; even were the connection an historical fact, they would not stand connected as art, for no one experiences raw history. The proof of the connection must lie, if anywhere, in the experienced conflict which is the poem itself. Since one set of references for the conflict is the historic Confederates, the poem, if it is successful, is a certain section of history made into experience, but only on this occasion, and on these terms: even the author of the poem has no experience of its history apart from the occasion and the terms.

It will be understood that I do not claim even a partial success in the junction of the two "ideas" in the poem that I am about to discuss. I am describing an intention, and the labor of revising the poem—a labor spread over ten years—fairly exposes the lack of confidence that I have felt and still feel in it. All the tests of its success in style and versification would come in the end to a single test, an answer, yes or no, to the question: Assuming that the Confederates and Narcissus are not yoked together by mere violence, has the poet convinced the reader that, on the specific occasion of this poem, there is a necessary yet hitherto undetected relation between them? By necessary I mean dramatically relevant, a relation "discovered" in terms of the particular occasion, not historically argued or philosophically deduced. Should the question that I have just asked be answered yes, then this poem or any other with its specific problem could be said to have form: what was previously a merely felt quality of life has been raised to the level of experience—it has become specific, local, dramatic, "formal"—that is to say, *informed*.

III

The structure of the Ode is simple. Figure to yourself a man stopping at the gate of a Confederate graveyard on a late autumn afternoon. The leaves are falling; his first impressions bring him the "rumor of mortality"; and the desolation barely allows him, at the beginning of the second stanza, the conventionally heroic surmise that the dead will enrich the earth, "where these memories grow." From those quoted words to the end of that passage he pauses for a baroque meditation on the ravages of time, concluding with the figure of the "blind crab." This creature has mobility but no direction, energy but from the human point of view, no purposeful world to use it in: in the entire poem there are only two explicit symbols for the locked-in ego; the crab is the first and less explicit symbol, a mere hint, a planting of the idea that will become overt in its second instance—the jaguar towards the end. The crab is the first intimation of the nature of the moral conflict upon which the drama of the poem develops: the cut-off-ness of the modern "intellectual man" from the world.

The next long passage or "strophe," beginning "You know who have waited by the wall," states the other term of the conflict. It is the theme of heroism, not merely moral heroism, but heroism in the grand style, elevating even death from mere physical dissolution into a formal ritual: this heroism is a formal ebullience of the human spirit in an entire society, not private, romantic illusion—something better than moral heroism, great as that may be, for moral heroism, being personal and individual, may be achieved by certain men in all ages, even ages of decadence. But the late Hart Crane's commentary, in a letter, is better than any I can make; he described the theme as the "theme of chivalry, a tradition of excess (not literally excess, rather active faith) which cannot be perpetuated in the fragmentary cosmos of today—'those desires which should be yours tomorrow,' but which, you know, will not persist nor find any way into action."

The structure then is the objective frame for the tension between the two themes, "active faith" which has decayed, and the "fragmentary cosmos" which surrounds us. (I must repeat here that this is not a philosophical thesis; it is an analytical statement of a conflict that is concrete within the poem.) In contemplating the heroic theme the man at the gate never quite commits himself to the illusion of its availability to him. The most that he can allow himself is the fancy that the blowing leaves are charging soldiers, but he rigorously returns to the refrain: "Only the wind"—or the "leaves flying." I suppose it is a commentary on our age that the man at the gate never quite achieves the illusion that the leaves are heroic men, so that he may identify himself with them, as Keats and Shelley too easily and too beautifully did with nightingales and west winds. More than this, he cautions himself, reminds himself repeatedly of his subjective

prison, his solipsism, by breaking off the half-illusion and coming back to the refrain of wind and leaves—a refrain that, as Hart Crane said, is necessary to the "subjective continuity."

These two themes struggle for mastery up to the passage,

> We shall say only the leaves whispering
> In the improbable mist of nightfall—

which is near the end. It will be observed that the passage begins with a phrase taken from the wind-leaves refrain—the signal that it has won. The refrain has been fused with the main stream of the man's reflections, dominating them; and he cannot return even to an ironic vision of the heroes. There is nothing but death, the mere naturalism of death at that—spiritual extinction in the decay of the body. Autumn and the leaves are death; the men who exemplified in a grand style an "active faith" are dead; there are only the leaves.

Shall we then worship death . . .

> . . . set up the grave
> In the house? The ravenous grave . . .

that will take us before our time? The question is not answered, although as a kind of morbid romanticism it might, if answered affirmatively, provide the man with an illusory escape from his solipsism; but he cannot accept it. Nor has he been able to live in his immediate world, the fragmentary cosmos. There is no practical solution, no solution offered for the edification of moralists. (To those who may identify the man at the gate with the author of the poem I would say: He differs from the author in not accepting a "practical solution," for the author's personal dilemma is perhaps not quite so exclusive as that of the meditating man.) The main intention of the poem has been to make dramatically visible the conflict, to concentrate it, to present it, in Mr. R. P. Blackmur's phrase, as "experienced form" —not as a logical dilemma.

The closing image, that of the serpent, is the ancient symbol of time, and I tried to give it the credibility of the commonplace by placing it in a mulberry bush—with the faint hope that the silkworm would somehow be implicit. But time is also death. If that is so, then space, or the Becoming, is life; and I believe there is not a single spatial symbol in the poem. "Sea-space" is allowed the "blind crab"; but the sea, as appears plainly in the passage beginning, "Now that the salt of their blood . . ." is life only insofar as it is the source of the lowest forms of life, the source perhaps of all life, but life undifferentiated, halfway between life and death. This passage is a contrasting inversion of the conventional

> . . . inexhaustible bodies that are not
> Dead, but feed the grass . . .

the reduction of the earlier, literary conceit to a more naturalistic figure derived from modern biological speculation. These "buried Caesars" will not bloom in the hyacinth but will only make saltier the sea.

The wind-leaves refrain was added to the poem in 1930, nearly five years after the first draft was written. I felt that the danger of adding it was small because, implicit in the long strophes of meditation, the ironic commentary on the vanished heroes was already there, giving the poem such dramatic tension as it had in the earlier version. The refrain makes the commentary more explicit, more visibly dramatic, and renders quite plain, as Hart Crane intimated, the subjective character of the imagery throughout. But there was another reason for it, besides the increased visualization that it imparts to the dramatic conflict. It "times" the poem better, offers the reader frequent pauses in the development of the two themes, allows him occasions of assimilation; and on the whole—this was my hope and intention—the refrain makes the poem seem longer than it is and thus eases the concentration of imagery—without, I hope, sacrificing a possible effect of concentration.

IV

I have been asked why I called the poem an ode. I first called it an elegy. It is an ode only in the sense in which Cowley in the seventeenth century misunderstood the real structure of the Pindaric ode. Not only are the meter and rhyme without fixed pattern, but in another feature the poem is even further removed from Pindar than Abraham Cowley was: a purely subjective meditation would not even in Cowley's age have been called an ode. I suppose in so calling it I intended an irony: the scene of the poem is not a public celebration, it is a lone man by a gate.

The dominant rhythm is "mounting," the dominant meter iambic pentameter varied with six,- four-, and three-stressed lines; but this was not planned in advance for variety. I adapted the meter to the effect desired at the moment. The model for the irregular rhyming was "Lycidas," but other models could have served. The rhymes in a given strophe I tried to adjust to the rhythm and the texture of feeling and image. For example, take this passage in the second strophe:

> Autumn is desolation in the plot
> Of a thousand acres where these memories
>   grow
> From the inexhaustible bodies that are not
> Dead, but feed the grass row after rich row.
> Think of the autumns that have come and
>   gone!—
> Ambitious November with the humors of
>   the year,
> With a particular zeal for every slab,
> Staining the uncomfortable angels that rot
> On the slabs, a wing chipped here, an arm
>   there:
> The brute curiosity of an angel's stare
> Turns you, like them, to stone,
> Transforms the heaving air
> Till plunged to a heavier world below
> You shift your sea-space blindly
> Heaving, turning like the blind crab.

There is rhymed with *year* (to many persons, perhaps, only a half-rhyme), and I hoped the reader would unconsciously assume that he need not expect further use of that sound for some time. So when the line, "The brute curiosity of an angel's stare," comes a moment later, rhyming with *year-there,* I hoped that the violence of image would be further reinforced by the repetition of a sound that was no longer expected. I wanted the shock to be heavy; so I felt that I could not afford to hurry the reader away from it until he had received it in full. The next two lines carry on the image at a lower intensity: the rhyme, "Transforms the heaving *air,*" prolongs the moment of attention upon that passage, while at the same time it ought to begin dissipating the shock, both by the introduction of a new image and by reduction of the "meaning" to a pattern of sound, the ere-rhymes. I calculated that the third use of that sound (stare) would be a surprise, the fourth (air) a monotony. I purposely made the end words of the third from last and last lines—*below* and *crab*—delayed rhymes for *row* and *slab,* the last being an internal and half-dissonant rhyme for the sake of bewilderment and incompleteness, qualities by which the man at the gate is at the moment possessed.

This is elementary but I cannot vouch for its success. As the dramatic situation of the poem is the tension that I have already described, so the rhythm is an attempt at a series of "modulations" back and forth between a formal regularity, for the heroic emotion, and a broken rhythm, with scattering imagery, for the failure of that emotion. This is "imitative form," which Yvor Winters deems a vice worth castigation. I have pointed out that the passage, "You know who have waited by the wall," presents the heroic theme of "active faith"; it will be observed that the rhythm, increasingly after "You who have waited for the angry resolution," is almost perfectly regular iambic, with only a few initial substitutions and weak endings. The passage is meant to convey a plenary vision, the actual presence, of the exemplars of active faith: the man at the gate at that moment is nearer to realizing them than at any other in the poem; hence the formal rhythm. But the vision breaks down; the wind-leaves refrain supervenes; and the next passage, "Turn your eyes to the immoderate past," is the irony of the preceding realization. With the self-conscious historical sense he turns his eyes into the past. The next passage after this, beginning, "You hear the shout . . ." is the failure of the vision in both phases, the pure realization and the merely historical. He cannot "see" the heroic virtues; there is wind, rain, leaves. But there is sound; for a moment he deceives himself with it. It is the noise of the battles that he has evoked. Then comes the figure of the rising sun of those battles; he is "lost in that orient of the thick and fast," and he curses his own moment, "the setting sun." The "setting sun" I tried to use as a triple image, for the decline of the heroic age and for the actual scene of late afternoon, the latter being not only natural desolation but spiritual desolation as well. Again for a moment he thinks he hears the battle shout, but only for a moment; then the silence reaches him.

Corresponding to the disintegration of the vision just described, there has been a breaking down of the formal rhythm. The complete breakdown comes with the images of the "mummy" and the "hound bitch." (*Hound* bitch because the hound is a hunter, participant of a formal ritual.) The failure of the vision throws the man back upon himself, but upon himself he cannot bring to bear the force of sustained imagination. He sees himself in random images (random to him, deliberate with the author) of something lower than he ought to be: the human image is only that of preserved death; but if he is alive he is an old hunter, dying. The passages about the mummy and the bitch are deliberately brief—slight rhythmic stretches. (These are the only verses I have written for which I thought of the movement first, then cast about for the symbols.)

I believe the term modulation denotes in music the uninterrupted shift from one key to another: I do not know the term for change of rhythm without change of measure. I wish to describe a similar change in verse rhythm; it may be convenient to think of it as modulation of a certain kind. At the end of the passage that I have been discussing the final words are "Hears the wind only." The phrase closes the first main division of the poem. I have loosely called the longer passages strophes, and if I were hardy enough to impose the classical organization of the lyric ode upon a baroque poem, I should say that these words bring to an end the Strophe, after which must come the next main division, or Antistrophe, which was often employed to answer the matter set forth in the Strophe or to present it from another point of view. And that is precisely the significance of the next main division, beginning: "Now that the salt of their blood . . ." But I wanted this second division of the poem to arise out of the collapse of the first. It is plain that it would not have suited my purpose to round off the first section with some sort of formal rhythm; so I ended it with an unfinished line. The next division must therefore begin by finishing that line, not merely in meter but with an integral rhythm. I will quote the passage:

> The hound bitch
> Toothless and dying, in a musty cellar
> *Hears the wind only.*
> > *Now that the salt of their blood*
> Stiffens the saltier oblivion of the sea,
> Seals the malignant purity of the flood. . . .

The caesura, after *only*, is thus at the middle of the third foot. (I do not give a full stress to *wind*, but attribute a "hovering stress" to *wind* and the first syllable of *only*.) The reader expects the foot to be completed by the stress on the next word, *Now*, as in a sense it is; but the phrase, "Now that the salt of their blood," is also the beginning of a new movement; it is two "dactyls" continuing more broadly the falling rhythm that has prevailed. But with the finishing off of the line with *blood*, the mounting rhythm is restored; the whole line from *Hears* to *blood* is actually an iambic pentameter with liberal inversions and substitutions that were expected to create a counter-rhythm within the line. From the caesura on, the rhythm is new; but it has—or was expected to

have—an organic relation to the preceding rhythm; and it signals the rise of a new statement of the theme.

I have gone into this passage in detail—I might have chosen another—not because I think it is successful, but because I labored with it; if it is a failure, or even an uninteresting success, it ought to offer as much technical instruction to other persons as it would were it both successful and interesting. But a word more: the broader movement introduced by the new rhythm was meant to correspond, as a sort of Antistrophe, to the earlier formal movement beginning, "You know who have waited by the wall." It is a new formal movement with new feeling and new imagery. The heroic but precarious illusion of the earlier movement has broken down into the personal symbols of the mummy and the hound; the pathetic fallacy of the leaves as charging soldiers and the conventional "buried Caesar" theme have become rotten leaves and dead bodies wasting in the earth, to return after long erosion to the sea. In the midst of this naturalism, what shall the man say? What shall all humanity say in the presence of decay? The two themes, then, have been struggling for mastery; the structure of the poem thus exhibits the development of two formal passages that contrast the two themes. The two formal passages break down, the first shading into the second ("Now that the salt of their blood . . ."), the second one concluding with the figure of the jaguar, which is presented in a distracted rhythm left suspended from a weak ending—the word *victim*. This figure of the jaguar is the only explicit rendering of the Narcissus motif in the poem, but instead of a youth gazing into a pool, a predatory beast stares at a jungle stream, and leaps to devour himself.

The next passage begins:

> What shall we say who have knowledge
> Carried to the heart?

This is Pascal's war between heart and head, between *finesse* and *géométrie*. Should the reader care to think of these lines as the gathering up of the two themes, now fused, into a final statement, I should see no objection to calling it the Epode. But upon the meaning of the lines from here to the end there is no need for further commentary. I have talked about the structure of the poem, not its quality. One can no more find the quality of one's own verse than one can find its value, and to try to find either is like looking into a glass for the effect that one's face has upon other persons.

If anybody ever wished to know anything about this poem that he could not interpret for himself, I suspect that he is still in the dark.

I cannot believe that I have illuminated the difficulties that some readers have found in the style. But then I cannot, have never been able to, see any difficulties of that order. The poem has been much revised. I still think there is much to be said for the original *barter* instead of *yield* in the second line, and for *Novembers* instead of *November* in line fifteen. The revisions were not undertaken for the convenience of the reader but for the poem's own clarity, so that, word, phrase, line, passage, the poem might at worst come near its best expression.

Wallace Stevens

THREE ACADEMIC PIECES: I (1947)

THE ACCURACY of accurate letters is an accuracy with respect to the structure of reality.

Thus, if we desire to formulate an accurate theory of poetry, we find it necessary to examine the structure of reality, because reality is the central reference for poetry. By way of accomplishing this, suppose we examine one of the significant components of the structure of reality—that is to say, the resemblance between things.

First, then, as to the resemblance between things in nature, it should be observed that resemblance constitutes a relation between them since, in some sense, all things resemble each other. Take, for example, a beach extending as far as the eye can reach, bordered, on the one hand, by trees and, on the other, by the sea. The sky is cloudless and the sun is red. In what sense do the objects in this scene resemble each other? There is enough green in the sea

to relate it to the palms. There is enough of the sky reflected in the water to create a resemblance, in some sense, between them. The sand is yellow between the green and the blue. In short, the light alone creates a unity not only in the recedings of distance, where differences become invisible, but also in the contacts of closer sight. So, too, sufficiently generalized, each man resembles all other men, each woman resembles all other women, this year resembles last year. The beginning of time will, no doubt, resemble the end of time. One world is said to resemble another.

A moment ago the resemblance between things was spoken of as one of the significant components of the structure of reality. It is significant because it creates the relation just described. It binds together. It is the base of appearance. In nature, however, the relation is between two or more of the parts of reality. In metaphor (and this word is used as a symbol for the single aspect of poetry with which we are now concerned—that is to say, the creation of resemblance by the imagination, even though metamorphosis might be a better word) —in metaphor, the resemblance may be, first, between two or more parts of reality; second, between something real and something imagined or, what is the same thing, between something imagined and something real as, for example, between music and whatever may be evoked by it; and, third, between two imagined things as when we say that God is good, since the statement involves a resemblance between two concepts, a concept of God and a concept of goodness.

We are not dealing with identity. Both in nature and in metaphor identity is the vanishing-point of resemblance. After all, if a man's exact double entered a room, seated himself and spoke the words that were in the man's mind, it would remain a resemblance. James Wardrop, in *Signature*, said recently:

The business of the press is to furnish an indefinite public with a potentially indefinite number of identical texts.

Nature is not mechanical to that extent for all its mornings and evenings, for all its inhabitants of China or India or Russia, for all its waves, or its leaves, or its hands. Its prodigy is not identity but resemblance and its universe of reproduction is not an assembly line but an incessant creation. Because this is so in nature, it is so in metaphor.

Nor are we dealing with imitation. The difference between imitation and resemblance is a nicety. An imitation may be described as an identity manqué. It is artificial. It is not fortuitous as a true metaphor is. If it is an imitation of something in nature, it may even surpass identity and assume a praeter-nature. It may very well escape the derogatory. If it is an imitation of something in metaphor, it is lifeless and that, finally, is what is wrong with it. Resemblance in metaphor is an activity of the imagination; and in metaphor the imagination is life. In Chinese metaphor, there is a group of subjects to which poets used to address themselves, just as early Western painters and etchers used to address themselves to such a subject as the Virgin crowned by Angels. The variations in these themes were not imitations, nor identities, but resemblances.

In reality, there is a level of resemblance, which is the level of nature. In metaphor, there is no such level. If there were it would be the level of resemblance of the imagination, which has no such level. If, to our surprise, we should meet a monsieur who told us that he was from another world, and if he had in fact all the indicia of divinity, the luminous body, the nimbus, the heraldic stigmata, we should recognize him as above the level of nature but not as above the level of the imagination. So, too, if, to our surprise, we should meet one of these morons whose remarks are so conspicuous a part of the folklore of the world of the radio —remarks made without using either the tongue or the brain, spouted much like the spoutings of small whales—we should recognize him as below the level of nature but not as below the level of the imagination. It is not, however, a question of above or below but simply of beyond. Level is an abbreviated form of level of resemblance. The statement that the imagination has no level of resemblance is not to be taken as a statement that the imagination itself has no limits. The imagination is deceptive in this respect. There is a limit to its power to surpass resemblance and that limit is to be found in nature. The imagination is able to manipulate nature as by creating three legs and five arms but it is not able to create a totally new nature as, for instance, a new element with creatures indigenous thereto, their costumes and cuisines. Any discussion of level is a discussion of balance as well. Thus, a false exaggeration is a disturbing of the balance between reality and the imagination.

Resemblances between one object and another as between one brick and another, one egg and another, are elementary. There are many objects which in respect to what they suggest resemble other objects and we may include here, as objects, people. Thus, in addition to the fact that one man resembles all other men, something about one man may make him resemble some other particular man and this is true even when the something about him is detached from him, as his wig. The wig of a particular man reminds us of some other particular man and resembles him. A strand of a child's hair brings back the whole child and in that way resembles the child. There must be vast numbers of things within this category. Apparently objects of sentiment most easily prove the existence of this kind of resemblance: something in a locket, one's grandfather's high beaver hat, one's grandmother's hand-woven blankets. One may find intimations of immortality in an object on the mantelpiece; and these intimations are as real in the mind in which they occur as the mantelpiece itself. Even if they are only a part of an adult make-believe, the whole point is that the structure of reality because of the range of resemblances that it contains is measurably an adult make-believe. Perhaps the whole field of connotation is based on resemblance. Perhaps resemblance which seems to be related so closely to the imagination is related even more closely to the intelligence, of which perceptions of resemblance are effortless accelerations.

What has just been said shows that there are private resemblances. The resemblance of the baby's shoes to the baby, by suggestion, is likely to be a resemblance that exists for one or two alone. A public resemblance, by contrast, like the resemblance of the profile of a mountain to the profile of General Washington, exists for that great class of people who co-exist with the great ferns in public gardens, amplified music and minor education. What our eyes behold may well be the text of life but one's meditations on the text and the disclosures of these meditations are no less a part of the structure of reality.

It quite seems as if there is an activity that makes one thing resemble another (possibly as a phase of the police power of conformity). What the eye beholds may be the text of life. It is, nevertheless, a text that we do not write. The eye does not beget in resemblance. It sees.

But the mind begets in resemblance as the painter begets in representation; that is to say, as the painter makes his world within a world; or as the musician begets in music, in the obvious small pieces having to do with gardens in the rain or the fountains of Rome and in the obvious larger pieces having to do with the sea, Brazilian night or those woods in the neighborhood of Vienna in which the hunter was accustomed to blow his horn and in which, also, yesterday, the birds sang preludes to the atom bomb. It is not difficult, having once predicated such an activity, to attribute it to a desire for resemblance. What a ghastly situation it would be if the world of the dead was actually different from the world of the living and, if as life ends, instead of passing to a former Victorian sphere, we passed into a land in which none of our problems had been solved, after all, and nothing resembled anything we have ever known and nothing resembled anything else in shape, in color, in sound, in look or otherwise. To say farewell to our generation and to look forward to a continuation in a Jerusalem of pure surrealism would account for the taste for oblivion.

The study of the activity of resemblance is an approach to the understanding of poetry. Poetry is a satisfying of the desire for resemblance. As the mere satisfying of a desire, it is pleasurable. But poetry if it did nothing but satisfy a desire would not rise above the level of many lesser things. Its singularity is that in the act of satisfying the desire for resemblance it touches the sense of reality, it enhances the sense of reality, heightens it, intensifies it. If resemblance is described as a partial similarity between two dissimilar things, it complements and reinforces that which the two dissimilar things have in common. It makes it brilliant. When the similarity is between things of adequate dignity, the resemblance may be said to transfigure or to sublimate them. Take, for example, the resemblance between reality and any projection of it in belief or in metaphor. What is it that these two have in common? Is not the glory of the idea of any future state a relation between a present and a future glory? The brilliance of earth is the brilliance of every paradise. However, not all poetry attempts such grandiose transfiguration. Everyone can call to mind a variety of figures and see clearly how these resemblances please and why; how inevitably they heighten our sense of reality. The images in Ecclesiastes:

                                    Or ever
the silver cord be loosed, or the golden bowl be broken, or the pitcher be broken at the fountain, or the wheel broken at the cistern—

these images are not the language of reality, they are the symbolic language of metamorphosis, or resemblance, of poetry, but they relate to reality and they intensify our sense of it and they give us the pleasure of "lentor and solemnity" in respect to the most commonplace objects. These images have a special interest, as a group of images in harmony with each other. In both prose and poetry, images come willingly but, usually, although there is a relation between the subject of the images there is no relation between the images themselves. A group of images in harmony with each other would constitute a poem within, or above, a poem. The suggestion sounds euphuistic. If the desire for resemblance is the desire to enjoy reality, it may be no less true that the desire to enjoy reality, an acute enough desire today, is the desire for elegance. Euphuism had its origin in the desire for elegance and it was euphuism that was a reason in the sun for metaphor. A school of literary ascetics denying itself any indulgence in resemblances would, necessarily, fall back on reality and vent all its relish there. The metaphorical school, in the end, does the same thing.

The proliferation of resemblances extends an object. The point at which this process begins, or rather at which this growth begins, is the point at which ambiguity has been reached. The ambiguity that is so favorable to the poetic mind is precisely the ambiguity favorable to resemblance. In this ambiguity, the intensification of reality by resemblance increases realization and this increased realization is pleasurable. It is as if a man who lived indoors should go outdoors on a day of sympathetic weather. His realization of the weather would exceed that of a man who lives outdoors. It might, in fact, be intense enough to convert the real world about him into an imagined world. In short, a sense of reality keen enough to be in excess of the normal sense of reality creates a reality of its own. Here what matters is that the intensification of the sense of reality creates a resemblance: that reality of its own is a reality. This may be going round a circle, first clockwise, then anticlockwise. If the savor of life is the savor of reality, the fact will establish itself whichever way one approaches it.

The relations between the ego and reality must be left largely on the margin. Yet Narcissus did not expect, when he looked in the stream, to find in his hair a serpent coiled to strike, nor, when he looked in his own eyes there, to be met by a look of hate, nor, in general, to discover himself at the center of an inexplicable ugliness from which he would be bound to avert himself. On the contrary, he sought out his image everywhere because it was the principle of his nature to do so and, to go a step beyond that, because it was the principle of his nature, as it is of ours, to expect to find pleasure in what he found. Narcissism, then, involves something beyond the prime sense of the word. It involves, also, this principle, that as we seek out our resemblances we expect to find pleasure in doing so; that is to say, in what we find. So strong is that expectation that we find nothing else. What is true of the observations of ourselves is equally true of the observations of resemblances between other things having no relation to us. We say that the sea, when it expands in a calm and immense reflection of the sky, resembles the sky, and this statement gives us pleasure. We enjoy the resemblance for the same reason that, if it were possible to look into the sea as into glass and if we should do so and suddenly should behold there some extraordinary transfiguration of ourselves, the experience would strike us as one of those amiable revelations that nature occasionally vouchsafes to favorites. So, when we think of arpeggios, we think of opening wings and the effect of the resemblance is pleasurable. When we read Ecclesiastes the effect of the symbols is pleasurable because as symbols they are resemblances and as resemblances they are pleasurable and they are pleasurable because it is a principle of our nature that they should be, the principle being not something derived from Narcissism since Narcissism itself is merely an evidence of the operation of the principle that we expect to find pleasure in resemblances.

We have been trying to get at a truth about poetry, to get at one of the principles that compose the theory of poetry. It comes to this, that poetry is a part of the structure of reality. If this has been demonstrated, it pretty much amounts to saying that the structure of poetry and the structure of reality are one or, in effect, that poetry and reality are one, or should be. This may be less thesis than hypothesis. Yet hypotheses relating to poetry, although they may appear to be very distant illuminations, could be the fires of fate, if rhetoric ever meant anything.

There is a gradus ad Metaphoram. The nature of a metaphor is, like the nature of a play, comic, tragic, tragic-comic and so on. It may be poetic. A poetic metaphor—that is to say, a metaphor poetic in a sense more specific than the sense in which poetry and metaphor are one—appears to be poetry at its source. It is. At least it is poetry at one of its sources although not necessarily the most fecundating. But the steps to this particular abstraction, the gradus ad Metaphoram in respect to the general sense in which poetry and metaphor are one, are, like the ascent to any of the abstractions that interest us importantly, an ascent through illusion which gathers round us more closely and thickly, as we might expect it to do, the more we penetrate it.

In the fewest possible words since, as between resemblances, one is always a little more nearly perfect than another and since, from this, it is easy for perfectionism of a sort to evolve, it is not too extravagant to think of resemblances and of the repetitions of resemblances as a source of the ideal. In short, metaphor has its aspect of the ideal. This aspect of it cannot be dismissed merely because we think that we have long since outlived the ideal. The truth is that we are constantly outliving it and yet the ideal itself remains alive with an enormous life.

William Carlos Williams

AN ESSAY ON *LEAVES OF GRASS* (1955)

LEAVES OF GRASS! It was a good title for a book of poems, especially for a new book of American poems. It was a challenge to the entire

concept of the poetic idea, and from a new viewpoint, a rebel viewpoint, an American viewpoint. In a word and at the beginning it enunciated a shocking truth, that the common ground is of itself a poetic source. There had been inklings before this that such was the case in the works of Robert Burns and the poet Wordsworth, but in this instance the very forms of the writing had been altered: it had gone over to the style of the words as they appeared on the page. Whitman's so-called "free verse" was an assault on the very citadel of the poem itself; it constituted a direct challenge to all living poets to show cause why they should not do likewise. It is a challenge that still holds good after a century of vigorous life during which it has been practically continuously under fire but never defeated.

From the beginning Whitman realized that the matter was largely technical. It had to be free verse or nothing with him and he seldom varied from that practice—and never for more than the writing of an occasional poem. It was a sharp break, and if he was to go astray he had no one but himself to blame for it. It was a technical matter, true enough, and he would stick it out to the end, but to do any more with it than simply to write the poems was beyond him.

He had seen a great light but forgot almost at once after the first revelation everything but his "message," the idea which originally set him in motion, the idea on which he had been nurtured, the idea of democracy—and took his eye off the words themselves which should have held him.

The point is purely academic—the man had his hands full with the conduct of his life and couldn't, if they had come up, be bothered with other matters. As a result, he made no further progress as an artist but, in spite of various topical achievements, continued to write with diminishing effectiveness for the remainder of his life.

He didn't know any better. He didn't have the training to construct his verses after a conscious mold which would have given him power over them to turn them this way, then that, at will. He only knew how to give them birth and to release them to go their own way. He was preoccupied with the great ideas of the time, to which he was devoted, but, after all, poems are made out of words not ideas. He never showed any evidence of knowing this and the unresolved forms consequent upon his be-

ginnings remained in the end just as he left them.

Verses, in English, are frequently spoken of as measures. It is a fortunate designation as it gives us, in looking at them, the idea of elapsed time. We are reminded that the origin of our verse was the dance—and even if it had not been the dance, the heart when it is stirred has its multiple beats, and verse at its most impassioned sets the heart violently beating. But as the heart picks up we also begin to count. Finally, the measure for each language and environment is accepted. In English it is predominantly the iambic pentameter, but whether that is so for the language Whitman spoke is something else again. It is a point worth considering, but apart from the briefest of notices a point not to be considered here. It may be that the essential pace of the English and the American languages is diametrically opposed each to the other and that that is an important factor in the writing of their poetry, but that is for the coming generations to discover. Certainly not only the words but the meter, the measure that governed Whitman's verses, was not English. But there were more pressing things than abstract discussions of meter to be dealt with at that time and the poet soon found himself involved in them.

Very likely the talk and the passionate talk about freedom had affected him as it had infected the French and many others earlier. It is said that, when as a young man he lived in New Orleans, he had fallen in love with a beautiful octoroon but had allowed his friends and relatives to break up the match. It is possible that the disappointment determined the pattern of his later rebellion in verse. Free verse was his great idea! *Versos sueltos* the Spanish call them. It is not an entirely new idea, but it was entirely new to the New York Yankee who was, so to speak, waiting for it with open arms and an overcharged soul and the example of Thomas Jefferson to drive him on.

But verse had always been, for Englishmen and the colonials that imitated them, a disciplined maneuver of the intelligence, as it is today, in which measure was predominant. They resented this American with his new idea, and attacked him in a characteristic way —*on moral grounds*. And he fell for it. He had no recourse but to defend himself and the fat was in the fire. How could verse be free without being immoral? There is something to it. It is the same attack, with a more modern tilt to it, that undoubtedly bothers T. S. Eliot. He is one of the best informed of our writers and would do us a great service, if free verse— mold it as he will—is not his choice, to find us an alternative. From the evidence, he has tried to come up with just that, but up to the present writing he has not brought the thing off.

The case of Mr. Eliot is in this respect interesting. He began writing at Harvard from a thoroughly well-schooled background and produced a body of verse that was immediately so successful that when his poem *The Waste Land* was published, it drove practically everyone else from the field. Ezra Pound, who had helped him arrange the poem on the page, was confessedly jealous. Other American poets had to take second place. A new era, under domination of a return to a study of the classics, was gratefully acknowledged by the universities, and Mr. Eliot, not Mr. Pound, was ultimately given the Nobel Prize. The drift was plainly away from all that was native to America, Whitman among the rest, and toward the study of the past and England.

Though no one realized it, a violent revolution had taken place in American scholarship and the interests from which it stemmed. Eliot had completely lost interest in all things American, in the very ideology of all that America stood for, including the idea of freedom itself in any of its phases. Whitman as a symbol of indiscriminate freedom was completely antipathetic to Mr. Eliot, who now won the country away from him again. The tendency toward freedom in the verse forms, which seemed to be thriving among American poets, was definitely checked and the stage was taken over for other things. I

shall never forget the impression created by *The Waste Land*; it was as if the bottom had dropped out of everything. I had not known how much the spirit of Whitman animated us until it was withdrawn from us. Free verse became overnight a thing of the past. Men went about congratulating themselves as upon the disappearance of something that had disturbed their dreams; and indeed it was so—the dreams of right-thinking students of English verse had long been disturbed by the appearance among them of the horrid specter of Whitman's free verse. Now it was as if a liberator, a Saint George, had come just in the nick of time to save them. The instructors in all the secondary schools were grateful.

Meanwhile, Mr. Eliot had become a British subject and removed himself to England where he took up residence. He became a member of the Church of England. He was determined to make the break with America complete, as his fellow artist Henry James had done before him, and began to publish such poems as *Ash Wednesday* and the play *Murder in the Cathedral*, and the *Four Quartets*. Something had happened to him, something drastic, something to do, doubtless, with man's duty and his freedom in the world. It is a far cry from this to Whitman's thought of man as a free agent. The pendulum had gone the full swing.

It is inevitable for us to connect the happenings in the world generally with what takes place in the poem. When Mr. Eliot quit writing, when he quit writing poems, it looked as if he had got to a point where he had nowhere else to turn, and as if in his despair he had given up not only the poem but the world. A man as clever and well informed as he was had the whole world at his feet, but the only conclusion that he reached was that he wanted none of it. Especially did he want none of the newer freedom.

Not that he didn't in his verse try it on, for size, let us say, in his later experiments, particularly in *Four Quartets*, but even there he soon came to the end of his rope. The accented strophe he had definitely given up, as Wagner in the prelude to *Parsifal* had done the same, but to infer from that fact that he had discovered the freedom of a new measure was not true. It looked to me, at least, as if there were some profound depth to his probing beyond which he dared not go without compromising his religious faith. He did not attempt it. It is useful to record the limits of his penetration and the point at which he gave up his attempts to penetrate further. Just how far shall we go in our search for freedom and, more importantly, how shall our efforts toward a greater freedom be conditioned in our verses? All these decisions, which must be reached in deciding what to do, have implications of general value in our lives.

The young men who are students of literature today in our universities do not believe in seeking within the literary forms, the lines, the foot, the way in which to expand their efforts to know the universe, as Whitman did, but are content to follow the theologians and Mr. Eliot. In that, they are children of the times; they risk nothing, for by risking an expanded freedom you are very likely to come a cropper. What, in the words of Hjalmar Ekdahl in *The Wild Duck*, are you going to invent?

Men, offering their heads, have always come up with new proposals, and the world of events waits upon them, and who shall say whether it were better to close one's eyes or go forward like Galileo to the light or wait content in the darkness like the man in the next county? Whitman went forward to what to him seemed desirable, and so if we are to reject him entirely we must at least follow him at the start to find out what his discoveries were intended to signify and what not to signify.

Certainly, we are in our day through with such loose freedom as he employed in his verses in the blind belief that it was all going to come out right in the end. We know now that it is not. But are we, because of that, to give up freedom entirely? Merely to put down the lines as they happen to come into your head will not make a poem, and if, as hap-pened more than once in Whitman's case, a poem results, who is going to tell what he has made? The man knew what he was doing, but he did not know all he was doing. Much still remains to discover, but that freedom in the conduct of the verses is desirable cannot be questioned.

There is a very moving picture of Whitman facing the breakers coming in on the New Jersey shore, when he heard the onomatopoeic waves talk to him direct in a Shakespearean language which might have been Lear himself talking to the storm. But it was not what it seemed; it was a new language, an unnamed language which Whitman could not identify or control.

For as the English had foreseen, this freedom of which there had been so much talk had to have limits somewhere. If not, it would lead you astray. That was the problem. And there was at about that time a whole generation of Englishmen, prominent among whom was Frank Harris, whom it did lead astray in moral grounds, just as there were Frenchmen at the time of the French Revolution who were led astray and are still being led astray under the difficult conditions that exist today. It is the reaction against such patterns of thought that moved Eliot and that part of the present generation which is not swallowed up by its fascination with the scene which draws them to Paris whenever they get the opportunity to go there. For in your search for freedom—which is desirable—you must stop somewhere, but where exactly shall you stop? Whitman could not say.

To propose that the answer to the problem should lie in the verse itself would have been to those times an impertinence—and the same would be the case even now. The Greeks had their Dionysia in the spring of the year, when morals could be forgotten, and then the control of life resumed its normal course. In other words, they departmentalized their lives, being of an orderly cast of mind, but we do not lend ourselves easily to such a solution. With us it is all or nothing, provided we are not caught at it.

Either we give ourselves to a course of action or we do not give ourselves. Either we are to be free men or not free men—at least in theory. Whitman, like Tom Paine, recognized no limits and that got him into trouble.

But the waves on the Jersey shore still came tumbling in, quieting him as their secret escaped him, isolating him and leaving him lonesome—but possessed by the great mystery which won the world to his side. For he was unquestionably the child of the years. What was the wave that moved the dawning century also moved him and demanded his recognition, and it was not to be denied. All the discoveries and inventions which were to make the twentieth century exceed all others, for better or worse, were implicit in his work. He surpassed the ritualistic centuries which preceded him, just as Ehrlich and Koch and finally Einstein were to exceed Goethe. It was destined to be so, and the New World of which he was a part gave him birth. He had invented a new way of assaulting fate. "Make new!" was to him as it was to Pound much later on an imperious command which completely controlled him.

If he was to enlarge his opportunity he needed room, in verse as in everything else. But there were to be no fundamental changes in the concepts that keep our lives going at an accepted pace and within normal limits. The line was still to be the line, quite in accord with the normal contours of our accepted verse forms. It is not so much that which brought Whitman's verse into question but the freedom with which he laid it on the page. There he had abandoned all sequence and all order. It was as if a tornado had struck.

A new order had hit the world, a relative order, a new measure with which no one was familiar. The thing that no one realized, and this includes Whitman himself, is that the native which they were dealing with was no longer English but a new language akin to the New World to which its nature accorded in subtle ways that they did not recognize. That made all the difference. And not only was it new to America—it was new to the world.

There was to be a new measure applied to all things, for there was to be a new order operative in the world. But it has to be insisted on that it was not disorder. Whitman's verses seemed disorderly, but ran according to an unfamiliar and a difficult measure. It was an order which was essential to the new world, not only of the poem, but to the world of chemistry and physics. In this way, the man was more of a prophet than he knew. The full significance of his innovations in the verse patterns has not yet been fully disclosed.

The change in the entire aesthetic of American art as it began to differ not only from British but from all the art of the world up to this time was due to this tremendous change in measure, a relative measure, which he was the first to feel and to embody in his works. What he was leaving behind did not seem to oppress him, but it oppressed the others and rightly so.

It is time now to look at English and American verse at the time Whitman began to write, for only by so doing can we be led to discover what he did and the course that lay before him. He had many formidable rivals to face on his way to success. But his chief opponent was, as he well knew, the great and medieval Shakespeare. And if any confirmation of Shakespeare's sacrosanct position in the language is still sought it is easily to be obtained when anything is breathed mentioning some alteration in the verse forms which he distinguished by using them. He may be imitated as Christopher Fry imitates him, but to vary or depart from him is heresy. Taken from this viewpoint, the clinical sheets of Shakespeare as a writer are never much studied. That he was the greatest word-man that ever existed in the language or out of it is taken for granted but there the inquiry ends.

Shakespeare presented Whitman with a nut hard to crack. What to do with the English language? It was all the more of a problem since the elements of it could not be presented at all or even recognized to exist. As far as the English language was concerned, there was only to use it and to use it well according to the great tradition of the masters.

And indeed it was a magnificent tradition. At the beginning of the seventeenth century it had reached an apogee which it had, to a great extent, maintained to the present day and of which it was proud and jealous. But when Shakespeare wrote, the laurels were new and had so recently been attained and had come from such distinguished achievements that the world seemed to pause for breath. It was a sort of noon and called for a halt. The man himself seemed to feel it and during an entire lifetime did no more than develop to the full his talents. It was noon sure enough for him, and he had only to stretch out in the sun and expand his mood.

Unlike Whitman, he was or represented the culmination of a historic as well as literary past whose forms were just coming to a head after the great trials which were to leave their marks on the centuries. There had been Chaucer, but the language had come of age since then as had the country. Now America had been discovered and the world could not grow much larger. Further expansion, except in a limited degree, was unlikely, so that the poet was left free to develop his world of detail but was not called upon to extend it. More was not necessary than to find something to do and develop it for the entire span of a long life. But as always with the artist, selection was an important point in the development.

For instance, as his sonnets show, Shakespeare was an accomplished rhymer, but he gave it up early. The patches of heroic couplet which he wrote for the Players in *Hamlet* are among the best examples of that form. Yet his main reliance was on blank verse—though he did, on occasion, try his hand at a triple accent which he rejected without more than a thought. The demands of the age called for other things and he was, above everything else, a practical man.

Practicing for so long a time upon the iambic pentameter, he had the opportunity to develop himself prodigiously in it. Over the years he shows a technical advance, a certain

impatience with restraint in his work which makes it loose and verges more toward the conformation of prose. There is a great difference between Shakespeare's earlier and later work, the latter being freer and more natural in tone.

A feeling for prose began to be felt all through his verse. But at his death the form began to lapse rapidly into the old restrictions. It got worse and worse with the years until all the Elizabethan tenor had been stripped away, or as Milton phrased it speaking of his illustrious predecessor:

> Sweetest Shakespeare, Nature's child,
> Warbled his native woodnotes wild.

With Milton came Cromwell and the English Revolution, and Shakespeare was forgotten, together with the secrets of his versification, just as Whitman today is likely to be forgotten and the example of his verses and all that refers to him.

The interest that drove Whitman on is the same one that drove Shakespeare at the end of his life in an attempt to enlarge the scope of written verse, to find more of expression in the forms of the language employed. But the consequences of such experimentation are always drastic and amount in the end to its suppression, which in the person of a supreme genius is not easy.

From what has been said thus far, you can see why it is impossible to imitate Shakespeare; he was part of a historic process which cannot repeat itself. All imitations of the forms of the past are meaningless, empty shells, which have merely the value of decorations. So that, if anything is now to be created, it must be in a new form. Whitman, if he was to do anything of moment, could not, no matter how much he may have bowed down to the master, imitate him. It would not have had any meaning at all. And his responsibility to the new language was such that he had no alternative but to do as it bade him.

Though he may not have known it, with Whitman the whole spirit of the age itself had been brought under attack. It was a blind stab which he could not identify any more than a child. How could he, no matter how acute his instincts were, have foreseen the discoveries in chemistry, in physics, in abnormal psychology, or even the invention of the telephone or the disclosure of our subterranean wealth in petroleum? He knew only, as did those who were disturbed by his free verse, that something had occurred to the normal structure of conventional aesthetic and that he could not accept it any longer. Therefore, he acted.

We have to acknowledge at once in seeking a meaning involving the complex concerns of the world that the philosophic, the aesthetic, and the mechanical are likely to stem in their development from the same root. One may be much in advance of the other in its discoveries, but in the end a great equalizing process is involved so that the discovery of the advance in the structure of the poetic line is equated by an advance in the conception of physical facts all along the line. Man has no choice in these matters; the only question is, will he recognize the changes that are taking place in time to make the proper use of them? And when time itself is conceived of as relative, no matter how abstruse that may sound, the constructions, the right constructions, cannot be accepted with a similar interpretation. It may take time to bring this about, but when a basic change has occurred in our underlying concern it brooks no interference in the way it will work itself out.

Whitman didn't know anything about this, nor does Mr. Eliot take it into his considerations nor Father Merton either, but if they had to construct a satisfactory poetic line it had and still has to be done according to this precept. For we have learned, if we have learned anything from the past, that the principles of physics are immutable. Best, if you do not approve of what writing has become, to follow

in Mr. Eliot's footsteps.

For it is important to man's fate that these matters be—if anything is important to man's fate in this modern world. At least, you cannot retrace steps that have been taken in the past. And you don't know, you simply do not know, what may come of it. No more than Whitman knew what his struggle to free verse may have implied and may still imply for us no matter how, at the moment, the world may have forsaken him. The books are not closed even though the drift in the tide of our interest may at the moment be all the other way. It cannot so soon have reversed itself. Something is still pending, though the final shape of the thing has not yet crystallized. Perhaps that is the reason for the regression. There are too many profitable leads in other associated fields of the intelligence for us to draw back now.

Where have the leads which are *not* aesthetic tended to take us in the present century? By paying attention to detail and our telescopes and microscopes and the reinterpretations of their findings, we realize that man has long since broken from the confinement of the more rigid of his taboos. It is reasonable to suppose that he will in the future, in spite of certain setbacks, continue to follow the same course.

Man finds himself on the earth whether he likes it or not, with nowhere else to go. What then is to become of him? Obviously we can't stand still or we shall be destroyed. Then if there is no room for us on the outside we shall, in spite of ourselves, have to go *in:* into the cell, the atom, the poetic line, for our discoveries. We have to break the old apart to make room for ourselves, whatever may be our tragedy and however we may fear it. By making room within the line itself for his inventions, Whitman revealed himself to be a worthy and courageous man of his age and, to boot, a farseeing one.

Dylan Thomas

NOTES ON THE ART OF POETRY (1951)

YOU WANT TO KNOW why and how I just began to write poetry, and which poets or kinds of poetry I was first moved and influenced by.

To answer the first part of this question, I should say I wanted to write poetry in the beginning because I had fallen in love with words. The first poems I knew were nursery rhymes, and before I could read them for myself I had come to love just the words of them, the words alone. What the words stood for, symbolised, or meant, was of very secondary importance. What mattered was the *sound* of them as I heard them for the first time on the lips of the remote and incomprehensible grown-ups who seemed, for some reason, to be living in my world. And these words were, to me, as the notes of bells, the sounds of musical instruments, the noises of wind, sea, and rain, the rattle of milkcarts, the clopping of hooves on cobbles, the fingering of branches on a window pane, might be to someone, deaf from birth, who has miraculously found his hearing. I did not care what the words said, overmuch, nor what happened to Jack and Jill and the Mother Goose rest of them; I cared for the shapes of sound that their names, and the words describing their actions, made in my ears; I cared for the colours the words cast on my eyes. I realise that I may be, as I think back all that way, romanticising my reactions to the simple and beautiful words of those pure poems; but that is all I can honestly remember, however

A reply to a student's questions.

much time might have falsified my memory. I fell in love—that is the only expression I can think of—at once, and am still at the mercy of words, though sometimes now, knowing a little of their behaviour very well, I think I can influence them slightly and have even learned to beat them now and then, which they appear to enjoy. I tumbled for words at once. And, when I began to read the nursery rhymes for myself, and, later, to read other verses and ballads, I knew that I had discovered the most important things, to me, that could be ever. There they were, seemingly lifeless, made only of black and white, but out of them, out of their own being, came love and terror and pity and pain and wonder and all the other vague abstractions that make our ephemeral lives dangerous, great, and bearable. Out of them came the gusts and grunts and hiccups and heehaws of the common fun of the earth; and though what the words meant was, in its own way, often deliciously funny enough, so much funnier seemed to me, at that almost forgotten time, the shape and shade and size and noise of the words as they hummed, strummed, jugged and galloped along. That was the time of innocence; words burst upon me, unencumbered by trivial or portentous association; words were their spring-like selves, fresh with Eden's dew, as they flew out of the air. They made their own original associations as they sprang and shone. The words, "Ride a cock-horse to Banbury Cross," were as haunting to me, who did not know then what a cock-horse was nor cared a damn where Banbury Cross might be, as, much later, were such lines as John Donne's,

"Go and catch a falling star, Get with child a mandrake root," which also I could not understand when I first read them. And as I read more and more, and it was not all verse, by any means, my love for the real life of words increased until I knew that I must live *with* them and *in* them always. I knew, in fact, that I must be a writer of words, and nothing else. The first thing was to feel and know their sound and substance; what I was going to do with those words, what use I was going to make of them, what I was going to *say* through them, would come later. I knew I had to know them most intimately in all their forms and moods, their ups and downs, their chops and changes, their needs and demands. (Here, I am afraid, I am beginning to talk too vaguely. I do not like writing *about* words, because then I often use bad and wrong and stale and wooly words. What I like to do is to treat words as a craftsman does his wood or stone or what-have-you, to hew, carve, mould, coil, polish and plane them into patterns, sequences, sculptures, fugues of sound expressing some lyrical impulse, some spiritual doubt or conviction, some dimly-realised truth I must try to reach and realise.) It was when I was very young, and just at school, that, in my father's study, before homework that was never done, I began to know one kind of writing from another, one kind of goodness, one kind of badness. My first, and greatest, liberty was that of being able to read everything and anything I cared to. I read indiscriminately, and with my eyes hanging out. I could never have dreamt that there were such goings-on in the world between the covers of books, such sand-storms and ice-blasts of words, such slashing of humbug, and humbug too, such staggering peace, such enormous laughter, such and so many blinding bright lights breaking across the just-awaking wits and splashing all over the pages in a million bits and pieces all of which were words, words, words, and each of which was alive forever in its own delight and glory and oddity and light. (I must try not to make these supposedly helpful notes as confusing as my poems themselves.) I wrote endless imitations, though I never thought them to be imitations but, rather, wonderfully original things, like eggs laid by tigers. They were imitations of anything I happened to be reading at the time: Sir Thomas Browne, de Quincey, Henry Newbolt, the Ballads, Blake, Baroness Orczy, Marlowe, Chums, the Imagists, the Bible, Poe, Keats, Lawrence, Anon., and Shakespeare. A mixed lot, as you see, and randomly remembered. I tried my callow hand at almost every poetical form. How could I learn the tricks of a trade unless I tried to do them myself? I learned that the bad tricks come easily; and the good ones, which help you to say what you think you wish to say in the most meaningful, moving way, I am still learning. (But in earnest company you must call these tricks by other names, such as technical devices, prosodic experiments, etc.)

The writers, then, who influenced my earliest poems and stories were, quite simply and truthfully, all the writers I was reading at the time, and, as you see from a specimen list higher up the page, they ranged from writers of schoolboy adventure yarns to incomparable and inimitable masters like Blake. That is, when I began, bad writing had as much influence on my stuff as good. The bad influences I tried to remove and renounce bit by bit, shadow by shadow, echo by echo, through trial and error, through delight and disgust and misgiving, as I came to love words more and to hate the heavy hands that knocked them about, the thick tongues that [had] no feel for their multitudinous tastes, the dull and botching hacks who flattened them out into a colourless and insipid paste, the pedants who made them moribund and pompous as themselves. Let me say that the things that first made me love language and want to work *in* it and *for* it were nursery rhymes and folk tales, the Scottish Ballads, a few lines of hymns, the most famous Bible stories and the rhythms of the Bible, Blake's Songs of Innocence, and the quite incomprehensible magical majesty and nonsense of Shakespeare heard, read, and near-murdered in the first forms of my school.

* * *

You ask me, next, if it is true that three of the dominant influences on my published prose and poetry are Joyce, the Bible, and Freud. (I purposely say my "published" prose and poetry, as in the preceding pages I have been talking about the primary influences upon my very first and forever unpublishable juvenilia.) I cannot say that I have been "influenced" by Joyce, whom I enormously admire and whose Ulysses, and earlier stories I have read a great deal. I think this Joyce question arose because somebody once, in print, remarked on the closeness of the title of my book of short stories, "Portrait of the Artist As a Young Dog" to Joyce's title, "Portrait of the Artist as a Young Man." As you know, the name given to innumerable portrait paintings by their artists is, "Portrait of the Artist as a Young Man"—a perfectly straightforward title. Joyce used the painting-title for the first time as the title of a literary work. I myself made a bit of doggish fun of the *painting*-title and, of course, intended no possible reference to Joyce. I do not think that Joyce has had any hand at all in my writing; certainly, his Ulysses has not. On the other hand, I cannot deny that the shaping of some of my "Portrait" stories might owe something to Joyce's stories in the volume "Dubliners." But then, "Dubliners" was a pioneering work in the world of the short story, and no good storywriter since can have failed, in some way, however little, to have benefited by it.

The Bible, I have referred to in attempting to answer your first question. Its great stories, of Noah, Jonah, Lot, Moses, Jacob, David, Solomon and a thousand more, I had, of course, known from very early youth; the great rhythms had rolled over me from the Welsh pulpits; and I read, for myself, from Job and Ecclesiastes; and the story of the New Testament is part of my life. But I have never sat down and studied the Bible, never consciously echoed its language, and am, in reality, as ignorant of it as most brought-up Christians. All of the Bible that I use in my work is remembered from childhood, and is the common property of all who were brought up in English-speaking communities. Nowhere, indeed, in all my writing, do I use any knowledge which is not commonplace to any literate person. I *have* used a few difficult words in early poems, but they are easily looked-up and were, in any case, thrown into the poems in a kind of adolescent showing-off which I hope I have now discarded.

And that leads me to the third "dominant influence": Sigmund Freud. My only acquaintance with the theories and discoveries of Dr. Freud has been through the work of novelists who have been excited by his case-book histories, of popular newspaper scientific-potboilers who have, I imagine, vulgarised his work beyond recognition, and of a few modern poets, including Auden, who have attempted to use psychoanalytical phraseology and theory in some of their poems. I have read only one book of Freud's, "The Interpretation of Dreams," and do not recall having been influenced by it in any way. Again, no honest writer today can possibly avoid being influenced by Freud through his pioneering work into the Unconscious and by the influence of those discoveries on the scientific, philosophic, and artistic work of his contemporaries: but not, by any means, necessarily through Freud's own writing.

To your third question—Do I deliberately utilise devices of rhyme, rhythm, and word-formation in my writing—I must, of course, answer with an immediate, Yes. I am a painstaking, conscientious, involved and devious craftsman in words, however unsuccessful the result so often appears, and to whatever wrong uses I may apply my technical paraphernalia. I use everything and anything to make my poems work and move in the direction I want them to: old tricks, new tricks, puns, portmanteau-words, paradox, allusion, paronomasia, paragram, catachresis, slang, assonantal rhymes, vowel rhymes, sprung rhythm. Every device there is in language is there to be used if you will. Poets have got to enjoy themselves sometimes, and the twisting and convolutions of words, the inventions and contrivances, are all part of the joy that is part of the painful, voluntary work.

Your next question asks whether my use of combinations of words to create something new, "in the Surrealist way," is according to a set formula or is spontaneous.

There is a confusion here, for the Surrealists' set formula *was* to juxtapose the unpremeditated.

Let me make it clearer if I can. The Surrealists—(that is, super-realists, or those who work *above* realism)—were a coterie of painters and writers in Paris, in the nineteen twenties, who did not believe in the conscious selection of images. To put it in another way: They were artists who were dissatisfied with both the realists —(roughly speaking, those who tried to put down in paint and words an actual representation of what they imagined to be the real world in which they lived)—and the impressionists who, roughly speaking again, were those who tried to give an impression of what they imagined to be the real world. The Surrealists wanted to dive into the subconscious mind, the mind below the conscious surface, and dig up their images from there without the aid of logic of reason, and put them down, illogically and unreasonably, in paint and words. The Surrealists affirmed that, as three quarters of the mind was submerged, it was the function of the artist to gather his material from the greatest, submerged mass of the mind rather than from that quarter of the mind which, like the tip of an iceberg, protruded from the subconscious sea. One method the Surrealists used in their poetry was to juxtapose words and images that had no rational relationship; and out of this they hoped to achieve a kind of subconscious, or dream, poetry that would be truer to the real, imaginative world of the mind, mostly submerged, than is the poetry of the conscious mind that relies upon the rational and logical relationship of ideas, objects, and images.

This is, very crudely, the credo of the Surrealists, and one with which I profoundly disagree.

I do not mind from where the images of a poem are dragged up; drag them up, if you like, from the nethermost sea of the hidden self; but, before they reach paper, they must go through all the rational processes of the intellect. The Surrealists, on the other hand, put their words down together on paper exactly as they emerge from chaos; they do not shape these words or put them in order; to them, chaos *is* the shape and order. This seems to me to be exceedingly presumptuous; the Surrealists imagine that whatever they dredge from their subconscious selves and put down in paint or in words must, essentially, be of some interest or value. I deny this. One of the arts of the poet is to make comprehensible and articulate what might emerge from subconscious sources; one of the great main uses of the intellect is to *select*, from the amorphous mass of subconscious images, those that will best further his imaginative purpose, which is to write the best poem he can.

And Question five is, God help us, what is my definition of Poetry?

I myself, do not read poetry for anything but pleasure. I read only the poems I like. This means, of course, that I have to read a lot of poems I don't like before I find the ones I do, but, when I *do* find the ones I do, then all I can say is "Here they are," and read them to myself for pleasure.

Read the poems you like reading. Don't bother whether they're important, or if they'll live. What does it matter what poetry *is*, after all? If you want a definition of poetry, say: "Poetry is what makes me laugh or cry or yawn, what makes my toenails twinkle, what makes me want to do this or that or nothing," and let it go at that. All that matters about poetry is the enjoyment of it, however tragic it may be. All that matters is the eternal movement behind it, the vast undercurrent of human grief, folly, pretension, exaltation, or ignorance, however unlofty the intention of the poem.

You can tear a poem apart to see what makes it technically tick, and say to yourself, when the works are laid out before you, the vowels, the consonants, the rhymes and rhythms, "Yes, this is *it*. This is why the poem moves me so. It is because of the craftsmanship." But you're back again where you began. You're back with the mystery of having been moved by words. The best craftsmanship always leaves holes and gaps in the works of the poem so that something that is *not* in the poem can creep, crawl, flash, or thunder in.

The joy and function of poetry is, and was, the celebration of man, which is also the celebration of God.

W. H. Auden

THE VIRGIN & THE DYNAMO (1962)

There is a square. There is an oblong. The players take the square and place it upon the oblong. They place it very accurately. They make a perfect dwelling-place. The structure is now visible. What was inchoate is here stated. We are not so various or so mean. We have made oblongs and stood them upon squares. This is our triumph. This is our consolation.
VIRGINIA WOOLF.

THE TWO REAL WORLDS

1) The Natural World of the Dynamo, the world of masses, identical relations and recurrent events, describable, not in words but in terms of numbers, or rather, in algebraic terms. In this world, Freedom is the consciousness of Necessity and Justice the equality of all before natural law. (*Hard cases make bad law.*)

2) The Historical World of the Virgin, the world of faces, analogical relations and singular events, describable only in terms of speech. In this World, Necessity is the consciousness of Freedom and Justice the love of my neighbor as a unique and irreplaceable being. (*One law for the ox and the ass is oppression.*)

Since all human experience is that of conscious persons, man's realization that the World of the Dynamo exists in which events happen of themselves and cannot be prevented by anybody's art, came later than his realization that the World of the Virgin exists. Freedom is an immediate datum of consciousness; Necessity is not.

THE TWO CHIMERICAL WORLDS

1) The magical polytheistic nature created by the aesthetic illusion which would regard the world of masses as if it were a world of faces. The aesthetic religion says prayers to the Dynamo.

2) The mechanized history created by the scientific illusion which would regard the world of faces as if it were a world of masses. The scientific religion treats the Virgin as a statistic. "Scientific" politics is animism stood on its head.

Without Art, we could have no notion of Liberty; without Science no notion of Equality; without either, therefore, no notion of Justice.

Without Art, we should have no notion of the sacred; without Science, we should always worship false gods.

By nature we tend to endow with a face any power which we imagine to be responsible for our lives and behavior; vice versa, we tend to deprive of their faces any persons whom we believe to be at the mercy of our will. In both cases, we are trying to avoid responsibility. In the first case, we wish to say: "I can't help doing what I do; someone else, stranger than I, is making me do it"—in the second: "I can do what I like to N because N is a thing, an x with no will of its own."

The pagan gods of nature do not have real faces but rather masks, for a real face expresses a responsibility for itself, and the pagan gods are, by definition, irresponsible. It is permissible, and even right, to endow Nature with a real face, e.g., the face of the Madonna, for by so doing we make nature remind us of our duty towards her, but we may only do this after we have removed the pagan mask from her, seen her as a world of masses and realized that she is not responsible for us.

Vice versa, the saint can employ the algebraic notion of *any* in his relation to others as an expression of the fact that his neighbor is not someone of whom he is personally fond, but anybody who happens to need him; but he can only do this because he has advanced spiritually to the point where he sees nobody as a faceless cypher.

Henry Adams thought that Venus and the Virgin of Chartres were the same persons. Actually, Venus is the Dynamo in disguise, a symbol for an impersonal natural force, and Adams' nostalgic preference for Chartres to Chicago was nothing but aestheticism; he thought the disguise was prettier than the reality, but it was the Dynamo he worshiped, not the Virgin.

PLURALITIES

Any world is comprised of a plurality of objects and events. Pluralities are of three kinds; crowds, societies and communities.

1) A *Crowd*. A crowd is comprised of $n > I$ members whose only relation is arithmetical; they can only be counted. A crowd loves neither itself nor anything other than itself; its existence is chimerical. Of a crowd it may be said, either that it is not real but only apparent, or that it should not be.

2) A *Society*. A society is comprised of a definite or an optimum number of members, united in a specific manner into a whole with a characteristic mode of behavior which is different from the modes of behavior of its component members in isolation. A society cannot come into being until its component members are present and properly related; add or subtract a member, change their relations, and the society either ceases to exist or is transformed into another society. A society is a system which loves itself; to this self-love, the self-love of its members is totally subordinate. Of a society it may be said that it is more or less efficient in maintaining its existence.

3) A *Community*. A community is comprised of n members united, to use a definition of Saint Augustine's, by a common love of something other than themselves. Like a crowd and unlike a society, its character is not changed by the addition or subtraction of a member. It exists, neither by chance, like a crowd, nor actually, like a society, but potentially, so that it is possible to conceive of a community in which, at present, $n = I$. In a community all members are free and equal. If, out of a group of ten

persons, nine prefer beef to mutton and one prefers mutton to beef, there is not a single community containing a dissident member; there are two communities, a large one and a small one. To achieve an actual existence, it has to embody itself in a society or societies which can express the love which is its *raison d'être*. A community of music lovers, for example, cannot just sit around loving music like anything, but must form itself into societies like choirs, orchestras, string quartets, etc., and make music. Such an embodiment of a community in a society is an order. Of a community it may be said that its love is more or less good. Such a love presupposes choice, so that, in the natural world of the Dynamo, communities do not exist, only societies which are submembers of the total system of nature, enjoying their self-occurrence. Communities can only exist in the historical world of the Virgin, but they do not necessarily exist there.

Whenever rival communities compete for embodiment in the same society, there is either unfreedom or disorder. In the chimerical case of a society embodying a crowd, there would be a state of total unfreedom and disorder; the traditional term for this chimerical state is Hell. A perfect order, one in which the community united by the best love is embodied in the most self-sustaining society, could be described, as science describes nature, in terms of laws-of, but the description would be irrelevant, the relevant description being, "Here, love is the fulfilling of the law" or "In His Will is our peace"; the traditional term for this ideal order is Paradise. In historical existence where no love is perfect, no society immortal, and no embodiment of the one in the other precise, the obligation to approximate to the ideal is felt as an imperative "Thou shalt."

Man exists as a unity-in-tension of four modes of being: soul, body, mind and spirit.

As soul and body, he is an individual, as mind and spirit a member of a society. Were he only soul and body, his only relation to others would be numerical and a poem would be comprehensible only to its author; were he only mind and spirit, men would only exist collectively as the system Man, and there would be nothing for a poem to be about.

As body and mind, man is a natural creature, as soul and spirit, a historical person. Were he only body and mind, his existence would be one of everlasting recurrence, and only one good poem could exist; were he only soul and spirit, his existence would be one of perpetual novelty, and every new poem would supersede all previous poems, or rather a poem would be superseded before it could be written.

Man's consciousness is a unity-in-tension of three modes of awareness:

1) A consciousness of the self as self-contained, as embracing all that it is aware of in a unity of experiencing. This mode is undogmatic, amoral and passive; its good is the enjoyment of being, its evil the fear of nonbeing.

2) A consciousness of beyondness, of an ego standing as a spectator over against both a self and the external world. This mode is dogmatic, amoral, objective. Its good is the perception of true relations, its evil the fear of accidental or false relations.

3) The ego's consciousness of itself as striving-towards, as desiring to transform the self, to realize its potentialities. This mode is moral and active; its good is not present but propounded, its evil, the present actuality.

Were the first mode absolute, man would inhabit a magical world in which the image of an object, the emotion it aroused and the word signifying it were all identical, a world where past and future, the living and the dead were united. Language in such a world would consist only of proper names which would not be words in the ordinary sense but sacred syllables, and, in the place of the poet, there would be the magician whose task is to discover and utter the truly potent spell which can compel what-is-not to be.

Were the second mode absolute, man would

inhabit a world which was a pure system of universals. Language would be an algebra, and there could exist only one poem, of absolute banality, expressing the system.

Were the third mode absolute, man would inhabit a purely arbitrary world, the world of the clown and the actor. In language there would be no relation between word and thing, *love* would rhyme with *indifference,* and all poetry would be nonsense poetry.

Thanks to the first mode of consciousness, every good poem is unique; thanks to the second, a poet can embody his private experiences in a public poem which can be comprehended by others in terms of their private experiences; thanks to the third, both poet and reader desire that this be done.

The subject matter of the scientist is a crowd of natural events at all times; he presupposes that this crowd is not real but apparent, and seeks to discover the true place of events in the system of nature. The subject matter of the poet is a crowd of historical occasions of feeling recollected from the past; he presupposes that this crowd is real but should not be, and seeks to transform it into a community. Both science and art are primarily spiritual activities, whatever practical applications may be derived from their results. Disorder, lack of meaning, are spiritual not physical discomforts, order and sense spiritual not physical satisfactions.

It is impossible, I believe, for any poet, while he is writing a poem, to observe with complete accuracy what is going on, to define with any certainty how much of the final result is due to subconscious activity over which he has no control, and how much is due to conscious artifice. All one can say with certainty is negative. A poem does not compose itself in the poet's mind as a child grows in its mother's womb; *some* degree of conscious participation by the poet is necessary, *some* element of craft is always present. On the other hand, the writing of poetry is not, like carpentry, simply a craft; a carpenter can decide to build a table according to certain specifications and know before he begins that the result will be exactly what he intended, but no poet can know what his poem is going to be like until he has written it. The element of craftsmanship in poetry is obscured by the fact that all men are taught to speak and most to read and write, while very few men are taught to draw or paint or write music. Every poet, however, in addition to the everyday linguistic training he receives, requires a training in the poetic use of language. Even those poets who are most vehemently insistent upon the importance of the Muse and the vanity of conscious calculation must admit that, if they had never read any poetry in their lives, it is unlikely that they would have written any themselves. If, in what follows, I refer to the poet, I include under that both his Muse and his mind, his subconscious and conscious activity.

The subject matter of a poem is comprised of a crowd of recollected occasions of feeling, among which the most important are recollections of encounters with sacred beings or events. This crowd the poet attempts to transform into a community by embodying it in a verbal society. Such a society, like any society in nature, has its own laws; its laws of prosody and syntax are analogous to the laws of physics and chemistry. Every poem must presuppose— sometimes mistakenly—that the history of the language is at an end.

One should say, rather, that a poem is a natural organism, not an inorganic thing. For example, it is rhythmical. The temporal recurrences of rhythm are never identical, as the metrical notation would seem to suggest. Rhythm is to time what symmetry is to space. Seen from a certain distance, the features of a human face seem symmetrically arranged, so that a face with a nose a foot long or a left eye situated two inches away from the nose would appear monstrous. Close up, however, the exact symmetry disappears; the size and position of the features vary slightly from face to face and, indeed, if a face could exist in which the symmetry were mathematically perfect, it would look, not like a face, but like a lifeless mask. So with rhythm. A poem may be described as being written in iambic pentameters, but if every foot in every line were identical, the poem would sound intolerable to the ear. I am sometimes inclined to think that the aversion of many modern poets and their readers to formal verse may be due to their association of regular repetition and formal restrictions with all that is most boring and lifeless in modern life, road drills, time-clock punching, bureaucratic regulations.

It has been said that a poem should not mean but be. This is not quite accurate. In a poem, as distinct from many other kinds of verbal societies, meaning and being are identical. A poem might be called a pseudo-person. Like a person, it is unique and addresses the reader personally. On the other hand, like a natural being and unlike a historical person, it cannot lie. We may be and frequently are mistaken as to the meaning of the value of a poem, but the cause of our mistake lies in our own ignorance or self-deception, not in the poem itself.

The nature of the final poetic order is the outcome of a dialectical struggle between the recollected occasions of feeling and the verbal system. As a society the verbal system is actively coercive upon the occasions it is attempting to embody; what it cannot embody truthfully it excludes. As a potential community the occasions are passively resistant to all claims of the system to embody them which they do not recognize as just; they decline all unjust persuasions. As members of crowds, every occasion competes with every other, demanding inclusion and a dominant position to which they are not necessarily entitled, and every word demands that the system shall modify itself in its case, that a special exception shall be made for it and it only.

In a successful poem, society and community are one order and the system may love itself because the feelings which it embodies are all members of the same community, loving each other and it. A poem may fail in two ways; it may exclude too much (banality), or attempt to embody more than one community at once (disorder).

In writing a poem, the poet can work in two ways. Starting from an intuitive idea of the kind of community he desires to call into being, he may work backwards in search of the system which will most justly incarnate that idea, or, starting with a certain system, he may work forward in search of the community which it is capable of incarnating most truthfully. In practice he nearly always works simultaneously in both directions, modifying his conception of the ultimate nature of the community at the immediate suggestions of the system, and modifying the system in response to his growing intuition of the future needs of the community.

A system cannot be selected completely arbitrarily nor can one say that any given system is absolutely necessary. The poet searches for one which imposes just obligations on the feelings. "Ought" always implies "can" so that a system whose claims cannot be met must be scrapped. But the poet has to beware of accusing the system of injustice when what is at fault is the laxness and self-love of the feelings upon which it is making its demands.

Every poet, consciously or unconsciously, holds the following absolute presuppositions, as the dogmas of his art:

1) A historical world exists, a world of unique events and unique persons, related by analogy, not identity. The number of events and analogical relations is potentially infinite. The existence of such a world is a good, and every addition to the number of events, persons and relations is an additional good.

2) The historical world is a fallen world, i.e., though it is good that it exists, the way in which it exists is evil, being full of unfreedom and disorder.

3) The historical world is a redeemable world. The unfreedom and disorder of the past can be reconciled in the future.

It follows from the first presupposition that the poet's activity in creating a poem is analogous to God's activity in creating man after his own image. It is not an imitation, for were it so, the poet would be able to create like God *ex nihilo*; instead, he requires pre-existing occasions of feeling and a pre-existing language out of which to create. It is analogous in that the poet creates not necessarily according to a law of nature but voluntarily according to provocation.

It is untrue, strictly speaking, to say that a poet should not write poems unless he must; strictly speaking it can only be said that he should not write them unless he can. The phrase is sound in practice, because only in those who can and when they can is the motive genuinely compulsive.

In those who profess a desire to write poetry, yet exhibit an incapacity to do so, it is often the case that their desire is not for creation but for self-perpetuation, that they refuse to accept their own mortality, just as there are parents who desire children, not as new persons analogous to themselves, but to prolong their own existence in time. The sterility of this substitution of identity for analogy is expressed in the myth of Narcissus. When the poet speaks, as he sometimes does, of achieving immortality through his poem, he does not mean that he hopes, like Faust, to live for ever, but that he hopes to rise from the dead. In poetry as in other matters the law holds good that he who would save his life must lose it; unless the poet sacrifices his feelings completely to the poem so that they are no longer his but the poem's, he fails.

It follows from the second presupposition, that a poem is a witness to man's knowledge of evil as well as good. It is not the duty of a witness to pass moral judgment on the evidence he has to give, but to give it clearly and accurately; the only crime of which a witness can be guilty is perjury. When we say that poetry is beyond good and evil, we simply mean that a poet can no more change the facts of what he has felt than, in the natural order, parents can change the inherited physical characteristics which they pass on to their children. The judgment good-or-evil applies only to the intentional movements of the will. Of our feelings in a given situation which are the joint product of our intention and the response to the external factors in that situation it can only be said that, given an intention and the response, they are appropriate or inappropriate. Of a recollected feeling it cannot be said that it is appropriate or inappropriate because the historical situation in which it arose no longer exists.

Every poem, therefore, is an attempt to present an analogy to that paradisal state in which Freedom and Law, System and Order are united in harmony. Every good poem is very nearly a Utopia. Again, an analogy, not an imitation; the harmony is possible and verbal only.

It follows from the third presupposition that a poem is beautiful or ugly to the degree that it succeeds or fails in reconciling contradictory feelings in an order of mutual propriety. Every beautiful poem presents an analogy to the forgiveness of sins; an analogy, not an imitation, because it is not evil intentions which are repented of and pardoned but contradictory feelings which the poet surrenders to the poem in which they are reconciled.

The effect of beauty, therefore, is good to the degree that, through its analogies, the goodness of created existence, the historical fall into unfreedom and disorder, and the possibility of regaining paradise through repentance and forgiveness are recognized. Its effect is evil to the degree that beauty is taken, not as analogous to, but identical with goodness, so that the artist regards himself or is regarded by others as God, the pleasure of beauty taken for the joy of Paradise, and the conclusion drawn that, since all is well in the work of art, all is well in history. But all is not well there.

Selective Index

Adams, Henry, 545
aesthetics, described by
Croce, 391–408; history of,
404–08
Aiken, Conrad, 522
Aldington, Richard, 29, 37
allegory, 189–91, 194, 237
ambiguity, 129–31
anagnorisis, 234
ananke, 197
anatomy, Frye's definition
of, 181, 214
apocalypse, 185, 215, 239–40
Apuleius, 212, 214
archetype, 183–84, 186,
191, 215–24
Aristotle, 33, 84, 85, 144,
164, 234, 280, 361, 381,
405, 408–09; "neo-
Aristotelianism," 254–55,
361–81
Arnold, Matthew, 63, 64,
66, 75, 81, 86, 95–101
(and Pater), 102, 103,
104, 108, 128, 200, 205,
208, 250, 252, 381
Auden, W. H., 219, 239,
494, 542
Auerbach, Erich, 388,
464–65
Austen, Jane, 209, 358, 364
autonomous art, 67, 182–84,
250, 403

Babbitt, Irving, 106, 253
Bachelard, Gaston, 432
Baker, Howard, 321

Balzac, Honoré de, 460, 463,
473, 475, 479–82
Bardi, Giovanni, 500
Baudelaire, Charles, 46,
87, 88, 89, 110–11, 115–18,
194, 485–87
Baumgarten, A. G., 406–07
Belgion, Montgomery, 103
Benedict, Ruth, 222
Benjamin, Walter, 387
Bentham, Jeremy, 165
Bible, as fictional form, 189–91,
215, 238, 541–42
Blackmur, R. P., 186, 249,
255, 256–58, 525
Blake, William, 182 ff.,
189–97, 202, 229–30,
232–34, 236, 237, 238,
424, 427, 501, 504, 518,
519, 541
Bloch, Ernst, 452–53
Boccaccio, 436, 438–41
Bodkin, Maud, 377
Boehme, Jacob, 197, 424
Boileau, 460–61
Booth, Wayne, 255
Borrow, George, 208, 209, 214
Bouilhet, Louis, 471, 486,
487, 489
Bourget, Paul, 479
Bradley, A. C., 294, 302
Bradley, F. H., 165
Brandes, Georg, 481
Brémond, Henri, 109, 116
Bridges, Robert, 23
Brontë, Emily, 209
Brooks, Cleanth, 131, 255,
282, 377

Brooks, Van Wyck, 276,
337
Browning, Robert, 9, 18,
35, 88, 92, 94, 154, 301,
328
Bunyan, John, 210
Burke, Edmund, 225
Burke, Kenneth, 255–56,
258
Burns, Robert, 498, 500–01,
533
Burton, Robert, 213–14
Butler, Samuel, 212–13
Byron, George Gordon, Lord,
227, 229

Carlyle, Thomas, 96, 99, 101
Cary, Joyce, 353
Catullus, 10, 18, 25, 59,
88, 89
Cavalcanti, Guido, 5, 17,
23, 34, 51, 59, 62, 94
Cervantes, 444
Cézanne, Paul, 43
Chapman, George, 193
Chapman, John Jay, 279
Chateaubriand, 477
Chaucer, 17, 25, 60, 538
Chesterton, G. K., 228
Classicism, contrasted with
Romanticism, 401–02,
510–11
Coleridge, S. T., 69–70, 81,
85, 89–90, 101, 102, 108,
128, 130, 131, 149, 162–
63, 169, 171–72, 177,
266, 374, 375, 381